COMPARATIVE DEVELOPMENT EXPERIENCES OF SUB-SAHARAN AFRICA AND EAST ASIA

Comparative Development Experiences of Sub-Saharan Africa and East Asia

An Institutional Approach

Edited by
MACHIKO NISSANKE and ERNEST ARYEETEY
African Economic Research Consortium, Nairobi

ASHGATE

Published by
Ashgate Publishing Limited
Gower House
Croft Road
Aldershot
Hants GU11 3HR
England

Ashgate Publishing Company
Suite 420
101 Cherry Street
Burlington, VT 05401-4405
USA

Ashgate website: http://www.ashgate.com

British Library Cataloguing in Publication Data
Comparative development experiences of Sub-Saharan Africa &
East Asia : an institutional approach
1.East Asia - Economic conditions - Congresses 2.Africa -
Economic conditions - 1960- - Congresses
I.Nissanke, Machiko II.Aryeetey, Ernest III.African
Economic Research Consortium
338.9'5

Library of Congress Cataloging-in-Publication Data
Comparative development experiences of Sub-Saharan Africa and East Asia: an institutional approach / edited by Machiko Nissanke and Ernest Aryeetey.
p. cm.
Includes bibliographical references and index.
ISBN 0-7546-3647-X
1.East Asia--Economic policy. 2.Africa, Sub-Saharan--Economic policy. 3.Economic development--Case studies. I.Nissanke, Machiko. II.Aryeetey, Ernest, 1955-

HC460.5.C635 2003
330.95--dc21 2003043715

ISBN 0 7546 3647 X

Printed and bound in Great Britain by MPG Books Ltd, Bodmin, Cornwall

Contents

List of Tables

List of Figures

List of Abbreviations

ADB	Asian Development Bank
AfDB	African Development Bank
ADMARC	Agricultural Development and Marketing Corporation (Malawi)
AE	Allocative efficiency
AERC	African Economic Research Consortium
AFTA	ASEAN Free Trade Area
APEC	Asia-Pacific Economic Cooperation
ASEAN	Association of Southeast Asian Nations
BIAO	International Bank of West Africa
BIN	State Industrial Bank (Indonesia)
BIPIK	Small Industries Development Programme (Indonesia)
BPM	Bank Pembangunon Malaysia
BOK	Bank of Korea
BOT	Bank of Thailand
CAR	Central African Republic
CBS	Central Bureau of Statistics
CEPD	Centre for Economic Planning and Development (Taiwan)
CFA	Communauté Financière Africaine
CFAF	CFA franc
COLS	Corrected ordinary least squares
CPI	Consumer price index
CRDB	Cooperative and Rural Development Bank (Malawi)
CSAE	Centre for the Study of African Economies
CTI	Confederation of Tanzania Industries
CVTOT	Coefficient of variation for terms of trade
DAC	Development Assistance Committee (of OECD)
DCGTX	Direction et Controle des Grands Travaux
DFI	Development finance institution
DMBs	Deposit taking banking institutions
DRC	Democratic Republic of Congo
DY	External debt to GDP ratio
EDB	Economic Development Board (Singapore)
EE	Economic efficiency
EEC	European Economic Commission
ENA	Ecole Nationale d'Administration
EPB	Economic Planning Board (Korea)
EPZ	Export processing zone
ESAF	Enhanced structural adjustment facility
ESEA	East and Southeast Asia
ESRF	Economic and Social Research Foundation

ETLR	Evolutionary Theory of Land Rights
EU	European Union
EUP	Economic Urgency Plan (Indonesia)
FAO	Food and Agriculture Organization
FDI	Foreign direct investment
FIIRO	Federal Institute of Industrial Research, Oshodi
FSC	Financial Supervisory Commission (Korea)
FTD	Food Technology Division
GATS	General Agreement on Trade in Services
GATT	General Agreement on Tariffs and Trade
GDP	Gross domestic product
GNP	Gross national product
HCI	Heavy and chemical industry
HIES	Household income and expenditure survey
HIID	Harvard Institute for International Development
HIV/AIDS	Human immuno-deficiency virus/Acquired immune deficiency syndrome
HOS	Heckscher–Ohlin–Samuelson model
HPAE	High performing Asian economy
ICOR	Input-capital output ratio
ICP	International Comparisons Project
ICRG	International Country Risk Guide
IFCT	Industrial Finance Corporation of Thailand
ILO	International Labour Organization
IMF	International Monetary Fund
INDEBANK	Industrial Development Bank (Malawi)
INDEFUND	Investment and Development Fund (Malawi)
JASPA	Jobs and Skills Programme for Africa
JETRO	Japan External Trade Organization
JMAFF	Japanese Ministry of Agriculture, Forestry and Fisheries
KERI	Korean Economic Research Institute
KIK/KMKP	Small Enterprise Development Programme (Indonesia)
KKU	The Feasibility Credit Scheme (Indonesia)
KLI	Korea Life Insurance
KOTRA	Korean Overseas Trade Organization
K-REP	Kenya Rural Enterprise Programme
KRW	(Korean currency)
KSY	Korea Statistical Yearbook
KUK	Small Enterprise Credit Scheme (Indonesia)
LAC	Latin America and the Caribbean
LDC	Least developed country
LIBOR	London inter-bank offer rate (of interest)
LIK	Small Industry Estates (Indonesia)
LIUP	Local industry upgrading programme
LNG	Liquid natural gas
LP	Linear programming

LTES	Long-Term Economic Statistics of Japan
M2	Broad money
M&A	Mergers and acquisitions
MARA	Majlis Amanah Rakyat (Malaysia)
MARDI	Malaysian Agricultural Research and Development Institute
Mbase	Monetary base
MDC	Malawi Development Corporation
MEs	Manufacturing enterprises
MEDEC	Malaysian Entrepreneurship Development Centre
MENA	Middle East and North Africa
MFCRI	Macro-financial crisis
MIDF	Malaysian Industrial Development Finance
MIEL	Malaysian Industrial Estates Limited
MITI	Ministry of Trade and Industry (Malaysia)
ML	Maximum likelihood
MSEs	Micro and small enterprises
MSTQ	Metrology, standardization, testing and quality assurance
MVA	Manufacturing value added
n.a.	Not available
NAFTA	North American Free Trade Agreement
NBFI	Non-bank financial institution
NCG	Not claims on government
NEA	Northeast Asia
NEC	Newly exporting country
NEP	New Economic Policy (Malaysia)
NFA	Not foreign assets
NFI	New forms of investment
NFS	Nursery factory scheme
NGNP	Nominal GNP growth rate
NGO	Non-government organization
NIEs	Newly industrializing economies
NPL	Non-performing loan
NTB	Non-tariff barrier
OECD	Organization for Economic Cooperation and Development
OLS	Ordinary least squares
PCE	Personal consumption expenditure
PPP	Purchasing power parity
PPR	Public Policy Research Working Papers Series (World Bank)
PUSTH	Relative consumer price indexes between the USA and Thailand
R&D	Research and development
RER	Real exchange rate
RGNP	Real GNP growth rate
ROSCA	Rotating savings and credit association
RPED	Regional Programme for Enterprise Development
SAF	Structural adjustment facility
SAL	Structural adjustment loan

SAP	Structural adjustment programme
SCAP	Supreme Commander for the Allied Powers
SCS	Savings and credit society
SD	Singapore dollar
SDF	Skills Development Fund (Singapore)
SE	Small enterprise
SEA	Southeast Asia
SECAL	Agricultural sector adjustment loans
SEDOM	Small Enterprise Development Organization of Malawi
SIFO	Small Industry Finance Office
SIFS	Small Industries Financing Scheme (Singapore)
SIRIM	Standards and Industrial Research Institute of Malaysia
SMEs	Small- and medium-scale enterprises
SMIs	Small- and medium-scale industries
SOAS	School of Oriental and African Studies
SOE	State-owned enterprise
SSA	Sub-Saharan Africa
SSNALF	Service share of the non-agricultural labour force
S&T	Science and technology
TDRI	Thai Development Research Institute
TE	Technical efficiency
TFP	Total factor productivity
TNC	Transnational corporation
TOT	Terms of trade
TRIM	Trade related investment measure
TRIPS	Trade related intellectual property rights
UN	United Nations
UNCTAD	United Nations Conference on Trade and Development
UNDP	United Nations Development Programme
UNECA	United Nations Economic Commission for Africa
UNESCO	United Nations Educational, Scientific and Cultural Organization
UNIDO	United Nations Industrial Development Organization
UNU/INTECH	United Nations University/Information Technology
UPT	Unit Pelayanan Teknis
UR	Uruguay Round
USA	United States of America
VAT	Value added tax
WDR	World Development Report
WIDER	World Institute for Development Economics Research
WPS	Working Paper Series
WTO	World Trade Organization

List of Contributors

Ali Abdel Gadir Ali, United Nations Economic Commission for Africa (UNECA), Addis Ababa, Ethiopia

Ernest Aryeetey, Institute of Statistical, Social and Economic Research, University of Ghana, Accra, Ghana

Anne Booth, School of Oriental and African Studies (SOAS), University of London, UK

Ha-Joon Chang, University of Cambridge, UK

Ibrahim A. Elbadawi, The World Bank, Washington, DC

Sung-Hee Jwa, Korea Economic Research Institute, Seoul, Korea

Toshihiko Kawagoe, Seikei University, Tokyo, Japan

Kwanghee Nam, Korea Economic Research Institute, Seoul, Korea

Benno J. Ndulu, The World Bank, Dar es Salaam, Tanzania

Njuguna S. Ndung'u, University of Nairobi, Kenya

Bhanupong Nidhiprabha, Thammasat University, Bangkok, Thailand

Machiko Nissanke, School of Oriental and African Studies (SOAS), University of London, UK

Ademola Oyejide, University of Ibadan, Ibadan, Nigeria

Hiey Jacques Pégatiénan, Université de Cocody, Abidjan, Côte d'Ivoire

Juro Teranishi, Hitotsubashi University, Tokyo, Japan

Erik Thorbecke, Cornell University, New York, USA

Samuel M. Wangwe, Economic and Social Research Foundation (ESRF), Dar es Salaam, Tanzania

Thee Kian Wie, Centre for Economic and Development Studies, Indonesian Institute of Sciences (PEP-LIPI), Jakarta, Indonesia

Acknowledgements

As the coordinators of this Collaborative Research Project on Comparative African and East Asian Development Experiences, we would like to express our appreciation to the African Economic Research Consortium (AERC) for entrusting the project to us and for supporting us throughout the long process of bringing the separate papers to the point of publication. We would also like to express our sincere gratitude to the Japanese government for providing generous financial support for the conference at which the draft papers were presented and discussed. We are equally grateful to the United Nations University in Tokyo, and the Korean Development Institute for their financial contribution towards the travel expenses of several conference participants.

The conference was organized by AERC in collaboration with United Nations University and held in Johannesburg on 3–6 November 1997. On that occasion we were especially honoured to have very distinguished guests as key speakers. They were Honourable Trevor Manuel, Minister of Finance of South Africa, Professor Shigeru Ishikawa, Hitotsubashi University, Tokyo, and Professor John Harris, Boston University, USA. We were also fortunate to have inspiring speeches by Ian Goldin and Stephen Gelb from the Development Bank of South Africa, who also kindly hosted a conference dinner.

We are most grateful to all the conference participants for their invaluable comments and lively participation. Besides the authors of the various chapters of this volume, participants included Toru Yanagihara, Howard Stein, Yilmaz Akyuz, Sung-Hee Jwa, Jane Harrigan, Olu Ajakaiye, Hal Hill, Jomo Sundaram, Colin McCarthy, Ben Fine, Anwar Nasution, Ponciano S. Intal, Laurence Harris, Yujiro Hayami, Hirohisa Kohama, Paul Collier, Mohammed Sadli, Tony Killick, Andrew Mullei, David Court, Kerfalla Yasane, Yasutami Shimomura, Abel Thoahlane, Naoyuki Shinohara, Atushi Hatakenaka, Jung Hoo Yoo, Alan Gelb, Julius Court and Beatrice Weder. They made valuable contributions to the conference as chairs of sessions, designated discussants or paper presenters.

Editorial constraints forced us to be selective in the process of shaping the final volume. All the papers included here were substantially revised and updated to incorporate the comments and discussions communicated in the conference and by other reviewers. Many of the papers were also revised to reflect the financial crisis that struck East and Southeast Asia in 1997–1998. We would like to express our great appreciation to everyone who provided their most useful written comments and for the other papers presented at the conference, from which we all benefited greatly for the revision and editorial work.

Machiko Nissanke and Ernest Aryeetey
Project Coordinators

Preface

The issues of how much divergence exists in the development paths of Africa and East Asia and how such divergence came about have been the subject of considerable speculation and some study in the last decade. It has turned out that the extent of the divergence has been much larger than initially believed, as it has become increasingly obvious that it goes well beyond simple economic performance after the application of capital, labour and technology. The divergence is reflected by institutional developments, influenced by a wide range of factors, that have varied from country to country in East Asia. Those varying factors were generally used to achieve a single purpose, however: a transformed economic structure. What has not been equally clear is how those varying factors were applied to achieve results that are so markedly different from developments in Africa.

The African Economic Research Consortium (AERC) instituted a research project in 1996 to investigate in a collaborative manner how the diverging developments of the two regions in the last four decades could be explained. The project was planned to take into account the institutional and structural features of economies alongside whatever policy differences there may be. Of crucial importance was the role of the state and markets in different areas and how they affected economic performance. The idea was to cover all the major sectors of the economies in the two regions within a historical context. By studying the same development themes in both Asia and Africa, AERC sought to highlight the specific areas in which the differences occurred and how they related to particular policy regimes and institutional arrangements, including changes in these over time.

To inform the collaborative research among Asian and African researchers, a number of framework papers were commissioned by the Consortium. These sought to throw light on relevant conceptual and empirical issues in addressing the specific thematic areas where the diverging developments could be observed. On the conceptual side, the papers sought to introduce African and Asian researchers to current debates and relevant literature seeking to explain those differences. They sought to distil from the myriad existing explanations those that had the most relevance for understanding the institutional and policy contexts of development in the two regions. On the side of empirics, the papers sought to show how various concepts had been deployed in earlier research and what their findings had been. They were expected to show the way forward for carrying out new research to explain situations across the two regions that had not been adequately explained.

This volume contains the edited framework papers, which were presented and discussed at a conference organized in Johannesburg in November 1997. Because the economic situation in East Asia changed considerably within months after the conference, the framework papers and the nature of the proposed research had to be revised and adjusted considerably to take into account those new developments. In this regard, it is important to observe that of particular importance to the project has been the issue of how institutions in East Asia could have been used to arrive at the remarkable achievements of the three decades prior to the difficulties of 1997/98, while the weaknesses of those same institutions led to that debacle and yet they were able to withstand the shocks in a manner that could not have been anticipated earlier. The inherent contradictions in the 'miraculous' East Asian achievements with admirable institutional arrangements over a relatively short period and the apparent fragility of those same institutions offer considerable opportunities for researchers to try to understand what works best when and where. It raises fundamental questions for African researchers as they attempt to understand their own environments better.

The commissioning of the papers and the conference in Johannesburg were organized with considerable financial support from the Japanese government through a trust fund at the World Bank. AERC appreciates this support enormously. We also appreciate the support of the United Nations University and the Korean Development Institute. And we cannot fail to mention the contributions of Benno Ndulu and Ibrahim Elbadawi, respectively the former AERC executive director and research director, who provided the initial guidance for the project. The project steering committee and coordinators also worked hard to mobilize resources for the project and to direct its intellectual development. These contributions are highly appreciated by AERC, as are those of the authors who made this publication possible. AERC is grateful to them all.

Delphin Rwegasira
Executive Director
African Economic Research Consortium

PART ONE

THE CONTEXT

Chapter 1

Introduction: Comparative Development Experiences in Sub-Saharan Africa and East Asia

Ernest Aryeetey and Machiko Nissanke

Before the Asian crisis of 1997/98, it was commonplace to juxtapose the dismal growth performance of the sub-Saharan Africa (SSA) economies against the rapid and sustained growth record of the East Asian economies, as the growth performances of the two regions began to diverge markedly in the 1970s. The East Asian development experiences were popularly presented to policy makers in Africa as an attractive example to draw lessons from. Indeed, many of the East Asian economies managed not only to register 'admirable' growth rates but also to accomplish relatively equitable income distribution with dynamically evolving changes in socio-economic structures. The sharp contrast in economic performance of the two regions prompted the examination of factors and conditions that gave rise to the diverse outcomes, in particular because both regions had been subject to the same turbulent global environment.

In their early attempts, mainstream economists attributed the divergence in economic performances between the two regions almost exclusively to policy differences, especially the difference in policies for international trade and investment. It is true that there has been a clear disparity in the degree of integration into the global economy between the two regions. Aggressively following an outward-oriented development strategy, most East Asian economies not only accelerated the process of integration into the world economy but also upgraded their linkages in the years of their rapid economic growth. In contrast, the majority of SSA countries failed to take advantage of the opportunities provided by the increasing international economic interactions. In the 1970s and 1980s, instead of becoming more integrated into the world economy, they were largely marginalized and experienced slow growth and stagnation. With growing recognition of their disadvantageous positions, over the past decade SSA counties have increasingly searched for ways to accelerate their participation in the world economy.

Interestingly, the East Asian crisis erupted in the wake of this gradual embrace of globalization by African countries. The crisis, which started as a financial crisis arising primarily as financial *excess*, not a crisis of fundamentals, clearly exposed the severe difficulties in managing national economies in highly regionally integrated and globalizing environments. The event has helped us to raise a critical question for sub-Saharan Africa: how to manage the process of *strategic integration* into the global economy. As Senbet (1998) notes, the lessons from the Asian crisis, if drawn correctly, can help SSA countries to draw a strategy towards sustainable globalization.

The Genesis of This Collection

The Asian Crisis of 1997/98 radically changed perceptions and assessments of the East Asian economies, held popularly as the 'Miracle' story until the very onset of the crisis. As the crisis fast unfolded into a deeper general economic crisis of the whole region through the contagion effects in 1998, some commentators started forcefully arguing that the Asian Crisis was specific to the East Asian model due to 'crony capitalism', riddled by insider dealings, corruption and non-transparent corporate governance. The region's economic policies, which were previously regarded as a key ingredient in creating the miracle, were suddenly written off as a 'curse' for engendering the disaster.

In our view, these simplistic interpretations of the causes of either the miracle or the crisis only obscure a much needed realistic understanding of the conditions and factors that could explain the very different growth and development experiences of SSA and East Asia in the last four decades. Such naïve assessments of the complex process of economic development cannot provide a satisfactory answer to the equally important question of why some East Asian economies have subsequently managed to engineer a rather quick turn-around from the crisis, compared with the historical experiences of other regions.

In a longer historical perspective, we suggest that there is no neat dichotomy between the broad policy frameworks adopted in the two regions alongside the well-established and clear divergence in outcomes. There have been, instead, some similarities in policy frameworks for significant periods, but varied in terms of implementation environments and in terms of sectors where some policies were targeted. By the same token, different countries in the two regions have adopted approaches that do not necessarily fit into a generalizable framework. Hence, it is necessary to go well beyond simple comparisons of policies at rather superficial levels and examine carefully the institutional implementation context within which growth and development have proceeded in the two regions.

In the past, we have often encountered casual remarks in which the experiences of the two regions are contrasted. This book intends to make amends for this by examining the processes that underlie each region's experiences. While we are not in a position to provide a comprehensive comparison of Africa and East Asia, we try here to present both African and Asian perspectives on what transpired in the two regions in specific areas, comparing policies, institutions and outcomes.

Specifically, this volume intends to bridge the knowledge gap that has arisen because researchers in the two regions actually know relatively little about each other's economies. Until now, African economists have had at best only a second-hand view of the economies of East and Southeast Asia, usually derived from the western scholarly literature. While these sources are useful, they do not sufficiently focus on the most relevant aspects of the Asian experience in terms of detailed policy design and implementation procedures. Similarly, Asian policy makers interested in making assistance to Africa more effective often have little knowledge of the economies of Africa and how best to situate the Asian experience in the African environment. Also, the recent negative conditions in such countries as Thailand, Indonesia, Malaysia, Korea and even Japan need to be well understood and placed within the proper development context.

The book is a collection of the selected papers that were first presented at an international conference in Johannesburg in November 1997[1] in the background of the early phase of the Asian Crisis. The Conference was organized by the African Economic Research Consortium (AERC) as the first programme workshop on the thematic topic of Comparative Institutional Analysis for its collaborative research programme, *Comparative Development Experiences in Africa and Asia.*

The programme was set up by AERC as an active research network to facilitate direct interactions and to conduct research on policy experiences among scholars and policy makers in Africa and Asia. The main objectives of this collaborative research programme were to establish interactive channels for sustained conveyance and interchange of relevant experiences (and unfiltered lessons to be drawn) between African and Asian scholars and policy makers, and to provide a regular forum for discussing economic policies and observing directly how policies are related to economic institutions/agents in the two regions.

Many revisions to these papers were made in 1998–1999, as the Asian Crisis gathered its pace and evolved into a global financial crisis. Instead of revising the papers in tandem with fast evolving events, the authors were asked to focus on long-term development issues and the sustainability of economic structures and relationships. Hence, individual chapters of this volume discuss the crisis only in relation to the long-term growth and development. We discuss the extent to which the crisis affected a comparison with Africa in the paragraphs that follow.

Development Performance in Sub-Saharan Africa in a Comparative Perspective

Following the spurt of economic growth enjoyed in the initial post-independence years, real GDP growth rates in SSA countries steadily declined over the more recent decades.[2] With growing populations, the economic growth performance in

[1] Conference on Comparative African and East Asian Development Experiences, held at Karos Indaba, Johannesburg, South Africa, 3–6 November 1997.

[2] It is important to note that sub-Saharan countries are by no means homogeneous in their economic performance as well as in other institutional, socio-political and civil characteristics. Given the scope of this book, however, we try to convey some general trends

SSA, measured by per capita growth, has consistently lagged behind that of the rest of the world, particularly East Asia (Table 1.1 and Figure 1.1). Thus, amid the severe economic crises the region experienced in the 1980s, many countries initiated large-scale economic reforms within the context of donor-supported structural adjustment programmes. Some improvements, admittedly fragile, in macroeconomic balances in 'adjusting' countries have been recorded (World Bank, 1994). But, after 15 years of economy-wide reform efforts, the region's growth performance remains far too modest to lead the economies along a self-sustaining path of economic development and erode growing levels of poverty.

Table 1.1 Growth in GDP per capita, per cent per annum

	1961–1972	1973–1980	1981–1990	1986–1996
Africa	1.3	0.7	-0.9	-1.0
East Asia	7.0	7.1	9.4	7.2
Southeast Asia	3.2	4.9	4.3	6.6*
South Asia	1.3	1.6	3.3	2.9

*Malaysia, Indonesia, Thailand only for 1985–1995.
Source: World Bank, Economic and Social Data Base.

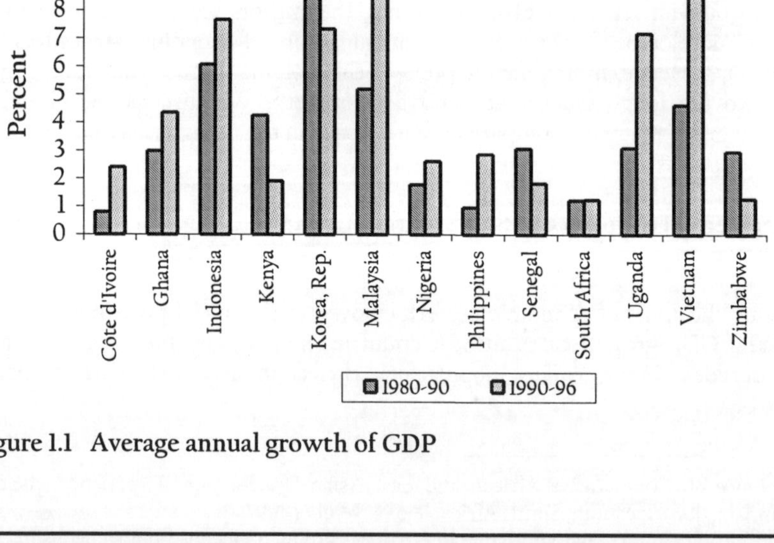

Figure 1.1 Average annual growth of GDP

---

observed across 47 countries in the region, while recognizing the diversity and heterogeneity of these economies.

Collier and Gunning (1997) note that during 1990–1994 the decline in African per capita GDP accelerated to 1.8 per cent per annum, 6.2 percentage points below the average rate attained by all low-income developing countries. Savings rates in most of sub-Saharan Africa remain at a depressed level (see Table 1.2). The low savings rates of these SSA countries suggest that investment and economic growth still depend heavily on foreign savings in the form of external finance. For many countries of the region, dependence on concessional aid flows for economic development has been high and rising. In the early 1990s, aid flows to Africa increased at 6 per cent per annum in real terms and aid constitutes about 9 per cent of African GNP, as compared with 2 per cent in South Asia (Collier, 1994). By 1994 aid had grown to 12.4 per cent of GDP. The aid dependence ratio is much higher for some countries. For example, gross concessional aid flows accounted for 49 per cent and 27 per cent of GDP in 1991 for Mozambique and Tanzania, respectively.

The differences in economic performance are probably most glaring with respect to participation in international trade and other external transactions. The ratio of world trade to GDP has doubled since the 1960s, with the ratio of merchandise exports to GDP rising from 11 per cent to 18 per cent and the share of primary products in total world trade being halved as that of manufactures rose.

Table 1.2 Comparative indicators on savings and investment

	Gross domestic investment as % of GDP		Gross domestic saving as % of GDP	
	1980	1998	1980	1998
Low and middle income countries	27	25	26	24
East Asia & Pacific	32	36	31	37
Europe and Central Asia	-	23	-	21
Latin America & Caribbean	24	22	22	20
Middle East & N. Africa	27	-	38	-
South Asia	21	22	15	17
Sub-Saharan Africa	24	18	26	15

Source: World Bank, *World Development Report* 1999/2000.

Among manufactured goods, there has been a decisive shift towards trade in intermediate goods and a major growth in intra-industry trade. About 20 per cent of the imports of many growing economies is for parts and components. It is estimated that close to half of the world trade in manufactures passes through multinational corporations. The trade in services has grown even faster as commercial service exports accounted for about 20 per cent of world trade in 1996. It is expected that the internationalization of these services will continue.

Africa has failed to be part of this dynamic growth of international trade in goods and services. The share of SSA in world trade has fallen from over 3 per cent in the 1960s to less than 2 per cent currently. Taking out South Africa, this share is only 1.2 per cent. There has been very little diversification. It is estimated that for SSA the erosion of the world trade share between 1970 and 1993 has meant a loss of $68 billion, or 21 per cent of GDP (World Bank, 1998). The poor integration of SSA economies into the global economy is reflected in Table 1.3, where we compare a number of SSA and East Asian economies. Trade as a percentage of GDP was as high as 70.2 per cent in Malaysia in 1996 and only 21.5 and 20.7 per cent in Nigeria and South Africa, respectively, two of SSA's largest economies.

Table 1.3 Integration with the global economy

	Trade % of PPP GDP		Trade in goods % of GDP		Growth in real trade less growth in real GDP Percentage points	Mean tariff – All products %	Gross private capital flows % of PPP GDP		Gross foreign direct investment % of PPP GDP	
	1986	1996	1986	1996	1986–96	1990–96	1986	1996	1986	1996
Côte d'Ivoire	36.0	32.0	118.5	151.6	0.7	4.8	4.9	3.4	0.5	0.1
Ghana	11.0	15.3	44.6	126.6	2.4	-	1.9	2.4	0.0	0.4
Indonesia	10.7	13.6	55.0	69.7	1.3	13.2	2.0	2.1	0.1	0.8
Kenya	16.8	17.9	67.1	115.2	5.5	-	2.9	2.5	0.2	0.0
Malaysia	33.6	70.2	163.5	269.0	7.8	9.1	2.8	4.6	0.7	2.0
Nigeria	17.2	21.5	65.0	98.6	-2.0	-	11.2	12.4	0.4	1.4
Senegal	22.6	16.1	108.6	98.9	-0.6	-	7.7	4.5	0.3	0.4
South Africa	17.4	20.7	93.4	105.4	3.8	8.8	2.2	3.5	0.1	0.1
Thailand	14.7	31.3	85.8	138.2	6.9	-	1.6	5.0	0.2	0.8
Uganda	10.1	6.3	28.9	32.6	-0.2	-	6.0	1.8	0.0	0.6
Zimbabwe	13.8	19.8	76.1	139.1	3.6	24.3	2.0	3.8	0.1	0.2
Korea	33.6	46.7	115.0	118.0	4.5	11.3	3.5	11.1	0.8	1.1

Source: World Bank (1998); World Development Indicators.

The growth in real trade as a percentage of GDP was fastest in Malaysia and Thailand. Only Kenya recorded a high growth rate among the SSA countries. For SSA, real trade as a share of GDP declined by an average 0.35 percentage points annually between 1980 and 1993, while it went up by 1.4 points for East Asia and the Pacific. However, export growth in East Asia began to slow markedly in the mid 1990s, and except in the Philippines, dropped sharply in 1996. The worst case was in Thailand where the nominal dollar value of exports actually fell. This has been attributed by Radelet and Sachs (1998) to over-valuation of exchange rates, the appreciation of the Japanese yen against the dollar after 1994, the competition effects of Mexico's participation in the North American Free Trade Agreement (NAFTA) and the peso devaluation, and the world-wide glut in semi-conductor production. This deterioration of export performance was one of contributing factors in the Asian crisis, as discussed below.

During the early decades Africa achieved some notable improvements in development indicators, including such social provisions as health and education. While life expectancy at birth increased from 40 years to 49–52 years and the infant mortality rate per 1,000 live births declined from 167 to 97 in the period 1960–1997, most of the gains in these indicators were made in the 1960s and 1970s, and the progress was halted in the 1980s and 1990s. As a result, Africa's achievement lags behind that of other developing countries (Table 1.4). The share of population having access to health services, safe water and sanitation is still very low. Provision of these services is also known to be urban-biased. About one third of children under five were assessed as underweight, showing no improvement on this score over the last 20 years. Diseases associated with poor sanitation and poverty claim many lives, while the AIDS epidemic and HIV infection have reached alarming levels.

Table 1.4 Selected development indicators

(a) GNP per capita, life expectancy, infant mortality

	GNP per capita		Life expectancy at birth (years)		Infant mortality rate (per 1,000 live births)	
	US$ 1998	Average annual growth (%) 1985–94	1960	1997 male / female	1960	1997
All developing countries	1,250	0.7	46	63 / 67	150	64
of which: Sub-Saharan Africa	480	-1.2	40	49 / 52	167	105
East Asia and Pacific	990	6.9	-	67 / 70	-	37
South Asia	430	2.7	-	62 / 63	-	77
Europe and Central Asia	2,190	-3.2	-	64 / 73	-	23
Middle East and North Africa	2,050	-0.4	-	66 / 68	-	49
Latin America and the Caribbean	3,940	0.6	-	66 / 73	-	32

(b) Access to services, nutritional status, education

	Per cent population with access to:				Underweight children under age 5		Adult literacy rate (%)			
	Health services 1985–95	Safe water 1975–80	Safe water 1990–97	Sanitation 1990–97	1975	1985–95	1970	1997	1997 Female	1997 Male
All developing countries	80	40	72	43	40	30	43	61	63	80
Sub-Saharan Africa	57	25	50	44	31	31	27	55	50	66

Source: World Bank, *World Development Report*; UNDP, *Human Development Report*.

The adult literacy rate increased in aggregate from 27 per cent to 55 per cent, but remains well behind the level attained by all developing countries combined. In 1997, there was still a gender discrepancy in the adult literacy rate: female adult literacy is 16 percentage points behind male literacy rate.

It is also estimated that the Africa region as a whole experienced a food deficit to the tune of 19.6 million tons of cereals in 1995. By 1997, some 37 countries were suffering from food deficits (United Nations, 1997). Indeed, food security remains a critical issue for SSA.[3] The most vulnerable to food security are smallholder farmers, pastoralists and households headed by women. The incidence of poverty is widespread, estimated to range between 40 and 66 per cent (Ali, 1995). To deal with this scale of human deprivation, not only must rates of growth be accelerated, but the development path has to be reoriented towards a broad-based and equitable one.[4]

Explaining the Divergent Growth and Development Patterns

Among several studies, the East Asian Miracle study (World Bank, 1994) is probably one of the most publicized attempts to examine key conditions for 'success' of economic management in eight East Asian countries[5] and draw lessons from the Asian experiences for the other developing countries. Classifying economic policies into fundamentals and selective interventions, the World Bank study acknowledges the prevalence of systematic government intervention (via multiple channels) to address market failures in these economies, in particular in Northeast Asia. It also notes that the success of selective intervention in Northeast Asian countries is attributable to the rigorously pursued performance-based, yet highly transparent contest framework, which has been pragmatic and adaptable to constantly changing internal and external circumstances.

However, the World Bank (1994) rejects the replicability and appropriateness of interventionist policies for other developing countries on two accounts. First, it

[3] The UN (1997) further reports that the number of hungry and undernourished people in the continent continues to increase. Some 35 percent (or 217 million people) of the total population in sub-Saharan Africa is estimated to be chronically malnourished. This number is projected to increase to 300 million by the year 2010, if the prevailing food situation continues unabated.

[4] Furthermore, there is growing evidence that environmental degradation has grown by alarming proportions in Africa. Ecosystems have shown signs of high stress: soil erosion and degradation, deforestation, and increased desertification are widely observed throughout Africa (Ellis, 1996).

[5] These are referred to as the High Performing Asian Economies; they are Japan, Hong Kong, the Republic of Korea, Singapore, Taiwan, Indonesia, Malaysia and Thailand. Thus, the eight countries are rather heterogeneous, where three quite distinct models can be observed, as Perkins (1994) suggests: a) the manufactured exports-led state interventionist models of Japan, Korea and Taiwan; b) the free port service commerce dominated model of Singapore and Hong Kong; and c) the natural resource rich model of Indonesia, Malaysia and Thailand.

argues that establishing the causality between growth and a specific intervention is difficult, and hence, measuring the relative impact of fundamentals and the interventions is virtually impossible. It infers that either government intervention in East Asia accounted for only a small fraction of total growth or growth in East Asia would have been as fast if the 'market-friendly' policies had been substituted for actual interventionist policies. Second, a prerequisite for pursuing contest-based resource allocation—a high quality civil service with the capacity to monitor in isolation from political interference—is typically absent in other settings. Therefore, the Bank study recommends that other countries focus on fundamentals and thereby create a market-friendly environment rather than on getting interventions to work. It concludes that 'the fact that interventions were an element of some East Asian economies' success does not mean that they should be attempted everywhere, nor should they be used as an excuse to resist needed market-oriented reform' (Page, 1994: 624; World Bank, 1994: 26).

The World Bank study has been severely criticized by a number of academics and practitioners for failing to understand the interdependence between fundamentals and selective interventions. They note that macroeconomic basics are in reality anchored in a policy formation and implementation context, and hence in 'micro-institutions that exhibit pervasive state interventions' (Amsden, 1994: 627). Thus, the study failed to assess seriously how elements of the East Asian model can be adapted to suit conditions in other countries.[6] For this, similarities and differences in locally prevailing conditions should be analysed in sufficient depth.

More importantly, policy measures themselves, as noted by Kwon (1994), are not the sole factor determining the success or failure of policies. Indeed, given frequent institutional failures in policy implementation, the selection of sound measures may not necessarily ensure the success of policies. Equally, the difference in the growth performances between East Asian economies and other regions cannot be explained only in terms of a fundamentally different set of policy choices such as export orientation or market liberalization (Woo-Cummings, 1996). The effectiveness and outcome of policies depend on multiple factors originating from internal domestic conditions and external environments.

The domestic conditions encompass the economic, socio-political and cultural environments as well as societal interests and historical constraints, which can be summarized by what institutional economics succinctly refers to as institutional structures and environments.[7] These conditions differ enormously by country and

---

[6] The study has also been criticized for its selective and incomplete references and presentation of empirical evidence and its tendentious and biased interpretation (Amsden, 1994; Kwon 1994; Lall, 1994). Rodrik (1994) criticized the study for failing to register the relative equality of income, wealth and schooling as an important initial condition, rather than a consequence, of economic development in East Asia.

[7] We discuss in Chapter 2 more precise definitions of institutional environments and governance structures found in the literature of institutional economics. In general, these include human skills and information endowment, institutional arrangements such as the structure of civil and political institutions and community organizations, organizational

by region. Equally disparate is the external environment facing a particular economy, i.e., the forms and extent of participation in the regional and global economy. We shall return to these questions in Chapter 2, where they are discussed in a framework provided by institutional economics.

Recent Developments in East Asia in Perspective

Since the Asian financial crisis broke in 1997, there has been speculation that whatever positive lessons might have been drawn from the East Asian economic history of the last 40 years would have to be tamed. It is our view that much as the recent developments provide additional lessons to be learned in terms of policy and institutional weaknesses, they do not take away significantly from the achievements of those economies in terms of the structures they erected and their performance potential. From this perspective, we present here a brief literature review that discusses the nature and causes of the Asian crisis and a number of policy implications.

The Conditions That Led to the Crash

Despite the attempts to attribute the causes of the Asian crisis to the East Asian model of crony capitalism, as mentioned earlier, most informed observers agree that what happened in East Asia was a financial crisis that could hit any economy when specific economic conditions hold and prevail for a long time without being attended to. The crisis was primarily twofold: a currency crisis and a financial sector crisis as interrelated phenomena (Corsetti et al., 1998). As such, it shares a commonality, in several critical aspects, with previous financial crises of recent decades, including those in the Southern Cone countries in the early 1980s and Mexico in 1994/95. Chang et al. (1998) also espouse the view that the crisis resulted primarily from market failures that are characteristic of (or endogenous to) under-regulated, over-liquid international financial markets.

This does not take away from the fact that for a number of years, the external real sector performance of several Asian countries had been weakened by the global glut of their highly specialized manufactured export goods as well as their declining competitiveness arising out of over-valued exchange rates in fixed peg systems. All of which occurred in an environment of fierce competition from China, Vietnam and other newly industrializing economies. Nor do we dispute the fact that the Asian economies have suffered from the fragility of the domestic financial system, associated with excessive risk-taking and over-lending under a lax regulatory/supervisory regime.

Indeed, a considerable current account deficit, which was predominantly financed with short-term capital inflows, had begun to develop prior to the crisis in several countries. This was not viewed at the time as a serious problem, however,

---

characteristics of factor and goods markets and production units, government–business relations, and regulatory environments and incentive structures.

since foreign borrowing was used to finance investment rather than consumption and the overall internal fiscal and monetary balance remained sound. Domestic credit continued to expand and foreign capital kept flowing into the economies right up to the onset of the crisis.

The crisis was indeed a direct outcome of this *over-investment by private agents*. Private agents, including financial institutions and corporations, were highly leveraged. There was a large build-up of short-term foreign liabilities on an unhedged basis by domestic financial institutions or corporations. Yet, the rate of return to investment was reported to have been rapidly deteriorating for some years (Harris 1998b). Corporate returns had slowed sharply in a number of countries (Pomerleano, 1998). The declining quality of investment must have reflected either the falling marginal rates of investment because of the very high investment rates that prevailed in these economies, or wrong investment decisions with regard to sectors and borrowers. Either way, these were the joint outcome of poor asset management by financial intermediaries and poor investment decisions by borrowers/corporations.

If the foregoing conditions were assumed to be known ex ante, a number of critical questions would come up: why had over-investment/over-borrowing been sustained for so long in these Asian economies, despite the 'long-standing' weaknesses? Why were these signs of the structural weaknesses, such as under-regulated financial institutions, fragile over-indebted corporate finance or poor investment quality, not detected or taken seriously earlier in order to arrest the problem in time or at least contain its scale? Why did it take a form of abrupt speculative attacks on pegged currencies and large-scale bank runs to wake up investors and policy makers, with the resultant deep crisis that shook the foundation of the regional economies and the global economic system?

McKinnon and Pill (1998) explain over-borrowing/over-investment and the twin crisis in terms of *moral hazard* problems inherent to weak financial systems. They suggest that over-borrowing occurs when the non-bank private sector becomes euphoric about the success of reform because of the overly optimistic signal about macroeconomic developments contained in loose credit conditions. Banks are likely to respond to this by extending credit recklessly in the absence of adequate bank supervision, but with public guarantee not to let banks fail. The problem becomes further exacerbated when domestic banks take unhedged foreign exchange positions in accessing international capital markets to meet credit demand, as they face not only real credit risks but also currency risks. Foreign lenders do not take a prudent position towards these borrowers, as they too believe they would be bailed out in the event of a crisis. Meanwhile, over-borrowing goes on unchecked with unlimited offer of credit.

Thus, in their thesis, the problem of over-borrowing is rooted in an institutional failure to manage the moral hazard problem introduced by implicit or explicit deposit insurance domestically as well as international rescue operations such as those organized by the International Monetary Fund (IMF). When credit booms eventually end in bust, with unrealizable expectations and increasingly risky bank assets, the probability of bank failure will be increased: banks would suffer additional capital losses following devaluation from the currency mismatch on their balance sheet, precipitating a general financial crisis. Thus, they conclude that under such circumstances, the magnitude of the boom–bust over-borrowing cycle is likely to be escalated both ex ante and ex post.

Following a similar line of arguments, Kane and Rice (1998: 24) suggest that 'bad banking regulation is made partly responsible for the extent of overvaluation in booms and for the suddenness of corrective downward swings in asset valuation. Hiding adverse information during economic booms allows prices to rise too high, while the abrupt surfacing of hidden information leads to a rapid downward revaluation of bank net worth. The root of the asset–price bubble and of its bursting is the self-interested attempt by banks and regulators to conceal adverse information from bank customers and taxpayers'.

Relating the irrational behaviour of investors to the panic model of banking crisis developed by Minsky (1978) and Kindelberger (1996), others suggest that over-investment/over-borrowing in the crisis-hit Asian countries was fuelled and sustained by excessive asset inflation in the boom years. According to this model, asset prices are inherently volatile, going through psychological boom–bust cycles: On one hand, the irrationally optimistic psychology of the boom renders loans, securities and real estate severely over-valued, and debt is often contracted to leverage the acquisition of speculative assets for subsequent resale. On the other hand, when fundamental valuation returns to asset pricing, investors overreact in the opposite direction to real or imagined adverse shocks to the repayment prospects of the borrowers. Panic ensues and asset prices experience ruinous declines. Thus, the market crashes with the collapse of speculative bubbles. Reflècting these highly volatile movements of asset prices, capital markets and financial systems (both domestic and international) are inherently unstable as surges of euphoria and despair alternate in shaping market conditions.

Miller and Luangaram (1998) observe that in many Asian countries currency crises have been preceded by a boom–bust cycle of prices for assets such as stocks and real estate. While noting that such cycles may exist without necessarily involving the financial sector, they suggest that there can be a close link between the performance of the financial sector and asset prices. For example, a banking crisis could arise from a sharp movement of asset prices if bank loans are tied to the market value of assets accepted as collateral. Over the cycle, excess credit creation can easily raise asset values above equilibrium; when this disequilibrium is being corrected, credit constraints can set in motion a vicious downward spiral in asset prices leading to financial collapse, as borrowers are forced to sell assets to repay loans. As Asian firms are known to be highly geared with financial institutions, this link between asset prices and banking performance may have prevailed in these East Asian economies.

In all cases, regardless of the direct causes, an eventual realization of banks' negative net worth triggers bank runs. Bank runs could induce, and escalate into, an open currency crisis, if the expected increased liquidity resulting from a government bailout is inconsistent with the fixed parity. Especially is a bank run more likely to lead to a currency attack, when foreign currency reserves reach below a threshold in relation to foreign denominated liabilities of banks and corporations. In turn, a speculative attack on the currency can give rise to a banking crisis if deposit money is used to speculate on the currency or banks are loaned offshore-borrowed funds without hedging currency risks. Thus, Miller (1998) notes that there are important linkages between bank solvency and currency stability and that causation may run in either direction.

Nevertheless, the two explanations for over-borrowing with an inevitable crash are built on a different set of behavioural assumptions: while the McKinnon–Pill model relies on the assumption of banks' privileged information advantage in the presence of deposit insurance to explain the pervasive moral hazard problem, the Minsky–Kindelberger model locates a primary explanation in a Keynesian-type herdism. Hence, there is a critical difference in the policy implications of the two theses. The first thesis, focusing on moral hazard as the common factor underlying the currency crisis and banking crisis, places a particular emphasis on the need for effective banking supervision and regulation with a much improved flow of timely and quality information.

In contrast, relating the financial crisis to the cyclical nature of market-based economies in general, the second thesis recommends a broader set of measures, including a policy of moderating the irrational swings in asset prices by controlling all avenues of monetary expansion at national and international levels (Kindelberger, 1996). Further, the second thesis doubts the risk-assessment capacity of market participants, even if relevant information is made available. According to Chang et al. (1998: 651), 'the key problem (in East Asia) was the *evaluation* of the information available: as in most of financial "mania", market operators were simply unwilling to focus on the downside risks as the upside was more attractive'.

In all these explanations of what triggered the crises in Asia, there appears to be a general agreement that the rapid pace of financial market deregulation and capital account liberalization contributed, as is the case with many other financial crises of recent decades. A sharp increase in nominal interest rates following liberalization tends to deteriorate the risk composition of banks' loan portfolios, giving rise to the problem of adverse incentive and selection as well as aggravating the moral hazard problem (Stiglitz and Weiss, 1981). An easier entry into financial sectors upon liberalization also leads to a proliferation of banking and non-banking financial institutions and places an excessive strain on the supervisory and regulatory capacity of the oversight agencies, which in many cases had not been strengthened as liberalization proceeded. Furthermore, in the absence of adequate supervision and regulation, close politico-business coalitions can be forged under liberalization through money politics and patronage, as has been observed in several crisis-hit economies in Asia and elsewhere in the world (McNeill and Bøckman, 1998).

In particular, liberalization of international capital transactions produces, under easy global liquidity conditions, a spurt of foreign capital inflows seeking higher short-term returns than are available elsewhere and willing to accept the higher risk that emerging markets are believed to carry. Goldstein (1998) notes that in a number of 'miracle' Asian economies a credit boom in the 1990s was stoked by large short-term private capital inflows, with a build-up of short-term foreign liabilities in the period leading up to the crisis. In Thailand, easy foreign money made available through the establishment of the Bangkok International Banking Facility in 1993 to domestic banks and financial houses was known to be used for the purchase of real estate and equities with high loan–collateral ratios. In Korea, too, banks borrowed aggressively offshore for on-lending to corporations as well as for large-scale holdings of equities (Chang, 1998; Goldstein, 1998). This undoubtedly contributed to asset price bubbles in boom as well as to price crashes in bust. Sterilization policies effected to neutralize the monetary impact of large-scale inflows aggravated the situation by inducing further an inflow of interest-sensitive capital, since interest on domestic debt paper had to be raised (Calvo, 1998). This also created an additional incentive for domestic borrowers to raise funds in international capital markets.

Because of the pegged exchange rate, little management of currency exposure was undertaken in most countries of the region despite the potentially hazardous currency/maturity mismatches between liabilities and assets. Speculative attacks on the currency, triggered by sudden reversals of market confidence, hit directly the vulnerable balance-sheet positions of Asian financial institutions. The net worth of these banks (and financial conditions of corporations such as those in Indonesia that had heavily contracted short-term foreign debt) rapidly deteriorated during the currency crisis due to a sharp rise in domestic interest rates effected to defend a currency, followed by an eventuality of large-scale devaluation. In many cases, this may have turned even those banks and corporations that were solvent in the pre-currency-crisis period to conditions of insolvency/bankruptcy.

Moreover, there is also some evidence that derivative contracts, which provide banks low-risk fee and commission income as well as possibilities to circumvent particular prudential regulations, played an integral role in the rise in short-term flows to the region (Kregel, 1998). In many cases, swap contracts and credit derivatives combine currency risk and market price risks, producing co-movement in these markets. This created a cumulative causation that produced unexpected declines and excessive instability in both currency and asset markets during the height of the crisis.

Thus, altogether it should be noted that the Asian crisis was very much a crisis of globalizing capital, with large contagion effects throughout the region and emerging markets at large. As soon as a wake-up call sounded in Thailand, a financial crisis was contagiously spread to countries with similarities in conditions or countries with spill-over effects via trade and financial linkages. A number of countries initially entered into a crisis partly due to the *herd* behaviour of international investors arising out of psychological or informational externalities. As portfolio managers were punished for continued exposure in regions with failing prospects, investors tended to use the behaviour of others as a proxy for accurate information, all heading for the exit by simply following the herd. This kind of behaviour creates a condition of overshooting, amplifying the effect of initial events and turning 'correction' into 'collapse'.

From this perspective, many suggest that foreign investors played a large role in creating conditions leading to the crises in East Asia. Radelet and Sachs (1998: 2) argue that the Asian crisis is as much a crisis of international financial markets as the earlier financial crises were. They note that 'each of financial crisis episodes displays elements of a self-fulfilling crisis, in which capital withdrawals by creditors cascade into a financial panic and result in an unnecessary deep contraction'. They go on to argue that 'international loan markets are prone to self-fulfilling crises, in which although individual creditors may act rationally, market outcomes produce sharp, costly and fundamentally unnecessary panicked reversals in capital flows. Initially, a liquidity crisis occurs if a solvent but illiquid borrower is unable to borrow fresh funds from capital markets in order to remain current on debt-servicing obligations. The unwillingness or inability of the capital market to provide fresh loans to the illiquid borrower is the nub of the matter. Bank runs are triggered by exogenous stochastic demands for liquidity by some depositors and not at all by fears of imprudent lending'. If this 'coordination failure' diagnosis is correct, what was required at the onset of the crisis was an orderly 'work-out' procedure or 'forced roll-over' arrangements to provide fresh liquidity.

Others disagree with the idea that ascribes the cause of the crisis to the problem of illiquidity. They argue that a root cause for the Asian financial crisis is of domestic origin, which is institutionally deeply embedded in these economies, rather than arising out of illiquidity conditions. In their view, the crisis should be treated essentially as one that is caused by the problem of insolvency, involving perverse financial incentives, distorted asset prices and misallocated resources, leading ultimately to a creditor panic. It is argued that the domestic banking system in the crisis-afflicted economies had long been infiltrated by the moral hazard problem in the absence of an effective regulatory/supervisory system, and that this condition had encouraged banks to gamble for resurrection.

For example, Kane and Rice (1998) argue that political loans were so pervasive in Asia that many banks must have been in effect 'zombie' banks, whose earning assets cannot generate enough income to pay the principal and interest due on their debts. These banks with negative net worth would favour highly speculative and highly leveraged loans that a well-capitalized bank would reject. In advance of the emergence of palpable crisis, distressed zombie banks in Asia had experienced a silent run and an influx of foreign bank debt. Eventually, the currency crisis forced the insolvency of these domestic zombie banks into the open.

Again, these two diagnoses offer a variety of policy reforms with different emphases. The illiquidity diagnosis stresses the need for international monetary reform towards: a) generalized orderly work-out arrangements, which could involve an establishment of the Emerging Financial Mechanisms, an equivalent of International Bankruptcy Court; and b) regulation and supervision over international capital flows, which could be effected at the national level as well as at the global level. The insolvency diagnosis tends to confine the discussion on policy reform to domestic measures. An utmost emphasis is placed on improvement of regulation of financial institutions in emerging economies, so as to ensure greater transparency and proper monitoring of bank portfolios.

Despite the differences in emphasis, few would disagree, on balance, that in order to prevent a recurrence of these crises, reforms are required at both the international and national levels, since a financial crisis such as the East Asian crisis is an outcome of the interface of global and domestic financial systems.

Further, while it is easier to agree on preventative measures ex post, there is an ongoing controversy surrounding the question of what constitutes appropriate policy actions once the economies are seized by the crisis conditions. In particular, a strong criticism has been voiced over the IMF policy conditionality attached to its initial financial assistance, which was seen as reflecting its misunderstanding of the true nature of the crisis. As in other crises involving fiscal disequilibrium, the IMF programme prescribed tight budget discipline and monetary policy with a sharp increase in interest rates to avert further capital outflows. Many critics have argued that combined with a mandatory closure of some banks and financial houses, these austerity measures of the IMF programme exacerbated the Asian Crisis by further aggravating financial strains of corporations and financial institutions and the real debt deflation problem with an increased expectation of defaults.

Indeed, once a crisis situation developed, as Stiglitz (1998a) notes, 'the irrational pessimism proved self-filling as capital outflows, and the accompanying depreciating currencies and falling asset prices exacerbated the strains on private sector balance sheets'. A vicious cycle set in, as financial sector problems led to severe credit crunch and borrowers' debt capacity was drastically reduced. The performance of the real sector sharply deteriorated, with increasing corporate failures and bankruptcies. Bank runs intensified, as public confidence was severely impaired. This in turn resulted in a further decline in currency and asset prices. Moreover, with a worsened access to trade financing facilities, a depreciation-assisted export-led recovery has been slow to materialize. Such economically weakened conditions have naturally fostered political and social instability, further deepening the crisis. Many argue that one of the primary explanations for the way in which the crisis unfolded and the unexpected severity of the collapse of the Asian economies lies in the inappropriate policy responses to the crisis by the governments and the international community because of their misperception of the nature of the crisis.

Lessons Drawn from the Crisis

Did the crisis wipe away the achievements of East Asia in the previous three decades? The crisis and the policy response to it (the standard instruments of monetary and fiscal tightening) led to major setbacks to growth immediately, which have been reflected in their social consequences.

> After decades of rising incomes and living standards, household earnings have fallen and unemployment has risen sharply in the Asian countries most affected by the Asian crisis. All income groups have been affected, including the rich, who have suffered a decline in net wealth due to the decline in stock and real estate prices. Of particular social concern, however, has been the impact of job losses on low-income urban workers and the second-round effects on the poor in urban and rural areas (UNCTAD, 1998).

The crisis showed that Asia had policy as well as institutional weaknesses that should have been addressed sooner. But Radelet and Sachs (1998) maintain that the basic infrastructure for expanding output still exists in East Asia. This is a position not too far removed from the view Stiglitz (1998a: 3) expresses when he writes that 'the East Asian crisis is not a refutation of the East Asian miracle. The more dogmatic version of the Washington Consensus does not provide the right framework for understanding both the success of the East Asian economies and their current troubles. Responses to East Asia's crisis in this (conservative) view of the world are likely to be, at best, badly flawed, and at worst, counterproductive'. In the early part of 1998, the IMF and the World Bank expected the East Asian economies to turn around their economies again only by 2002. However, some of these economies surprised commentators with a much swifter recovery than these gloomy predictions.

One of the immediate lessons that can be drawn from the East Asian financial crisis for Africa is the need for countries to make themselves less vulnerable to speculative flows and attacks by opening up their economies in a much more careful manner than the East Asian countries did. Thus, an issue of strategic integration into the global economy is presented with a renewed urgency to policy makers of the two regions.

The question of strategic integration is important for several reasons. First, while there has undoubtedly been an accentuated tendency for the world economy to move towards greater interaction and integration between national economies, what has emerged from this trend is a degree of *fractured globalization* rather than a unified globalized economy (Harris, 1998a). A fully integrated world economy, one that an ineluctable process of globalization is popularly assumed to produce, has not emerged. As globalization is not a process proceeding neutrally in a policy vacuum, there is a significant degree of discretion in policies towards integration. The forms of integration are likely to be greatly affected by national policies towards the multi-dimensional process of integration, including policies on trade, finance, technology, industrial structure, competition and migration. The optimal level of openness may differ for each aspect, which itself depends critically on the stage of development among other factors. This leads to a strategic question: what is the best policy mix to achieve integration or what is a measured and properly sequenced set of policies towards trade, foreign direct investment and capital flows.

Second, the benefits of globalization are unevenly distributed. It has been observed that income levels tend to diverge rather than converge among participating national economies and across regions as globalization proceeds. There are winners and losers from the on going process and income inequality tends to be amplified. Moreover, net benefits from globalization are not necessarily guaranteed. Depending on the nature and forms of integration, countries may benefit from dynamism and growth within the international economy, but integration into the international economy by itself does not ensure these benefits. If they are achieved, the initial adjustment costs may include worsening poverty for some groups. The risks and costs involved can be large for fragile economies. Opening up the economies to the powerful external forces shaping the globalization process requires careful strategic thinking about the forms, pace, sequencing, phasing and time-frame for integrating the economy more fully into the world economy.

The excessive pace and incorrect sequencing of liberalization in an attempt to reap greater benefits from the globalization process can result in severe difficulties. The severity of problems that can arise from mismanagement of financial policies in particular has been amply demonstrated by the Asian financial crisis. There is consensus that while the institutional and fundamental problems that could slow down growth already existed in the East Asian economies, they alone could not have disrupted growth so abruptly had there not been a rapid liberalization of financial systems and a hasty opening of the capital account.

The Asian crisis has shown that the risks associated with financial liberalization are high, as international capital flows are inherently volatile, which has exposed vulnerable and fragile economies to highly volatile external forces. However, the East Asian crisis does not suggest by any means that well-orchestrated programmes backed with strategic policies for economic growth and diversification do not pay off. This book will show how some of those long-term gains were made.[8]

Synopsis of This Book

The subsequent chapters attempt to examine and discern differences (and similarities) in prevailing conditions in Asia and Africa under various macro and sectoral themes, in order to provide in-depth explanations for the divergent development experiences in the two regions. Accordingly, the book is structured under the following topics:

- Macroeconomic management and the development process
- Trade, industry and technological development
- Financial policies and financial sector development
- Rural development, income distribution and poverty alleviation

The discussions in these four distinct areas of African and East Asian development are preceded by a cross-cutting paper on broad development issues in the two regions. The elements of all of these chapters are discussed below.

Chapter 2, by Nissanke and Aryeetey, serves as thematic paper by setting the tone for the subsequent chapters. The authors present the overall framework of the comparative institutional *analysis*. To this aim, the chapter first discusses several key analytical concepts useful for comparative institutional analysis in the light of East Asian experiences. These include: institutional environments and organizational governance structures; markets, evolution of markets and market failures; the roles of government, the nature of the state and state failures; and governance structures and mechanisms. Against this analytical and comparative perspective, the chapter then

[8] The issue of strategic integration into the global economy is taken up more explicitly in a separate conference volume under our co-editorship to be published by UNU Press (forthcoming 2003).

tries to delineate the main characteristics of key economic and civic institutions in sub-Saharan Africa (governments, financial institutions and private agents, private firms, and households), and the forms and nature of their interactions.

Thus, Chapter 2 examines the interface among the different institutions, including government–private sector relationships, incentive structures, and the patterns and extent of information flows among different economic agents. Other facets are mechanisms for monitoring and contract enforcement, resolution of agency problems, information sharing and cooperation, and institutional innovation, as well as overall coordination capacity of institutions. The authors examine the effects of recent economic reforms on institutional structures and the processes of reform themselves. In all this, Nissanke and Aryeetey note the careful use of state structures to support private sector initiatives in Northeast Asia and suggest that it is the development of conducive interfaces at the policy and institutional levels between the state and private agents that explains the more sustained level of investments and growth in Asia. The inadequacy of this in Africa would by default explain the latter's difficulties. They caution, however, that attempting to replicate relationships that helped Asia's development in Africa will not necessarily be helpful in view of the path-dependent nature of those relationships, anchored in history and culture. Africa would have to carve out its own path, after drawing critical lessons from its history and assessing carefully its own institutional structures and environments.

Part Two contains four chapters that discuss *macroeconomic management and the development process.* The first of these discussions is by Ndulu, Elbadawi and Ndung'u in Chapter 3, which attempts to explain Africa's relatively poor long-term macroeconomic performance. The authors do this by analysing the mechanisms through which the variable categories of macroeconomic policy environment, macroeconomic instability, external shocks, human capital and regional spillover effects, and institutional and policy uncertainties affect growth, exports savings and private investments. Using this framework they draw a comparison among sub-Saharan African, East Asian and Latin American economies for stated policy variables and other fundamentals. Using panel regressions they then undertake simulations to assess the relative contributions of the various factors to the differential performance of the regions.

Their findings indicate that policy-induced risks are important in explaining the slow response of investment to economic reforms in SSA, much more important than in East Asia. They also suggest that the same policy environment explains the differential in growth performance in the two regions. For savings, they suggest that variables under the categories of growth and human capital development are significant explanators. In addition to these, various policy variables also account for poor savings in SSA: high inflation, negative real interest rates, current account deficits and financial depth. The poor export performance of SSA is affected by similar policy and institutional factors including terms of trade shocks and exchange rate misalignment.

Pégatiénan writes about macroeconomic management and the development process in francophone Africa in Chapter 4. Francophone Africa is shown to have performed quite well with respect to inflation compared with other African economies, despite its overall worse growth performance. The good performance with respect to inflation is explained by the role of the regional central bank, which limits the financing of the fiscal deficit to 20 per cent of the previous year's tax revenue. Pégatiénan shows that export performance was worse in this subregion than in other parts of the region, which he attributes to exchange rate appreciation in the subregion prior to the major devaluation in 1994.

In addition to some macroeconomic policy lapses that underpin the slow growth, Pégatiénan suggests that institutional considerations may be more important explanatory factors for slow growth in francophone Africa. He discusses such phenomena as the 'limited horizons of economic agents', the extended family system and its impact on savings and investment, the human capital of the subregion, including leadership and social attitudes to work and efficiency, the role of the state and its relationship with the private sector, individual property rights, the rule of law, and the quality of public administration. By and large, the conclusion from this chapter is that francophone Africa has not been able to capitalize on the window of opportunity created by the presence of an external agency of restraint in the form of a regional central bank because the institutions for economic management in the region are very weak.

In Chapter 5, Sung-Hee Jwa and Kwanghee Nam discuss Korea's experiences in macroeconomic management and stabilization. They first provide an overview of macroeconomic policies beginning in the 1960s and emphasize the strong government-led approach to export expansion under the first economic development plan (1962–1966). They shows how the government of Korea throughout the 1960s and 1970s did not limit its role to facilitating the mobilization of resources, but was actively involved in their allocation through the use of macroeconomic policies (mainly through foreign exchange and credit allocation) that directed resources to selected industries. The 1980s saw a more focused attempt to achieve stabilization objectives following the higher inflation that accompanied the major drive to develop the heavy and chemical industries sectors in the 1970s.

These fundamental macroeconomic issues were soon overtaken by a boom induced by low interest rates internationally, favourable exchange rate movements and low oil prices, all of which facilitated some stability in domestic prices and economic growth. This also forced the postponement of a significant overhaul of the system of economic management with regard to the roles of the state and the private sector. Serious macroeconomic management had to wait till after 1989 when the economy once again suffered a downturn following deteriorating external economic conditions. The authors discuss at length the approaches and outcomes of the economic reform programme with its focus on liberalization of the financial market and shows how this facilitated growing capital inflows. To sustain the growth rates of the early 1990s, while advocating greater participation for the private sector in resource allocation, they argue for greater independence in monetary and exchange rate determination with indirect policies, and also calls for 'exchange market intervention and policy mix under a more open environment'.

A parallel appraisal of macroeconomic experience is undertaken for Southeast Asia by Nidhipraba in Chapter 6. Nidhipraba's discussion focuses on the period after 1981 and also discusses the experience of the financial crises of 1997/98 in the region. He draws our attention to the fact that while there is a tendency to discuss the high growth rates for the region as a whole, there are important differences among the countries in the patterns of the trade-off between growth and price stability. Thus, while Singapore managed to achieve an average growth of 8.5 per cent in 1991–1995 with very low inflation at 2.6 per cent, similar growth in Thailand and Malaysia came with higher inflation, while somewhat higher inflation rates in Indonesia and Philippines led to a more modest growth.

Nidhipraba explores the macroeconomic stance that made the high growth possible. He suggests that prudent fiscal policy throughout the 1980s led to a reduction of the fiscal deficit. This prepared a favourable ground for the growth in foreign direct investments that had in turn contributed to acceleration of the growth rates. The fiscal prudence is shown to have cut across all countries. This happened alongside rapidly improving financial deepening indicators and a growth in savings as household incomes rose, while the exchange rate was kept stable and fixed in many cases. Nidhipraba discusses the macroeconomic stance and the institutional framework for developing policy to attract foreign investment. He turns to investigate what went wrong with policy-making in the second half of the 1990s that led to the financial crisis of 1997/98. The thesis here is that economic management in Thailand had become lax, leading to a rapid build-up of debt at the same time that growth was beginning to slow down. Indecisiveness crept in, precipitating a loss of credibility for the government. The close ties between the capital markets of the region then forced a contagion effect in economies that were themselves not entirely prepared.

Part Three discusses *trade, industry and technology* in the two regions. In Chapter 7, Oyejide and Wangwe examine the policies that have been deployed for industrial development in SSA since the 1960s and responses to them, as well as their effects on industrial growth in the region. They observe a two-way interactive relationship between trade and industrial policies. Thus, they contend that the pace and pattern of industrialization have been influenced by a protective trade regime for most of SSA's history, while the dynamism of the export sector has depended on the industrialization policies. After highlighting SSA's industrial development experience, essentially revolving around import-substitution in the early decades that led to some noticeable manufacturing growth, they show that this began to decline by the beginning of the 1970s.

They discuss the public–private sector relationships that existed at the time and whatever influence this had on policy and outcome. Here they distinguish between the experiences of East Asia and SSA. In the former, the state essentially played the role of an active facilitator and promoter, while the state's role in the latter was that of direct owner and regulator applying very restrictive policies to private agents. To highlight this point, the chapter examines how the state related to the private sector in the development of industry and the application of technology in several African country examples. The authors also discuss the issues of networking, industrial linkages and contracting arrangements, as well as human capacity and institutional strength for industrial development. They conclude that the main difference between East Asian economies and SSA does not lie in the policies themselves, but in their design and implementation, as well as in stability and credibility of institutions and the incentive structures they created. The human capacity element is strongly emphasized here.

In Chapter 8, Thee Kian Wie considers similar issues for the ASEAN countries, while Ha-Joon Chang does the same for Northeast Asia in Chapter 9. Thee argues that industrialization in the ASEAN countries was considered to be a matter of urgency even before the advent of the 1960s, since governments believed the development of industry was the key to economic welfare and greater economic power. In the early years, they emphasized import-substitution with some success in initiating rapid growth as in SSA. However, the pace began to slacken by the mid 1960s, thus prompting a shift to export-promotion in a number of countries.

Throughout all this, ASEAN countries had a much more open trading system than African countries did, with relatively few tariff and non-tariff barriers. Indonesia is described here as having had the most inward-looking industrial development strategy at the time, but this was more open than in many SSA countries. The 1980s saw a more radical emphasis on openness and export promotion than before, with the introduction of wide-ranging trade reforms. Thee focuses on the export promotion efforts of the region with a discussion of policies and programmes including the setting up of export processing zones, the role of foreign direct investment, support for small and medium-scale industries, and the promotion of industrial and technological upgrading. Thee emphasizes the need for a conducive incentive system to achieve a breakthrough, which will include macroeconomic stability and a 'neutral or only mildly protectionist trade regime'. These have to be aided by strengthened human capital through appropriate education support.

Ha-Joon Chang presents what he sees as misconceptions of the Northeast Asian trade and industrial development experience, especially in contrast with the Southeast Asian experience. He argues, for example, that the contrast in the degree of intervention in north and south (which makes the north more interventionist) is misleading since there were varying degrees of intervention within all the countries for specific aspects of trade and industrial development that may have been more similar than is often considered to be the case. There are also major variations in the state–private sector relationships that have been misrepresented in the literature, as well as a wrongful application of mainstream trade theories to explain the Northeast Asian experience. For example, in relation to infant industry arguments, Chang suggests that their failure in many developing countries was a result of inadequate attention to developing supporting export promotion strategies.

Chang also explains the relative success of Northeast Asia's industrial policies compared with the other regions in terms of political economy questions surrounding policies towards scale economy and competition. Under scale economy, he throws light on entry regulation, consumption control and export promotion, where the state played an active role in developing export markets for firms that were deliberately built large in relation to domestic markets, through provision of export subsidies, marketing information service and export financing facilities. Under competition policy, Chang examines how public agencies provided support for mergers and negotiated market segmentation, subsidies for capital equipment, subsidies for R&D, and the spread of technological information by public agencies. Chang concludes his chapter by contending that the arguments against non-replicability are based on false premises.

In **Part Four** the focus is on the development of *financial sector policies and market response* in SSA and in Japan in the Meiji period. Aryeetey and Nissanke discuss trends in financial sector development in many African countries in Chapter 9. They suggest that SSA's inability to achieve significant investment growth is in large part related to the poor mobilization of domestic savings, which is partly an outcome of a dysfunctional financial system. The dysfunctional financial system dates back to the beginnings of the modern economy in most SSA economies when institutions for banking were created only to support primary commodity trade for colonial governments. The early post-independence initiative was to lead to active state participation in terms of ownership and credit allocation through policies of financial repression.

The authors argue that while recent attempts to reform financial systems are welcome and essential, they do not adequately address many of the structural problems facing the financial systems of the region. With the main focus on market liberalization and bank restructuring, the authors assert that the effects of reforms were limited because of the lack of attention to structural features of the market and the institutional constraints to financial market operations in SSA. They illustrate the extent to which informational deficiencies as well as other structural characteristics of the markets led to the creation of significant gaps in financial products and services for real sector development. Wide-ranging liberalization may need to be muted, but with some intervention to enhance the operation of financial markets for real sector development.

The financial market failures that have plagued many developing economies lately, and the policy and institutional development options that these economies confront, are likened by Teranishi in Chapter 10 to the experiences of Meiji Japan (1868–1912). He suggests that faced with the same problems SSA economies currently experience, Meiji Japan opted for the development of its system, relying extensively on indigenous elements in the financial system alongside the development of modern institutions. This was done by devoting significant resources to the development of those modern financial institutions but adapting them to existing socio-economic conditions by relying heavily on links with traditional financial mechanisms. The Meiji Japan experience shows a significant involvement of the state in the development of banks, but this was done primarily through a system of incentives to the private sector. It was also a system that later led to interlocked ownership of banking and other businesses.

Part Five is devoted to the subject of *rural poverty, income distribution and rural development*. There are three chapters here: Ali Ali and Erik Thorbecke for SSA (Chapter 11), Toshihiko Kawagoe for Northeast Asia (Chapter 12) and Anne Booth for Southeast Asia (Chapter 13). Ali and Thorbecke provide a socio-economic profile of the rural sector with indicators on income and consumption, food output, and employment, as well as income distribution and inequality measures across the region. They compare SSA with other developing regions in terms of the extent and incidence of poverty to reveal that poverty in SSA is much more persistent. Factors behind this poverty profile are manifold, encompassing all aspects of institutional environments that have shaped rural development paths in sub-Saharan Africa: physical, technological and legal environments (including access to land, the quantity and quality of infrastructure, markets, etc.), policies and institutions, as well as culture and social code. They suggest that in SSA, a geographical condition has contributed to the persistence of poverty as it makes the provision of the required infrastructure difficult. In addition, however, poor policies (such as villagization in Tanzania in the 1970s) did not help, while the institutional framework for addressing rural development issues remains inadequate in most cases.

In contrast with SSA, Kawagoe suggests that Northeast Asia has basically established a more equitable distribution of income than SSA and other developing regions, largely a consequence of agrarian reforms pursued at the beginning of the post-war period. He discusses the institutional features of rural communities in Northeast Asia by examining the mode of rural economic organizations, activities and communal rules. He also looks at income distribution and poverty alleviation measures. Kawagoe further considers how rural development measures such as human capital development, public agricultural research and rural infrastructure investment have contributed to the region's economic growth, labour supply, exports and food supply. From a comparative perspective, Kawagoe suggests that while Asian rural production operates within a structure of collectivist input arrangements and the harnessing of individualized output, the reverse is supposedly the case in SSA where individuals make input decisions and whole communities share in the output. The issue of whether communalism is the bane of rural production in SSA obviously requires a further careful study.

Anne Booth's chapter on Southeast Asia effectively complements the discussion on Northeast Asia as it seeks to draw out differences between the two regions. Drawing attention to the considerable heterogeneity within each region, she explores the growth and distributional experiences of the major agricultural economies of Southeast Asia in order to bring out both the differences within the region and the differences between Southeast Asia and other parts of East Asia. There is no doubt that agricultural productivity and rural production have been far higher in East Asia than in SSA, although the rate of growth in the former has slowed considerably since the mid 1980s. One of the critical explanations for this relative performance can be found in East Asia's greater attention to the use of higher-yielding varieties of specific crops in appropriate bio-physical conditions. The 'East Asian experiences' cannot be regarded as a universal success story, however, as the record of agricultural and rural development policies is a very mixed one, producing both successes and failures.

In terms of policies and institutions for agricultural development, there has been considerable variation across countries and over time in the region. While public interventions and direct support may be observed for specific crops in different countries, it is difficult to observe a much more generalized approach to state intervention for rural production. Thus, she argues that no country in Southeast Asia can claim to have pursued an integrated rural development policy as such. Rather, they have adopted an uncoordinated bundle of crop-specific policies that have varied considerably over time.

Notwithstanding this, the rapid agricultural growth of the 1970s, as well as the subsequent process of industrialization, definitely led to substantial reduction in poverty levels while producing a mixed picture for income inequalities in the region with considerable variation in the Gini coefficient across and within countries and over time. Booth discusses in detail trends in income distribution and inequality across sectors and regions by examining the pattern and growth rates of productivity, the distribution of wealth, and the incidence of poverty. The slowdown in the growth of agricultural production did not lead to lower incomes overall as the rural economies underwent a structural change to accommodate more off-farm activities.

By evaluating the impact of various reform programmes such as land reform with its effect on land titling, and the structural adjustment and affirmative action programmes, she also considers how accelerated growth and structural transformation affected poverty and inequality. Her literature survey suggests strong evidence confirming the importance of access to land as a determinant of rural poverty. She concludes that broader, economy-wide policies can play a crucial role in raising rural incomes, while the results of targeted poverty-reduction programmes have been mixed throughout the region. Despite the serious setback in the poverty profile in countries affected by the recent financial crisis, such as in Indonesia, the poverty trends are much more positive in Southeast Asia than in SSA.

References

Ali, A. 1995. 'The challenges of poverty alleviation in sub-Saharan Africa'. Paper presented at the World Congress of the International Economic Association, Tunis, December.

Amsden, A.H. 1994. 'Why isn't the whole world experimenting with the East Asian model to develop?: Review of *The East Asian Miracle*'. *World Development*, vol. 22, no. 4: 627–33.

Calvo, G.A. 1998. 'Capital flow volatility: Issues and policies'. Paper presented at the Plenary Session, AERC Biannual Research Workshop, Nairobi, December 1998.

Chang , H.J. 1998. 'Korea: The misunderstood crisis'. *World Development*, vol. 26, no. 8.

Chang, Ha-Joon, Gabriel Palma and D. Hugh Whittaker. 1998. 'The Asian crisis: Introduction'. *Cambridge Journal of Economics*, 1998, 22: 649–52.

Collier, P. 1994. 'The marginalization of Africa'. Mimeo. Centre for the Study of African Economies, University of Oxford, Oxford.

Collier, P. and J.W. Gunning. 1997. 'Explaining African economic performance'. Mimeo. Centre for the Study of African Economies, University of Oxford.

Corsetti, G., P. Posenti and N. Roubini. 1998. 'What caused the Asian currency and financial crisis? Part I and II'. Mimeo.

Ellis, S. 1996. *Africa Now: People, Policies and Institutions*. London: James Currey; Paris: Heinemann.

Goldstein, M. 1998. 'The Asian financial crisis: Origins, policy prescriptions and lessons'. Paper presented at the Plenary Session, AERC Biannual Research Workshop, Nairobi, December 1998.

Harris, L. 1998a. 'The dynamics of globalization: Eight sceptical theses'. Paper presented at the UNU-AERC Conference. Tokyo, 3–4 August.

Harris, L. 1998b. 'Something fundamental'. Paper presented at the Plenary Session, AERC Biannual Research Workshop, Nairobi, December 1998.

Kane, E. and R. Rice. 1998. 'Bank runs and banking policies: Lessons for African policy makers'. Paper presented at the Plenary Session, AERC Biannual Research Workshop, Nairobi, December 1998.

Kindelberger, C. 1996. *Maniacs, Panics and Crashes*, Third edition. London and Basingstoke: Macmillan.

Kregel, J.A. 1998. 'Derivatives and global capital flows: Applications to Asia'. *Cambridge Journal of Economics*, vol. 2: 667–92.

Kwon, J. 1994. 'The East Asian challenge to neo-classical orthodoxy'. *World Development*, vol. 22, no. 4: 635–44.

Lall, S. 1994. 'The East Asian miracle study: Does the bell toll for industrial strategy'. *World Development*, vol. 22, no. 4: 645–54.

Miller, V. 1998. 'The double drain with a cross-border twist: More on the relationship between banking and currency crises'. *American Economic Review*, vol. 88, no. 2 (May).

Miller, M. and Pongsak Luangaram. 1998. 'Financial crisis in East Asia: Bank runs, asset bubbles and antidotes'. *National Institute Economic Review*, no. 165, July.

Minsky, H. 1978. 'A theory of systematic fragility'. In Edward Altman and Alan Sametz, eds., *Financial Crises: Institutions and Markets in a Fragile Environment*. New York: Wiley International.

McKinnon, R. and P. Huw. 1998. 'International overborrowing: A decomposition of credit and currency risks'. *World Development*, vol. 26, no. 7: 1267–82.

McNeill, D. and H. Bøckman. 1998. 'Introduction to the special section of viewpoints on the Asian Financial Crisis'. *World Development*, vol. 26, no. 8: 1529–33.

Page, J. 1994. 'The East Asian miracle: An introduction'. *World Development*, vol. 22, no. 4: 615–25.

Perkins, D.H. 1994. 'There are at least three models of East Asian development'. *World Development*, vol. 22, no. 4: 655–61.

Pomerleano, M. 1998. 'The East Asian crisis and corporate finances: The untold micro story'. Mimeo.

Radelet, S. and J. Sachs. 1998. 'The East Asian financial crisis: Diagnosis, remedies and prospects'. *Brookings Paper on Economic Activity*, No. 1.

Rodrik, D. 1994. 'King Kong meets Godzilla: The World Bank and the East Asian Miracle'. In *Miracle or Design*, Overseas Development Council Policy Essay No. 11, Washington, D.C.

Stiglitz, J. 1998. 'Macroeconomic dimensions of the East Asian crisis'. In *Financial Crisis and Asia*. CEPR Conference Report No. 6.

Stiglitz, J. 1998. 'More instruments and broader goals: Moving towards the post-Washington Consensus'. The 1998 WIDER Annual Lecture, Helsinki, January 1998.

Stiglitz, J. and A. Weiss. 1981. 'Credit rationing in markets with imperfect information'. *American Economic Review*, 71: 393–410.

United Nations. 1997. 'Food security in Africa in the context of the World Food Summit'. An Issues Note, Sixth Meeting of the Panel of High-Level Personalities on Africa Development. United Nations, New York, 13–14 March.

UNCTAD, 1998. 'International financial instability and the East Asian crisis'. *Trade and Development Report 1998*. New York and Geneva: UN Conference on Trade and Development.

Woo-Cummings, M. 1996. 'The political economy of growth in East Asia: A perspective on the state, market and ideology'. In M. Aoki, H. Kim and H. Okuno-Fujiwara, eds., *The Role of Government in East Asian Economic Development.* Oxford: Clarendon Press.
World Bank. 1994. *The East Asian Miracle: Economic Growth and Public Policy.* A World Bank Research Report. Oxford and New York: Oxford University Press.
World Bank. 1998. 'The challenge of globalization for Africa'. Paper for Dakar Conference.

Chapter 2

Comparative Institutional Analysis: Sub-Saharan Africa and East Asia

Machiko Nissanke and Ernest Aryeetey

In many developing countries, there is a considerable gap between policies as designed to achieve certain objectives and the institutional environments for policy implementation. This gap is wider in sub-Saharan Africa, in particular, as there are severe problems and bottlenecks in the way policies are formulated and then implemented, which have been exacerbated by high uncertainty, lack of information and the policy makers' bounded rationality. Yet, to ensure efficacy of policy measures, policy formulation and design must explicitly allow for the specificity of the implementation context. The issue of transferability of development models or relevance of development experiences from other regions should be examined in the light of these conditions and environments. How to build appropriate institutions and social capacity over time to implement economic policies effectively is another equally critical question to be kept in the forefront in examining 'relevant experiences'.

The growing acknowledgement of the reality of the importance of the policy context has been matched by two new developments in the discipline of development economics: a) the formation of *endogenous growth models* in theoretical and empirical literature; and b) a growing application of *institutional economics*, pioneered by Coase, North and Williamson among others, as an analytical framework for understanding the process of economic development and reform.

Framework for Analysis – Institutional Economics

Explicitly allowing for the path-dependent nature of economic growth, the endogenous growth literature attempts to explain the cross-country difference in aggregate economic performance in terms of initial endowments, policies and institutional variables, in addition to conventional variables such as factor inputs and productivity growth.

While an empirical verification of the importance of institutional variables rests largely on hypothesis testing through regression analyses in this first group of literature, institutional economics embraces an interdisciplinary and historical approach to the analysis of institutional features and structures of economies. It draws our attention to the critical role that different institutions and organizations play in determining economic performance. Locating the micro-foundations of economies in the institutional environments and organizational governance structures, and viewing the development process as the evolution of institutions, it stresses the centrality of dynamics and evolution to an understanding of economics (Toye, 1995).

Within this alternative framework to the conventional neoclassical equilibrium analysis, the sources of the inefficient resource allocation and the low-growth path of an economy can be identified with its inability to transform institutional structures in response to new technological and market opportunities. Under such circumstances institutions could become critical constraints to economic performance. In a more dynamic and adaptive institutional environment, institutions can play a major role in reducing uncertainty and transaction costs and in promoting the acquisition of knowledge and technology. Thus, institutional economics is increasingly seen to offer a coherent account of institutional changes necessary for economic development, and hence a set of tools to inform institutional design and policy alternatives.

There are two schools of institutionalism in economics: the old institutional economics and the new institutional economics (Harriss et al., 1995; Stein, 1995). The old institutional economics rejects the neoclassical assumption of rational-maximizing atomistic agents and takes organizations and entities, operating in a complex historically specific environment of social, economic and legal institutions, as a unit of analysis. It views economic systems as having evolved out of adjustments to existing institutions, provoked by technical change (Harriss et al., 1995).

In contrast, the new institutional economics adopts the neoclassical choice theoretical approach for the starting point of its microeconomic analysis. It does criticize the neo classical model, however, for failing to include the role of transaction costs in exchange or to explain the nature of institutions in supporting the formation and operation of markets, minimizing transaction costs, and reducing uncertainty.[1] In the new institutional economics, institutions are seen to be created and refined to deal with market failures, imperfect and costly information, and the agency and incentive problems. From this perspective, Bates (1995) argues that institutions provide the mechanisms whereby rational individuals can transcend social dilemmas.

Importantly, institutional economics views both market and state as one of many institutions that shape patterns of economic activity and recognizes the existence of state failure as well as market failure as part of the general occurrence of institutional failures. As we have witnessed over recent decades, the conventional academic and policy debate has often been governed by sharply dichotomous approaches to the role of the state and the market in resource allocation and in the resolution of market failures and imperfections. This trait is still evident in the study of the East Asian Miracle, which nonetheless signifies, in some crucial aspects, a noticeable departure from the official positions taken by the World Bank in the 1980s.

In contrast, institutional economics recognizes that neither state nor market is invariably the best way to organize the provision of goods and services. As Bates

[1] Transaction costs include the costs of search, screening, monitoring and enforcement; of negotiation; of transfer of property rights; and of coordination and safeguarding (Coase, 1992).

(1995: 36) notes, '[v]iewed from the perspective of the new institutionalism, this debate (i.e., state or market) appears impoverished. For the new institutionalism highlights the role of institutions that are neither fully centralised, as is the state, or fully decentralised as is the market'.

Market Enhancing View as Applied to East Asian Economic Development

Parallel to the new surge of interest among development economists in the New Institutional Economics, a similar view on this question has been advanced by the recent collective attempts to redefine and identify the role of government in East Asian economic development, following immediately on *The East Asian Miracle* (Aoki et al., 1996; Ishikawa 1996; Hayami, 1996; Yanagihara, 1997). The new approach is referred to as 'the market enhancing view' as opposed to the traditional contrasting views of the role of the government, i.e., the 'market friendly view' and the 'developmental state view'.[2]

The *market enhancing view* emphasizes the interplay between institutions and markets, recognizing the role of institutions in supporting the market deepening process in East Asian economic development. Instead of viewing the role of government and that of markets as mutually exclusive substitutes, the emerging perspective is one of complementarity between the two for the resolution of market failures and coordination problems. One of the critical roles of government is indeed identified as enhancing market functioning and mechanisms (Aoki et al., 1996).

Here, each economy is explicitly viewed as a system of interdependent institutions, and the government is regarded as a coherent and endogenous cluster of these institutions, which, together with the private sector, constitute an economic system. Private agents and institutions as productive units such as industrial firms comprise the core of this economic system, the evolution of which proceeds primarily with the enhancement of organizational capabilities of firms and the expansion and deepening of inter-firm relationships. Markets are where coordination among decisions made by private agents should take place. The functioning of the system depends on the productive and organizational capacities of its constituent economic agents and the institutional arrangements governing the relationships among them.

The process of institutional development and learning, i.e., the strengthening of organizational capabilities of economic agents and market deepening, is explicitly recognised as one of the critical aspects of economic development. Market deepening is interpreted here as the process of intensification of interactive interrelationships among agents and institutions, as individual agents undergo their own organizational evolution. It involves the development of institutional arrangements for network relationships among agents. This perception of markets is similar to that found in the

[2] Yanagihara (1996) presents an 'economic system approach', distinct from the 'market enhancing approach' advanced by Aoki. Though there are subtle differences between the two new approaches, they both emphasize the importance of institutional arrangements and organizational characteristics in shaping the path of economic development. Therefore, in our discussion below, both are treated as one approach broadly conforming to perspectives of institutional economics.

general institutional economics literature and, hence, conceptually different from the perspective that underlies the conventional neoclassical paradigm. In the latter, individual agents merely respond to the prevailing incentive structure embedded mostly in relative price signals through competitive market interfaces in their utility maximizing efforts.

Private institutions are viewed as having comparative advantages in their flexible ability to provide appropriate incentives and to process locally available information. They are potentially able to respond to market failures by making the changes in institutional arrangements and organizational coordination that allow them to internalize externalities, risks and decisions. In this set-up, the prime role of government policy in relation to these agents/institutions and markets is to facilitate and promote this process of private sector coordination, and to shape the institutional environment. 'The government could act to complement the market mechanism, rather than as a substitute to the latter' (Aoki et al., 1996: 1), wherein joint coordination by both the government and the private sector could ensure farsighted cooperation among institutions through risk- and information-sharing.

In this interpretation of East Asian economic development, economic performance is explicitly treated as the outcome of interactions among different (both economic and non-economic) public and private institutions. There is a great convergence of understanding the development process between this approach and that taken by the institutional economics reviewed above.

African Policy Debate and Comparative Institutional Analysis

In the context of the development policy debate applied to sub-Saharan Africa, there has long been a tendency to attribute the cause of the region's poor development performance, exclusively, *either* to the historically evolved unequal relations with the West, *or* to the large-scale prevalence of government policy failure.

Naturally, we must caution that it is difficult to place the economic policies that African countries pursued soon after independence within the general framework. While they all seemed to have the common goal of accelerating the pace of economic growth and development, they tended to diverge on such issues as the role of the state, the degree of openness that could be accommodated, the desirable pattern of investments (i.e., investments in social services versus economic services), government–private sector relations, etc. The fact that irrespective of the approach used, the long-term results were not very dissimilar suggests that the failure is the outcome of a wrong mix of policies, institutions, external environments and societal preparedness.

Nonetheless, the gravity of opinion has over time shifted generally towards a diagnosis that failure of the African state is the chief culprit (Adam and O'Connell, 1997). Reflecting this sentiment, Elbadawi and Ndulu (1995) conclude that 'SSA has been more severely impacted by adverse external shocks but it has also failed to deliver a growth enhancing policy environment—be it at the economic level or in terms of stable and effective governance structure'.

In the 1980s, at the time of the external financial crisis and the surrounding discussion about the conditionality attached to the structural adjustment loans, the predominant view was that at the root of African problems were the *dirigiste* economic policies. However, faced with the 'slowness' of expected supply responses of private agents to new liberalized and deregulated policy environments of the donor-sponsored structural adjustment programmes, the recent debate has acquired a much needed subtlety. Indeed, academics and policy makers alike, in and out of Africa, have to climb a rather steep learning curve to realize what is the best way to address Africa's development challenge. Along this learning curve, the aid relationship between the donor community and African countries has evolved, as Adam and O'Connell (1997) note, from the 'capital shortage' diagnosis in the 1960s and 1970s, to the 'policy failures' diagnosis in the 1980s, and finally to the 'institutional failures' diagnosis in the 1990s.

Reflecting this trend, a body of literature has just begun to emerge that looks at the situation in a more comprehensive framework than was previously done, by attempting to explain Africa's economic performance in this institutional perspective, encompassing such aspects as the quality of public and private economic institutions, particular governance structures (or polity), and the extent of social capital or civic engagement (Aron, 1997).

Our discussion above points to the need for detailed empirical research to examine different development experiences in Asia and Africa in the *comparative institutional perspective*. In particular, the different outcomes of economic policies in the two regions can be analysed in terms of the capacity and possibility of the respective economic systems and their institutions and organizations to: a) resolve not only coordination and market failures but institutional failures; and b) coordinate activities so as to expand the production possibility frontier.

Objectives and Structure of the Framework Chapter

The objective of this framework chapter is to set the tone for the subsequent chapters by: 1) presenting several key analytical concepts of institutions for our comparative analysis and main features of institutions found in East Asian economies; and 2) summarizing some critical issues emerging from the existing literature regarding the interrelationships between institutions, policies and development in sub-Saharan Africa. Because so many heterogeneous institutions are involved in determining a trajectory of economic development, given its scope, this chapter will confine its analysis and discussion to two institutions, i.e., markets and governments, and the relationships between them. Through our discussion we hope to delineate the critical differences in the government–private agents relationships in East Asia and sub-Saharan Africa, focusing on institutional arrangements, and governance structures and mechanisms.

The remainder of this chapter is structured as follows: The next section examines and discusses several concepts useful for comparative institutional analysis in the light of East Asian experiences. These include: institutional environments and organizational governance structures; markets, evolution of markets and market failures; the roles of government, the nature of the state/government and its failures; and governance structures and mechanisms.

Then, after accounting for external environments (i.e., the nature, forms and extent of international links of African countries), we delineate the main characteristics of key economic and civic institutions in SSA (governments, financial institutions and private agents, private firms, and households), and the forms and nature of their interactions. Finally, we offer concluding remarks and a further research agenda for comparative studies.

Institutions and Development: Analytical Concepts and East Asian Experiences

Institutions are defined in institutional economics as regulatory systems comprising formal rules and laws as well as informal conventions and norms of behaviour, which in combination constrain and govern agents' behaviour and their interactions.[3] Therefore, institutions condition and structure opportunities and incentives in human exchanges to ensure individual compliance with collective decisions through appropriate incentives and sanctions. Largely influenced by polities, institutions are seen to serve as mechanisms and means to deal with a whole set of market failures (e.g., public goods, externalities, wedge between social and private benefits/returns, etc.), and to reduce transaction and information costs and uncertainties.

Institutional Environment and Governance Structure

Organizations, i.e., individual agents, firms, collective bodies such as employers' organizations and labour unions, can be also regarded as part of institutions, since they provide sets of rules governing the relationships both among their members and between members and non members (Nabli and Nugent, 1989). Some authors, however including North (1990, 1995), define organizations separately from institutions, as ongoing interest groups bound by common purpose to assure the perpetuation of certain institutional structures. According to this view, institutional arrangements create the framework, but collective action takes place within organizations.

The close symbiotic relationships and inter-dynamics between institutions and organizations are increasingly recognized by all as among the critical forces for social change. Thus, distinct institutional arrangements can shape organizational behaviour, while alternative sets of organizational responses and modes may affect institutions (Harriss et al., 1995). Indeed, organizational and institutional innovations constitute an important element of technological progress that engenders economic growth. A dynamically evolving economy, taking advantage of new market and technological

---

[3] In the literature of institutional economics, several definitions of institutions are given, broadly depending on whether they are approached from a behavioural perspective or a rules perspective (Nabli and Nugent, 1989).

opportunities, is likely to be constantly subject to these innovations. Thus, many institutionalists emphasize the role of organizational coordination relative to market coordination in responding to a series of market and coordination failures.

In contrast, a stagnant economy is more likely to be characterized by structural and transition failures of its institutions and organizations. Under such conditions, the economy is, as a rule, impaired by high transaction cost institutions, and agents are encouraged to be driven by bounded rationality and opportunism, which in turn produce instability and inefficiency (Khan 1995). Thus, North (1995: 9) notes:

> statist regulation, ill-defined property rights and other constraints restrict rather than stimulate economic activity. These conditions result in rent-seeking and redistribution, not rising productivity. Organisations that operate within the Third World institutional frameworks are not inefficient; they are efficient at making a society more unproductive.

Needless to say, institutions and organizations are constantly exposed to both domestic and external regional and global conditions. How an economy is integrated into the international economic system has a critical bearing on the evolutionary path of institutions and organisations. In addition to the usual channels of external trade and financial flows, such factors as geopolitics and politics surrounding foreign aid, strategic positions taken by multinational corporations and offshore financial institutions have all affected and even shaped domestic institutional and organizational structures. At the same time, as Woo-Cummings (1995) suggests in relation to the economies in Northeast Asia, the manner of articulation between the domestic and external societies tells us much about the efficacy of the state in restructuring the domestic society. Equally, it is well acknowledged that Southeast Asian economies have greatly benefited from the regional dynamism developed over the last two decades or so. Foreign institutions and organizations such as multinational corporations, offshore financial institutions and overseas Chinese business communities are known to be active agents in deciding directions and outcomes of economic activities in those economies.

Now, for our comparative institutional analysis, the conceptual line drawn by Williamson (1995) between a macro analytic perspective and a micro analytic perspective may be most pertinent and attractive. Using the two-part definition proposed earlier by Davis and North (1971), Williamson makes a useful distinction between the concept of *institutional environment* and institutional arrangement, which is referred to as the *institutions of governance:*

> Institutional environment is the set of fundamental political, social, legal ground rules that establishes the basis for production, exchange and distribution. ... An institutional arrangement is an arrangement between economic units that governs the ways in which these units can cooperate and/or compete.

On the one hand, the institutional environment is regarded as a background condition and can be analysed in the macro analytical perspective. On the other hand, the micro analytic approach to the institutions of governance is particularly useful in examining critical aspects of intra- and inter-institutional relationships in terms of governance structures and mechanisms, wherein the economic theories of agency, contract and incentives can be ingeniously applied. In this chapter, 'institutions' are broadly defined to include both aspects of institutional environments and organizational governance structures. We examine below several concepts of key institutions with frequent reference to the East Asian economic development experience.

Markets

In the neoclassical economic model, markets are seen as a realm where rational utility-maximizing atomistic individual agents interact in exchange of goods and services. It is assumed that while coordination takes place centrally and instantaneously in the minds of an abstract Walrasian auctioneer (the 'invisible hand'), this instantaneous process of relative price adjustments is to be accomplished in an extremely decentralized manner in the absence of such a coordinator. Institutions are exogenously given to the pricing system, which is viewed as the main coordinating mechanism, and exchanges involve no transaction costs. It is claimed that markets free from distortions will produce Pareto efficient prices and resource allocation. Structural adjustment programmes and the 'market-friendly view' of states rest their central reform blueprints on this premise of markets.

In contrast, institutional economics—old and new—sees markets as broad institutional structures and arrangements that support and govern the process of exchange with an aim of minimizing transaction costs.[4] Coase (1992: 717) notes that 'what are traded on the market are not physical entities, but the rights to perform certain actions and the rights which individuals possess are established by the legal system.... As a result, the legal system will have a profound effect on the working of the economic system....' This gives rise to the concept of efficient property rights, since the institutional setting that governs the exchange process, including an appropriate system of property rights, becomes an important prerequisite for the efficient functioning of markets.[5] The efficient system of property rights is the one that results in minimizing transaction costs for market operation.

Another important departure from the Walrasian world is an explicit recognition that real markets are institutionalized in environments characterized by imperfect, costly and incomplete information, and that players in real markets are not atomistic, fully informed individuals, which could ensure an outcome of perfect competition. An analysis of market structures with unequal distribution of market power, then, becomes important for our understanding of market operations. Markets also require appropriate governance mechanisms and arrangements to prevent agency problems arising out of opportunistic behaviour such as moral hazard and adverse incentives.

---

[4] Stiglitz (1989) also defines markets as an important set of institutions.

[5] In a similar vein, old institutionalists define markets as social institutions that structure, organize and legitimate contractual agreements and the exchange of property rights.

Evolution of markets as institutions Further, as social institutions, markets evolve and transform over time as increasing specialization and division of labour proceed. North (1989) notes this evolution of markets as a movement from personal exchange towards impersonal exchange of modern economies. Personal exchange involves local trade where specialization and division of labour are extremely limited and where individuals often engage in repeated dealings among themselves in a geographically and socially confined community setting. The measured transaction costs are low, because transactions are governed by social codes and norms with minimum monitoring and enforcement costs.[6] Personal exchange then evolves into limited impersonalized exchange that involves some long distance and cross-cultural trade. This type of exchange requires governance mechanisms such as kinship links, bounding, the exchange of hostages or merchant codes of conduct.

Finally, there emerges the advanced impersonal exchange of modern economies, which requires third-party enforcement rules and other elaborate institutional structures to reduce transaction costs with effective formal systems of monitoring and mechanisms of enforcing contracts and property rights. An extensive information network that can provide market participants timely and comprehensive information is another critical prerequisite for market development. For markets to operate efficiently, access to information should not be discriminatory, and the rules governing market operations should be transparent and comprehensible to all market participants.

However, North (1989 and 1990) notes that an economy does not necessarily graduate automatically from the first stage of personalized exchange towards the modern impersonal mode of exchange. From a perspective of institutional economics, 'markets require more than simply the absence of any hindrances to individual maximisation decisions. Markets require an institutional structure that supports the exchange process' (Stein, 1995: 116). To support the process of market transformation, an appropriate institutional environment and governance structure should be developed to reduce uncertainties and transaction costs.

The history of commerce illustrates how this requirement led to the formation and rise of city states initially, and nation states later on, that were capable of specifying property rights and enforcing contracts (North, 1989, 1990). Institutional structures of markets must also evolve with minimum *transformation* costs to assist the process of market expansion and deepening.[7] Thus, Stein (1995: 116) notes the need for policies of institution building that 'will expedite the transformation of type one and two markets into a third type, which would assist in the expansion of growth and accumulation'. The transformation costs are often determined by the nature of the state and its relationship with the society governed, as discussed in the case of sub-Saharan Africa.

---

[6] See Nissanke and Aryeetey (1998) for measured transaction costs for informal finance in sub-Saharan Africa.

[7] Here, we define transformation costs in relation to market transformation, as costs involved in transforming the form and nature of modes of market exchanges. Thus, they are different from those given by North (1990: 6). North's transformation costs are referred to the traditional production costs of capital, labour, technology and natural resources.

Furthermore, in developing economies, where a modern institutional structure was superimposed on a traditional society, informal market institutions and formal modern institutions tend to coexist side by side. This condition often results in an extreme form of market fragmentation and segmentation with few effective linkages among them. To address this kind of low-equilibrium situation, the institutional environment including the polity and social norms and codes, which works in favour of perpetuating fragmentation and segmentation, has to be analysed in depth. As a part of policy actions, integrative measures designed to overcome market fragmentation may be considered for fostering market development and deepening.[8]

Market failures The discussion above leads us to consider the cases and sources of market failures. In our view, there are three kinds of market failures that require a different set of policy actions: 1) market failures associated with early stages of development, which take the form of missing and incomplete markets and market-supporting institutional infrastructure; 2) market failure associated with diffuse externalities and public goods arguments; and 3) market failure caused by incomplete and costly and asymmetric information. Stiglitz (1989) asserts that identifying the precise source of each type of market failure is of great importance for devising an appropriate policy action.

As Aoki et al. (1996) note, there are noticeable differences among economists in their perceptions of the scale of market failures observed in practice and the ability of different institutions to resolve market failures. The 'developmental state view' (e.g., Amsden, 1989; Wade 1990) defines market failures in relation to specific development goals set by the government rather than in relation to 'Pareto' optimal efficient allocation of resources. This view takes the position that market failures in developing economies are pervasive indeed and government could play a critical role in overcoming the problem by adopting proactive interventionist policies to accelerate the process of late industrialization. Thus, Amsden (1989:14) argues that 'economic expansion depends on state intervention to create price distortions that direct economic activity toward greater investment'. The emphasis is on the trade-off between short-term allocative efficiency and long-run dynamic efficiency, with the acknowledgement market-determined prices are not appropriate as signals for enhancing dynamic efficiency.

It is well emphasized in their original writings that the likelihood of success or failure of intervention rests critically on the quality and forms of the intervention. However, policy prescriptions put forward by some proponents of this view appear to be based on a rather naive claim that the presence of market failures by itself provides a justification for government intervention and that government can act as a benevolent and omni competent institution well suited to serve public interests with its developmental motivation.

The 'market-friendly view' is more sceptical of the ability of government intervention to produce a positive outcome and proposes that the role of government

[8] See Nissanke and Aryeetey (1998) for an analysis of the nature and scale of fragmentation observed in financial markets in sub-Saharan Africa.

should be confined to the 'minimalist', since a danger of government (state) failure is much more prevalent. Government intervention is viewed as a most damaging source of distortion to the market mechanisms. The third approach, proposed as an alternative to these opposing views, has been gathering a much needed acceptance in recent years. In reality, '[w]e need to recognise both the limits and strengths of markets, as well as the strengths, and limits, of government interventions at correcting market failures' (Stiglitz, 1989: 202). One of these recent attempts to take up this question further is the 'market enhancing view' advanced by Aoki et al. (1996).

As discussed earlier, the market-enhancing view emphasizes the complementarity between market and state (or private sector institutions and public sector institutions) in resolving market failures and coordination problems. It recognizes that under competitive environments, markets have comparative advantages in quickly and flexibly responding to changing conditions. First of all, markets are equipped with built-in self-regulating features such as free entry and exit. Second, private agents have better access to detailed local information.

Further, this approach points out that private institutions have the potential to respond to emerging market failures through non-market solutions such as intra-firm coordination and control or hierarchy on the strength of their organizational adaptability and flexibility. The approach recognizes that the ability of private firms to find such non-market solutions is severely limited in developing economies, however, and market failures in these countries are far more prevalent because of incomplete and missing markets and inadequate institutional environments.

Since economic development is viewed as a process of system changes, this new approach singles out coordination problems, among all other forms of market failure, as the most critical for the system's capacity to evolve dynamically. This is because coordination among firms becomes of paramount importance in determining an economy's evolutionary path when investment decisions are being made. Coordination failure arises because of complementarity among industries, economies of scale, and incomplete information available to private firms about new market and technological opportunities. While it is conceivable for coordination failures to be resolved through decentralized experiments by firms, private market and non-market coordination may involve high transaction costs for negotiation, monitoring and enforcement, particularly when institutional environments and private sector institutions are not sufficiently developed.

It is also noted that the presence of coordinating externalities does not always imply and justify policy activism and that government coordination is not always superior to private coordination, since governments also face information and incentive problems, as discussed below. This school of thought (Aoki et al., 1996) emphasizes that state activism per se does not contribute to economic growth. However, East Asian experiences show that governments' positive involvement in the coordination process, if skilfully conducted, could reduce transaction costs and hence enhance the coordination capacity of private institutions. Above all, government action is viewed as 'more credible because it can assure the credibility of commitments made not only by itself but also by other economic agents through its powers of enforcement'.

The complementarity between actions taken by government and those by private sector institutions, illustrated in the example above, is the central thesis of the market enhancing view. According to this view, government actions and policies should be directed at improving the ability of private institutions to solve coordination problems and to overcome other market failures. It is important to note, however, that this market-enhancing role of government is viewed as contingent upon the stage of development. In other words, a boundary for government activism and intervention depends on the level of economic development. Evidently, market-enhancing interventions are most useful when late industrializing countries are eager to catch up. Thus, Gerschenkron (1962) noted that the state could compensate for lack of prerequisites for industrialization. As an economy matures, private institutions develop, appropriate institutional environments are established and the importance of this role of government recedes.

Now, whether or not governments could indeed play such a vital role for economic development depends crucially on the capability of government, the nature of the state, and the interrelationships between government and private institutions, including governance mechanisms and structures characterizing their relationships. The institutional context and organisational structure within which government operates is itself also increasingly acknowledged as having immense consequences on the efficacy of government policy.

Governments (States)

In the contemporary world, it is the sovereign nation state that is supposed to set an overall institutional and governance framework within which all other institutions operate.[9] However, beyond this broad understanding, the actual roles that the state (government) is supposed to play in economic development have been a controversial issue in the policy debate. The neoclassical school confines the role of government essentially to that of provider of basic public goods and the guarantor of macroeconomic stability and property rights. In addition to these, the regulatory function of government is increasingly seen as critical for efficient market operation carried out otherwise by decentralized private agents and institutions. However, it is argued that government intervention in other forms is bound to generate unproductive rent-seeking activities and the opportunity for predation.

[9] As globalization has proceeded at a gathering pace, however, many political, economic and social issues have to be addressed, beyond the boundary of nation states, at the level of regional and global institutions. Indeed, the recent financial crises epitomize an acute need for credible and effective institutional governance and regulatory mechanisms at the global level.

The Roles of Government

According to the institutionalists, the role of government in economic development is much wider. In addition to its role in specifying and enforcing formal rules, including property rights, contracts and commitments that are not self-enforcing, the state plays a critical role in the support and development of markets and other institutions.[10] In relation to markets, Okuno-Fujiwara (1996) suggests that there are two distinguishable roles for government: market-*sustaining* and market-*guiding*. While these two roles can be executed in a complementary manner, the prime objectives of the two are different:

- *The market-sustaining role* aims to uphold the working of the market by providing proper incentive systems for innovation and R&D.
- *The market-guiding role* aims to help the economy to move in a certain direction by providing incentives and coordinating private activities.

Obviously, the second, guiding, role is more interventionist than the first, sustaining, role. In the first role, government confines its function to encouragement of private innovative activities, but in the second one, government tries to steer the course and pace of economic development through active intervention both in macro resource allocation in favour of designated sectors and in micro corporate strategies by dissemination of vital information. Effective mechanisms, policy instruments and institutional governance structures may differ, depending on which one of these roles governments are expected to play. In short, it is important that policy objectives be clearly set.

Many institutionalists argue further that given the right environment and the capacity of appropriate governance structures, the state can act as the primary agent of institutional innovation and that it has the potential to stabilize and transform other institutions including markets. That is, the state can play the role of a prime institution to promote development, which is similar to the view held by the developmental state proponents. Indeed, East Asian development experiences as such are often cited as historical evidence of 'developmental states', while such states have been difficult to create and sustain in other developing regions in the post independence periods. This gives rise to a number of critical questions for comparative analysis across regions:

- Under which circumstances and conditions can the state act as developmental, i.e., what determines the nature and behavioural patterns of a state?
- Why are government failures so pervasive, preventing government from acting as a prime lagent of development?
- Which intervention mechanisms and policy instruments are most effective to enable government to perform a developmental function?

---

[10] Institutionalists recognize the state as a political institution, often representing the dominant economic interest groups within a nation society.

- Which institutional and governance structures encourage sustainable conditions for survival of developmental states?

We discuss these questions in turn.

The nature of the state One of main arguments of the market-friendly view for minimalist government is that government intervention policies create rents that would certainly propagate unproductive rent-seeking activities, resulting in large-sale government failures.[11] However, one of most striking findings from analysis of East Asian development experiences suggests that this is not always the case and government intervention can, under specific conditions, facilitate economic growth, accelerate the accumulation process and make a positive contribution towards more equitable, growth-sharing patterns of rent distribution. What accounts for the differential outcome from seemingly similar policies? An important clue to this question may be found in the institutional implementation context of policies, namely the nature of the state and the actual governance mechanisms used for rent creation and rent distribution.

Several commonly observed conditions in Japan, Korea and Taiwan have been frequently regarded as characteristics of the so-called East Asian developmental states. These conditions can be summarized as follows:

- Governments are capable of mobilizing support and resources for collective goals of 'catching up': There was a strong national desire to engineer an upward movement in the international system even at the cost of welfare loss in the short run. In short, a strong impetus for catching up has to exist. Thus, Evans (1998) notes that in East Asian economies the sense of a national project of economic development constituted one of the most important collective goods provided by the state.

  These national characteristics are the outcome of historically evolved external conditions such as geopolitics and the way the states have been articulated into international economic systems.[12] They are also undeniably the results of historically conditioned domestic political settlements. At the end of the Second World War, many of the economies were characterized by a relatively egalitarian social structure without a politically powerful dominant economic class. After the post-war land reforms, a relatively low level of inequity

[11] Government failures also result from government coordination failure due to imperfect information or information dilemmas (Aoki et al., 1996).

[12] Woo-Cummings (1996: 338) notes that 'economic growth in East Asia is not culturally determined, but developed out of a particular late-developing regional context at a particular time called the Cold War'. He contrasts the strong East Asian states with the weak Latin American states, where a 'showcase modernity' was created, aimed not at self-sustaining development but at satisfying a set of elite consumption patterns for powerful agrarian interest groups. The insertion of national economies into the international system has been mainly via trade in natural resources, which was characterized by its dependent status.

was observed in wealth distribution, particularly in agricultural landholdings. This initial equitable condition has been largely maintained by the 'associated tendency toward assimilation in educational and income opportunities in the subsequent years' (Aoki et al., 1996).

- Economic policies of governments are effectively run by highly disciplined bureaucrats, who are insulated from political pressures and influences: In these East Asian economies, 'there are both a bureaucracy with the ability to analyse, design, and implement an appropriate economic plan and also the social system and the bureaucratic culture that maintains the moral discipline within the government' (Okuno-Fujiwara, 1996).

  Evans (1998: 66) also concludes that 'a highly capable, coherent economic bureaucracy, closely connected to, but still independent of, the business community, has been an essential institutional prerequisite for successful policy formation and implementation'. Yet, East Asian bureaucracies are by no means perfect and there are a variety of ways to create a coherent bureaucracy. Importantly, however, it has to be supported by a decision making structure that resolves issues of jurisdiction and coordination. The rules and mechanisms governing distribution of economic rents must be performance-based and accountable, as discussed in detail below.

- It is worth noting that the East Asian economies are by no means free from corruption. On the contrary, corruption has been rampant and remains a central concern in these economies. However, corruption in these economies features more in the relationships between politicians and large private business groups than in the forged patron–client relationships between bureaucrats (patrons) and middle- and lower-middle-class interest groups (clients), as observed in other developing regions.[13]

  Overall, it can be claimed in relative terms that in the East Asian economies, there have been several counteracting governing mechanisms in place to prevent rent-seeking activities from shifting the production possibility frontier inwards. Consequently, their economic performances have not been overwhelmed too much by wasteful corruptive activities.

- Motivated private entrepreneurs and institutions are encouraged and fostered to grow and develop by government policies: Entrepreneurs are often provided with both ex ante incentives and ex post renegotiation facilities that allow adjustments for unravelled uncertainties and newly revealed information in the context of a *relation-based* government structure.[14] There are many channels and

[13] Khan (1995) makes a conceptually useful distinction between corruption and clientelism. He notes an example of clientelism affecting the economic performance in patron–client relations in Bangladesh. In the latter, the client bargains for resources on the basis of an organizational ability to disrupt income flows to the patron. Due to weak asset rights owing to limited state enforcement capacity, this results in a loss of resources besides constraining the state to a low level of efficiency.

[14] Okuno-Fujiwara (1996) identifies, in the framework of contract theory, several types of government on the basis of government–private sector relationships: rule-based, relation-based and authoritarian. He suggests that the post-war Japanese government was charac-

> forums such as deliberation councils through which government bureaus and private business representatives exchange and share information about technological best practice and market opportunities and collectively try to find a cooperative outcome. Evans (1998) regards the close business–government ties as 'the *sine qua non* of being able to maintain credibility over time in spite of the policy failures and reversals which must inevitably afflict even the most capable policy makers', Evans (1988: 68). The 'support/performance bargain' has been implemented with 'mutual confidence that predictions and commitments were credible', Evans (1998: 75). Again, it can be noted that government-business relations did not emerge spontaneously in either Korea or Taiwan, but were initially based on the deliberate policy 'synthesis of scepticism and enlistment' (Evans, 1998).

In contrast to developmental states, predatory states are usually characterized by the rationing of *divisible benefits* on the basis of favouritism to buy political support or to appease various interest groups (Bates, 1981, 1983: Teranishi, 1996). Such patron–client relationships are more likely to result in much unproductive rent-seeking activity. Viewing government as a strategic agent maximizing fiscal revenue, Aoki et al. (1996: 17) note that 'whether government chooses to act as a predator or to promote the private sector depends critically on the quality of its tax apparatus.... A revenue-maximising government with a poor tax apparatus will always choose to act as a predator'. Thus, in order to restrain government from acting as a predator on the private sector, it should be equipped with a high-quality tax collection apparatus and an information-processing capability.

With their weak tax base, predatory states try to hold up private agents, i.e., to extract extra income as much as possible from them. Responding to such government behaviour, the private agents refrain from making risky, forward-looking investments. Private firms and rural households have no incentive to carry out investments of their own unless such investments are supported by the government and they are assured that they can keep a substantial portion of returns from undertaking risky investments.[15]

It may be worth presenting a few caveats about some of our oversimplified statements concerning such complicated issues in the domain of political economy. First of all, it should be emphasized that an authoritarian government and a predatory state are not necessarily synonymous, although the two regime concepts are often used interchangeably in the literature. While under an authoritarian regime, private

---

terized by a relation-based bureau-pluralism, which has comparative advantages in the market guiding role. In contrast, a rule-based government system such as found in the United States is superior in the market-sustaining role. He suggests that post-war Japanese industrial policy used government 'management' of competition among private firms with the help of relation-based policy implementation on one hand, and government provision of various incentive mechanisms to realize the intended macroeconomic resource allocation on the other.

[15] We illustrate below how such a low-equilibrium situation has developed in sub-Saharan Africa.

agents are accorded no bargaining power in negotiations, the state can be 'developmental', as many successive East Asian governments are more accurately characterized as successful developmental authoritarian regimes.

Like a relation-based government, an authoritarian government may carry out the market-guiding role rather successfully. However, it is usually not good in its market-sustaining role, as it fails to offer a clearly defined business environment with the guaranteed protection of civil and political rights (Okuno-Fujiwara, 1996). There is always a threat that an autocratic regime may change the rules governing economic activity in one stroke and turn into a predatory state. The difficulty in predicting the political future of some of the repressive regimes in sub-Saharan Africa and Latin America is one factor, among many, that holds back economic development, by increasing uncertainty and dampening incentives for investments in the long run.

Second, East Asian economies are by no means homogeneous in many aspects, including in the nature of the state. Again, there appears to be a critical difference between the Northeast Asian states and the Southeast Asian states, as well as within each subregion. Booth (1995) notes that while in Northeast Asia, the success of the states has been due in considerable measure to the very active guidance provided by government agencies, in Southeast Asia successive governments have found the process of policy reform hampered by the need to appease different constituencies based on different regional, religious or ethnic groups. She suggests the process through which states evolve away from the predatory model to produce an efficient, growth-promoting regime with property rights has not been completed, further giving a verdict for Indonesia, 'the developmental state may in fact be simply a front for a predatory state' (p. 304).[16]

In their analysis of rent distribution mechanisms in Malaysia, Jomo and Gomez (1996) argue that a substantial part of rents created in its industrialization drive has either accrued mainly to foreign investors, or has been instrumental in proliferating political patronage and clientelism. With minimum transparency of the rent allocation process, timber politics, resource politics and land politics have been rampant in many economies of Southeast Asia during the high-growth period.

Governance structures and mechanisms Among all other policy instruments, tax-cum-subsidies and trade policies are commonly used means for coping with various forms of market failures. However, in Northeast Asian economies, a more innovative device was needed to facilitate the catching-up process with the overriding imperative for fast upgrading of production and technology capabilities. In order to alleviate government coordination failures, a main approach adopted by governments of East Asia was to place limits on competition, so as to keep the number of players in each sector to a manageable size (Kim and Ma, 1996).[17]

Kim and Ma (1996) recount how the petrochemical industry was promoted by imposition of strict controls over market entry and technology imports during the early stages of the industry development. At the very outset, it was clearly envisaged

---

[16] This verdict has been most plainly validated by the events that unfolded in Indonesia in 1997–1998.

[17] This approach was particularly characteristic in the Japanese and Korean cases.

that as the industry matured, the government would embark on the gradual process from strict government controls to liberalization.[18] These intervention policies for technology acquisition as well as policy of addressing information problems can be seen as saving transaction costs by changing incentives or enabling coordination and monitoring. Thus, Chang (1994) concludes that state intervention in South Korea reduced transaction costs by enabling the coordination of technology acquisition at a lower cost.

A solution to the other form of government failures, i.e., unproductive rent-seeking activities, was found in the use of *contingent rents* as incentive mechanisms, whereby rent opportunities are created by a set of interventionist policies and these policy-induced economic rents are distributed contingent upon the relative economic performances of private firms.[19] Indeed, this 'performance-based rents' policy was a key instrument for corporate governance and industrial policy in East Asia.[20] Hellmann et al. (1996) argue that if this instrument provides an increasing return to activities that are underprovided in a competitive equilibrium, it is a welfare enhancing policy. While rent transfers realized by a direct subsidies policy would alter the distribution of income without directly altering the incentives of the competing parties, contingent rents provide private firms with incentives for improved performance and induce them to build their reputation.

The policy of *financial restraints* in East Asia is often cited as one of successful examples of contingent rents applied for institution building in the financial sector (Hellmann et al., 1996). It is based on the premise that in the absence of rent opportunities, banks do not have sufficient incentives to provide the socially efficient level of financial services due to information-related problems. The objective of a policy of financial restraint is to create rent opportunities in the private sector through a set of financial policies such as interest rate control, entry regulation and managed competition. The size of rents captured by banks is proportionate to their efforts in expanding their business, i.e., rent opportunities are performance-indexed rewards to banks. Thus, rents create incentives for banks to step up their vigorous

---

[18] Kim and Ma (1996) list the mechanisms for minimizing the possibility of government coordination failures and creating incentives for innovation; these include: contingent and staggered entry through the technology-licensing policy; ensuring economies of scale and avoiding excessive competition; securing favourable terms and conditions for domestic firms in technology transfers; promoting 'unpackaging' of imported technologies; and promoting R&D activities.

[19] Policy induced economic rents are returns in excess of those generated by a competitive market, while contingent rents are the realization of rents contingent upon performance (Aoki et al., 1996).

[20] While *The East Asian Miracle* study claims that distribution of rents in East Asia has been conducted in a highly transparent and well-specified contested framework, others such as Rodrik (1994) emphasize that many of the interventions have been non-uniform, discretionary and firm-specific. An important point to note, however, is that while there is much room for creative flexibility and discretion in policy application vis-à-vis individual firms, the basic rules are laid out clearly as performance-based in a contested framework.

efforts to expand their deposit base and improve their loan portfolio by more diligent monitoring.

Furthermore, given rent opportunities, banks are induced to provide services that are not supplied under perfectly competitive markets. For example, term loans are usually under-supplied, because banks are reluctant to engage in long-term lending due to agency problems, inflation risk and the lack of liquidity that accompanies long-term lending.[21] Once interest rate control reduces the agency problems, however, banks are given incentives to forge a close link with firm-borrowers. Banks may try to build reputational capital by rescuing firms that are viable in the long run. Under such circumstances, banks are more likely to take an active role in corporate governance. Relation-specific capital thus developed between firms and banks could further reduce agency costs related to financial intermediation.

As banks become long-run agents, firms could be induced to adopt long-term business perspectives and the time horizon for firms' investment decisions could be extended. Governments in Japan and Korea are known to have effectively used the financial restraint policy coupled with credit policy as a powerful industrial policy instrument in their heavy industrialization drive. In both countries, since the financial structures of industrial firms were highly leveraged, relational banking activities evolved under this policy environment could serve as a useful instrument for corporate governance and risk management (Nissanke, 1996). Risks facing otherwise vulnerable industrial firms were practically shared and socialized. Thus, under financial restraint, co-insurance schemes and effective governance structures can be established in the tripartite government–industrial firms–banks relationships.

However, it is important to stress the critical difference between the policies of financial repression and financial restraint. On the one hand, financial repression arises under a specific condition, where excessive regulation and controls that undermine competition for efficiency and growth are combined with high and growing inflation. In particular, under a regime of financial repression, governments chronically in a fiscal crisis are prone to extract rents from the private sector: A number of measures such as interest rate controls or high reserve requirements are often viewed as a form of implicit taxation on the domestic financial system, whereby the government with the weak general tax base has access to a readily available source for financing fiscal deficits at low cost.[22]

---

[21] Credit guarantee schemes were established in many countries as mechanisms to manage risks associated with term loans. However, their effectiveness is usually undermined by agency problems. Credit guarantee schemes give rise to moral hazard for both banks and borrowers, as none of these parties engaged in credit relations takes full responsibility for defaults and losses. The tendency is for borrowers to engage in riskier projects, while banks have less incentive to monitor.

[22] Several studies provide estimates of the size of government revenue resulting from financial repression. Giovannini and De Melo (1990) measured the revenue from repression as the difference between the foreign and domestic costs of government borrowing. The unweighted average of 'financial repression tax revenue' thus calculated for 24 countries across the different continents amounted to 2 per cent of GDP for the period of 1974–1987. Chamley and Honohan (1990) included currency tax (seigniorage), reserve requirements and the quasi-tax effects of interest rate ceilings in their measurement of the size of implicit taxation of financial

Under this regime, the household sector doubly loses out due to control on the deposit rate as well as to the inflation tax, the combination of which typically results in highly negative returns to households' financial assets. Borrowers tend to engage in rent-seeking activities in their search for rent transfers created by preferential lending rates and direct credit allocation. Banks are discouraged from engaging vigorously in deposit mobilization and financial intermediation to the private sector and their incentives to build an institutional capacity in liquidity and assets management are severely impaired because of the high financial repression tax imposed on them. Nissanke and Aryeetey (1998) recount how financial system development has been retarded in sub-Saharan Africa under the financial repression regime.

On the other hand, the policy of financial restraints was implemented successfully in stable macroeconomic environments with clearly defined policy objectives to foster the competitiveness and technological capability of domestic industrialists. Under a regime of financial restraints, though similar measures such as low interest rates or entry restrictions were used, government acts to create and distribute rents *within* the private sector. Rent opportunities are first accrued to banks, but eventually rents are distributed and shared within the private sector for higher social benefits. In particular, financial risks are practically shared between the government and banks, as the government does bear inflation risk through sound macroeconomic management while banks are left to bear credit risk through prudent portfolio management. Importantly, under this framework, the government acts as a risk-taking partner at the critical stage of economic development.[23]

This is a clear example of how comparable policies such as interest rate controls and direct credit allocation could produce diverse outcomes. Thus, Hellmann et al. (1996: 169) note, 'The institutional arrangements that are responsible for how rents are created and captured have an important influence on their ultimate efficacy in promoting financial efficiency'. It is, therefore, not surprising to note their cautionary remarks in this regard: 'financial restraint could be badly implemented or corrupted for other purposes and there is a danger for financial restraint turning into financial repression' (p. 196). The policy implementation context—in particular, the governance structure under which policies are carried out and the relationships between the government and the private sector—are so decisive to ensure positive outcome from intervention policies. The actual outcome from policies is essentially contingent upon the government's institutional capacity to set clear policy objectives and to design appropriate governance structures for implementation.

---

intermediation for five African countries. Between 1978 and 1988, explicit and implicit 'financial repression tax' jointly accounted for an average 4 per cent to 7 per cent of GDP in Ghana, Nigeria and Zambia, while for Kenya and Côte d'Ivoire, it was estimated to be close to 2 per cent.

[23] Aoki et al. (1996) note various risk-sharing schemes and institutions that unfolded in postwar Japan. While some of them such as many labour market institutions evolved autonomously, others were created by the government for specific purposes in the general context of facilitating fast growth and industrial restructuring as well as for redistribution objectives.

Apart from this strict prerequisite condition, it should be emphasized that like all other interventionist policies, the policy of financial restraint to create an institutional basis for relational banking is a time-specific instrument, applicable and pertinent only to a particular stage of economic development. Given the path-dependent nature of institutional evolution, financial policies should be evolved in the light of stages of financial market development. In both Japan and Korea, many aspects of financial restraints have been dismantled over the recent years in waves of economic and financial liberalization. Moreover, some of their traditional modes of governance such as relational banking and corporate governance have become increasingly antiquated, and in certain cases, impediments to the new environments and different policy objectives.[24]

Nevertheless, the conceptual distinction between the policy of financial restraint and financial repression, advanced lucidly and forcefully by Hellmann et al. (1996), has made an important contribution to our understanding of the process and mechanisms of economic development in some of the Northeast Asian economies.

Equally, it is important to note that in East Asia, some mechanisms, either autonomously unfolded or policy induced, are in place for redistribution of economic rents to sustain the pattern of shared growth over an extended period. Thus, in addition to the price support policy of the major agricultural crop or standard tax subsidy policies for distribution, Aoki et al. (1996) note the redistribution mechanism referred to as *bureau-pluralism*, whereby economic rents are widely shared within the Japanese society.[25] This has in turn contributed to rapid economic growth through the fast expansion of domestic markets for consumption goods as well as the sustainment of willingness to share both risks and return on the part of private agents.

Institutions and Development in Sub-Saharan Africa: Governments and Private Agents

Most countries in sub-Saharan Africa are still locked into the pattern of international division of labour forced upon them during the colonial period. The weak foundation of their economies can be most vividly illustrated by their modes of international linkages.

External Conditions and International Linkages

African economies in general are uncomfortably heavily dependent for export earnings on a very limited number of primary commodities—unprocessed agricultural

[24] Indeed, many commentators cited one of main factors in the recent banking crisis in the East Asian economies as the relation-based banking practices and corporate governance.

[25] Bureau-pluralism is defined as a mechanism whereby pluralistic interests are protected by the mediation of government bureaucracy. Through this mechanism, quasi-rents acquired through organizational and technological innovation by the advanced and high-productivity sectors are redistributed to backward, low-productivity sectors.

and mineral products—that are vulnerable to externally determined price and volume movements. The export sector often remains an enclave, generating very limited consumption–production linkages in the economies and failing to provide either a stable or growing source of revenue. Exports of manufactured goods represent only about 5 per cent of total exports. Africa's competitiveness in world markets of traditional exports has also declined. As the rate of growth in trade for manufactured goods and services was much faster than that for primary commodities (twice for mining products and four times for agricultural products), Africa's share in world exports fell from 2.4 per cent in 1970 to 1 per cent in 1992.

Moreover, agricultural production in Africa has not benefited from any technological breakthrough such as the green revolution on such a scale as observed in other parts of the world to ensure a minimum level of food security on a sustainable basis. Food imports have risen to the equivalent of one-third of domestic food production in recent decades. Further, the pattern of industrialization in the early post-independence years also created an industrial and manufacturing sector with high import dependence for spare parts, equipment and raw materials. Thus, the import dependence of African economies remains high, while their import capacity has dwindled.

The continuous turbulence in the international economic system in the 1970s and 1980s took a disproportionately large toll on the fragile, low-income African economies. In addition to a series of internal shocks such as the severe droughts of 1973/74 and 1984/85 and the civil strife incessantly inflicted on many parts of the continent, these economies were affected by a series of external shocks: the major oil price increases of 1973 and 1979; the worldwide stagnation and recession following restrictive demand management in the developed countries in the early 1980s; and the collapse of commodity prices and substantial declines in the continent's terms of trade.[26] There were also the steep rise in international interest rates, the capital crunch and the debt crisis of the early 1980s, which ensued in the rapid build-up of Africa's debt overhang.

The increase of Africa's debt burden has resulted in obligations well beyond its capacity to repay on contractual terms. Voluntary capital inflow, both portfolio and foreign direct investment, which had never been of a substantial size, came to an almost complete halt. An option of gaining access to international capital markets as a means of softening the immediate impacts of shocks has become nonexistent because of the sharp fall in creditworthiness of African countries. Many countries turned to the only available source to finance growing balance of payments deficits—official foreign assistance and loans, which were increasingly tied to the implementation of stabilization policies and structural adjustment programmes (SAPs).[27] Access to desperately requested debt rescheduling facilities has also become conditional upon the acceptance of SAPs.

---

[26] See Maizels (1992) for the extent of the terms of trade deterioration for the region in the 1980s.

[27] Africa received 37 per cent of official aid supplied by OECD DAC members in 1993.

Under the prevailing international economic system, African countries were left with no alternative to the implementation of stabilization-cum-adjustment under SAPS. However, serious concerns were raised that adjustment programmes designed and implemented in the context of desperate crisis management of external payments have not given sufficient attention to building the solid institutional capacity indispensable for the continent's long-term development prospects.

The present narrow base for raising fiscal and export revenues also means the continuing implementation of short-run stabilization policies on a perpetual basis, leaving the economies constantly exposed to large external shocks, as primary commodity prices in the world market exhibit not only declining long-term trends but also excessively volatile fluctuations that are detrimental to growth and development. Sub-Saharan African countries have to undertake continual adjustments to their deteriorating, and highly unstable, position in current account of external balance. The scale of adjustment required has often far exceeded the capacity of these economies to absorb volatilities and manage associated high uncertainty and aggregate systemic risks. As Table 2.1 shows, African economies, along with Latin American countries, were characterized by high macroeconomic instability throughout the period of 1970–1990.

Table 2.1 Macroeconomic instability by major world regions

	1970–1990
Developing countries	1.19
Africa	1.22
LAC	1.25
Other LDCs	1.03
OECD	0.26
World	0.99

Notes: The four regions are sub-Saharan Africa, noted as Africa; Latin America and the Caribbean, noted as LAC; North Africa, Middle East and Asia, noted as other LDCs; and OECD member countries. Macroeconomic instability index is calculated on the basis of four indicators: the annual inflation cost measure; the coefficient of variation of the real exchange rate; the total foreign debt to GDP ratio; and the percentage black market premium over the official exchange rate.

Source: Schmidt-Hebbel et al.

Though some improvements are reported to have been achieved in macroeconomic balances in terms of fiscal and monetary indicators in 'adjusting' countries (World Bank, 1994), a viable and sustainable position in balance of payments is much harder to attain. Conditions and prospects facing many countries have actually worsened because of their growing debt servicing burden and much reduced export earning capacity. The failure to diversify export structures and attract foreign direct and portfolio investment flows has left the continent virtually bypassed by the dynamic forces that have swept the international trading and financial systems with the aid of advanced information and telecommunication technology. While most of the African economies have not been directly affected by the global financial crisis by virtue of non-active participation in the international capital market, there is a real danger that Africa will be further marginalized by recent waves of the process of global integration and formation of a new international order.[28]

Government and Public Institutions

Today, many economists have begun to locate a compelling reason for the 'surprising' failure of supply response to market liberalization and economic reforms in Africa in the continent's cumulative institutional impoverishment (Aron, 1996). This diagnosis is probably most readily applied to some distinctive attributes of African governments. To discern the root of the problems, it is necessary to understand how African states have evolved in recent history.

As Brett (1995: 203) notes, the colonial state introduced a distorted set of economic structures that blocked indigenous opportunities for autonomous growth and reinforced many of the regressive characteristics of traditional institutions. The attempts to democratize the state before independence failed because of the non-existence of autonomous political and social structures in civil society. Traditional values and structures survived at the societal level, distorted by their coexistence with the dominant modern system. Modern political and economic institutions were based on monopolistic principles that guaranteed the power of those who controlled the state and marginalized the interests of the great majority. The conditions created during the colonial transition discouraged the development of universal value systems that would support a nationally oriented political and economic order.

Thus, the institutional arrangements at independence were dominated by dualism and monopoly. At independence, the state was structured around the top political leaders in the executive branch who could act as benevolent social guardians (Teranishi, 1996). However, this was soon replaced by authoritarian and highly centralized governments, often led by military officers. Governance structures have evolved in a such manner that the state in Africa has been typically portrayed as autocratic: 'authoritarian in its character with enormous power often concentrated in the person of the President, and yet weak in institutional and administrative capacity, with limited material means (indebted) and little control over peripheral regions in some cases'.[29]

More often than not, private agents/institutions were viewed as nascent, fragile, technologically backward, incapable of creating the dynamism needed for autonomous development. The state was therefore assumed to play a central role in economic development. Economic policies often embedded a strong bias against the private sector and rural farmers. They usually included expropriation of private property; the favoured direct allocations of foreign exchange, trade licenses and subsidized credit to parastatals and rent-seekers; and the very high taxation of the traditional export sector. Generally, it is estimated that in Africa, taxes and tax-like

[28] In the 1980s and 1990s, Africa's share of foreign direct investment to developing countries was under 1 per cent of the estimated total of around $200 billion per annum (Collier, 1994).

[29] This is an extract from Buijtenhuis and Rijinierse, *Democratisation in Sub-Saharan Africa, 1989–92, African Studies Centre Research Report 52, 1993:19.*

distortions have been higher, more widespread and more volatile than elsewhere, if wide-ranging implicit forms of taxation are taken into account (Adam and O'Connell, 1997). These include the tax on exporters induced by the over-valuation of the real exchange rate; financial repression tax; other forms of partial or complete expropriation (such as nominal price controls or monopsony by commodity boards); and the cost of macroeconomic volatility.

The dominance of a small elite in the political process often made the majority, especially in rural areas, de facto disenfranchized. Poor education reduced the worth of the franchise of many people. Many governments have been characterized as being hostage to their narrow urban support base (Collier and Gunning, 1999). Some governments engaged in fiscal profligacy, as the politically-connected poorly-organized private sector forged a 'covenant' with the state to promote the interests of particular factions such as military cliques and ethnic groups (Aron, 1996, 1997). The intensity of controls increased the opportunities for corruption. Furthermore, corruption in Africa is known to be much more decentralized than elsewhere. Clientelism based on the patron-client relationships, as discussed earlier, is reported to have been pervasive in every form of public sector institutions. Though patron–client relationships cannot characterize the entirety of the relationships between economic agents, they are certainly more pronounced where the failure of the state is endemic. Further, many African states are known to have held, if not a hostile, then a non-facilitating attitude to foreign and domestic private business (Aron, 1997).

These centralized, authoritarian governments rapidly became overextended in the light of their limited administrative capacity, with its dysfunctional judicial and regulatory systems. Government offices, including many oversight (monitoring and regulatory) agencies for public sector institutions such as parastatals, have been made ineffective due to political appointments, politically controlled funding, multiple and conflicting objectives, or low morale with few incentive schemes in place. The transparency and accountability of these public institutions and government offices have been minimal, resulting in the lack of effective agencies of restraint on government policies and actions (Collier, 1995). Africa comes in the bottom group in cross-regional comparison in terms of an index of bureaucratic efficiency, which combines lack of corruption and perceived independence of the judiciary, or measures on bureaucratic delays and the enforceability of contracts (Adam and O'Connell, 1997).

Thus, many find that one of the primary causes for Africa's development tragedy is the absence of robust, morally-anchored public institutions, and in particular, the predatory nature of African states. For example, Adam and O'Connell (1997) argue that African governments have sacrificed broad-based economic development for other, more *venal* objectives, as governments that are captive to a favoured group tend to trade growth for transfers and to use discretionary taxation to make transfers to themselves or their supporters. Bates (1991) explains this condition, arguing that a system of discretionary taxes or selective subsidization is highly rationalized at the political level if not at the economic level, as it emerges from the need of governments to buy support. Divisible benefits distributed to finance various costs, discussed earlier, became an increasing burden on public finance in many African states.

Similarly, Collier and Gunning (1999: 64–111) conclude that 'African governments have behaved in ways which are damaging to the long term interests of the majority of their populations because they have served narrow constituencies. They have been damaging partly through "sins of commission", such as agricultural taxation, and partly through "sins of omission", such as a failure to provide adequate infrastructure'. Collier and Gunning (1999) rank the low-income African countries according to three conditions that can be accepted as necessary for growth: a minimum degree of social stability; a minimum degree of macroeconomic stability; and a minimum degree of allocative efficiency. They estimate that 12 per cent of the population in Africa live in conditions of inadequate social order (i.e., without peace); 46 per cent in economies without a minimum adequate macroeconomic environment; and a further 12 per cent in economies without a minimum adequate resource allocation environment. Cumulatively, 70 per cent of African populations live without a minimum adequate social-economic environment.

We believe, however, that it is an over-simplification and naive to describe the African state as typically predatory. The development goals of such countries as Ghana, Tanzania, Côte d'Ivoire, Kenya, Zambia and many others at independence were motivated by a high sense of the need to improve the living conditions of the people. Most of the economic policies they adopted were informed by the intellectual debate on development at the time, which emphasised the need for rapid industrial growth and was ambiguous on the ownership of the investment capital (Lewis, 1964). Industrial growth was expected to achieve higher incomes and lead to modernisation of agriculture.

The failure of many such plans was the result of placing these well-intentioned policies in the 'wrong' institutions. The development policies were not quite in tandem with available resources and existing societal norms and capabilities. In many countries, the state overestimated its ability to implement development plans with the human capital available. The overstretched public institutions could not appropriately develop a framework for attracting investment capital and distributing the benefits from early investments. The resulting chaos is characterized by massive corruption and inept public institutions. Africa, probably more than any region, has failed to adapt policies to prevailing conditions at any given time. Consequently, it is entrapped in a vicious circle, which has further intensified the failure of the state.

The SAPs are designed to confine the role of the state to minimalist with an overriding responsibility for prudent fiscal and monetary management and provision of essential social services only. The role designated to the state therein reflects the market-friendly view, including investing in human capital formation; delivering a stable macroeconomic environment; creating an enabling and supporting environment for the private sector; and deregulating domestic markets and liberalizing trade and financial transactions.

Therefore, measures attached to structural adjustment loans as policy conditionalities typically encompassed: reducing budget deficits by cutting subsidies to urban consumers and protected, inefficient parastatals; civil service reform and retrenchment; and state asset privatization. Other measures were promoting exports; maintaining tight control over monetary policy to reduce high levels of inflation;

ridding the economy of the vast range of controls on economic activity; deregulating foreign exchange and credit markets and a variety of products and factor markets; and restructuring the financial sector.

In practice, the looming fiscal crisis (often resulting in a near complete revenue collapse) and external debt overhang problems have necessitated a sharp reduction in the size of the state through a series of austerity measures. However, this has also resulted in a fragile state with a reduced institutional capability to function: the scope and quality of public social services and infrastructure provision has progressively deteriorated. Aron (1996) concludes that the state in Africa has come full circle to the *small* government of pre-colonial days, but with a seriously depleted and impaired institutional capacity to deliver social services and to build physical and social infrastructure.

Yet, despite the severe retrenchment in capital and social expenditure endured over many years, the fiscal position in many African countries remains fragile and overly aid-dependent. For the region as a whole, overall fiscal deficits excluding grants increased from 8.9 per cent of GDP in 1981–1986 to 9.8 per cent of GDP in 1991–1992. Despite the increased share of foreign official grants from 1.4 per cent of GDP in 1981–1986 to 3.1 per cent of GDP in 1991–1992 and the sharp reduction in *primary* fiscal deficits, the revenue–expenditure gap has not been reduced because of the steep rise in debt service payments. Thus, while Africa is the most indebted developing region in terms of debt ratios, despite repeated rescheduling, the fiscal condition in SSA continues to be highly vulnerable to changes in foreign aid. It is increasingly argued that the quality, rather than the size, of governments does matter more for effective governance, but the current condition of the 'demise' of the state in SSA raises a serious concern.

The ongoing transition from systems of personal or authoritarian rule—characterized by infrequent but often violent turnover of incumbents—to democratic regimes with a multi-party system since the turn of the 1990s is seen as a starting point for creating governments committed to broad-based, equitable economic development.[30] For this to happen, however, the current trend towards the drastic impairment of state capacity should be reversed. Instead, every effort is required to encourage the emergence of capable, strong developmental states with fair, participatory and transparent governance structures, which will be truly accountable to the populace. A whole set of new democratic institutions may have to be enacted in some cases, while in other cases existing institutions should be completely renovated for new environments.

[30] Collier and Gunning (1999) estimate that even by 1991 only 13 per cent of the population in SSA was living in states in which legislators had been chosen in contested multi-party elections, and only 10 per cent in states in which the chief executive had been so chosen.

Risks, Financial Markets and Private Agents' Responses

Our discussion so far[31] confirms the generally held view that African economies are continuously exposed to large aggregate external and policy generated shocks as well as to high political instability, civil strife and natural calamity (Collier, 1996; Adam and O'Connell, 1997). As shown in Table 2.2, African economies have been characterized by relatively high levels of macro financial volatility and relatively frequent periodic crisis, compared with other developing countries except Latin American countries. The risk-rating index used by institutional investors places Africa as the most risky region in the world.

Table 2.2 Aggregate risk indicators by major world regions

	Macro-financial volatility 1960–94	Macro-economic crisis index 1960–94	Institutional investor risk rating index 1979–94	Capital flight stock as per cent of GDP 1980–90	Civil liberty index 1960–89
Sub-Saharan Africa	1.05	1.14	1.62	90	5.65
Latin America and Caribbean	1.12	1.69	1.21	30	3.7
East Asia	0.73	0.55	0.56	18	4.9
South Asia	0.73	0.55	0.56	20	4.2
OECD	0.46	0.33	0.32	0	1
Other (Oceania and Mid East)	-	-	-	110	5.15

Notes: Elbadawi and Schmidt-Hebbel's index of macro-financial policy volatility is an ex post measure defined as the equally-weighted sum of the standard deviations of the public deficit to GDP ratio, the current account deficit to GDP ratio, the inflation rate and the real exchange rate. The measure of macroeconomic crisis is proxied by the one-sided deviation of outcomes from sustainable threshold levels of the macroeconomic policy indicators.

Source: Adam and O'Connel (1996).

It is abundantly clear that economic transactions in Africa are conducted in highly uncertain and risky environments, which engender eminently more volatile returns to investment and income streams than in other parts of the world. This characteristic has critical bearings on economic performance and management for this region (Nissanke and Aryeetey, 1997).

Financial market performance First, the high-risk environment and the frequent incidence of large income shocks heighten demand for mechanisms and institutions for risk management, if only for sheer survival. When insurance markets are missing and insurance possibilities are limited, an act of intertemporal trade to effect resource transfers over time such as saving and credit becomes vitally important for

[31] This section is drawn heavily from Nissanke and Aryeetey (1997, 1998).

consumption-smoothing (Besley, 1995). There is potentially immense demand for financial intermediation as an effective device of risk-pooling and risk-sharing in sub-Saharan Africa.

However, the risk-management capacity of financial institutions in the formal sector is very restricted indeed (Nissanke and Aryeetey, 1997, 1998). This partly reflects one of the key characteristics of these economies, i.e., the less diversified, commodity dependent nature. The portfolio structure of these institutions is typically narrowly concentrated with little risk diversification, making it difficult to offset financial loss in one activity against the gains from another over spatial risk-pooling. A wave of loan defaults can be propagated throughout the financial system due to the high risk-covariance. In times of negative aggregate shocks, banks' net worth can rapidly turn negative. Thus, they are ill-equipped to deal with high aggregate systemic risks. With a general crisis in the *real* economy, which impairs borrowers' net worth drastically, financial distress ensues.

Moreover, the long history of widespread political interference and control in banks' operations has undoubtedly impaired the risk handling capacity of these institutions. Critically, the manner in which repressive policies have been implemented in sub-Saharan Africa has hindered development of the institutional capacity of financial institutions. The rationale of commercial viability has been largely subsumed by the dictates of governments' other policy objectives as well as political goals. Many banks failed to develop the capacity for risk assessment and monitoring of their loan portfolio. Savings mobilization was often not actively pursued. There was neither active liquidity and liability management nor any incentive to increase efficiency, often result in increased costs of financial intermediation. Financial repression has discouraged banks from investing in information capital, crucial for the development of financial systems. Institutions are typically burdened with severe agency problems in dealing with idiosyncratic risks, i.e., the problems caused by costly and imperfect information—adverse selection, moral hazard and contract enforcement.

In information-constrained economies such as those in sub-Saharan Africa, informal financial market segments have long developed devices and mechanisms for coping with the agency problems within geographically and socially confined community settings. These mechanisms, used by heterogeneous informal associations and agents, are firmly rooted in indigenous social codes and norms. They insist less on presentation of physical assets as collateral, relying instead on interlinked credit contracts with land, labour or product markets,[32] social pressure, reputation, and personal knowledge of borrowers for screening, monitoring and contract enforcement. They possess a competitive edge in risk management and transaction cost in credit provision within local networks as well as in small and short-term savings mobilization, which is difficult for formal institutions to tap because of size-sensitive cost considerations.

The financial products and services offered by formal institutions do not easily correspond to those required by the majority of potential borrowers and savers—the

---

[32] Product-related loans can be output-tied or input-tied loans, or loans from market agents (Germidis et al., 1991).

provision of small and short-term liquidity and savings facility. In contrast, informal financial activities usually specialize in small and short-term transactions or seasonal requirements, i.e., cash-flow and liquidity management, albeit in a fragmented manner.

Generally, in conjunction with the policy-based explanation embedded in the financial repression hypothesis (Fry, 1982, 1988; Roe, 1991), the type of market segmentation observed in developing countries can be explained by structural differences in the cost and risk characteristics of different types of transactions (Hoff and Stiglitz, 1990).[33] Nissanke and Aryeetey (1998) confirm that each market segment clearly has some potential comparative advantage in serving specific market niches. However, they also suggest that there has emerged a specific market structure in Africa, whereby structural and institutional barriers can be binding obstacles to interaction across segments and hence provide the opportunity to exploit market power in each segment, thus perpetuating *fragmentation.* In fragmented markets, flows of funds and information are insignificant between segments and access by clients to financial instruments is extremely limited, with little substitution and overlapping demand. Under such conditions, formal and informal sectors often form almost discrete financial enclaves.

Market segmentation could, however, result in efficient specialization for market niches by different segments of informal and formal finance, with comparable risk-adjusted returns across segments, where each unit's comparative advantage is fully exploited. Under such conditions, differences in interest rates reflect differences in cost of funds, transaction costs and risk. This may closely approximate market conditions observable in some Asian countries, where a heterogeneous and dynamic informal financial sector continues to exist as a part of financial systems, reflecting specialization in financial services by each sector (Biggs, 1991; Ghate, 1990). Yet, market integration has taken place therein and the intermediation efficiency of the system as a whole has increased over time. For example, Biggs (1991) suggests that decentralization of lending optimizes screening and monitoring of loans and hence can reduce an economy's overall intermediation costs and increase investment efficiency.[34]

In sub-Saharan Africa, with its various structural and institutional constraints, the range of clientele selected by each lender, in attempts to mitigate the information problems and to contain risks and transaction costs, is both narrow and polarized at

[33] The financial repression hypothesis is mainly concerned with parallel market activities stimulated by pervasive government controls and regulations, while market specialization in credit transaction is more effectively explained by the imperfect information economics.

[34] In his analysis of Taiwan, Biggs (1991) found that the high opportunity cost of investible funds, determined by informal market rates, kept the efficiency of aggregate investment high. This deterred entrepreneurs from undertaking low-yield investments, even when they had access to cheap bank funds. He concludes that the development of a dualistic financial system—with the formal sector serving 'full-information' borrowers and the informal lenders serving 'information-intensive borrowers—'helped credit intermediaries allocate funds to `information-intensive' borrowers at a lower cost and more efficiently than would have been possible if all investible resources were channeled through formal sector banks' (p. 168).

the extreme market-ends. Market-based reforms and liberalization measures have not obviated the effects of these structural and institutional constraints, which have become binding impediments to improving the intermediation efficiency of financial systems.

The portfolios of banking institutions continue to be dominated by two characteristics: an extremely high incidence of non-performing loans and an excess of liquidity. Banks have not changed their operational practice, as their portfolio decisions are a function of many parameters, such as risk averseness, net worth, asset quality and intermediation efficiency measured in terms of loan transaction costs. In addition, decisions are affected by externally imposed factors, such as a poor information capital base and policy uncertainty and creditability. The lack of changes in these parameters explains the paucity of savings mobilization efforts, the 'low-lending trap' in the presence of latent excess demand for credit and loans, and the de facto crowding out of private finance by public financial requirements. These factors have combined to form a general *post-liberalization credit crunch* in many countries, encouraged by the presence of high-yielding government papers or bank bills.

While many informal segments grew along with demand for their services, they face difficulties moving beyond their particular sphere of specialization. In effect, they hardly perform a function of effective financial intermediation. In general, informal lenders' liability base is narrow, being limited to deposits taken from a specific group of people or from surplus income earned by the lender from other economic activities. This severely constrains informal units' ability to meet growing demand for loans and credits. Consequently, both formal and informal segments of the financial system continue to serve a distinct clientele and a narrow market niche.

Private agents' response The high degree of uncertainty and instability is also known to have a powerful deterrent effect on the rate of private investment and economic growth. As the Theory of Investment under Uncertainty postulates, with partial (with high cost) or complete irreversibility of fixed investment, the critical threshold that must be reached by expected returns, required to trigger investment, can become inhibitively high in an extremely uncertain environment (Dixit and Pindyck, 1994; Schmidt-Hebbel et al., 1996; Serven and Solimano, 1993; Serven, 1996; Scaramozzino, 1997). Investors have an incentive to postpone commitment and wait for new information. Thus, the option value of waiting increases. Firms will be more reluctant to invest, as they try to avoid getting caught with too much capital, should the future turn out worse than expected. Hence, the new approach concludes that the uncertainty and instability can be seriously harmful to fixed investment decisions and that changes in uncertainty can have a strong effect on aggregate demand.

The persistently low level of *private* investment in Africa can be evaluated in the light of this new investment theory. The poor rate of private investment growth can be compared with reasonably high and stable rates of aggregate total investment, which is nevertheless below that of other regions (Table 2.3). This reflects partly the fact that in Africa, the state-owned enterprise sector, which accounted on average for

18 per cent of GDP, was responsible for over 30 per cent of total investment.[35] This can be somewhat related to another stylized fact of African investment, i.e., it has been markedly less efficient. Adam and O'Connell (1997) estimate that measured by the incremental output–capital ratio, investment in Africa is about one-quarter of that achieved in East Asian economies and around one-half to two-thirds of the efficiency levels in other developing countries. In particular, the rate of return on African public projects is significantly lower than that of other regions. Collier and Gunning (1999) argue that in Africa, growth has been reduced mainly through low returns on investment rather than a low level of investment. Overall, private investment has typically received less supportive treatment than public investment. Adam and O'Connell (1997) go even further to argue that in Africa government behaviour has contributed to, rather than ameliorated, the risk and uncertainty faced by the private sector.

The recent survey carried out by the World Bank in Africa (World Bank, 1994) identified several conditions as major deterrents to investment. They are: political and economic policy uncertainty; the lack of currency convertibility; poor infrastructure and regulation; rudimentary financial and business services; breach of contract; and high taxation. Collier (1995) also lists three major deterrents to African private investment: endemic corruption; the uncertain economic reputation of governments due to a finite possibility of policy reversal; and the illiquidity of firms' fixed assets, attributed to the breakdown both of the private audit profession in verifying firms' accounts, and of the civil legal system in establishing and enforcing legal title. This points out that weak institutions can be the principal explanation for holding back private investment.

Table 2.3 Distribution of total investment 1960–1980 (as % of absorption)

Region	Total investment	Public sector share of total investment	Private investment	Public investment
Sub-Saharan Africa	15.2	45	8.4	6.8
Latin America	20.1	35	13.1	7.0
East Asia	23.8	30	16.7	7.1
South Asia	14.1	35	9.2	4.9
OECD	22.4	17	18.6	3.8

Source: Adam and O'Connell (1997).

Furthermore, as Adam and O'Connell (1997) emphasize, it is critically important to note that greater uncertainty has significantly affected the *composition* of investment

[35] However, it can be argued that the poor performance of state-owned enterprises cannot be attributed to the question of ownership per se and it may be more meaningfully examined in terms of governance structures and organizational incentives affecting the management of these enterprises.

in Africa in favour of reversible and safe investments that have a self-insurance character. Thus, it is argued that safe and liquid assets are systematically chosen over less liquid but high-yielding assets. Aryeetey (1994) shows that in the environment of high uncertainty about the sustainability of reforms in the medium to long term, private investors in Ghana chose to put their capital in short-term assets in sectors of the economy with relatively lower sunk costs and shorter turnover periods, such as trading, rather than in long-term physical investments. Consequently, the distributive trade subsector became the fastest growing sector during 1984–1991. Thus, instead of embarking on the steady path towards industrialization and diversification, 'Ghana has become a nation of traders. There have been newspaper reports of investors obtaining international loans to import inputs for their manufacturing plants with public guarantees, and then diverting these to import finished consumer items for retailing' (p. 1218).

In a similar vein, the unstable and high-risk political and economic environment, in particular the level and expected trajectory of the inflation rate, and expectations about exchange rate depreciation, has had a significant effect on the asset composition of the savings portfolio held by private agents. Private agents adjusted their asset holdings away from domestic currencies in favour of non-financial assets or foreign currencies. *Demonetization, currency substitution* (or *dollarization)* and *capital flight* are known to have been as prevalent on as large a scale in much of sub-Saharan Africa during the economic crisis of the 1980s as in Latin America (Nissanke, 1997).

In a number of African countries, demonetization has taken place, as more rural households have retreated into the subsistence economy in crisis periods. Foreign currencies are also used as a hedge and a refuge against losses in real wealth under high and persistent domestic inflation combined with financial repression. A substantial difference in the real expected rates of return on domestic- and foreign-denominated assets has emerged due to the recent tendency in many African countries for frequent and large devaluations necessitated by unviable positions in their balance of payments. In some countries foreign exchange is also held for acquiring restricted imports. During the pre-liberalization period, in response to extensive controls on foreign trade and capital transactions, many private agents operated in parallel markets for foreign exchange and tradeable goods.

In the case of currency substitution, cash balances in foreign currencies, originated in under-invoicing and smuggling of exports, over-invoicing of imports, foreign tourism, and diversion of remittances through non-official channels, are held by private agents within national borders, in order to make transactions in the parallel foreign exchange market or for illegal underground transactions in goods and foreign exchange. In the presence of large and increasing demand for foreign currency, several countries have allowed domestic residents to open and operate foreign currency deposits within the domestic financial system.

However, residents, particularly wealthy elites, may still prefer to hold assets abroad in foreign currency deposit accounts, or in other forms of financial and real assets, which is known as *capital flight*. On the basis of estimates by Claessens and Naude (1993), Adam and O'Connell (1997) speculate that capital flight from sub-Saharan Africa by the beginning of the 1990s might have reached A size that is equivalent to 90–100 per cent of GDP. Collier and Gunning (1999) reckon that African wealth owners have chosen to locate 37 per cent of their portfolios outside Africa. This share is compared with 29 per cent for the Middle East, 17 per cent for Latin America, 4 per cent for South Asia and 3 per cent for East Asia. Chang and Cumby (1991) estimate that 36 sub-Saharan countries experienced capital flight, amounting to $32–$40 billion from 1976 to 1987. Nigeria and Sudan alone accounted for more than half of total capital flight.[36] Chang and Cumby (1991: 162) suggest that several African countries have exhibited capital flight on par with countries such as Argentina or Mexico in the 1980s, and that 'as in the case with the large Latin American debtors, there are often two-way capital flows, with the private sector increasing its external assets at the same time that the public sector is increasing its external liabilities'.

Both demonetization and capital flight can have significant influence on the conduct of monetary and fiscal policy by reducing government revenues through a loss of seigniorage and inflation tax on the holdings of domestic cash balances. They also constitute a large proportion of the substantial *leakage* of domestic savings that could have been intermediated for productive investment at home.

Interestingly, as Aron et al. (1997) note:

> In the aftermath of stabilisation (in Latin America and SSA) it has been observed that capital (new or flight capital) does not substantially return, and even if it does, it is usually placed in liquid form rather than in irreversible productive assets. The recent repatriation of capital flight and the flow of new private capital in SSA may be substantially characterised by speculative behaviour. This is because investors have the option of waiting, until the front-loading of investment returns is sufficient to compensate them for the risk of relinquishing the liquidity option of a wait and see position.

Apart from the leakage effect, the political and economic environments in Africa have kept the economic activities of a significant proportion of private agents away from the official economy. The so-called *informal* economy, sometimes also referred to as the underground or second economy, is indeed firmly anchored in African traditional values and social structures, which are characterized by a dominance of relatively autonomous networks bound by kinship, tribe, religion or community ties. Further, these networks span rural/urban boundaries (Aron et al., 1997). Over time, as economic conditions have deteriorated, the 'second economy' has become an important source of employment and income for most households. The size of the informal sector in Africa is estimated to be substantial. For example, Bagachwa and Naho (1994) estimate that the second economy in Tanzania has grown from 20 per cent of official GDP in the late 1960s to a sizeable 40 per cent of GDP since the mid 1980s.[37]

[36] Nigeria accounts for nearly half the SSA region's total capital flight, and Sudan accounts for another 20 per cent. Other countries that experienced capital flight of over $1 billion were Gabon, Zambia, Zaire, Congo, Liberia, Ghana and Uganda (Chang and Cumby, 1991).

[37] Their estimates can be compared with the size of the underground economy, estimated to be 20–30 per cent of officially measured GDP for some developing countries (Montiel et al., 1993).

Upon liberalization of trade and foreign exchange transactions, some of these activities have come out in the open, having led to one-off phenomena such as the urban construction boom or the sudden spur of consumer demand, widely observed in many SSA countries in the initial phase of the adjustment period. Wuyts (1997), for example, describes the process whereby the own-funded import scheme introduced in Tanzania has allowed the importation of cheap consumer goods, resulting in the cheapening of wage goods and hence the growth of the informal sector.

In addition to being forced to cope with unstable political and macroeconomic environments, both farm households and micro and small-scale enterprises face difficult conditions for economic transactions: high risk, emanating from less diversified activities prone to frequent large shocks; poor public provision of transport, storage facilities, telecommunication and other social extension services in health, training and education; and lack of social capital such as institutions for enforcing contracts and property rights, or regulatory and auditing systems. Under such conditions, costs of entering into transactions beyond small communities can be excessively high. The underdeveloped market network and business relationships must be partly responsible for substantial inventory accumulation. Firms and farmers in Africa are often compelled to accumulate large inventories at high cost to cope with shocks and risks.

Operating in such high-risk environments, without effective insurance and credit markets, private agents have relied extensively on traditional social institutions and mechanisms, which are based on village and kinship groups, for informal insurance arrangements. These have provided informal social safety nets and redistribution mechanisms, serving as a social and economic stabilizer and displaying a quite remarkable degree of resilience and dynamism in some cases. Living in close proximity enables agents to reduce the costs of contract enforcement and other transaction costs and to mitigate the moral hazard problems with the socially and geographically confined set-up.

In the absence of functioning formal institutions, however, economic exchange is restricted to interpersonal exchanges in small-scale production and local trade, to obviate the contract enforcement problem through repeated dealing and cultural and social homogeneity. African economies appear to lock into a low developmental equilibrium, wherein 'a dense social network leads to the development of fairly stable informal structures, such as customs, trust and normative rules which give an informal institutional framework for organising activities' (Aron, 1997). In this equilibrium condition, kinships are important for insurance, protection and law enforcement.

Institutional economics as discussed in the sections above suggests that economic development proceeds when social enforcement mechanisms move up *from* unwritten taboos, customs and traditions at one end *to* third-party enforcement under written constitutions at the other end. The latter higher form of enforcement mechanisms facilitates complex, long-term and multi-contract impersonal exchanges,

---

Montiel et al. (1993) also cite the findings of studies that claim that in virtually all countries—both industrial and developing—a parallel or informal economy operates alongside the more visible and better-recorded official economy.

since the increasing specialization and division of labour associated with more complex societies raise the rate of return to *formalization*.

A critical question to be addressed in relation to African economic development is whether and how to create a condition whereby private agents operating in informal institutional set-ups feel ready to graduate and transform these arrangements into effective formal institutions to engage in productive activities promising high social and private returns. A key to this may be found in searching for ways and mechanisms to reduce both risks and costs associated with such transformation (i.e., the *transformation risk* and *costs*) and transaction costs. This can be achieved only when African countries as nation states are able to commit to long-term investment in social, human and information capital in order to build institutional frameworks and endowments for sustainable development.

Conclusions and Further Research Issues

In this paper, we have tried to highlight the critical differences in the government –private agents relationships in East Asia and sub-Saharan Africa, focusing on institutional arrangements and governance structures and mechanisms. It is hoped that our discussion corroborates the relevance and usefulness of institutional analyses to deepen the understanding of the differences in economic performances in a dynamic analytical context.

Indeed, institutional economics has comparative advantages over the standard static economic theory in dealing with the determinants of change over time, as it places the nature and sources of dynamism at the centre of analysis (Harriss et al., 1995; Bardhan, 1989). It treats institutional development as an evolutionary process, emphasizing its path-dependent nature. Hence, it well recognizes that 'transferring the formal political and economic rules of successful economies to other settings is not a sufficient condition for good economic performance'.

Indeed, a simple replication of policies and systems that have worked rather well under specific historical conditions in one country or another may not produce a best outcome in other countries. Certainly, the positive outcome from the application of interventionist policy in some Northeast Asian economies during the period of their industrialization drive does not suggest that sub-Saharan countries should adopt it as a framework of economic policy regardless of their institutional environment and policy implementation context. As Evans (1998: 79) reminds us, 'superimposing similar policies on inadequate institutional foundations could well have perverse effects', as the efficacy of economic policy depends critically on the institutional context. Furthermore, not only similar policies but also similar organizational forms can give rise to different outcomes under different institutional settings because of the wide divergence in behavioural patterns.[38] Therefore, the appropriateness of any

[38] We are grateful to Yilmaz Akyuz for drawing our attention to this important point.

policy action or development strategy has to be carefully judged and evaluated in light of locally prevailing conditions and specific policy objectives.

Each developing and reforming country has its own specific circumstances, experiences, institutions and history, all of which should be taken into account in designing its own architecture of institutional arrangements and development policies. Thus, institutionalists warn directly that 'each society is different in its own way...and it takes only a small change in pay-offs to render a particular strategy profile unqualified equilibrium. Such sensitive dependence on small (and perhaps imperceptible) differences raises the question of replicability of the experiences of others' (Evans, 1998: 79). For all these reasons, the issue of replicability and transferability cannot be examined in its mechanical interpretation. Instead, for our comparative institutional analysis, 'the idea of 'transferable lessons' should be understood as an invitation to indigenous innovation that takes advantage of the underlying analytical logic of East Asian institutions' (Evans, 1998: 79).

Importantly, institutional perspectives direct our attention to the need for identifying the causes and consequences of institutional changes, and conditions for adaptive efficiency as opposed to allocative efficiency. Thus, North (1995: 26) notes:

> It is adaptive rather than allocative efficiency which should be the guide to policy. Allocative efficiency is a static concept with a given set of institutions; the key to continuing good economic performance is a flexible institutional matrix that will adjust in the context of evolving technological and demographic changes as well as shocks to the system.

Killick et al. (1995) further suggest that it is adaptability and flexibility that explains, at least partially but in an important way, the differences in economic performances between East Asian economies on one hand and East European and African economies on the other hand. As a critical part of these explanations, a further microanalysis of differences in governance structures and mechanisms is required for our in-depth comparative studies, since these intra- and inter-institutional governance structures may prove to be a key to our understanding of the determinants of national economic flexibility and sources of innovative flexibility.

References

Adam, C. and S. O'Connell. 1997. 'Aid, taxation and development: Analytical perspectives on aid effectiveness in sub-Saharan Africa'. Working Paper Series (WPS/97–5). Centre for the Study of African Economies, University of Oxford.

Ali, A. 1995. 'The challenges of poverty alleviation in sub-Saharan Africa'. A contributed paper presented at the World Congress of the International Economic Association, Tunis, Tunisia, December 1995.

Amsden, A.H. 1989. *Asia's Next Giant: South Korea and Late Industrialization*. New York: Oxford University Press.

Amsden, A.H. 1991. 'The diffusion of development: The late-industrializing model and greater East Asia'. *The American Economic Review*, vol. 81, no. 2: 282–87.

Amsden, A.H. 1994. 'Why isn't the whole world experimenting with the East Asian model to develop? Review of *The East Asian Miracle*'. *World Development*, vol. 22, no. 4: 627–33.

Aoki, Masahiko, Hyung-Ki Kim and Masahiro Okuno-Fujiwara, eds. 1996. *The Role of Government in East Asian Economic Development*. Oxford: Clarendon Press.

Aron, J. 1996. 'The institutional foundation of growth'. In Stephen Ellis, ed., *Africa Now: People, Policies and Institutions*. London: James Currey/Heinemann; and Paris: Karthala.

Aron, J. 1997. 'Political, economic and social institutions: A review of growth evidence (with an Africa focus)'. Background paper for the *World Bank World Development Report 1997* on 'The State in a Changing World'.

Aron, J., I.A. Elbadawi and B. Ndulu. 1997. 'The state and development in sub-Saharan Africa'. Background paper for the *World Bank World Development Report 1997* on 'The State in a Changing World'.

Aryeetey, E. 1994. 'Private investment under uncertainty in Ghana'. *World Development*, vol. 22, no. 8: 1211–21.

Bagachwa, M.S.D., and A. Naho. 1994. *A Review of Recent Developments in the Second Economy in Tanzania*. Special Paper No. 16. African Economic Research Consortium, Nairobi.

Bardhan, P. 1989. *The Economic Theory of Agrarian Institutions*. Oxford: Clarendon Press.

Bates, R.H. 1981. *Markets and States in Tropical Africa: The Political Basis of Agricultural Policies*. Berkeley, Los Angeles and London: University of California Press.

Bates, R.H. 1983. *Essays on the Political Economy of Rural Africa*. Cambridge: Cambridge University Press; and Berkeley, Los Angeles and London: University of California Press.

Bates, R.H. 1991. *Beyond the Miracle of Markets: The Political Economy of Agrarian Development in Kenya*. Cambridge: Cambridge University Press.

Bates, R.H. 1995. 'Social dilemmas and rational individuals: An assessment of the new institutionalism'. In J. Harriss, Janet Hunter and Colin M. Lewis, eds., *The New Institutional Economics and Third World Development*. London: Routledge.

Besley, T. 1995. 'Savings, credit and insurance'. In J. Behrman and T.N. Srinivason, eds., *Handbook of Development Economics III*. New York: North Holland.

Biggs, T.S. 1991. 'Heterogeneous firms and efficient financial intermediation in Taiwan'. In Michael Roemer and Chris Jones, eds., *Markets in Developing Countries*. San Francisco: ICS Press.

Booth, A. 1995. 'The state and the economy in Indonesia in the nineteenth and twentieth centuries'. In J. Harriss, Janet Hunter and Colin M. Lewis, eds., *The New Institutional Economics and Third World Development*. London: Routledge

Brett E.A. 1995. 'Institutional theory and social change in Uganda'. In J. Harriss, Janet Hunter and Colin M. Lewis, eds., *The New Institutional Economics and Third World Development*, London: Routledge.

Buijtenhuis, R. and E. Rijnierse. 1993. 'Democratisation in sub-Saharan Africa 1989-1992'. *African Studies Centre Research Report* 51.

Chang, Ha-Joon. 1993, 1994. *The Political Economy of Industrial Policy*. New York: St. Martin's Press; and Basingstoke: Macmillan.

Chang, K. and R. Cumby. 1991. 'Capital flight in sub-Saharan Africa'. In I. Husain and J. Underwood, eds., *African External Finance*. Washington, D.C.: The World Bank.

Claessens, S. and D. Naud. 1993. 'Recent estimates of capital flight in developing countries'. *Policy Research Working Paper Series* No. 1186. Washington, D.C.: The World Bank

Coase, R.H. 1992. 'The institutional structure of production'. *American Economic Review*, vol. 82, no. 4: 713–20.

Collier, P. 1994. 'The marginalisation of Africa'. Centre for the Study of African Economies, University of Oxford, September 1994.

Collier, P. 1995. 'The role of the African state in building agencies of restraint'. Centre for the Study of African Economies, University of Oxford, February 1995.

Collier, P. 1996. 'The role of the state in economic development: Cross-regional experiences'. Paper presented at the Plenary Session of the AERC Biannual Research Workshop. Nairobi, December 1996.

Collier, P. and J.W. Gunning. 1999. 'Explaining African economic performance'. *Journal of Economic Literature,* March 1997, vol. 37, no. 1: 64–111. Centre for the Study of African Economies, University of Oxford.

Davis, L.E. and D.C. North. 1971. *Institutional Change and American Economic Growth.* Cambridge: Cambridge University Press.

Dixit, A.K. and R.S. Pindyck. 1994. *Investment under Uncertainty.* Princeton, New Jersey: Princeton University Press.

Elbadawi, I.A., and B.J. Ndulu. 1995. 'Growth and development in Sub-Saharan Africa: Evidence on key factors'. Paper presented at the 1995 World Congress of the International Economic Association. Tunis, December 1995.

Evans, P. 1998. 'Transferable lessons? Re-examining the institutional prerequisites of East Asian economic policies'. *Journal of Development Studies,* Special Issue: New Perspectives on East Asian Development, vol. 34, no. 6: 66–86.

Fry, M.J. 1982. 'Models of financial repressed developing economies'. *World Development,* vol. 10, no. 9, 731–50.

Fry, M.J. 1988. *Money, Interest, and Banking in Economic Development.* Baltimore and London: Johns Hopkins University Press.

Germidis, D., D. Kessler and R. Meghir. 1991. 'Financial systems and development: What role for the formal and informal financial sectors?' OECD, Development Centre Studies, Paris.

Gerschenkron, A. 1962. *Economic Backwardness in Historical Perspective.* Cambridge, Massachusetts: Harvard University Press.

Ghate, P.B. 1990. 'Interaction between the formal and informal financial sectors'. Paper presented at the UN International Conference on Savings and Credit for Development. Denmark, 28–31 May 1990.

Harriss, J., J. Hunter and C.M. Lewis. 1995. *The New Institutional Economics and Third World Development.* London: Routledge.

Hayami, Yujiro. 1996. 'Towards an East Asian model of economic development'. Paper presented at Round Table Conference, International Economic Association. Tokyo, 16–19 December 1996.

Hellmann, T., K.C. Murdock and J. Stiglitz. 1996. 'Financial restraint: Toward a new paradigm'. In M. Aoki, H. Kim and M. Okuno-Fujiwara, eds., *The Role of Government in East Asian Economic Development.* Oxford: Clarendon Press.

Hoff, K. and J.E. Stiglitz. 1990. 'Imperfect information and rural credit markets – Puzzles and policy perspectives'. *The World Bank Economic Review,* vol. 4, no. 3: 235–50.

Ishikawa, Shigeru. 1996. 'From development economics to policy of development aid policy'. Institute of Developing Economics, Tokyo.

Jomo, J.S., and T. Gomez. 1996. 'Rents and development in multi-ethnic Malaysia'. In M. Aoki, H. Kim and M. Okuno-Fujiwara, eds., *The Role of Government in East Asian Economic Development.* Oxford: Clarendon Press.

Khan, M. 1995. 'State failure in weak states: A critique of new institutionalist explanations'. In J. Harriss, Janet Hunter and Colin M. Lewis, eds., *The New Institutional Economics and Third World Development.* London: Routledge.

Killick, T. 1995. *The Flexible Economy.* London and New York: Routledge.
Kim, Hyung-ki and Jun Ma. 1996. 'The role of government in acquiring technological capability: The case of the petrochemical industry in East Asia'. In M. Aoki, H. Kim and M. Okuno-Fujiwara, eds., *The Role of Government in East Asian Economic Development.* Oxford: Clarendon Press.
Kwon, J. 1994. 'The East Asia challenge to neoclassical orthodoxy'. *World Development*, vol. 22, no. 4: 635–44.
Lewis, A. 1964. 'Economic development with unlimited supplies of labour'. The Manchester School, volume 22.
Lall, S. 1994. 'The East Asian miracle study: Does the bell toll for industrial strategy?' *World Development*, vol. 22, no. 4. 645–54.
Maizels, A. 1992. *Commodities in Crisis.* Oxford: Oxford University Press.
Matsuyama, Kiminori. 1997. 'Economic development as coordination problems'. In M. Aoki, H. Kim and M. Okuno-Fujiwara, eds., *The Role of Government in East Asian Economic Development.* Oxford: Clarendon Press.
Montiel, P.J., P-R. Agenor and N. Ul Haque. 1993. *Informal Financial Markets in Developing Countries - A Macroeconomic Analysis.* Oxford: Blackwell.
Nabli, M.K., and J.B. Nugent. 1989. 'The new institutional economics and its applicability to development'. *World Development*, vol. 17, no. 9: 1333–47.
Nissanke, M. 1996. 'Raising finance for private enterprise investment'. Background paper for UNIDO's *Global Report 1997.*
Nissanke, M. 1997. 'Africa: Institutions, policies and development'. International Development Centre of Japan, Tokyo.
Nissanke, M. and E. Aryeetey. 1998. *Financial Integration and Development in Sub-Saharan Africa.* London and New York: Routledge.
Nissanke, M. and E. Aryeetey. 1997 'Financial risks and market structure in sub-Saharan Africa'. Paper presented at the 10th Anniversary Conference of the Centre for the Study of African Economies. University of Oxford, 17–18 April 1997.
North, D.C. 1989. 'Institutions and economic growth: An historical introduction'. *World Development*, vol. 17, no. 9.
North, D.C. 1990. *Institutions, Institutional Change and Economic Performance.* Cambridge: Cambridge University Press.
North, D.C. 1995 'The new institutional economics and Third World development'. In J. Harriss, Janet Hunter and Colin M. Lewis, eds., *The New Institutional Economics and Third World Development.* London: Routledge.
Okuno-Fujiwara, M. 1996. 'Toward a comparative institutional analysis of the government business relationship'. In M. Aoki, H. Kim and M. Okuno-Fujiwara, eds., *The Role of Government in East Asian Economic Development.* Oxford: Clarendon Press.
Page, John M. 1994. 'The East Asian miracle: An introduction'. *World Development*, vol. 22, no. 4: 615–25.
Perkins, D.H. 1994. 'There are at least three models of East Asian development'. *World Development*, vol. 22, no. 4: 655–61.
Rodrik, D. 1994. 'King Kong meets Godzilla: The World Bank and the East Asian Miracle'. In *Miracle or Design*, Overseas Development Council Policy Essay No. 11. Washington, D.C.
Scaramozzino, P. 1997. 'Investment irreversibility and finance constraints'. *Oxford Bulletin of Economics and Statistics*, Oxford, vol. 59, no. 1.

Schmidt-Hebbel, K., L. Serven and A. Solimano. 1994. 'Saving, investment and growth in developing countries'. *The World Bank Economic Review*, vol. 6 (September).

Schmidt-Hebbel, K., L. Serven and A. Solimano. 1996. 'Savings and investment: Paradigms, puzzles and policies'. *The World Bank Research Observer*, vol. 11, no. 1: 87–117.

Serven, L. 1996. 'Irreversibility, uncertainty and private investment: Analytical issues and some lessons for Africa'. Paper presented at the AERC Biannual Research Workshop. Nairobi, May 1996.

Serven, L. and A. Solimano, eds., 1993. *Striving for Growth after Adjustment: The Role of Capital Formation*. Washington, D.C.: The World Bank.

Stein, H. 1995. 'Institutional theories and structural adjustment in Africa'. In J. Harriss, Janet Hunter and Colin M. Lewis, eds., *The New Institutional Economics and Third World Development*. London: Routledge.

Stiglitz, J. 1989. 'Markets, market failures and development'. *American Economic Review*, vol. 79, no. 2 (May): 197–203.

Teranishi, J. 1996. 'Sectoral resource transfer, conflict and macro-stability in economic development: A comparative analysis.' In M. Aoki and M. Okuno-Fujiwara, eds., *Role of Government in East Asia: A Comparative Institutional Analysis*. Oxford: Oxford University Press.

Toye, J. 1995. 'The new institutional economics and the implication for development theory'. In J. Harriss, Janet Hunter and Colin M. Lewis, eds., *The New Institutional Economics and Third World Development*. London: Routledge.

United Nations Development Programme. *Human Development Report*. Various Years.

United Nations. 1997. 'Food security in Africa in the context of the World Food Summit' (An issues note). Sixth Meeting of the Panel of High-Level Personalities on African Development. United Nations, New York, 13–14 March 1997.

Wade, R. 1990. *Governing the Market: Economic Theory and the Role of Government in East Asian Industrialization*. Princeton, N.J.: Princeton University Press.

Williamson, O. 1985. *The Economic Institutions of Capitalism*. New York: Free Press.

Williamson, Oliver E. 1995. 'The institutions and governance of economic development and reform'. Proceedings of the World Bank Annual Conference on Development Economics, 1994.

Woo-Cummings, M. 1996. 'The political economy of growth in East Asia: A perspective on the state, market and ideology'. In M. Aoki, H. Kim and M. Okuno-Fujiwara, eds., *The Role of Government in East Asian Economic Development*. Oxford: Clarendon Press.

World Bank. 1993. *The East Asian Miracle: Economic Growth and Public Policy*. A World Bank Policy Research Report. Washington, D.C.: The World Bank.

World Bank. 1994. *Adjustment in Africa: Reforms, Results and the Road Ahead*. A World Bank Policy Research Report. Washington, D.C.: The World Bank.

Wuyts, M. 1997. 'Informal economy, wage goods and the changing patterns of accumulation under structural adjustment'. Paper presented at the UNCTAD workshop. Mauritius, December 1997.

Yanagihara, T. 1997. 'Economic system approach and its applicability'. In Toru Yanagihara and Susumu Sambommatsu, eds., *East Asian Development Experience*. Tokyo: Institute of Developing Economies.

PART TWO

MACROECONOMIC MANAGEMENT AND THE DEVELOPMENT PROCESS

Chapter 3

Macroeconomic Performance in Sub-Saharan Africa in a Comparative Setting

Ibrahim A. Elbadawi, Benno J. Ndulu and Njuguna S. Ndung'u[1]

A strong recovery in growth occurred in sub-Saharan Africa (SSA) during 1995 and 1996, with real GDP growth averaging slightly over 4.3 per cent. What is also notable about this recovery is that it has been very broad in occurrence—with most countries taking part. Moreover, 11 of the 44 countries in the region achieved growth rates in excess of 6 per cent,[2] and only two countries continued to register declines in real incomes. Furthermore, this growth recovery has been accompanied by a strong expansion in exports, declining inflation and relatively stable currencies. Export earnings grew at an average of 8 per cent in 1996, with export volume expanding at the rate of 4 per cent. Low inflation is a feature the Franc Zone countries have persistently maintained; the median inflation for these countries has been in the range of 5–8 per cent for more than two decades now. Several non-CFA countries have recently been able to reduce inflation from levels in excess of 30 per cent to less than 17 per cent, with some maintaining it at below 10 per cent (Uganda, Kenya, Guinea, Lesotho, Gambia) over this two-year period. A significant number of countries have signed Article VIII with the International Monetary Fund, completely freeing up external current account transactions. In addition, Uganda and Kenya have also freed up their external capital accounts.

Although this strong recovery pales in comparison with the stellar performance of East Asian countries, where real growth averaged in excess of 7 per cent during the past decade, such growth has not occurred in this region since 1970. Various observers have expressed doubt over whether it can be sustained and some attribute it to good luck associated with good weather and a strong rise in world market prices. These fortunate incidents may have played an important role, but they did not occur for the first time. In fact, prices of commodities in the world market were lower in the two years in question than in 1990, and much lower than

---

[1] We acknowledge research assistance from Aida Kimemia and Radha Ruparel. We further appreciate comments from Jane Harrigan, Olu Ajakaiye and participants of Johannesburg meeting, November 1997. The usual disclaimer still applies.

[2] In 1996 countries that registered the strongest growth performance included Rwanda (13.3 per cent), Ethiopia (12.4 per cent), Malawi (10.4 per cent), Angola (8.6 per cent), Uganda (7 per cent) and Côte d'Ivoire (6.5 per cent) (IMF, 1997a).

at the peaks that occurred in 1976/77. Others attribute this recovery more to the past decade of adjustment and economic reforms, complemented by a relative decline in civil unrest and opening up of political systems. This is confirmed by improvements of investor perceptions as supported by the findings from recent surveys.

The worrying factor in the sustainability of this recovery is that the response of savings and investment has continued to be slow, thus limiting the expansion of productive capacity. Savings remain very low even among the strongest reformers, at 9.5 per cent during 1991–1995 for countries with structural adjustment and enhanced structural adjustment facilities (SAF/ESAF); this is a marginal increase from about 8 per cent during the crisis period of 1981–1985. Similarly, investment was at approximately 19 per cent for this group of countries during 1991–1995 compared with 17 per cent in the crisis period (IMF, 1997b). What is more striking is that African countries have hardly benefited from the recent vast expansion of international capital flows even though the measured returns to investment were in sub-Saharan Africa (unadjusted for risk) compare very favourably against the rest of the developing world (25 per cent vs. 15 per cent). Yet during 1990–1994, foreign flows as a proportion of private fixed investment were actually negative (–1 per cent), indicating the dominance of net repayment in equity investment. This contrasts sharply with 11 per cent for East Asia and 15 per cent for Latin America over the same period (Jaspersen et al., 1995).

There are some encouraging developments since 1994, however. Investors in Wall Street and in Europe have begun including Africa in the flotation of funds targeting Africa. Over a dozen African funds now exist, with a total investment in excess of $1 billion, in New York and Europe. Although Africa's share in emerging markets represents only 4 per cent of the total, the region is now being viewed as the 'last frontier' for international portfolio investment (Senbet, 1997).

Against this background, this chapter seeks to throw some light on Africa's relatively poor long-term macroeconomic performance. Even with the recent evidence of economic recovery, indicators show that poverty is still pervasive, with head-count ratios close to 40 per cent when an international poverty line is applied, and it is more severe as measured by the mean distance from this line or the mean poverty gap index (Ravallion and Chen, 1997). The perspective we adopt is that of a high ambition for growth in order to reduce both the breadth and depth of poverty. Our counterfactual analysis for growth and its determinants uses the stellar performance of East Asia as a comparator. We begin by reviewing existing evidence and literature to filter out the main wisdom to explain the links between macroeconomic performance in SSA and its determinants. Our focus will be on growth, savings, investment and exports.

A Background Survey

For the past two and a half decades African economies have grown at a third of the pace of East Asian economies, with the difference in growth performance widening during the 1980s before narrowing marginally in the 1990s. Because of the more rapid population growth of sub-Saharan Africa the difference is much wider in real per capita income terms, as vividly illustrated in Table 3.1.

Table 3.1 Comparative macroeconomic performance: SSA, East Asia and Latin America (medians)

	SSA	Latin America	East Asia
Real GDP growth (%)			
1970–79	4.37	4.27	7.81
1980–84	1.78	1.69	7.26
1985–94	2.68	3.43	7.95
Real per capita GDP growth (%):			
1985–94	-0.30	0.80	5.60
Real per capita GDP ($)			
1960–69	335.00	1,107.00	555.00
1970–79	425.00	1,333.00	923.00
1980–89	374.00	1,267.00	1,393.00
1990–94	361.00	1,372.00	2,048.00
Investment to GDP (%)			
Total fixed investment			
1970–79	17.36		
1980–84	19.46		
1985–94	17.40	16.13	28.71
Private fixed investment (%)			
1970–79	7.89		
1980–84	8.90		
1985–94	8.40	11.15	20.90
Investment productivity			
1970–79	21.00		30.00
1980–84	8.00		20.00
1985–94	12.00		22.00
Exports to GDP (%)			
1960–79	24.00	20.00	19.20
1970–79	26.20	21.60	28.40
1980–89	23.10	22.30	30.10
1990–94	22.30	23.70	38.40

Source: Compiled by authors.

A median economy in East Asia has maintained a real GDP growth of about 7.5 per cent since 1970. In contrast, the real GDP of a median African economy expanded at an annual rate of 2.2 per cent over the same period, slightly less than a third the speed of the East Asian economy. When we make the comparison in real per capita terms the difference in real growth for the past one and a half decades

(1985–1994) is nearly 5.9 percentage points. If we include the 1970s, when Africa registered higher growth than in the subsequent period, this difference narrows to 4.7 percentage points.

The long persistence of these differences in growth explains the very large widening of the gap in the levels of per capita incomes over this period, from 2:1 in the 1970s to 5:1 in the 1990s. Latin America faired marginally better than SSA for the period as a whole in terms of growth performance, but given Latin America's much higher initial income per capita, the growth difference has not translated into the large gap in the levels of incomes with East Asia as in the case of SSA. Nevertheless, the median country in Latin America now has two-thirds of real income per capita compared with a median economy in East Asia, reversing the situation that obtained in the 1970s when the median income per capita in Latin America exceeded that of East Asia by nearly 40 per cent. Relative to Africa the gap in income per capita has been maintained, in fact widening slightly from 3:1 to about 4:1. What is quite obvious in these data is how fast the relative fortunes of nations can change through differences in the levels of economic growth.

Next we look at investment, which in the absence of deterioration in investment productivity would invariably form the key base for growth. This qualification is important since, as Table 3.1 shows for SSA, the region has experienced periods of fixed investment expansion (1980s compared with 1970s) combined with declines in real growth. The only plausible explanation for such an anomaly from received wisdom is a downturn in efficiency, whether caused by a sharp drop in the utilization of capacity, foreign exchange constraints or policy misalignment. The persistence of these adverse conditions for investment productivity can lead to protracted periods of growth decline. This qualification notwithstanding, empirical evidence from cross-country studies confirms the critical role of investment in spearheading growth in the long term (De Long and Summers, 1991, 1992; Easterly and Rebelo, 1993).

Fixed investment in SSA stayed in the narrow range of 17–19.5 per cent through the period 1970–1994 (Table 3.1). The peak was reached during 1980–1984 in spite of the biting economic crisis prevalent then. Since that period it has not recovered despite significant improvements in the policy environment. This presents perhaps the biggest challenge to exploiting the benefits of reforms into a virtuous circle, from better policy conditions to sustained growth. Elbadawi et al. (1997b) provide a range of explanations for this disturbing situation, which we take up in greater detail in the next section. Suffice to mention at this stage that they are mainly related to uncertainties about the sustainability of reforms and risks associated with political instability and civil disorder. Investors are suspicious of policy reversals associated with inability to service sovereign debt in the future, with a probable recourse to high inflation tax to effect the required internal transfers. The absence of requisite physical infrastructure to support high investment returns, and weak legal structures to safeguard property aggravate the situation. In any event, investors have decided to wait for reassurance.

Compared with East Asia, the fixed investment rate in SSA pales considerably, although it compares well with that in Latin America. During 1985–1994 a median economy in East Asia maintained an investment rate of nearly 30 per cent, compared with 17.4 per cent for SSA. The region also maintained investment productivity at nearly twice the level obtaining in SSA, at 22 per cent compared with SSA's 12 per cent. It therefore comes as no surprise that the differences in long-term growth rates have been what they are. A major area of learning from the experience of East Asia rests in the region's ability to sustain both high levels of investment and its productivity.

There are two sources of finance for investment: domestic savings and foreign savings. In 1994, SSA's average domestic saving as a share of GDP was estimated at 16 per cent, in great contrast with East Asia's 37 per cent and Latin America's 20 per cent. In terms of gross national saving (i.e., after adjusting for net factor income and net private transfers), SSA's saving rate is much lower, averaging 13 per cent in 1993. This rate has experienced a steady decline on average since the 1970s, although significant country variations do exist. The World Bank (1994) shows that the average national saving rate for SSA declined from 19.7 per cent in 1975–1979 to a low of 13.0 per cent during 1986–1993, in contrast with the performance for the rest of the developing world, which saw the rate decline much less steeply. These rates include net official transfers (public) from abroad. The most significant source of this deterioration is the persistent decline in public saving. Government dissaving in a median SSA country, as measured by fiscal deficit to GDP, widened from −2.69 per cent during 1970–1979 to −4.78 per cent and −4.33 per cent during 1980–1984 and 1985–1994, respectively. For the period 1970–1994 as a whole the comparative medians are −4.1 per cent for SSA, −1.8 per cent for East Asia and −1.2 per cent for Latin America (Table 3.1).

The consequence of these developments has been a growing reliance on foreign saving or low levels of investment when such inflows remain inadequate to sustain higher levels of investment. In SSA's case there is virtually total reliance on official sources of foreign finance, unlike Southeast Asia and Latin America, where private sources currently dominate foreign inflows. With growth pressures on the levels of official development assistance, unless diversification into private capital inflows is effected, investment may seriously suffer in the future. Therefore, focus has to be primarily on creating conditions for raising domestic saving and reducing the flight of such savings once mobilized. Improved conditions for attracting private foreign capital will complement this effort.

Exports play a crucial role in supporting faster growth. In a foreign exchange-constrained economy and indeed one that depends heavily on imports for intermediate and capital goods, both the expansion and utilization of productive capacity depend on the adequacy of export earnings to finance imports. SSA's share of world exports has been declining in the context of unprecedented expansion of world trade; the share has dropped from approximately 3 per cent in the mid 1950s to the current 1 per cent (Yeats et al., 1997). Although this might itself reflect the much slower growth of African economies, the decline in the export orientation during the 1970s and the 1980s when world trade was growing faster than output is an important explanation. Decline in export volumes between the mid 1970s and the mid 1980s was precipitate in many SSA countries, and linked to excessive taxation both explicit and implicit. A modest recovery has been in progress since 1986, with countries engaged in reforms being able to reverse the downward trend and actually register an average growth in export volume of 3.2 per cent during 1986–1993 (Hadjimichael et al., 1994). Due to the strong downward trend of world commodity prices, however, export earnings did not fair as well. This rate of recovery remains inadequate as imports continued to expand at an annual rate of 6.4 per cent over the same period, and for many poorer countries debt servicing requirements expanded rapidly.

In a comparative sense East Asia's export performance was again far above SSA's; from 19 per cent during 1960–1969, Asia's export share of GDP rose sharply and persistently to 38.4 per cent during 1990–1994. The share of exports for a median country in SSA in fact declined from 24 per cent in the 1960s to 22 per cent in the 1990. That for Latin America increased slightly over the same period, from 20 per cent to 24 per cent (Table 3.1).

Initial Conditions and Long-Term Growth

There is now a growing literature that attempts to explain the slow growth performance as well as low savings and investment responses to policy reforms in SSA. All these studies use cross-country regressions involving a wide range of developing countries and conduct counterfactuals to explain the distinct performance of SSA by way of measured differences in growth determinants. Most notable among the group of studies on Africa are those that focus on explaining long-term growth.

A common feature of these studies is the finding that initial conditions for growth do matter. Although the income convergence effect has been found to be relatively weaker in SSA in spite of lower incomes than for middle-income countries, it is nevertheless significant (Easterly and Levine, 1996). The underlying convergence effect is predicated on the potential for higher returns in capital-starved low-income countries. The initial quality of human capital and infrastructure has also been shown to be a significant explanatory variable for long-term growth through its influence on the marginal product of private investment. On this aspect SSA countries have the lowest status compared with other developing regions.

The main focus of the earlier studies explaining the slow growth in SSA countries was to isolate the influence of policy from the background of wide pursuit of reforms since the early 1980s. World Bank (1994), Elbadawi (1992), Elbadawi and Ndulu (1995), and Easterly and Levine (1994) are among the most prominent of these. The studies confirmed the strong influence of macroeconomic instability and the misalignment of the real exchange rate on slow growth, along with the much weaker influence of external shocks, predominantly terms of trade (TOT) effects. However, these studies invariably found that after accounting for fundamentals, external shocks and policy influence, there remained a large and significant unexplained difference with the expected relationship (the Africa dummy).

The effort was then turned to unpackaging this dummy by searching for what else matters or how to measure better what matters. The effort took three directions. The first was to determine whether geography matters. In the context of studies on African growth, Chua (1993a/b) pioneered the work on neighbourhood growth contagion effects, around the hypothesis of growth poles, and the negative spillover effects of civil unrest and bad reputation associated with it. The study's findings were successful in turning the dummy statistically insignificant. The most recent effort in this area is that by Sachs and Warner (1997), which includes the effects of tropical climate and land-lockedness on growth, finding both features influence growth negatively. The neighbourhood effect in this study weakens, however.

The second direction of effort has been on the influence of political instability, corruption and institutional quality. These exert their influence largely by raising investors' risk perceptions and reducing the effectiveness of resource application via waste and leakages. The works by Aron (1996), Sachs and Warner (1995, 1997), Elbadawi et al. (1997a), Easterly and Levine (1996), Rodrik (1997), Collier and Gunning (1997), and Collier (1996) all confirm the importance of these factors in limiting the realization of growth potential. The recent *World Development Report* (1997) treats these weaknesses most comprehensively in the context of the role of the state, singling out the critical role of citizens' voices for more accountable governance, technocracy and better quality of institutions as key to evolving a strong state.

The third direction has been in pursuing better measures of the influence of external shocks and trade openness on long-term growth. The influence of debt overhang through discouraging private investment and putting pressure on sustaining macro stability is one of these. Elbadawi et al. (1997a) find a very strong negative and significant influence of the debt to GDP ratio beyond a threshold of 97 per cent by estimating a debt–growth Laffer curve. A very large proportion of SSA countries exceeds this threshold and faces retardation of growth. This effect supplements the crowding-out of current expenditures via external transfers to service debt, which was also found to be significant their study.

The effect of trade openness on long-term growth was found to be insignificant in a large number of previous cross-country growth studies. However, Sachs and Warner (1995, 1997) and Collier and Gunning (1997) have found openness to be a very significant explanatory variable of long-term growth performance. In fact, Sachs and Warner (1997) and Collier (1995) rate lack of openness to trade the top ranking reason for the slow growth performance of African countries. Results from Rodrik (1997) place it considerably lower on the scale and attribute its effects on growth much more to the strategic complementarity of the influence of macroeconomic policies and investment. Using an Africa only sample, Rodrik conducts a source of growth decomposition by categories of performance. For the high growth performers in the region, the most important contributors to growth were public savings, demography, human resources and a catch-up effect. Export taxation was a significant factor for explaining growth in the worst performers.

Drawing these studies together, a clear conclusion has been reached that the included factors now explain growth in SSA, and the previously significant 'Africa dummy' virtually disappears. There are no distinct features (unknown) that fail to explain the response of growth to policy, structural elements or external shocks. This allows us to perform much more comprehensive counterfactuals using other regions' data to determine the scope of growth performance in SSA if similar conditions were replicated. To this end, it is instructive to note the important conclusions from studies by Easterly and Levine (1996) and Sachs and Warner (1997), which are presented in Table 3.2.

Table 3.2 How much would African economies grow?

	Sachs & Warner (1997)	Easterly & Levine (1996)
Policy environment		
Openness	2.1	
Government surplus	0.1	0.4560
Institutional quality	0.6	0.6100
Assassinations (political instability)	-	0.0093
Black market premium	-	0.6040
Structural features		
Human capital		
Life expectancy	-	-
Initial schooling	-	0.32
Growth of active population	-	-
Financial depth	-	0.288
Infrastructure (telephones/worker)	-	0.632

Source: Sachs and Warner (1997); Easterly and Levine (1996).

The conclusions from the Sachs and Warner (1997) study restrict the simulations to only the policy environment; their openness variable includes the level of black market exchange rate premium, which Easterly and Levine account for separately. The second simulation by Easterly and Levine (1996) includes all categories of variables in the counterfactual:

- The policy environment, particularly appropriate exchange rate regimes, low inflation, openness to trade, low fiscal balances, institutional quality and political instability, account for 56 per cent to 85 per cent of the difference in long-term growth performance between SSA and East Asia. When East Asian levels of performance in these are substituted for, keeping all other growth-influencing factors constant, SSA growth could have been between 1.7 and 2.8 percentage points higher or two to three times above predicted growth performance of 0.9 per cent during the period 1970–1994.

- Structural features and geography, including human capital, quality of institutions and economic infrastructure, account for 20 per cent to 44 per cent of growth difference. Replacing African structural features with those of East Asia, the estimated rise in long-term growth would have been 1.24 percentage points higher or 1.4 times more than the predicted level with African structural features.

External shocks do not feature significantly in the differences in these two studies. But as we shall see later in this chapter, these become important when the effects of debt overhang are included. Simulations pertaining to Africa's performance in savings, investment and exports are taken up in the following section, together with the additional factors that help explain growth.

In the meantime, the treatment of the main determinants of growth, savings, investment and exports in SSA categorizes these into four major groups: macroeconomic policy environment, external shocks, human capital and regional spillover effects, and institutional and political uncertainty. The discussion identifies the main channels of influence by these factors and assesses outcomes of attempts to improve them for better growth performance. This forms the basis of comparing the simulation results and the discussion of the institutional underpinnings of successful transition to high growth.

Macroeconomic Policies and Outcomes: Regional Comparisons

Empirical literature suggests that economic growth and other related macroeconomic targets (e.g., exports and private investment) are associated with five broad categories of variables:

- Macroeconomic policy environment, mainly reflecting the extent of departure from fundamental macroeconomic balances or the degree and quality of intermediate macroeconomic public sector policies and outcomes, such as public investment policy.
- Macroeconomic instability.
- External shocks.
- Human capital and regional spillover effects.
- Institutional and political uncertainty variables.

The theoretical strand of the endogenous growth literature and the recent investment-irreversibility literature provide the rationale, as well as suggest the channels of influence of these variables, especially those in the category of non-traditional determinants such as macroeconomic uncertainty and institutional, political and regional variables. However, it should be noted at the outset that only a smaller set of policy variables and other fundamentals have been shown to be robustly and significantly associated with the three macroeconomic performance variables. Moreover, the econometrics methodology of this literature, mainly based on decadal averages of cross-country regressions, is subject to criticism related to the ability of the methodology to identify adequately the various individual effects.

In what follows we discuss a preliminary framework for analysing the mechanism through which the five categories of variables affect growth, exports, savings and private investments. To complement the analysis, as well as to partially take the criticism of cross-country analysis into consideration, we discuss some country-specific experiences and briefly review ten successful transitions (to high sustained growth and low macroeconomic instability) recently analysed by Elbadawi and Schmidt-Hebbel (1996).

Overview of Cross-Regional Evidence

Using the framework described, we draw a brief comparison among SSA, Latin America/Caribbean (LAC) and East Asia for a select set of policy variables and other fundamentals. This will motivate the analysis of the next section, which provides some simulations, based on the estimated results of panel regressions. The panel regressions help to assess the relative contribution of the various factors in explaining the differential performance of East Asia relative to SSA for each of the three performance variables, in addition to private savings.

Macroeconomic policy environment Starting with fiscal policy, three channels of influence can be identified: the financing implications of fiscal deficits; the macroeconomic uncertainty of large fiscal deficits; and the degree of complementarity (or substitutability) between public and private investment. High fiscal deficits may be financed internally by domestic credit creation, which reduces real money balances and pushes up real interest rates, or by forced savings by the private sector through financial repression. Either directly or indirectly, the result in both cases is crowding-out of private investment, and possibly a slowdown in exports and overall economic growth. Furthermore, to the extent that the rate of monetary expansion is high enough to accommodate both private and public investment demands, the ensuing economic instability associated with inflation should have a negative impact on economic performance. If, on the other hand, public sector deficits are financed by external debt, increased indebtedness could be another source of economic uncertainty with similar negative consequences.

The central role of fiscal reforms in the context of structural adjustment programmes (SAPs) should in principle have enhanced macroeconomic performance in reforming countries. However, the highest and most sustainable pay-offs of fiscal adjustment were usually associated with deeper and more structural reforms that went beyond reducing the overall fiscal deficits (see, for example, Easterly and Schmidt-Hebbel, 1991). In particular, it has been noted by many observers that fiscal consolidation often takes the form of reduced public investment, which may be complementary to private investment (see, for example, Blejer and Khan, 1984; Serven and Solimano, 1993b).

As argued by Schmidt-Hebbel and Muller (1991: 12), 'public infrastructure, communications and transport services are often underpriced with long waiting times and other administrative measures which inhibit both efficient use by the private sector and lead to sub-optimal public investment levels in these areas. This contributes to rationing of public services with very high urban land prices in areas that have access to the rationed public services. Increased availability of public services through higher public investment raises the profitability of private investment'. Even though the evidence on the complementarity of public and private investment is mixed,[3] the more recent evidence seems to suggest that there are certain categories of public investment (especially in the areas of infrastructure, human capital, and law and order) that tend to strongly crowd in private investment, as well as enhance private sector exports and overall growth. Furthermore, there appear to be lower (and upper) thresholds below (above) which public investment may not be effective (Serven, 1996b).

The evidence on fiscal policy and its implications for interest rates and monetary policy across the three regions suggests the following (Table 3.3):

- Fiscal deficits have always been higher in SSA than in the other two regions, and in 1985–1994 the ratio of fiscal deficits to GDP in SSA (at an average rate of 4.33 per cent) was more than four times the ratios in East Asia and LAC. On the other hand, public investment ratios have been consistently higher in SSA relative to other regions. The very disappointing growth performance in SSA suggests that the returns to public investment in this region must be very low indeed (e.g., Collier, 1996).
- The rate of growth of domestic credit, an imperfect but good indicator of availability of investment finance, slowed steadily in both SSA and LAC throughout 1970–1994. On the other hand, the rate of credit expansion in East Asia remained high and steady throughout: 14.2 per cent, 13.4 per cent and 10.4 per cent in the three consecutive periods. The combination of single-digit inflation and average per capita GDP growth in excess of 5 per cent since 1970 allowed considerable financial deepening to take place in East Asia. In the case of SSA the absence of vigorous growth meant that a tight monetary policy was required to keep inflation under control.
- The cost of borrowing, reflected by the real lending rate, rose steadily during the period in the three regions. Even though the real rates were still negative in SSA during the last period, they have been positive and very large since.

---

[3] While Serven (1996a), Mlambo and Kumar (1995), Blejer and Khan (1984), Serven and Solimano (1993b), Greene and Villanueva (1991), and Oshikoya (1994) found complementarity using cross-country data, Balassa (1988) found that public investment crowds out private investment.

Table 3.3 Endogenous macroeconomic indicators

	E Asia	LAC	SSA
Period 1: 1970–1979			
Public investment (as a % of GDP)	6.79	7.23	9.47
Of which: Infrastructure	1.77	2.20	1.80
Human resources	0.65	0.56	0.72
Real exchange rate (RER)	138.13	165.77	149.42
Fiscal balance (as a % of GDP)	-2.11	-1.02	-2.69
Growth in domestic credit (%)	14.24	8.08	15.34
Inflation (%)	7.95	22.91	10.42
Real interest rate (%)	-3.16	-3.03	-4.71
RER variability (%)	6.66	6.10	6.60
Inflation variability (%)	64.77	39.78	56.68
Period 2: 1980–1984			
Public investment (as a % of GDP)	9.77	6.10	10.56
Of which: Infrastructure	0.65	1.64	1.24
Human resources	1.16	0.32	0.86
Real exchange rate (RER)	134.02	197.45	124.97
Fiscal balance (as a % of GDP)	-2.48	-3.46	-4.78
Growth in domestic credit (%)	13.36	9.14	5.12
Inflation (%)	9.98	25.07	12.14
Real interest rate (%)	2.09	2.52	-2.79
RER variability (%)	7.14	11.68	6.83
Inflation variability (%)	68.44	40.69	47.68
Period 3: 1985–1994			
Public investment (as a % of GDP)	7.79	4.98	9.00
Of which: Infrastructure	0.89	1.31	1.82
Human resources	1.13	0.32	0.78
Real exchange rate (RER)	105.55	119.01	102.09
Fiscal balance (as a % of GDP)	-1.05	0.96	-4.33
Growth in domestic credit (%)	10.38	0.81	1.85
Inflation (%)	6.45	43.85	9.86
Real interest rate (%)	3.15	2.44	-1.03
RER variability (%)	7.25	12.99	11.50
Inflation variability (%)	42.64	32.70	53.56

Notes: E Asia = East Asian countries; LAC = Latin American countries; SSA = Sub-Saharan Africa

Source: Compiled by authors.

Foreign exchange policies affect real macroeconomic target variables through the real exchange rate, which is the economy-wide relative price affecting inter-sector resource flows. A major real exchange rate disequilibrium, especially real exchange rate over-valuation, could be very harmful to overall economic competitiveness and eventually investment and economic growth. In the short run, however, corrective real devaluation to eliminate real exchange rate over-valuation can have a contractionary effect on private investment in countries where prices of capital goods have been made artificially cheaper by the over-valued currency. On the other hand, real depreciation will also cause the relative domestic currency price of exportables to rise. Despite the possible contractionary effects of real exchange rate depreciation on investment and growth in the short run, the ensuing initial positive incentive effects for exportables and the subsequent resource reallocation towards the export sector should eventually lead to an export-led spur to private investment and growth. Two observations emerge:

- Using the real exchange rate as a measure of international competitiveness—in terms of producing comparable tradeable goods at lower costs compared with other countries—SSA countries have achieved significant strides on this score. For example, between the first and third periods, the real exchange rate depreciated (declined) by 31 per cent in SSA, compared with 24 per cent and 33 per cent for East Asia and Latin America (Table 3.3).
- Strictly speaking, however, the appreciation (depreciation) of the real exchange rate can only be harmful (beneficial) to competitiveness if the evolution of its fundamentals (i.e., its equilibrium value) suggests that the rate should depreciate rather than appreciate. The significant deterioration in the terms of trade, especially in SSA and LAC, suggests that the real exchange rate depreciations appear to have been driven by the adverse evolution of the terms of trade. However, more recently and due to surges in private capital inflows mainly attracted by high real interest rates precipitated by requirements for non-inflationary finance of fiscal deficits, the gains in competitiveness in many leading African reforming countries have been severely compromised (Elbadawi, 1996).

Macroeconomic uncertainty As has been argued in the recent literature, the importance of uncertainty arises from the nature of the investment process itself: that capital equipment takes time to build and that it is partially irreversible or sector specific.[4] It has been shown that under conditions of uncertainty, risk-averse firms associate uncertainty with greater variability in expected profits, and may curtail their investment altogether. Risk-neutral firms, on the other hand, may prefer the 'waiting option' to undertaking physical investment and instead invest in information gathering to reduce the uncertainty. Two sources of economic policy based risk and uncertainty affecting private investment decisions can be identified. One stems from the risk associated with economic variables that are important determinants of overall economic stability. This is captured by the

[4] See, for example, Pindyck (1993), Rodrik (1990) and van Wijnbergen (1992).

volatility of these variables such as terms of trade, inflation and real exchange rate. High volatility in the last two variables reduces the information content of prices as coordinators of economic activity, and hence increases the riskiness of long-term investment. Two comments can be made:

- SSA has fared well in terms of inflation, unlike LAC; inflation remains in single digits for most of the period and is comparable to the Asian rates. However, East Asia distinguished itself as a much more stable region compared with the other two in terms of trade and real exchange rate variabilities (Tables 3.3 and 3.4). Moreover, in terms of inflation variability, SSA has been the least stable of the three regions for most of the 1970–1994 period, including 1985–1994.
- The aggregate African macroeconomic instability analysis masks a very important divide between the CFA and non-CFA countries. Due to the monetary discipline of the CFA zone, this group of countries has been able to maintain low and stable inflation, compared with the flexible exchange rate regime economies of SSA, which have experienced much higher inflation and inflation variability than the overall African median (Elbadawi, 1996). On the other hand, the CFA countries have been much more prone to higher real exchange rate variability, mainly due to the their inflexible exchange rate regime (Hoffmaister et al., 1997).

The other source of economic uncertainty is the potential for future policy reversals or lack of policy implementation. In this case, uncertainty is caused by low credibility of the current policy framework, which induces a postponement of the investment decision. This source of uncertainty is likely to dominate cases of highly indebted countries undergoing far-reaching structural reforms,[5] or cases of reforming countries with a long history of policy reversals (Collier, 1996). Following other studies in the literature,[6] we have approximated this policy uncertainty by one variable, which strongly contributes to it, without being its only determinant: the external debt to GDP ratio. In addition to its effect on the type of uncertainty described above, high external debt can affect private investment and hence growth and exports through three additional channels:

- A high stock of debt signals the negative 'debt overhang effect' on private investment, due to higher expected future taxes required to service foreign debt payments;[7]

---

[5] In a recent paper, Serven (1996b) shows that even small probabilities of policy reversal in a model with entry and exit costs for capital can deter private investment by considerable amounts.

[6] See, for example, Schmidt-Hebbel and Muller (1991), Mlambo and Kumar (1995), and Serven (1996b), among others.

[7] Several of the most recent studies find significant and negative influence of outstanding foreign debt on private investment; see, for example, Serven (1996b), Serven and Solimano

Table 3.4 Exogenous effects and human capital indicators, by region

	E Asia	LAC	SSA
Period 1: 1970–1979			
Terms of trade (TOT)	111.74	140.04	129.19
TOT variability	7.66	14.20	12.31
External debt (as a % of GDP)	27.57	22.97	23.79
Debt service (as a % of exports)	14.23	24.29	5.48
Schooling (1960-1965)	1.44	1.39	0.82
Real per capita GDP growth	5.47	1.92	1.95
Regional GDP growth	4.82	2.55	1.37
Period 2: 1980–1984			
Terms of trade (TOT)	113.84	121.20	110.98
TOT variability	6.05	8.41	8.98
External debt (as a % of GDP)	38.78	43.66	49.61
Debt service (as a % of exports)	19.30	43.20	14.94
Schooling (1970–1975)	1.56	1.54	0.85
Real per capita GDP Growth	4.41	-1.38	-1.21
Regional GDP Growth	4.14	4.02	0.70
Period 3: 1985–1994			
Terms of trade (TOT)	98.86	101.53	99.92
TOT variability	4.77	8.80	8.14
External debt (as a % of GDP)	44.25	63.10	81.24
Debt service (as a % of exports)	18.36	33.71	17.08
Schooling (1980–1985)	1.70	1.78	1.01
Real per capita GDP growth	5.62	0.79	-0.40
Regional GDP growth	3.45	-0.38	-0.86

Notes: Countries: E Asia = East Asian countries; LAC = Latin American countries; SSA = Sub-Saharan Africa. Schooling: Log of 1 + average years of school attainment. Regional GDP growth: Weighted average for the growth of per capita GDP real GDP of the neighbours of the country. Weights used are GDP in 1960.
Source: Compiled by authors.

- A high stock of debt increases the cost of fresh new debt and therefore acts as a credit rationing mechanism in the international capital market, which reduces the rate of capital accumulation; and finally,
- There is a crowding-out effect, where servicing of a growing stock of debt will

(1993b), Mlambo and Kumar (1995), and Schmidt-Hebbel and Muller (1991).

reduce the national saving available for investment. This effect is reflected by the ratio of debt service to exports (or to GDP). Both the stock and flow effects are expected to have negative effects on private investment.

One observation that emerges is that between the last two periods the stock of external debt for SSA almost doubled (from 49.6 per cent in 1980–1984 to 81.2 per cent in 1985–1994). The result was that these countries were the most highly indebted of the three groups; the debt ratio was 44.3 per cent for East Asia and 63.1 per cent for LAC in the last period (Table 3.2). In terms of debt service to export ratios, the burden in the most recent period is low for SSA (at 17.1 per cent), mainly due to a dysfunctional debt situation in which some of these countries were likely to have defaulted on their debt payment obligations.

Human Capital and Regional Effects

The importance of human capital for creating knowledge and technology-based externalities, which could permit significant increases in the productivity of capital, is now very firmly established in the new growth literature,[8] and appears to be strongly corroborated by the recent East Asian 'miracle' performance. It can be argued that in a country endowed with a high stock of human capital, and hence a highly skilled and educated labour force, expected returns from investment would in general be higher, especially in skill-intensive industries. This is because the overall cost of training would be lower, and it would be easier to introduce more advanced equipment and processes to raise productivity and reduce unit costs. This argument is consistent with the evidence from the empirical growth literature, which finds the stock of human capital to be among the major determinants explaining cross-country differences in growth, exports and investment.[9] For example:

- SSA has always lagged behind the other two regions on this score. In 1980–1985, the school enrolment ratios in LAC and East Asia were higher by 77 per cent and 69 per cent, respectively, relative to those in SSA (Table 3.4). An additional indicator of human capital is life expectancy at birth. Again the same patterns obtain. The expected age in 1985–1994 was 69.7 in East Asian countries and 68.3 in LAC, compared with only 51.1 for SSA.
- The challenge of enhancing the stock of human capital in SSA is mainly in the area of cost effectiveness and mode of delivery, where the private sector could play an important role in the case of higher (post-secondary) education and curative medical services. However, given that the efficiency of public service delivery in SSA is generally lower than in other developing regions (Collier,

[8] The formal theoretical rationalization of this argument is provided by Lucas (1988).

[9] For example, studies by Barro (1991), Mankiw, Romer and Weil (1992), and Khan and Kumar (1993) have found a positive effect of the initial stock of human capital on per capita GDP growth.

1996), higher expenditure on education and health may be required as well in order for the state to provide adequate levels of service in basic education and health.

Economic cooperation has a potential positive impact on national policy credibility, and hence investment and subsequently growth and export performance, because it can provide a mechanism for collective commitment to economic reform in a context of a reciprocal threat-making arrangement (e.g., Collier, 1991). Deeper economic integration in a given region may also permit expansion of the regional economy to generate the threshold scales necessary to trigger the much needed strategic complementarity. Furthermore, it helps attract the levels of investment required for the development of modern manufacturing cores and the transfer of technology within the region (e.g., Krugman, 1991). The empirical strand of the literature also supports the investment and growth enhancing effects of economic integration. This literature finds that spillover effects (proxied by regional investment, regional political instability or regional growth) are significant and robustly linked to variations in investment and growth across countries (e.g., Chua, 1993a/b; Easterly and Levine, 1996).

An approximate measure of the regional spillover effect for a country is given by the average growth of its neighbours. Comparisons based on this measure reveal the lack of growth poles in SSA and LAC relative to East Asia. For example, the average annual per capita growth rates of the immediate neighbours of the median country from SSA (LAC) in 1985–1994 were a dismal −0.86 per cent (−0.38 per cent), compared with 3.4 per cent for East Asia (Table 3.2).

External shocks External shocks can affect national economies through several channels: terms of trade, capital flows or international interest rates. Given the dominance of the first of these effects and that the other two are reflected through the effect of external debt (see above), we confine ourselves here to the discussion of the terms of trade effect. Fluctuations in the terms of trade can affect macroeconomic performance through two possible channels:[10] first, and as has happened in many African countries (Table 3.4), a decline in terms of trade reduces incomes and the profitability of the export sector and hence export growth. If profits are positively correlated across sectors, the fall in incomes and the profitability of the export sector will have a negative effect on overall investment and growth. Second, terms of trade deterioration may affect investment, exports and growth indirectly, through a worsening of the current account. Countries have responded to a deteriorating current account by increasing controls on imports, devaluing the exchange rate, or tightening fiscal and monetary policies. Controls on imports of intermediate or capital goods may have a direct adverse effect on private investment. Tight fiscal policies may reduce public investment, while monetary restraint would result in credit rationing, both of which could adversely affect private investment.

[10] See, for example Cardoso (1993).

Institutional and political uncertainty The other source of uncertainty that affects economic performance is institutional uncertainty or instability in the political environment. Political instability judged to be harmful to investment ranges from rapid government turnover, which affects policy credibility and leads to unstable incentive and policy frameworks, thus raising the value of the 'waiting' option, to more extreme forms of social and political unrest, such as widespread political violence or civil wars, that create more fundamental aspects of uncertainty such the collapse of institutions of government and civil society (macro insecurity) and the loss of life, physical property or property rights (micro insecurity) (Collier, 1996). The latter takes place when, for example, violent change of governments involves a radical redefinition of the basic 'rules of the game', raising the risk of expropriation and nationalization.

Investors require more than formal statements in which states commit themselves to the role of *impartial* enforcers of contracts. The presence of an efficient and impartial bureaucracy to implement the declared policies is equally important. Hence recent cross-country studies find bureaucratic or institutional quality (in addition to political stability) to be strongly associated with investment performance (e.g., Knack and Keefer, 1995).

Two sets of indicators are used to assess the likely impact of institutional and political factors on investment and growth. The first is a *subjective* composite measure of the degree of institutional quality, absence of corruption, enforcement of contracts and protection of property rights. The other set of indicators reflects various aspects of political instability such as civil and regional wars, unconstitutional and violent attempts at change of governments, riots, and purges of civil and military employees. The evidence from the literature suggests that these two sets of indicators are systematically associated with investment and growth, and therefore appear to account adequately for the variables that matter: investment risk and property rights. Other important but more subtle indicators, such as the degree of human rights, democracy or erosion of civil rights, were not found to be robustly associated with investment (see Aron et al., 1996). The indicator of institutional quality suggests that SSA provides the worst institutional support among the three regions (Table 3.5).

Historically SSA has been one of the most violence-prone regions of the world. From 1970 to 1994 there were 19 civil wars, more than twice as many as in East Asia and almost three times the number in LAC. SSA also has by far the highest number of revolutions (violent attempted change of government). Given this disturbingly high degree of political instability, and the strong association among political stability, transparency and accountability, and economic performance, it can be argued that perhaps the most rewarding form of investment African countries could make is in the areas of national and regional peace by building mechanisms for conflict resolution and introducing national political reforms to bring about more open, enfranchising, accountable and transparent governments.

Table 3.5 Institutional and political indicators, 1970–1994

	E Asia	LAC	SSA
Indicators of corruption			
Corrupt (1)	3.2	3.0	2.8
Corrupt (2)	5.1	6.5	4.1
Quality of institutions	6.3	5.1	4.5
Political environment			
Number of regional wars	0.0	1.0	6.0
Number of civil wars	9.0	7.0	19.0
Number of purges	15.0	10.0	9.0
Number of riots	20.0	40.0	28.0
Number of revolutions	8.0	14.0	21.0

Notes: Countries/regions: E Asia = East Asian countries; LAC = Latin American countries; SSA = Sub-Saharan Africa.

Institutions: Average of (a) government repudiation of contracts, (b) risk of expropriation, (c) Rule of law (first multiplied by 5/3) and (d) bureaucratic quality (first multiplied by 5/3) over the 1980s.

Sources: Corrupt (1) Knack and Keefer (1995); original source: International Country Risk Guide (ICRG). Corrupt (2) Mauro (1995).

The Experiences of Ten Successful Transitions

Elbadawi and Schmidt-Hebbel (1996) analyse the patterns of macroeconomic and financial instability/growth transitions for a group of ten countries that managed to achieve successful transformations to low instability and high growth. Six of these successful countries are in the East Asian region,[11] one is in Latin America and three are in SSA. The length of the post-transition period—where high growth and low instability were achieved—varies from 7 years in the case of Uganda to 29 years in the cases of Korea and Singapore.

The transitions to a high growth plateau have been quite remarkable in all ten countries. Korea stands out as the most spectacular, where annual per capita growth rates averaged more than 7.6 per cent for 29 years (1966–1994). Singapore achieved an annual average growth rate of 8.2 per cent for 17 years (1966–1982) and another average rate of about 6 per cent for 13 years (1982–1994). Botswana managed a staggering 11.2 per cent annual per capita growth rate for 10 years (1969–1979), followed by a 6.8 per cent annual growth rate for another 10 years (1980–1990). Other countries achieved major turnarounds from negative or low to very high and sustained growth: Indonesia from −0.23 per cent in 1961–1967 to 5.1 per cent in 1968–1994; Chile from 1.0 per cent in 1971–1986 to 5.2 per cent in 1987–1994; Mauritius from 0.93 per cent in 1961–1971 to 5.9 per cent in 1972–1979 and 3.9

[11] Two other successful East Asian countries (Taiwan and Hong Kong) are excluded from the analysis due to lack of data.

per cent in 1980–1994; and Uganda from –2.6 per cent in 1971–1987 to 3.5 per cent in 1988–1994. The remainder of the countries (China, Malaysia, Thailand) have managed to graduate from fair to spectacular by almost doubling their initial growth rates (of 3–4 per cent) over the two periods.

Elbadawi and Schmidt-Hebbel's analysis suggests three important characteristics of these remarkable transformations. First, the relationship between growth and growth volatility across phases was negative; in particular low growth volatility is necessary for sustained average growth in the post-transition period. Save for Thailand, Botswana and Korea (for the 1961–1965 and 1966–1982 comparison), the very impressive growth transitions have also been associated with considerable declines in growth volatility. The fall in growth volatility between the two phases has been quite dramatic—ranging from around 50 per cent in Korea (from 1966–1982 to 1983–1994), Singapore, Mauritius and Uganda, to more than 60 per cent for Chile, more than 70 per cent for China, and almost 80 per cent for Malaysia. The exception to this regularity was Indonesia, which achieved a dramatic transition from an average negative per capita growth rate of –0.23 per cent during 1961–1967 to more than 5 per cent annual growth rate throughout 1968–1994, while growth volatility fell only modestly from 2.5 per cent to about 2 per cent. On the other hand, compared with other transition cases, growth was relatively stable in Indonesia before the recovery period.

The results suggest that the majority of successful transitions have been achieved by limiting the frequency of occurrence of very low growth 'outliers' that appear to have derived both low and more volatile average growth outcomes during the pre-transition periods. This finding is consistent with the evidence obtained by Hausman and Gavin (1995: Figure 2), which shows a negative relationship between long-run growth rate and the volatility of real GDP for a sample of about 130 countries. Hausman and Gavin also find that terms of trade volatility, monetary policy volatility and pegged exchange rate regimes, in addition to capital flow volatility and political instability, tend to exacerbate volatility of real GDP. They also find that financial depth played the role of a 'shock absorber', suggesting that deep financial markets provide adequate insulation for the real economy and hence permit effective adjustment to shocks. This finding is very important for explaining the successful experiences of the high performing Asian economies (HPAEs), as well as for drawing lessons for other developing countries from the HPAEs' successful transitions.

Second, the experiences of successful transitions corroborate the widely held view in the literature that inflation crises beget reforms and recovery,[12] even when the more general and overall indicator of macro-financial crisis (MFCRI)[13] is used. According to Elbadawi and Schmidt-Hebbel's results, most of the ten countries

[12] Bruno and Easterly (1995) provide very strong evidence that an inflation crisis usually results in higher and longer growth in post-crisis episodes.

[13] As defined in Elbadawi and Schmidt-Hebbel (1996), this indicator measures the extent of expansive macroeconomic and financial policies, relative to benchmark levels deemed to be sustainable or consistent with macroeconomic equilibrium.

that achieved major turnarounds in their growth performance were clearly affected by a major crisis in the initial period. Moreover, the success of these countries on the growth front during the post-crisis period was strongly linked to their ability to avoid subsequent major crises. Even for the countries such as Korea and Indonesia, where data are not available to allow comparison of MFCRI indexes in the initial periods with those of subsequent periods, there is ample evidence that considerable economic and political crises affected these countries during these pre-take-off periods (e.g., Haggard, 1994). In fact, Haggard argues that severe economic and political crises not only triggered good policies in several East Asian countries during the 1950s and 1960s, but have also shaped the institutions in these countries and facilitated some of the major strategic initiatives, such as land reforms in Korea and Taiwan. This latter aspect of the Asian initial conditions is believed to be the missing ingredient that eluded many developing countries attempting an 'Asian miracle' of their own (Rodrik, 1994).

Third, higher and sustained growth has always been associated with better financial and macroeconomic policy performance. Aside from avoiding crisis-proportions macroeconomic disequilibrium, restoring growth on a sustained basis also requires good macroeconomic and financial policy performance, in terms of both levels and volatility of key policy variables. As indicated above, the relevance of macroeconomic policy to growth is justified in the theoretical strand of the endogenous growth literature, which was strongly corroborated by empirical research (e.g., Easterly and Rebelo, 1993; Fischer, 1993; Schmidt-Hebbel, 1995). For example, consistent with their spectacular growth record, Korea and Singapore excelled over all other countries in terms of overall macro-financial performance. The same story holds for almost all other successful transitions. Elbadawi (1996) reaches similar conclusions when he compares African macroeconomic economic policy stances with the policy frontier (Southeast Asia: Indonesia, Malaysia and Thailand),[14] and argues that Africa needs further adjustment (see also World Bank, 1994).

Comparative Analysis of Performance Indicators

It has been shown that for two consecutive years, 1995 and 1996, real GDP growth for a number of countries in SSA has signalled a measure of economic recovery. The question that arises is the sustainability of this recovery. This is because the response to investment and savings has been slow and this has slowed the expansion of productive capacity. It should be noted that because of data limitations these two years have not been incorporated into our analysis and simulations.

The section draws its contribution from estimated cross-country panel regressions that attempt to explain growth, investment, savings and export supply

---

[14] Elbadawi (1996) compares Southeast Asia in 1980–1990 with SSA in 1991–1992, in an attempt to capture the later and more consolidated stages of African economic reforms.

in these countries over 1970–1994. We use the estimated equations to calculate the relative contributions of each block of variables in the two regions (East Asia and SSA). As stated in the introductory part of the chapter, the objective is to explain links between macroeconomic performance in SSA and their determinants by using the stellar performance of East Asia for comparison. In this way, we tentatively help to account for SSA's relatively poor macroeconomic performance when taking a long-term view.

Four indicators of performance are used in this section: private investment, real output growth, savings and export supply. Using these indicators and a range of their determinants we compare the performance of East Asia with that of sub-Saharan Africa, and show what accounts for differences in their performance by simple simulation. The simulations use the means of each variable in the panel regressions for East Asia, net of that of SSA and multiplied by the estimated coefficient. The idea is to assess the relative importance of the explanatory variables in explaining SSA's performance in relation to the variables in the model by way of contrast with the sample as a whole and with East Asia in particular. The main question asked in these computations is what explains SSA countries' economic performance relative to the overall sample of developing countries and the best performers in East Asia.

To accomplish this, the sample means of the explanatory variables are computed, together with the means for the SSA and East Asian regions. We then use the regression coefficients of the respective variables from the panel regressions to obtain the contribution of each variable in explaining the differential performance effects. We subtract the SSA mean of the variable from the sample mean (and East Asian means) and multiply by the coefficient from the regression results. The percentage contributions thus show which region is better off or worse off. These results are discussed in the following sections.

Private Investments

A range of variables were analysed in the investment equation as determinants of investment. The major question asked in the panel regression equations is what contributed to the slow investment response even after almost a decade of economic reforms. The other question asked, and one that bears extreme importance in the comparative analysis with East Asia, is why even when investments have been seen to increase, has output growth fallen, implying inefficiency of investment. We attempt to shed light on these issues by looking at the relative contributions of the variables outlined.

The first category of determinants of private investment is external factors (external debt and terms of trade). This category of variables includes a measure of the ratio of current debt stock to GDP and a debt overhang measure, which is debt stock lagged and squared. The effects from debt overhang will discourage private investments, as argued in the previous section, depending on how the respective governments are expected to raise fiscal revenue necessary to finance external debt service obligations. Thus, inflation tax and excessive government expenditure will contribute to increased domestic inflation, which also discourages private investment. The perception here is that a high debt service burden is viewed by potential investors both as a threat to sustaining reforms and as a potential source of higher inflation tax to meet future debt service requirements (Elbadawi, 1996). In addition there is a liquidity constraint coming from debt service obligation. These three variables thus encompass the effects through which external debt affects investments through various channels. Terms of trade, on the other hand, affect savings and hence investment. It is argued in the literature that a decline in terms of trade reduces the income and profitability of the export sector, which reduces export growth and investments. In the panel regression, these effects are accounted for not just by the level of the terms of trade, but also by its volatility in influencing private investment (see Elbadawi et al., 1997a).

The simulations from the estimated panel regression (for 1970–1994) show that SSA is better off than East Asia when current external debt stock to GDP is considered, but worse off when the measure of debt overhang is considered. However, the effect of debt overhang is minimal at 0.06 per cent following the size of the estimated coefficient. The results from debt service to exports also show that SSA is better off than East Asia. This gives an overall effect that showing that external debt variables have worsened the investment performance in East Asia by a proportion of 6.4 per cent compared with SSA. These results are contradictory when one looks at the magnitude of external debt and debt overhang; it is clear that SSA has been associated with more severe difficulties in relation to external debt (debt crisis) than has East Asia. As argued in the introductory part of the chapter, this shows the heavy reliance of public investment on external financing (see Table 3.6).

The terms of trade effect, which enters both in variability adjusted by the level of terms of trade and in terms of trade shock clearly shows that SSA is much more negatively affected by terms of trade than is East Asia. These results are consistent with cases of primary exports, which are subject to wide fluctuations. Terms of trade affect investment through the saving channel since income levels are affected. Thus, this offers one explanation of the better performance in investment in East Asia.

The next group of variables combines institutional, political, real output growth and regional indicators. These are shown in Table 3.7. The simulation results for both categories of variables that determine private investments for East Asia have a better performance than those for SSA. Investment performance in Africa seems to be hampered by quality of institutions, civil wars and low output growth. This is consistent with the fact that a country at war or in recession cannot stimulate private investments and thus growth is low. The overall effect shows that the policy environment in East Asia explains the investment differential in the two regions.

Table 3.6 Impact of external factors on private investments

	Means of variables		Coefficient	Contribution (%)
	E Asia	SSA		
External debt				
External debt to GDP ratio (DY)	0.352	0.719	0.171	-6.39
Dy_{t-1}^2	0.167	1.074	-0.001	0.06
Debt service to exports	0.176	0.155	-0.024	-0.05
Overall effects				-6.38
Terms of trade effects:				
Log (CVTOT/TOT)	-2.190	-1.970	-0.125	2.75
TOT SHOCK	0 .048	-0.005	-0.022	-0.10
Overall effects				2.65

Table 3.7 Growth and social-political variables

	Means of variables		Coefficient	Contribution (%)
	E Asia	SSA		
Institutional and policy variables:				
Quality of institutions	0.782	0.656	0.087	1.10
Dummy for SSA revolutions	0.000	0.223	-0.001	0.02
Dummy for SSA civil wars	0.000	0.133	-0.001	0.02
Overall effects				1.14
Growth and regional conditions:				
Regional per capita GDP	795.5	549.0	0.001	-0.01
Real GDP growth	0.073	0.033	0.102	0.41
Overall effects				0.39

The next class of variables includes those related to the policy environment. Not surprisingly, and consistent with our prediction, the policy environment affords a significant explanation for investment performance in the two regions. As argued in Elbadawi et al. (1997a), policy-induced risks are very important in explaining the slow response of investment to economic reforms. This is captured by variables indicating policy instability, which is much higher in SSA than in East Asia. The overall effect shows that the policy environment in East Asia accounts for the differential in private investment in the two regions. This explains why the private investment ratio (as a percentage of GDP.) is 20 per cent on average in East Asian countries compared with an average of 9.6 per cent in SSA countries.

In summary, the poor performance of SSA in investment is explained by external indebtedness, terms of trade, poor institutions, political upheavals, recessions and a hostile policy environment (Table 3.8).

Table 3.8 Impact of policies on private investment

	Means of variables		Coefficient	Contribution (%)
	E Asia	SSA		
Policy variables:				
Real interest rate variability	-0.303	2.164	-0.055	10.31
Financial depth	0.579	0.293	0.028	0.80
Fiscal balance to GDP ratio	-0.016	-0.048	0.040	0.13
Change in public investment	.001	0.001	0.393	0.02
Overall policy contribution				11.26
Policy outcome:				
Inflation variability	0.043	0.318	-0.001	0.02
Unexplained residual				1.28
Investment ratio	20.0%	9.6%		10.36

Real Output Growth

The next indicator of performance looks at determinants of growth in these two regions. Evidence from panel regression is again used and the means of key determinants compared. Table 3.9 shows the contribution from external debt and terms of trade. The most noticeable is the variability of terms of trade, which is much higher in SSA than in East Asia. Although the level of the coefficient is low, and thus the overall differential contribution to growth is low at 0.001 per cent, it does help to explain differences in growth performance.

Table 3.10 shows the next set of growth determinants. These are human capital indicators and the policy environment. East Asia seems to have favourable human capital indicators: higher levels of initial schooling, higher levels of initial income, low population growth and higher life expectancy than the SSA region. The growth differential is thus consistent with the arguments that initial conditions matter for long-term growth and that growth in the long run tends to enhance the performance of these indicators. The contribution to growth performance by these determinants shows that SSA is worse off.

The policy environment clearly explains the differential in growth performance in the two regions. The category of variables explains a sizeable proportion of the observed per capita growth of 9 per cent for East Asia compared with 5.1 per cent for SSA on average. Some key variables, like financial depth, exchange rate misalignment and inflation, clearly distinguish SSA from East Asia and help explain the poor growth performance between 1970 and 1994 for SSA countries.

Table 3.9 Contributions to growth from external factors

	Means of variables		Coef- ficient	Contri- bution %)
	E Asia	SSA		
External debt:				
External debt to GDP ratio (DY)	0.352	0.719	5.380	-1.98
Dy_{t-1}^2	0.146	0.783	-2.770	1.76
Debt service to export ratio	0.176	0.155	-0.057	0.00
Overall contribution				0.22
Terms of trade:				
Terms of trade variability	0.069	0.111	-0.019	0.001

Table 3.10 Contribution to growth: Human capital and policy variables

	Means of variables		Coef- ficient	Contri- bution (%)
	E Asia	SSA		
Human capital:				
Log of initial schooling	1.678	0.939	0.0016	0.012
Initial income	7.671	6.715	0.006	0.006
Population growth rate	0.018	0.028	-0.001	0.000
Life expectancy ratio	66.297	48.608	-0.001	0.18
Overall contribution				0.036
Policy variables:				
Fiscal balances to GDP ratio	-0.016	-0.048	-0.312	-0.01
Lagged fiscal balances GDP	-0.016	-0.048	-0.001	0.00
Public investment ratio	0.085	0.0111	0.234	-0.01
Financial depth	0.579	0.293	2.957	0.81
Real exchange rate misalign- ments	0.104	0.525	-0.012	2.63
Overall contribution				3.43
Policy outcome:				2.16
Inflation	0.084	0.522	-3.760	1.65
Dummy for inflation >40%	0.010	0.132	-1.220	0.51
Unexplained residual				1.39
Per capita GDP growth	0.090	0.051		3.84

Savings Performance

Table 3.11 reports the simulation results for savings performance in the two regions. Three categories of variables are considered. Terms of trade changes, which clearly have negative effects on savings in both regions, are slightly higher in SSA. The differential in impact is negligible due to the low value of the coefficient.

Table 3.11 Contribution to savings: 1970–1994

	Means of variables		Coef-ficient	Contri-bution (%)
	E Asia	SSA		
Terms of trade effects:				
Terms of trade changes	-1.05	-1.16	-0.09	-0.01
Growth and human capital:				
Dependency ratio	73.19	92.64	0.11	-2.11
Per capital income	3.99	1.18	3.09	8.67
Per capital income squared	20.38	1.95	-0.05	-0.97
Per capita growth	10.35	5.25	1.66	8.44
Overall contribution				14.03
Policy variables:				
Public saving/GDP	7.19	2.97	-1.13	-4.76
Government consumption/GDP	11.51	13.89	0.30	-0.72
Social security/Govt. expenditure	2.49	1.25	-0.92	-1.14
Real interest rate	0.35	-42.10	-0.01	-0.34
M2/GDP	58.17	25.15	-0.38	12.65
Private credit/domestic credit	97.90	81.77	0.01	0.14
Current account deficit/GDP	-4.02	-8.34	0.16	5.65
Overall contribution				11.48
Policy outcome:				
Inflation	8.24	48.60	0.00	-0.18
Unexplained residual				-11.48
Private serving rate	18.09	9.90		8.19

The next category of variables that determine savings is growth and human capital development. All the variables in this category favour East Asia and thus create a favourable saving environment and performance. This category of variables accounts for the huge performance differential of 14 per cent between the two regions in favour of East Asia.

Policy variables are the next category of determinants. The results clearly show that East Asia's policy environment is conducive for savings and this explains why the savings rate is twice that of SSA. Several factors explain this difference in performance: public savings are higher in East Asia, government consumption is lower and spending on social security is higher. Moreover the real interest rate is positive in East Asia and negative (-42.10 per cent) on average in SSA. Even though there have been arguments to the effect that savings in poor countries do not respond to real interest rates, the huge differences in real interest rates are spectacular and the large negative real interest in SSA cannot enhance a savings culture.

The other factors that stand out clearly are inflation, current account deficits and financial depth as measured by broad money (M2) to GDP ratio. The current account deficit is twice as high in SSA as in East Asia, which compounds the effect of terms of trade; together these explain the low investment and poor export performance discussed below. All these factors help to account for the difference in performance of savings in East Asia and sub-Saharan Africa, and explain why East Asia has done better in investment and thus growth than sub-Saharan Africa.

Export Performance

The final performance indicator in this section is export supply. A panel regression for export supply was estimated with lagged export supply, terms of trade shocks, export price index, real output growth, GDP per capita, policy variables and a dummy for civil wars in SSA.

The simulation results comparing these two regions are shown in Table 3.12. The results confirm the substantial differential in performance in export supply in the two regions, which can be explained by the export culture (lagged effects), terms of trade, and institutional, growth and policy variables. In particular, the policy variables that are significant in the panel regression show that real exchange rate misalignment has been higher in SSA and average export duties are also higher. These variables have negative and significant effects on export performance and they show that East Asia has a better performance (12.44 per cent) than SSA. These effects confirm the overall poor export performance in SSA, which is half that of East Asia as a percentage of GDP.

Table 3.12 Contribution to export performance

	Means of variables		Coef-ficient	Contri-bution (%)
	E Asia	SSA		
Lagged effects	44.6	20.0	0.207	5.11
Price and terms of trade:				
Terms of trade shocks	0.034	0.005	0.0618	0.18
Export price index	91.47	91.68	0.0285	-0.622
Overall effects				4.668
Institutional variables:				
Dummy of SSA civil wars	0.00	0.1302	0.222	2.89
Output growth variables:				
Per capita GDP growth	5.359	0.578	0.0922	51.85
Speed of growth of GDP	0.0733	0.0343	0.6713	2.62
Overall contribution				54.47

Table 3.12 (contd)

	Means of variables		Coef-ficient	Contri-bution (%)
	E Asia	SSA		
Policy variables:				
Real exchange rate	-0.0085	-0.0190	0.0705	0.0742
RER misalignment	0.08979	0.4825	-0.0932	3.660
Export duties	0.00127	4.6112	-0.0121	4.047
Overall contribution				12.44
Export to GDP ratio	44.611	20.109		24.502

The Institutional Underpinnings of Successful Transition

The reform experiences of the ten countries reviewed earlier show very clearly that these countries managed to achieve the transition to low instability and high growth on a sustained basis, yet almost all other developing countries did not. This 'win–win' achievement rests with the role of institutions. Almost all of these successful transitions have been effected by relatively capable, sufficiently mandated and adequately insulated institutions—institutions that have also been subject to some measure of accountability. The key challenge in the process of institutional design is to strike the appropriate and delicate balance between 'rules' and 'discretion'.

Rules are necessary for ensuring transparency and accountability, and hence policy credibility; too many rules, however, may lead to suboptimal executive discretion, which will necessarily stifle flexibility and responsiveness to uncertain and changing internal and external environments. Understanding the nature of the institutions that underlie these successful transitions is critical for drawing policy lessons for current and future reforming countries, especially those in SSA. An 'effective' institutional design is a product of and contingent upon the broader socio-political context, which appears to be very much shaped by initial conditions and history.

Success in East Asia

The consensus view in the literature[15] is that the success of the high performing Asian economies (HPAEs) in developing the right kind of institutions to support their remarkable transition can be credited to a combination of four factors:

- Clever institutional design that allowed concentration of key policy functions in the hands of independent bureaucratic organizations, which provided the much needed insulation for the technocratic elites from political capture.

[15] See, for example, World Bank (1993) and Rodrik (1994).

- An overarching and strategic commitment in all of these countries to the principle of 'equally shared growth', which aided the objective of bureaucratic insulation by reducing the inclination toward 'pressure group' type politics (Amazonas, 1995; Haggard, 1994).
- The presence of an honest, highly motivated and capable civil service sustained by 'merit-based recruitment and promotion, competitive remuneration, and generous rewards to those who make it to the top' (Rodrik, 1994: 43).
- The creation of modalities ('deliberation councils' in the terminology of the World Bank's 1993 report) for overall consultation as well as for exchange of views and information between government and the private sector. These councils have served several useful purposes. For example, in addition to helping address market imperfections by acting as a signalling device for future government policy directions, they have also been instruments for applying pressure on the government bureaucracy to be responsive to as well as accountable for outcomes of economic polices.

While these institutional characteristics of the HPAEs may appear to be consistent with an a priori abstract 'winning' institutional framework, their ability to become a winning combination was very much conditioned by the initial economic conditions and the socio-political history of these countries[16] (more on this below). In addition, the policy institutions in the HPAEs appear to be orthogonal to the mainstream principles of economic theory (for example, dynamic inconsistency in policy, investment under irreversibility and rent-seeking), which generally favours 'rules' over 'discretion'. Indeed, throughout the history of the HPAEs many government interventions have been at the firm level, highly complex and non-uniform, where bureaucracies have been accorded considerable executive discretion (Rodrik, 1994).

An important distinction needs to be drawn between the institutional underpinnings for implementation of macroeconomic policies and those for sectoral and microeconomic policies. In implementing macroeconomic policies, successful Asian bureaucracies have in fact operated under fairly explicit rules, buttressed by both traditions and politics (see Haggard, 1994). For example, as early as the late 1940s—following the hyperinflation crisis—substantial independence was granted to the central bank in Taiwan, in the context of an overall policy emphasis on economic stability. This orientation was further strengthened and extended to other areas of economic policy making institutions in the late 1950s, when it

[16] For example, Rodrik (1994) argues that deliberation councils have been used in many countries as an instrument of repression to impose government policies on a reluctant private sector. He also points out that like the HPAEs, many countries have attempted to implement a centralized style of policy making, but could not achieve the same success, to say the least. And finally, other countries (such as India) have inherited a very well educated cadre of civil service that has deep traditions of professional excellence and merit, yet they fail to deliver a level of performance comparable to that of the bureaucracies in the HPAEs.

became clear that the generous levels of U.S. aid would be cut down. This pattern is even clearer in the case of the Southeast Asian economies. In Indonesia, a key stabilization plan introduced in 1966 included, among others, a constitutional balanced budget provision, which decreed that expenditure could not exceed the sum of revenue plus counterpart funds generated by the aid programme. The salient feature of macroeconomic policy institutions in Malaysia has been the independence of the central bank since the post-independence period, which grew out of the currency board tradition established under British rule. More recently, the bureaucratic discretion in Thailand, which is credited for the strong economic recovery that began in the 1980s despite frequent changes in government, in turn 'was circumscribed by a number of rules that limited the government's capacity to spend, and by a central bank with a long tradition of independence' (Haggard, 1994: 90).

The Experiences of Other Successful Countries

The evolution of institutions in two successful non-Asian countries—Chile and Uganda—appears to be much more influenced by the concern for establishing policy credibility following the deep economic and political crises that affected both countries prior to the launch of economic reforms. In the case of Chile, the emerging Chilean—indeed the Latin American—development model necessarily calls for more emphasis on rules rather than discretion. Corbo (1996: 1) provides a succinct description:

> the new model has strengthened the role of the state in setting the rules for the development of a competitive market economy in the form of incentives, private property laws and their enforcement, and contractual law. As the government is moving out of the production of private goods, it is taking also an increasing role in insuring equality of opportunities in primary education, nutrition and primary health as well as in reducing extreme poverty.

The institutional reforms consistent with this vision in Chile included deep structural reforms of tax and revenue institutions and a change in the rule of operation of the central bank. These changes allowed the bank to run as an independent monetary and exchange rate policy institution, explicitly aimed at maintaining low and stable inflation. An important point to note is that like the Asian economic programme, the new Chilean development model is very much committed to the principles of shared growth, even though it will not benefit from the initial conditions of relatively equitable income and asset distribution that prevailed in East Asia.

The Ugandan reform programme mainly reflects the mainstream institutional structure prescribed by the Washington Consensus (Williamson, 1994), where a statutory cash budget, independent revenue authority and central bank are the main ingredients in the institutional set-up of the programme. The creation of these institutions, in addition to strong commitment by the political leadership to low and stable inflation, must be credited for the quick and decisive elimination of hyperinflation that affected the country prior to 1986.

Botswana, on the other hand, represents a case of a generally conservative, if not minimalist, state that does not seem to have been inspired by the presence of a major crisis in its recent history. The key test of the macroeconomic stance of the authorities in Botswana was provided by the challenge of managing the boom in the mining sector (diamonds). In the words of Norberg and Blomstrom (1993: 176–77):

> Also the spending effects of the diamond boom have been small, something which is mainly due to government policy. Since the diamond industry is state owned, the government controls the revenues. The revenues have mainly been used to promote national income, rather than to subsidize different sectors (such as import-substituting manufacturing) and support various interest groups. To maximize national income, a large proportion of the revenues from diamonds have been invested, not in Botswana, but in foreign banks and firms. By sterilizing revenues abroad and executing a non-expansive monetary policy at home, the inflationary pressure has diminished and the negative effect of the diamond boom have been reduced.

Mauritius is SSA's closest example to the East Asian models. Unlike in Uganda, for example, structural adjustment conditionality did not play a major role in shaping the policy making institutions in Mauritius, neither did the country experience major crises comparable to those in Uganda and other African countries. While there is no formal or informal institutional independence for policy institutions (such as the central bank, for example), the strong private sector tradition has been effective in limiting macroeconomic expansionism by the public sector.

Lessons for SSA

Until recently—and notwithstanding the experiences of the HPAEs—conventional wisdom suggested that 'successful programs are likely to:

- Apply simple and uniform rules, rather than selective and differentiated ones;
- Endow bureaucrats with few discretionary powers;
- Contain safeguards against frequent, unpredictable alteration of the rules; and
- Keep firms and other organizational interests at arm's length from the policy formulation and implementation process' (Rodrik, 1994: 44).

These principles are motivated by concerns about excesses of executive policy institutions as well as a strong desire to establish credibility of economic policy. In terms of the institutions entrusted with the design and implementation of macroeconomic policy, even the East Asian countries have adhered to some institutional measures that ensure macroeconomic stability, albeit in a context that allows considerable discretionary initiatives. Three considerations appear to be tilting the balance in SSA towards recommending more emphasis on institutional measures for enhancing the credibility of policy reforms (as well as sustainability of transitions from war to peace), and less emphasis on discretion.

First, the East Asian countries have rather unusual backgrounds of initial economic conditions and socio-political history. Many of these countries emerged from extreme political crisis that facilitated or triggered major strategic measures (such as the land redistribution in Korea and Taiwan), which resulted in relatively more equitable income and asset distribution compared with other developing countries. Moreover, these countries also had a much more educated labour force relative to their levels of incomes in the early 1960s (Rodrik, 1994). It has been argued that these initial conditions were critical to the emergence of capable institutions that are relatively free from political capture, which in turn was made possible by the relatively well educated civil service, while the relatively equitable income and wealth distribution reduces the payoffs for pressure group politics (Amazonas, 1995; Haggard, 1994). Moreover, the presence of intense military and ideological threats faced by these countries up to the 1970s facilitated the emergence of 'developmental' states in the East Asian region (Gunnarsson and Lundahl, 1996).

Second, this conclusion suggests that the East Asian institutional model may not be generalizable, especially in SSA, where institutions as well as states are particularly weak. Too much discretion along the East Asian model could be quite risky.[17] Indeed, the concern about the fragility of Africa's states and institutions may have been the motivation for as well the attraction of recent proposals that call for Africa to 'tie its hands' and pre-commit itself to reciprocal threat-making trade and policy coordination arrangements with dominant trading partners (such as the European Union), as a means for ensuring national policy credibility (see Collier, 1991). As a further articulation of this idea, in a more recent paper Collier (1996) addresses three core roles for the state:

- The delivery of security and regulation
- The creation of economic policy environment
- The provision of services

The central theme of the paper is that unlike successful economic development experiences from other regions (most notably East Asia), reforming African countries face problems of *bad reputation* and the perception of being part of a *high-risk* region. The paper provides a detailed and insightful analysis to establish this claim as well as to draw the implications in terms of the 'appropriate' role of the African state in each of the three areas. Based on his analysis, Collier recommends that a typical reforming African state should make its central objective to shorten the time required for *living down its history*, which was typically

[17] For example, a composite measure of quality of institutions during the 1980s assigns (on a scale of 1 to 10) a score of more than 8 each for Hong Kong, Taiwan and Singapore (and a median of 6.5 for East Asia), compared with a median score of 4.5 for SSA.

marred by bad security (including civil wars) as well as economic policy reversals. To achieve these the author proposes that the African state should attempt to *lock in* to credible external and internal *agencies of restraint* as a means for ensuring the sustainability and credibility of economic and political reforms.

Third, more recent evidence suggests that external and policy-induced volatilities have been on the rise in Latin America (as well as SSA) and that they have substantial economic cost in terms of growth, investment and social welfare (e.g., Hausman and Gavin, 1995; Serven, 1996a/b). This evidence has prompted some authors to recommend even further tightening of some rules, such as minimizing the risks faced by the fiscal accounts through much more regimented tax and revenue policy and setting precautionary fiscal targets. Other measures are the institution of 'contingent fiscal rules', which specify automatic fiscal response to large macroeconomic shocks, as well as change in the areas of public debt management and adjustment to terms of trade shocks (Hausman and Gavin, 1995). However, the recommendation from this literature also emphasizes the importance of designing policy institutions that allow sufficient flexibility and executive discretion in response to shocks. At least in the context of macroeconomic policy making institutions, this provides a convergence of sorts towards the East Asian models.

In summary, then, if Africa is to achieve a transition to sustained high growth, the appropriate institutional design should be one that emphasizes rules more than discretion, especially in the area of macroeconomic policy. As opposed to the rather peculiar initial conditions of the HPAEs, and with the recent evidence that external and policy-induced volatilities have been on the rise, there is more need for Africa to focus on shortening the time required to 'live down' its unusual history of bad security and policy reversals, by building domestic and external agencies of restraints. However, this proposition is very different from advocating a weak or even a 'disengaged' state. Indeed, we strongly agree with Haggard (1994: 98) that 'rather than warn that such policies cannot work in other settings because of administrative weakness, it makes more sense to emphasize the importance of a strong and competent state for the formulation and implementation of coherent public policy'.

Moreover, it has been argued that evidence from developing countries suggests that economy-wide macroeconomic reforms are more important than microeconomic and sectoral policies—aimed at achieving microeconomic efficiency and structural reforms—in terms of the effects of the two sets of policies on economic performance in general and on whether countries manage to avoid crisis, specially following external shocks such as the debt crisis of 1982 (Rodrik, 1996).[18]

---

[18] Furthermore, in evaluating the policies adopted by two of the most successful East Asian miracle countries (Republic of Korea and Taiwan) according to the 'Washington Consensus' paradigm, Rodrik (1996) shows that their records were far from outstanding in the areas of regulation, trade liberalization, privatization, elimination of barriers to DFI and financial liberalization. However, they truly excelled in establishing macroeconomic stability, maintaining macroeconomic competitiveness and securing property rights.

The upshot of this analysis is that macroeconomic stability and macroeconomic competitiveness should be secured and maintained on a sustained basis. However, other microeconomic and sectoral reforms constitute a development strategy and hence could be applied with varying degrees of intensity, sequencing and policy mix, depending on the nature of institutions, polity and the external environment.

Concluding Observations

SSA's strong recovery and registered high growth during 1995–1996 is still low compared with that of East Asian countries. This chapter compared the performance indicators for the two regions for 1970–1994. It was argued that the task facing SSA countries is determining how to achieve high growth, high private investment, high savings ratios and high export performance, and how to sustain these performances. The comparative analysis asks why this has not been possible in SSA and what lessons can be learned from East Asian experiences.

The analysis focused on four key indicators: growth, investment, savings and export supply. It was argued that investment, in the absence of deteriorating investment productivity, should form the basis for future growth and the challenge for SSA. At the same time a lesson from East Asia is to sustain both the high levels and the productivity of investment.

Some lessons for SSA countries can be drawn from the results of estimated panel regressions for the differences in the performances of the two regions:

- The differences in growth explain the very large and widening gap in the levels of per capita income over the period. What is quite revealing in the discussions is how fast the relative fortunes of nations can change through differences in the levels of economic growth.
- Because of low saving levels, there has been a growing reliance on foreign savings or low levels of investment when such inflows are inadequate to sustain higher levels of investment in SSA countries. In SSA, there is virtually total reliance on official sources of foreign finance, in contrast with East Asia, where private sources currently exceed foreign inflows. The lesson to be learned by SSA countries is that there is need to focus on creating conditions for raising saving rates and levels and to reduce the flight of such savings. In addition, there should be improved conditions for attracting private capital to complement this effort.
- Exports play a crucial role in supporting faster growth. East Asia's performance in this respect was again far above SSA's. This has been recognized in Africa as evidenced by the wave of trade liberalization, regional integration and trade agreements in the region, yet export diversification has not taken place.
- Initial conditions do matter. The initial quality of human capital and infrastructure determine long-term growth through their influence on the marginal product of private investment. On these aspects, SSA countries have the

lowest status of any developing regions. The question asked, then, is why did those countries in East Asia manage to achieve a high and sustained growth. The argument in this paper is that the economic and social transition in East Asia effected by relatively capable, sufficiently mandated and adequately insulated institutions that were also subject to some measure of accountability. Understanding the nature of the institutional designs that underlie these successful transitions is critical for drawing policy lessons for current and future reforming countries, especially in SSA, but initial conditions and history shape these institutions.

Four factors on institutional success in East Asia can be distilled from the literature:

- Institutions with key policy functions in the hands of an independent bureaucratic organization that insulated technocratic elites from political capture.
- Principle of 'shared growth', aided by the objective of bureaucratic insulation, which reduced the payoffs to the pressure groups' type of politics.
- A civil service guided by 'merit-based' recruitment and promotion, competitive remuneration, and a competitive reward structure.
- Modalities for consultation as well as for exchange of views and information between the government and the private sector.

Three considerations appear to be tilting the balance towards recommending more emphasis on institutional measures for enhancing the credibility of SSA policy reforms and less emphasis on discretion:

- Initial conditions and socio-political history in East Asia seem to have created a more favourable institutional environment than what obtained in SSA.
- East Asian institutional models may not be generalizable, but can provide important and crucial lessons. For example, Collier (1996) suggests that African countries should attempt to 'lock in' credible external and internal 'agencies of restraint' as a means of ensuring the sustainability and credibility of economic and political reforms.
- Such measures work to reduce external and policy-induced volatilities that have substantial economic costs in terms of growth, investment, savings and export performance.

In summary, for SSA countries to achieve a transition to sustained high growth, the appropriate institutional design should be one that emphasizes rules more than discretion, especially in macroeconomic policy. We have shown that a combination of policy environment, human capital development and institutional factors account for the huge differences in economic performance between East Asia and sub-Saharan Africa.

References

Amazonas, A. 1995. 'A reassessment of the relative economic performance of Brazil and Korea'. Paper presented at the Development Studies Association Meeting, City College, Dublin, 7–9 September.

Aron, J. 1996. 'Political, economic and social institutions: A review of growth evidence'. Background paper for the *World Development Report*, 1997.

Aron, J., I. Elbadawi and B. Ndulu. 1996. 'State and development in sub-Saharan Africa'. Mimeo. Background paper for the World Bank 1997 *World Development Report*, 'The State in a Changing World'.

Balassa, B. 1988. 'Public finance and economic development'. PPR Working Paper No. 31, The World Bank, Washington, D.C.

Barro, R. 1991. 'Economic growth in a cross-section of countries'. *Quarterly Journal of Economics*, vol. 106, May: 407–44.

Blejer, M. and M. Khan. 1984. 'Government policy and private investment in developing countries'. *IMF Staff Papers*, vol. 31, no. 2: 379–403.

Bruno, M. and W. Easterly. 1995. 'Inflation crises and long-run growth'. Mimeo. The World Bank, Washington, D.C.

Cardoso, E. 1993. 'Macroeconomic environment and capital formation in Latin America.' In L. Serven and A. Solimano, eds., *Striving for Growth after Adjustment: The Role of Capital Formation.* Washington, D.C: The World Bank.

Chua, H. 1993a. 'Regional spillovers and economic growth'. Center Discussion Paper No. 700, Economic Growth Center, Yale University.

Chua, H. 1993b. 'Regional public capital and economic growth'. Unpublished mimeo. Economic Growth Center, Yale University.

Collier, P. 1991. 'Africa's external economic relations 1960–90'. Chapter 6 in D. Rimmer, ed., *Africa 30 Years On*. London: The Royal Africa Society in association with James Currey.

Collier, P. 1996. 'The role of the state in economic development: Cross regional experience'. Paper presented at AERC Biannual Research Workshop. Nairobi, December.

Collier, P. 1995. 'The marginalization of Africa'. *International Labour Review*, 134(4–5).

Corbo, V. 1996. 'The market and the government in Latin America: The emerging model'. Paper presented at the International Conference on the World Economy in Transition, Hitotsubashi University, Japan.

Delong, J.B. and L.H. Summers. 1991. 'Equipment investment and economic growth'. *Quarterly Journal of Economics*, 106(2): 445–502.

Delong, J.B. and L.H. Summers. 1992. 'Equipment investment and economic growth: How robust is the nexus?'. *Brookings Papers on Economic Activity*.

Easterly, W., and R. Levine. 1996a. 'Africa's growth tragedy: Policies and ethnic divisions'. The World Bank, February.

Easterly, W., and R. Levine. 1996b. 'The tragedy of African growth'. Policy Research Working Paper, The World Bank, Washington, D.C.

Easterly, W., and R. Levine. 1994. 'Africa's growth tragedy'. The World Bank (later in 1995 appeared as *Policy Research Working Paper* No. 1503.

Easterly, W., and S. Rebelo. 1993. 'Fiscal policy and economic growth: An empirical investigation'. *Journal of Monetary Economics*, 32(3): 417–57.

Easterly, W., and K. Schmidt-Hebbel. 1991. 'The macroeconomics of public sector deficits: A synthesis'. Paper presented at the World Bank Conference on Macroeconomics of Public Sector Deficits, Washington, D.C., June.

Elbadawi, I. 1996. 'Consolidating macroeconomic stabilization and restoring growth in sub-

Saharan Africa'. In B. Ndulu and N. van de Walle, eds., *Policy Perspectives on African Development Strategies*. Washington D.C.: Overseas Development Council.

Elbadawi, I. 1992. 'World Bank adjustment lending and economic performance in sub-Saharan Africa in the 1980s: A comparison of early adjusters, late adjusters and nonadjusters'. Working Paper Series No 1001. Washington, D.C.: The World Bank.

Elbadawi, I., and B. Ndulu. 1995. 'Growth and development in Sub-Saharan Africa: Evidence of key factors'. Invited paper presented at the World Congress of the International Economic Association, Tunis, December.

Elbadawi, I., and K. Schmidt-Hebbel. 1996. 'Macroeconomic policies, instability and growth in the world'. Paper presented at AERC Biannual Research Workshop. Nairobi, December.

Elbadawi, I., B. Ndulu and N. Ndung'u. 1997a. 'Debt overhang and economic growth in sub-Saharan Africa'. In Z. Iqbal and R. Kanbur, eds., *External Finance for Low Income Countries*. IMF Institute. Washington, D.C.: International Monetary Fund.

Elbadawi, I., B. Ndulu and N. Ndung'u. 1997b. 'Risks, uncertainties and debt overhang as determinants of private investment in SSA'. Paper presented at the Conference on Investment, Growth and Risk in Africa, Centre for the Study of African Economies (CSAE), Oxford University.

Fischer, S. 1993. 'The role of macroeconomic factors in growth'. *Journal of Monetary Economics*, 32(3): 485–511.

Greene, J., and D.Villanueva. 1991. 'Private investment in developing countries: An empirical analysis'. *IMF Staff Papers*, March.

Gunnarsson, C., and M. Lundahl. 1996. 'The good, the bad and the wobbly: State forms and Third World economic performance'. In M. Lundahl and B. Ndulu, eds., *New Directions in Development Economics: Growth, Environmental Concerns and Government in the 1990s*. New York: Routledge.

Haggard, S. 1994. 'Politics and institutions in the World Bank East Asia'. In A. Fishlow et al., eds., *Miracle or Design: Lessons from the East Asian Experience*. Oversees Development Council, Policy Essay No. 11, Washington, D.C.

Hadjimichael, M., D. Ghura, M. Muhlesien, R. Nord and E. Ucer. 1994. 'Effects of macroeconomic instability and economic growth in sub-Saharan Africa: An empirical investigation'. *IMF Working Paper*, 1994/98.

Hausman, R., and M. Gavin. 1995. 'Macroeconomic volatility in Latin America: Causes, consequences and policies to assure stability'. Mimeo. Inter-American Development Bank, Washington, D.C.

Hoffmaister, A.W., J.E. Roldos and P. Wickhan. 1997. 'Macroeconomic fluctuation in Sub-Saharan Africa'. *IMF Working Paper* WP/97-82.

IMF. 1997a. *World Economic Outlook*. Washington, D.C.: International Monetary Fund

IMF. 1997b. 'ESAF at ten years: Economic adjustment and reform in low income countries'. Summary report (September).

Jaspersen, F.Z., A.H. Aylward and M. Sumlinski. 1995. 'Trends in private investment in developing countries: Statistics for 1970–94'. *IFC Discussion Paper 28*. Washington, D.C.: International Finance Corporation.

Khan, M., and M. Kumar. 1993. 'Public and private investment and the convergence of per capita incomes in developing countries.' *IMF Staff Papers*/WPS 193/51, June.

Knack, S., and P. Keefer. 1995. 'Institutions and economic performance: Cross country tests using alternative institutional measures'. *Economics and Politics*, 7(3): 207–27.

Krugman, P. 1991. *Geography and Trade*. Cambridge, Massachusetts: MIT Press.

Lucas, R. 1988. 'On the mechanics of economic development'. *Journal of Monetary Economics*, 22, June.
Mankiw, N., D. Romer and D. Weil. 1992. 'A contribution to the empirics of economic growth'. *Quarterly Journal of Economics*, May.
Mauro, Paulo. 1995. 'Corruption and Growth.' *Quarterly Journal of Economics* (August): 681–712.
Mlambo, K., and M. Kumar. 1995. 'Determinants of private investment in sub-Saharan Africa: An empirical investigation'. Presented at the World Congress of the International Economic Association. Tunis, December.
Norberg, H., and M. Blomstrom. 1993. 'Dutch disease and management of windfall gains in Botswana'. Reprint Series No. 111, Department of International Economics and Geography, Stockholm School of Economics.
Oshikoya, T. 1994. 'Macroeconomic determinants of domestic private investment in Africa: An empirical analysis'. *Economic Development and Cultural Change*, The University of Chicago.
Pindyck, R. 1993. 'A note on competitive investment under uncertainty'. *American Economic Review* 83: 1 (March): 273–77.
Ravallion, M., and S. Chen. 1997. 'What can new survey data tell us about recent change in distribution and poverty?' *World Bank Economic Review*, vol. 11, no. 2: 357–82.
Rodrik, D. 1990. 'How should structural adjustment programs be designed?' *World Development*, vol. 18(July): 933–47.
Rodrik, D. 1994. 'King Kong meets Godzilla: The World Bank and the East Asian miracle'. In *Miracle or Design*, Overseas Development Council Policy Essay No. 11. Washington, D.C.
Rodrik, D. 1996. 'Understanding economic policy reform'. *Journal of Economic Literature*, vol. XXXIV: 9–41, March.
Rodrik, D. 1998. 'Trade policy and economic performance in sub-Saharan Africa'. *National NBER Worling Paper* no. W6562.
Sachs, J., and A. Warner. 1995. 'Economic reform and the process of global integration'. *Brookings Papers on Economic Activity*, 1995/1.
Sachs, J., and A. Warner. 1997. 'Sources of slow growth in African economies'. HIID, March.
Senbet, L. 1997. 'The development of capital markets in Africa: Constraints and prospects.' Paper prepared for the Conference of African Finance Ministers, UNECA and AERC,
Schmidt-Hebbel, K, 1995 *Fiscal Adjustment and Growth: In and Out of Africa*. Special Paper No. 19 African Economic Research Consortium, Nairobi, Kenya.
Schmidt-Hebbel, K., and T. Muller. 1991. 'Private investment under macroeconomic adjustment in Morocco'. Policy Research Working Paper No. 787. The World Bank, Washington, D.C.
Serven, L. 1996a. 'Does public capital crowd out private capital? Evidence from India'. Policy Research Working Paper No. 1613. The World Bank, Washington, D.C.
Serven, L. 1996b. 'Irreversibility, uncertainty and private investment: Analytical issues and some lessons for Africa'. Paper presented at the AERC Biannual Research Workshop. Nairobi, Kenya, May.
Serven, L., and A. Solimano. 1993. 'Economic adjustment and investment performance in developing countries: The experience of the 1980s'. In Serven and Solimano, eds., *Striving for Growth after Adjustment: The Role of Capital Formation.*, Washington, D.C.: The World Bank.
Van Wijnbergen, S. 1992. 'Trade reform, policy uncertainty, and the current account: A non-expected utility approach'. *American Economic Review*, vol. 75: 626–33.

Williamson, J., ed. 1994. *The Political Economy of Policy Reform*. Washington, D.C.: Institute for International Economics.

World Bank. 1994. *Adjustment in Africa: Reforms, Results and the Road Ahead*. New York: Oxford University Press.

World Bank. 1993. *The East Asian Miracle: Economic Growth and Public Policy*. New York: Oxford University Press.

World Bank. 1997. *World Development Report, 1997*. New York: Oxford University Press.

Yeats, A., A. Amjadi, U. Eincke and F. Ng. 1997. *Did Domestic Policies Marginalize Africa in the World Trade*. Directions in Development Series, The World Bank.

Chapter 4

Macroeconomic Management and the Development Process: A Perspective of Francophone Africa

Hiey Jacques Pégatiénan

The objective of this chapter is to determine the relative importance of macroeconomic management and institutional quality in economic development, understood as the permanent increase of per capita income and of individual well-being. Francophone Africa has a record of poor economic performance compared with other parts of sub-Saharan Africa and other less developed countries, probably because efforts to improve efficiency, savings and investment, the main sources of economic growth, have not been fostered. Such efforts cannot be stimulated unless economic institutions create adequate incentives; these institutions are: the rule of law, protection of property rights, respect for contracts and efficiency of public administration.

Investigation of determinants of savings, investments and foreign direct investment strongly suggests that macroeconomic policy and risk play an important role. Institutions are linked to savings, investment and foreign direct investment through transaction costs and risk. Simulations show that the effects of small changes of institutional quality on savings, investment and foreign direct investment may dominate effects of macroeconomic policies. Therefore, policies that combine macroeconomic management and institutional changes are desirable.

The economic performance of Africa has been disappointing and the bulk of its increasing population still lives in poverty. The continent has not yet taken advantage of the globalization of the economy, yet other parts of the developing world attract significant flows of foreign direct investment and of other types of capital. The situation has not changed much despite reforms implemented everywhere since the early 1980s. The objective of this paper is to determine the relative role of macroeconomic management and institutional quality in these economic difficulties. The analysis focuses on francophone Africa. In doing so we must bear in mind that francophone Africa is not a homogeneous group, but has significant diversities. This diversity of situations could not be reflected in this paper; the specific situation of Côte d'Ivoire was extensively used to illustrate problems and hopes. In many ways using Côte d'Ivoire as a showcase, positive or negative, is warranted because this country is taken as a model for its past good performances as well as for its wrongdoings, which must not be repeated elsewhere.

Economic Performance

This section gives an indication of how well francophone Africa performed in comparison with other parts of sub-Saharan Africa and the rest of developing world. This relative performance is evaluated in terms of growth rate, inflation, current account deficit and financial policies.

Growth and Inflation

Table 4.1 shows that over 1986–1993, the growth performance of francophone Africa was poor compared with all of sub-Saharan Africa in terms of both real income level (-0.6 per cent versus 1.7 per cent) and per capita real income (-3.4 per cent versus -1.6 per cent); its situation is also less favourable when contrasted with that of non CFA African countries (3.9 per cent for real income and 0.9 per cent for per capita real income growth). Côte d'Ivoire holds a special place among francophone African countries; its growth performance is even worse than that of overall francophone Africa.

Table 4.1 Economic performance in Africa (1986–1993)

	Sub-Saharan Africa	CFA countries	Non CFA countries
Growth and inflation			
Real GDP growth	1.7	-0.6	3.9
Per capita GDP growth	-1.6	-3.4	0.9
Inflation rate	83.4	1.4	29.2
External sector			
Current account balance/GDP (estimation 1993)	-2.6	-7.6	-3.8
Public external debt			
% GDP	54.9	85.8	92.6
% exports	244.8	407.5	329.9
Real effective exchange rate growth (%)	-2.6	-3.3	-4.6
Terms of trade growth (%)	-4.2	-1.0	-2.5
Exports growth (%)	1.7	0.4	1.2
Imports growth (%)	4.3	2.8	4.6
Financial policies (estimation 1993)			
Fiscal deficit/surplus as % of GDP			
Overall	-8.1	-7.1	-7.5
Primary	-2.7	-1.2	-1.3
Money supply growth	125.0	3.0	25.5
Inflation rate (change in %)	197.7	0.8	32.3
Real interest rate (change in %)	-181.5	7.5	-9.6
Nominal effective exchange rate (change in %)	-5.7	6.9	-18.0

Table 4.1 (contd)

	Sub-Saharan Africa	CFA countries	Non CFA countries
Savings/investment equilibrium			
Private savings/GDP	11.3	11.1	11.5
Public savings/GDP	-0.7	-2.3	2.2
Private investment/GDP	9.9	11.6	9.1
Public investment/GDP	6.3	6.0	9.5
(Savings-investment)/GDP			
Public balance	-2.0	-1.3	-0.9
Private balance	1.5	1.9	-0.5
Overall	-0.5	0.6	-1.4

Source: IMF (1996).

Indeed, Table 4.2 shows that over 1986–1993, real income and per capita real income fell in Côte d'Ivoire by 1.6 per cent and 8.1 per cent, respectively, and that this negative trend continued through 1995. In comparison, over 1986–1992, real income and per capita real income grew, respectively, by 7 per cent and 5.3 per cent in Southeast Asia and by 2.3 per cent and 0.2 per cent, respectively, in Latin America (IMF, 1996). This comparison with other parts of the developing world highlights the growth problems faced by francophone Africa in general and by Côte d'Ivoire in particular.

It is clear that this poor situation is not explained by inflation. Indeed, francophone African countries performed extremely well on the inflation front; in 1986–1993, their inflation rate was only 1.4 per cent on average versus 83.4 per cent for sub-Saharan Africa and 29.2 per cent for non CFA African countries (Table 4.1). We know that the main reason for this is the rule set by the monetary union and the regional central bank that limits the monetization of fiscal deficit to 20 per cent of previous year's fiscal revenues. The monetary discipline responsible for this successful control over inflation is one of the major achievements of Franc Zone institutional arrangements.

Table 4.2 Economic performance of Côte d'Ivoire (1980–1995)

	1980–1986	1986–1993	1993–1995
Growth and inflation			
Real GDP growth	-0.20	-1.60	-1.6
Per capita GDP growth	-3.90	-8.10	-8.2
Inflation rate	7.26	3.80	3.8
External sector			
Current account balance/GDP	-9.87	-9.10	-3.61
Public external debt			
% GDP	93.40	111.30	164.10
% exports	235.80	345.90	446.30
Real effective exchange rate growth (%)	3.66	-1.80	-1.80

Table 4.2 (contd)

	1980–1986	1986–1993	1993–1995
Exports growth (%)	8.87	-6.80	-6.80
Imports growth (%)	3.82	-2.70	-2.70
Financial policies			
Deficit/surplus as % of GDP			
Overall	-16.00	-5.20	-6.80
Primary	-5.50	1.30	1.50
Money supply growth	7.60	-1.50	-1.50
Real interest rate (% change)	347.00	-18.50	643.00
Nominal effective exchange rate (% change)	2.76	6.90	6.90
Savings /investment equilibrium			
Private savings/GDP	4.08	6.92	8.50
Public savings/GDP	4.52	-5.85	-1.42
Private investment/GDP	9.10	4.82	5.79
Public investment/GDP	10.04	5.17	4.66
Gross domestic savings/GDP	8.60	1.06	7.07
Gross domestic investment/GDP	19.14	10.00	10.45
(Savings-investment)/GDP	-10.53	-8.93	-3.38
Private balance	-5.01	2.10	2.70
Public balance	-5.52	-11.02	-6.10

Source: Author's computations from diverse sources.

External Position

Over 1986–1993, the current account deficit of francophone Africa was larger (-7.6 per cent of GDP) than that of sub-Saharan Africa (-2.6 per cent) and of non CFA countries (-3.8 per cent). The situation of Côte d'Ivoire (-9.1 per cent) was even worse than that of francophone Africa, but its deficit declined during 1993–1995 (-3.6 per cent) because of devaluation.

One reason for the deterioration of the current account is trade balance. In francophone Africa, the value of exports and imports increased less (0.4 per cent and 2.8 per cent, respectively) than in sub-Saharan Africa (1.7 per cent and 4.3 per cent, respectively) and in non CFA countries (1.2 per cent and 4.6 per cent, respectively). Thus net exports fell less in francophone Africa than in sub-Saharan Africa and in non CFA countries; therefore the larger current account deficit of francophone Africa compared with that of non CFA countries cannot be explained by the trade balance deficit. The trade balance situation of Côte d'Ivoire is different from that of other African countries; indeed, both exports and imports declined instead of growing at a smaller pace. Over the 1986–1993 period, exports declined (-6.8 per cent) faster than imports (-2.7 per cent); thus net exports fell faster than elsewhere in Africa, and this trend continued over the 1993–1995 period.

The major reasons for the current account deficit could be the deterioration of the terms of trade and the appreciation of the real exchange rate. The terms of trade deteriorated in francophone countries less (−1 per cent) than in sub-Saharan Africa (−4.2 per cent) and non CFA countries (−2.5 per cent). The real exchange rate appreciated in francophone Africa more (−3.3 per cent) than in overall sub-Saharan Africa (−2.6 per cent), but less than in non CFA countries (−6 per cent); This is probably an indication that macroeconomic policies were somehow better in francophone countries than in their non CFA counterparts. As for Côte d'Ivoire, its terms of trade deteriorated less and its real exchange rate appreciated less than in other African countries.

Since net exports declined less, apparently, because the terms of trade deterioration and real exchange rate appreciation were less than in non CFA countries, the question is why the current account deficit grew worse than in non CFA countries. The possible explanation is the heavier debt burden of francophone Africa; as far as Côte d'Ivoire is concerned, in addition to the debt burden explanation, there is a structural reason. Indeed, Côte d'Ivoire's production system is strongly dependent on external production factors whose payments are traditionally larger than the traditional trade surplus.

Public external debt is another indicator of external position; that position was not good for Africa over 1986–1993. Indeed, public external debt represents 55 per cent of GDP and 245 per cent of exports for sub-Saharan Africa; those figures were 86 per cent and 407 per cent, respectively, for francophone Africa. Relative to GDP, francophone Africa had a better situation than non CFA countries, but when this indicator is computed relative to exports, its position is worse than that of non CFA countries. Since the debt burden in terms of exports is really what matters for daily financial management, the debt burden of francophone countries is heavier than that of other African countries. Côte d'Ivoire's debt burden in terms of exports was lighter than that of overall francophone countries because its export performance has always been better than that of most francophone countries, but it was heavier than that of non CFA countries. Over 1993–1995 Côte d'Ivoire's debt burden increased.

Financial Policies

The economic performance of francophone Africa measured in terms of growth rate, inflation and current account deficit has something to do with the financial policies pursued. The cornerstone of the financial policies is fiscal policy, the net situation of which is given by fiscal deficit. The overall fiscal deficit of francophone Africa (−7.1 per cent) is smaller than that of sub-Saharan Africa (−8.1 per cent) and non CFA countries (−7.5 per cent). Primary fiscal deficit is much lower and has the same trend as the overall (−1.2 per cent, 2.7 per cent and −1.3 per cent for francophone Africa, sub-Saharan Africa and non CFA countries, respectively). The difference between overall and primary deficit gives the extent of external debt service. The situation of Côte d'Ivoire is worse than that of other African countries; over 1986–1993, the country produced an overall fiscal deficit of 5.2 per cent of GDP and a primary fiscal surplus of 1.3 per cent of GDP. The discrepancy between the overall and the primary fiscal deficit highlights the particularly severe debt problem that Côte d'Ivoire faces. Table 4.2 also shows the relative success of the economic reforms implemented in that country since the early 1980s.

Large fiscal deficits are dangerous because the money creation that is used to finance them fuels inflation. On this particular front francophone Africa escaped that criticism since its money growth (3 per cent) during 1986–1993 was substantially less than that of sub-Saharan Africa (125 per cent) and of non CFA countries (25.5 per cent). In Côte d'Ivoire the situation is even better than that of all other African countries since the money creation declined by 1.5 per cent over 1986–1993. As indicated earlier, this performance is due to the restrictive nature of monetary institutions put in place in the Franc Zone. On the other hand, interest rate policies were less restrictive in francophone Africa than in other parts of the continent, since its real interest rate increased by 7.5 per cent while it fell by 181 per cent and 9.5 per cent in sub-Saharan Africa and in non CFA countries, respectively. In Côte d'Ivoire, over 1986–1993, real interest rates declined (–18.5 per cent) more than in non CFA countries, meaning that its financial repression was more severe than in those countries.

Over 1986–1993, the nominal exchange rate increased by 6.9 per cent in francophone Africa and in Côte d'Ivoire, while it fell by 5.7 per cent and 18 per cent in sub-Saharan Africa and in non CFA countries, respectively. As indicated earlier changes in the nominal exchange rate do not mean policy change in francophone Africa; rather they represent an exogenous shock that totally reflects the relative performance of France's economy.

On most accounts, except monetary policy and performance—which is by no means trivial—francophone Africa fares worse than its non CFA homologues. Why is that so? The rest of the chapter tries to answer this question by a look at institutions.

Institutional Foundations and Capabilities for Economic Performance

In industrialized countries economic agents have for centuries had all the basic ingredients that make individuals and nations grow and develop economically. At the individual level, these ingredients are: positive attitudes towards economic effort and risk taking, education, market information, and technical knowledge and skills; these ingredients have empowered private individuals to take advantage of new opportunities generated by economic incentives. At the national level, adequate physical infrastructure and institutions built by the state create the right economic environment for private agents to perform in markets. Mainstream economic analysis and adjustment policy prescriptions for decision making in Africa routinely take these prerequisites for granted and very often downplay or ignore their action in the transmission process of incentives and in the conversion of these incentives into actual goods, services and economic growth. It is argued that the results of 'policies to move from stabilization to growth' (Dornbusch, 1990) have been disappointing because analysts took quality of institutions for granted at both individual and national levels, when in fact this link has always been missing (Pégatiénan, 1990). It is also argued that the debate over public/private sector boundaries has been wrongly targeted.

Institutional Foundations

Development has to do with the increase per se of real income and well-being on one hand, and the process whereby this increase spreads among as many individuals or groups of individuals in the society as possible and sustains itself permanently, on the other hand. Development is growth plus institutional innovation designed to make growth deepen and sustainable. Attempts to promote growth without conscious institutional innovation in francophone Africa have generated unnecessary costs and have turned out to be a waste of energy and resources. The institutional perspective of economic development in Africa concerns the following issues: attitudes and behaviour, efforts to improve economic efficiency, the role of the state, colonial and neo-colonial factors, and markets.

Attitudes and behaviour These issues range from the limited exposure of economic agents to outside ideas, to the self-serving perspectives of African leaders.

Limited horizons of economic agents: Economic progress in francophone Africa has been minimal and disappointing basically because of the limited horizons of the majority of the population who have little or no access to new ideas, goods and services, to better ways of doing usual or old things. Since the majority of the population is rural in all francophone African countries, new ideas concern non agricultural products and activities; new ways of doing usual or old things relate to methods of cultivation and animal breeding, food processing, and marketing of agricultural and animal products. The basic reason for the limited horizon is the lack of education and information, and as a consequence limited contacts with the outside world. It is notable that francophone countries generally fare poorly compared with their African homologues in terms of adult education; the illiteracy rates are relatively high. The poor performance in terms of adult educational coverage is explained by the strong reluctance in francophone countries to use local languages as a vehicle of instruction, partly because very little linguistic research exists. In that respect Côte d'Ivoire is even more narrow; indeed, virtually no effort has ever been made to improve the literacy rate of adults through local languages—'ivorian French' or 'Musa's French' is the universal communication vehicle in urban as well as in rural areas among illiterates.

Since the lack of resources prevents a universal formal education in francophone Africa, adult education was a necessity. By not systematically using local languages or 'Musa's French' as instruments for adult education, opportunities to broaden the information base for the majority of the population, and to open their minds to new ideas and better ways of doing things, were lost. Since those new ideas and better ways of doing things hardly reach ordinary people because of the deficiencies and inefficiencies of government extension systems, it is small wonder that progress is either slow or nonexistent in rural areas.

Extended family system: All individuals in African countries, no matter the scope of their horizons, are burdened with the extended family system, the constraints of which complicate economic decision making. The extended family system does have its positive aspects, one of which is family solidarity. The solidarity of the group is a built-in income distribution mechanism whereby the person who works and earns a living pays for the expenses of the whole family, direct and indirect. Through that system it is possible to survive without working or without earning an income. The system also serves as health insurance for almost all members of the extended family since their health bills, including funerals, are paid for by those members of the family who actually earn an income. Thus the extended family system cushions the hardships of policy failures and of adjustment measures. It actually works as a natural safety net. Although this system guarantees an equitable distribution of income for all members of the extended family, it tends to bring the equilibrium level of personal income down.

One negative side of the system is the parasite mentality that develops within society. We have come to a point where there is no shame or guilt for an able person to be taken care of without compensation. It has even gone as far as to be considered a right or an obligation since some senior member of the extended family once took care of today's income earners. The large propensity to consume implicit in the analysis leaves out a low or sometimes negative savings, hence a low or zero investment rate. Another negative consequence of the extended family system is the drive of civil servants for active and/or passive corruption as an avenue to generate additional income in order to balance their budget. It is hypothesized that the positive consequences of the extended family system are more than compensated for by the negative consequences of low saving and investment and corruption so that the net impact is negative.

Intellectuals: Change, progress and even revolutions are sparked by new ideas usually generated by intellectuals. African intellectuals shoulder heavy responsibilities for the lack of visible change and progress in francophone Africa. Their major achievement was their participation in the winning of political independence from colonial powers; in post independence years, however, they failed to play a significant role in the stimulation of the development process since their production of creative ideas was minimal. This happened despite their access to a large spectrum of experiences and technologies in the developed world where they studied, on one hand, and their daily contacts with African realities, constraints and expectations, on the other hand. From the commingling of their inside understanding of those realities and the actual needs of the people, they were expected to sort out these complex issues and come up with operational suggestions and advice to decision makers. They actually produced no innovative solutions because they lacked ambition for the subcontinent, hence they did not fight for excellence and quality. Their thinking remained backward instead of forward-looking and prospective; it could not help shift the frontier of knowledge on African issues outward.

Not only could they not shift the frontier outward, they even could not be on that frontier. Instead, they were behind it, misusing and wasting their creative abilities and actually generating fewer new and useful ideas than they possibly could. One major reason for this inefficiency in knowledge production is the lack of demand for different opinions from African political classes, which actively went firmly against any expression of dissent. The other major reason is the necessity for intellectuals to supplement their low civil servants' salaries by hunting desperately for 'greener pastures' through political sinecures or executive positions in parastatals. This feeding mentality (*politique du ventre* in French) cost Africa the substitution of politicized thinking for professionalism, hence slow progress.

Political leaders: African political classes can also be blamed for the slow progress of the continent because they wasted many opportunities to help countries and people develop. This was achieved by mere selfishness, absence of vision (short-term action, no strategic thinking) and limited ambition (help to be on the frontier, to get ready, and to go out and compete with the best) for the subcontinent.

The basic flaw in African politicians and leaders is that their attitudes are more self-serving than focused on the public interest; their genius and creativity gear the organization of local institutions toward the attainment of their personal goals. A prominent francophone political figure and leader, President Houphouët Boigny, once said: 'You do not inspect the mouth of a person who roasts peanuts'. There is no concern as long as peanuts are private property; it becomes a big issue, however, if the peanuts are taxpayers' or communities' money. Across all francophone Africa 'peanut roasting' rules as a system of economic and political management; responsibilities of roasting peanuts are not allocated randomly according to professionalism, excellence and performance; rather, the allocation is discretionary, made along tribal and political lines.

'Peanut roasting' as a management system has both macroeconomic and microeconomic consequences. At the micro level, the first impact is clientelism and dependency attitudes towards the authority that grants the duties such as loyalty, absence of dissent, and no objectivity or independence in thinking. To the extent that the grantee is not highly educated there is little waste for the country. The opportunity cost of skills becomes high when it is the human capital embedded in highly trained intellectuals that is misused or underused in this way. The second effect is the wrong signals sent to all civil society and especially to African youth's imagination; the message is the following: big and quick money gained without toil. The third effect is the legitimization of corruption in everybody's mind as a normal avenue to be part of the 'peanut roasting' or to get access to some sort of 'public peanuts'.

Intellectuals and politicians try to make private and special interests flourish, while public interests are deemed well served by civil servants with frequent moonlighting—and 'sunlighting' as well. These asymmetric attitudes and behaviour weaken the state and introduce inefficiencies into the overall economy.

Efforts to improve economic efficiency Basic truths of economics are that individual and national well-being cannot be taken for granted; rather work effort and sweat are required to extract goods and services from nature. In doing so production units, although rational, used to actually extract less than the maximum quantity possible of these goods and services (technical inefficiency), and at costs well above the minimum cost ruling (allocative inefficiency). Therefore production units are routinely located below the frontier; the inefficiencies generated translate into losses of growth points to the national economy. These two truths may not be independent, and it can be hypothesized that production and cost inefficiencies are caused by the size and intelligence of effort applied to work. The crucial problem then is to identify appropriate institutions that are favourable to the promotion of effort (Lewis, 1955) to move individuals, production units and overall economy up to the frontier or to improve both technical and allocative efficiencies of all economic agents.

Work effort and efficiency: A certain quantity of physical effort devoted to work is necessary in order to get goods and services in quantities sufficient to cover the needs of the society. The usual problem is that people provide what is necessary to cover subsistence needs and little effort is devoted to produce surpluses for markets. The efforts for subsistence depend on the size of the household and of the extended family. Extra work effort will depend on the adequacy of incentives to produce surpluses for markets. Is the quantity of physical work of francophone Africans adequate, or above or below adequate levels? According to popular beliefs, quantities of physical effort applied to work might not be adequate in all parts of francophone Africa. In fact, what matters most is not the quantity of work effort but the intelligence that is used to do the work. Indeed, the productivity of work is associated less with quantity of physical effort than with intelligence. Given the large illiteracy rate of francophone Africans, especially peasants, the quality of their work would lean more toward physical content than toward intelligence; this may be one of the major determinants of observed inefficiencies. Only empirical studies can determine the average quantity of physical effort devoted to work and the average efficiency ratios, especially in agriculture, and justify any judgement about its adequacy.

Available empirical evidence from three francophone countries (Benin, Burkina Faso and Côte d'Ivoire) shows that peasants seem to be more efficient allocatively than technically; technical efficiency is rather low for traditional food production. (Refer to Table 4.3.) Technical efficiency is much higher for animal production in Côte d'Ivoire. For small-scale food processing technical efficiency (around 80) is higher than allocative efficiency (30). We must be very concerned about the low technical efficiency in traditional agriculture; francophone peasants have a long road to walk until they can reach the frontier, they are far from using best practices. Efforts required in order to improve technical efficiency are bigger than those necessary to reach allocative efficiency; at least one case study suggests that technical and exogenous factors have a bigger role to play than others (Zonon, 1996).

Table 4.3 Economic efficiency in francophone Africa

Authors	Methods	Country	Type of goods	TE %	AE %	EE %
Kouadio and	LP	Côte d'Ivoire	Multi products	40	-	-
Pokou (1991)	COLS	Burkina Faso	Cereals	44	-	-
Kaboré (1996)	LP	Côte d'Ivoire	Banana	72	-	-
Nuama Ekou (1996)	COLS	Côte d'Ivoire	Banana	67	-	-
Zonon (1996)						
- zone 1	COLS	Burkina Faso	Cereals	36	58	21
- zone 2	COLS	Burkina Faso	Cereals	32	76	25
- zone 3	COLS	Burkina Faso	Cereals	47	62	30
- zone 4	COLS	Burkina Faso	Cereals	37	30	11
Kacou and	ML	Côte d'Ivoire	Cow and oxen	75	98	26
Nuama (1997)			Sheep	68	-	-
			Poultry	70	17	88
Medjigbodo (1997)	ML	Bénin	Cereal processing	79	30	24
Pégatiénan (1997)	ML	Côte d'Ivoire	Manufactured products	80	57	45.6

TE = technical efficiency; AE = allocative efficiency ; EE = economic efficiency.
ML = maximum likelihood; COLS = corrected ordinary least squares; LP = linear programming.

As for industry, preliminary results of a study on Côte d'Ivoire's manufacturing industry show that average technical efficiency ratio (80) is comparable to what is observed elsewhere technical efficiency ranges between 64 and 90 (Caves and Barton, 1990); while allocative efficiency is less comparable (57) (Pégatiénan, 1997). These findings suggest that between 28 per cent and 68 per cent of additional economic growth is possible in agriculture without new resources, between 25 per cent and 32 per cent of additional growth is possible in animal production in Côte d'Ivoire with existing resources, and 20 per cent of extra growth is possible in food processing (Benin) and in manufacturing (Côte d'Ivoire) without new resources. Therefore, in situations where new investment is impossible because of lack of resources, economic growth is still possible through improvements in technical efficiency.

Incentives are necessary to stimulate efforts that foster economic efficiency; the most important incentives are: reward for work effort, the possibility of exchanging goods and services with anybody, and the economic freedom to allocate resources freely.

Property rights: The right to own resources and to appropriate the fruit of one's work is a strong stimulus to work harder and smarter. There is, however, a big problem with property rights, that is, the divide between private and public sector. It is essential to protect public property from the invasion of private individuals; it is similarly crucial to protect private property from an expansionist state. Unless this divide is clearly designed and strictly enforced, efforts to work harder and smarter will not be forthcoming; we come back to this issue in more details later in the paper. The 'peanut roasting' management system clearly illustrates the confused nature of the divide between public and private property rights; indeed, one can witness daily in francophone countries actions or initiatives of private individuals invading public property and simultaneously expansionist states legally expropriating the property of private individuals. This simultaneous crossing of the divide occurs not so much because of the absence of the law, but rather because law enforcement is generally very poor.

Exchange and trade: The possibility of exchanging goods and services produced with anybody locally and outside the country is an essential corollary to work effort and to reward for work effort. Exchange or trade with others makes goods and people move around in different places; these movements induce circulation of new ideas and new ways of doing things. By bringing together producers with a larger number of possible buyers, exchange or trade enlarges existing markets. By moving around new goods, new wants for consumption as well as new ideas and techniques for production, exchange or trade generate new profitable opportunities that boost work effort and efficiency.

Economic freedom: Economic freedom is another strong incentive that fosters effort to work and intelligence in work; indeed, it is essential for performance that economic agents feel free to use their financial resources and skills in the most profitable ways. Therefore, it is crucial that local institutions be favourable to freedom to choose where to apply work effort, to decide the kind of work, activity or profession, to allocate resources in ways that push production to its maximum or reduce costs to the minimum. Adequate institutions are also needed that facilitate the pulling of resources out of unprofitable activities or their injection into endeavours that look more profitable. To the extent that individuals are certain to personally capture the benefits of their work, freedom to choose will increase their confidence in the economic system, hence boost their excitement for new ideas to improve their economic performance. Freedom to choose raises the question of the relative role and importance of individual or private enterprise as opposed to public enterprise; it is argued that efficiency is really what matters and that the public/private divide is a real but secondary issue. We need to build institutions that are favourable to these incentives.

The role of the state Since the inception of modern economic theory, the role of the state has always been an essential and very controversial issue. For capitalist as well as socialist countries in francophone Africa, this debate has been going on for years; it became even hotter with the introduction of adjustment policies and programmes implemented since the early 1980s in all Francophone countries. Specific issues of this debate dealt with here are: the private/public divide, democracy, basic features of a strong state, and building trust among social partners.

Private/public divide and democracy: What dominates the current debate about private/public divide is policy prescriptions aimed at enforcing the reduction of the size of state and public enterprise to the benefit of more private enterprises. The theoretical justification for these prescriptions is the low efficiency with which the state delivers goods and services resulting from its direct involvement in their production and the distortions introduced in other sectors of the economy by this involvement. The usual recommendation is to stick to the provision of public goods such as education, health and economic infrastructure. Efficiency is really what matters, irrespective of the sector of activity; if a state enterprise manages to become efficient in the production of particular goods or services, why should the state pull out and the private sector take over? Similarly, if appropriate arrangements can be made to attract private investment in economic infrastructure, why should not it be possible. Financial resources are the major constraint; since those resources are limited, the state should limit its interventions to niches where it can invest most productively and efficiently. Therefore selectivity is an important policy prescription. Unfortunately it takes a good quality administration in order for the state to be selective; not very many francophone countries can afford good and efficient administrations.

Today the debate about the role of the state stresses the necessity of democratization. The theoretical justification is that political democracy has economic benefits; it improves policy understanding by civil society and better implementation and investment choices by policy makers. Again, efficiency is what matters. Does democracy per se guarantee efficiency in a state's operations? Does it automatically improve the quality of administration that actually runs the economy and performs investment choices? Success stories of Southeast Asian 'dragons' do not show a straightforwardly positive correlation between economic performance and political democracy.

In most francophone countries the states and ruling political regimes are autocratic and allow little dissent. But despite the force they use in dealing with their constituencies, they actually look very weak for the following reasons: lack of performance in terms of economic growth, inefficiencies in delivering public goods, and high transaction costs and economic risks generated by their operating systems. Force is used as a substitute for economic performance. The strength of the state is not correlated with formal elections, not even with true democracy. A non elected or a non democratic state can still be strong if it legitimizes its hold on power by generating positive economic growth rates and by efficiently delivering whatever goods and services it has chosen to produce. Economic performance and efficiency in a state's operations have something to do with quality of institutions; therefore, it is hypothesized that the strength of the state derives from the quality of economic institutions.

Institutions and strength of the state: The state has an exclusive responsibility for creating the institutions required to foster work effort, efficiency improvements and capital formation, all of which contribute to the building of confidence or trust among economic agents and social partners. These institutions are the rule of law, the protection of property rights, respect for contracts, family, and the quality of administration.

Rule of law: It cannot be said that the rule of law prevails in all circumstances in francophone countries. In most of these countries, Côte d'Ivoire in particular, the law exists—although it is very often outdated and badly in need of revision to accommodate local and worldwide changes in economic structure. In popular opinion the enforcement system of existing laws is neither always effective nor efficient; law is routinely enforced differently according to family and political connections in ways that tend to exclude unconnected people from good quality legal services. Since complaints by vocal circles about these inefficiencies rarely have expected consequences, corruption is the only adjustment mechanism left to individuals. Corruption is fed by those who have family and political connections; those who cannot afford connections pay for this public good with money or in kind. How favourable is the rule of law to incentives (reward for effort, exchange of goods and services, freedom to choose) to improve economic efficiency? Where the rule of law prevails there is a guarantee for property rights, in general, and for the right to reward for work effort, in particular; in that environment, conflicts about contracts generated by trade and exchange with different people and in different markets can be resolved to everybody's satisfaction. Freedom to choose can also be fully exercised in countries where the rule of law prevails. Countries where the rule of law does not prevail have difficulties stimulating work effort and improving economic efficiency.

Protection of property rights: It was noted above that reward for effort is not an effective incentive unless it is captured by individuals who actually perform the job. Institutions that expropriate the property of economic agents existed in countries that opted for socialism and were theoretically absent in those with capitalist options. Since most francophone countries officially choose mixed economic regimes, with private sector living side-by-side with public sector, it can be said that expropriation of private property is not something that has been very frequently observed.

Does expropriation foster incentives to increase work effort and to improve economic efficiency? It is very clear that rules, mechanisms or arrangements that deprive private agents, local or foreign, of the ownership of their resources and of the reward for their work cannot stimulate effort nor can they boost efforts to improve efficiency.

Respect for contracts: In places where there are checks and balances in political powers, legislation can guarantee that private ownership is protected against government intrusion and prevent exploitation of private individuals by other private individuals. But in contexts where government has little or no respect for law it may be difficult to prevent a government from repudiating contracts regularly signed between nationals, including the government itself, and foreigners either private or public. Possibilities of contract repudiation by a local government do not stimulate foreign capitalists already in the country or willing to invest in the country to increase their work effort. Mechanisms and arrangements that give room to contract repudiation by governments cannot be favourable to incentives to improve economic efficiency.

Quality of public administration: Administration is the way the government organizes itself in order to discharge its duties, the most important of which is setting up the appropriate institutions necessary to generate adequate economic growth rates and improve the well-being of the majority of people. We have indicated that guarantee of the rule of law, protection of property rights, respect for contracts by government and the institution of the family create the premises for the attainment of these goals. The creation of institutions capable of accommodating changes occurring in society is a big challenge that requires good quality administration. An evaluation of the performance of Côte d'Ivoire's administration is presented here with the hope that it features sufficiently well the profile of administration in most francophone countries. The following issues are examined: management styles, structures, tools available, and skills and performances of individuals in the system.

The management style of Ivorian administration can be characterized by the following problems (Burgess, Carrier and Pégatiénan, 1990): the weight of tradition, with its battery of rules, principles, norms, attitudes, mentalities and individual privileges, and an array of statutes with sometimes substantial rent situations. These problems are probably universal and not specific to Côte d'Ivoire. The following items, however, may be more Côte d'Ivoire specific: Management is purely administrative and not strategic in the sense that there is no focus on objectives, performance and results; besides this, centralization of responsibilities by the hierarchy is commonplace, and there is little space for delegation of power.

The structure of administration is characterized by the diversity and complexity of missions (large number of ministries). There is little, or even no, consultation and coordination between administrative bodies at the same hierarchical level, resulting in duplication and overlapping of responsibilities and missions.

There are plenty of management tools such as data banks, statistical information and specific studies, but they are underutilized for daily management. Administrative procedures are applied routinely with an orientation that is more legalistic than efficiency focused. The administrative system is outdated and slow, sanctions are not effective, and tolerance is widespread.

The skills level of the management staff may be high in absolute terms, but they usually are not adequate for strategic management of the economy. Civil servants have respect for administrative procedures and norms, but lack analytical competence for economic and financial management. Supervision is minimal. Besides the lack of adequacy of basic skills other problems are lack of motivation due to low salaries, the absence of delegation and the inhibition of individual initiative by the hierarchical structure.

Three main lessons can be learned from the discussion of style, structure, management tools and skills. First, administration does not focus on objectives, performance and results. Second, administrative actions are not well coordinated. Third, skills and human resources are geared towards respect for norms and procedures, and there is little competence in using analytical tools for policy formulation in economic and financial management. It must be added that during the crisis years absence of resources to work with was common as a consequence of constraints imposed by financial stabilization. Finally, it must be noted that the administration usually lacks vision, strategic thinking or forward-looking attitudes; instead, daily decisions are made on the basis of short-run thinking. We cannot say that administration in francophone countries in general, and in Côte d'Ivoire in particular, has the required quality to foster work effort and to boost economic efficiency.

Private institutions: The foregoing discussion emphasized public institutions; obviously, this should not mean that private institutions play no role in economic performance of African countries. There are key private institutions that play a crucial role, such as the extended family system, strategies against risks and strategies to get access to factors of production. It must be determined whether these institutions can explain the performance differential between francophone countries and the rest of Africa. The extended family system is a private institution created by individuals and privately ruled without government's interference; its nature and impact were discussed earlier. Economic agents face many constraints and risks created either by nature or by policies pursued by governments; their strategies are developed to avoid constraints and to reduce risks. Among the typical strategies to avoid constraints on factor markets are pooling of the family labour force and rotating labour services to avoid hiring of costly labour to meet demands for labour in peak periods. Other strategies are informal savings and banking systems. In traditional Africa, risk management strategies on goods and labour markets are intercropping on the production side and large family size on the labour market side. These private institutions exist everywhere in Africa, irrespective of the colonial power; they cannot, per se, explain differences between francophone and non francophone countries. However, the environment within which these institutions function may make a difference, as argued in the following sections.

Colonial and neo-colonial factors France's colonial rule was exogenously imposed by history on francophone countries, but in many ways its neo-colonial attitudes are endogenously driven by African leadership. The French touch affects economic institutions and performance. Some issues related to that touch are schooling and training, quality of public administration, and overall economic management.

Schooling and training: Schooling and training systems open up and mould people's minds; they also broaden their horizons. Access to new ideas and to new ways of doing things is made partly through formal training received at school. To the extent that new ideas and new ways of doing things affect intelligence applied to work, school has impacts on economic efficiency, provided the skills taught are relevant and effectively transmitted. The major problem with the school inherited from France is that it generally does not teach work skills; moreover skills learned are not relevant for actual market jobs. The main reason why it does not teach work skills is the dichotomy between general education, including university, on the one hand, and technical and engineering training, on the other. The bottleneck is the inadequacy or even absence of communication networks between these two blocks. Up to today, most francophone countries have been unable to blend or properly sequence general and technical education at either primary or secondary levels. In Côte d'Ivoire, in particular, all attempts to formulate and implement such structural and institutional changes to improve education (Usher Assouan Reform of Education) failed. No attempt has ever been made to reconcile general higher education given by universities with the technical and engineering training for which special schools or *grandes écoles* are responsible. Therefore, there is no engineering training taught in francophone universities; similarly, *grandes écoles* cannot offer a regular university curriculum including graduate programmes, hence francophone countries do not offer graduate training in engineering. It is essential to mention that there is a special *grande école* for administration (Ecole Nationale d'Administration, ENA), and as a consequence there is no graduate training in public administration or government, which means that analytical capabilities for public management at master's and PhD or doctorate levels are routinely nonexistent.

Skills taught at schools are not relevant for actual market jobs because of the complete absence of communication between the formal school and work environments and also because there is inadequate strategic planning at the government level. The typical example is the lack of agricultural skills at primary or secondary levels in countries where agriculture is the dominant economic activity. For non agricultural activities, graduates from secondary school and especially from university have to be trained again for the job, before they become usable and productive. At the level of public administration, the lack of graduate training may be part of the explanation why policy dialogue with Bretton Woods institutions and other external agencies is sometimes difficult; indeed civil servants may not have graduate training or skills without consequences for project management, but they cannot do without graduate training when they have responsibilities of formulating macroeconomic frameworks and implementing and monitoring adjustment policies and programmes.

Public administration: We argued earlier that coordination and strategic management are central to the quality of administration. Public administration in Côte d'Ivoire bears the footprints of French influence. In periods when coordination and strategic management were effective, the quality of administration was high, when they disappeared quality of administration declined; it is interesting to note that in both instances, French expatriates were heavily involved. The Ministry of Planning played a crucial role in the evolution of public administration, from 1965 to 1977. It was the coordinating body through which every other ministry had to go for their financial needs and programmes; it set goals and priorities, built the framework, and made investment choices after resolving different trade-offs. Strategic management was routinely used at that time by this ministry; objectives, performance, and results or outcomes were items of consideration as a method of dealing with problems at hand. The Ministry of Planning was staffed with expatriates—either civil servants, contract holders seconded by French consultant firms or individual contract holders. Even when the executive positions were held by locals, they used to be reinforced by expatriates. During that period, the high quality of Côte d'Ivoire's administration was praised even by the World Bank (Ouayogode and Pégatiénan, 1994).

In 1977, there was a government reshuffle and the Ministry of Planning was merged with the Ministry of Economy and Finance; most experienced Ivorians working with the Ministry of Planning in the golden years left for the private sector. From that period up to 1994, coordination and strategic management were progressively transferred to a parallel administration, the *Direction et Controle des Grands Travaux* (DCGTX), with almost a hundred French expatriates (half the total staff) having control over all executive positions. DCGTX was originally in charge of technical and architectural control of public works and infrastructure, but its competence shifted progressively to incorporate other technical projects as well. The glory of that parallel administration reached a climax in 1987, when the president took from technical ministries the responsibility of formulating and implementing all projects and programmes including adjustment and stabilization policies and programmes.

Technical ministries were left with no intellectual input in projects; their area of intervention was limited to broad political orientations. In the early 1990s, DCGTX had full responsibility on behalf of Côte d'Ivoire to negotiate adjustment and stabilization loans with World Bank; during that period DCGTX had antagonistic relations with technical ministries because of its direct access to the president. The regular administration's strength was actually reduced by the very prominence of DCGTX and by lack of structural or institutional communication between the technical (DCGTX) and political wings of the same administration. After DCGTX took over in 1987, the relatively poorer quality of the management of projects financed by the World Bank, including structural adjustment loans, began to show up (Ouayogode and Pégatiénan, 1994) as regular administration gave up the battle.

Economic management: French influence on economic management of Côte d'Ivoire is overwhelming. Issues worth discussing in that connection are the role of the state and public enterprise, adjustment policies, and 'external influences'. The role of the state and public enterprise has been traditionally large or prominent in Côte d'Ivoire as it always has been in France. It is noteworthy that the first Minister of Economy and Finance of independent Côte d'Ivoire was a Frenchman who served until 1965. The chosen strategy of state capitalism had an official justification, that is, substituting temporarily for the missing Ivorian private sector. This strategy was implemented through involvement in public enterprise in almost all sectors of the economy: agriculture, industry and services (transport, telecommunications, energy, banking, etc.) State capitalism was also indirect through participation in the equity capital of private firms of all sectors of activity. The basic idea is that some activities and sectors of activities should not be left in the hands of private capital or the market because they are part of the state's responsibilities.

France always dominated the economic scene in Côte d'Ivoire until adjustment policies and programmes came. Indeed, before 1981, the Bretton Woods institutions, especially the World Bank, had far less financial exposure and influence in the country than did France. Indeed, up until 1981, these institutions intervened through individual and sector projects. The project approach, even with macroeconomic impacts, did not require prior changes in macroeconomic framework and policies. The situation changed drastically with stabilization and structural adjustment policies, as they not only required changes in the macroeconomic framework, but also reversals in fiscal, monetary, trade and industrial policies, as well as transformation of structures and institutions.

Changes in economic incentives affected the overall economy, including interests of special groups; formulation and monitoring the implementation of policies responsible for these changes gave external actors a hold and a heavy involvement and interference in policy actions. Policy dialogue between the World Bank and Côte d'Ivoire was not much affected by France, the third party in World Bank–Côte d'Ivoire relations, as long as the Bank's financial exposure was concentrated in individual projects in infrastructure and agriculture, and French firms, working in construction and processing of agricultural raw materials, were the main beneficiaries. With the advent of adjustment policies, policy dialogue between the World Bank and Côte d'Ivoire's government became much more difficult, partly because of the third party's strong disagreement about policies themselves, and partly because of its different approaches to the analyses of these policies (Ouayogode and Pégatiénan, 1994).

We already mentioned antagonistic relations between the French-run parallel administration DCGTX and the technical ministries; these antagonistic relations were extended to the World Bank about adjustment policies and programmes in the early 1990s. The preference of real adjustment over monetary adjustment in francophone countries in general has something to do with the fear of Ivorian leaders, particularly President Houphouet Boigny, of the negative consequences of devaluation; it is noteworthy that devaluation became possible after President Boigny's illness and death. But to say that France had also a lot to do with it, when devaluation was taboo in francophone political and economic circles, and for it to happen in January 1994, would be an understatement.

In international economic relations, France has always wanted to protect francophone countries; in compensation, it has been very keen on shielding their domestic markets against 'external influences' and predators through the monopoly on public investment contracts and strong barriers to entry of 'foreign' firms in the Ivorian market. Francophone political leaders probably have no doubt about the sign of the net economic effects of these paternalistic relations, but it is worthwhile asking whether the globalization movement under way will accommodate these particular relationships.

The tenure of French technical assistance: The analysis above should not give the false impression that francophone leaders in general, and those of Côte d'Ivoire in particular, had no responsibility in this evolution; actually, internal reasons explain why French technical assistance prevailed for so long. The first reason is that in the golden years of the country's economic 'miracle', Ivorian executives in ministries, public administrations and parastatals used much of their time and energy for moonlighting. While they were physically or mentally away from work, substantive and technical content of official business was taken care of by technical assistants. The second reason is the generation conflict that existed between senior Ivorian executives and junior professionals freshly graduated with higherlevel degrees from Western schools and universities. These youngsters desired to demonstrate their competencies and get credit for their on-the-job performances; understandably, their performances and the implicit competition with existing management were not always welcome by senior executives. Hence, expatriate technical assistants were used as a shield against in-house competition.

The most important reason for the tenure of technical assistance in Côte d'Ivoire was probably President Houphouët Boigny's will not to remove the French from public administration and parastatals too soon in order to avoid a hasty 'Ivoirization'; he himself did not believe too much in experts, though. He probably was not right, since nothing in the system forced expatriates to actually transfer their skills and competencies to locals.

An important qualification to the foregoing argument is in order. That is, the tenure of this assistance was also self-serving—indeed, being a technical assistant in Côte d'Ivoire was a lucrative adventure for a Frenchman or woman, since they earned around three times more than in Europe (Ouayogode and Pégatiénan, 1994). The regular tools for lengthening their contract and stay were their failure to train locals and the tight control over the information networks.

Institutional foundations are generally weak in francophone countries because the state and its administration failed to put in place legal schemes, administrative procedures and strategic management systems favourable to the increase of work effort and the promotion of economic efficiency. Despite its autocratic and monolithic nature, the state is actually weak since it delivers neither adequate growth rates nor good quality public services. These weaknesses transpire specifically in macroeconomic management and in development strategies.

Impact of the colonial factor: In several ways, the nature of French colonization may be a major long-lasting factor in the poor economic performance of francophone Africa. The reasons for this may be: import cost, limited openness to other commercial alternatives, the heavy reliance on the public sector and the rigidity of the education system. We already mentioned the weight of France's influence on the economy of francophone countries. There is no doubt that the bulk of the bilateral trade is based more on cultural ties than on purely commercial ones, given that most imports come from France. Higher costs are induced, thereby, contributing to make francophone countries an expensive commercial area, despite the relatively low inflation due to more restrictive monetary policies.

The fact that the majority of enterprises are owned by nationals from the former colonial power limits opportunities for choosing the best technological alternatives available on world markets. The traditionally heavy reliance on the inherited public sector helped strengthen the rigidity of the structure of the economy; the negative consequences of this rigidity on the economy's ability to respond to exogenous shocks were compounded by the limited management capacities of the administration. Finally, the educational system in francophone countries is excessively geared towards administrative skills and insufficiently towards scientific and technical skills; the current skill structure does not give economic agents the aptitude to adapt and adjust promptly to changes and shocks.

At the individual level, there is a strong impression that people in francophone are less prone to take private initiative. They seem reluctant to take care of themselves through self-employment in the private sector, preferring to rely heavily on civil service. This attitude is partly the result of the excessive reliance on state intervention and assistance, and partly the result of biases in the skills content of the education system in francophone countries. As a consequence, many profitable economic opportunities are missed.

Institutional Capabilities and Human Resources

A close look at organizational capacities for development strategies and macroeconomic management capacities reveals that most often resistance to reforms and to their efficient implementation can be blamed on the poor quality of human resources in macroeconomic management and in institutional innovation. Ultimately, human resources are the instruments that actually make things move and cause changes to happen. Economic agents need information and an entrepreneurial spirit in order to perform; efficient market development is something that is also needed.

Information Human resources consist not only of skills and techniques available in public administration and in private enterprises but also of one crucial item, information. We are concerned with economic information about markets, and markets are about opportunities for profitable activities leading to the creation of new goods and services. Access to economic information and appropriate interpretation of incentives require some level of education; economic agents whose horizons are limited by lack of education have difficulties surviving competition in markets. Obstacles in the way of access to market information may not be due to lack of education but rather to monopoly of special interest groups. Therefore, to make information about profitable opportunities flow to everybody, the state must not only provide minimal education but more importantly prevent special interest groups from confiscating information networks.

Entrepreneurship Some level of education is necessary in order to be able to interpret correctly the incentives contained in economic information, but it is far from being sufficient; the necessary and sufficient condition for economic information to be fully used is an entrepreneurial input. An entrepreneur is the economic agent who loves converting new ideas and techniques into new goods and services; since exploration of new horizons and new markets is risky, entrepreneurs are people who love risk taking. They need not have themselves the appropriate skills and techniques since they can buy them from the market at any time; what is needed, rather, is aptitude to combine in appropriate ways information, existing goods and services, and skills and techniques in order to create new goods and services and to be in a position to adopt best practices. An awareness of appropriate ways of combining inputs is what makes entrepreneurs unique and indispensable. A society that manages to increase the proportion of its people who love to take the risk of converting new ideas and techniques into new goods and services at lower costs engages effectively in the development process.

There is a lack of entrepreneurs in francophone Africa able to convert available skills and techniques into new goods and services at lower cost. The kinds of entrepreneurs who do exist invest mainly in trade, transport, real estate and housing; they do not take risks either in large-scale industry or in small-scale processing of agricultural products. The case of Côte d'Ivoire is special; indeed, the huge wealth extracted over decades from the marketing of cocoa and coffee beans could not constitute start-up capital for an industrial sector controlled by private Ivorians. One possible excuse for that lacuna may be high transaction costs and policy induced risks (Collier and Gunning, 1997), but we also think that political leaders in francophone countries have limited expectations for their countries, hence they have no workable strategies to foster local industrial entrepreneurship.

Political Leadership

Francophone Africa failed to generate enlightened political leaders capable of inventing economic institutions favourable to work effort, market development and local private entrepreneurship. The political leaders Africa has are unable to improve the efficiency of the state and of public administration in particular; they seem not to be aware of the transaction costs that their policies and the ways they live create for other economic agents. They also seem not to understand the risks that are generated by their policies. The inability of political leaders to transform existing institutions and adapt them to new circumstances, and to increase the speed of that transformation, is a significant obstacle to growth. Even Côte d'Ivoire, blessed for decades with outstanding political leadership, was not saved from the lack of quality of institutions (den Tuinder, 1978). Indeed, in the midst of economic prosperity total factor productivity growth was highly negative because the quality of economic institutions was deteriorating (Pégatiénan, 1994, 1996; Kouassy and Pégatiénan, 1995). Unfortunately, improvements in total factor productivity during the adjustment years were not large enough to compensate for the collapse of capital accumulation and to maintain positive economic growth.

Information, skills and techniques, entrepreneurs, and political leadership are essential elements of human resources. They condition the actual response of economic agents to incentives. No market can function only with goods and services and without human resources and response: market development proceeds necessarily through improvements of human resources and response.

Market Development

Markets are made of the following items: goods and services, incentives, institutions and structures, and human resources (information, skills and techniques, entrepreneurs, and political leaders). Each element is important, but taken in isolation, it cannot make markets operate; for markets to work, each element has to play its complementary role. Experience shows that in less developed countries, economic incentives are generally not right, and that in those cases, markets function in ways that are wrong but nevertheless adapted to ruling real and relative prices. Individuals who get the right information change attitudes and behaviours on one hand, and entrepreneurs find required combinations of skills and techniques that generate mixes of goods and services suited to actual incentive structures.

There are frequent complaints about inadequate incentives, low efficiency, and slow or negative economic growth. Unless human resources (policy makers and public administration) intervene to transform institutions and structures and reset them in ways that are favourable to improvements in economic efficiency, markets and growth performance will continue to be disappointing. Economic incentives may be right after economic reform, but human response to these incentives—impossible without the action of entrepreneurs—may be hindered by quality of institutions or structures (like corruption of civil servants or poor infrastructure, both of which generate high transaction costs and risks), confiscation of information by special interest groups, inadequacy of skills and techniques, or prohibitive acquisition costs on factor markets. Hence, expected mixes of goods and services may not be forthcoming, or, when they are the coefficients of their supply elasticities may be well below expectations. Actions on economic incentives only through macroeconomic policies (stabilization) will not suffice to start the engine of growth—there is a need for a simultaneous move on institutions and structures.

The foregoing analysis argues that incentives, institutions or human resources taken in isolation will not succeed in moving an economy ahead in the right direction. Rather, an integrated view of the role of each individual element is the right direction to take, with each actor having a distinct role to play. Invisible hands may play a significant role in the existence of markets and in the coincidence of individuals' and society's interests, but humans—that is, individuals, the state and entrepreneurs—have something crucial to contribute to the smooth functioning of markets. Indeed, economic institutions and the state are integral parts of markets; as we argued before, efficiency is what really matters, therefore the state can intervene anywhere in markets provided it performs well and its own actions are efficient. We do have instances of East Asian dragons where this happy change has occurred. The state can contribute significantly by transforming institutions and adapting them to rapidly evolving circumstances and by preventing monopolies or oligopolies from confiscating economic information. Commitment of political leaders and the state to the development of efficient markets in francophone countries is a crucial part of their development process.

The importance of institutions has led us to try to measure their quality and determine whether this quality improved or deteriorated over the years. This useful but risky exercise is done for Côte d'Ivoire.

Index of Institutional Quality

We tried to measure the level of quality of individual elements of these institutions mentioned earlier. A grade was given on a scale from 1 to 5 of increasing level of quality (Table 4.4). Weights were given to each element according to its perceived relative importance.

Evaluating institutional quality in Côte d'Ivoire Quality of administration ranks first (50 points) because we think that administration is the arm of the state that thinks and implements, its performance commands all the functioning of the legal and procedural system. Rule of law is ranked second (30 points) to administration and ahead of other elements; protection of property rights and respect for contracts by the government have the same weight. Rule of law was good in the first decade, started deteriorating in the mid 1970s and became a real problem beginning in 1990; this was evidenced particularly with the political turmoil of the early 1990s and with the electoral process in 1995. it can be said of Côte d'Ivoire that respect and protection of property rights have generally been guaranteed, but the grade of 3 assigned reflects unsatisfactory ways in which commercial disputes have been resolved. The government has had the reputation of fulfilling its contractual responsibilities. Administration quality was fairly good during the first decade and average in the second; it became poor in the third decade but has upgraded to average since 1990, with an acceleration of structural adjustment. Overall quality of economic institutions was fairly good in the first 15 years, but has deteriorated ever since, even after devaluation.

Table 4.4 Quality of economic institutions in Côte d'Ivoire

	Rule of law	Protection of property rights	Respect of contracts	Quality of administration	Overall economic institutions
Weight	30	10	10	50	100
1960–65	4.0	3.0	5.0	3.0	3.5
1965–70	4.0	3.0	5.0	3.0	3.5
1970–75	4.0	3.0	5.0	2.8	3.4
1975–80	3.0	3.0	5.0	2.1	2.7
1980–85	3.0	3.0	5.0	1.7	2.5
1985–90	3.0	3.0	5.0	1.3	2.3
1990–95	2.0	3.0	5.0	2.1	2.4
1995–97	1.0	3.0	5.0	2.2	2.2

The index of institutions, quality is the following: 1 = Poor; 2 = Average; 3 = Fairly good; 4 = Good; 5 = Very good/excellent.
Source: Author's best guesses.

Administration quality was determined by computing the weighted average of the grades given the following different components (Table 4.5): Corruption and fraud, efficiency of public investment, democracy, conflict of competence, coordination, strategic management and skills and techniques. Again the weight measures the relative importance of each component. Corruption and fraud rank first (25 points) because it is the most important element in determining the efficacy of public administration; if corruption and fraud are low administration can still have a good quality even though other elements are poor. Efficiency of public investment ranks second (20 points) because, the government being the most important investor, the quality of public investment has a crucial impact on the rest of the economy. Coordination and conflict of competence are next and on the same footing (15 points); administration cannot be efficient if its actions are not coordinated or if there is a conflict of competence of its different centres of decision or action. Democracy ranks fifth because we think that what really matters is the efficient delivery of services, and this is possible even if democracy is nonexistent—provided the administration is keen on legitimizing its hold on power by the efficient delivery of services. Strategic management and skills and techniques should not be marginalized despite their lower grades.

The scores of the administration on corruption and fraud have never been good; they were average in the first 15 years and have deteriorated since the mid 1970s. Efficiency of public investment deteriorated over the last 30 years, with only marginal improvement over the 1990–1997 period. Coordination and conflict of competence were not a problem over 1960–1975, but then they deteriorated steadily as explained earlier. Democracy was always poor until 1990 when expression of political opinion became legal and possible through increased number of journals and pamphlets. Strategic management goes hand-in-hand with coordination.

Table 4.5 Quality of public administration in Côte d'Ivoire

	Skills and technical qualification	Strategic management	Coordination	Conflict of competence	Democracy	Efficiency of public investment	Corruption and fraud	Total / Average score
Weight	5	10	15	15	10	20	25	100
1960–65	4.0	5.0	5.0	4.0	1.0	2.0	2.0	3.0
1965–70	4.0	5.0	5.0	4.0	1.0	2.0	2.0	3.0
1970–75	4.0	5.0	5.0	4.0	1.0	1.0	2.0	2.8
1975–80	3.0	4.0	4.0	3.0	1.0	1.0	1.0	2.1
1980–85	1.0	2.0	3.0	2.0	1.0	2.0	1.0	1.7
1985–90	1.0	1.0	2.0	1.0	1.0	2.0	1.0	1.3
1990–95	1.0	1.0	3.0	2.0	2.0	4.0	1.0	2.1
1995–97	1.0	1.0	4.0	3.0	2.0	3.0	1.0	2.2

Source: Author's best guesses.

Changes in institutional quality, transaction costs and risks We constructed a quantitative index of institutional quality with 1975–1980 as the base year because, at this period, quality of administration was highest; the rate of change was then computed to determine its evolution. Results (Table 4.6) show the steady degradation of overall institutional quality as well as quality of public administration; 1990–1995 is an outlier in this general tendency because public administration improved by 38 per cent over the previous periods. The first years of the 1990–1995 period correspond to the institution of the premiership in Côte d'Ivoire and in particular to the implementation of a set of adjustment programmes the synergy of which explains that improvement. But it is very clear that this improvement is fragile since, despite devaluation, new waves of deterioration have set in.

The steady degradation of general institutional quality, and of public administration in particular, generated or accelerated transaction costs and risks that are already embedded in African economies because of the smallness of markets and the high costs of goods and services. These transaction costs are due to the rise of corruption and fraud and to arbitrary justice, which cost unnecessary time and money to economic agents.

Table 4.6 Index of institutional quality in Côte d'Ivoire (1975–1980 = 100)

	Public administration	Overall economic institutions	Change of quality (%) Public administration	Change of quality (%) Overall economic institutions
1960–65	143	129		
1965–70	143	129	0	
1970–75	133	126	-7	-2.8
1975–80	100	100	-25	-20.6
1980–85	81	92	-19	-8.0
1985–90	62	85	-23	-7.6
1990–95	100	89	38	4.7
1995–97	105	81	5	-9.0

Source: Authors' computations.

Recent Experiences of Macroeconomic Management

The following sections discuss Côte d'Ivoire's actual experiences in macroeconomic management. Issues to be covered are: the flexibility and adaptability of policies, the management of external shocks and net capital flows, public expenditure and the management of public finance, and impact of reforms on macroeconomic management and performance.

Flexibility and Adaptability of Policies

Issues of flexibility and adaptability concern macroeconomic and sector policies (agricultural pricing, public and private investment, privatization, industrial and trade policy, social policy). In this context, we must distinguish the period before devaluation, which coincides with the long reign of President Houphouet Boigny, and the post devaluation period. Most of this discussion is an account of evaluations of the policy dialogue between Côte d'Ivoire and the World Bank (Ouayogode and Pégatiénan, 1994).

Macroeconomy Public investment was the engine of growth in Côte d'Ivoire before the crisis of the 1980s and early 1990s, but investment programmes were very ambitious relative to available financial resources. Problems raised by these ambitious programmes were the size of the fiscal deficit and the quality of public investment; the dialogue was then about the need to reduce the volume and pace of public investment in order to increase public saving and improve the quality of public investment.

The government steadily resisted advice to increase public saving and to improve the process of investment selection and allocation. It held its positions for a long time, despite the sharp decline of the country's financial credibility and prestige on international markets. The dialogue was marked by the weakening of technical administration after 1977, as already mentioned, but the resistance to change was also due to the President's rigid vision of the matter. Disagreement with the government about macroeconomic and institutional reforms led to the interruption of the World Bank' s financial assistance in fiscal year 1988.

Sector policy issues Direct and indirect agricultural policies have always taxed Ivorian peasants, but incentives have remained reasonable. As far as agricultural pricing is concerned, the government of Côte d'Ivoire has maintained for a long time an asymmetrical behaviour; indeed, the government is ready to increase producer prices when world prices are high but, for social and political reasons, resists reducing producer prices when world prices are falling. More generally there has been confidence in market forces as long as they were favourable, but suspicion about them generated by unfavourable turns. The government agreed with the World Bank to increase producer prices in 1984 when the world market paid good prices, but resisted the advice to reduce them after 1987, when the world market was unfavourable; this was a major reason for interruption of the Bank's financial assistance in 1988. Constrained by huge financial losses, the government finally agreed to reduce producer prices, for the first time, in July 1989. The government also held a rigid position about the role of the price stabilization fund (Caisse de Stabilisation); even now, it resists a complete dismantling of the institution, which shields peasants from the world market and, in many ways, also from private dealers and brokers.

The government of Côte d'Ivoire always believed that state intervention is necessary in order for the private sector to develop, but state capitalism was meant to be a temporary substitute for the Ivorian private sector. Government's conviction of the crowding in effect of public investment on private investment has always been strong and this is the reason why public investment, in particular through public enterprise, sharply increased over the years. The importance given by Ivorians to the role of the state—public investment and public enterprise—in the economy explains why it was so difficult to change policies when financial constraints became severe; privatization and reduction of public investment were difficult policy reforms to accept and to implement.

Nonetheless, it was believed that the existing extensive outward orientation of Côte d'Ivoire's economy was not sufficient, and that further liberalization was required. One instance of the problem encountered is the 1984 simulated nominal devaluation through a simultaneous export subsidy and import duty surcharges. The implementation of this policy was poor, as export subsidies could not be paid, and the administration found the reform to be an academic exercise, hence its lack of credibility. Liberalization efforts or attempts kept going back and forth, indicating obstacles in the way.

Over the last 30 years Côte d'Ivoire has implemented elitist social policies in education, health and housing; these policies have been costly and generally not poverty sensitive until very recently. The unit cost of education and health was very high because of the small size of targeted populations, overdosing and architectural extravagance. Policy choices in education favoured secondary and higher education relative to primary education; in health care, they emphasized curative instead of preventive care. The location of schools and health centres favoured urban areas and left the rural majority with limited access to social services. As for employment and immigration policies, Côte d'Ivoire is the most open country in francophone Africa, with more than a quarter of its population being foreign. As a result of inherent policy biases, social and political considerations and constraints slowed the pace and limited the content of economic reforms, especially in the early 1990s.

What has happened since the death of President Boigny and the advent of new leadership? Devaluation has been successful as far as inflation is concerned; the initial disappointment experienced with private investment in being reversed. Yet, after the euphoria of significant improvements of macroeconomic equilibrium, there are still many signs of continued weaknesses in central administration. Substantial areas of structural and institutional reform, like the redefinition of the role of the agricultural price stabilization fund, remain to be resolved.

The overall characterization of the flexibility and adaptability of policies to changing circumstances is that Côte d'Ivoire's government was obstinate in its policy stances; it had the fortune that, for decades, economic and political events vindicated those policy stances. Was it mere luck, or the foresight of a gifted leader? Probably both. If Côte d'Ivoire is not fortunate enough to have this luck in the near future, then problems will be compounded as significant weaknesses in central administration precludes foresight.

Public Debt Management

The obstinacy of Côte d'Ivoire's government in keeping too ambitious investment programmes created a debt overhang that led the country into the financial and economic crisis that started in the late 1970s and lingered for 13 years. Ambitious public investment programmes and some luck produced Côte d'Ivoire's 'economic miracle', but the challenges of that success could not be met by timely and adequate policy changes; one of these challenges was efficient debt management.

Acceleration of public investment occurred in the early 1970s, where investment programmes were financed by external and internal resources. Over the 1971–1980 period the stock of external debt increased from CFAF 136.4 billion to CFAF 1,265 billion, a rise by a factor of 9; over 1980–1993, the stock increased from CFAF 971.65 billion to CFAF 4,196.8 billion; this stock doubled, between 1994 and 1996 reaching CFAF 8,637 billion in 1996 (Kouassy, 1997b). Internal debt started increasing in the 1980s; from CFAF 601.5 billion in 1988 it reached CFAF 1,025.5 billion in 1992 and CFAF 1,102.8 billion in 1996. A substantial proportion of the internal debt was made of arrears stemming mainly from the agricultural price stabilization fund's deficit, as producer prices were not reduced when world prices fell; this debt was also explained by rescheduling of debt services owed the central bank.

In the 1960s and 1970s foreign donors were bilateral, and even up to the early 1980s private donors dominated. Since the 1980s the share of multilateral donors has dominated. The structure of external debt is dominated by medium- and long-term debt, and the rise of payments arrears between 1986 and 1994 relates to private debt contracted in the 1970s. Up to 1985, the share of Bretton Woods institutions financing was only 10 per cent, but their share increased to 15 per cent in 1987 and to 20.5 per cent in 1995. This steady increase is linked to the adoption of structural adjustment programmes. Debt on nonconcessional terms was low for Côte d'Ivoire, but it increased from 5.7 per cent in 1980 to 14 per cent in 1994. The weight of debt service represented 25.9 per cent, 37.3 per cent and 22.1 per cent, respectively, in 1980, 1983 and 1996. The fall of the weight of debt service after 1983 is explained by improved export competitiveness and also by the debt alleviation mechanism after devaluation. As for internal debt, banking and non-banking agents were major donors.

Debt rescheduling was important for public finance, representing 60 per cent of annual regular debt service. In 1994, debt rescheduling and alleviation gains were larger than debt services actually paid; this was a gain from the devaluation. Internal debt service represents 2 per cent to 3 per cent of GDP and 13 per cent of total public revenues. Payments of internal arrears, which are of concern to non-banking private agents, represented 10 per cent of public revenues in 1994 and more than 7 per cent in 1995 and 1996.

In conclusion, Côte d'Ivoire has never systematically studied the actual or future impact of debt and of the structure of the financing of the economy on overall performance. Instead, short-run considerations have been the major management horizon.

Structure of Public Expenditure, Provision of Public Infrastructure and Management of Public Finance

For a long time, the size and structure of public expenditures have been matters for concern. Problems created by these expenditures are fiscal deficit and the differential impacts of alternative modes of financing that deficit.

One-fourth of GDP was made of primary expenditures in 1990, but this share declined over the years to 19 per cent in 1996. The GDP share of debt service fell faster, from 10 per cent in 1990 to 6.1 per cent in 1996. Current expenditures constitute the bulk of primary expenditures; before devaluation they represented over 80 per cent and went up to 85.5 per cent in 1993; this share fell to 71 per cent after devaluation. Personnel expenses took the bulk of current expenditures—more than 50 per cent before devaluation and around 41 per cent in 1995 and 1996.

Discretionary expenses are important items as they show the leverage of the government outside of controlled processes; they declined from 17 per cent of total primary expenditures to 9 per cent in 1993 and to 7.1 per cent in 1996. To show the importance of discretionary expenses, they can be compared with volume of public investment; they were very high before devaluation, constituting 90 per cent of public investment on average, and declining from 155 per cent in 1990 to 63 per cent in 1993. Discretionary expenses declined sharply after devaluation to reach 30 per cent of public investment; in 1996 the share was still high at 25 per cent.

The GDP share of public investment declined during the crisis years, from 12 per cent in the 1980s to 2.5 per cent in 1990, but rose slightly to 3 per cent in 1993. After devaluation, this share climbed to 5.2 per cent on average, from 4.7 per cent in 1994 to 5.5 per cent in 1995 and 1996. In terms of total primary expenditures, public investment increased from 11 per cent of primary expenditures in 1990 to 14.3 per cent in 1993; sharp increases occurred after devaluation, from 24 per cent in 1994 to 28 per cent in 1995 and 1996. Thus after devaluation there was a restructuring of public expenditures in favour of public investment, although its GDP share remains historically low compared with that of the mid 1970s and 1980s. As the GDP share of public investment shows, the provision of public infrastructure was poor before devaluation, as the government was forced to reduce its investment expenditures in order to accommodate personnel expenditures; new investments were impossible and even maintenance was not guaranteed.

Impact of Reforms

Côte d'Ivoire's economy has been under reform since the early 1980s. For 12 years these reforms took the turn of real adjustment with a combination of stabilization and institutional and structural changes. In January 1994, the devaluation of CFAF occurred. How have these reforms affected macroeconomic management and performance?

Reforms and macroeconomic management Reforms in this area focused on changes in three directions:

- Size, structure and efficiency of public expenditures
- Liberalization of trade and industry and of the overall incentives systems
- Devaluation of the CFAF

We investigate the effects of these reforms on efficiency of investment, on management of public finance, on trade liberalization and on total factor productivity.

Investment efficiency The ICOR in the private sector is smaller than public sector ICOR, demonstrating that private investment is more efficient than public investment. Within the public sector, public investment financed with private finance or project loans is more efficient than public investment financed with budgetary support. ICORs in 1995 and 1996, after devaluation, are consistently smaller than in 1994. Since devaluation, management of investment has been much better than before devaluation.

Public finance management Public revenues linked with external trade grew steadily and substantially up to 1987, but declined over 1987–93, probably because of the change in liberalization policies (Kouassy, 1996); post devaluation revenues have not increased much despite the renewed liberalization. As for total revenues, there are a steady decline up to 1993 and a small rise after devaluation; the reason for the small changes after devaluation is probably that other components of public revenues declined as a response to liberalization. For example, indirect taxes fell by 23 per cent between 1983 and 1986 and by 33 per cent between 1987 and 1993. As far as expenditures are concerned, there was a steady decline over the entire period of reforms except in 1987–1988; this temporary increase of expenditures may be linked to the disbursement of export subsidies.

Changes in expenditures and revenues are reflected in fiscal deficits and debt. Public debt accelerated between 1984 and 1993. Global fiscal deficit remained larger than 10 per cent of GDP over the period, with a surge to 16 per cent of GDP over 1987–1988. If these results are interpreted as adverse outcomes of trade liberalization policies, it can be understood why the liberalization process slowed between 1989 and 1993.

Trade liberalization policies Having sketched episodes of trade liberalization earlier, we now consider empirical indicators of these policies. One element to appreciate is the importance of non-tariff barriers to trade, as indicated by the number of products subject to those barriers. On the basis of these numbers, it can be seen that protection increased between 1976 and 1982 (+142 per cent products subjected to these measures); it declined between 1984 and 1987 (−24 per cent products subjected), which is equivalent to liberalization. In 1988 protection increased with the number of products subjected to non-tariff barriers; after devaluation, there was a renewed liberalization process, with a reduced number of products subjected to non-tariff barriers (Kouassy, 1996).

Another indicator of liberalization is the degree of openness estimated by GDP share of exports and GDP share of imports. These indicators show that the Côte d'Ivoire economy is open through exports and imports, and that openness by exports is always greater than openness by imports (Kouassy, 1996). Until 1982 openness by imports was stable, ranging between 20 per cent and 36 per cent; after 1982 openness by imports declined from 20 per cent in 1981 to 12.5 per cent in 1991. Openness by exports evolved in two phases. In the first phase (1960–1974) the degree of openness was 25–35 per cent; openness declined in the second phase (1974–1982) to 20–25 per cent.

Degree and nature of openness depend on sectors of economic activity. Four categories of sectors can be considered: marginally open, open by exports, open by imports, open by export and import. Food agriculture and services have degrees of openness lower than 10 per cent. Sectors open by exports are export and industrial agriculture, with rates sometimes higher than 100 per cent, food processing industries (rates of 30–60 per cent) and wood industries (87 per cent in 1991). Sectors open by import are fisheries and petroleum products with rates higher than 2 per cent in 1991, grain processing and beverages (20–30 per cent in 1991), and industrial equipment (100–300 per cent in 1976 and 15–130 per cent in 1991). Sectors open by export and import are textiles and footwear, chemical and rubber products, building materials, and metal work (30–300 per cent in 1991). Thus Côte d'Ivoire's economy is open by exports for primary products, food processing industries and other agro-allied industries; it is open by imports for cereals, fisheries, manufactured goods and industrial equipment. Products that are open by export and import are textiles, chemicals and metal goods.

Total factor productivity growth One indicator of changes in macroeconomic management as a consequence of economic reforms is total factor productivity (TFP) growth. Despite its analytical and estimation problems and shortfalls, this indicator helps to highlight growth potentials of improvements of efficiency in macroeconomic management. In difficult times, it is worth knowing the existence of possibilities in which improvements of TFP can more than compensate for lack of resources to finance capital accumulation and maintain reasonable growth rates. It is very clear that the biggest challenge of Côte d'Ivoire's past success was the steady and rapid decline of its TFP growth over 1960–1989 period, especially in years of economic prosperity (Table 4.7).

Table 4.7 Relative contribution of factors of production to growth in Côte d'Ivoire

	Growth of (%)			Relative contribution to growth (%)	
	Real income	Volume of input	TFP	Volume of input	TFP
1962–1989	3.7	6.7	-3.0	181	-81
1962–1981	6.5	12.8	-6.3	197	-97
1981–1989	-2.1	-6.1	4.0	290	-190
1981–1986	1.2	-8.3	9.5	-692	792
1986–1989	-4.2	-3.5	-0.7	83	17

Source: Pegatiénan (1994).

The average real growth rate over the study period was 3.7 per cent with growth of volume of factors and TFP contributing +6.7 per cent and -3 per cent, respectively (Table 4.7). In prosperity years (1960–1980) average real growth rate was 6.5 per cent with the volume of factors growing at 12.8 per cent and TFP falling at an average rate of 3.3 per cent; during crisis and adjustment years (1981–1989) the negative growth of 2.1 per cent was explained by the negative growth of volume of factors (-6.1 per cent) and a positive growth of TFP (+4 per cent).

Over the 1960–1989 period, then, the contribution of volume of factors to overall growth was +181 per cent while TFP contributed -81 per cent. In comparison, contribution of TFP growth in developed and all less developed countries was 49 per cent and 31 per cent, respectively (Chenery, Robinson and Syrquin, 1986); more recent estimates show that in all less developed countries, Africa, Asia and Latin America, this contribution was 25 per cent, 5.9 per cent, 40 per cent and 12.5 per cent, respectively (Hadjimichael et al., 1995). While African macroeconomic management looks very poor, by all standards Côte d'Ivoire's situation, inferred from TFP growth, is even worse than that of the continent.

Thus, empirical evidence demonstrates that efficiency of macroeconomic management in Côte d'Ivoire is poor; reforms helped fix what was wrong, but could not do much prior to devaluation. Not much can really be said before impact of these reforms is evaluated.

Reforms and Macroeconomic Performance

Impact evaluation will be made at several levels: public expenditures and the tax system on one hand, and impact of investment efficiency and of trade liberalization, on the other.

Differential impact of structure of public expenditures Changes in structures are important elements of reforms for one reason: that is, the different components have different impacts on performance. The different components of public expenditures are current expenditures, public investment and total expenditures. The impact of these components is evaluated in terms of their impact on total income, exports and private investment. There are direct effects (on total income) and indirect effects (on exports and private investments); indirect effects may be more important than direct effects. The distinction between direct and indirect effects is important for policy formulation. These impacts are evaluated in terms of elasticities.

In general, Côte d'Ivoire public expenditures are productive or efficient; current expenditures are more efficient or productive than public investment, especially in terms of exports; they are also productive relative to non-tradeable output or public investment. After devaluation, efficiency of current expenditures increased. Public investment is efficient, especially relative to exports, but less than current expenditures; its efficiency relative to production and exports falls after devaluation. The different components of public expenditures are efficient in terms of private investment and exports after devaluation, demonstrating the favourable effects of reforms as tending to promote private investment and exports as accompanying measures of devaluation. The relatively lower efficiency of public investment relative to private investment is noteworthy and points to more management efforts. Total expenditures have a stronger impact on exports than on private investment, again showing the need to improve incentives directed at private investment.

Differential impact of taxes Côte d'Ivoire faces many problems at the level of revenue collection. Two indicators of efficiency are used, one is the elasticity of different taxes, the other is the average tax rate. It is clear from the table that tax efficiency is low—and indeed very low, less than one in all cases—especially for indirect taxes. Even after devaluation, tax efficiency is still low although more stable. Smallness and variability of fiscal revenues reflect weaknesses of fiscal administration. Indeed, coordination is insufficient among different revenue collection centres and there are also conflicts of competence, highlighting the fact that institutions are crucial to macroeconomic performance.

GDP share of fiscal revenues shows the tax burden that economic agents have to bear; this burden does not seem to be too heavy: it is around 16.5 per cent on average in 1995 and around 19 per cent in 1996. Actually, these figures underestimate actual tax rate and inclusion of tax evasion would lead to higher rates.

Impact of trade liberalization Lack of time and resources precludes a rigorous evaluation of the impact of trade liberalization on the economy; instead, only an interpretation of some performance indicators is done in relation to different liberalization episodes.

We can see that GDP share of increases with trade liberalization in early 1980s, the deficit falls from −6.3 per cent in 1980 to −3 per cent in 1981–1983, and there is a surplus over 1984–1993 period, with a surge of 17 per cent over 1984–1986 period as a consequence of the first phase of liberalization. After devaluation there is a deficit estimated at 2.5 per cent in 1995.

Relative export prices fell steadily from 1980 to 1993, showing degradation of incentives to produce export goods. Competitiveness of local goods relative to imports steadily deteriorated over 1980–1993. As far as efficiency is concerned, there was a steady improvement in capital productivity, very impressive in the 1984–1986 period when liberalization was very active. Although the increase in productivity can be partly explained by the fall in investment due to lack of resources, it is also true that the active liberalization can be credited with a significant additional contribution. Despite the renewed liberalization process, capital productivity fell. Import substitution progressed over 1980–1993, increasing from 60 per cent in the early 1980s to around 70 per cent between 1984 and 1993. This progress can be explained by the contraction of financial resources as a consequence of adjustment. The fall of import substitution after devaluation shows that local production was not that strong. In summary, the impact of liberalization on exports is ambiguous (positive in first phase of liberalization and negative in second phase of liberalization, after devaluation); its impact on import competitiveness is more unfavourable.

No doubt reforms in Côte d'Ivoire had a generally positive impact on macroeconomic management and performance. Structures seem to have had differential impacts on the efficiency and performance of public expenditures, but we can also see that deeper or more radical institutional reforms are still needed for a significant improvement of internal revenue collection. In many and significant ways structures and institutions determine macroeconomic management and performance.

Capital Accumulation, Macroeconomic Management and Institutions

So far our discussion has disregarded technical progress, which can be defined as outward (inward) shifts of the production (cost) frontiers; these shifts are not possible without capital accumulation. The occurrence of technical progress and capital accumulation induces the production and consumption of more goods and services with a positive impact on economic growth. This positive economic growth results from the increase of the productivity of given volumes of labour and capital and from the generation of positive externalities that make increasing returns to scale possible. Since sources of technical progress are outside francophone Africa, the main objective of this section is to explore the implications for the subregion. In particular, the section will determine the relative role of macroeconomic policy and institutions in investment and saving decisions.

Capital Accumulation and Savings/Investment Equilibrium

Why and how does technical progress happen, and what impact does it have on economies of francophone countries? To answer these questions, we examine the role of knowledge and capital goods in shifts of production and cost frontiers. Then the impact of technical progress on efficiency and competitiveness is discussed. The major requirements of capital accumulation—the transmission mechanism of technical progress—are saving and investment.

The production frontier gives the maximum quantity of goods and services that can be produced given the level of technology and knowledge. The cost frontier gives the minimum cost combination of factors used in producing one unit of goods and services. To the extent that francophone Africa does not have the same level of technology and knowledge as the rest of the world, its production (cost) frontier is well inside (above) that of the rest of the world and especially that of industrialized countries. The distance between the observed position of francophone Africa on its production frontier and the position of the rest of the world on its own production frontier measures the technological gap of francophone Africa. Outward (inward) shifts of the production (cost) frontier of the rest of the world increase this technological gap. Since daily experience shows that these shifts in the rest of the world are steady and very rapid, while at the same time technical change is slow or nonexistent in francophone Africa, the technological gap is widening fast.

Technical progress does not result from the mere passage of time. Rather it is a deliberate, conscious change induced by improvements of basic scientific knowledge as well as by applications of this basic knowledge to transform nature, eliminate obstacles to an easier life and in many ways make old dreams come true. Transformation of these scientific principles into goods and services is made possible by the construction of successive generations of capital goods, the use of which facilitates the production of streams of new goods and services at lower cost. Capital goods are the concrete link or bridge between knowledge and actual goods and services. Only research and development can build this bridge—the possession of these capital goods is possible only through capital accumulation or investment. Hence countries that do not have internal capacity to invent new capital goods, because of lack of basic scientific knowledge or abilities to apply this basic knowledge through research and development, can buy it from the market through investment. The technological gap of francophone Africa is basically explained by its lack of investment or the slow pace of that investment. Since this gap is widening rapidly, francophone Africa cannot cope with technical progress unless its rate of investment is at least as fast as the rate of the outward (inward) shift of production (cost) frontier in the rest of the world.

For francophone Africa to be able to compete in world markets, it must find ways to reduce its technological gap. In this globalization era, competition is not an option but an obligation for the subregion to avoid marginalization or even disappearing from the world map. Unfortunately this risk is real, since francophone Africa is positioned not on its own frontier but somewhere inside it; hence the actual technological gap is greater than that measured by the distance between Africa's production frontier and the rest of the world's. There is an inefficiency problem added to the technological one; indeed, the gap also includes the quantity of goods and services that francophone Africa forgoes by not producing the maximum possible of goods and services with techniques at its disposal today. Again relative to the world production frontier, the inefficiency is greater than that suggested by its own production frontier. In order for francophone Africa to compete (in terms of cost, price and quality) in world markets it must reduce both inefficiency and technological gaps. With duality properties, similar reasoning is valid with cost frontier.

While below or inside the production frontier, shifting that frontier outward may be a resource wastage since existing possibilities or opportunities are not exhausted. It is better first to try to be on the frontier by imitating local best practices, that is by reducing the efficiency gap. For countries that adopt aggressive export strategies external competition requires a rapid improvement in efficiency (both technical and allocative), simultaneously with a reduction of the technological gap, by investing more than countries that concentrate on local markets. Globalization and international competition require that francophone Africa adapt its institutions and transform them in ways that are favourable to efforts to improve efficiency as well as efforts to invest productively.

Efforts to Save and to Invest Productively

Increase of proportion of savers and investors A lot of investment has taken place in Africa during the last 30 years, but compared to what should have been done, it is still below expectations. The volume of investment per se is less important than the productivity of that investment, no matter how little it may be. What really matters is the ability of a society to generate people who can invest productively; therefore the increase of the proportion of economic agents who can invest productively is crucial.

We already indicated the need to have entrepreneurs who take risks in order to try new ideas and techniques and create new goods and services. It is crucial then to increase the proportion of entrepreneurs who will invest productively. In particular, it is essential to increase the proportion of entrepreneurs who accept to invest productively an increasing share of their income or personal savings.

Finding entrepreneurs may be difficult, not because the entrepreneurial abilities are lacking but because the financial resources necessary to pay for the investment do not exist locally. Therefore, for investment to be possible, countries must have some local savings that can be lent. The other financial problem that francophone Africa faces, then, is the ability to generate an increasing proportion of economic agents who save a growing proportion of their income.

However, a society is likely to be able to generate an increasing proportion of such people unless conducive local institutions exist. Francophone countries are not yet endowed with quality economic institutions. It was argued earlier that the extended family system in operation in this part of the continent does not favour savings and investment because little disposable income is left after the expenses of the family have been taken care of. Lack of adequate and efficient financial institutions also has a significant role to play.

Financial institutions The major role of financial institutions is to provide loanable funds in order to make investment possible. These financial institutions have problems of scope and efficiency, but their operations are also influenced by the overall institutional climate. Francophone financial institutions face several problems (Marchés Tropicaux, 1996, 1997). Prior to reforms in 1990–1991 the basic problem was lack of liquidity and solvency, hence uncertainties about clients' rights to their deposits; after reforms the situation in West Africa improved while that in Central Africa failed to change. The second problem relates to the inability of the banking system to convert short-term resources into loans to finance medium and long-term investment; rather, the system concentrates on short-term commercial activities. One variant of this institutional inadequacy is the complete lack of financial services to accommodate the needs of agriculture, small and medium-scale enterprises, and microenterprises in the informal sector. The last problem is the monopolistic structure of a banking system dominated by only three to five large banks. In particular, barriers to entry are significantly high for non French candidates.

Côte d'Ivoire's formal financial sector (Bamba, 1997) is dominated by banking activities; the banking sector represents 95.6 per cent of employment in the sector and 88.9 per cent of resources. Within the banking sector, 4 banks out of 11 make 80 per cent of total loans and receive the same proportion of deposits. The non-financial banking sector is dominated by the stock exchange (Bourse des Valeurs d'Abidjan) with 57 per cent of activities and by the public treasury, with 34 per cent. The informal financial sector is dominated by social funds (84.5 per cent of activities), NGOs (12.6 per cent), and credit and savings cooperatives (2.9 per cent). The structure of domestic credit shows that 58 per cent of total credit is short term, 23 per cent is medium term and 11 per cent is long term. The share of long-term credit increased from 27 per cent in 1995 to 51 per cent in 1996. In general, the formal financial sector does not give long-term credit for the following reasons: insufficient personal contribution, inadequacy of collateral, absence of collateral for young investors, low or uncertain profitability with high risks, inadequate medium- and long-term resources at the banking system, lack of risk capital. Despite financial liberalization programmes, rates of bank interest margins and costs of financial intermediation are on the high side; this tendency of financial prices to rise is explained by personnel costs.

Financial intermediation is poor because financial institutions are not adapted to the needs of the economy. There is a lack of trust between the bank and its client not only because the bank is unable to provide funding when and where needed for profitable activities, but also because of corruption and the arbitrariness of local justice.

Evolution of Savings/Investment Equilibrium in Francophone Africa

In this section efforts to save and invest are evaluated and compared with efforts elsewhere in the developing world.

Investment and savings rates In 1986–1992 total investment effort in francophone Africa (IMF, 1996) was estimated to be 17.8 per cent of GDP and was smaller than that of overall sub-Saharan Africa (18.3 per cent) and non CFA African countries (18.6 per cent). These efforts in francophone Africa represented 58 per cent of those in Southeast Asia (30.4 per cent of GDP in 1986–1992) and 86 per cent of those in Latin America (20.6 per cent of GDP). As far as total savings is concerned, francophone countries saved 8.8 per cent of GDP in the same period, a relatively smaller effort compared with overall sub-Saharan Africa (12 per cent) and especially non CFA countries (13.7 per cent). Again, these savings performances are short of those in other parts of developing world; they represent only 29 per cent of those in Southeast Asia (30 per cent of GDP) and 46 per cent of those in Latin America (19.1 per cent of GDP). Thus it can be seen that the savings efforts in francophone Africa are smaller than the investment efforts; it is also clear that francophone countries still have a long journey before they can perform as well as Southeast Asia.

As savings and investment behaviours of the private and public sectors differ it is important to evaluate them. In 1986–1993 the private sector in francophone countries invested 11.6 per cent of GDP, an effort larger than that of sub-Saharan Africa (9.9 per cent) and non CFA countries (9.1 per cent). (See Table 4.1.) In the same period the private sector in francophone countries saved 11.1 per cent of GDP, an effort comparable to that of sub-Saharan Africa (11.3 per cent) and non CFA African countries (11.5 per cent). Thus, compared with other parts of Africa, relative efforts and performances of francophone Africa in investment were better than in savings, which means that its investment saving equilibrium showed a deficit. The public sector in francophone countries invested 6 per cent of GDP over 1986–1992 period, less than in sub-Saharan Africa (6.3 per cent) and in non CFAF countries (9.5 per cent). The situation is worse for savings; public sector dissaved (−2.3 per cent of GDP), a situation worse than that observed in sub-Saharan Africa (−0.7 per cent of GDP) and in non CFA countries (+2.2 per cent of GDP); thus the savings performance of the public sector is worse than that of other parts of Africa.

The situation of total investment being greater than total saving is probably explained by public investment that is larger than public saving.

The situation of francophone countries may hide differences between individual countries; examples of Senegal and Côte d'Ivoire will be taken. In Senegal (IMF, 1996), the total investment rate was estimated to be 12.9 per cent of GDP in 1986–1993, while the total savings rate was 7.2 per cent of GDP. Senegal's total investment was 71 per cent of that of overall francophone countries, whereas its total savings rate represented 82 per cent of that of the subregion. Thus, globally Senegal's performances were worse than those of all francophone countries. Government investment and savings rates were 4.4 per cent and 2.6 per cent, respectively, while private sector investment and savings were 8.5 per cent and 4.6 per cent, respectively, in the same period. Senegal's private and public sector performances are below those of overall francophone countries, and Senegal's savings and investment situation is worse than that of overall francophone countries.

The investment and savings situation in Côte d'Ivoire is not good. A general feature is that the investment rate is greater than the savings rate; the total investment rate declined from 19 per cent in 1980–1986 to 10 per cent in 1986–1993 and stagnated at 10.4 per cent in 1993–1995 (Table 4.2). This performance is worse than those of sub-Saharan Africa and even of overall francophone Africa—it is 77 per cent of that of Senegal. Finally, Côte d'Ivoire's investment rate represents one-third of that of Southeast Asia and 52 per cent of that of Latin America. Total savings fell from 8.6 per cent of GDP in 1980–1986 to 1 per cent in 1986–1993 and to 7 per cent in 1993–1995 (Table 4.2). This savings performance is well below that of sub-Saharan Africa (12 per cent in 1986–1992) and of non CFA countries (14 per cent in 1986–1992). It is also inferior to that of francophone countries (9 per cent in 1986–1992) (Table 4.1); in particular it represents only 14 per cent of Senegal's savings rate.

Since 1980 private and public investment rates have fallen together and at approximately the same pace. The private investment rate fell from 9 per cent in 1980–1986 to 4.8 per cent in 1986–1993 and 5.8 per cent in 1993–1995; public investment was 10 per cent, 5 per cent and 4.7 per cent in 1980–1986, 1986–1993 and 1993–1995, respectively (Table 4.2). During a long period government invested more than the private sector but the situation reversed after 1993–1995 with the decline of government size. The private investment situation in Côte d'Ivoire is very unfavourable compared with the rest of world; over 1986–1992 period the private sector in Côte d'Ivoire invested two times less than private sector in overall sub-Saharan Africa (10 per cent); its investment performance represented 45 per cent of that of overall francophone countries and 56 per cent of that of Senegal. Unlike investment, private savings rose from 4 per cent in 1980–1986 to 7 per cent in 1986–1993 and 8.5 per cent in 1993–1995 (Table 4.2); it was 64 per cent of that observed in the rest of Africa and 152 per cent of that of Senegal. Since 1993 Côte d'Ivoire public sector has invested more than the private sector, whereas since 1980 the private sector has saved more than the public sector. The implications for fiscal deficit, inflation, real exchange rate and balance of payments are clear.

Savings and investment equilibrium Differences between savings and investment rates measure the equilibrium between the aggregates. We observe (Table 4.1) that globally the savings/investment balance in francophone countries is favourable since they generated a savings surplus over 1986–1993 period (0.6 per cent of GDP), whereas other parts of Africa produced savings deficits (−0.5 per cent and −1.4 per cent of GDP in sub-Saharan Africa and in non CFA countries, respectively). In 1986–1993, both Senegal and Côte d'Ivoire generated a global deficit representing 5.8 per cent and 8.9 per cent of GDP, respectively, with Senegal performing better. Private sector savings/investment equilibrium in francophone countries was responsible for the savings surplus; this surplus was greater in francophone countries (1.9 per cent of GDP) than in sub-Saharan Africa (1.5 per cent) and non CFA countries (−0.5 per cent). There was a savings deficit in the public sector; in 1986–1993; this public sector deficit was smaller in francophone Africa (−1.3 per cent of GDP) than in sub-Saharan countries but larger than that in non CFA countries (−0.9 per cent). In Senegal both private and public sectors show a saving deficit, but private deficit (−4 per cent of GDP) was larger than public deficit (−1.8 per cent); in Côte d'Ivoire the private sector shows (Table 2) a savings surplus (2.1 per cent of GDP) while public sector generates a large savings deficit (−11 per cent of GDP) over 1986–1993. The situation improved in 1993–1995 since the private sector's savings surplus increased slightly to 2.7 per cent of GDP, while the public sector savings deficit significantly declined to −6.1 per cent of GDP.

In francophone countries the private sector refrains from investing, leaving idle its savings, which are small by developing world standards. In contrast, governments invest too much. Not only is the government unable to mobilize idle private savings (much of which is exported through capital flight), but more importantly, it generates public debt. This structural weakness of government finance is particularly striking in Côte d'Ivoire. That is why it is essential to investigate the determinants of private investment and savings.

Institutional Change and Private Investment and Savings

We need to investigate the relative role in private sector decisions to save and invest of two groups of factors: macroeconomic policy and institutions. Since external finance has to substitute for local savings, it is also crucial to search for determinants of foreign direct investment. Recent empirical work (Hadjimichael et al., 1995) shows that macroeconomic policies and uncertainties play a significant role, positive and negative, respectively, in private investment and savings decisions in Africa. In particular, these studies show that not only are savings and investment rates in francophone countries significantly lower than the African average, but also that the coefficient of the francophone dummy is large. The institutional quality was not directly included in that exercise. We will do the same exercise for Côte d'Ivoire; the 'risk variable' will be used to integrate institutional quality indirectly through simulations.

The results of this exercise are given in Table 4.8; we concentrate on the risk factor. How important is risk? In the current study risk is measured by a three-year moving average coefficient of variation of real exchange rate. Investigation shows that risk has a negative impact on private investment but this influence is not always decisive. Indeed, when tax rate is associated with the risk variable in the same equation, risk becomes significant while the influence of public investment is simultaneously dampened and becomes insignificant. Thus, when the increase of public investment is financed by increased taxes, public investment is less of an incentive for private investment, whereas the negative impact of risk is confirmed and strengthened. Risk has a negative impact on private savings and on foreign direct investment, but its role is not significant.

Table 4.8 **Determinants of private investment, savings and foreign direct investment in Côte d'Ivoire, 1963–1995 (Estimation method: OLS)**

	1	2	3
Constant	0.02717	0.10082	-0.013561
	(0.4988)	(1.9341)*	(-2.42951)**
Per capita real income (t-1)	0.28214	0.162399	0.02095
	(3.1907)***	(1.26533)	(2.7362)**
Debt ratio (t-1)	-0.26759	-	-0.01932
	(-3.8282)***		(-3.1678)***
Infrastructures (t-1)	0.174818	-	0.01432
	(0.825)		(0.90515)
Inflation	-0.01911	-1.66488	-0.010879
	(-0.3275)	(-2.7635)**	(-1.60790)
Real exchange rate	0.074190	--	0.00942
	(2.3640)**		(2.9486)**
Risk	-0.000597	-0.000109	-3.790E-05
	(-2.2976)**	(-0.37494)	(-1.40780)
Tax rate (t-1)	-0.33114	-	0.01000
	(-2.9852)**		(0.82137)
Education expenditure (t-1)	-	-	-
Labour cost (t-1)	-	-	-
Foreign saving rate (t-1)	-	0.22696	-
		(-1.694)	
Public saving rate (t-1)	-	-0.32288	-
		(-1.8839)*	
Real interest rate on deposit	-	-0.01706	-
		(-2.8744)**	
Monetization (t-1)	-	0.12955	-
		(0.67910)	
$\overline{R^2}$	0.8461	0.4812	0.4654

Table 4.8 (contd)

	1	2	3
DW	2.07	1.910	2.75
F	21.00	5.108	4.8564
RHO	0.1841	-	-
	(0.644)		
N	32	32	32

Notes: 1 = Private investment/GDP
2 = Private savings/GDP
3 = Per capita foreign direct investment
t statistics in parentheses
* 10 per cent level of significance
** 5 per cent level of significance
*** 1 per cent level of significance

In order to evaluate the relative role of macroeconomic management and institutional quality in the development process, we use simulations. Links between institutions and economic growth are not direct but indirect; they play out their effects through savings and investment. In turn, influences of institutions on the savings/investment nexus are transmitted by transaction costs and risks as discussed earlier. This exercise, however, is limited not only by the lack of empirical evidence on these transmission mechanisms, but also by its partial equilibrium nature; therefore, the results are only illustrative of the problems and should be taken with caution.

The basic financial problem of Côte d'Ivoire and similar countries is that the private savings rate is higher than the investment rate; therefore private investment must match private savings. Our simulations horizon is 1996–2005. The base case scenario indicates that this catch up will not occur until 2002; beyond, the deficit of private savings that shows can be compensated for by foreign direct investment. Inappropriate macroeconomic policies are detrimental to this already worrisome savings/investment situation. Indeed, the investment rate declines steadily and rapidly, while the savings rate increases at a very modest speed. Excess savings is maintained for a long time and the catching up of investment does not occur until 2005, the last year of the period; besides, foreign direct investment is deterred and declines rapidly. By contrast, adequate macroeconomic policies produce modest improvements of the investment rate; the same policy package reduces the savings rate, but the improvement of investment is modest compared with the fall in savings; the result is an early catch up of private investment in 1997.

The macroeconomic policy scenario highlights two important problems. The first is the difficulty in changing the savings rate probably because omitted variables such as dependency ratio play a more important role than macroeconomic management. The second problem relates to the fact that the same set of policies may not suit investment and saving simultaneously; for example, increasing public savings in order to foster public investment is a policy move that is favourable to private investment but it deters private savings. Therefore, it is better to design specific policies for each of these aggregates. This applies also to foreign direct investment.

We argued all along that changing the quality of institutions in directions that are favourable to economic incentives will promote work effort, improvements in efficiency, and efforts to save and invest. Since efficiency and investment are major determinants of economic growth, institutional quality will promote growth. This was verified with a politico institutional scenario. Again, the influence of institutions on savings and investment work through the 'risk variable'.

A fall in institutional quality reduces investment and savings rate. The catch up does not occur before 2004, two years after the time prescribed by the base case scenario, and foreign direct investment also falls. A modest improvement in institutional quality raises investment and savings, but investment grows faster than savings and the catch up occurs in 2001, one year earlier than in the base case scenario. Foreign direct investment is also favourably influenced by this quality improvement. It is remarkable that small changes in institutional quality produce significant effects on private savings and investment.

A combination of macroeconomic policies and institutional changes was also investigated. We found that the negative effects of inadequate macroeconomic policies can be significantly dampened by small improvements in institutional quality—the catch up occurs in 2003 instead of 2005. A deterioration of institutional quality can wipe out the positive effects of good or appropriate macroeconomic policies. In this case the catching up never occurs.

Simulations show that institutional quality may matter more than macroeconomic policies. This can be explained by the fact that if public administration is good, institutional quality will also be good. Wrong macroeconomic policies are inconsistent with good administration. When institutional quality is poor, public administration is not good, and poor administration cannot design and implement good macroeconomic policies. This raises the problem of coexistence between good economic performance and autocratic or non-democratic regimes or governments. A non-democratic regime can maintain a very efficient public administration that produces good institutional quality.

Conclusions

The principal objective of this paper was to determine the relative role of macroeconomic management and institutional quality in economic development understood as the permanent increase of per capita income and of individual well-being. Francophone Africa has a record of poor economic performance compared with other less developed countries; this is so because efforts to improve efficiency, savings and investment, the main sources of economic growth, have not been fostered. Such efforts cannot be stimulated unless economic institutions are favourable to the basic incentives that determine them. These institutions are: rule of law, protection of property rights, respect for contracts and efficiency of public administration; only the state has this responsibility. Focusing on Côte d'Ivoire, the analysis shows that macroeconomic policies faced problems caused not so much by lack of appropriate skills and techniques as by lack of coordination and strategic management. Recent experiences of macroeconomic management indicate the existence of efforts to reform and of significantly positive yields of these reforms.

The investigation of determinants of savings and investment strongly suggests that macroeconomic policies and risk factors play a role. Institutions are linked with savings, investment and direct foreign investment through transaction costs and risks; their effects are explored by simulations. These simulations show that the effects of changes of institutional quality on savings, investment and foreign direct investment may dominate the effects of macroeconomic policies. Results suggest the implementation of integrated policies combining macroeconomic management with changes in institutional quality. Efforts to improve institutional quality must start with public administration, and within public administration, they should focus on corruption and fraud. Once the government wins the battle on this front other elements of the administration will work fine. For example, there will be a better enforcement of the rule of law as soon as corruption and fraud are reduced and justice becomes less arbitrary. Unfortunately, strategies to improve the quality of institutions must rely heavily on the willingness of African people and leaders to change. Civil society must press for this change through education and the realization that people must be responsible for their own fate.

References

Abdoulaye, Z. 1996. Analyse comparée de l'efficacité de la production céréalière au Burkina Faso: Case de quatre zones agroalimentaires. Thèse de doctorat 3ème cycle, CIRES, Université de Cocody, Abudjan, non publiée.

Albert, H. and H.J Pégatiénan. 1989. Revue des systèmes de suivi et d'évaluation en République de Côte d'Ivoire. Programme des Nations Unies pour le Développement.

Jacques, A. 1996. Le CIAN attire l'attention sur l'évolution récente du système bancaire et financier en Afrique francophone. *Marchés tropicaux*, 252, Février 1996.

Bamba, N. 1997. 'La politique de financement du secteur privé'. Rapport de recherche, CAPEC, Université de Cocody, Côte d'Ivoire.

Burgess, P., A. Carrier and H.J. Pégatiénan. 1990. 'Pour le renforcement des capacités de gestion du secteur public de la Côte d'Ivoire'. Mission d'identification. Programme des Nations Unies pour le Développement.

Collier, P., and J. Gunning. 1997. 'Explaining economic performance.' Working Paper Series WPS/97-2, Centre for the Study of African Economies.

Chenery, H., S. Robinson and M. Syrquin. 1986. *Industrialization and Growth.* A World Bank research publication. New York: Oxford University Press.

den Tuinder. 1978. *Ivory Coast: The Challenge of Success.* A World Bank country economic report. Baltimore: The Johns Hopkins University Press.

Dornbush, R. 1990. *Policies to Move from Stabilization to Growth. Proceedings of the World Bank Annual Bank Conference on Development Economics.* Washington, D.C.: The World Bank.

Ekou, N. 1996. Analyse de l'efficacité des systèmes de production de banane poyo en Côte d'Ivoire. Thèse de doctorate 3ème cycle, CIRES, Université de Cocody, Abidjan, non publiée.

Hadjimichael et al. 1995. *Sub-Saharan Africa: Growth, Savings, and Investment, 1986–93*. Washington, D.C.: International Monetary Fund.

IMF. 1996. *International Financial Statistics Yearbook*. Washington, D.C.: International Monetary Fund.

Kabore, T.S. 1996. Innovations techniques et efficacité économique dans les système de production des provinces du Bulkiendé et du Sanguié au Burkina Faso. Thèse de doctorat 3ème cycle, CIRES, Université de Cocody, Abudjan, non publiée.

Kouassy, O. 1996. 'Liberalisation du commerce extérieur et performance de l'économie ivoirienne'. Rapport de recherche. CIRES, Université de Cocody, Côte d'Ivoire.

Kouassy, O. and H.J. Pégatiénan. 1995. Productivité et croissance en Côte d'Ivoire. Document de travail, CAPEC, Université de Cocody, Abidjan.

Kouassy, O. and H.J. Pégatiénan. 1997a. 'Le financement public de l'économie'. Rapport de recherche. CAPEC, Université de Cocody, Côte d'Ivoire.

Kouassy, O. and H.J. Pégatiénan. 1997b. 'L'impact de l'endettement sur le financement de l'économie en Côte d'ivoire'. Rapport de recherche CAPEC, Université de Cocody, Côte d'Ivoire.

Lewis Arthur. 1955. *The Theory of Economic Growth*. French translation. Paris: Payot, 1967.

Ouayogode and H.J. Pégatiénan. 1994. Relations between The World Bank and Côte d'Ivoire. The World Bank History Project. Forthcoming.

Pégatiénan, H.J. 1990. Comments on 'Policies to move from stabilization to growth' by Dornbush. Proceedings of the World Bank Annual Conference on Development Economics.

Pégatiénan, H.J. 1994. 'Les sources de la croissance économique en Côte d'Ivoire'. Document de travail CAPEC. Université de Cocody, Côte d'Ivoire.

Pégatiénan, H.J. 1996. 'Pourquoi la crise économique s'est prolongée en Côte d'Ivoire?' Politique Economique en Bref. CAPEC. Université de Cocody, Côte d'Ivoire.

Pégatiénan, H.J. 1997. L'efficacité technique dans l'industrie manufacturière de la Côte d'Ivoire, CAPEC, Document de travail, Université de Cocody, Abidjan.

Pierre Pelletier. 1997a. Les unions régionales en Afrique Subsaharienne. Les avancées de 1996 et l'échéancier de 1997. *Marchés tropicaux*, 597.

Pierre Pelletier. 1997b. Les unions régionales en Afrique Subsaharienne. *Marchés tropicaux*, 266.

Chapter 5

Korea's Experience in Macroeconomic Management and Stabilization Policy

Sung-Hee Jwa and Kwanghee Nam

Korea has achieved a remarkably high economic growth during the last 30 years. In an economic development process that followed a government-led export promotion strategy. The government has been actively involved in almost every important aspect of economy-wide decision-making, and the private sector has followed signals given by the government. Government-led order has always dominated over the spontaneous market order.

In consequence, the active role of government in resource mobilization has been emphasized in Korea. In the developing period, Korea came up with a very peculiar macroeconomic management pattern. While the economy was subject to inflationary pressure stemming from the concern of maximum resource mobilization, macroeconomic policy instruments were unavailable. As a result, direct controls on important individual prices and even on economic activities within the private realm were widely used as the main instruments for maintaining macroeconomic stability. In sum, the macroeconomic stabilization function was performed by micro regulations.

However, in contrast to this legacy, Korea's more recent macroeconomic policy environment has undergone a drastic change. The Korean economy is becoming increasingly open and integrated with the global economy through financial liberalization, including capital flow liberalization. Korea can no longer rely on direct regulations for macroeconomic management given the increasing openness of the economy. Furthermore, globalization and the increasingly borderless economy will tend to limit the feasibility of the government's control of the domestic economy and will force the adaptation of a market order-led economic management system.[1]

This chapter reviews past experiences in macroeconomic management and stabilization and seeks a new system of macroeconomic management in Korea, in light of new developments in the macroeconomic policy environment such as

[1] The increasingly borderless economy in a globalized world market implies the high international mobility of economic agents and resources, such as firms, capital and other economic factors, which, in turn, implies that any regulatory and discriminatory domestic economic policy will become ineffective since economic agents and resources under unfair treatment by the government policy will move away. Therefore, economic policy should be based on the market mechanism in a nondiscriminatory way.

liberalization and globalization of the domestic economy. The chapter first briefly reviews Korea's experience of macroeconomic management over the last three decades and then looks at the legacies of the past regime of excessive government involvement in economic management. Next it discusses possible changes forthcoming in the macroeconomic policy environment, suggests a new regime of macroeconomic management that would enable Korea to successfully adapt to newly emerging economic environments, both international and domestic, and sheds light on the roles the government should assume in order to promote sustainable economic development led by private sector initiatives. The chapter also assesses Korea's financial crisis in 1997 and discusses the reforms undertaken after the crisis, as well as lessons from the recent reforms.

Overview of Korea's Past Macroeconomic Management and Performance

The turning point in Korean economic development came in 1961 when President Park began a series of major changes in economic policy. Since then Korea has been under strong government-led economic management to undertake industrialization. The scope of government intervention extended to a wide range of activities such as direct involvement in resource allocation and the designation of the private sector for nurturing strategic industries.

The Export Drive since the 1960s

The primary goal of industrial policy in the 1960s was to promote exports. This was an important shift in strategy from the import substitution policy undertaken in the 1950s. The export-drive policy focused on labour intensive industries, using the relatively well educated and abundant labour force.

To implement the export-drive strategy, the government launched the first five-year economic development plan (1962–1966) designed by the Economic Planning Board (EPB, 1961), which served as the major policy coordinator. For credit allocation, the government also undertook measures to strengthen 'state control over finance', such as the revision of the Bank of Korea Act (1962) to subordinate the central bank to the government. Exchange rate reform (1964) was undertaken to adopt the system of a unitary rate and devalue the Korean won.

Macroeconomic statistics show that the Korean economy successfully took off under the government-led plan: during the 1960s, Korea's economic growth reached an annual rate of 8.5 per cent with annual export growth at 39 per cent. During this period, inflation was relatively mild, reaching an annual rate of 13.7 per cent (see Table 5.1).

Table 5.1 Trend of M2, GNP, inflation and effective exchange rate from 1961 to 1994 (rate of increase, per cent)

	1961–70	1971–79	1980–85	1986–88	1989	1990	1991	1992	1993	1994
M2[a]	44.78	30.36	20.49	17.94	18.26	21.67	19.57	19.22	17.71	15.16
M2 velocity[a]	-8.87	-0.04	-2.59	0.33	-4.77	-0.97	0.52	-6.54	-5.51	-0.95
Nominal GNP	27.67	30.14	17.10	18.33	12.61	20.49	20.18	11.42	11.23	14.07
Real GNP	8.52	8.52	6.06	12.08	6.87	9.58	9.09	5.03	5.84	8.22
GNP deflator	17.64	19.94	10.71	5.58	5.38	9.96	10.17	6.09	5.09	5.40
CPI[b]	13.71	15.23	10.91	4.30	5.70	8.58	9.33	6.22	4.80	6.26
Nominal export	39.01	39.19	12.59	26.40	2.77	4.23	10.54	6.63	7.31	16.75
Nominal import	23.36	28.89	7.71	19.21	18.63	13.63	16.72	0.31	2.48	22.13
Nominal effective exchange rate[c]	13.71	8.22	8.44	4.74	-11.79	5.98	5.95	9.49	5.75	3.43
Nominal effective exchange rate[c]	1.15	0.82	2.38	3.06	-9.68	4.81	1.36	7.42	3.74	0.83

Notes: a. The end-of-period data prior to 1970 and the average of period data thereafter are used.

b. Prior to 1967, data refer to consumer prices in Seoul.

c. Based on Korea's trade weights with its four major trading partners, the US, Japan, Germany, and the UK. A positive rate of increase means a depreciation.

Source: Ministry of Finance and Economy.

The Heavy and Chemical Industry Drive in the 1970s

The 1970s have been described as Korea's period of heavy and chemical industry (HCI) promotion. Korea introduced the HCI strategy in 1973, to address concerns about transforming from labour intensive to capital intensive industry, reducing the mounting current account deficits caused by an ever-increasing import demand for capital and intermediate inputs for export production, and even the non-economic consideration of improving the self-defence capability through heavy industry. It was, however, essentially an import substitution policy in the heavy and chemical industry sector. Of course, even under the HCI drive, the export promotion policy was not abandoned but remained a general pillar of Korea's development strategy. In this effort, a more active government role in resource mobilization was inevitable to support the HCI drive.

The central bank's rediscount window as well as commercial banks' credit supply were all geared to support the heavy and chemical industry in addition to the export industries. However, this policy resulted in excessive expansion in the money supply, which, in turn, produced high inflation with various signs of microeconomic resource misallocation and macroeconomic imbalances. In addition, the two oil price shocks experienced in this decade, in 1973 and 1979, aggravated the inflationary situation. During this period, Korea achieved economic growth at an annual rate of 8.5 per cent, which is commendable, but also experienced high annual inflation at 15.2 per cent. This generated the concern that the growth could not be sustained without some strong corrective measures to curb inflationary pressures.

Economic Stabilization Policies since the 1980s

In Korea, the 1980s started with strong anti-inflationary policy measures. Monetary growth was decelerated, fiscal expenditures were tightened and efforts were made to change the degree of government intervention in resource allocation. The HCI drive was toned down and attempts were made to alleviate the structural problems it created through various adjustment measures. Deregulation and market opening were also adopted as a part of the general economic policy stance. The economic management pattern changed from strong government intervention in resource allocation characterized by various regulations on prices, quantities, entries, imports and other important economic activities to a more market-oriented resource allocation and mobilization system. The stabilization programme was firmly maintained in spite of the low growth performance in the first half of the 1980s. Consequently, Korea succeeded in curbing inflationary pressures.

During the period from 1986 to 1988, after a five-year fight against inflation, Korea experienced a strong economic boom thanks to favourable external conditions, such as the so-called 'three lows': the low dollar and won vis-à-vis the yen, low international interest rates, and low oil prices. Korea enjoyed a double-digit growth rate of 12 per cent and low, single-digit inflation of 5.6 per cent. This success was not without costs, however. Extraordinary economic performances actually reduced the government's and private sector's perception of the need for structural adjustment and for changes in the policy pattern. That is, the good economic environment failed to motivate either the government or private firms to make serious efforts towards structural adjustment and a shift in policy regime.

The economic downturn in 1989, due to the deterioration in external economic conditions and the economic fluctuations since then, brought back the typical interventionist role of the government in economic management, although this time for different purposes. The popular view was that the economic downturn and sluggish export performance were due to the weakness of Korea's industrial competitiveness primarily caused by the concentration of economic activities in the *chaebol* relative to the small and medium-sized firms. Therefore, the necessity to promote small and medium size firms and to curb the *chaebol*'s excessive business diversification activities began to receive popular support. The so-called balanced industrial structure was thought of as an important element for industrial competitiveness. Of course, the anti-*chaebol* sentiment that had gained momentum since the democratization process in 1987 also provided a good environment for this popular view. Now, financial support for small and medium-sized firms has been emphasized as the most important lending priority at every financial institution. (See Table 5.2 for the trend of the central bank's loans and discounts to support the commercial banks' policy loans.) In this way, the activist and interventionist government role in economic management patterned during the 1960s and 1970s was subdued during the first half of 1980s under the efforts to stabilize the macro economy, but regained momentum, though for different reasons, towards the end of the 1980s.

Table 5.2 Trend of loans and discounts of the Bank of Korea (%)

	1973–81	1982–86	1987–91	1992	1993	1994
Loans under the aggregate credit ceiling system[a]	-	-	-	-	-	64.2
Rediscounts on real bills	72.6	45.6	35.7	42.1	39.2	-
Loans for foreign trade	60.3	28.7	7.8	6.3	6.6	-
Rediscounts on commercial bills[b]	12.3	16.9	27.9	35.8	32.5	-
Loans for agriculture, fishery & livestock	3.9	2.2	3.6	3.0	3.2	3.5
General loans	20.7	50.6	60.4	37.4	41.3	22.7[c]
Others	2.7	1.5	0.2	17.6	16.3	9.7[c]
Loans & discounts of the BOK (A)	100.0	100.0	100.0	100.0	100.0	100.0
A / Monetary base	63.2	160.4	93.2	90.7	68.9	53.4

Notes: 1. The aggregate credit ceiling system was newly introduced in 1994 to control the aggregate size of the central bank's loans and discounts, which had been major sources of the commercial banks' policy loans but had become a burden on the central bank's monetary control as shown in the last row of this table. Loans under the aggregate credit ceiling system included some of the general loans and other loans, in addition to loans for foreign trade and rediscounts on commercial bills.

2. Rediscounts on commercial bills to large firms were abolished in 1988. Therefore, all rediscounts since then are for small and medium-sized firms.

3. Certain categories have shifted to the aggregate credit ceiling system.

Source: Ministry of Finance and Economy.

Efforts to upgrade industrial competitiveness by increasing investment through easy financial credits over a short time period, in addition to financial support for small and medium-sized firms, inevitably created an expansionary economic situation. The inflation rate again turned out to be around 10 per cent in 1990 to 1991, but is considered to be actually much higher since the measured inflation rate necessarily underestimated the true rate due to the price index management through widespread price regulation.

In recent years, price indexes have shown that inflationary pressures have been subsiding but various regulations on individual prices are still ubiquitous. The government's propensity to favour maximum growth even with some inflation and rapid political democratization, which has activated various interest groups' voice for governmental favour, could result in an ever expansionary economic situation. There still seems to exist plenty of reason to expect a resurgence of inflationary pressure in the future.

Macroeconomic Performance Evaluation

Korea's past economic development experience reveals very interesting aspects of macroeconomic management. One is that the Korean economy has shown outstanding economic growth as well as investment rates. The investment rate has risen considerably and steadily. In the 1961–1972 period, the investment ratio was 19.4 per cent; this rose to 30.1 per cent in 1973–1980 and to 33.4 per cent since 1981. Expansion of investment helps the economy to accumulate capital. As is well known, the neoclassical growth theory argues that capital accumulation is a key factor in economic growth. According to a growth accounting study, capital accounts for 3.68 per cent of total GDP growth of 8.6 per cent a year for the 30 years between 1960 and 1990.[2] Total factor productivity and labour accounts for 2.46 per cent each. Capital thus appears to be the most important growth factor in the past 30 years.

As shown in Table 5.3, both domestic investment and the national savings ratio rose rapidly. But, for the most part, the former has been higher than the latter with the exception of the late 1980s. The difference is financed by foreign savings. Current account balances were in deficit during most of the period, sometimes causing worry about a foreign debt crisis. In addition, over-investment accelerated the financial problems of firms during the recent recession period.

Table 5.3 Investment and savings ratio (%)

Year	Ratio	Savings ratio	Year	Ratio	Savings ratio	Year	Ratio	Savings ratio	Year	Ratio	Savings ratio
1960	10.0	9.0	1970	24.3	18.1	1980	31.9	23.2	1990	37.1	35.9
1961	12.0	11.7	1971	24.8	16.1	1981	29.9	22.9	1991	39.1	36.1
1962	11.8	11.0	1972	20.9	17.3	1982	28.9	24.4	1992	36.8	34.9
1963	17.0	14.4	1973	25.2	22.6	1983	29.4	27.6	1993	35.2	35.2
1964	13.2	14.0	1974	31.8	20.3	1984	30.6	29.9	1994	36.2	35.4
1965	14.1	13.2	1975	28.6	18.1	1985	30.3	29.8	1995	37.4	36.2
1966	20.4	16.6	1976	26.5	24.2	1986	29.2	33.7	1996	38.6	34.6
1967	20.9	15.4	1977	28.3	27.5	1987	30.0	37.3			
1968	24.9	18.2	1978	32.5	29.9	1988	31.1	39.9			
1969	27.9	21.4	1979	35.8	28.5	1989	33.8	36.2			

Source: The Bank of Korea.

[2] According to Perkins (1997), Korean data produces the following results:

$$g_Y = a + \omega_K * g_K + \omega_L * g_L$$

0.086 0.0246 0.0297 * 0.124 0.703 * 0.035

where g denotes the growth rate of GDP (Y), Capital (K) and Labour (L), respectively.

Another interesting aspect of macroeconomic management is monetary neutrality. In spite of the Korean government's continuous efforts to support economic development with an ever-increasing credit creation, the long-run neutrality of money seems to hold as shown in Figure 5.1. Money supply (M2) growth and inflation (in the GNP deflator) seem to move very closely, showing a correlation coefficient of 0.98 during the period from 1976 to 1994 (see Table 5.4). However, the real GNP growth rate seems to have no strong relationship with monetary growth and the correlation coefficient between them actually turned out to be −0.34 for the same period. This could be taken as strong supporting evidence against the fine-tuning of counter-cyclical macroeconomic policy.

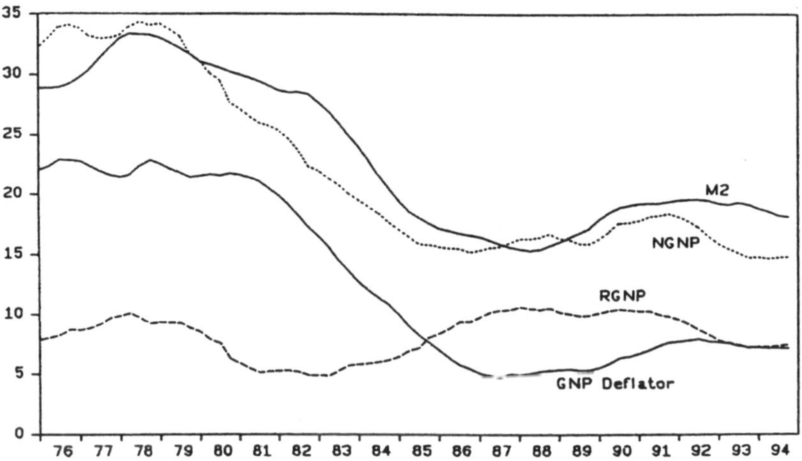

Figure 5.1 Trends of monetary growth, GNP growth and inflation in Korea

Notes: 1. M2 growth rate.
2. NGNP: nominal GNP growth rate.
3. RGNP: real GNP growth rate.
4. GNP deflator: inflation in GNP deflator.
5. All data are in five-year moving averages.

Table 5.4 Correlation coefficients among monetary growth, GNP growth and inflation from 1976 to 1994

	M2	RGNP	NGNP
RGNP	−0.3368		
NGNP	0.9406	−0.0669	
GNP deflator	0.9824	−0.3624	0.9520

Note: The data used are same as the data in Figure 5.1.

Existing Patterns of Macroeconomic Management

Any macroeconomic policy instrument must contribute to the effective control of the total size of aggregate demand but have minimal effects on the relative price structures, and therefore the resource allocation in the economy. However, Korea's macroeconomic management has relied heavily on the direct regulation of prices, as well as particular economic sectors or behaviours, as suggested above, distorting the relative price structures and leading to resource misallocation.

The main reason for this pattern is that traditional macroeconomic policy instruments, such as monetary and fiscal instruments, have not been readily available since financial resource mobilization for industrial development has been a prime concern under the government-led development strategy. It is not the purpose of this paper to evaluate in detail the overall merits and demerits of government-led strategy in economic development, but it can be observed that Korea's development strategy produced a distorted macroeconomic management pattern.

Concerning monetary policy, the central bank has directly controlled the commercial bank credit policy as well as the interest rates, setting them below market equilibrium levels. 'Money supply for economic growth' has been the prime concern; as a result, the central bank's high-powered money is almost automatically provided to targeted industrial sectors. Therefore, monetary policy has inevitably been reduced simply to a money multiplier management policy with differential effects on various economic and financial sectors. At the same time, interest rates have not been allowed to play their most important role of financial resource allocation mechanism because the provision of low-cost funds to the targeted industrial sector has been the major concern.

Policy loans with low interest rates became a stumbling block to the introduction of the indirect monetary policy instrument, i.e., open market operations, by retarding the development of financial instruments and markets. Korea's monetary policy was characterized by interest rate regulation, direct credit control, non-market allocation of government and central bank bonds to the financial sector, frequent changes of the reserve requirement ratio, and other regulatory measures.[3] Fiscal expenditure policy has been an area devoid of macro-stabilization concerns. Korea does not even have a consolidated and consistent data set on the total size of the nation's fiscal budget. The consolidated government budget, inclusive of the central government's general account, special funds and special accounts, does not include the budget of the provincial

---

[3] For example, Korea's banking sector has heavily relied on the practice of compensating balances to evade the long-standing regulations on the lending rates that could artificially inflate money supply figures such as M2. The central bank forces commercial banks to reduce the balance of deposits by canceling compensating balances with lending balances, thereby intending to reduce the M2 figures. However, it has been shown that the compensating balances would not affect the aggregate deposit balance. See Jwa (1992) for the nature and effects of the compensating balances in the context of monetary policy.

government in a timely way. Therefore, Korea has not been in a position to effectively use fiscal expenditure policy for macroeconomic stabilization.[4]

Exchange rate policy has also been devoid of macroeconomic stabilization concerns and has always been constrained by the concern for maintaining export competitiveness. The real exchange rate has from time to time appreciated but has generally been under relatively stable and depreciating trends. Also, it was found that exchange rate depreciation had been used to boost exports especially during the recession period. In this way, the exchange rate has been rigidly managed and therefore, especially when appreciation pressure was felt became subject to large and sudden discrete changes at the last minute after a stubborn resistance to the pressure for exchange rate changes[5] as experienced in the mid 1980s.

Therefore, macroeconomic management had to rely on other non-traditional instruments, i.e., direct regulations. For example, in order to manage the aggregate investment expenditures, the construction industry (with the largest share in domestic investment) has been regulated, and even the investment decisions in the manufacturing sector of large business groups has been subject to government influence through informal moral suasion, of course in addition to the effort of controlling the total money supply.

A national campaign appealing to the public to refrain from extravagant consumption and the temporary imposition of high taxes and import restrictions on certain consumer goods were the frequently used instruments for the management of aggregate consumption expenditure. On the other hand, in order to reduce current account deficits, import restrictions were frequently used, sometimes with campaigns for import substitution by the domestic goods.

Furthermore, individual price controls were widely used to 'manage the price index'. Not only the important key industrial products in the manufacturing sectors but also public utilities and various service products in the non-tradeable sectors have long been subject to government price regulations. Even factor price restraints such as interest rate regulation and a campaign for wage and land price restraints were regarded as important policy instruments for controlling inflationary pressures, and it has not been kept in mind in devising anti-inflationary policy measures that such factor prices as interest rate, wage and land price tend to be driven up by the economy-wide inflationary pressure rather than the other way around.

Short Horizon in Macroeconomic Management

For economic management, Korea has used two sets of management plans: annual macroeconomic management plans and five-year economic and social development plans.

In the early period of economic development, the five-year plan was taken as a strict action programme and therefore provided a guideline for annual as well as

[4] See Cho and Park (1994) for a similar view.

[5] See Jwa (1988) for similar points on Korea's exchange rate policy.

medium-term investment projects to achieve the growth target for the plan period. As the economy grew and became more complex, the economic development plan extended to include the social sector and turned into an economic and social development plan. At the same time, the nature of the plan also changed from a directive to an indicative plan. However, in order to respond effectively and in a timely way to the rapidly changing foreign as well as domestic economic environments, an annual review of the economic performance became inevitable.

Therefore the annual economic management plan began to be actively used as a concrete directive for annual economic management, replacing the five-year plan. Of course, the five-year plan continued to be in effect officially, but the actual management of the economy tended to be directed by the annual plan; even quarterly economic management plans have been regularly announced and reviewed, thereby weakening the medium- or long-term concern in economic management.

A short horizon in macroeconomic management can produce many problems. Most significantly, it can create macroeconomic instability since annual management plans tend to be based on the idea of fine-tuning, possibly leading to a stop-go policy pattern. Furthermore, fine-tuning policy patterns and a short horizon in economic management tend to create time inconsistencies in economic policy and therefore tend to lead to short-sightedness in the investment decisions of the private sector. And because the possibility of frequent redirection of the policy stance tends to encourage powerful interest groups in the economy, such as the associations of big business groups, and of small and medium-size firms to lobby for expansionary policy, it can also create an inflation-prone macroeconomic policy stance. Once the importance of the share of those interest groups in a national economy is realized, it becomes very difficult to take a macroeconomic policy stance against their interests. In Korea's recent economic history, it is interesting to observe that genuine and lasting anti-inflationary policy has been a very rare occurrence, having been exercised only once during the first half of the 1980s.

Political Democratization and Political Economy in Macroeconomic Policy Making

Since the mid-1980s, Korea has experienced rapid political democratization. As a result, labour unions, small and medium-size firms and other socio-economic interest groups that claim to be underprivileged rose as powerful lobbying groups adding to the already powerful big business groups. In general, these groups, have a common short-term interest in maintaining an ever expanding economy and so tend to push for an inflationary macroeconomic policy stance: high wage growth, low interest rate, easy monetary policy, and so forth.

So far, it seems to be the case that this political force has not been strong enough to produce a serious macroeconomic imbalance, even though it sometimes poses a constraint to macroeconomic policy making. In the future, however, it is possible that political economy in macroeconomic policy making, due to political democratization and the short horizon for policy making, noted above, can produce the process toward an inflationary economy unless some counteracting safety nets are set in place.

Changing Prospects in Macroeconomic Policy Environments

National economies are becoming increasingly integrated into a global economy, moving from shallow integration under the General Agreement on Tariffs and Trade (GATT) to deeper policy integration under the new World Trade Organization (WTO) system.[6] In addition to such international efforts among national economies through official bodies of international cooperation, the private sector initiative for globalizing economic activities has always been an even more important driving force for economic integration. Thus, political and geographical borders of national economies are no longer effective hindrances to the international flow of economic activities. Globalization implies the expansion of economic activities across politically defined national and regional boundaries through the increased movement of goods and services, which include labour, capital, technology and information, via trade and investment.

The Implications of Globalization for Economic Management

What does globalization imply for national economic policy making? Most importantly, any preferential or discriminatory policy will become increasingly ineffective under a globalized economic environment due to the increased mobility of economic goods and services, factors and agents and to the resulting inability of the national economic authority to hold these elements within national boundaries.

From this perspective, a government-led economic development strategy and the policy instruments for it will also become less effective. In this context, one can easily see that many existing regulations to promote or protect targeted industries would become obstacles to further economic development. Quantity and price regulations, which are administrative conveniences to control the 'price index', would also burden the economy in the global competition.

Therefore, the prospect of the Korean economy being globalized implies that economic policy making and implementation should be guided by principles of non-discrimination and the market mechanism.

Economic Liberalization and the Problems of Direct Regulation

In the coming decades, as globalization expands, domestic economic liberalization and reform will gain a new momentum. As a result, economic management based on direct regulation in macro and microeconomic policies will tend to lose effectiveness and become inconsistent with the general philosophy of economic liberalization.

---

[6] See Lawrence et al. (1994) for detailed discussion on the possibility as well as the necessity of deeper policy integration under the new world economic order.

Interest rates will be fully deregulated, and banking management will be given more freedom. Credit allocations by non-market mechanisms and preferential loans for targeted industrial sectors will be neither effective nor consistent with the liberalized policy stance. Management of private investment, consumption and imports by regulatory measures will not be available as instruments for macroeconomic stabilization policy. Price regulations will be lifted and 'price index management' will also be unavailable.

Therefore, macroeconomic management should rely on traditional macroeconomic stabilization policies based on indirect control methods through the market system.

Capital Flow Liberalization and Its Implications for Macroeconomic Management

Korea is continuously opening its banking and capital markets. Foreign banks and securities firms are expanding their branch networks in Korea, and the stock market has been opened since 1992. Since Korea became a member of the Organization for Economic Cooperation and Development (OECD) in 1996, its capital flow liberalization has widened. After the financial crisis in 1997, Korea eventually lifted regulations on international capital flow, following the restructuring programme proposed by the International Monetary Fund (IMF).

Korea's capital account is almost fully opened to levels comparable to the advanced OECD countries. In addition, the Korean won is freely floated. The Korean economy is integrated more fully with world economies and has strengthened its macroeconomic linkages with major economies.

The immediate implications of these changes for macroeconomic policy making that the so-called domestic policy cannot be concerned only with domestic issues, but must give careful consideration to the possible repercussions to and from the major foreign economies. In addition, the autonomy of monetary policy and exchange rate policy cannot be simultaneously guaranteed under the open economy setting. Furthermore, Korea has to take into consideration the international political economy in macroeconomic policy making, as a member of OECD and must prepare for the active participation in international macroeconomic policy coordination when necessary.

Democratization and the Political Business Cycle

As political pluralism and a democratic political system are developing in Korea, the possibility of political business cycles will increase. As a result, macroeconomic policy may become contaminated from political manipulation by the ruling political party as well as lobbying by interest groups.

Until recently, Korea's political system has been rather authoritarian; therefore, the chance of the ruling group losing its election was almost nil. Under these circumstances, there was little incentive for the ruling group to implement short-term economic policies to increase its re-election probability. Of course, the authoritarian government saw merit in improving the economic performance to justify its seizure of power, but possibly with a much longer horizon than a five-year, one-term democratic government would have. This seems to be Korea's experience thus far since the beginning of the more democratic system in 1987. The current political situation, with presidential elections every five years, national assembly elections every four years and the newly begun local elections every four years, should generate a good environment for political business cycles in the future.

In order to provide a stable macroeconomic environment for continued high economic development, certain safety devices will be necessary in the macroeconomic management system to prevent political factors from distorting the macroeconomic policy stance.

Reforms in Macroeconomic Policy Regime

One important condition under which macroeconomic stabilization functions become beneficial to economic development is that macroeconomic management should not distort relative price structures and therefore resource allocation. Macroeconomic management should stabilize the aggregate economy and inflationary pressures, but should not disturb micro resource allocation.

Indirect Macroeconomic Management System

Korea's macroeconomic management has relied on direct price and quantity regulations and distortion of the relative price structures; money and credit supply and tax and fiscal expenditure measures have usually been geared to support targeted industries. As a result, the effectiveness of macroeconomic stabilization policy has increasingly worsened, and actual inflationary pressure has always been felt more severely than the managed and officially announced price index suggests. At the same time, the distortive impact on the relative price structure must have been larger.

The most urgent reform needed in macroeconomic management is the active development and use of traditional macroeconomic policy instruments and the establishment of an indirect macroeconomic management system. First, the function of macroeconomic policy should be normalized, using macroeconomic policy instruments not to support development policy but for genuine macroeconomic stabilization.

Next, all regulated prices should be liberalized, not only major service prices including those of public utilities, but also major industrial product prices. Through this reform, Korea should be ready to discard the so-called price index management practices and pave the way for a genuine macroeconomic policy system. At the same time, various quantity regulations should also be liberalized.

And then, Korea should try to avoid a macroeconomic management system that relies heavily on various regulatory measures purported to encourage or discourage economic activities of specific sectors not for resource allocation purposes but for macroeconomic stabilization. Reforms should also be carried out in the direct regulations imposed on individual firms' investment projects to stabilize the aggregate investment level and on imports for current account management.

Finally, it should be kept in mind that it will not be advisable to actively use macroeconomic policy in a counter-cyclical manner. As shown in Figure 5.1, what Korea, as well as the OECD countries, have learned from the experience with counter-cyclical macroeconomic policies during the past two decades is that these policies have not been very effective, falling short of expectations, and even worse, have often been destabilizing. Note that the correlation between the real GNP and monetary growth rates for Korea was actually negative for the last 30 years (see Figure 5.1 and Table 5.4). Therefore, while Korea should establish a macroeconomic management system in which genuine monetary and fiscal measures rather than direct regulation measures are developed for macroeconomic stabilization purposes, if necessary, the actual operation of these measures should be guided by lessons learned from past experiences of active counter-cyclical macroeconomic policy. As the economic environment becomes increasingly uncertain and the requirements for the government's superior information for successful stabilization policy more difficult to satisfy, a stable macroeconomic policy may be a better choice than a counter-cyclical policy. In addition, Korea is in the midst of various economic reforms. In this regard, one should also remember an important lesson from the New Zealand economic reform, which, while still ongoing, has been praised as one of the most successful reforms in recent history.

Counter-cyclical demand management policies were largely eschewed during the reform period. Fiscal policy was focused largely on reducing the fiscal deficit in a progressive, credible manner, while monetary policy was aimed at reducing inflation steadily over time, with neither responding significantly to the state of the economic cycle (Evans et al., 1996).

Reform of Monetary Policy Practices

Korea's monetary policy practices can be characterized as a mixture of money multiplier manipulation and money demand control. To see this, suppose the money supply and the aggregate expenditure are expressed as follows:

Money supply equation: $M = \mu B$ (1)

Aggregate expenditure equation: $Y = M V$ (2)

where M, μ, B, Y and V are monetary aggregate, money multiplier, high-powered money, aggregate nominal expenditure and income velocity, respectively. Equation 1 is a simple money supply equation and Equation 2 is a simple form of the quantity of money equation. Indirect monetary management means controlling B through open market operation given a relatively stable μ. On the other hand, monetary control under the regime of macroeconomic management with direct regulation usually takes the form of manipulating μ without controlling *B*. In Korea, the base money has been used as a source of policy loan almost beyond the central bank's control. Therefore, the central bank has no choice but to rely on direct regulation of μ to control money supply, such as direct controls on commercial bank credit behaviour and frequent manipulations of the required reserve ratio. In addition, if M is not effectively controlled, the next resort is to manage Y, which should be the direct regulations on *V* (i.e., money demand behaviour) as has been the case in Korea. Controlling consumption, business investment and import behaviour with direct regulatory measures is a typical form of money demand (velocity) manipulation practice. In this sense, the money multiplier and velocity management play a major role in aggregate demand management in the so-called direct monetary and macroeconomic control regime.

Concerning the specific measures for establishing the indirect macroeconomic management system, an introduction of indirect monetary control system will be the most urgent step. Instead of relying on commercial bank credit control, direct manipulation of interest rates, frequent changes of required reserve ratio and non-market allocation of government bonds to the private sector financial institutions, open market operations should be given the highest priority as a monetary policy instrument. To this end, the central bank's burden in supporting the priority sectors with base money creation should be relieved, with increasingly less emphasis on industrial promotion policy and policy loans. The central bank's discretionary power to manage the base money supply could be strengthened with this approach. In addition, as regards interest rate regulation, securities markets should be liberalized at the earliest possible time to help the development of the money market as a market for open market operation. Also, efforts should be made to broaden the variety of the securities traded as objects for open market operations.

With these reforms, monetary policy can operate indirectly through the control of central bank's base money without causing distortions in financial resource allocation.

Reform of Fiscal Policy Practices

Fiscal policy as a macroeconomic policy has been virtually nonexistent in Korea. According to Cho and Park (1994), the International Monetary Fund (IMF) fiscal impulse measures suggest that fiscal policy was procyclical for 11 out of 20 years from 1974 to 1993, and especially procyclical for four consecutive years in the 1990s.[7] They trace their findings to the following three reasons: First, the stance of

[7] The IMF's fiscal impulse measure is obtained by dividing the difference of the actual fiscal deficit (or surplus) and the cyclically neutral one by the actual nominal GNP where the neutral one is calculated by subtracting the expenditure proportional to the potential nominal GNP from the actual tax revenue proportional to actual nominal GNP, with the proportions given by the ones in the base year. See Cho and Park (1994).

fiscal policy itself was wrongly set. Second, the rigidity of fiscal policy management forced a belated procyclical policy response in subsequent years to the demand from the public in previous years. Third, the government concentrated only on general accounts of the central government, overlooking a consolidated budget including various special accounts and funds, as well as provincial government budgets.

Therefore, there remains ample room for fiscal policy to be reformed to play a more useful role as a macroeconomic policy. Above all, as already argued, the government's industrial supporting policy for economic development should be de-emphasized, except for the necessary cases of government involvement such as social infrastructure investment, R&D support, etc. It is also necessary to improve the flexibility of fiscal expenditures by lengthening the expenditure planning horizon beyond the yearly span but not to succumb to political pressure for fiscal expansion due to the increased flexibility.

In addition, to improve the capability to monitor fiscal stance correctly and to take proper policy actions, Korea should be able to prepare a consolidated account of central government and public sector data on a quarterly basis with the least possible time lag. Local government account should be included in the public sector data.

Reform of Exchange Rate Policy

Korea's exchange rate system was liberalized in March 1990. The central value of the Korean won/US dollar exchange rate is determined as an average of individual exchange rates weighted with respective foreign exchange volumes of all exchange transactions executed during a previous market day. Initially, the band around the central value within which the market rate was allowed to fluctuate was 0.4 per cent, but it has gradually been expanded to 1.5 per cent. After the financial crisis in 1997, the government eventually adopted a free-floating exchange rate system.

However, Korea does not yet seem fully prepared to use exchange rate policy genuinely as a macroeconomic policy. The exchange rate was strongly emphasized as a critical factor affecting export performance, especially since the late 1980s, after the experience of chronic current account deficits in the earlier period of economic development.

The major concern in exchange rate management has been to maintain export competitiveness. A typical example was the reluctance to appreciate the Korean won during 1986–1988 when the economy was rapidly expanding due to the sharp real depreciation caused by the strong yen. Korea paid a due price for mismanagement in the form of inflation and loss in international competitiveness from a belated exchange rate overshooting. However, it still seems to be the case that the concern for achieving current account surpluses looms larger than the one for macroeconomic stabilization, while recently the importance of the exchange rate as a macroeconomic variable has begun to be newly evaluated.

As Korea's economy gets more open and further integrated with the world economy, exchange rate policy cannot be confined to the role of export promoter but should also promote macroeconomic stabilization and act as a buffer against foreign shocks.

Maintaining a Macroeconomic Policy Stance Free from Politics

During the last 30 years, Korea has succeeded in achieving a relatively stable macroeconomic environment even with the full-hearted support for industrial development through the central bank's base money and commercial banks' policy loans. However, the degree of central bank autonomy in Korea has been relatively low in terms of legal independence, governor's turnover rate, and the overall independence index given by the weighted average of both measures.[8] In spite of the relatively low central bank independence, the Korean government's inflation consciousness has helped achieve relatively low inflation even under rapid economic growth. In this sense, the Korean government seems to have placed priority on national economic considerations over any other political concerns. Not only the Bank of Korea but also the Ministry of Finance (now merged to the Ministry of Finance and Economy) have, to some extent, actually been functioning just like any other staunch inflation-fighting central bank, even if the independence of the Bank of Korea was relatively low.

However, the political environment has changed towards further democratization so that interest groups and political parties will seek their own interests more actively. Interest groups such as national federations of big businesses as well as small and medium-sized firms and labour unions will lobby the political parties, which in turn will put pressure on the government to change the macroeconomic policy stance for their own interests. Furthermore, the political parties, concerned with re-election and staying in power, will try to manipulate macroeconomic policy to increase their chances of re-election. As a result, one can see that the so-called political business cycle may not be a remote possibility.

To prepare for the worst possible case of political economy of macroeconomic management, Korea has to introduce some safety nets to prevent political forces from influencing the macroeconomic policy stance. Here, one can think of two possible directions: emphasizing on rule-based policy making; and lengthening the policy horizon.

Emphasis on Rule-Based Economic Policy Making

The main reason for interest groups to lobby the government directly or through political parties is because they see the possibility that the policy stance can be changed. Therefore, the surest way to protect economic policy making from political influences is to convince the public that policy stances cannot be changed except for very special and rare cases.

---

[8] See Cukierman et al. (1992) for this international comparison of central bank independence.

The issue of rule versus discretion in economic policy making has been raised in the context of how to maintain time consistency in economic policy making and implementation after experiencing high inflation under the discretionary macroeconomic policy regime.[9] A rule-based policy is recommended as a substitute for a fine-tuning, discretionary policy. The underlying reason why a fine-tuning, discretionary policy regime tends to become time inconsistent is the economic agents' conception that government policy making is endogenous or can be made to become endogenous. Therefore, the issue of maintaining time consistency in policy making is exactly the same as protecting the economic policy from interest group politics. In this sense, not only to improve the time consistency of macroeconomic policy but also to avoid the distortion in macroeconomic policy stance due to lobbying by interest groups, the government should make itself less free in policy change, thereby signalling to the public the government's commitment to the given policy stance. Once the public is convinced that the government has no choice but to stick to the given stance under any circumstances, then the leadership of the government policy over the public can be improved.

For this purpose, it will be necessary to introduce some characteristics of a rule-based policy in macroeconomic management. In order to protect the monetary policy stance from political pressure, it is important to have an independent central bank, but it is even more important to emphasize rule-based policy in monetary policy making. In the past, the government announced a monetary growth target annually but, often, the target was not kept or was changed in the course. Therefore, the growth target of money supply has not constrained central bank behaviour in the usual sense.

Lengthening the Economic Policy Horizon

Rule-based policy making is an important step towards the improvement of macroeconomic policy environment but may not be enough to achieve its intended purposes unless the horizon of rule making is set long enough. As already mentioned, Korea has used a series of five-year economic development plans, but recently the horizon of economic policy making has been shortened even to the quarterly length. Furthermore, the tradition of making five-year plans was discontinued when the current government recently launched the so-called New Economy Plan to replace the then existing seventh five-year economic plan, and the current government seems to have no further intention to return to the traditional practice of making five-year plans for the subsequent period. It seems that Korea has lost the long-term policy horizon, with the result that the government will be perceived less stalwart about its policy stance. In principle, economic policy stance can be changed once in a quarter at the shortest or in a year at the longest.

---

[9] See Kydland and Prescott (1977), Taylor (1985), Barro and Gordon (1983), and Fischer (1990) for discussions of this issue.

Under this situation, there is no room for even a rule-based policy to be beneficial if it is adopted on a quarterly basis. If a monetary growth target is adopted as a strict rule but can be easily and regularly changed in a quarter, the rule cannot be effective protection against the political economy forces. Therefore, it will be beneficial to incorporate a policy horizon of at least longer than not only a quarter but also a year into the nation's economic policy making. For this purpose, it may be useful to have a long-term development strategy other than the typical five-year economic plan that had been used in Korea, because the latter type of plan will be increasingly ineffective as the size and complexity of the economy grow.

A Search for a New Development Strategy: The Role of Government vs. Market in Economic Management

This section first looks at lessons from the Korean experiences of government-led economic development in the past 30 years by reviewing the policy patterns, defining their characteristics and noting the legacies. Korea's experiences suggest that government intervention in endogenous decision variables created many problems, such as the unfair rules of the game and the private sector's reluctance to economize. It will be argued that such intervention will inevitably be unsuccessful because the size and complexity of the Korean economy have reached a point where the government's information superiority cannot be guaranteed anymore.

The section also provides a basic framework to discuss the optimal role of the government in a general context. It does this by invoking the Hayekian philosophy (Hayek, 1984[1968]), of interpreting market competition as a discovery procedure of the optimal solutions to the economic resource allocation problems. The section concludes that government's role should be confined to preserving the spontaneity and endogeneity of the market order and to cultivating a better economic environment for the working of the market order. The government determines exogenous variables for the market order, while the determination of endogenous variables should be left to the market.

Korea's Experiences

Korea's government-led export promotion strategy for economic development has seen the government's active involvement in almost every important aspect of economy related decision-making. The private sector has followed the signals given by the government. The government-led order has always taken precedence over the spontaneous market order.

In the context of maximum utilization of economic resources, the economic development process usually entails two interrelated aspects of resource utilization. One is how to mobilize economic resources, and the other is how to allocate them. There has been a lively discussion on the optimal degree of government intervention in resource allocation, and the consensus seems to be that the market order is generally superior to government intervention, except in the special cases of the so-called 'market failures'. Practically speaking, however, it is very difficult to resolve the issues of the extent and method of government intervention exercised for optimal promotion of resource allocation for economic development.

The Korean government intervened directly in the microeconomic resource allocation through discriminatory policies, such as favouring certain sectors and certain groups of economic agents. The government controlled financial resource allocation by regulating on interest rates and lending activities of financial institutions. In the earlier stage of development—until the 1970s—the large business groups and heavy and chemical industry sector were favoured, but now small and medium-size firms are relatively favoured. The government has been a substitute for the role of the market competition as a discovery procedure in making the important allocation decisions such as what business lines the large business groups can engage in and what kind of businesses the financial institutions can lend money to. This pattern of direct intervention into the private decision areas has been ameliorated through the liberalization process in recent years, but generated far-reaching and lasting negative effects on the mindset of the policy makers regarding the role of the market order.

On the other hand, little attention has been paid to the possible side effects of emphasizing the active role of government in resource mobilization. It has been the case that the mobilization drive tended to create a detrimental environment for macroeconomic management. In general, once priority is given to domestic resource mobilization, then even macroeconomic measures such as monetary, fiscal and exchange rate policies tend to be 'mobilized' as instruments to support economic development, thereby eroding the macroeconomic stabilization role. Low interest rates, base money creation, and tax and expenditure instruments all tend to be used to support policy loans for important industries. Exchange rate management also tends to be constrained by the concern for export promotion. How to mobilize available macroeconomic policy instruments to support economic development becomes the dominant concern rather than how to improve macroeconomic stability.

Broadly speaking, it can be said that Korea has not been an exception in emphasizing the active role of government in resource mobilization even though the degree has, of course, fluctuated during the development period depending on the situation faced by the country. In this process, Korea came up with a very peculiar macroeconomic management pattern. While the economy was subject to inflationary pressure stemming from the base money and credit expansion out of the concern for maximum resource mobilization, monetary policy instruments such as the control of the base money became inoperative. As a result, direct controls on important individual prices and even on economic activities within the private realm became widely used as the main instruments for maintaining macroeconomic stability. In sum, macroeconomic policy functions were performed by micro regulations.

In contrast to such legacies in the economic management pattern of government-led development, Korea's economic policy environment has undergone a drastic change in recent years, forcing the reform of the existing economic management system. The Korean economy is becoming increasingly open and integrated with the global economy through financial liberalization including capital flow liberalization. Given the increasing openness of the economy, Korea can no longer rely on direct regulations for macroeconomic management. Furthermore, globalization and the increasingly borderless world economy tend to limit the feasibility of the government's control over the domestic economy and will force the adoption of a market-led economic management system. Globalization also implies the high international mobility of economic agents and resources such as firms, capital and other economic factors. This, in turn, suggests that any regulatory and discriminatory domestic economic policies will become ineffective since economic agents and resources subject to unfair treatment by the government policy will move away. Therefore, the economic policy should be based on the market mechanism in a non-discriminatory way.

Characteristics of Government-Led Economic Management

One should be aware that it is very difficult to precisely define the concept of government-led economic management. Here, the concept is loosely and broadly defined. A government-led economic management regime is an economic policy regime in which the government determines major endogenous economic variables within the realm of private economic agents by imposing its will on the market as an outsider rather than as a participant in the market process. In this regime, the government predetermines the outcome that would otherwise be determined endogenously through market processes.

Government-led economic management defined in this way tends to exhibit the following characteristics: At the level, it tends to rely on direct regulations, such as credit rationing, over open market operations for money supply control and on wage–price controls over aggregate demand management for anti-inflationary policy. In addition, microeconomic policy takes the form of picking the winners before the market process works itself out and of providing the means (such as financial support) necessary for the chosen to win.

In order for this type of economic management to be successful without causing distortions in resource allocation, the government must have informational superiority over private market participants and should have a complete set of solutions ready to be put into action against a host of difficult economic policy issues.

The requirements that must be fulfilled for government intervention to be beneficial are difficult to satisfy, however, especially as the economy grows in size and complexity. Unless a complete recipe of solutions to various economic problems is readily available, the degree of government intervention should be reduced in order to benefit the economy.

Korea seems to have already entered this stage of economic development and is in need of active private sector initiatives for further sustained economic development.

Legacies of Government-Led Economic Management

More than 30 years of active government intervention into private economic matters has created many legacies that pose serious stumbling blocks to the policy regime shift toward greater private sector participation.

Even as the informational requirements for efficient economic policy making become increasingly difficult to satisfy, economic policy makers, including economists who are accustomed to the mindset of the past regime, still think that they can and should manage the economy down to the finest details. This mentality poses a serious stumbling block to economic reform and liberalization. They even think they can and should regulate the deregulation.

To compound this problem, many private economic agents have lost their sense of independence and fear that liberalization may create chaos. Therefore, they often seek government intervention, even in the affairs of the private sector, and even ask the government to control the process of economic liberalization.

In addition, active government economic management has created various barriers to entry that have produced monopolistic and oligopolistic economic structures. The tendency to rely on direct regulations for economic management has also produced widespread regulations of prices and quantities that has distorted in the economic incentive structure. As a result, these phenomena have tended to discourage the individual economic agent's will to economize and the broader motivation for innovation.

Finally, as government intervention becomes more widespread, thereby creating an excess demand for intervention beyond its true capability or necessity, the effectiveness of economic management by the government is rapidly declining.

Market Order and the Role of Government Economic Policy

The basic viewpoint concerning the role of government economic policy taken in this section derives from the Hayekian philosophy: there exists a market order in the economy that arises endogenously and spontaneously, independent of any outside intervention. Competition in the market order is a process of discovering the optimal outcome, and one cannot discover or dictate the market outcome in advance without going through the competition process.

According to this view, the government role should be confined to preserving the spontaneity and endogeneity of the market order and cultivating a better environment for the working of the market order. To this purpose, the government should establish a regime of fair competition in the economic and social system so that the discovery function of the market order can be used to the maximum.

In this framework, the role of government should be limited to defining the economic and social environments, that is, determining the exogenous variables for the market order, while the determination of the endogenous variables should be left to the market order. If the government wants to influence the endogenous variables, it must participate in the market order in the same manner as the private economic agents, or change the environments or incentive structure for the market order in such a way as to influence the endogenous variables in the desired direction. In any case, the government should refrain from directly intervening in the market order and dictating the endogenous variables.

Macroeconomic stability as an exogenous environment One of the most important economic conditions for the private market order is the macroeconomic environment. Maintaining macroeconomic stability is understood as a precondition for efficient long-term economic decisions and is therefore regarded as the most important responsibility of a government. In the debate on the role of the government in economic development, World Bank (1993) has consistently contended that the most important contributing factor in the East Asian economic miracle was macroeconomic stability. One can also argue in the current context that maintaining macroeconomic stability is just like providing a better exogenous environment for the market order and should be part of the government's active policy function.

Globalization and the role of the government in economic resource allocation Recently, national economies have become increasingly integrated into a global economy, moving from shallow integration under the GATT system to deeper policy integration under the new WTO system. Under the globalized economic environment, any preferential or discriminatory policy will become increasingly ineffective because of the increased mobility of economic goods and services, factors, and agents, as well as the resulting inability of the national economic authority to hold these elements within national boundaries.

Accordingly, the government-led economic development strategy and the policy instruments for it will also become less effective. In this context, one can easily see that direct regulations to promote or protect targeted industries would become obstacles to further economic development. In general, the prospect of any economy being globalized implies that economic policy-making and implementation should be guided by principles of non-discrimination and the market mechanism. Furthermore, in the coming decades, as globalization expands, domestic economic liberalization and reform will also gain a new momentum; as a result, economic management based on direct intervention in microeconomic resource allocation will tend to lose effectiveness and become inconsistent with the general philosophy of economic liberalization.

It seems to be increasingly popular for rational governments to try to implement one form or another of an industrial policy similar to that adopted by successful East Asian economies such as Japan, Taiwan, and Korea. A lengthy discussion on the nature and characteristics of the so-called industrial policies in those East Asian economies can be found in the World Bank (1993). This study suggests that while government intervention was helpful under certain conditions, the most important factors in the East Asian Miracle are the macroeconomic stability and market conforming economic policies followed by these economies.

This tendency becomes even more conspicuous when talking about the possible policy response to the so-called 'unlimited competition' resulting from globalization. An increasingly common view seems to be that the government should help business firms successfully compete in the international market. The government should intervene, to a large extent, in adjusting the industrial structure to the globalized competitive environments.

However, the basic stance concerning the role of government taken in this note suggests the following implications, which are diametrically opposite to this new trend of industrial policy. Above all, globalization is basically a diversified and sometimes conflicting phenomenon that has different economic implications depending on the context.

Oman (1993) identifies the globalization phenomenon as not only a market extension but also as a mixture of market deregulation, the spread of new information technologies, the intermeshing of financial markets, and the innovation of industrial and production systems. Therefore, it is especially difficult for a government to design a particular industrial structure that is supposed to be optimal for its economy. In this sense, one can further conjecture that the economists' search for an alternative industrial organization among the so-called American Fordist, German Craft, and even lean and flexible production systems will not yield any definitive, single structure of industrial organization. Jwa (1997) analyses the implications of globalization on the optimal industrial structure.

Therefore, instead of adopting an active interventionist industrial policy that requires a tremendous volume of information and does not easily produce the right solutions, an effective response to globalization may be to let the market order prevail in discovering an optimal business structure and, for this, to let the private sector freely make structural adjustments.

The Korean Financial Crisis: Midterm Evaluation

Many economists believed that the immediate key cause of Korea's financial crisis was a combination of measures taken by the Korean government in 1997 rather than just a single particular policy measure implemented during the second half of that year.[10] The most important cause of the crisis was the near depletion of foreign currency reserves. Needless to say, the latent structure of the crisis stems from other more fundamental factors. The domestic origin of the crisis can be traced back to the long-standing structural weaknesses of the Korean economy, although one should acknowledge the exogenous effect of the contagion of the Southeast Asian crisis.

We further believed that Korea's failure to keep up with the rapid pace of globalization was one of the main contributors to the crisis. Korea was ill-prepared for the changes in the global economic environment. The country's over-exposure to short-term external debt made it particularly vulnerable to cyclical shocks as well as to changes in market expectations. The Korean economy has long

---

[10] For a thoughtful review of what caused the Korean financial crisis, see Jwa and Huh (1998).

been plagued by pervasive moral hazard problems; under the umbrella of government protection, financial institutions indulged in questionable lending practices. Yet for every reckless lender, there was also a reckless borrower and reckless supervisors.

Korean corporations pursued excessively leveraged expansions into less profitable business areas and were consequently brought down by heavy debt burdens and substantial investment losses. This, in turn, resulted in the staggering accumulation of non-performing loans (NPLs) in the financial sector and the erosion of financial institutions' capital base. A string of *chaebol* bankruptcies starting with the Hanbo Group began in early 1997. One immediate impact was the sharp drop in investor confidence. In fact, the abrupt outflow of short-term foreign portfolio investments between September and November 1997 initiated a sudden capital flight and the currency collapsed as a result. The Won plunged 27.5 per cent against the US dollar in November 1997, and by December 1997 had lost 40.3 per cent of its value from a year earlier.

Under such circumstances, it was inevitable for the Korean government to seek assistance from the IMF. An official request for an emergency liquidity arrangement was made on 21 November 1997. Korea finalized the stand-by arrangement with the IMF on 3 December, and as of February 1999 had had nine 'Reviews for the Economic Programme'.

Midterm Evaluation of Korea's Reforms

Under the difficult economic circumstances arising from the foreign exchange reserve depletion and the recession, the new government has been accelerating reform efforts in four major areas. From the onset of the crisis, the D.J. Kim government, whose economic policies are rooted in the interlocked principle of democracy and market economy, understood the main causes of the crisis and set out to restructure entire sectors of the economy. Recognizing that squandering of loans and corrupt lending and borrowing practices were at the core of the structural failure, the new government prioritized the restructuring of the financial and corporate sectors simultaneously. In addition, labour and public sector restructuring has also been pursued to give each sector the flexibility and efficiency necessary to keep up with other sectoral reforms.

As a result of these efforts, the government seems to have overcome the immediate crisis through a sharp increase in the country's foreign currency reserves and stabilization of the foreign exchange rate. It may, however, be a little bit early to say that the foundation for the revival of the nation's economy was laid with rising credit ratings and an improved environment for foreign investment. Moreover, the current macroeconomic recovery looks fragile. It is time to look back at what the Korean economy tried to achieve and evaluate the progress.

Reassessing the government's role The Korean economic crisis at the beginning was characterized as a short-term liquidity problem. It soon became apparent, however, that the basis of the problem was the inability of the Korean government.

During the one and one-half years following the crisis, the primary concern in Korea was to overcome the financial crisis. The macroeconomic policies adopted by the Korean government to accomplish this have been assessed as successful in the sense that the Korean economy showed such a quick recovery. The impressive short-term success, at least in terms of macroeconomic variables, is mainly the result of the quick recognition by Korean authorities of the need for such measures. Korean authorities were well aware of the Japanese government's experience, whereby problems in the financial sector were not tackled in time, eventually leading to the long-run stagnation of the Japanese economy.

There exists a basic dilemma, however. On the one hand, as we have discussed, the crux of the structural problems beneath the current difficulties lies in the Korean government's active role in all facets of economic life, leaving various market institutions weak. On the other hand, an active governmental role was inevitable during the crisis. Besides, there is a need for a responsible 'monitor' who can ensure the implementation of genuine reform measures addressing past mistakes. The government may at present be the only player in a position to step in and control the speed as well as the magnitude of economic recovery, but it is time to put the government back in its place by reassessing its role in preparing for the future.

The active role assumed by the government raised concerns in some corners, even with a strong consensus on the need for a substantive reform of the Korean economy. For example, active government participation in commercial bank credit allocation gave rise to the weak condition of the banking sector. Such government-led practices have provided an ideal background for a moral hazard problem. A firm blanket guarantee for the safety of banks liabilities was not matched at all in terms of prudent supervisory efforts to ensure the soundness of bank assets.

The major reasons public sector reforms are in disarray are that the Korean government is adrift between interventionism and free market principles and its basic stance toward both the reform and a conducive fiscal policy is contradictory. The proposed public sector reform programs call for the privatization of some government organizations and elimination of unnecessary regulations. Meanwhile, the government intends to retain control of most aspects of the economy and society. Absence of a clear-cut perspective on the government's role makes it difficult to have faith in the substance of the proposed reforms.

Re-establishment of the financial sector The measures taken so far have been adequate to stabilize financial markets. They have also been instrumental in convincing international capital markets of a positive near-term outlook. By facing the NPL problem squarely, the Korean government is not only cleaning up the financial sector's balance sheets but also removing the key source of uncertainty about the fair valuation of Korean financial institutions for potential customers and investors. Major changes have already been made in the financial and corporate sectors to transform institutional settings with the aim of introducing a new paradigm of free market-based economic activities.

The function of banks' boards of directors has been widened. For example, most Korean banks have adopted a new system that segregates executive directors from the board of directors, which comprises a majority of non-executive directors. Executive directors can now carry out only what has been decided by the board of directors. In addition, the auditing function is enhanced by the introduction of an audit committee, which will help the auditor maintain a level of independence. Other measures, such as accounting rules and prudential regulations, have also been strengthened to the level of global standards. These new measures will definitely improve the governance of financial institutions. The most important thing is not the adoption of new measures, however, but their application. Despite the visible progress of financial sector restructuring, five problems can be pointed out.

First, we must worry that the fruitful effects of restructuring may be diminished by the government's impetuosity, which has been displayed in the case of Korea Life Insurance (KLI). In the process of dealing with the troubled KLI, the Korean government tried to nationalize KLI by pouring in public money. However, the government's decision to cancel the managerial rights of the troubled firm's major shareholders and its chair has run into a roadblock. The court has ordered the Financial Supervisory Commission (FSC) to scrap plans to burn the outstanding stocks and replace the insurance company's management. The court pointed out that the FSC did not follow due procedures before issuing administrative orders. Despite this ruling, the FSC will proceed with its plan to nationalize troubled financial institutions such as Seoul Bank and others. The pace of restructuring will slow down, however, as the court ruled that the Korean economy was not in an emergency situation and therefore the FSC did not follow the proper rules in addressing troubled financial institutions.

Second, despite the Korean government's firm intent to sell off ailing banks and complete the financial sector reform this year, the proposed sale of financial institutions such as Korea First Bank and Seoul Bank has been delayed. The main visible reason for the delay is the disagreement about the real value of the banks' assets and the amount of bad loans. Furthermore, Daewoo's liquidity crisis not only delays but also threatens the deals. The more realistic reason for the delay, however, is that Korean government officials do not want to be the target of criticism for selling financial institutions at scrap value. No Korean wants to see domestic financial institutions sold at giveaway prices to foreigners, even though one should not underestimate the learning effect from foreign institutions or managers. Besides, the Korean government should acknowledge that the sooner it sells financial institutions to foreigners or the private sector, the more taxpayer money it can save.

Third, there were worries that political judgement would prevail over economic principle in the restructuring process. The concerns that general elections in April would distort the restructuring process are not too farfetched. The government's handling of Korea Life Insurance gave us some doubts about political influences. Why the Korean government chose quick nationalization rather than sale to foreign or domestic buyers is not clear at this moment.

Fourth, it can be agreed that the government's restructuring policy lacks consistency. The government adopted different rules each time important decisions were needed, using circumstantial necessity as an excuse. An example is the government's plan to bring in foreign experts to manage Seoul Bank after breaking off talks with The Hong Kong and Shanghai Banking Corporation (HSBC). The government explained that the purpose of selling financial institutions to foreigners is to learn advanced financial techniques and that either selling to foreigners or bringing in foreign experts is thus basically the same. Why then had the Korean government been trying so hard to sell Seoul Bank to foreigners at that time?

Finally, after several mergers and acquisitions (M&As) encouraged by the Korean government to restructure the financial sector, the average size of financial institutions has increased. There were five cases of M&As among commercial banks and more are currently ongoing in other sectors. However some of these M&As were not a result of market mechanisms or client demand, but of the regulatory commission's pressure. Therefore, there are doubts as to whether they will really result in increased competitiveness and efficiency. Besides, these M&As failed to reflect the real value of the firms undergoing the M&A process. It does not improve the competitiveness of M&Aed financial institutions, since these M&As are not market driven.

Corporate sector restructuring Corporate sector reform has emerged as a key task since the onset of the 1997 currency crisis. However, much of the discussion surrounding the implementation of such a reform has not been based on a systematic understanding of the corporate governance structure, which has a direct bearing on how businesses behave. Too much attention is being paid to changing outward symptomatic characteristics rather than fixing the underlying institutional and incentive structures. It has to be pointed out that recent Korean corporate restructuring has proceeded under strong government guidance, in a style that is reminiscent of the government's industrial restructuring attempts of the 1970s and 1980s.

For example, the terms of the big deals were set by the government, which determined the acquiring and acquired firms in advance and gave them the guidelines and deadlines to be accomplished. These big deals raise doubts as to the consistency of government policies. First of all, they might lead to an increase in economic concentration rather than efficiency. After the big deals are over, there remains the problem of whether the government should allow new entries into the industries where big deals have happened. If the government allows them, then it raises the question of why the big deals were ordered in the first place. If it does not, it has to find a logical explanation for why it cannot.

Current efforts by banks and the government to improve financial conditions, such as eliminating cross guarantees between group subsidiaries, will eventually help the corporate sector. However, the policy of lowering firm's debt/equity ratio also raised doubts on its propriety. The government applied a 200 per cent debt/equity ratio guideline to each of the five big *chaebols* and did not give any consideration to the diversity of each *chaebol* and industry. Taking into consideration each *chaebol*'s different business characteristics and managerial styles, it is very questionable whether the uniform application of the same numerical target and deadline to each *chaebol* can be effective. Besides, it also creates a problem of policy inconsistency. If the Korean government continues with the same guideline after 2000, it will restrict the freedom of the firms in managing financial options.

Above all else, corporate restructuring should proceed on the basis of market principles. As such, the government needs to adopt a non-interventionist policy. In other words, the government should not bail out ailing firms as it did in the past. Instead, it should allow creditor banks to voluntarily evaluate the viability of firms and decide on debt restructuring. Transparency of corporate management through enhanced disclosure of business performance is the basis upon which management should be held accountable. In order to achieve this, the financial statements of listed companies have to satisfy international financial standards. For the affiliates of large business conglomerates, their consolidated financial statements are to be disclosed by the end of this year.

Improvement of corporate governance and management transparency in the corporate sector have been promoted as specified in the 'Five Major Tasks' for corporate restructuring, which includes the elimination of cross guarantees, the establishment of core competence and the improvement of the capital structure. Last year, remarkable progress was made in the area of corporate governance. The accountability of *chaebol* owners was increased considerably by forcing them to register as a director of their leading affiliates. As such, they will no longer be free from the consequences of management misconduct.

Korea has merely laid the basic framework to improve corporate governance as from 1998. From this year onwards, more efforts should be made to induce proper institutional settings. Institutional investors, including banks and other financial institutions, have started to exercise voting rights at shareholders' meetings. Previously, institutional investors, even in cases where they held a greater stake than the largest individual shareholder, were not able to use their voting rights to influence decisions. The appointment of more than a quarter of the total number of directors from outside was made mandatory for all publicly traded companies. Minority shareholders' rights were strengthened. These new measures have proved to be efficient in advanced countries. During the course of corporate restructuring, corporate governance is expected to improve gradually either by sharing ownership with foreign firms or by transferring ownership to creditor banks through debt/equity conversions.

Financing resolution costs The recent macroeconomic recovery was mostly attributable to the government's active counter cyclical monetary and fiscal policies. The core problem of the restructuring process has not been solved, however. In addition to the banking sector, there are more financial institutions waiting for public funds, such as investment trust companies and insurance companies. The greatest difficulty facing structural reform is to find a way to finance the huge volume of resolution costs for restructuring the financial system. In May 1998, the government estimated that it would cost the public KRW64 trillion to purchase bad loans, pay deposit liabilities on behalf of financial institutions and participate in the institutions' recapitalization. This amount accounts for about 15 per cent of the current GDP in 1997 prices.

The government plans to raise the needed resources by having the Non-performing Assets Resolution Fund and the Deposit Insurance Fund issue public bonds in the market. However, the absorption of such a large quantity of bonds is not easy. If these bonds were issued in the domestic market, market interest rates would surge, pushing up firms' financial costs. Furthermore, it would not be easy for the fiscal budget to shoulder the burden of servicing the interest. The government is now trying to come up with appropriate measures to solve this problem. For example, it is considering making payments in bonds when buying up bad loans or recapitalizing financial institutions. Along with this, it intends to recycle support funds by promptly selling off bad assets, and to secure sufficient money for servicing bonds by privatizing public enterprises and cutting government spending.

However, the total amount of bad loans to be cleared out during the entire restructuring period is likely to be higher than the government's initial assessment of KRW120 trillion. The Korean government will introduce new standards for categorizing bad loans. After having the problems of the Daewoo group exposed, if the loans on the 'watch list' include those for which interest has not been paid for 1-3 months, the amount of bad loans will increase sharply. If the category of bad loans is extended to include normal loans given to businesses that will be unprofitable in the future, the amount of bad loans to be cleared out is expected to increase even more.

If the amount of bad loans increases, the estimation of the fiscal burden following financial reform rises sharply. Despite the improved economic environment due to the rapid economic recovery and a reduction in interest rates, about 25–30 per cent of total loans are estimated to be bad loans. If this is the case, about KRW30 trillion of financial resolution cost is needed in addition to the KRW64 trillion that the government established originally.[11] The total national debt/GDP ratio was 32.2 in 1998 and expected to increase to 38 per cent at the end of 1999. When we include the debt in the public sector and government guaranteed payments, the total national debt/GDP ratio will reach about 50 per cent, which is not low, and will act as a burden to the Korean economy and policy makers.

Lessons to Be Learned

Thanks to the government's efforts to overcome the short-term currency crisis, Korea can now afford to concentrate on economic recovery. Growth for 1999 is expected to be higher than 7 per cent, compared to a 5.8 per cent contraction in

---

[11] Nam and Kwon (1999) estimated that the additional amount of public resources reach about KRW27 trillion, under reasonable assumptions.

1998. Usable foreign exchange reserves were substantially increased to record levels. Many analysts believe that the Korean economy had already bottomed out of the trough either in the fourth quarter of 1998 or in the first quarter of 1999. Either way the Korean economy is headed for a full recovery this year and the next. The worst part of the currency crisis has passed without inflicting too much structural damage. Although at the early stages of recovery the high interest rate policy regime imparted a huge negative impetus on the Korean economy, we could say that the macroeconomic situation so far has been good enough to stabilize the economy and influential in recovering international confidence. Cautious optimism for the future of the Korean economy is rising, although the global environment is still full of uncertainties and instabilities.[12]

Since this recent recovery is very dramatic, we could insist that the fundamentals of the Korean economy have not been damaged severely.[13] That is, an easy monetary policy along with a fiscal policy stimulus can play an important role in reshuffling all the nominal variables. The unprecedented low interest rates helped improve the financial status of the business sector. The National Assembly passed supplementary budgets twice each year for both 1998 and 1999, increasing the budget deficit to more than 5 per cent of GDP in two consecutive years. This increasing budget deficit also helped boost aggregate demand. Namely, the current economic recovery is sustained by this kind of governmental stimulus policy and could be a quite fragile one, not based on productivity increase and new investment. Therefore, it is very important to nurture the growth potential of the Korean economy, despite the pressing demands to solve immediate difficulties.

Keeping this in mind, what lessons can Korea draw from its harshest economic ordeal since the launch of industrialization in the early 1960s? Under the D.J. Kim government's policy of joint development of market economy and democracy, the meaning of market economy has turned out to be vague. The process of economic reform has so far led to a maze of complicated political considerations that may even hinder a speedy transition to a new system. The most important lesson we can draw from the recent ordeal is that it is absolutely vital to construct and manage an economic system in tune with liberalization and globalization. Although Korea had pursued liberalization and market opening since early in the 1990s, the sophistication of the economic system and the mentality of economic agents had failed to keep pace with these trends. That is, it can be said that the Korean economy has stumbled in the course of globalization. From an historical perspective, the current crisis might be viewed as the necessary

---

[12] Troubled economic conditions in Latin America and Russia, the real possibility of a Chinese currency devaluation, and questions about the state of the American stock market all shroud the atmosphere.

[13] Cho (1999) used the time-series methodology of Blanchard and Quah to show the decomposed magnitude of the demand shock in last year's recession. According to his analysis, 4 per cent of GDP's decline out of −5.8 per cent can be attributed to the aggregate demand shock. The implication of this decomposition is that an aggregate demand driven recession can be cured rather easily through expansionary fiscal and monetary policies.

price of transition and renewal for the coming century. In that sense, what is happening in Korea is developmental in nature. In some sense the Korean financial crisis can be a blessing for the future as long as the ongoing reforms continue to bring about a new economic order. This new economic system should provide the ground on which free competition will prevail, and all economic players better do their best for themselves and for society. The whole matter relies on how successfully Korea carries out true reforms in all the sectors concerned.

In the past, market principles necessary for liberalization and internationalization were not put into practice. The supervisory system for financial institutions and corporate governance and exit procedures were ineffective so that they could not prevent moral hazard-type problems. In addition, there was a clear failure to understand the prevailing culture of international financial markets. Therefore, in order to ride out of the current crisis and build up medium- and long-term growth potential, market principles should be enshrined in the economy through the pursuit of market-oriented policies. Similarly, systems to secure the efficient supervision of financial institutions and to ensure the transparency of corporate management must be prepared so that they can be put in place as soon as possible. Meanwhile, it is important to make an effort to cooperation with other countries' financial authorities and keep international financial market participants well informed as to what is really happening in Korea by strengthening communications with them.

Another lesson learned from this crisis is a renewed recognition of the importance of the financial industry to the overall economy. In the process of economic development from the 1960s, the basic functions of the financial industry, such as credit screening, had been largely neglected because the financial sector had been regarded simply as a means of supporting the real sector. This eventually became a cause of the crisis. When many large firms collapsed, it led to a severe bad loan problem for financial institutions. Thus, the crisis has taught Koreans the importance of an efficient financial system.

Throughout the long haul of recovery from the crisis, non-viable financial institutions have been leaving the market on an unprecedented scale. Financial institutions have been forced to desist from practices that involve moral hazard and must now operate their businesses in accordance with market discipline, which requires transparent financial statements and profit-oriented, sound and accountable management. Only the first round of financial restructuring has been completed so far. There still remain problems such as a need for more public funds.

In the process of overcoming the financial crisis, both the financial and corporate sectors are now learning and realizing what direction the Korean economy should take. The Korean corporate sector, through the implementation of rigorous reform, has taken a step towards improving competitiveness in the future. In order for Korea to surmount the present crisis and regain the momentum of sustained growth, there seems to be no alternative other than swift and intensive structural reforms. Reforms always go hand in hand with pain in the short run, however. In the process of putting reform policies into practice, various challenges and dilemmas may well arise. Therefore, a problem we must solve is how to minimize the side effects and pain without wavering from the fundamental thrust of structural reform.

Many efforts need to focus on implementing any structural reform that is beneficial to the Korean economy in the long run. The recent experience heightened awareness about the need to reform various segments of the Korean economy. Indeed, one beneficial legacy of the financial crisis is that the experience will have increased the awareness of firms, the government, the press and the general public of the need to improve efficiency in all areas. As we explain in this paper, Korea has undergone significant institutional changes since the implementation of the IMF package that would never have been enacted in the absence of such developments.

As the newly rejuvenated financial sector equips itself with the more advanced management skills and the software aspect of restructuring, the momentum built by the stimulus should be fuelled by financial sector liquidity support and support recovery into the second half of the year. Nonetheless, Korean's will to reform should be adamant, and complacency should not be allowed to set in. In order to do this, reform and restructuring can only be implemented faster. There is no reverting back to the old days of inefficiency, squandering of resources, and moral hazard. Onward and upward, the march should go on.

In conclusion, the general direction of Korean government's economic reform after financial crisis seems adequate. However, what worried is the muscular role assumed by the Korean government despite the existence of a strong consensus regarding the need for substantive reforms. We clearly remember that active governmental participation in bank credit allocation led to a feeble banking sector. We also acknowledge that such government-led practices have been ideal ground for moral hazard problems. Even facing an immediate need for reforms, the government should not intend to keep control of most aspects of the economy and society. A clear-cut perspective on the government's role is needed to successfully implement the proposed reforms.

Evaluation of the reform measures taken by the Korean government will also be precious to both policy makers and academicians here and abroad. The next crisis will almost definitely be of a different variety. Nonetheless, a clear understanding of the experience of the Korean economy cannot but help give us an advantage in preparing for the future. Korea is drawing invaluable lessons from the current turmoil. However it must foot the bill, a huge one, for the crisis. It is absolutely vital to construct and manage a sound economic system in tune with liberalization and globalization. Another positive aspect is a renewed recognition of the importance of the financial industry, which Korea had neglected for a long time. These lessons will serve as a recipe for Korea to construct a more advanced and efficient economic system.

Concluding Remarks

A brief summary of the arguments made in this chapter is in order. First, the chapter reviewed Korea's macroeconomic management and development strategy since the 1960s, and evaluated Korea's macroeconomic performance during the period of 1960s–1990s.

Then, the chapter discussed many issues related to Korea's macroeconomic management in the coming decades. It argued that macroeconomic management by direct regulation measures which was dictated by the economic development strategy of financially supporting the targeted industries, short policy horizon, and political distortion in macroeconomic policy stance as being problematic patterns of Korea's macroeconomic management. It also argued that globalization and integration of the world economies, economic liberalization, capital flow liberalization, and rapid political democratization are characteristics of the new economic environment that will dictate the necessary changes in macroeconomic management.

With regard to the direction of reforms in the macroeconomic policy regime, it is emphasized that the philosophical orientation concerning the role of governmental economic policy should be shifted from the government led intervention to the private sector led market economy in which competition as a discovery procedure replaces the government role of interventionist economic policy for the efficient resource allocation. This may be the precondition for the genuine shift from the old regime of macroeconomic management to the new regime.

The chapter argued that under the new paradigm of governmental economic function, Korea should reform the practices of monetary, fiscal, and exchange rate policies, so that indirect macroeconomic management systems are easily introduced. Monetary policy should rely more on open market operations; fiscal policy should be cultivated as effective means of macroeconomic stabilization, and; the exchange rate should be given more flexibility with exchange market liberalization. In addition, the need for a safety net to protect the macroeconomic policy stance from the political manipulation by political parties as well as socio-economic interest groups was also recognized. The safety net may include enhancement of the central bank independence, rule-based economic policy making and lengthening of the economic policy horizon.

Next, the chapter evaluated the Korean experience of government-led economic development strategy in the past 30 years, and searched for an optimal role of the government in general. Korea's experience suggests that intervention into endogenous decision variables creates many problems and will not be successful because the size and the complexity of Korean economy are such that the informational superiority of the government cannot be guaranteed. Based on the lessons of the Korean experience, it argues that the government role should be confined to preserving the spontaneity and endogeneity of the market order and to cultivating a better economic environment for the working of the market order. The government determines exogenous variables for the market order while the determination of endogenous variables should be left to the market.

Finally, the chapter reviewed Korea's financial crisis of 1997 and discussed the restructuring of the financial, corporate, labour and public sector and lessons from the recent reforms undertaken after the crisis.

References

Amsden, A. 1989. *Asia's Next Giant: South Korea and Late Industrialization.* New York: Oxford University Press.

Barro, R.J. and D.B. Gorden. 1983. 'A positive theory of monetary policy in a natural rate model'. *Journal of Political Economy*, vol. 91, no. 4: 589–610

Cho, Dongchul. 1999. 'A year after the Korea economic crisis: What next?' Working Paper No. 9902, Korea Development Institute.

Cho Yoon Je and Woo-kyu Park. 1994. 'Fiscal policy in an open economy'. Staff paper, Korea Institute of Public Finance (in Korean).

Choi, Kwang. 1999. 'Public sector reform and fiscal policy in Korea'. Paper presented to Australia and Korea into the New Millennium: Political, Economic and Business Relations' Conference .

Corsetti, G., P. Pesenti and N. Roubini. 1998. 'What caused the Asian currency and financial crisis?' National Bureau of Economic Research Working Paper No. 6833–6834, December.

Cukierman, A., S. Webb and B. Neyapti. 1992. 'Measuring the independence of central banks and its effects on policy outcomes'. *World Bank Economic Review*, 6: 353–98.

Edison, H.J. 1993. 'The effectiveness of central bank intervention: A survey of the literature after 1982'. Department of Economics, Princeton University.

Evans, L., A. Grimes and B. Wilkinson. 1996. 'Economic reform in New Zealand 1984–95: The pursuit of efficiency'. *Journal of Economic Literature*, vol. 34, no. 4: 1856–1902.

Fischer, S. 1990. 'Rules versus discretion in monetary policy'. In Benjamin M. Friedman and Frank H. Hahn, eds., *Handbook of Monetary Economics*, Vol. II. Amsterdam: North-Holland.

Fleming, J.M. 1962. 'Domestic financial policies under fixed and under floating exchange rates'. *IMF Staff Papers*, vol. 9: 369–80.

Hayek, F.A. von. 1984. 'Competition as a discovery procedure'. In Nishiyama Chiaki and Kurt R. Leube, eds., *The Essence of Hayek*. Stanford, California: Hoover Institute Press.

Hwang, I. 1998. *Market Structure and Social Efficiency*. Seoul: KERI Press.

IMF. 1987. 'Theoretical aspects of the design of fund-supported adjustment programs'. Occasional Paper No. 55. International Monetary Fund, Washington, D.C.

Jwa, Sung-Hee. 1988. 'The political economy of market-opening pressure and response: Theory and evidence for the case of Korea and the United States'. *Seoul Journal of Economics*, vol. 1, no. 4: 387–415.

Jwa, Sung-Hee. 1992. 'Economic rationale of compensating balance requirements and its impact on money supply'. *Korea Development Review*, vol. 14, no. 1: 89–119 (in Korean).

Jwa, Sung-Hee. 1997. 'Globalization and industrial organization: Implications for structural adjustment policies'. Regionalism vs. Multinational Trade Arrangement, NBER-East Asia Seminar on Economics, Vol. 6.

Jwa, Sung-Hee and Chan Guk Huh. 1998. 'Korea's 1997 currency crisis: Its causes and implications'. *Korean Journal of Economics*, vol. 38, no. 2: 5–33.

Jwa, Sung-Hee and Insill Yi. 1999. 'Korean financial crisis: Evaluations and lessons'. Paper presented to Australia and Korea into the New Millennium: Political, Economic and Business Relations' Conference.

Kim, Dae Il. 1998. 'The social impact of the crisis in Korea'. Paper presented at the EDAP Regional Conference on Social Implications of the Asian Financial Crisis organized by the KDI and UNDP, Seoul, Korea, 29–31 July.

Kydland, F.E. and E.C. Prescott. 1977. 'Rules rather than discretion: The inconsistency of optimal plans'. *Journal of Political Economy*, vol. 85: 473–91.

Lawrence, R.Z., A. Bressand and T. Ito. 1994. *A New Vision for the World Economy*. Brookings Project on Integrating National Economies, Brookings Institution, Washington, D. C.

Lee, Kye-Sik and Young-Sun Koh. 1995. 'The macroeconomic impact of budgetary items'. *The KDI Journal of Economic Policy*, vol. 17, no. 2 (Summer). Korea Development Institute (in Korean).

Ministry of Finance and Economy. 1999. *Djnomics: A New Foundation for the Korean Economy*.

Ministry of Finance and Economy. 1999. *The Economic Crisis in Korea and the Role of Fiscal Policy*, OECD/PUMA SBO Meeting, June.

Ministry of Finance and Economy. 1999. *One Year of People's Government*, February.

Mundell, R.A. 1968. *International Economics*. London: Macmillan.

Nam, J. and K. Jaejung. 1999. 'Estimating the size of non-performing loans and public supporting costs after Korean financial crisis'. Mimeo.

OECD. 1990. 'Liberalization of Capital Movements and Financial Services in the OECD Area'. Organization for Economic Cooperation and Development.

OECD. 1985. 'Exchange Rate Management and the Conduct of Monetary Policy'. OECD Monetary Studies Series.

Oman, C. 1993. 'Globalization and Regionalism: The Challenge for Developing Countries'. OECD Development Centre.

Perkins, D.H. 1997. 'Structural transformation and the role of the state: Korea, 1945–1995'. In Dong-Se Cha, Kwang Suk Kim and D.H. Perkins, eds., *The Korean Economy 1945–1995: Performance and Vision for the 21st Century*. Seoul: Korea Development Institute.

Planning and Budget Commission. 1998. *The Budget of the Republic of Korea - Fiscal Year*, December.

Taylor, H. 1985. 'Time inconsistency: A potential problem for policymakers'. *Business Review, Federal Reserve Bank of Philadelphia*, March/April, pp. 3–12.

Wade, L.L. 1989. 'The economic role of government'. In Warren J. Samuels, ed., *Fundamentals of the Economic Role of Government*. Greenwood Press.

Weber, W.E. 1986. 'Do sterilized interventions affect exchange rates?' *Quarterly Review*, Summer.

World Bank. 1993. *The East Asian Miracle*. New York: Oxford University Press.

Chapter 6

Macroeconomic Management and the Development Process: The Southeast Asian Perspective

Bhanupong Nidhiprabha

The Southeast Asian countries shared the success of achieving high economic growth rates with price stability and external balances between 1990 and 1995. However, their success began to fade away rapidly in 1997. This chapter attempts to explain the relevance of macroeconomic management in contributing to the success in the economic development process in past decades and to analyse the causes of the failure at present.

The chapter begins with a brief presentation of the characteristics of economic growth in Southeast Asia between 1981 and 1985. It then discusses the stylized facts of their development pattern, which are linked with macroeconomic management, where the roles of foreign direct investment, public investment in human capital, and the monetary and fiscal polices are the main focuses. The reasons for the recent disappointing performance of the economies in terms of decelerating growth rate and plunging exchange rates are examined and the contagion effect of the currency crisis is analysed. Finally the conclusion ponders lessons for African countries.

Southeast Asian Growth Characteristics: 1991–1995

High economic growth rates in the last decade were the hallmark of countries in this region, but there are some differences in the pattern of growth and in the trade-off between growth and price stability. These differences can be related to macroeconomic policy management. Between 1991 and 1995, GDP in Singapore, Malaysia and Thailand expanded by 8.5 per cent on average, while the Indonesian economy grew by 7.8 per cent. During the same period, the Philippine economy began to recover from recession and was able to register a 2.2 per cent growth rate (Table 6.1). Although the countries in this group have some differences in terms of country sizes, resource endowments, number of population, social and political structure, they were able to manage their economies to achieve rapid growth with internal and external stability.

Table 6.1 Selected aspects of economic development in Southeast Asia

Country	Per capita nominal GDP (US$) 1996	Population (million) 1997	Annual average GDP growth rate 1991–95	Savings rate (% of GDP) 1995	Investment rate (% of GDP) 1995	Budgetary balance/ GDP (%) 1991–95	Average annual inflation rates 1991–95
Indonesia	1,147	200	7.8	35.8	37.8	-0.3	8.9
Malaysia	4,637	21.2	8.6	37.2	40.6	-0.3	4.1
Philippines	1,197	71.5	2.2	14.7	22.3	-0.6	10.5
Singapore	30,564	3.1	8.5	52	33.2	4.7	2.6
Thailand	3,058	60.8	8.5	36.5	43.1	2.9	4.8

Source: Economic and Social Survey of Asia and the Pacific 1997, United Nations (Table 11.1, 22).

Singapore's high growth rate was associated with a low inflation rate of 2.6 per cent, while in Thailand and Malaysia, with comparable growth rates, the cost of high growth in terms of price stability loss was about 2 percentage points higher than in Singapore. High inflation rates in Indonesia and the Philippines were associated with lower growth rates. The inflation rate in the Philippines was almost 6 percentage points higher than that of Thailand and its growth rate was 6 percentage points lower than Thailand's average GDP growth. The important question is whether the Philippines would have had higher economic growth had it been able to reduce inflation. Compared with the Philippines, Indonesia was more resilient in terms of the ability to sustain high growth rate of 7.8 per cent, despite the high inflation rate of almost 9 per cent. The cost of the trade-off between growth and inflation in Malaysia and Thailand was lower than Indonesia's. Both countries experienced high growth with lower inflation.

In general, there seems to be a negative relationship between growth and inflation in the region. During the period 1990–1995, there were no external shocks from commodity and oil prices. The rising price level was mainly due to demand expansion. The different trade-off relationships between economic growth and inflation seem to be related to the differences in economic structure and the macroeconomic policy applied in these Southeast Asian countries.

The rapid growth generated rising standard of living as well as increased ability to save. Thus Thailand and Malaysia were able to save more than 40 per cent of their GDP, while the saving ratio in the Philippines was only 14.7 per cent of GDP, due to the lower growth rate. Indonesia, with a per capita income similar to the Philippines, was able to raise the saving rate to 36 per cent, because of high growth of real GDP. The very fact that per capita income in Singapore was almost 10 times higher than that in Thailand explains Singapore's very high saving ratio of 52 per cent in 1995, despite the same rate of economic expansion with other countries in the region. Figure 6.1 illustrates the rising trend of saving ratios in Singapore, which was contributed by forced savings of the private sector, through provident funds. The high saving ratios in other countries levelled off after 1990. It is noted that for the case of Thailand, the household saving rate declined during that period, while the public sector's savings increased due to budget surplus. The Thai government budget surplus was sufficiently large enough to offset the decline in private saving, thereby maintaining high total saving rate. Financial liberalization was carried out in Thailand in the early 1990s. It is possible that the relaxation of households' liquidity constraints after financial deregulation can lead to consumption booms, as was observed by Bayoumi (1993) for the case of the United Kingdom. Speight and White (1995) also found that liquidity constraints are a pervasive feature of developing country consumption behaviours. Financial liberalization that is taking place in developing countries therefore may contribute to the consumption booms and lead to undesirable effects in the development process.

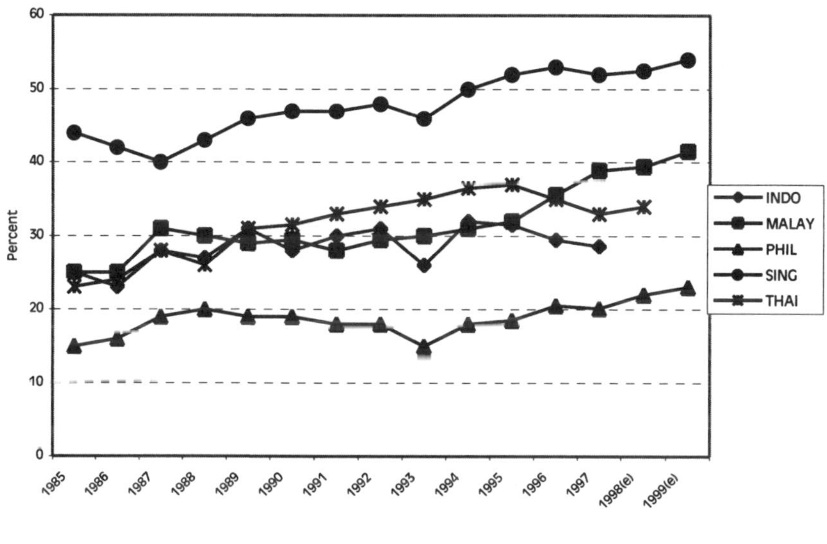

Figure 6.1 High savings rate in Southeast Asian economies

Capital formation requires financing from domestic savings and foreign savings. Thailand's capital expenditure was the highest among the countries in the group (Table 6.1) in terms of investment to GDP ratio. The rapid capital accumulation was made possible by foreign savings. Malaysia, to a lesser extent, was also dependent on foreign capital flows for domestic investment. Indonesia was able to finance its rapid capital formation by relying mainly on its high domestic savings, thereby relying less on foreign savings. In the case of the Philippines, investment was constrained by the low level of domestic savings. Singapore is the only country in the region that has surplus in the current account; its high saving rate far exceeded the investment rate in 1995. It is noted that while the growth of some other countries' in the region was driven mainly by both investment and exports, Singapore's recent rapid growth was due more to the contribution of export expansion than due to domestic investment booms.

With rapid economic expansion, the Southeast Asian governments were able to control their fiscal deficits. In the cases of Singapore and Thailand, fiscal balances showed surplus at 4.7 per cent and 2.9 per cent of GDP between 1991 and 1995 (Table 6.1). The budget deficits in the remaining countries were less than 1 per cent of GDP. With high economic growth and low inflation, fiscal imbalances were unlikely to complicate the management of external imbalances.

Southeast Asian Development Patterns

Between 1980 and 1995 there was a substantial change in the output structure in Southeast Asian countries. The share of agriculture in total output declined sharply in these countries, except for the Philippines, where there was a marginal decline from 23.5 to 21.5 per cent in GDP (Table 6.2). The rapidly rising share of industry output was evident in Indonesia, Malaysia and Thailand. The share of industrial output in Thailand and Indonesia rose from 30 per cent in 1980 to 42 per cent in 1995, while Malaysia's share of industrial output increased from 36 per cent to 47 per cent during the same period. In contrast, the relative importance of industrial output declined in Singapore and the Philippines as a result of a rising share of output from the service sector in both countries to 63 and 43 per cent, respectively.

Because of the rising importance of the industrial sector, the growth momentum of the Southeast Asian countries has been dictated by the growth of industrial output rather than agricultural output as it was in the early 1960s. This changing pattern of output has become a stylized fact in the development process. GDP growth rates of these countries in the period 1991–1995 were consistently higher than in the period between 1981 and 1990 (Table 6.2). For example, Indonesia was able to raise the average growth rate from 5.7 per cent between 1981 and 1990 to 7.8 per cent during the period 1991–995. Malaysia's growth rate increased from 6 to 8.6 per cent during the corresponding period. Thailand, Singapore and the Philippines also experienced higher growth rates in the early 1990s than in the 1980s. The reason behind this rapid growth is the expansion in exports of manufacturing products, made possible by outward-oriented development policies that reduced the bias against external trade.

It should be noted that export structures of these countries are also changing: the share of manufacturing output in total exports has been increasing at the expense of the share of agricultural exports. The changing structure of exports reflects the changing degree of comparative advantage. Capital formation concentrated mainly in the manufacturing sector, thereby raising the productivity of industrial workers higher than those in the agricultural sector. The rise in real wages in the urban sector attracted unskilled labour from rural areas to the industrial sector. The structure of employment also changed from the last decade: a rising share of industrial workers in total employment at the expense of the share of labour in the agricultural sector. This—another stylized fact in the development process—is clearly demonstrated in Table 6.2. A high income country such as Malaysia has only 18 per cent of the labour force working in the agricultural sector, while in Indonesia almost 50 per cent of the labour force are so employed. The share of agricultural labour in Thailand and the Philippines was still 42 per cent or more in 1994. The wage pressure on the industrial sector in these three countries was not as severe as in Malaysia and Singapore, because they have relatively more abundant

Table 6.2 Growth and structure of real GDP (%)

Country	Average Annual growth rate of real		Sectoral share of gross domestic product						Sectoral share of economically active population			Sectoral productivity (ratio to overall average product)		
	GDP		Agriculture		Industry		Services		Agriculture	Industry	Services	Agriculture	Industry	Services
	1981–90	1990–95	1980	1995	1980	1995	1980	1995	1995	1995	1995	1995	1995	1995
Indonesia	5.7	7.8	30.7	16.1	31	41.9	38.4	42	54.9	14.1	31.1	0.29	2.97	1.35
Malaysia	6	8.6	22.9	13.5	35.8	47.4	41.3	39.1	18	35.6	46.3	0.75	1.33	0.84
Philippines	1.8	2.2	23.5	21.5	40.5	35.5	36	43	44.7	15.8	39.5	0.48	2.25	1.09
Singapore	7.4	8.5	1.1	0.2	38.8	36.9	60	62.9	0.3	32.7	67	0.67	1.13	0.94
Thailand	7.9	8.5	20.2	10.8	30.1	42.4	49.7	46.8	41.6	23.7	34.7	0.26	1.79	1.35

Source: Economic and Social Survey of Asia and the Pacific 1997, United Nations (Table 11.2).

labour supply from the agricultural sector. The percentage share of agricultural labour in these five countries has the same rank as the number of population shown in Table 6.1. Countries with relatively abundant labour supply would have a higher share of agricultural employment.

The low wage rate in the agricultural sector is caused by low productivity. One can calculate sectoral productivity relative to the average product of each country by simply dividing the sectoral share of output by the sectoral share of employment. Table 6.2 demonstrates that the average product of agricultural labour in Indonesia, the Philippines and Thailand was lower than the national average product (since the ratio is less than unity), but these countries' labour productivity in industrial sector was substantially higher than the average product for all sectors. It is argued here that the high growth rates experienced by these countries were the result of the rapid expansion of output in the industrial sector, which can be explained by both quality and quantity of labour forces employed in this sector. In other words, the Southeast Asian economy grew rapidly not only because of the increase in factor inputs, but also because of the increased productivity of labour.

Macroeconomic Management

This section we addresses the question of what kind of macroeconomic management led to high growth rate with stability between the 1980s and 1995. First we discuss the nature of the internal and external balances of the Southeast Asian nations. The role of foreign direct investment in building up export capacity of industrial sector is emphasized, while the role of public spending on education is discussed in terms of the process of human capital investment. The monetary and fiscal policies applied in various countries are compared.

Internal and External Balances

Between 1981 and 1990, the problem of widening resource gaps for the Southeast Asian countries was not serious. Thailand was the only country in the group that experienced a shortage of domestic savings. Between 1991 and 1995, however, domestic saving in Malaysia, Philippines and Thailand, albeit high, was not sufficient to finance domestic investment. Heavy reliance on foreign savings was made in the Philippines and Thailand, whose resource gaps widened considerably to 7.4 and 5.3 per cent, respectively (Table 6.3). To maintain high growth rate of GDP, the process of capital formation must not be disrupted. One of the key ingredients for growth in these countries is the ability to attract foreign capital flows to maintain a high investment rate.

Table 6.3 exhibits the prudent fiscal policy adopted by these countries across the board. In the 1980s, most countries, except Singapore, ran a budget deficit. During the period 1981–1990, Malaysia's budget deficit amounted to 8.2 per cent of GDP, but this was reduced to 0.3 per cent of GDP in the early 1990s. The increasing degree of fiscal prudence can be observed for all countries between 1991 and 1995. All countries in Table 6.3 were able to reduce the size of the fiscal deficit relative to GDP. In the case of Thailand, the reduction in government spending led to a budget surplus of almost 3 per cent of GDP between 1991 and 1995. Singapore even experienced an increased budget surplus from 1.2 to 4.7 per cent of GDP.

The rising per capita permanent income in the last 15 years in these countries implies that the ability to save has increased enormously. The income elasticity for demand for broad money is greater than unity, suggesting that the demand for financial savings at commercial banks would rise more rapidly than income level. As Table 6.3 indicates, the ratio of M2/GDP increased sharply for all countries from 1981 to 1995. The rising degree of financial deepening as measured by the ratio of M2/GDP can be observed in Figure 6.2. From 1985 to 1995, the financial deepening process took place rapidly in all countries. The high M2/GDP of Singapore was surpassed only by Malaysia in 1995. This is not surprising, since in a highly developed financial market like Singapore, means of financial savings are not limited to bank deposits. It has been argued that a high degree of financial deepening is a prerequisite for growth, since the availability of financial savings would reduce financial constraints for domestic investment. Empirical evidence from 71 developing countries from the 1960s and 1980s indicates that financial intermediation promotes growth and its contribution to growth is as significant as export expansion and capital formation (Odedokun, 1996). The macroeconomic management that leads to a positive real interest rate would contribute to high level of financial intermediation, which in turn promotes growth by ensuring the availability of credit to finance investment.

Table 6.3 Macroeconomic indicators of balance and stability

Country	Resource gap[a]		Budgetary balance/ GDP[b]		Average annual M2/GDP		Interest rates[c]	Exchange rates[d]	Average annual inflation rates[e]	
	1981–90	1991–95	1981–90	1991–95	1981–90	1991–95	1991–95	1986–95	1981–90	1991–95
Indonesia	1.7	1.2	-3.0	-0.3	25.2	44.4	13.5[f]	-2.75	8.6	8.9
Malaysia	2.6	-1.3	-8.2	-0.3	67.2	83.6	2.9	-2.3	3.3	4.0
Philippines	0.5	-7.4	-3.1	-0.6	30.0	41.8	1.2	1.1	14.7	10.5
Singapore	1.7	13.3	1.2	4.7	77.0	89.7	1.2	2.4	2.3	2.6
Thailand	-2.9	-5.3	-2.1	2.9	55.8	77.1	4.4	-0.6	4.5	4.8

Notes: a. Resource gap is defined as gross domestic savings/GDP minus gross domestic investment/GDP
b. Budgetary balance/GDP of Indonesia and Malaysia excludes grants
c. Real interest rate on time deposits of 12 months
d. Refers to trend growth rate of real effective exchange rate
e. Refers to changes in consumer price index
f. 1991–1992

Source: Economic and Social Survey of Asia and the Pacific 1997, United Nations (Table 11.3: 46).

Since all real interest rates on time deposits of 12 months in Southeast Asian countries were positive (Table 6.3), there has been no disincentive for savings. And despite high inflation rates in Indonesia and the Philippines, both countries still maintained positive real interest rates between 1991 and 1995, resulting in the increasing degree of financial deepening in Indonesia, as measured by M2/GDP, from 25 per cent between 1981 and 1990 to 44 per cent in the first half of the 1990s.

The corresponding figures for the Philippines are 30 to 42 per cent. As the financial deepening ratio suggests, Singapore has the highest degree of financial development, followed by Malaysia and Thailand.

It should be noted that the responsiveness of savings to rising real interest rates may be relatively small in low-income countries, since their inter-temporal elasticities of substitution are low because of large shares of necessities in household budgets. As a result, interest rate liberalization may not produce a substantial increase in savings in the least developed countries. In the case of Thailand, the share of food expenditures in household budgets is around 39 per cent. Ogaki et al. (1996) found evidence supporting the hypothesis that saving sensitivity to the interest rate is a function of rising income.

Exchange rate stability is another factor that contributes to continuous flows of foreign capital. The percentage change in real effective exchange rates of the Southeast Asian countries remained minimal between 1986 and 1995. The average annual rate of depreciation and appreciation was less than 2.8 per cent (Table 6.3). In the case of Thailand the average appreciation rate was only 0.6 per cent per year. Despite high inflation in Indonesia and the Philippines, both countries managed to let their currency depreciate so that their international competitiveness would not be lost by high inflation.

While inflation rates in the Philippines declined to some extent in the early 1990s, other Southeast Asian countries experienced higher inflation in the 1990s than in the 1980s. As discussed earlier, the rising price level was the result of demand factors. Nevertheless, their inflation rates in the last five years cannot be regarded as excessive by international standards. The macroeconomic management that aimed to maintain fiscal balances and exchange rate stability led to low inflation and sustainable current account deficits in the Southeast Asian economies from 1981 to 1995.

The Role of Foreign Direct Investment

The recent upsurge in foreign direct investment in this region can be characterized by strong concentration on export production. Singapore received the largest share of inflows of foreign direct investment among countries in the region between 1984 and 1989, averaging US$2.2 billion per year. Foreign direct investment in Singapore more than doubled in the early 1990s (Table 6.4). While more over 50 per cent of foreign direct investment in the region went to Singapore in the late 1980s, its share declined to 33.7 per cent in the early 1990s. Singapore's loss was Malaysia's gain; Malaysia's share of foreign direct investment rose from 17.9 per cent between 1984 and 1989 to 31.3 per cent in 1990–1995. During the latter period, Malaysia already received a larger volume of foreign direct investment than Singapore in 1992 and 1995.

It can be said that foreign direct investment in Southeast Asia contributed to changing the structure of the economy by transforming predominantly agricultural countries into industrializing countries. The speed of the transformation depends partly on the flows of foreign direct investment. The level of direct investment flows into the Philippines and Vietnam between 1984 and 1989 was not large enough to enable these two countries to catch up with their neighbours.

Table 6.4 **Foreign direct investment inflows, 1984–1995**

Country	Average		Share (%)		1990	1991	1992	1993	1994	1995
	1984–89	1990–95	1984–89	1990–95						
Indonesia	406	2,161	91	15.2	1,093	1,482	1,777	2,004	2,109	4,500
Malaysia	798	4,453	17.9	31.3	2,333	3,998	5,183	5,006	4,398	5,800
Philippines	326	881	7.3	6.2	530	544	228	1,025	1,457	1,500
Singapore	2,239	4,785	50.3	33.7	5,575	4,879	2,351	5,016	5,588	5,308
Thailand	676	1,873	15.2	13.2	2,444	2,014	2,116	1,726	640	2,300
Vietnam	2	58	0.0	0.4	16	32	24	25	100	150
China	2,282	19,635	-	-	3,487	4,366	11,156	27,515	33,787	37.500

Source: Economic and Social Survey of Asia and the Pacific 1997, United Nations (Table IV. 5, p. 148).

Real wage rates in the region have been rising, because the Southeast Asian countries have entered that stage of development where the era of unlimited supply of labour has long gone. Countries with relatively more abundant supplies of labour became more attractive to foreign investors than the Southeast Asian countries. By 1992, the amount of foreign direct investment into China had nearly equalled the combined amount of the total direct investment flows into Southeast Asian countries (Table 6.4). The positive effect of foreign direct investment on the balance of payments leads to accumulated international reserves in host countries, which is likely to have a strong impact on the stability of their currencies.

Foreign direct investment is also a vehicle for technology transfer for multinational corporations to developing countries. Firms in developed countries may relocate their plants to the area where cheap labour is available, as predicted by the product cycle hypothesis. Countries that receive huge amounts of foreign direct investment would be able to pull labour from the agricultural sector faster than countries that receive low levels of foreign direct investment. Thailand, Indonesia and the Philippines received smaller amounts of foreign direct investment than Singapore and Malaysia, leaving the substantial difference in sectoral productivity between agriculture and industrial sectors (Table 6.2). On the other hand, the productivity gap was much smaller in the case of Singapore and Malaysia. Since real income depends on labour productivity, as long as productivity differentials among sectors remain high, economic development would not lead to an improvement in income distribution.

Human Capital Investment

Government can improve income distribution by raising public spending on education. As a result, the achievement of high economic growth can be realized without sacrificing equity. In a recent study by Jha (1996), there is evidence supporting the view that secondary schooling can improve income distribution in developing countries by raising the income share of the lowest 40 per cent of the population at the expense of those in the top 20 per cent. If social unrest is detrimental to the process of economic development by creating risks and uncertainty, public spending on education can indirectly reduce social tensions from income inequality. Education budgets can be regarded as public investment in human capital so as to smoothen the transformation of a traditional agricultural sector to a modern industrial sector.

Growth can be indirectly enhanced by public investment in human capital. In various cross-economy studies such as Lucas (1988), King and Levine (1993), and Levine and Zervos (1996), the secondary school enrolment rate was included, among other explanatory variables such as financial development proxy, in the regression explaining growth differentials among developing countries. Empirical evidence suggests that growth can be affected by investment in human capital in the long run by raising the marginal productivity of labour.

Table 6.5 indicates that although the 1995 adult literacy rate of countries in the region is quite high, the secondary school enrolment rates in Thailand and Vietnam were substantially below those in neighbouring countries. Shortages of skilled labour have become more serious as Thailand cannot compete in international markets for unskilled labour intensive products from countries at the lower development ladder, nor can Thailand push forward to replace the markets that once belonged to Asian tiger countries that have graduated to exporting more advanced technology intensive products. Malaysia and the Philippines would have no difficulty in forging ahead with exporting skilled labour intensive products. The slowdown in the Thai economy can be regarded as a structural problem, since there would be a substantial time lag before Thailand can reap the benefits from the investment in human capital.

Table 6.5 Gross enrolment ratios and adult literacy rates

Country	Year	Enrolment ratios				Adult
		Primary	Secondary	Tertiary	All level (1993)	Literacy rate (1995)
Indonesia	1992	114	43	10	61	84
Malaysia	1993	93	59	-	61	83
Philippines	1993	111	79	26	77	95
Singapore	1991	107	68	-	68	91
Thailand	1992	98	37	19	54	94
Vietnam	1993	111	35	2	51	94

Source: Economic and Social Survey of Asia and the Pacific 1997, United Nations (Table 11.8, p. 78).

The share of Thailand's education spending in GDP was 3.8 per cent in 1985; this declined to 2.9 per cent in 1990, probably due to the failure of the government to understand the importance of the role of human capital in the process of economic development. Nevertheless, the education spending share in 1995 rose to 3.1 per cent of GDP (Table 6.6). Countries at a higher development ladder such as Malaysia and Singapore have put great emphasis on the role of government in providing education. Especially in Malaysia, government spending on education was more than 5 per cent of GDP on the average. It should be noted that the Malaysian government budget allocated to education was always higher than defence spending. With a strong commitment to human capital development throughout the last decades, Malaysia and Singapore have achieved a higher standard of education than other countries in the region, giving rise to the comparative advantage in producing high value added products and skilled labour intensive products for export.

Table 6.6 Government expenditure on defence and education

	1985	1990	1995
Defence/GDP:			
Indonesia	2.238	1.279	0.991[a]
Malaysia	5.042	4.266	4.162
Philippines	1.330	2.164	1.962[a]
Singapore	6.107	4.818	4.235[a]
Thailand	4.430	2.750	2.41
Education/GDP:			
Indonesia	2.199	1.725	1.603[a]
Malaysia	5.603	5.789	4.962
Philippines	2.254	3.317	2.931[a]
Singapore	5.866	4.063	4.233
Thailand	3.820	2.884	3.145

Note: a. 1993.

Sources: Asian Development Bank, Government Finance Statistics Yearbook, and office of the National Economic and Social Development Board, Thailand.

In 1985, the allocated budget for defence in Thailand was 4.4 per cent of GDP, whereas the education budget represented only 3.8 per cent of GDP. Nevertheless, my feeling of the subject is that, given the total budget, if the government spends more on defence, they would have less to spend on education and other social expenditures. The latter might contribute to higher marginal social benefit than additional dollar on defence spending. The trade-off between education and defence spending was less pronounced in Malaysia and Singapore, but there seems to be such trade-off in Indonesia and the Philippines. The share of Southeast Asian. governments' defence spending in GDP has been declining since 1985 (Table 6.6). With the increase in international cooperation of the countries in the Southeast Asian region, there has been less political tension and there is a lesser need to build up military capability to defend national territories. Indonesia has the lowest share of defence spending in the region, yet managed to further reduce the relative size of the defence budget in 1995. Singapore's share of defence spending declined from 6.1 per cent of GDP in 1985 to 4.2 per cent in 1993. Thailand has made a remarkable reduction in defence spending, from 4.4 per cent in 1985 to 2.4 per cent in 1995.

Singapore has the highest level of defence spending (relative to GDP) among the Southeast Asian countries, while Indonesia has the lowest. It seems that higher-income countries would tend to have higher military expenditures than lower-income countries. Malaysia, with the second highest per capita income, also has the second highest military expenditure. Thailand and the Philippines are also in descending order in terms of per capita income and in terms of defence spending. From Table 6.6, we may conclude that perhaps defence spending is a luxury good for Southeast Asian countries. This observation is quite in contrast to recent findings by Wall (1996), who studied 65 developing countries between 1984 and 1988 and concluded that the share of military spending would decrease with a rising level of GDP.

As argued by Knight et al. (1996), since military spending is economically unproductive and distorts resource allocation, an increase in military spending has an unambiguously negative and large direct impact on economic growth. There is also an indirect impact on growth through its negative impact on productive investment. A sustained long-run growth through higher capacity output can be obtained by military spending cuts by all countries in the region. There are other policy implementation measures that are not directly related to macroeconomic management, but the following contribute to rapid economic development: the market friendly policy, which implies less intervention by government in the market mechanism, and the reduction in trade barriers, which implies a lesser degree of protection and a higher efficiency in consumption and production.

Monetary and Fiscal Policy

As mentioned earlier, Southeast Asian governments are fiscally conservative and prudent. More importantly, when they ran budget deficits, the deficits were not financed by printing money. The claims on government by the Philippine central bank increased only 3.4 per cent in 1990 and by 2.6 per cent in 1995 (Table 6.7). Other countries relied less on borrowing from their central banks. Thailand's, budget deficit, for example, was financed by selling government bonds to commercial banks and the private sector. In effect, these governments switched from inflationary means of deficit financing through borrowing from the central bank or using treasury cash balances to non-inflationary means of deficit financing. When the budget was in surplus, the governments reduced their debts with the central banks rather than using the available budget for extra public consumption and investment. Therefore the Southeast Asian countries did not regard the surplus in the budget as an increase in permanent income; rather, they treated the surplus as transitory income. This approach has an advantage since engaging in large public investment projects may lead to inefficiency and to the possibility of using money to finance the projects during the period of experiencing a shortfall in tax revenues.

Table 6.7 Fiscal and monetary indicators

	Claims on governments and other public entities annual per cent growth		Money and quasi money annual per cent growth		Private investment per cent of gross domestic fixed investment		Credit to private sector per cent of GDP		Seignorage per cent of GDP	Spread over LIBOR (lending rate minus percentage points)	
	1990	1995	1990	1995	1980	1995	1990	1995	1993–95	1990	1995
Indonesia	-6.7	-	44.6	-	56.5	76.0	8.8	-	-	8.2	13
Malaysia	-1.2	-0.6	10.6	20.0	62.5	65.1	49.9	129.5	3.9	-1.1	1.6
Philippines	-3.4	2.6	22.5	24.2	68.9	80.1	42.2	45.0	1.4	15.8	8.7
Singapore	-4.9	-8.1	20.0	8.5	-	-	81.0	106.7	1.1	-0.9	0.4
Thailand	-4.0	-2.9	26.7	17.0	68.1	77.1	41.7	139.9	1.4	8.2	9.7

Source: World Development Indicators 1997, World Bank.

Thailand adopted this approach even though its budget was in surplus between 1988 and 1996. In 1997 when the Thai economy slowed down, tax revenues fell sharply and the government had difficulty balancing the budget. Public investment was the first item to be cut. In other words, fiscal flexibility must exist so that fiscal policy can be applied to changing conditions. Thailand experienced large budget deficit after 1976. While tax revenue continued its increasing trend throughout the 1980s, government spending increased faster, causing a considerable deficit as a share of GDP. This deficit did not fuel inflation because the Thai government avoided selling bonds to the Bank of Thailand. Commercial banks absorbed the larger part of the government bonds; was a requirement for commercial banks that wanted to open new branches that they must satisfy the condition of holding at least 16 per cent of their deposits as government bonds. Consequently, inflation in Thailand was moderate during the period of budget deficit.

The flexibility of fiscal policy is illustrated clearly in Figure 6.3. To reduce the deficit, government spending (as a ratio to GDP) fell sharply between 1985 and 1990; capital and defence spending were reduced substantially, producing a turnaround in the fiscal position from deficit to surplus by 1988. The ability to phase out or postpone public investment and to reduce the defence budget is crucial to the success of a sound fiscal policy. Unfortunately, fiscal discipline can only be implemented by political will, or perhaps with the conditions imposed by international lending agencies such as the World Bank or the International Monetary Fund (IMF).

The change in monetary base as a percentage of GDP, or the seigniorage, is shown in Table 6.7. Both the Philippines and Thailand's seigniorage amounted to only 1.4 per cent of GDP between 1993 and 1995. The governments in Southeast Asia do not use inflation tax as a means to raise tax revenue. It is possible that the revenue from issuing seigniorage can be low, for the demand for money might be sensitive to the inflation rate.

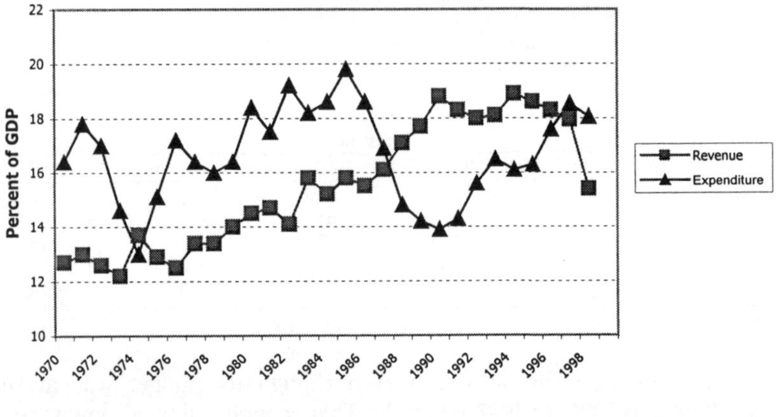

Figure 6.3 Thailand's fiscal flexibility

With low inflation, these Southeast Asian countries can enhance savings by promoting incentives for the accumulation of financial assets. In Malaysia and the Philippines M2 grew by 20 and 24 per cent, respectively. Thailand's growth rate of M2 slowed down from 26.7 per cent in 1990 to 17 per cent in 1995. The fact that the demand for money rose more rapidly than nominal income suggests that the velocity of money must have been declining over time. As a result, the declining velocity would mitigate the inflationary impact of capital inflows. The surplus budget of the Thai government helped decelerate the growth of the monetary base (Mbase) during the period of rapidly increasing international reserves (Figure 6.4). Since the net claims on government (NCG) by the central bank continuously declined they offset the rise in net foreign assets (NFA), despite the fact that the Bank of Thailand still provided credits to the financial sector (CF).

Thus fiscal prudence can reduce the pressure from massive capital inflows during economic booms. The capital inflows to Southeast Asian economies were partly due to borrowing from the private sector. In the case of Thailand, the spread of the commercial banks' lending rates over the LIBOR was substantial, reaching 8.2 per cent in 1990 and 9.7 per cent in 1995. The large spread, coupled with a minimal foreign exchange risk, induced excessive foreign borrowings from the private sector in Thailand.

Bank credit as a percentage of GDP rose from 41.7 per cent in 1990 to 140 per cent in 1995 (Table 6.7). With the availability of bank credit, the share of private investment as a percentage of total investment in Thailand rose from 68 to 77 per cent. In the Philippines, the share of private investment in total capital formation was even higher, at 80 per cent in 1995; the interest spread was 8.7 per cent in 1995. Although the interest spread in Malaysia was low, bank credit amounted to almost 130 per cent in 1995, a substantial increase from 50 per cent in 1990. Indonesia's share of private investment in total investment also increased between 1990 and 1995, reaching the high level of 76 per cent in 1995.

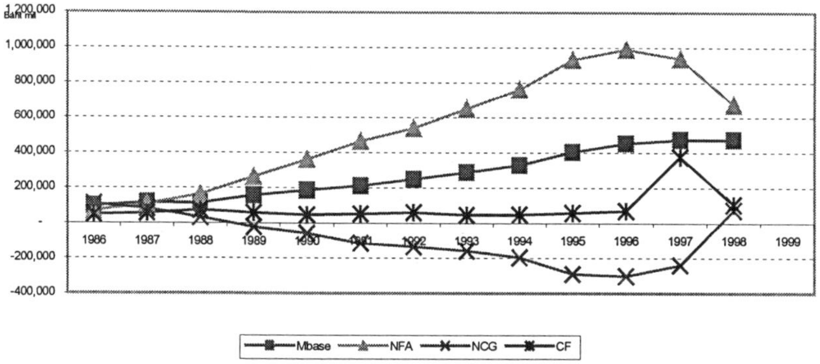

Figure 6.4 **Changes in Thailand's monetary base components**

It appears that the Southeast Asian countries undertake measures to stimulate private investment and try to reduce the role of public investment. Khan and Kumar (1997), using data from 95 developing countries over the period 1970–1990, found evidence supporting the view that private investment has a higher productivity than public investment. They also found that the difference in the impact of growth between public and private investment is most apparent in Latin America and Asia, but much less pronounced in Africa. However, Ram (1996) found contradictory evidence from 53 developing countries, suggesting that public investment may be more productive than private investment. In the case of Southeast Asian countries, public investment projects can have a positive impact on growth if they complement private investment. On the other hand, the impact on growth should be considered in both the quantity and the quality of investment. A rapid increase in private investment in the wrong sector may stimulate only short-run growth, while high quality public investment may contribute to growth in the long run.

What Went Wrong?

Thailand has accumulated foreign debt rapidly since the early 1990s, most of it created by the private sector. Foreign debts in 1995 doubled from the level in 1990, which more than tripled the foreign debt level in 1980. The size of Thailand's foreign debt was enormous, compared with other countries shown in Table 6.8. In 1990, the amount of foreign debt in Thailand was still below that in Indonesia and the Philippines. The Indonesian foreign debt in 1990 was four times higher than the debt level in Malaysia, and twice as large as the level in the Philippines.

In the case of Thailand, these external debts were created by both private corporations and local commercial banks that took advantage of low levels of international interest rates. With the rather stable exchange rate, the cost of foreign borrowing seemed to be cheap because there was no foreign exchange risk, as long as the baht was still pegged to the US dollar. This was the reason large parts of foreign borrowings were not hedged against future exchange rate depreciations. Thai commercial banks' foreign borrowing began to rise rapidly in 1993 during the boom period and the size of their banks' foreign liabilities began to exceed the level of monetary base in 1994. As Figure 6.5 shows, the ratio of commercial banks' borrowings relative to the monetary base (the foreign liability relative to the monetary base kept rising until 1995. It became impossible for the Bank of Thailand to sterilize the capital inflows. The open market operation measure was limited by the small size of the government bonds, due to the continued budget surplus of the Thai government. The Bank of Thailand also issued bonds, but the amount was insignificant compared with the level of capital inflows. Besides, the cost of sterilization is high as long as the Bank of Thailand has to pay high interest rates on the BOT bonds. Furthermore, the sterilization process may not work in the long run where capital mobility is high due to capital control liberalization.

Table 6.8 also reveals that Thailand's external debt consists of a relatively high ratio of short-term loans with the ratio rising from 42 per cent in 1980 to 47.6 per cent in 1995. Malaysia and Indonesia had a less liquid debt structure; their short/long-term debt ratio was around 27 per cent. Nevertheless, the increasing trend of reliance on short-term financing was seen in all three countries. On the contrary, the Philippine's reliance on short-term financing has been declining, judging from the ratio of short/long-term financing, which fell from 85.7 per cent in 1980 to only 15.8 per cent in 1995. Mismatching of maturity between borrowing and lending would create severe liquidity shortage if the short-term borrowings cannot be rolled over.

Some of these short-term foreign borrowings were extended to speculation in the property sector and the stock market during the boom period from 1990 to 1995. Because the Bank of Thailand has limited capacity to supervise financial institutions and because prudent financial regulations are lacking, bank credit grew rapidly and was allocated to speculative, unproductive and inefficient sectors. These sectors' performances are pro-cyclical and highly sensitive to business cycles. Since 1988, inflation in Thailand has been higher than that in the United States. As a result, the US consumer price index relative to the Thai price index (PUSTH) continued its declining trend (Figure 6.5). The large inflows of foreign borrowings led to rising price levels of non-traded goods. With the fixed nominal exchange rate between the baht and the dollar, the real exchange rate appreciated, causing a loss in the competitiveness of the Thai exports.

Table 6.8 Total foreign debt outstanding and disbursed (Million US$)

Country	Total foreign debt outstanding and disbursed			(1) Long-term			(2) Short-term			(2)/(1) (Percent)		
	1980	1990	1995	1980	1990	1995	1980	1990	1995	1980	1990	1995
Indonesia	20,938	69,872	107,831	18,163	58,242	85,481	2,775	11,135	22,350	15.3	19.1	26.1
Malaysia	6,611	16,421	34,352	5,256	14,514	27,078	1,355	1,906	7,274	25.8	13.1	26.9
Philippines	17,417	30,615	39,445	8,817	25,277	33,438	7,556	9,157	5,279	85.7	36.2	15.8
Singapore	2,071	4,204	8,405	1,870	3,468	7,181	201	736	1,214	10.7	21.2	16.9
Thailand	8,297	28,088	56,789	5,646	19,765	38,476	2,303	8,322	18,312	40.8	42.1	47.6

Source: Asian Development Bank (1997).

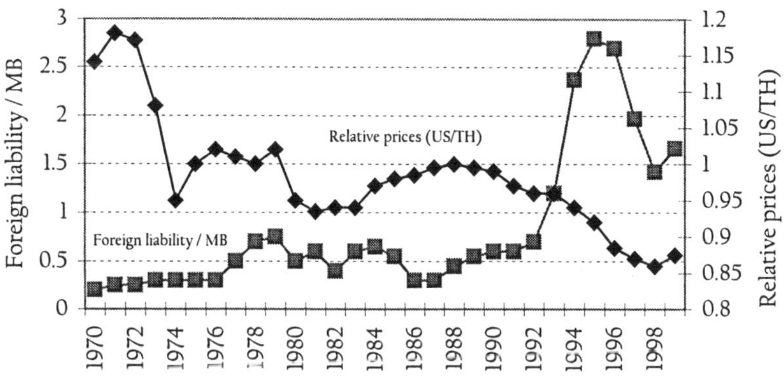

Figure 6.5 Thailand: Banks' foreign borrowing and relative prices

In 1996, the Southeast Asian economies were still expanding rapidly, except for Thailand (see Table 6.9). The output in the Philippines rose by 5.7 per cent—a considerable increase from the average growth of 2.2 per cent during 1991–1995. Singapore, Indonesia and Malaysia were able to maintain a near 8 per cent growth path, despite the regional slowdown in exports in 1996. Thailand was less resilient than other countries in the preparation for the export slowdown; GDP growth rate declined by 2 per cent to 6.7 per cent in 1996. The economic slowdown in Thailand was also brought about by the contractionary monetary policy. In an attempt to reduce the inflation and the current account deficit caused by overheated economy, the Bank of Thailand set the maximum credit expansion, which constrained domestic investment. Thus both exports and investment, which had been Thailand's growth driving forces in the past, were not functioning.

In 1997, the amount of foreign debt outstanding in the Philippines rose to $42.6 billion, while that in Malaysia declined to $29 billion. Both Thailand and Indonesia increased their foreign debts, to $93 billion and $108.8 billion, respectively. A large part of the debt in Thailand was created by the private sector. According to the Lawson Doctrine (Lord Nigel Lawson, former British Chancellor of the Exchequer), foreign borrowing by the private sector to finance the current account deficit reflects rational investment decisions made by private individuals. Therefore it should pose no problems as long as the public sector does not run a budget deficit. In Thailand, however, private firms tend to over borrow since they cannot anticipate foreign exchange risk and, as well, Thai commercial banks anticipate that the government may bail them out when they face difficulty. Moreover, if those foreign debts have short maturity, the private sectors would have trouble securing funds when hot money comes and goes rapidly once unfavourable news hits the markets. For example, Moody's Investor Service downgraded Thai commercial banks' ratings by one step, with the result that the cost of obtaining additional funds from abroad may be raised 50 basis points—if they can still obtain the loans.

Table 6.9 **Recent macroeconomic indicators**

Country	Per cent change on year earlier			International reserves (billion US$)		Interest rate
	GDP 1997	Inflation 1997	Currency units per US$ (22 Oct 1997)	1997	1996	Short-term per cent p.a.
Indonesia	+8.0*	+6.9 Sep	-36.65	19.3 Aug	15.50	30.50
Malaysia	+8.4Q2	+2.3 Sep	-26.18	26.1 Feb	23.10	8.60
Philippines	+5.7Q2	+5.3 Sep	-24.86	10.0 May	8.00	12.63
Singapore	+7.8Q2	+2.3 Aug	-10.13	80.7 Jun	72.20	3.89
Thailand	+6.7*	+7.0 Sep	-34.45	25.0 Aug	38.30	16.00

*Figures are for 1996.
Source: *The Economist*, 25–31 October 1997.

Because of the slowdown in economic growth, rising non-performing loans and political instability, the baht was under a massive attack by speculators on 14–15 May 1997. The Bank of Thailand tried to defend the baht exchange rate by selling dollars in the forward markets in Singapore and Hong Kong. Singapore also intervened to defend the baht. The interest rate was raised to prevent speculation in domestic markets (Figure 6.6), while the Bank of Thailand also controlled the outflows of baht so that speculators in the forward markets would be able to close their positions when the forward contract matured. In effect, the Bank of Thailand created a two-tier system for the exchange rate between the onshore and offshore markets. Consequently, the exchange rate between domestic and offshore markets can be widely different, depending on the availability of the two currencies. On 2 July 1997 Thailand yielded to market pressure and let the baht float; the Bank of Thailand had come to the important realization that they could not successfully defend the baht. The level of international reserves fell from $38.3 billion in August 1996 to only $25 billion in August 1997 (Table 6.9). The baht floating was a de facto devaluation, carried out when the financial sector was beset by non-performing loans and large foreign debts. After the float, the baht/dollar exchange rate tended to converge. Nevertheless, disparity is apparent when expectations of the two markets change with the arrival of good and bad news from Thailand.

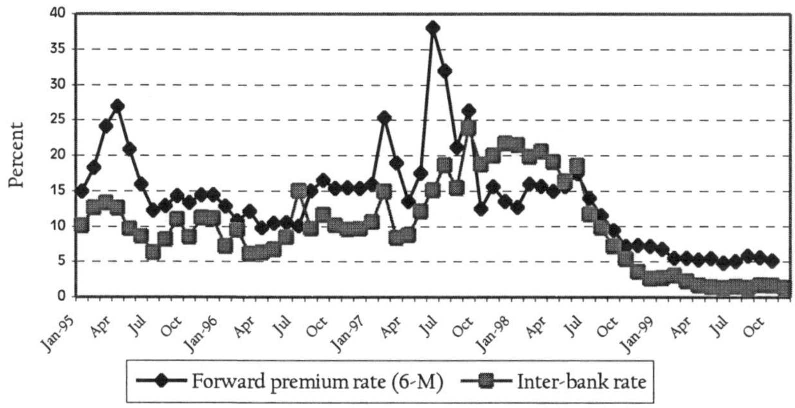

Figure 6.6 Thailand: Inter-bank rate and forward premium (6-month)

The existence of a large volume of debt relative to GDP in Thailand prolonged the economic recovery period. The short-term interest rate went up to 16 per cent in October 1997, while the year-on-year inflation rate rose to 7 per cent in September. The impact of devaluation on the price level is not fully felt due to lag adjustments and some price controls.

To make matters worse, the government has no credibility left in launching any economic measures to address the problem. A gasoline tax increase was abandoned after two days in effect because the government could not resist the pressure from the public. The Thai prime minister assured the country in a televised address on 30 June, 1997 that there would be no devaluation; the announcement of a managed float of the baht came only two days later. Credibility is the key to the success of economic policy and can significantly increase its effectiveness. Before floating the baht, the exchange rate between the baht and the US dollar was extremely stable; confidence about the exchange rate stability helped reduce uncertainties and risk in international trade. When the fixed exchange rate is abolished, volatility sets in especially when there is no credibility to anchor the exchange rate. Thai corporations rushed to protect themselves by buying dollars in the forward markets, while some Thai exporters were not willing to bring in dollars after receiving payments, anticipating a further depreciation of the baht. Because of the capital flight, Thailand experienced a deficit in the balance of payments in 1997, the first time since 1984, the year Thailand devalued the baht by 14.7 per cent. Four months after the float, the baht had depreciated by 34.5 percent from the exchange rate of 22 October 1996 (Table 6.9) and was heading toward the psychological barrier of 40 baht to the dollar.

The Contagion Effect

When the baht was under severe attack on 14 May 1997, the Philippines felt the pressure. The central bank of the Philippines raised the overnight interest rate by 1.75 per cent to 13 per cent to deter speculators. When Thailand's finance minister, who opposed devaluation, resigned on 19 June, the Philippines was also affected; the central bank had to raise the short-term interest rate to 15 per cent. When the baht was on the managed floating system on 2 July, it effectively depreciated by 20 per cent to a record low of 28.8 baht per US dollar. The central bank of the Philippines was forced to intervene heavily to prop up the peso, while the overnight lending rate was raised to 24 per cent on 3 July.

Five days later Malaysia's Bank Negara intervened aggressively to defend the ringgit. The move was a success since the ringgit reached a high of 2.51 against the US dollar after a low level of 2.524 on 8 July. The Philippines allowed the peso to move in a wider band against the dollar on 11 July and asked for an extension of the IMF's external fund facility. Indonesia also widened its rupiah trading band from 8 per cent to 12 per cent on the same day when its currency started to be affected. The IMF offered the Philippines $1.1 billion in financial support under the fast track regulation drawn up after the 1995 Mexican crisis. On 24 July, the ringgit dropped sharply to a three-year low of 2.653 to the dollar. Within one month after Thailand's de facto devaluation, other currencies in the region were affected. It was reported that Hong Kong spent US$1 billion on an intervention to defend the HK dollar during a period of two hours on an unspecified day in July.

The rupiah came under pressure again on 13 August, when it hit a historical low of 2,682 to the dollar. The central bank intervened heavily to rescue the rupiah to 2,655. Finally on 14 August, Indonesia abolished its system of a managed float through a band, plunging the rupiah to 2, 7555. On 20 August, the IMF approved the bailout package of $17.2 billion to Thailand. The ringgit continued to depreciate, breaking through the 3.0 ringgit to the dollar barrier on 4 September. The ringgit fell further in October, when the market was wary about tighter control on foreign exchange transactions. Indonesia also asked the IMF for financial assistance. On 14 October, Vietnam was not able to resist market pressure and widened the trading band of the dong from 5 per cent to 10 per cent either side of the daily official rate.

By 22 October, the Southeast Asian currencies had depreciated substantially against the US dollar. Thailand (-34.5 per cent) and Indonesia (–36.7 per cent) were the most severely affected, followed by Malaysia (–26.2 per cent) and the Philippines (–24.9 per cent). Singapore, with its more robust growth rate and $80 billion in international reserves, was the least affected in the region. The Singapore dollar fell by 10 per cent from the level in the same period a year earlier. Singapore's short-term interest rate still remained below 4 per cent, but other countries such as Indonesia, Thailand, and the Philippines had to resort to high interest rate policies to prevent currency speculation. The short-term interest rate in Indonesia and Thailand increased to 30 per cent and 16 per cent respectively. As long as the exchange rate remains volatile, a central bank would not be willing to inject liquidity into the market to drive down interest rates, but maintaining high interest rate for a long time would result in a slowdown in domestic spending and can lead to a severe contraction after devaluation.

Before the baht float, the stability of Southeast Asian currencies seemed to be the order of the day. After 2 July, the volatility of the exchange rates against the US dollar has been more pronounced. As can be see from Table 6.10, by using daily data from 130 observations from 1 January to 1 July 1997, the size of the standard deviation relative to the mean value of all currencies except the baht was rather small, less than 1 per cent The coefficient of variation of the baht exchange rate against the US dollar was among the highest, but its standard deviation represents only 2.4 per cent of its mean. All countries in the region adhered to the principle of exchange rate stability as an important macroeconomic objective.

Table 6.10 Stability and volatility of Southeast Asian currencies against the US$

	1 Jan – 1 Jul 1997					2 Jul – 17 Oct 1997				
	Baht	Peso	Ringgit	Rupiah	Sing dollar	Baht	Peso	Ringgit	Rupiah	Sing dollar
Mean	25.64	26.35	2.50	2405.26	1.43	33.24	30.83	2.86	2892.56	1.50
Maximum	26.13	26.39	2.53	2444.00	1.45	37.30	35.80	3.37	3692.50	1.56
Minimum	23.15	26.28	2.47	2361.48	1.40	28.65	26.38	2.49	2431.00	1.43
SD.	0.628	0.025	0.016	24.882	0.013	2.512	2.604	0.250	376.214	0.036
CV=SD/Mean	0.024	0.001	0.006	0.010	0.009	0.076	0.084	0.087	0.130	0.024
Jaques–Bera	139.23	9.10	10.21	9.72	9.07	5.83	3.83	4.67	7.69	4.47
(Probability)	(0.000)	(0.011)	(0.006)	(0.008)	(0.010)	(0.054)	(0.147)	(0.097)	(0.021)	(0.107)

Source: Author's calculations.

Daily exchange rate data on each currency from 78 observations between 2 July and 17 October 1997 yielded a completely different picture, where exchange rates of all currencies had become more volatile. The rupiah became the most volatile currency, while the Singapore dollar was the least volatile. The Jacques–Bera statistics for testing the normality of exchange rate movements over the period of the study indicated that the normal distribution of all currencies could be rejected only in the first period during the first half of the year. The implication of the finding is that the Southeast Asian countries constantly intervened in currency markets to achieve a certain degree of stability with the result that the movements of the exchange rate were not distributed normally. However, the Jacques–Bera statistics from the period 2 July to 17 October were not statistically significant for all currencies, except the rupiah. Thus the movements of the baht, ringgit, Singapore dollar and peso seem to be normally distributed. The exchange rates change randomly every day according to news and events. After the baht float, governments in Southeast Asian countries intervened less frequently and let the market forces decide the daily market exchange rates.

Abrupt change in the exchange rate regimes would exert a fundamental impact on the Asian economies. If the exchange rates became more volatile, inflation rates would also fluctuate more widely. Since the welfare cost of inflation depends on whether the inflation rate can be anticipated, fluctuations of the price level would lead to higher welfare cost of asset holders. Furthermore, cost of foreign borrowing would be high, reflecting foreign exchange risks.

The age of cheap imports of foreign capital may have ended on 2 July 1997. Domestic saving mobilization is needed to replace foreign savings so as to regain the long-term pre-shock growth path. It is expected that the Southeast Asian economies are unlikely to experience the 8 per cent growth rate enjoyed earlier in the decade. The Malaysian government introduced severe austerity measures by tightening the budget to reduce the country's current account deficit and to restore confidence in the ringgit. Similarly, the Thai government cut the fiscal budget by 100 billion baht in order to meet the IMF's lending conditionality, which required a surplus budget in 1998 by at least 1 per cent of GDP. The sharp reduction of public spending further aggravated the purchasing ability in the Thai economy and may lead to a severe recession.

The contagion effects of currency realignments can be seen in Figure 6.7. The baht devaluation on 2 July triggered the fear of speculative attacks in other countries with characteristics similar to those of the Thai economy. Countries that are susceptible to currency attacks generally have the following in common: over-valued exchange rate as a result of pegging the domestic currency to the US dollar for too long, large current account deficits, domestic investment financed by short-term external borrowings, high interest rate policies to defend currencies, and over-lending by financial sectors to real estate. Although some countries in the region (such as Singapore) do not share these characteristics with Thailand, the Singapore dollar was also hit.

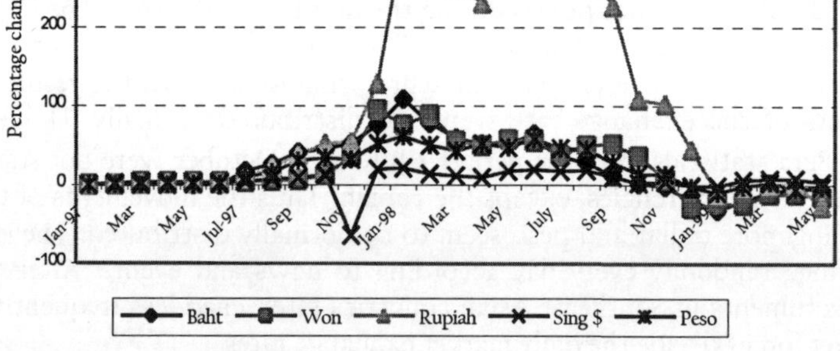

Figure 6.7 Contagion effect

Some economists advance the hypothesis of asymmetric information to explain the contagion effect: international investors do not have perfect information about countries in faraway regions and tend to view them as a group sharing similar characteristics. Moreover, since these countries have similar export structures and large volume of intra-regional trade, Thailand's devaluation would affect other countries' competitiveness if their countries do not depreciate their currencies in tandem with the baht.

A slowdown in the growth rate of one country in the region thus translates into a slowdown in imports of that country from other countries in the region. It is not surprising, therefore, to see that devaluation in one country can have a widespread contagion effect into other countries. The degree to which a country would suffer more or less depends on the responsiveness of the tradeable sector that can take advantage from currency depreciation, and the strength of the financial sector, which must be able to withstand the financial distress from enlarging non-performing loans caused by recession. Jardine Fleming International Securities estimates that non-performing loans will peak at a combined $73 billion in Malaysia, Thailand, Indonesia and the Philippines, representing 15 per cent of outstanding loans of these countries and 13 per cent of their combined GDP. The non-performing loans in Thailand will peak in 1998 at $27 billion (20 per cent of GDP), while Malaysia's non-performing loans will peak $19 billion (23 per cent of GDP). In Indonesia, NPL will reach 11 per cent of GDP or $19 billion.

Table 6.11 shows the correlation matrix of the prices of the US dollar in terms of Southeast Asian currencies in two periods: before and after the baht floating on 2 July 1997. The correlation coefficients were relatively low; the baht value has a negative correlation with the peso, the ringgit and the rupiah before 2 July. But these negative correlation coefficients changed to positive between 1 July and 20 October 1997. The coefficients also increased sharply and were approaching 0.95 for all currencies.

Table 6.11 Correlation matrix of the price of the US dollar, 1 Jan–1 Jul 1997

	Baht	Peso	Ringgit	Rupiah	Sing dollar
Baht	1.00				
Peso	-0.3777 (0.9203)	1.0000			
Ringgit	-0.4779 (0.9408)	0.5494 (0.9372)	1.0000		
Rupiah	-0.3783 (0.8948)	0.8505 (0.9005)	0.5633 (0.9377)	1.0000	
Sing dollar	0.1521 (0.9316)	0.5923 (0.8768)	0.1649 (0.9277)	0.7002 (0.9185)	1.0000

Note: Figures in parentheses indicate correlation coefficient between 2 July and 20 October 1997.

Other currencies in the region such as the ringgit and the Singapore dollar, which used to have a very low correlation coefficient of 0.16, began to move closely to each other. The correlation between the two currencies increased to 0.93. The rupiah and the peso, which previously had strong correlation of 0.85, moved even closer to each other with the higher correlation coefficient of 0.9. The correlation coefficient between the ringgit and the peso increased from 0.59 to 0.87. The increasing degree of the co-movements of the Southeast Asian currencies makes it difficult for traders and investors to diversify their risks by using different currencies and assets in their portfolio allocations.

The performance of the stock market is related to the foreign exchange market. Government attempts to prop up the existing exchange rate by raising domestic interest rates would result in a decline in stock prices. Furthermore, higher interest rates would affect stock prices by retarding economic growth and reducing corporate profits and dividends. During the economic booms before 1995, foreign investors were attracted to Southeast Asian markets and allocated more funds to the region. The stock prices were bid up and created a positive wealth effect on demand for consumption and investment. Since it is less costly to finance investment through equity than through borrowings, firms in the region took advantage of high price–earning ratios of their new shares. The booms in the stock markets gave rise to higher expectations for further asset price appreciation. Commercial banks and finance companies also extended credit to finance the purchase of assets such as real estate and stocks and pushed the asset prices up further. With the arrival of the unfavourable news of a slowdown in exports, rumours on devaluation and political uncertainty, the bubbles burst and caused a sharp decline in stock prices (Figure 6.8).

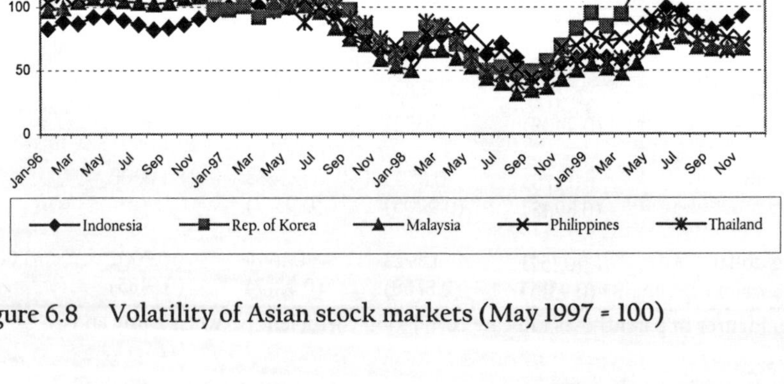

Figure 6.8 Volatility of Asian stock markets (May 1997 = 100)

The substantial fall in asset prices led to a sharp decline in wealth, causing a slump in domestic consumption. The sales of department stores in Bangkok have been falling over the last 14 months, reflecting a severe decline in wealth and a loss in consumer confidence. As Singh (1997) has argued, stock market developments in developing countries provide a poor guide to efficient investment allocation and the excessive volatility in the wake of unfavourable economic shocks may cause macroeconomic instability and reduce long-term growth.

Concluding Remarks

African countries can learn some valuable lessons from the rise and fall of Southeast Asian economies. It can be argued that macroeconomic stability was the cornerstone of the rapidly rising per capita income in Southeast Asian economies between the 1980s and the early 1990s. Successful financial liberalization requires price stability in terms of low and controllable inflation rates. Inflows of foreign direct investment, which enhance factor productivity through technology transfer, require a stable macroeconomic environment in host countries in the forms of sustainable current account deficit and stable exchange rates. The cost of external funds can be reduced by establishing exchange rate stability, since the forward premium of the exchange rate would be small. Thus macroeconomic stability facilitates rapid growth for developing countries, even if some developing countries are constrained by low level of domestic savings. Economic growth in Southeast Asia was driven mainly by rapid expansion of the industrial sector, which was stimulated by foreign direct investment. The output growth was the result of increasing both the quantity and productivity of labour.

In the past decade the Southeast Asian countries carefully implemented conservative macroeconomic policy to achieve stability in terms of the exchange rate, price levels, fiscal balances and moderate growth in money supply. Fiscal flexibility is demonstrated by the ability to trim public spending when needed. The sustained high growth path for the Southeast Asian economies was therefore related to the macroeconomic policy applied. However, sustaining high growth for too long can pose a problem. As long as the system of fixed exchange rate is not prohibiting high income growth, there is less need for the central bank to alter the exchange rate system. Nevertheless, rising tides of capital inflows would cause real exchange rate appreciation if the central bank wished to maintain exchange rate stability.

Since most central banks cannot effectively sterilize huge capital inflows in the long run, fiscal surplus must be used to mitigate the expansionary monetary base. Furthermore, excessive loan expansion of commercial banks to pro-cyclical sectors turns into non-performing loans and bad debts during an economic downturn. Once the stability of the financial system is threatened, confidence in the stability of the exchange rate or the financial reform policy package will simply collapse.

Floating the baht exchange rate should have been carried out during the period of balance of payment surplus; there would have been less pressure on the price of non-traded goods and the Thai economy could have avoided a hard landing. Since growth was viewed as the price objective of the monetary authorities, it was not surprising that they hesitated to let the baht appreciate since it would dampen export growth during the boom years.

Interest rate hikes should never be used to defend the exchange rate. The cost of defending the existing exchange rate is too high in terms of output loss. Moreover, the attempt is likely to fail in an environment of instantaneous international capital movements. When the impact of market expectations is quite strong, any deviations from the market's anticipation would cause further exchange rate depreciation. The sizes of the international reserves held by some Asian central banks are too small to protect their existing exchange rate level from voracious foreign speculators and panicked domestic corporations that have accumulated huge foreign debts.

Financial liberalization in the capital account and the banking sector should be delayed until both macroeconomic stability and prudent financial regulation and capable supervision are firmly established. Selective controls on capital inflows should be applied to make sure the inflows are persistent, less volatile and channelled to productive sectors.

Furthermore, financial deregulation may lead to a consumption boom by households as their liquidity constraints are relaxed. Timing, sequencing and the pace of the financial liberalization are crucial to the success of policy implementation. Competition among newly established financial institutions can lead to weaknesses of the entire financial system. Efficiency gains from competition may not be large enough to offset the loss in financial stability. The most urgent problem for Southeast Asian countries right now is the issue of the continued exchange rate depreciation, which is mostly related to policy credibility and public confidence in the financial system.

Foreign debts in Thailand and Indonesia have been created by the private sector. Since the exchange rate depreciation, the ratios of foreign debt to GDP in both countries are now comparable with those in African countries. At the same time, the ratios of market capitalization to GDP in Southeast Asian countries have declined sharply as a result of the stock market crashes. One of the important lessons learned is that high growth financed by short-term capital flows, such as portfolio investment and short-term foreign borrowings, is not sustainable and the benefits from financial liberalization may be elusive, unless the institutional developments are accompanied by strong supervision and prudential banking regulations.

A strong and independent central bank is necessary to create effective monetary policy. In general, the central banks in developing countries are assigned various policy objectives. The duty of defending the exchange rate can be a goal that is incompatible with conducting monetary policy to stabilize a financially opened economy. Fearing that bank runs may be intensified into a system-wide collapse of the whole financial system, the central banks have to consider whether they should bail out some ailing banks. The lessons from the Southeast Asian countries indicate that the fear of the contagion effect of bank runs may be overestimated. The central bank should refrain from bailing out some troubled banks since taxpayers should not be the ones who have to bear the cost of mismanagement of financial institutions. Instead, bank shareholders, creditors and some depositors, in descending order, should pay the price of undertaking risky behaviours. The problem of moral hazard can then be mitigated and the central bank can focus its role on stabilizing the economy, rather than trying to save some excessive-risk-taking financial institutions. When financial crisis and currency crisis are intertwined, the economic recession will be more severe and over a prolonged period of time.

The IMF bailout packages for Thailand and Indonesia also included conditionalities on good governance. Indeed, one of the factors that contributed to the collapse of these economies was the lack of policy credibility. When transparency and accountability are established in government organizations and the central bank, when authorities are under public scrutiny, and when the rule of law prevails, the effectiveness of macroeconomic policy can be enhanced considerably as a result of the enhanced degree of policy credibility.

References

Asian Development Bank. 1997. *Key Indicators of Developing Asian and Pacific Countries.* New York: Oxford University Press.

Bayoumi, T. 1993. 'Financial deregulation and household savings'. *Economic Journal*, vol. 103, no. 421 (November): 1432–43.

Jha, S.K. 1996. 'The Kuznets curve: A reassessment'. *World Development*, vol. 24, no. 4: 773–80.

Khan, M.S. and M.S. Kumar. 1997. 'Public and private investment and the growth process in developing countries'. *Oxford Bulletin of Economics and Statistics*, vol. 59, no. 1: 69–88.

King, R. and R. Levine. 1993. 'Finance and growth: Schumpeter might be right'. *Quarterly Journal of Economics*, August: 717–37.

Knight, M., N. Loayza and O. Villanueva. 1996. 'The peace dividend: Military spending cuts and economic growth'. *IMF Staff Papers*, vol. 43, no. 1: 1–37.

Levine, R. and S. Zervos. 1996. 'Stock market and long run growth'. *The World Bank Economic Review*, vol. 10, no. 3: 33–339.

Lucas, R.E. 1988. 'On the mechanics of economic development'. *Journal of Monetary Economics*, vol. 22, no. 1 (July): 3–42.

Odedokun, M.O. 1996. 'Alternative econometric approaches for analysing the role of the financial sector in economic growth: Time-series evidence from LDCs'. *Journal of Development Economics*, vol. 50: 119–46.

Ogaki, M., J. Ostry and M. Reinhart. 1996. 'Saving behaviors in low and middle-income developing countries'. *IMF Staff Papers*, vol. 43, no. 1 (March): 38–71.

Ram, Rati. 1996. 'Productivity of public and private investment in developing countries: A broad international perspective'. *World Development*, vol. 24, no. 8: 1373–78.

Singh, Ajit. 1997. 'Financial liberalization, stock markets, and economic development'. *Economic Journal*, vol. 107 (May): 771–82.

Speight, A.E. and M.J. White. 1995. 'Private consumption, public consumption and liquidity constraints in developing countries: Some empirical evidence'. *Applied Economics*, vol. 27: 925–33.

United Nations. 1997. Economic and Social Survey of Asia and the Pacific. New York.

Wall, Howard J. 1996. 'Is a military really a luxury good? An international panel study of LDCs'. *Applied Economics*, vol. 28: 41–44.

World Bank. 1997. World Development Indicators.

PART THREE

TRADE, INDUSTRY AND TECHNOLOGY

Chapter 7

Trade, Industry and Technology Development in Sub-Saharan Africa: Policies, Response and Effects

Ademola Oyejide and Samuel M. Wangwe

Economic development is closely associated with industrialization. Industrialization is, in turn, closely linked with technological development and productivity increase.

Trade and trade policies interact, in various ways, with both industrialization and technological development in the process of overall economic growth. Typically, industrialization is started off and often sustained through the importation, adoption and adaptation of foreign technology. Thus technology trade can contribute to both technological development and industrialization by augmenting local capabilities, particularly through the provision of learning opportunities. Recent development experience assigns a critical role to trade and outward-oriented trade policy in the development process. In particular, a policy focused on exports serves to induce domestic firms to acquire the capabilities for facing foreign competition by adopting international standards and technology.

The pace and pattern of industrialization have been influenced by the trade regime (e.g., protective trade policies), while the dynamism of export sectors has often been maintained through industrialization. The process of deepening industrialization has been associated with increasing complexity of products and of the technologies used. Policies that mediate the interactions among trade, industrialization and technology operate at different levels: macroeconomic policies, sectoral policies and micro-level policies, influence firm level responses.

This chapter focuses on the inter-relationships among trade, industrialization and technological development in the context of the overall process of economic development in sub-Saharan Africa (SSA) countries. The discussion pays particular attention to policies intended to positively enhance these inter-relationships, enterprise-level responses to these policies and their effects. It brings out some pertinent differences and similarities in prevailing conditions in Asia and Africa, providing an account of the divergent development experiences in the two regions in the area of trade, industry and technological development and addressing relevant institutional arrangements and organizational characteristics.

Sub-Saharan Africa's Development and Industrialization Experience

Economic performance in the SSA region has varied over time and across countries from the early 1960s to the mid 1990s. In broad terms, however, economic growth in the region was moderate and generally below the average rate for other developing countries in the early 1960s. After this time, SSA's average gross domestic product (GDP) growth rate accelerated, so that in the 1965–1973 period, its growth performance of 5.9 per cent was virtually the same as the 6 per cent recorded for all developing countries. SSA's growth rate faltered from the mid 1970s, however, and declined further into the 1980s. Thus, the region's average annual GDP growth rates of 2.5 per cent and 0.6 per cent during the 1973–1980 and 1980–1987 periods compare poorly with the corresponding growth rates of 4.6 per cent and 61 per cent turned in by all developing countries over the same time periods (World Bank, 1989). SSA's annual GDP growth rate averaged about 2 per cent between 1988 and the mid 1990s.

SSA's manufacturing sector grew significantly in the 1960s; the more than 8 per cent annual average growth rate of manufacturing value added was substantially higher than the corresponding GDP growth rate, although the base of the manufacturing sector from which this growth derived was quite small. In any case, by 1965, this sector contributed 15 per cent or more of the GDP of 12 countries (Botswana, Cameroon, Chad, Côte d'Ivoire, Ghana, Kenya, Madagascar, Mauritius, Senegal, Togo, Zaire and Zimbabwe).

This growth performance could not be sustained. It decelerated sharply in the 1970s and was virtually stagnant in the 1980s. Manufacturing output declined in SSA countries during the 1970s and in another 11 countries by the mid 1980s, with capacity utilization rates in manufacturing well below 35 per cent in many SSA countries (World Bank, 1989).

The growth of manufacturing value-added (MVA) over 1980–1993 was only 3 per cent per annum in real terms, and the rate declined steadily over time, from 3.7 per cent in the first half of the 1980s to 2 per cent between 1989 and 1994. The trend persisted within the latter period, with MVA growth falling from 3.3 per cent during 1989–1990 to 0.4 per cent in 1991–1992 period, then registering a modest recovery, to 1.7 per cent, in 1992–1994 (World Bank, 1996). This growth in fact conceals the continued stagnation or falls in MVA in many African countries—Africa has suffered the most serious 'deindustrialization' in recent times in the developing world. Average per capita income has declined by 1.1 per cent per annum, and SSA's share of manufacturing fell from 1.5 per cent of world MVA in 1980 to 0.8 per cent in 1994 (World Bank, 1997). During the early 1990s, the average contribution of SSA's manufacturing sector to the region's GDP averaged 16 per cent while its share of exports averaged 12 per cent (World Bank, 1995). These averages mask wide country variations. Among the more industrialized SSA countries (such as Mauritius, South Africa and Zimbabwe), the share of the manufacturing sector in GDP lies in the range of 23–39 per cent. But the broad picture confirms certain key features of SSA's manufacturing sector.

Clearly, most SSA countries have not succeeded in developing a technologically dynamic and internationally competitive industrial base.

The structure of industrial activity in SSA remains underdeveloped. It is dominated by the (minimal) processing of local natural resources and simple consumer goods industries, unlike those in Asia and Latin America, which have broadened and deepened into a range of more complex activities. Moreover, only a few African industrial activities have 'matured' to full competitiveness by international standards (Lall and Wangwe, 1997).

As a result, the region's import dependence remains high while its share of world exports of manufactured product has been low and falling. A recent assessment (World Bank, 1995: 50) concludes that 'African manufacturing has not reached a critical mass and scale at which it can take off...'

Failures of public policy have routinely been identified as the major reason for the unsatisfactory performance of SSA's GDP and manufacturing sector. In particular, it is suggested that SSA countries clung to import substitution industrialization policies for too long—well beyond the point at which the protected industries could make any significant contribution to growth. As a result of this strategy, most SSA industries were isolated from world markets and new technology; hence, they were under no real pressure to approach 'best-practice' operational frontiers in other parts of the world. Elbadawi (1996: 1) offers this summary:

> SSA's failed development strategies ... emphasized a dominant role for the state in the development process but ignored the drawback of badly managed state-provided incentives (rent-seeking, inefficiency, etc.) and belittled the roles of the private sector and market discipline in the development process.

The industrialization experience in SSA is associated with investments taking place under protection that has not only been high but has also been persistent over time. The sectors like agriculture and infrastructure, which would be supportive to industrial development, have lagged behind industrial requirements. Exports have remained undiversified, undynamic and insufficiently competitive. Technological development is central to the process of attaining international competitiveness. Yet technology adoption and innovations have not been pressured by competition either from domestic actors or from international trade.

The Government and the Private Sector

State intervention in economic development in post-colonial Africa was thought necessary to make up for market failures (distorted markets and missing markets) and the need to redress the socioeconomic imbalances cultivated during the colonial administration. Development planning was adopted in many African countries as one response to perceived market failures and imbalances in society (e.g., Asians in Eastern Africa, Lebanese in West Africa).

The Role of Government

Against this background, during the 1960s and 1970s many SSA countries tried to use various forms of government intervention to rectify obvious market failures and to promote specific industries and sectors. Thus, they acted in ways that reflected their belief in the ability and right of government to orchestrate the actions of both private and public economic agents and coordinate entrepreneurial decisions in support of economic growth objectives and targets established by the government. These interventions resulted in high levels of protection and isolation from the world markets, with the result that the whole economy was not closely linked into the global economy.

Since 'countries with better integration performance enjoyed not only higher but also more stable growth' (World Bank, 1996:25), the inadequate integration of SSA countries into the global economy is also held partly accountable for the region's poor performance in overall economic growth and industrialization. On this count, too, it has been recommended that SSA's development strategy should shift from an inward to an outward oriented one. Thus, the explicitly expressed intent of the structural adjustment programmes designed for and implemented in virtually all SSA countries since the early 1980s has been not only to 'get the fundamentals (i.e., prices and macroeconomic stability) right' but also to sharply curtail the role of government in the development process.

The idea of a 'hands-off' minimalist government sits rather uncomfortably with the wide recognition that on both theoretical grounds (market failures arising from missing and underdeveloped markets, learning and other externalities associated with modern manufacturing and technological development) and the lessons emanating from the development experience of other regions, government could and should play an important role in assisting the development of new and dynamic comparative advantage using selective intervention measures.

The response is expressed in the justifiable concerns about the weak or inadequate capacity of the typical SSA state to effectively design and manage such measures (World Bank, 1994, 1995; Lipumba, 1994). Thus, based largely on their record of past failures, their current lack of adequate capacity for implementing and monitoring selective interventions, and a political economy that is, apparently, highly susceptible to rent-seeking and corruption, SSA countries are enjoined to forgo the use of such measures. For instance, Winrock (1991) counsels that SSA countries should stick to policies that are simple and transparent and that require the least amount of technical know-how, while the World Bank (1994) advises SSA countries to use their limited state capacity sparingly by minimizing unnecessary government involvement in markets. The same considerations lead (Thorbecke, 1994: 70) to conclude that for SSA countries, 'it may be wiser to rely on more market and free trade-oriented policies and minimize interventionist policies'.

This admonition leaves several critical questions unanswered: to whom and how will the obvious growth-retarding market imperfections and failures be addressed? To what extent can the 'simple policies' work when the most relevant markets are absent to underdeveloped? Would seeking refuge in a 'minimalist' state rather than building the necessary capacity for the state to more carry out its functions effectively not amount to abandoning the quest for rapid and sustainable growth—or throwing out the baby with the bath water?

Some lessons from Asia may be useful here, as is shown in the chapters on Asia. However, at this point it may suffice to mention that while the principle of state intervention in economic development was also adopted in East Asia, substantial qualitative differences can be observed. The experience of most countries in East Asia shows that policy choices could not be treated as exogenous and political institutions had an important influence on the coherence of policy while bureaucracy came in for closer scrutiny. Overall, the intervention of SSA states in economic management tended to lean more towards controls and restrictions while the East Asian states tended to lean more towards promotion and facilitation (Rhee and Westphal, 1986). State intervention in Southeast Asia has relied more on market based instruments of industrial policy using market mechanisms and signals rather than negating them as was done in some of the post-colonial economies of 'intermediate regimes' (Jomo, 1996). State intervention in Africa negated this approach and in many cases relied on administrative controls, that operated against the market rather than through the market.

The experience of the second-tier countries suggests that state intervention is needed (Jomo, 1996) in the areas of technology (e.g., to deal with imperfections in market information), finance (e.g., to deal with market imperfections arising from risk and uncertainty), human resource training (e.g., to tap externalities in the labour market) and trade (e.g., to impose export targets in return to protection in the domestic market).

Public–Private Interactions and Relationships

State intervention in the African context was associated with varying relationships with the private sector. A study of six African countries (Côte d'Ivoire, Nigeria, Kenya, Tanzania, Zimbabwe and Mauritius) addressed the relationship between government and the private sector and found varying relations between them (Wangwe, 1995).

The system of controls in the then Rhodesia was made to operate effectively and the highly protected system that they constituted did not lead to the gross inefficiency that has characterized other import substitution regimes. The need to adapt and innovate led to the development of a wide range of technical skills, particularly in various branches of engineering. The strong orientation to market requirements led to a proliferation of products, often produced within large, vertically integrated conglomerates (Ndlela and Robinson, 1995).

In the case of Mauritius the government and the enterprise sector cooperated in many ways and held consultations on matters affecting industry. Government policy facilitated the process by which local entrepreneurs continuously gained control of industrial development (Lamusse, 1995). In Côte d'Ivoire the government worked with and was supportive of enterprise sector development in a way that did not threaten the main actors in industry, even if they were non-Ivorians (Ousou and Bouabre, 1995).

In the other three countries (Tanzania, Kenya and Nigeria) and post-independence Zimbabwe, the relationship between government and the enterprise sector (or significant parts of it) was less cordial. Government intervention in industrial development was perceived as intending to address imbalances in society, as a result of which some leading actors in industrial development could be losers. In Tanzania the nationalization policy and the socialist policy were perceived as a threat to the private sector. In Kenya the way the Africanization policy was introduced and practiced was perceived as a threat to the Asian community, who were the leading local private-sector industrialist group.

The indigenization policy in Nigeria posed a threat to some foreign investors. In post-independence Zimbabwe, too, the relationship between government and sections of the enterprise sector became less cordial as the government began to address some imbalances in society. The leading white community entrepreneurs perceived that they would be the losers. The application of controls in the absence of the rapport with the private sector that had existed under the previous regime, and the introduction of new controls on wages and labour relations, led to a situation in which bureaucracy became one of the obstacles to the running of any kind of economic enterprise.

The relationship between government and the private sector in Asia is closer to the relationship exhibited in the Mauritian case, which differs in many ways from many typical African countries.

Governments in East Asia pursued policies aimed to reduce uncertainty by addressing market failures and problems stemming from organization of industry (e.g., scale economies, entrepreneurial skills), structure of public institutions and rent-seeking behaviour. A set of institutions, institutional ties and more informal individual networks that connect the public and private sectors were put in place to keep policy makers connected to business, allowing information to flow between business and government without reducing the ability of the government to tackle interrelated institutional and structural bottlenecks that would otherwise hold back investment, technological progress and export development (UNCTAD, 1996: 128). In some cases mergers were encouraged and entry into specific industries was restricted, while cartels were promoted for specific purposes (e.g., standardization, specialization and exports) and direct public investments were undertaken. The East Asian experience demonstrates the complementarity between export promotion and import substitution as the policy packages contained both protectionist and export promotion measures for industries at varying degrees of maturity.

Government policies need to be designed to shape market responses so as to enhance their contribution to development. In the 1950s, when the manufacturing sector was not competitive internationally, governments promoted exports through a variety of subsidies (tariff rebates, tax exemptions, preferential export credits and export credit insurance). These provided the foundation for a reinforcement of such policies in the 1960s through more systematic promotion of manufactured exports. For instance, the Republic of Korea introduced a series of institutional reforms such as a monthly export promotion conference, the Korean Trade Promotion Corporation and the export targeting system. Government in most East Asian countries exercised considerable discipline over business; in order to meet export targets, through tax penalties, withdrawal of import licenses and reduced access to credit (UNCTAD, 1996: 129).

Networking, Linkages and Subcontracting

It may be unnecessary to possess all essential capabilities in-house if some of them can be obtained outside the firm. However, in such cases the firm needs at least to have the capacity to identify the kinds of capabilities it needs to buy from elsewhere and how best to use inputs and services provided by others.

Few firms in Africa have pursued networking and linkages as a policy issue. In fact, these linkages seem not to exist significantly in Africa, where the contracting and subcontracting culture is apparently undeveloped. Other types of linkages such as inter-firm linkages financial institution linkages and business support linkages, do exist, but they have mainly been used on an ad hoc basis.

Subcontracting activities among engineering and clothing firms, for instance, is limited, reflecting both the simple level of production undertaken by most firms (thus there was little need for subcontracting) and lack of 'competent' firms capable of undertaking subcontracting work.

The study of six African countries found that internal linkages (i.e., within the country) are limited (Wangwe, 1995). While there were some linkages among firms that shared premises in the industrial estates, there were only isolated cases of subcontracting arrangements outside these networks. There is little subcontracting or local procurement of manufactured inputs in the exporting firms. Large firms have only infrequent relations with small firms except for the purchase of some repair and maintenance services. Information and technology diffusion among firms is minimal except for very informal channels.

The study suggested that several factors explain this situation. First, import dependence over a long time has pre-empted the search for local alternative linkages. The lack of linkages reflects the pattern of import substitution industrialization, which emphasizes import-dependent assembly. Second, access to tied donor finance reduced the need to search for local sources of supply. Third, the capability to search for various local suppliers had not been developed. Fourth, some firms competed with their potential suppliers of technological services rather than being assisted by them. For instance, Themi of Tanzania produced farm implements, some of which were also being produced for the domestic market by two research and development institutions. The competitive relationship between the firm and the institutions that are supposed to provide technological services was not conducive to the development of technological linkages between them.[1] Lastly, poor inter-sectoral linkages may reflect poor infrastructural facilities for small firms, biases in policies and in credit markets, and the lack of an extension network.

Industry associations had made attempts to promote interactions among local firms by harmonizing production processes (e.g., identification of excess capacity in individual firms and possibilities of subcontracting, trading in spares, joint quality control, etc.). The case studies showed that in isolated incidents firms that receive large export orders have subcontracted some of the work to other firms (Wangwe, 1995). Inter-firm trade in unfinished products is very rare.

The creation of linkages and establishment of input-producing activities have been influenced by government policy. For instance, in the case of textiles and brewing, the establishment of some input-supplying activities was influenced by government policies discouraging imports (e.g., yarn and malt in Nigeria). Some of these firms have achieved such tremendous expansion that they now export as well as sell on the local market. In the case of the brewing industry in Nigeria, the search for local alternatives was intensified with the introduction of restrictions on importing barley (Oluremi, 1995). Increasing success with local substitutes for barley malt improved the capacity utilization rate for the industry, with the search for local substitutes involving most of the firms in investment in R&D as well as substantial plant conversion. Their efforts were complemented by the independent research endeavour at the Federal Institute of Industrial Research, Oshodi (FIIRO), which through some of its research report series demonstrated that lager beer could be produced using only sorghum. Today, most of the more successful firms use maize and sorghum in their beer production process.

The case studies of the six countries found that buyers and consumers of the firms' products provided useful market information. They were very instrumental in inducing product quality improvements. The interaction with export markets, which are more demanding, was particularly effective in this respect (Wangwe, 1995).

Linkages and subcontracting are much more prevalent in Asia. It would be useful to understand what it would take to replicate some of the positive experiences with subcontracting and other inter-firm linkages and relationships. The role of marketing agents had been observed to be important in South Korea but there seems to be one difference: Korean firms selectively let foreign buyers do much of the marketing during the early stages of export development, but this role was gradually transferred to the firms or to local trading institutions. This progressive transfer process does not seem to have taken place in Africa as yet except for some firms in Mauritius.

The trade–production nexus exhibited interesting linkages. The six country case studies in Africa found that the trade–production nexus was manifested in two forms. First, the contacts made in the trading phase with consumers or with suppliers enabled firms to accumulate capabilities and knowledge about the

[1] R&D institutions are often squeezed financially and one response is to engage in production.

characteristics of the markets and of suppliers. These contacts were a useful asset when the firms entered the manufacturing stage. Second, as some firms shifted from trading to manufacturing, part of the family continued with trading activities and some of them were located abroad. The local manufacturing firms then made use of the family connections, who acted as trusted agents and 'marketing offices' abroad. Networking with family members in foreign countries has been useful in getting access to information about market opportunities and sources of technology. Such family connections were found very effective in Mauritius, in Zimbabwe within the white community, and in Tanzania and Kenya within the Asian community. A large number of these contacts were retained and operated as networks through which new ideas about changing technological and marketing conditions were disseminated, contributing to the improvement of firms' positions in export markets.

Exporting firms that are subsidiaries of transnational corporations (TNCs) have benefited from a production–trade nexus of a different kind. Through their global networks of companies, TNCs in resource-based activities have engaged in the production and processing of primary resources and trading in the final products. Either they control the source of raw materials by developing their own plantations or, by establishing processing activities at the source of the raw materials, they have priority over procurement. For instance, the production of cotton is highly dispersed worldwide but its marketing is concentrated in the hands of a few big traders (notably 15 cotton traders, of whom two are European companies, eight are US companies and five are Japanese trading houses). The coffee market is dominated by a few trading companies (General Foods, Nestle, Suchard).

Capability building at firm level is expected to take place in the context of a network of linkages and relationships (formal and informal) with suppliers, customers, competitors, consultants, and technology R&D and educational institutions (UNCTAD, 1996). In this process of capability building, access to foreign technology and other organizational assets (e.g., marketing and distributional skills) is essential.

Recent developments in technology and the consequent TNC strategies have made it possible for TNCs to locate and relocate specific activities in the production chain according to specific locational advantages. With such geographically dispersed production sites, the spillovers from hosting TNCs are reduced but the chances of attracting some aspects of TNC activity is increased. The policy challenge may be to complement FDI with other forms of promoting upgrading and building of capabilities. In particular, development of domestic linkages (e.g., with suppliers) is important in increasing domestic value added of FDI activities.

The study of exporting firms in six countries in Africa addressed the issue of linkages between local and foreign firms. The positive role of foreign investment in building local technological capabilities has come out quite clearly in Mauritius, where local private capital has been progressively buying out foreign capital. This harmonious nationalization of investments has been facilitated by the existence of an entrepreneurial class that developed from the local plantocracy during the years when sugar production was dominant. The surpluses accumulated then were invested in industry. In addition, the macroeconomic environment and the climate for investments have been conducive for both local and foreign investment. For instance, one of the leading exporting firms in Mauritius, the knitwear firm, was established initially by Hong Kong investors with a minority Mauritian participation. After a few years the Hong Kong shareholders were bought out by Mauritians, and since 1977 the company has had an entirely local shareholding. The bulk of the shares are held by a local investment company belonging to a large sugar group. The existence of a capital market and a group of local individuals and institutions who are willing to invest seems to have favoured the process of nationalization in Mauritius.

The transfer of control from foreigners to indigenous owners has sometimes been far from smooth and possibly more destructive than constructive. One such case is Nigeria. The indigenization programme in Nigeria was carried out in 1974 and, together with further phases that were implemented before 1980, resulted in Nigerians taking over the control of several businesses hitherto controlled by foreigners. However, it would appear that the policymakers overlooked the economic side effects of the indigenization programme, especially its possible negation of the goal of economic independence. The substitution industries that had been established were acquiring the capability to manufacture for export but this development was thwarted by the workforce dislocation caused by the indigenization programme. Several of the newly established activities experienced personnel problems and some failed as a result.

The contribution of foreign investment in building local capabilities has not always been positive. The case studies showed that some locally controlled firms were bought out by TNCs in response to the threat of competition (e.g., Trituraf of the Côte d'Ivoire). Another multinational, Saco, had a monopoly for about ten years, after which many state-created companies started trading in the Côte d'Ivoire. But in the middle of the 1980s nearly all of these newcomers disappeared or were taken over, leaving Saco in control of most of the local cocoa-bean processing and by-product production (Ousou and Bouabre, 1995).

In discussions of the role foreign investment could play in industrialization and in building technological capabilities within firms it is important to recognize the changing forms of foreign investment. This study has shown that exporting firms in Africa have benefited in different ways from various forms of relationships with foreign firms. Foreign investment is increasingly taking forms other than the traditional direct foreign investment. There is considerable evidence that new forms of investment (NFI) will continue to gain importance in developing countries, superseding traditional FDI in some areas and complementing it in others (OECD, 1989). The implication of the debt crisis and foreign exchange shortages for the balance between FDI and NFI is likely to vary policies (macroeconomic policies and policies on foreign investment), the host-country's market potential, perceived degree of bureaucratic red tape, political stability and the availability of local managerial skills and skilled labour. However, it is likely that as some developing countries acquire various capabilities, they may want to bring in only those assets cannot obtain locally in order to minimize foreign exchange losses (through remissions abroad and payments for various services). Such long-term financial and foreign exchange considerations may lead to more selective pursuit of NFI, with government attitudes and policies tending to be more industry-specific, reflecting long-term benefits from learning by doing (OECD, 1989).

The changing perceptions of TNCs may continue to favour a relative increase in NFI, on the grounds that it increases leverage on firm-specific assets and that it has risk-shedding advantages over traditional FDI. In future, the balance between traditional FDI and NFI is likely to be influenced more by the global dynamics of inter-firm competition and by the interplay between those dynamics and host-government policies than by the latter's unilateral decisions (OECD, 1989). This underscores the importance of understanding global trends within specific industries.

The evidence presented by the OECD (1989) suggests that there is a long-term trend in the division of risks and responsibilities among TNCs, host countries and international lenders, which is characterized by increasing emphasis by TNCs on flexibility and the development of capabilities in relatively protected industry segments (where profit potentials are high), operating upstream of production (as suppliers of technology and management) in some industries and downstream (in marketing) in others. Host-country investors are increasingly retaining partial or total ownership of investment projects, while the degree of effective control depends increasingly on factors other than host-country ownership of equity. International lenders are likely to continue to play a central role in channelling financial capital to developing countries (in the form of new loans and debt rescheduling) and in that way will exert significant control over the international investment process (OECD, 1989).

The East Asian region exhibits a diversity of experiences with FDI. In Singapore and second-tier newly industrializing economies (NIEs), FDI accounted for 40–50 per cent manufacturing (1986–1988) and even higher in electrical machinery and electronics (about 70 per cent) compared with about 20 per cent in Korea (1986) and 2.2 per cent in Japan (1986) (UNCTAD, 1996). The share of FDI in gross fixed capital formation during 1991–1993 ranged from 0.1 per cent in Japan and 0.5 per cent in Korea to 24.65 per cent in Malaysia and 37.4 per cent in Singapore. In all countries the share of FDI increased in the last two decades, except in Japan where it remained constant (UNCTAD, 1996).

In terms of enhancing domestic capabilities successful upgrading has been exhibited in the first-tier NIEs whereby moves into design and product development gradually reduced dependence on TNCs (UNCTAD, World Investment Report, 1995). The second-tier NIEs have taken a less restrictive stance on FDI; they have not developed a diversified manufacturing base with intermediate and capital goods industries and have not put in place a well-developed local supplier network and adequately trained workforce. FDI originating in the first-tier into second-tier NIEs has been considerable. The evolution of industrial output and exports in the second-tier NIEs is raising concern about increasing reliance on FDI and insufficient technological and supply linkages between the TNC-dominated export sectors and the rest of the economy. There is concern about the need to take measures to deepen the domestic industrial base and improve the quality of the labour force, management and infrastructure (UNCTAD, 1996: 123). In fact, in recent years, there is evidence that second-tier NIEs have introduced more targeted measures such as local content agreements, more selective incentives to attract higher value-added activities, and greater efforts to capture FDI spillovers in the areas of training and R&D (UNCTAD, 1996:133).

Policy and Reforms

A policy package designed to deliberately raise the speed of growth and structure of a developing country's manufacturing sector in close association with technological development will, almost by definition, assign a significant role to the public sector. This arises partly from the fact that in the typical developing economy, the market system is unable to effectively transmit necessary information through price signals due to various imperfections, as a supplement to the market system, to facilitate and enhance information flow.

The prevalence of various scale economies and externalities associated with both modern manufacturing and the acquisition, assimilation and use of technology also justify a significant role for government in the development process. At the same time, the dynamism that invigorates the development process is expected to come primarily from the production decisions and investment choices that private enterprises make as they deploy their capabilities in attempts to seize perceived market opportunities. A development strategy that reflects this reality should have something to say about cooperation and collaboration between the public and private sectors, without which the design and implementation of development policy could be deficient.

Restructuring State Enterprises

Reform of the state sector enterprises is one of the key elements of government economic reforms programmes in Africa, whose objectives are to improve the operational efficiency of enterprises, reduce fiscal burden to the government, and broaden participation by nationals in the ownership and management of business and economic activities. The experience with privatization so far has shown that it takes more than change of ownership to spur long-term competitiveness in industry. This points to the fact that in Africa's industrialization there are other critical constraints to competitiveness that cannot necessarily be solved by mere privatization. Issues such as adequate and appropriate skills, entrepreneurship, technology, fiscal and monetary policy, competition and infrastructure problems will still play a deterring role in the achievement of higher manufacturing competitiveness. Purposeful policies to address these constraints are called for.

The process has encountered several problems, including slow investment response by the prospective private investors due to, among other things, bad state of the parastatals, inadequate resources and capacity of the concerned government machinery to expedite the process, and the fear and state of indecision the stakeholders about the validity of the privatization.

Reforms and Institutional Constraints

Institutional constraints In order for policies that enhance manufacturing competitiveness to be effective, institutions in many African countries have to be transformed to enable them to assume new roles and face new challenges. A reformed legal framework is needed that can provide investors (domestic and foreign) with stable and predictable economic and political environment that has legal backing and ensures confidence. This discussion implies that the need for institutional reforms is even more urgent. Since after economic reforms government objectives and modalities have changed, it is necessary to change the implementing institutions that were created in a new policy environment. A change in government bureaucracies is needed, likewise changes in corporate structures that allow companies to meet the challenge of changing, competitive market conditions. Good governance and political stability are instrumental in stimulating investment and production.[2]

Drags from previous regimes There are problems in Africa that are deeply embedded in the economic and political structures and attitudes carried over from previous regimes, which were characterized by bureaucracies that hindered the smooth workings of economic activities and efficient use of resources. Institutional reforms cannot be complete without inculcating a new kind of thinking and way of doing things that are commensurate with the new socioeconomic and political conditions. This emphasizes the importance of changing the attitude and behavioural codes of stakeholders in the previous regime to fit the new environment.

Learning by doing in policy reforms Learning by doing in policy formulation will enable the countries in question to wisely prioritize their needs, and in the case of industrial policy, to better design sustainable policies to enhance skills and local entrepreneurship, thus contributing to manufacturing competitiveness. Many firms in Africa lack the knowledge, time and resources to identify their technological needs. They often seek assistance to resolve pertinent issues underlying their own development. There is little effort to learn systematically from past experiences and from the experience of other countries.

---

[2] Legal reform in Africa is another important underpinning for the envisaged improvement in economic performance, especially in inducing investors and entrepreneurs. Without some realistic expectation that the legal system is sufficiently insulated from the locus of political authority, investors will consider the risk of legal conflict exceptionally high.

Administrative capacity and managerial cadres In many reforming African countries, constraints to the effectiveness of the policy changes is the lack of adequate administrative and managerial cadres to steer the economies away from the working of the old regimes to the new ones. The obstacles of human capacities including managerial and entrepreneurial deficiencies are manifested in the lack of adequate response to new investment and trade opportunities. To ensure manufacturing competitiveness in this era of globalization, managers in the enterprises have to be equipped with knowledge and expertise to manage in a new market and technology environment in which competitiveness, flexibility and adaptation to new situations are more important than in the past.

Resistance to change by economic agents The importance of governance in the context of policies, strategies and instruments of the manufacturing sector arises from a number of considerations. First, the discretionary use of promotional instruments may give rise to rent-seeking behaviour. Second, there is need for government intervention to shift its thrust from regulation to promotion. Third, administrative efficiency, accountability and transparency are of critical importance for the success of policy implementation and instruments thereof. The long history of protection and dictatorial regimes combined with rent-seeking behaviours is associated with interests in society that respective groups tend to strive to safeguard.

Changing Approaches to Policy Formulation

The environment in which policies are made is undergoing a continuous and rapid process of change. Recently, however, these changes have been even faster and more far-reaching. Individually and interactively the changes are necessitating the need to review the ways in which individuals and institutions carry out their activities and businesses. This presents enormous challenges as individuals and institutions alike devise mechanisms and build the capacity to cope with an increasingly dynamic environment.

The demand for more informed, more participatory and more precise policy making has similarly increased in the past one and half decades. The domain of economic management has expanded to encompass more rigorously the demands for continued macroeconomic stability, foster supply response and enhance efficiency of resource use. The dual transitional processes of economic and political liberalization have not only generated their own high demands for changes in the way they are doing business; further complications have arisen from the effect of the interactions of the two processes. Five main recent developments that influence the conduct of policy formulation, analysis and implementation, as well as economic management, can be identified:

- The transition from closed political regimes operating along patron–client networks to more open and liberalized political systems that allow for a more explicit articulation of interests of various groups in society.

- The transition from controlled and interventionist to more open and market-oriented economies.
- Donor attitudes that are increasingly changing towards promoting the recipient ownership of policies and development strategies as one way of enhancing aid effectiveness and the broad based accountability and transparency of policy action.
- The influence of the media, which has increased considerably in bringing policy issues to the public domain and enhancing public scrutiny of policy performance.
- Intensified challenges from changing world market conditions and rapid technological advances.

Political changes have emerged in the form of democratization and political liberalization. Various groups in society have greater freedom to articulate their positions on issues and hence make an impact on policy analysis and the policy making process. Under the new multiparty politics in many African countries political parties are free to articulate a variety of positions and policies, while social groups such as the, private sector, the civil society, youths and women are better placed to articulate their own interests. This has been accentuated by the significant increase in the freedom of the press which propelled greater media involvement in the process of bringing policy issues to the public domain thus enhancing public awareness and facilitating public scrutiny of policy performance. It is becoming politically more risky and costly to make policy mistakes and to ignore the views of these groups, which are slowly but surely gaining the strength and ground to affect the policy making process.

It is increasingly clear that in this new socio-political environment, policy making is no longer the monopoly of the government. Greater attention is being paid to devising the most appropriate ways through which all actors can be given the opportunity to present their views on policy proposals so that they can be incorporated into the policy making process. In the case of Tanzania, for instance, the role of the business community in policy formulation increased considerably in the 1990s. In 1994 the Confederation of Tanzania Industries (CTI) submitted an industrial policy proposal to the government. Subsequent initiatives by the government to formulate an industrial policy took into account the proposals from CTI, and in various stages of formulating the policies the government consulted the business community. In another important policy area, the budget, the business community submitted their inputs into the 1996/97 budget. Some of their proposals were incorporated into the budget and during 1996 and 1997 consultations have continued between the government and the business community on matters of fiscal policy. Similar consultations are found in several other countries (e.g., Ghana, Uganda).

These developments indicated that there is greater room now for various stakeholders to express their interests in policy making processes in Africa. However, this is an area where experience from Asian countries would be very useful. The long experience of involving the private sector in policy formulation in many Asian countries and the way the interactions between business and government have been evolving over time deserve closer scrutiny and understanding.

Conclusion

As in other developing regions, SSA countries have focused on industrialization as a key component of their development process over the last four decades or so. But compared with these other regions, SSA countries have had little success in building dynamic manufacturing sectors. The blame for this lack of success is typically placed at the door of poor macroeconomic and sectoral policies emanating from basically faulty development strategy.

While not necessarily de-emphasizing poor policy as a cause of SSA's generally unsatisfactory performance, it should be noted that the difference between SSA and other developing regions is probably not so much in the specific policy instruments used. The design and implementation of the policies, as well as their stability and credibility are important components of policy effectiveness. Other factors are the incentive (positive and negative) and institutional structures created around the policies, and how the policy package is adjusted to take account of changing circumstances. In addition, and in comparison with other developing regions, SSA had the smallest base of technical and managerial capital to work with. Yet, the promotion and enhancement of the technological capabilities of private enterprises received very little policy attention in many SSA countries. Finally, the deep distrust and virtual confrontation between the public and private sectors in many African countries have not created a conducive environment for either one to play their different but interlocking and complementary roles in the development process.

Recent institutional and policy reforms in many SSA countries have addressed some of the key macroeconomic and sectoral policy deficiencies. They have not, however, recognized that a number of constraints will continue to frustrate African industrialization aspirations even after SSA countries have managed to 'get the prices right'. The constraints relate, first, to market imperfections, externalities and scale economies that do not allow the market system to provide correct price signals and hence call for government intervention. Second is the need for African industry to receive a degree of protection, which should be time-bound and closely related to objective performance criteria, as assistance over a learning period. This is particularly important given the very low base of human capital and technological development from which African private enterprises generally start. Third is the need to create and strengthen collaborative arrangements and mechanisms that would enable African public and private sectors to work together achieve the common goal of rapidly enhancing social welfare.

The traditions of subcontracting, networking and engaging in linkages of various kinds between producers and consumers are not developed in Africa as they are in Asia. This is one area where useful lessons can be drawn from Asia. In particular, as many countries are opening up the policy making process to permit the participation of the private sector and other actors, the Asian experience in this area would be useful. The longer tradition of involving the business sector and other actors in the policy process in many Asian countries can provide relevant lessons for Africa.

References

AfDB. 1996. *African Development Report 1996*. Abidjan: African Development Bank

Biggs, T. et al. 1995. *Technological Capabilities and Learning in African Enterprises*. World Bank Technical Paper No. 288, African Technical Department Series. Washington, D.C.

Elbadawi, I.A. 1996. Market and Government in the Process of Structural Adjustment and Economic Development in Sub-Saharan Africa. International Conference on the World Economy in Transition, Hitotsubashi University, Tokyo, 8–10 February.

Evenson, R.E. and L.E. Westphal. 1994. *Technological Change and Technology Strategy*. UNU/INTECH Working Paper No. 12.

Harrold, P., et al (1996), *Practical Lessons for Africa from East Asia in Industrial and Trade Policies*, World Bank Discussion Papers, Africa Technical Department Series. Washington, D.C.

Lall, S., G.B. Navaretti, S. Teitel and G. Wignaraja (1994), *Technology and Enterprise Development*. London: Macmillan.

Lall, S. and S. Wangwe. 1997. 'Industrial Policy and Industrialization in Sub-Saharan Africa'. Paper presented at AERC Biannual Research Workshop, Nairobi, Kenya, 25 May.

Lamusse, R. 1995. 'Exporting Africa: Country studies – Mauritius'. In S.M. Wangwe, ed., *Exporting Africa: Technology, Trade and Industrialization in Sub-Saharan Africa*. UNU/INTECH. Studies in New Technology and Development. London: Routledge.

Ndlela, P. and P. Robinson. 1995. 'Exporting Africa: Country studies – Zimbabwe'. In S.M. Wangwe, ed., *Exporting Africa: Technology, Trade and Industrialization in Sub-Saharan Africa*. UNU/INTECH. Studies in New Technology and Development, London: Routledge.

Lipumba, H.H.I. 1994. *Africa Beyond Adjustment*. Washington, D.C.: Overseas Development Council.

OECD. 1992. *Technology and the Economy: The Key Relationships*. Paris: Organization for Economic Cooperation and Development.

Rodrik, D. 1992. 'Coordination failures and government policy: A model with applications to East Asia and Eastern Europe'. *Journal of International Economics*, 40: 1–22.

Rodrik, D. 1996. 'Conceptual issues in the design of trade policy for industrialization'. *World Development*, vol. 20(3): 309–20.

Stiglitz, J.E. 1996. 'Some lessons from the East Asian Miracle'. *The World Bank Research Observer*, vol. 11 (2): 151–77.

UNCTAD. 1993. *Trade Development Report*. New York and Geneva: United Nations.

UNCTAD. 1995. *Trade Development Report*. New York and Geneva: United Nations.

UNCTAD. 1996a. *Trade Development Report*. New York and Geneva: United Nations.

UNCTAD. 1996b. *The TRIPS Agreement and Developing Countries*. New York and Geneva: United Nations.

UNCTAD. 1996c. *World Investment Report*. New York and Geneva: United Nations.

UNIDO. 1996. *Industrial Development: Global Report 1996*. Oxford: Oxford University Press.

Wangwe, S.M., ed. 1995. *Exporting Africa: Technology, Trade and Industrialization in Sub-Saharan Africa*. UNU/INTECH. Studies in New Technology and Development. London: Routledge.

Winrock. 1991. *African Development: Lessons from Asia*. Arlington, Virginia: Winrock International.

World Bank. 1989. *Sub-Saharan Africa: From Crisis to Sustainable Growth*. Washington, D.C.: The World Bank.

World Bank. 1993. *East Asian Miracle: Economic Growth and Public Policy*. New York and Oxford: Oxford University Press.

World Bank. 1994. *Adjustment in Africa: Reforms Results and the Road Ahead*. New York: Oxford University Press.

World Bank. 1997. *World Development Indicators*. Oxford: Oxford University Press.

World Bank. 1997. *World Development Indicators 1997*. Oxford: Oxford University Press.

World Bank. 1995. *A Continent in Transition: Sub-Saharan Africa in the Mid-1990s*. Washington, D.C.: The World Bank.

World Bank. 1996. *Global Economic Prospects and the Developing Countries 1996*. Washington, D.C.: The World Bank.

Chapter 8

Trade, Industry and Technology Policies in Northeast Asia

Ha-Joon Chang

The area of trade, industry and technology policies has been the most controversial aspect of the so-called 'East Asian miracle', especially the Northeast Asian experience, by which we mean Japan, South Korea (henceforth Korea) and Taiwan. In the various versions of the trade policy debate during the 1970s and 1980s (e.g., import substitution vs. export promotion, inward vs. outward trade orientation, free vs. managed trade), the experiences of Korea and Taiwan (if not Japan) were first used as proofs of the superiority of, variously, laissez faire, open or pro-export trade regimes, only to be identified later as examples of a strategically-open (or strategically-closed, depending on your emphasis) and highly interventionist trade regime (Helleiner, 1990, is the best summary of these debates).

Since the early 1980s, various debates on industrial policy have raged, earlier around the Japanese case and later involving Korea and Taiwan as well. The debates involved heated exchanges on the nature of industrial policy in Northeast Asia and its impacts on economic performance (Johnson, 1984, best summarizes the early phase of this debate; Chang, 1994, Chapter 3, reviews the more recent literature). The debate on technology policy in Northeast Asia has been less mired in 'unproductive' controversies than those on trade and industrial policies have been, but is still far from settled (Nelson, 1993, contains useful articles on Northeast Asian technology policy).

This chapter reviews the experiences of the Northeast Asian countries in these policy areas, and highlights some policy issues that have been neglected or misunderstood. Inevitably, due to space limits, what we present here will be a rather schematic picture, one that cannot adequately address the recent policy changes, especially in the case of Korea.[1] After making some comments on the contrast between Northeast Asia and Southeast Asia, we review the Northeast

[1] Contrary to the popular conception, which believes that Korea's current economic crisis shows the limitations of the kind of interventionist industrial, trade and technology policies that I talk about in this chapter, I argue that it was actually the weakening of such policies, combined with ill-designed financial deregulation, during the 1990s (but especially since 1993, when the then new government of Mr. Kim Young Sam took power) that created the country's current crisis. See Chang (1998).

Asian experience in the areas of trade policy, industrial policy and technology policy, and then discuss the replicability of the Northeast Asian model, highlighting the question of institutional capabilities and the changes in the world trading system.

On the Contrast between Northeast Asia and Southeast Asia

One important theme in the most recent phase of the debate that is of particular concern in terms of both its thematic emphasis on institutions and the way in which 'regions' are delineated) is the contrast between Northeast Asia (henceforth NEA) and Southeast Asia (henceforth SEA: Malaysia, Indonesia and Thailand).

The crux of this theme, which was most explicitly brought out by the so-called 'East Asian Miracle Report' (World Bank, 1993), is that regardless of whether the 'selective industrial policy' of the Northeast Asian variety has been successful,[2] it is not applicable to other contexts, especially places like many sub-Saharan African countries, because it takes a government with very high administrative capabilities to make such policy work. Accordingly, the Southeast Asian countries, which have allegedly conducted much less interventionist industrial policies in line with their lower capabilities, are then presented as more 'realistic' models for other 'less capable' developing countries. I will deal with the issue of institutional capability more explicitly later in the chapter, but a few remarks on the alleged contrast between NEA and SEA may be in order at this point.

First, while it is true that the SEA countries have been, on the whole, less interventionist than the NEA countries, it is not possible to say that the SEA countries have been less interventionist on all accounts (Jomo et al., 1997). For example, in SEA there were sharp distinctions in trade policies between the domestic market-oriented industries, which were often much more heavily protected than their equivalents in NEA, and the export industries, which were under much 'freer' trade regimes than their NEA equivalents.

Second, there are signs that as they lose competitiveness in resource-related industries and labour-intensive assembly operations, the SEA countries have been feeling the need to 'upgrade' their industrial structure through more activist industrial policies, but have found it difficult to do so in the absence of NEA-style trade, industrial and technology policies (see the articles in the special symposium on Southeast Asia in *Journal of International Development*, 1995, vol. 7, no. 5). The fact that these countries are relying very heavily on (mostly illegal) immigrant workers at relatively early stages of development—Malaysia, with an 8-million-person

---

[2] The 'Miracle Report' believes that it did not, but many studies have pointed out the flaws in the Bank study's methodology and its use of evidence. For example, see the articles in the special symposium in *World Development*, 1994, vol. 22, no. 4 (especially the ones by Amsden, Kwon and Lall), Fishlow et al. (1994), and Chang (1995a, Appendix).

official workforce, is estimated to have 2–3 million such workers—is an indication that their upgrading efforts have not been very successful.

Third, it should not be forgotten that over the long run, the Northeast Asian countries have performed much better than the Southeast Asian countries. Although the exact result will depend on which periods and which countries are compared, per capita incomes in the NEA countries have grown something like 2 per cent per annum faster than those of the SEA countries. Accumulated over 30 years or so, the difference is significant (Table 8.1 gives some idea about the dimension of this). To paraphrase George Orwell, some 'miracles' are more miraculous than others!

Table 8.1 Relative economic performance: Northeast Asia vs Southeast Asia (income ranking among the sample Asian countries in parentheses)

	1961 per capita GNP (current $)	1993 per capita GNP (current $)	1961 relative to Korea	1993 relative to Korea
Indonesia	49 (8)	740 (7)	0.60	0.10
Korea	82 (7)	7,660 (3)	1.00	1.00
Thailand	88 (6)	2,110 (5)	1.07	0.27
China	117 (5)	490 (8)	1.43	0.06
Taiwan	122 (4)	10,600 (2)	1.49	1.38
Philippines	200 (3)	850 (6)	2.43	0.11
Malaysia	215[a] (2)	3,140 (4)	2.62	0.41
Japan	402 (1)	31,490 (1)	4.90	4.11
USA	2,308	24,740	28.14	3.23

Sources: All figures for 1961 are from Kindleberger (1965: Table 1.1) except the one for Korea, which is from the Korean national account statistics. All figures for 1993 are from World Bank (1995: Appendix Table 1) except the figure for Taiwan, which is from CIA (1994).

All of this suggests that despite the distraction created by the somewhat misleading dichotomy between NEA and SEA, the NEA model still remains the most important challenge to the orthodoxy. Needless to say, it should also be noted that there are important differences among the NEA countries themselves in a number of ways. These include:

- State–business relationship (a much more aloof relationship in Taiwan than in Japan or Korea).
- Corporate governance ('managerial capitalism' of Japan, family-owned large business groups in Korea, large state–owned enterprise sector coexisting with a vigorous small and medium-scale enterprise sector in Taiwan).
- Financial institutions (state ownership of banks absent in Japan and dominant in the other two).
- State ownership of manufacturing industries (very important in Taiwan, important in Korea, relatively unimportant in Japan).

- R&D spending pattern (the dominance of publicly-funded R&D in Taiwan due to the absence of large private sector firms).
- Macroeconomic policy stance (much more aversion to inflation in Taiwan for historical reasons).

There are enough similarities among these countries, however, especially between Japan and Korea, to warrant a talk of the NEA 'model', especially in the areas of trade, industrial and technology policies. Bearing these points in mind, let us discuss the trade, industrial and technology policies of the NEA countries.

Trade Policy

In the early days of international fascination with the East Asian 'miracle', say, during the 1970s and the early 1980s, the export successes of the NEA countries were often touted as living proof of the validity of the doctrine of the Heckscher–Ohlin–Samuelson model of comparative advantage (henceforth the HOS model). It was argued that thanks to their free trade policies, these countries had been able to specialize in labour-intensive products in which they had comparative advantages, and thus to reap the 'gains from trade'. These countries, it was said, therefore provided a conclusive refutation of the (in my view somewhat misleadingly characterized) 'import substitution industrialization' policies prevalent in other developing countries at that time (classic examples include Ranis and Fei, 1975; Balassa, 1982).

When subsequent research showed that the trade regimes of these countries were full of tariff protections and quantitative restrictions and therefore could not be described as 'free trade' regimes, some orthodox trade economists invented the notion of so-called 'virtual free trade' to save the core policy conclusions of the HOS model (Little, 1982; Lal, 1983; World Bank, 1987). It was argued that the anti-export biases of import substitution policies in the NEA countries were cancelled out by export subsidies, thus resulting in a 'neutral' incentive regime that 'simulated' the free trade outcome.

There are a number of serious problems with this argument, which we do not have time to go into (for a more detailed criticism, see Chang, 1993; also see Yusuf and Peters, 1985; Wade, 1990), but there are two main issues. The first is the assertion that the incentive structure of the trade regime of protection-cum-export-promotion is the same as that under a free trade is not true, and therefore that it is not possible to say that the former 'simulates' the latter.[3] Second, the

---

[3] The point is that it is the variance in the rates of protection across industries that matters rather than the average rate of protection. Following the logic of the 'virtual free trade' argument, we would recommend to Londoners moving to New York that they bring the same clothes they wear in London, because New York has 'virtually mild weather', because its average temperature is similar to that in London, which has genuinely mild weather.

argument ultimately relies on the HOS model, which had already been rejected in the earlier round of the debate.

The fact that these neoclassical renditions of the NEA trade policy are flawed, however, does not mean that the HOS model on which they are based is completely useless. Within its limited confine, the HOS model is hard to criticize, and, as we shall see later, can serve as an important tool in the design of trade policy. The problem is that when it comes to understanding the relationship between trade policy and development, the HOS model has very little to say, as it will be argued in the following.

Late Development, Infant Industry and Exports: Beyond the Conventional Version

If we reject the HOS framework, how should we understand the relationship among trade,.trade policy and development? I propose that the framework of 'late development', which includes the infant industry argument, is the superior alternative (Gerschenkron, 1966, is the classic work; Freeman, 1989, gives the most succinct summary of the framework; also see Fransman, 1986, and Dosi et al., 1989). But don't we all know, it may be asked, that infant industry promotion did not work in so many developing countries? My answer to this question is that infant industry promotion failed in many developing countries not because of the flaws in the basic logic of the infant industry argument, but mainly because of the failure of those countries to come up with a viable export strategy that should be an integral part of a successful infant industry programme (also see Section 8.4). Let me elaborate on this statement.

Industrial development in a backward country requires importing technologies from more advanced countries and adapting them to the local needs *and* capabilities, unless the country is willing to re-invent the wheel, so to speak. And this is the process by which all countries after the first industrial nation, that is, Britain, industrialized—a process known as 'catching up'. As it is widely accepted, when the backward country is above a certain threshold in terms of 'social capability' (Abramovitz, 1986), it has the opportunity to grow faster than the leader countries, as it can draw on the knowledge stock they have accumulated.

However, being a follower (or a latecomer) also has its drawbacks, which seem frequently insuperable, as testified to by the absence of widespread 'convergence' (e.g., see Pritchett, 1997). The trouble is that when a backward country tries to move into a new industry, it finds that its firms have to compete with the already well-established firms from developed countries with vastly superior technologies, managerial skills, financial abilities and even intangible assets (such as brand name loyalty). In the face of such competition, it is necessary for the poor country to protect the new, or 'infant', industry from international competition before its national firms can attain internationally competitive levels of productivity. The success of the NEA countries in effectively promoting the infant industries is too well known to document in any detail (Amsden, 1989; Wade, 1990; Chang, 1993; more on this later), but at this point it is worth noting that this is how most other now-developed countries developed too—including the United States, which was the most protected economy in the world in the late nineteenth and early twentieth centuries (see Table 8.2).

Table 8.2 Tariff rates for selected developed countries in their early stages of development (the rates are for manufactured goods except for Japan, which are for all goods)

	1820	1875	1913	1925
Austria	n.a.	15–20	18	16
Belgium	7	9–10	9	15
France	n.a.	12–15	20	21
Italy	n.a.	8–10	18	22
Japan	n.a.	4a	20	13
Sweden	n.a.	3–5	20	16
United Kingdom	50	0	n.a.	5
United States	40	40–50	25	37

Notes: a. Before 1899, Japan was made to keep low tariff rates through a series of 'unequal treaties' with the European and North American countries.
Source: World Bank (1991: 97, Box Table 5.2).

What was missing in the infant industry programmes in many developing countries was the export side of the story. The continued development of infant industries requires the ability to maintain the level of export earnings that is necessary in order to acquire new technologies (mainly in the form of buying the machinery that embodies such technology but also of paying for technical licenses and technical consultancies).[4] Without a stable supply of foreign exchange and hence of new technologies, a developing country that has no independent R&D capability is likely to end up reproducing the obsolete technologies that it imported in the past—the most extreme case being North Korea. In other words, export success is a vital element in successful infant industry promotion, rather than some antithesis of it as depicted in the conventional criticisms of the infant industry doctrine. Given these considerations, the importance of export in a late-developing context cannot be over-emphasized.

At this point, it is important to remember that unlike the conventional wisdom, the importance of export success does *not* mean that the country should adopt a 'free trade' policy. As the experience of NEA shows, achieving export

[4] Needless to say, there are sources other than exporting for foreign exchange, such as foreign aid and foreign direct investments. However, experience tells us that except for a small number of exceptionally placed countries, neither of these will be sufficient in the long run. Even for countries like Korea and Taiwan, whose strategic importance in the early Cold War brought them some of the highest per capita US aid in the world during the 1950s, foreign aid dried up quite quickly in the 1960s with changes in US economic and political priorities. In most countries, FDI accounts for less than 5 per cent of total investments anyway, but the NEA countries have all been below average in this respect (discussed in further detail below).

growth in the earlier stage of development can be greatly helped by government intervention.

For one thing, a continued export success requires the emergence of enough new industries so that the introduction of new, cheaper competitor countries does not compromise the country's foreign exchange earning capability. In theory, of course, these new industries could emerge through the market process, but the fact that a lot of developing countries, despite their great 'potential' to benefit from the catch-up process, remain stuck in a limited range of low-productivity activities testifies to the unlikelihood of such possibility in reality. Hence the importance of infant industry promotion for export success, which establishes a two-way interaction loop between the two. The NEA governments have promoted successive generations of infant industries both through trade protection and through other measures, some of which we will discuss in the next section of the chapter.

In addition, informational and financial help from the government can be crucial in helping the firms to export. Producers from developing countries usually lack the information and financial capabilities needed to enter export markets. Again, in theory, there could emerge private sector organizations (e.g., producer cooperatives, consulting firms, specialized banks) to provide these inputs, but this is unlikely, given that the lack of informational and financial capabilities in exporting firms to a large extent reflects the absence of such capabilities in the society at large. In order to help the exporting firms, therefore, the NEA governments provided export subsidies in forms such as subsidized loans for exporters, tariff rebates on export inputs, or generous 'wastage allowances' to the exporters using domestically scarce imported inputs (so that they could sell some of the 'wastes' in the domestic market at a premium). The NEA governments also provided information on foreign markets, usually through the government trading agency (such as JETRO in Japan and KOTRA in Korea) but sometimes through the diplomatic service. There were also efforts to promote the development of private sector organizations that could perform some of such functions (such as exporters' associations, various industry associations or the so-called general trading companies).

Especially in the early stage of development, the government can also help exporters by ensuring that there is adequate quality control for exported goods. This is because few exporting firms in a developing country possess well-recognized brand names, and consequently products are associated with country name, rather than the producers themselves. Therefore, a developing country firm producing substandard products will cause an 'externality' in the sense that it tarnishes not just its own reputation, but the reputation of all the producers from its country. Given such consideration, the NEA governments have waged campaigns to promote awareness among exporters of the importance of quality control, and have sometimes made quality control exercises mandatory among certain exporters.

Infant Industry and Comparative Advantage

So is there any place for the doctrine of comparative advantage in our story? I think there is. As the supporters of the doctrine point out, by protecting infant industries where it does not have comparative advantage, a developing country forgoes the gains from specialization and reduces its current income. Thus, the principle of comparative advantage helps us figure out how much sacrifice a country is making in order to develop certain new industries, and therefore helps us avoid infant industry promotions of excessive magnitude and duration.

The difficulty is that in translating this into policy action, there is a lot of room for disputes as to what exactly is 'excessive'. While the 'price' a country is paying for the protection of an infant industry may be relatively (but only relatively) clearly predicted using the HOS theory, the 'return' from such protection (i.e., higher productivity in the future) cannot be predicted by the theory. So, for example, when Korea was moving into industries like steel, shipbuilding and automobiles, many international lenders, including the World Bank and a consortium of European steelmakers, thought that the government supports proposed for these industries were nowhere near justifiable, because they were pessimistic about the returns from the proposed investment projects—a projection that was badly disproved later by the enormous success of many of these industries.

The upshot is that the HOS theory is useful in giving us some idea about the costs of protection, but it is hardly useful in letting us predict the 'returns' from the protection. This is because the principle of comparative advantage is a static framework, which tells us how much we can gain by specialization, given our current factor endowments, but not very much about what we have to do in order to improve our position over time, even as some leading neoclassical trade economists admit (Krueger, 1980). It can help us to know what sacrifices we are making *now* by protecting certain industries, but it does not help us predict what good (or bad) will come out of it *in the long run*. The whole point about infant industry protection is not to ignore the principle of comparative advantage altogether, but to *deliberately* violate it, knowing that this will reduce the country's current income, because some sacrifice in current income *is* necessary to develop new industries that can put the country on a higher growth trajectory in the medium to long run.

Infant Industries and Technological Capabilities

Now, the comparative advantage consideration is not the only reason why a poor country should not, and indeed cannot, support any infant industry it wants. Another consideration is related to the importance of 'technological capability' in industrial development (Fransman and King, 1984; Fransman, 1986; Abramovitz, 1986). This is an issue that we will come back to later, but let us discuss how it relates to the story of infant industry promotion.

Technology, unlike what is assumed in standard economics, can never be fully 'codified' (to borrow Hayek's terminology) in formal instructions. Therefore, making an imported technology work requires the ability on the part of the user to 'fill in the gaps' that are not covered by the formal instructions. This ability is what is called 'technological capability'. Poor countries, partly because of their lack of skilled workers but also because of their very inexperience in such industries, lack the capabilities to start up technologically demanding industries and run them well. And such technological capabilities can be accumulated only through a process of 'learning' over time.

Therefore, a poor country needs to start with technologically less demanding industries, which are usually labour-intensive but can also include some relatively capital-intensive industries like cement and fertilizer (where the capital equipments embody a particularly large portion of technology and are not too difficult to run), and *gradually* move into technologically more demanding industries. And this is exactly how the NEA countries developed their infant industries.

Let us emphasize, however, that, by saying 'gradually', we are *not* denying that the transition from simple industries to sophisticated industries can happen rather quickly, as in the case of countries like Korea, which moved from, say, producing cheap garments and plywood to being one of the world's leading producers of semiconductors, ships and automobiles within less than a single generation. However, this *does* mean that there are certain steps a poor country has to go through—a country cannot suddenly jump from, say, processing shrimps to biotechnology overnight—and the infant industry programmes should be designed accordingly.

Summary

So, to summarize, the secret of NEA trade policy is in its simultaneous and coordinated pursuit of infant industry protection and export promotion (sometimes one and the same industry was subject to both at the same time). These two policies are, contrary to the conventional wisdom, *not* mutually exclusive. They depend on each other. A successful infant industry programme needs continued export success if it is to be sustained by a continued inflow of advanced technologies. In turn, a continued export success needs successful infant industry programmes that can sustain the continued upgrading of export industries, as well as other state interventions in areas of finance, market information and product quality control. In designing a successful infant industry programme, the principle of comparative advantage can help, as it can give the policy makers some sense of what price their economy is paying by protecting a certain industry. However, the usefulness of the principle of comparative advantage stops just about there, as it does not tell us much about how the economy can maximize its 'returns' from such protection. Last but not least, in designing a successful infant industry programme, it is necessary to select the 'target' industries from among the ones that are within the reach of the country's present level of technological capability.

Industrial Policy

If it were only trade protection and some export support policy that were necessary for a successful infant industry promotion, there may have been many more 'miracles' other than the East Asian ones after all, as most developing countries have engaged in some form of trade protection for infant industries. Therefore, in order to understand what made the NEA countries particularly successful, we need to look beyond trade policy and dig further into how their industrial policy was conducted.

Managing the 'Rents': Discipline and State Autonomy

Providing trade protection and various forms of subsidies to the firms in infant industries amounts to creating 'rents' for them. Such rents provide *both* the incentives for the firms to move into the industries *and* the resources they can invest in improving their productivities (investments in physical capital, human capital and other sources of productivity growth), and therefore are central to the story of industrial upgrading in late-development contexts (for a more detailed exposition, see Chang, 1993).

Except for some extreme pro-market economists, there has been rather widespread acceptance that there are justifications for the state to 'distort' market signals and create rents to promote industrial development in developing countries. First of all, there are many standard 'market failure' arguments, such as public goods and externalities, that justify some kind of state intervention, although there are still debates about the exact methods of intervention. Second, there is the well-known argument for investment coordination across industries with demand complementarity (the so-called 'big push' argument; see Rosentein-Rodan, 1943, and Scitovsky, 1954). Third, we have the infant industry argument, which does not really fit within the standard 'market failure' framework but, as we discussed in the previous section, has been central to the industrial upgrading efforts of all late-developing countries.

As is by now well known, the NEA governments were engaged in all three types of intervention. Their governments played central roles in the provision of physical infrastructure, education, and R&D, which can be justified according the standard 'market failure' arguments (more on education and R&D below). They were also engaged in 'big push' efforts, with impressive records—as exemplified by the cases of Japan during the immediate postwar years and Korea during its heavy and chemical industrialization programme during the 1970s (see Okazaki, 1996, on Japan, and Chang, 1993, on Korea). The success of the NEA countries in nurturing infant industries in general is also well known, and we have already talked about it in some length in the preceding section.

Now, given that many other governments were ostensibly using similar arguments in order to justify their interventions, why have the NEA governments been more successful than others in their industrial policy? Or in other words, if there are enough *theoretical* justifications for selective industrial policy, why do some countries do it better than others *in practice*? In order to explain the difference, the recent literature has emphasized the *political economy* of policy 'implementation'.

The political economy arguments hold that the exceptional autonomy of the NEA governments enabled them to prevent the process of deliberate creation and management of rents from degenerating into a 'clientelistic' redistribution binge (Toye, 1987; Amsden, 1985, 1989; Wade, 1990; Chang, 1993). The logic behind this argument is the following. When the rents have been created by state intervention, rather than, say, superior technology as in the case of Schumpeterian 'entrepreneurial profit' (Schumpeter, 1961) (or for that matter the Marxian 'surplus profit', which is a precursor to the Schumpeterian notion; see Marx, 1981: 373–4), the disciplinary power of the market is weakened and therefore the state needs to supply that discipline.

Against this background, it has been frequently argued that a typical developing country state, being a 'soft' state, has the incentive and the political pressure to use these rents as the resources to buy up political supports rather than as the tool for a 'rational' infant industry programme, and that therefore only 'hard' states like those in NEA can create and manage rents with a substantial degree of rationality. More recently, it has been further emphasized that the business–state relationship in the NEA states is distinguished from those found in other countries in that it is 'embedded' in social relationships (the term is due to Evans, 1995). This embeddedness, it is argued, gives government agencies easier access to the information that is necessary for intelligent intervention (e.g., Evans, 1995, Akyuz et al., 1990).

As someone who has been a part of this literature, I have no fundamental problem with this argument. However, having a 'hard state', even of the 'embedded' kind, won't be of much use, if the disciplinary mechanism is poorly designed. State autonomy cannot fully substitute for good policy design. Then we must ask whether there really were so few differences between the industrial policy in NEA and those in other developing countries that we can confidently say that it all boils down to the question of state autonomy. In the following, I want to explore two areas of industrial policy where I think there existed some important differences between NEA and many other developing countries—namely, the policy regarding scale economy and the competition policy.

Dealing with Scale Economy: Entry Regulation, Consumption Control and Export Promotion

Many industries that have driven modern industrial development are subject to significant scale economy, without which it becomes difficult to achieve international competitiveness. However, the late-developing countries normally have small domestic markets due to low income, a fact that is often exacerbated by small population size, and this puts a serious limit on their firms' ability to exploit scale economy. The problem is sometimes exacerbated by the well-known tendency for consumers to want 'excessive' product variety (regarding products like passenger cars). Moreover, at the earlier stages of development, many of the products from these industries fall into the 'luxury' category, and allowing a rapid expansion of domestic demand for them may hurt capital accumulation, as they are basically consumed by the investing classes. The dilemma is that while the control of luxury consumption may be necessary in the earlier stages of development to promote capital accumulation (as it was done in the NEA countries), such control restricts the domestic market size for many industries even further (on the issue of luxury consumption control, see Chang, 1997a).

All these mean that infant industry programmes in the late-developing countries will have to operate under severe constraints on the ability of domestic firms to exploit scale economy. Faced with this problem, many late-developing country governments have imposed controls on entry and capacity expansion in the industries concerned, and the NEA countries have not been exceptions in this regard. Their governments have managed extensive regimes to regulate entry and capacity in many industries with scale economy. The problem, however, is that even with such regulations, many domestic markets are still too small to fully realize scale economy. Given this, even when technological learning occurs in the infant industries with the expected speed (which may not be the case), it is very difficult for them to achieve internationally competitive levels of productivity, as they cannot operate above the minimum efficient scale.

The only way to relax the constraint on productivity set by domestic market size in a late-developing country is for the firms in the infant industries to start exporting as soon as possible. However, the problem is that the governments had to impose trade protection in these industries in the first place because their firms could not compete with the already established producers from the advanced countries, whether at home or in the export markets. So the developing countries trying to promote infant industries with scale economy are faced with a dilemma—they cannot become competitive in the world market without exporting, but they cannot export before they become competitive.

The typical response by a developing country government to this dilemma has been to give up the export option but keep the protection on the grounds that the firms cannot compete with imports—a policy stance that was exacerbated by the ill-guided pursuit of 'technological self-sufficiency' and undue export pessimism. The problem with this solution is that this way the firms never 'grow up' and are likely to remain 'infants' for life. Needless to say, this has happened in certain industries in NEA. The Taiwanese passenger car industry, where few of the ten or so producers assemble more than several thousand cars per year, is perhaps the best such example. However, the Northeast Asian policy makers often took different courses of action. Occasionally, they would 'gamble' by encouraging, or even forcing, domestic firms to build world-class capacities from the beginning, giving them both the opportunity to realize scale economy and the extra push to export for fear of being stuck with an enormous excess capacity. The best examples here may be the Korean steel and shipbuilding industries in the 1970s, each of which started, due to state policy, with capacities that were many multiples of the domestic demands. More typically, however, the countries initially accepted sub-optimal production scales, but used a range of policy measures intended to bring forward the day when these firms could export and thus produce at more than the minimum efficient scale. We can talk about two groups of policies here.

The first group of policies, as we discussed earlier was aimed at directly helping exporters (e.g., marketing information service, export subsidies, export financing facilities). The second group of policies focused on raising the productivity of specific industries and included:

- Organizing mergers and negotiated market segmentation in industries with too many producers with suboptimal scale so that maximum (politically) possible scale of production could be achieved.
- Subsidizing capital equipment upgrading through 'rationalization' or 'modernization' programmes aimed at specific industries.
- Subsidizing R&D or training in specific industries directly or indirectly through the operation of public research or training institutes.
- Spreading information on best practice technologies in particular industries by public or semi-public agencies.

Our discussion shows that on the whole, the NEA countries have struck a difficult balance between scale economy considerations and the need to protect infant industries, through a mixture of export promotion policies, sector specific productivity policies and luxury consumption control—a policy dimension that was frequently missing in industrial policies of other developing countries. The need to achieve scale economy compels the government to control entry into many industries, but frequently even this is not sufficient to bring the domestic firms' productivities to the world level. The logical solution to this problem will be either to abandon the industry altogether, as the mainstream economists argue, or to make the firms start exporting as soon as possible, as the East Asian policy makers did. As the NEA experience shows, export success by infant industries cannot be achieved under a 'free trade' policy, but requires policy interventions that will raise productivity of the firms as well as policies to help them export.

Managing Competition: Allocative Efficiency vs. Productivity

If the scale economy problem is taken seriously by the policy makers of a late-developing country with small domestic markets, and accordingly the number of producers in each industry is restricted, an obvious problem that follows is the emergence of oligopolistic, or even monopolistic, markets. While there is no one-to-one relationship between the number of firms in an industry and the intensity of competition among them (in fact East Asia provides many examples of fierce competition in oligopolistic markets), oligopolistic markets pose a greater challenge to the designers of competition policy. And in countries with serious infant industry programmes, the resulting absence of competition from imports makes competition policy even more challenging.

In the mainstream discourse on competition policy, the allocative inefficiencies created by the market power of by oligopolistic firms are regarded as the most serious problem facing the competition policy makers, and thus a vigorous Anglo-Saxon (or rather American) style anti-trust policy is recommended to deal with the problem. Thus, even many neo-liberal supporters of far-reaching deregulation would concede that anti-trust policy is one area where government activism is legitimate and necessary (for further discussions on deregulation, see Chang, 1997b). Restricting the abuse of power by the dominant firms through anti-trust action has certainly been an issue in NEA, but the focus of competition policy in NEA was clearly elsewhere.

Many commentators have interpreted the 'lax' attitude of the NEA governments towards anti-trust policy as a product of corrupt collusion between the state and big business. While it would be foolish to argue that there has been no such collusion, it is important to recognize that such a policy stance largely emanated from the particular view of competition held by the NEA policy makers, rather than from corrupt political deals. Broadly, the view of competition held by the NEA policy makers is close to what I call the 'Continental' (mainly Germanic) view of competition (Chang, 1994). This view is represented by some politically unlikely bedfellows such as Marx, Schumpeter and Hayek, and starkly contrasts with the view of competition in neoclassical economics (for some classic works on this contrast, see Hayek, 1949, and McNulty, 1968; Chang, 1994, provides a more updated discussion on this issue).

As Hayek (1949) very aptly put it, neoclassical economics views competition as a 'state of affairs', in the perfect version of which no individual agent has market power (that is, the power to change the overall market outcome through unilateral action). Thus, according to this view, the existence of any market power implies lack of competition and thus inefficiency in resource allocation, and therefore requires the introduction of regulation and other measures by the government that 'simulate' the competitive outcome.

In contrast, the Continental tradition sees competition as a 'process' through which new information about technology and organization is constantly discovered and transmitted. In this view, market power is something that is constantly created and destroyed as new information is discovered. Moreover, according to this view, the social costs from the allocative inefficiencies created by the market power possessed by the firms expanding due to their new innovative ideas are often, if not necessarily, more than cancelled out by the benefits from productivity growth that such new ideas produce, or even by the gains from scale economy that can, by definition, only be reaped by firms with market power. Unlike the Anglo-Saxon tradition in which competition is seen as always beneficial, the Continental view admits that there can be such thing as 'excessive', 'wasteful' or 'destructive' competition.[5] Such a view of competition gave the following characteristics to the NEA competition policy.

First of all, as we pointed out earlier, the NEA governments have deliberately created oligopolistic, or even monopolistic, market structures, in order to exploit scale economy, if that was regarded as important in the particular industry concerned. Mainstream economists frequently ignore this point, but many estimates of the allocative inefficiencies arising from 'non-competitive' markets suggest only modest figures (1–2 per cent of GNP usually), whereas the cost increase that follows from sub-optimal scale of production is known to be very significant. In other words, scale economy consideration was given clear priority over market power consideration in the competition policy regimes of NEA.

Second, the NEA governments have been deeply concerned with 'excessive', 'wasteful' or 'destructive' competition. The idea of 'excessive' competition has often been dismissed as a notion based on irrational fears of competition by ignorant bureaucrats, but it makes perfect sense once we acknowledge the importance of dedicated physical and human assets in modern industries (or 'specific assets' in the words of Williamson, 1985). Given the existence of specific assets, any failed project that follows an 'excessive' entry (compared with what is warranted by the demand condition) leads to a 'waste' of resources in the sense that the specific assets used in the failed project may not be transferred to other activities without significant losses in their economic values (for a more systematic discussion of this issue, see Chang, 1994). As a result, the NEA governments have tried to coordinate investments ex ante in order to prevent excess entry, but when excessive entry materialized for whatever reason (e.g., erroneous projection, sudden changes in world market conditions, some firms defying the government plan, etc.), it organized and encouraged (explicit and implicit) cartels, negotiated capacity scrapping arrangements, or even forced merger and market-sharing programmes, to reduce the 'wastes' from excessive competition (see Chang, 1994, for further details).

Third, the NEA governments have willingly suspended anti-trust actions and allowed collusive behaviours by firms, when it was thought that a suspension of competition was necessary to raise the productivity in the industry concerned (for a more detailed theoretical account, see Chang, 1994).[6] For example, the Japanese state has frequently allowed, and often took initiatives in organizing, various types of cartels—to weather recession, to coordinate capacity expansion, to encourage

---

[5] More recently, some authors writing in the neoclassical tradition have also noted this phenomenon (for example, see Pindyck, 1991), but it is not possible to say that it is yet part of the theoretical 'core' of neoclassical economics.

[6] The German anti-trust legislation, which has served as a model for the Japanese legislation since the latter's 1953 amendment away from the Anglo-Saxon elements imposed earlier by the American Occupation Authority, also provides many similar 'escape' clauses to cartel and other collusive behaviours, especially by small firms, when they are related to aims like 'rationalization', 'specialization' (i.e., negotiated market segmentation), joint export activities and structural adjustments (Shin, 1994: 343–55).

joint R&D, to allow collusion in export markets, to promote technological upgrading by small firms, to phase out declining industries, to name just a few (Magaziner and Hout, 1980; Dore, 1986). In Korea, there existed no anti-trust legislation until 1981, and even after that collusive behaviours were explicitly allowed in 'promising industries', which needed to 'increase R&D, improve quality, and attain efficient production scale', and in 'declining industries' which needed to 'scale down their capacities' (the quotes are from the sixth Five-Year Plan [1987–1991] document; for further details, see Chang, 1993). In Taiwan, where many large firms were public enterprises, anti-trust policy has had a different dynamic, but the Taiwanese state did not hesitate to promote mergers if they were deemed necessary for exploiting scale economy (see Wade, 1990). Similar policies in other countries frequently ossified the cartels and resulted in industrial stagnation, but the NEA countries avoided such danger to a large extent, because the suspension of competition was regarded as a temporary measure to achieve relatively well-specified goals deemed necessary for productivity enhancement (although it can sometimes last quite long), and thus did not result in a general suspension of competition and was terminated when the stated objective was achieved.

The 'lax' anti-trust policy regimes in the NEA countries have traditionally been interpreted as examples of corrupt collusion between big business and the government. In this section, however, we have tried to point out that the view of competition that underlies these regimes is very different from the one behind the neoclassical recommendations for tough anti-trust policy, and therefore describing these regimes as simply serving the interest of dominant firms can be misleading. The view of competition that lay behind the NEA competition policy regimes was concerned less with the exercise of market power by the dominant firms, and more with the importance of scale economy to productivity, the need to avoid 'wasteful' competition, and the need to shelter firms from competition for a limited period in order to allow them time for technology upgrading and/or smooth phase-out. These concerns meant that competition policies in the NEA countries were designed in such a way that they were probably very 'inefficient' from the neoclassical point of view, but were quite effective in raising productivity and facilitating industrial restructuring. Once we cast away the conventional wisdom about competition policy, which equates competition policy with anti-trust policy, the NEA experience provides us with a lot of hitherto unrecognized lessons on how to build an effective competition policy regime.

Summary

Noting the importance of state autonomy in determining the success or otherwise of an activist industrial policy in a developing country, we asked whether there are no important differences between the successful and the unsuccessful countries in terms of industrial policy design. We argued that there are at least two important areas in which industrial policy in NEA differed from that in other developing countries: policies regarding scale economy and competition policy. We argued that the failure to achieve scale economy has been a major source of low productivity in many infant industries in other developing countries, while the problem was overcome in NEA through the governments' deliberate policies to promote export by these industries and raise their productivities more directly. Competition policy in NEA also differed from that practiced in many other developing countries, where it was more or less equated with anti-trust policy. Competition policy in NEA went much beyond anti-trust policy, and was mainly concerned with achieving scale economy, avoiding 'wasteful' competition and implementing precisely-targeted suspension of competition for limited durations in order to promote productivity growth.

Technology Policy: Regulating Inflows and Developing Capabilities

The importance of technology in determining the competitiveness of a country needs no further mention. And the recent developments in the literature on economics of technology have shown that, in contrast to the early neoclassical treatment of technological progress as an 'autonomous' process, policy actions matter greatly for technological progress (see essays in Dosi et al., 1988; Lundvall, 1992; Nelson, 1993; Fagerberg, 1996). However, there is one important note of caution here.

When we hear the word 'technology policy', we tend to think about investing money into grandiose R&D projects. But this is only a part of technology policy. Even for an advanced country, the accumulation of technological capabilities on the shop floor through production experience and on-the-job training plays a very important role, and for a poor country, its importance is much greater than R&D. For a poor country, special emphasis should be put on the adaptation (or assimilation) and incremental improvements of imported technology (especially at the shop floor level), rather than on original R&D. We should remember that until as late as the early 1960s, one-third of what was called 'R&D' in Japan, which was by then already a highly industrialized country, was essentially activities to adapt imported technology.

Now, the problem is that even assimilating imported technology is not easy and takes time. This means that the firms in a developing country starting new activities using newly imported technologies will have to be supported by the government before they can master the technologies and become competitive enough to deal with foreign firms at home and abroad. So in this sense, a well designed infant industry promotion programme is the most important technology policy in a developing country. A successful technology policy requires much more than an infant industry programme, however, and the NEA experience offers a lot of food for thought in this regard.

Unlike some other developing countries that pursued the elusive goal of 'technological self-sufficiency' only to end up reproducing obsolete technologies imported earlier, the NEA countries have always been keen to gain access to the most advanced technologies that they could handle. However, they have also been acutely aware of the need to regulate technology inflows in line with broad industrial strategy and with specific sectoral needs. So, for example, the government allowed or restricted the imports of a certain machine, depending on whether the industry producing that machine was being promoted as a strategic industry, whether the sector using the machine could meet the urgent need for technological upgrading only with imported machines, whether the machine did not embody overly obsolete technology, and so on.

Technology licensing was also carefully controlled in order to ensure that the right kind of technologies were imported on the right terms. Investments by transnational corporations (TNCs) were also heavily regulated, in the belief that accepting a 'package' of finance, technologies, managerial skills and other capabilities offered by TNCs was not as good for long-term industrial development as encouraging the national firms to construct their own packages, using their own managerial skills—obviously with some necessary outsourcing (on this point, see Helleiner, 1989; Lall, 1993; Chudnovsky, 1993).

The NEA policies towards TNCs deserve a special mention, given the current enthusiasm about globalization and the role of TNCs in it (for criticisms of the globalization thesis, see Hirst and Thompson, 1996; Wade, 1996; Chang, 1997c). The restrictive attitude of Japan towards TNCs is well known, but it should be noted that Taiwan and especially Korea have also maintained rather restrictive regulatory regimes vis-à-vis TNCs, with the result that the contribution of TNCs to investments in these countries was clearly below the international average (see Table 8.3; also see Chang, 1998, for further details). Thus, there were restrictions on the areas where TNCs could enter. And even when entry was allowed, joint ventures, preferably under local majority ownership, were encouraged over wholly-owned subsidiaries in an attempt to facilitate the transfer of core technologies and managerial skills.[7]

---

[7] For example, in the case of Korea during the 1970s, even in sectors where FDI was allowed, foreign ownership above 50 per cent was prohibited except where FDI was deemed to be of 'strategic' importance, which covered only about 13 per cent of all the manufacturing industries (EPB, 1981). These included industries where access to proprietary technology was considered essential for further development of the industry, and industries where the capital requirement and/or the risks involved in the investment were very large. The ownership ceiling was also relaxed if: (a) the investments were made in the free trade zones; (b) the investments were made by overseas Koreans; or (c) the investments would 'diversify' the origins of FDI into the country—namely, investments from countries other than the USA and Japan, which had previously dominated the Korean FDI scene (for further details, see EPB, 1981). As a result of such policies, as of the mid 1980s, only 5 per cent of TNC subsidiaries in Korea were wholly-owned, whereas the corresponding figures were 50 per cent for Mexico and 60 per cent for Brazil, countries that are often believed to have had much more 'anti-foreign' policy orientations than that of Korea (Evans, 1987). Due to the scarcity of large private sector domestic firms, the Taiwanese government had to be more flexible on the ownership question (33.5 per cent of the TNC subsidiaries were wholly-owned as of 1985; Schive, 1993), but Taiwan's reliance on FDI on the whole was for most of the time below the developing country average (see Table 8.3).

Table 8.3 The ratio of FDI inflows to gross domestic capital formation for various regions and selected countries (annual averages, in %)

	1971–75	1976–80	1981–85	1986–90	1991–93
All Countries	n.a.	n.a.	2.3	4.1	3.8
Developed	n.a.	n.a.	2.2	4.6	3.3
European Union	n.a.	n.a.	2.6	5.9	5.6
Austria	1.8	0.9	1.3	1.5	1.5
France	1.8	1.9	2.0	4.1	7.7
Germany	2.1	0.8	1.2	2.0	1.4
Netherlands	6.1	4.5	6.1	13.3	10.6
Sweden	0.6	0.5	1.6	4.0	9.5
UK	7.3	8.4	5.6	14.6	10.0
Switzerland	n.a.	n.a.	2.3	5.3	3.1
USA	0.9	2.0	2.9	6.9	3.2
Canada	3.6	1.7	1.0	5.8	4.3
Japan	0.1	0.1	0.1	0.0	0.1
Developing	n.a.	n.a.	3.3	3.2	5.7
Africa	n.a.	n.a.	2.3	3.5	4.6
Latin America	n.a.	n.a.	4.1	4.2	6.5
Argentina	0.1	2.1	5.0	11.1	37.6
Brazil	4.2	3.9	4.3	1.7	1.5
Chile	-7.3	4.2	6.7	20.6	8.5
Mexico	3.5	3.6	5.0	7.5	6.8
Asia	n.a.	n.a.	3.1	2.8	5.5
Bangladesh	n.a.	n.a.	0.0	0.1	0.2
China	0.0	0.1	0.9	2.1	10.4
Hong Kong	3.9	4.2	6.9	12.9	3.7
India	0.3	0.1	0.1	0.3	0.4
Indonesia	4.6	2.4	0.9	2.1	4.5
Korea	1.9	0.4	0.5	1.2	0.6
Malaysia	15.2	11.9	10.8	11.7	24.6
Pakistan	0.5	0.9	1.3	2.3	3.4
Philippines	1.0	0.9	0.8	6.7	4.6
Singapore	15.0	16.6	17.4	35.0	37.4
Taiwan	1.4	1.2	1.5	3.7	2.6
Thailand	3.0	1.5	3.0	6.5	4.7
Turkey	n.a.	n.a.	0.8	2.1	3.2
Eastern Europe	n.a.	n.a.	0.0	0.1	12.2

Source: UNCTAD (1993: Annex Table 3) for the 1971–1980 data; UNCTAD (1995: Annex Table 5) for the rest.

Policy measures other than the ones concerning entry and ownership were also used to control the activities of TNCs. For example, the technology that was to be brought in by the investing TNCs was carefully screened, and checked whether it was not overly obsolete or whether the royalties charged on the local subsidiaries, if any, were not excessive. For another example, in order to maximize technology spillover, investors that were more willing to transfer technologies were preferred, unless they were technologically too far behind, and local content requirements were quite strictly imposed.[8]

Policies that regulate the inflows of technology in NEA would not have been so effective without the policies to enhance the capabilities of the domestic firms to absorb the imported technologies. At one level, there have been those policies that do not involve industry-specific or skill-specific measures, such as government funding and management of general education and basic R&D. However, for the purpose of more specialized capability enhancement, the NEA governments also used a range of measures (with certain country variations). These included: (a) deliberate channelling of funding into science and engineering departments in universities, especially those related to 'strategic' industries (e.g., electronics engineering);[9] (b) public provision of specialized industrial training; (c) introduction of compulsory training schemes for large industrial firms (which are generally in those industries that were promoted as 'strategic industries'); and (d) introduction of a (German-style) skill certification system that encourages workers to acquire specialized skills whose possession cannot be easily verified.[10]

Even before a late-developing country reaches the world's technological frontier, there comes a stage when it must engage in some R&D, because as the

---

[8] One thing to note, however, is that the targets for localization were set realistically, so that they would not seriously hurt export competitiveness of the country. It was in fact the case that in some industries they were less strictly applied to the products destined for the export markets than those destined for the domestic market.

[9] Korea provides a particularly interesting example here. The country had a strong Confucian tradition, which encourages bright people to become government officials or lawyers rather than engineers or scientists. In the early 1960s, the vast majority of Korean university students were studying humanities, and there was an acute lack of engineers and scientists (the ratio between the two groups was 1 to 0.43 in 1962). The Korean government went out of its way during the following two decades to remedy this situation by putting tough restrictions on the expansion of humanities departments and encouraging the expansion of science and engineering departments (by 1980, the ratio turned 1 to 1.07). Although this policy was somewhat reversed in the 1980s (by 1989, it was down to 1 to 0.72 again), such policy succeeded in radically altering the supply pattern of university graduates (for further details, see You and Chang, 1993).

[10] Needless to say, many studies have emphasized the role of certain 'unique' labour institutions, such as lifetime employment and company unionism, in the East Asian countries in encouraging specialized skill formation. However, except for pointing out that the evolution of some of these institutions has actually been heavily influenced by their governments, the issue need not detain us here. On the role of labour institutions in skill formation in East Asia, see Dore (1987) for Japan and You and Chang (1993) for Korea.

imported technologies become more and more sophisticated, even mere absorption of a technology may require some independent R&D activities. And as is well known, when they reached this stage, the NEA countries all engaged in highly organized efforts to promote R&D (for the country details, see the country chapters in Nelson, 1993). What is notable is that even when they started spending significant amounts on R&D, the efforts were concentrated in 'applied' areas, often very precisely targeted by the government at particular end products with clear marketability, rather than in 'basic' areas. Although this practice attracted criticisms from certain quarters for not leading to 'genuinely creative' R&D, others argue that this 'market-oriented' nature is a strength, rather than a weakness, of the East Asian R&D policies, as it means that R&D spending gets directly and quickly translated into advantages in product markets.

The importance of enhancing the level of technology to promote economic development cannot be overemphasized. However, the kinds of things that a late-developing country has to do in order to increase its technological level are rather different from what the countries on the frontier have to do. The latecomers need to put more efforts into monitoring and controlling what kinds of technologies are imported by whom on what terms, and into enhancing skills on the shop floor. Technology policies in the NEA countries neither aimed at achieving some imaginary technological self-sufficiency nor blindly followed market forces. They were based on a clear programme of gradual technological upgrading, which involved a careful control over the paths of technological evolution through controls over technology inflow and over the formation of the capabilities to absorb imported technologies.

The Question of Replicability

The question of replicability has been a persistent theme in the debate on East Asia. In the early days of the debate, when the mainstream economists recommended the supposedly 'free market, free trade' model of East Asia to other developing countries, many dependency theorists pointed out that there were too many historical, geopolitical and perhaps cultural idiosyncrasies that made the model generally inapplicable. These theorists did not question the mainstream characterization of the model itself (on the curious similarities between the early mainstream and the dependency interpretations of the East Asian experience, see Chang, 1990; for criticisms of the 'East Asian idiosyncrasy' arguments, see Chang, 1995b). Later, when it became clear that the East Asian countries did *not* succeed on the basis of 'free market, free trade' policy, the mainstream economists adopted the dependency-style argument that they had so disparaged earlier and argued that the Northeast Asian model cannot be replicated, because its success was based on certain unique 'initial conditions' that other countries do not possess (World Bank, 1993, is the best example).

Two currently popular arguments in this vein are particularly relevant for the issues that we are looking at in this paper. The first argument emphasizes the importance of competent bureaucracy (and more broadly high human capital endowment) in successfully administering the kinds of 'sophisticated' trade, industrial and technology policies that the NEA countries have used. The second emphasizes the difficulty of using the NEA style 'non-market-conforming' policy instruments in the new international trading regime that came out of the Uruguay Round. How plausible are these arguments?

Bureaucracy, Human Capital and Institutions

It is true that a competent bureaucracy is needed for the effective administration of NEA-style trade, industrial and technology policies. However, it is not clear whether administering such policies necessarily requires more bureaucratic capabilities than other supposedly 'easier' policies such as macroeconomic policy. This would certainly depend on the extent of intervention and the sophistication of policy tools used—for example, the deft management of exchange rate or interest rate may be more difficult than running a few industry-specific technology upgrading schemes.

Moreover, the conventional argument mistakenly believes that the well-developed bureaucracy of the East Asian countries was a part of their historically determined 'initial conditions'. These countries' bureaucratic capabilities were, however, things that were 'built' through conscious organizational reform and personnel training, rather than things that were historically inherited (Cheng et al., 1996).[11] It is instructive to note in this context that Korea was sending its bureaucrats for training to the Philippines and Pakistan until the late 1960s.

More broadly, the common argument that the NEA countries started with an exceptionally favourable 'initial condition' regarding human capital endowment should also be qualified. From Table 8.4, we can see that Korea, and Taiwan to a lesser extent, may have had good human capital endowments around 1961 (given their income levels), but that this was not necessarily the case even 10–15 years before that. For example, the literacy ratio in Korea in 1945 (22 per cent) was lower than that of Zaire (now Democratic Republic of Congo) (31 per cent) and Ghana (27 per cent) in 1961, and not much better than what Kenya (20 per cent) or Tanzania (17 per cent) had that year. So the high human capital base of the NEA countries was not really an 'initial' condition, in the sense that it was something that was deliberately built over a relatively short period of time.

At a more general level, we should realize that the emphasis on bureaucratic capability and other human capital endowments as binding 'initial conditions' stems from the mistaken mainstream belief that while markets, as 'natural' phenomena, can be transplanted anywhere, 'institutions' (including the modern

[11] The World Bank, which put great emphasis on the impossibility of replicating NEA-style industrial policy in other countries on the grounds of their weak bureaucratic capabilities in the so-called 'East Asian Miracle' Report (World Bank, 1993) has recently come around to accepting, although somewhat reluctantly, the importance of capability 'building' (World Bank, 1997).

bureaucracy), as things constructed by humans, cannot. However, recent developments in institutional economics have persuasively demonstrated, first, that the conventional market–institutions dichotomy is misleading, as markets themselves are institutions, and second that markets are *not* natural phenomena that develop spontaneously, and like other institutions, have to be deliberately constructed.

Table 8.4 How 'initial' were the initial conditions? – Human capital endowments circa 1945 and circa 1960

	1961 per capita income (current $)	Literacy ratio circa 1960 (%)	Literacy ratio circa 1945 (%)
Indonesia	49	47	n.a.
Tanzania	50	17	n.a.
Pakistan	54	16	18 (1951)
Zaire	67	31	n.a.
India	69	24	19 (1951)
Kenya	72	20	n.a.
Korea	82	71	22 (1945)
Thailand	88	68	53 (1947)
Sri Lanka	122	61	n.a.
Taiwan	122	54	50 (1950)
Brazil	129	61	43 (1940)
Ecuador	143	67	n.a.
Ghana	179	27	n.a.
Philippines	200	72	52 (1948)
Malaysia*	215	23	38 (1947)
Mexico	279	62	57 (1950)
Chile	377	84	77 (1940)
Argentina	378	91	86 (1947)
South Africa	396	57	n.a.
Singapore	n.a.	n.a.	46 (1947)
Japan	402	98	n.a.
USA	2,308	98	n.a.

Sources:
1. Income figures for 1961 are from Kindleberger (1965: Table 1.1), except the one for Korea, which is from the Korean *National Account Statistics*.
2. Literacy figures for circa 1945 are from UNESCO, *Statistical Yearbook*, UN, *Statistical Yearbook*, various years; McGinn et al. (1980: Table 17). Literacy figures for circa 1960 are from World Bank, *World Development Report*, various years.

Indeed, if the market-based Anglo-Saxon model is so easy to replicate, why is it the case that most of the 'success stories' were based on some 'deviant' model, be it the Japanese, the German, the Swedish or the Italian? The difficulty that many developing and transitional economies are currently experiencing with their neoliberal reforms is just another testimony to how hard it actually is to replicate the predominantly market-based Anglo-Saxon model. In fact, the establishment of market institutions required a lot of government intervention even in the Anglo-Saxon economies themselves in their early days (see Polanyi, 1957, on Britain, and Kozul-Wright, 1995, for the USA).

The problem with the argument that the NEA model cannot be replicated elsewhere because of these countries' unique institutions is that it sees the institution as something immutable and thus underestimates the possibility of institutional adaptation and innovation. Like technologies, institutions, and indeed 'culture' as a set of informal institutions, are subject to adaptation and innovation, and therefore should not be seen as something immutable that a country inherits from its past. Especially from the point of view of the late-developing countries, adapting imported institutions to local conditions is as important as adapting imported technologies—if not more so.

The early Japanese experience is particularly instructive here. When the Japanese first embarked on the industrialization process, they had to import a lot of foreign institutions, picking what they thought were the most suitable among the 'best practice' ones. So if we look at Japan in the early Meiji period, we find an institutional patchwork. The commercial law system was from France, their criminal law from Germany, the central bank from Belgium, the navy from Britain, the army from Germany, the education system first from America but later from Germany, and so on (for more details, see Westney, 1987). It was only over time that they modified these imported institutions so that they could work together better and came up with some 'innovations' (e.g., lifetime employment) that made the system 'unique'. While the difficulty of making imported institutions work should not be underestimated, the scope for institutional innovation and adaptation should not be underestimated either.

The New World Trading Environment

How serious a constraint is the post Uruguay Round (henceforth post-UR) world trading regime on the adoption of the policy tools that the NEA countries used? Three points can be made here (for further details, see Akyuz et al., 1998).

First, the conventional wisdom overestimates the policy freedom that existed in the pre Uruguay Round (henceforth pre-UR) GATT system. Even in its old version, the GATT system imposed many restrictions on the kinds of policy tools that could be used. And, as a result, 'the [North] East Asian countries had to exercise a considerable amount of policy ingenuity and administrative and diplomatic skills to maintain some of their policies [even the pre-UR GATT system]' (Akyuz et al., 1998).

Second, while the post-UR GATT system does put more constraints on the scope of policy tools that can be used, the constraints are not as widespread and binding as they are usually argued to be. For example, the 'balance of payments' clause, which, instead of the 'infant industry' clause, had been the main justification for quantitative restrictions imposed by the developing countries (including NEA) for infant industry promotion before the UR, still exists under this new regime. Also, subsidies may be more strictly sanctioned against in the post-UR system, but there are still 'non-actionable' subsidies,[12] and even when it comes to 'actionable' subsidies, they do not have to be abolished immediately (eight years are allowed for their phasing-out). In the case of the poorest countries, some subsidies prohibited for richer countries, notably export subsidies, are still allowed. Last, the agreements on so-called TRIPS (trade-related intellectual property rights) and TRIMs (trade-related investment measures) may constrain the scope for things like local content requirements or compulsory technology licensing, but exceptions can be made,[13] and a wide range of other measures that can serve similar purposes are not affected by these agreements (e.g., export performance requirements on TNC subsidiaries).[14]

Finally, it needs emphasizing that the new trading regime does not prohibit many policy measures that have been fruitfully used in NEA. Strategic credit rationing by the state, the use of domestic taxes to encourage or discourage particular activities, dissemination of information on export markets and best practice technology by state agencies, direct and indirect controls on competition in strategic industries, and policies to encourage the formation of specialized skills are only some of the more important examples.

Some Final Thoughts on the Question of Replicability

I would agree with those who express scepticism about the replicability of the NEA model, if all they mean is that countries with different political and institutional conditions may have to find different solutions to similar economic problems. However, there is more to their argument that, wittingly or unwittingly, makes it an intellectually dishonest and biased discourse.

Those who express scepticism about the replicability of the NEA model often have a very exaggerated view about the superiority of the initial conditions of the East Asian countries, and have an unduly pessimistic view about other countries changing their conditions. So they believe that the initial institutional and political (and even cultural) conditions are almost perfectly binding and therefore that countries that do not start with the NEA sort of initial conditions cannot emulate them. One curious thing, however, is that most of the same people seem to be oblivious to the fact that the initial conditions may be equally binding when countries try to imitate the Anglo-Saxon model.

The same sort of exaggeration, narrowness of views and prejudices prevail in the discussions of the effect of the post-UR trading regime. The pre-UR trading regimes are described as somehow very permissive, the constraints imposed by the

---

[12] They mean subsidies against which retaliatory action cannot be taken, and include subsidies to promote basic research, agriculture and regional development.

[13] Local content requirements can be invoked under the balance of payments clause. Compulsory licensing is also allowed under special circumstances.

[14] It also needs pointing out that how strictly these agreements will be, and can be, implemented, especially in the case of TRIPS, still needs to be seen.

post-UR regime are highly exaggerated and the role of policy ingenuity in getting around these constraints is completely ignored.

The intention here is not to deny the importance of questioning the replicability of the NEA model. This is essential if other countries want to learn real lessons from NEA. However, more balanced and open-minded discussions that are more grounded in a hard look at the facts will be necessary if the question of replicability of the NEA model is not to degenerate into a convenient avenue for some to denounce the relevance of a socioeconomic model that they do not like.

Concluding Remarks

The debates surrounding the trade, industrial and technology policies in NEA during the last two decades or so have slowly but now very perceptibly shifted the 'average' opinion towards the 'heterodoxy'—the 1997 report from the World Bank is a good example (World Bank, 1997). However, there are still areas where the intellectual limitations of the conventional economic theory are impeding our understanding of what the Northeast Asian model is really about and the lessons we can draw from it for other countries. This means that despite the incredible number of books and articles written on this area, there are still many important issues that are poorly understood (e.g., failure to recognize the 'non-orthodox' view of competition behind NEA competition policy), or worse, hardly discussed (e.g., control of luxury consumption comes to mind). Trying to cover a vast area of trade, industry and technology in a single chapter, I could not include all the points that deserve further attention nor could I adequately cover all the issues that I did raise. However, I hope the chapter has raised enough doubts in people's minds that they realize that the research in the area is far from complete.

References

Abramovitz, M. 1986, 'Catching up, forging ahead, and falling behind'. *Journal of Economic History*, vol. 46, no. 2: 385–406.

Akyuz, Y., H-J. Chang and R. Kozul-Wright. 1998. 'New perspectives on East Asian development', *Journal of Development Studies*.

Amsden. A. 1985. 'The state and Taiwan's economic development'. In P. Evans, D. Rueschemeyer and T. Skocpol, eds., *Bringing the State Back In*. Cambridge: Cambridge University Press.

Amsden, A. 1989. *Asia's Next Giant*. New York: Oxford University Press.

Balassa, B. 1982. 'Development strategies and economic performance'. In B. Balassa et al., *Development Strategies in Semi-Industrial Economies*. Baltimore: The Johns Hopkins University Press.

CIA (Central Intelligence Agency). 1994. *World Fact Book*. Washington, D.C.: Central Intelligence Agency.

Chang, H-J. 1990. 'Interpreting the Korean experience – Heaven or hell?' Research Paper Series, No. 42, Faculty of Economics and Politics, University of Cambridge.

Chang, H-J. 1993. 'The political economy of industrial policy in Korea'. *Cambridge Journal of Economics*, vol. 17, no. 2: 131–157.

Chang, H-J. 1994. *The Political Economy of Industrial Policy*. London and Basingstoke: Macmillan.

Chang, H-J. 1995a. 'Explaining "flexible rigidities" in East Asia'. In T. Killick, ed., *The Flexible Economy*. London: Routledge.

Chang, H-J. 1995b. 'Return to Europe? – Is there anything that Eastern Europe can learn from East Asia?'. In H-J. Chang and P. Nolan, eds., *The Transformation of the Communist Economies – Against the Mainstream*. London and Basingstoke: Macmillan.

Chang, H-J. 1997a. 'Luxury consumption control and industrialisation in East Asia'. Mimeo. Background paper prepared for *Trade and Development Report 1997*. Geneva: UNCTAD.

Chang, H-J. 1997b. 'The economics and politics of regulation'. *Cambridge Journal of Economics*, vol. 21, no. 6: 703–28.

Chang, H-J. 1997c. 'Transnational corporations and strategic industrial policy'. In R. Kozul-Wright and B. Rowthorn, eds., *Transnational Corporations in the World Economy*. London: Macmillan Press.

Chang, H-J. 1998. 'Globalization, transnational corporations, and economic development – Can the developing countries pursue strategic industrial policy in a globalizing world economy?' In D. Baker, G. Epstein and R. Pollin, eds., *Globalization and Progressive Economic Policy: What are the Real Constraints and Opportunities?* New York: Cambridge University Press.

Cheng, T., S. Haggard and D. Kang. 1996. 'Institutions, economic policy, and growth in the Republic of Korea and Taiwan Province of China'. Paper prepared for the UNCTAD Conference on 'East Asian Development: Lessons for a New Global Environment', Kuala Lumpur, Malaysia, 29 February – 1 March 1996.

Chudnovsky, D., ed. 1993. *Transnational Corporations and Industrialisation*. London: Routledge.

Dore, R. 1986. *Flexible Rigidities: Industrial Policy and Structural Adjustment in the Japanese Economy 1970–80*, London: The Athlone Press.

Dore, R. 1987. *Taking Japan Seriously – A Confucian Perspective on Leading Economic Issues*. London, The Athlone Press.

Dosi, G., C. Freeman, R. Nelson, G. Silverberg and L. Soete, eds. 1988. *Technical Change and Economic Theory*. London: Pinter Publishers.

Dosi, G., L. Tyson and J. Zysman. 1989. 'Trade, technologies and development: A framework for discussing Japan'. In C. Johnson, L. Tyson and J. Zysman, eds., *Politics and Productivity*. New York: Harper Business.

EPB (Economic Planning Board). 1981. *Oegoogin Tooja Baeksuh* (White Paper on Foreign Investment). Seoul, Korea: The Government of Korea (in Korean).

Evans, P. 1987. 'Class, state, and dependence in East Asia: Lessons for Latin Americanists'. In F. Deyo, ed., *The Political Economy of the New Asian Industrialism*. Ithaca: Cornell University Press.

Evans, P. 1995. *Embedded Autonomy – States and Industrial Transformation*. Princeton: Princeton University Press.

Fargerberg, J. 1996. 'Technology and competitiveness'. *Oxford Review of Economic Policy*, vol. 12, no. 3: 39–51.

Fishlow, A., C. Gwin, S. Haggard, D. Rodrik. and R. Wade. 1994. *Miracle or Design? Lessons from the East Asian Experience.* Washington, D.C: Overseas Development Council.

Fransman, M. 1986. *Technology and Development.* London: Frank Cass.

Fransman, M. and K. King, eds. 1984. *Technological Capability in the Third World.* London: Macmillan.

Freeman, C. 1989. 'New technology and catching-up'. *European Journal of Development Research*, vol. 1, no. 1: 3–11.

Gerschenkron, A. 1966. *Economic Backwardness in Historical Perspective.* Cambridge, Massachusetts: Belknap Press.

Hayek, F. 1949. 'The meaning of competition'. In F. Hayek, *Individualism and Economic Order.* London: Routledge & Kegan Paul.

Helleiner, G. 1989. 'Transnational corporations and direct foreign investment'. In H. Chenery and T.N. Srinivasan, eds., *Handbook of Development Economics*, vol. 2. Amsterdam: Elsevier Science Publishers, B.V.

Helleiner, G. 1990. 'Trade strategy in medium-term adjustment'. *World Development*, vol. 18, no. 6: 879–97.

Hirst, P. and G. Thompson. 1996. *Globalisation in Question.* Cambridge: Polity Press.

Johnson, C. 1982. *MITI and the Japanese Miracle.* Stanford: Stanford University Press.

Johnson, C., ed. 1984. *The Industrial Policy Debate.* San Francisco: Institute for Contemporary Studies.

Jomo, K.S., et al. 1997. *Southeast Asia's Misunderstood Miracle–Industrial Policy and Economic Development in Thailand, Malaysia, and Indonesia.* Boulder and Oxford: Westview Press.

Journal of International Development. 1995, vol. 7, no. 5.

Kindleberger, C. 1965. *Economic Development*, 2nd edition. New York: McGraw-Hill.

Kozul-Wright, R. 1995. 'The myth of Anglo-Saxon capitalism: Reconstructing the history of the American state'. In H-J. Chang and B. Rowthorn, eds., *Role of the State in Economic Change.* Oxford: Oxford University Press.

Krueger, A. 1980. 'Trade policy as an input to development'. *American Economic Review*, vol. 70, no. 3: 288–92.

Lal, D. 1983. *The Poverty of Development Economics.* London: The Institute of Economic Affairs.

Lall, S., ed. 1993. *Transnational Corporations and Economic Development.* London: Routledge.

Little, I. 1982. *Economic Development.* New York: Basic Books.

Lundvall, B-Å., ed. 1992. *National Systems of Innovation: Towards a Theory of Innovation and Interactive Learning.* London: Pinter Publishers.

Magaziner, I. and T. Hout. 1980. *Japanese Industrial Policy.* London: Policy Studies Institute.

Marx, K. 1981. *Capital*, vol. 3. Harmondsworth: Penguin Books.

McGinn, N., R. Snodgrass, Y-B. Kim, S-B. Kim and Q-Y. Kim. 1980. *Education and Economic Development in Korea.* Cambridge, Massachusetts: Harvard University Press.

McNulty, P. 1968, 'Economic theory and the meaning of competition'. *Quarterly Journal of Economics*, vol. 82, no. 4: 639–56.

Nelson, R., ed. 1993. *National Innovation Systems.* New York: Oxford University Press.

Okazaki, T. 1996. 'The government–firm relationship in post-war Japanese economic recovery: Resolving the co-ordination failure by co-ordination in industrial rationalisation'. In M. Aoki, H-K. Kim and M. Okuno-Fujiwara, eds., *The Role of Government in East Asian Economic Development–Comparative Institutional Analysis.* Oxford: Oxford University Press.

Pindyck, R. 1991. 'Irreversibility, uncertainty, and investment'. *Journal of Economic Literature*, vol. 29, no. 3: 1110–48.
Pritchett, L. 1997. 'Divergence, big time'. *Journal of Economic Perspectives*, vol. 11, no. 3: 3–17.
Polanyi, K. 1957. *The Great Transformation*. Boston: Beacon Press.
Ranis, G. and J. Fei. 1975. 'A model of growth and employment in the open dualistic economy: The cases of Korea and Taiwan'. In F. Stewart, ed., *Employment, Income Distribution and Development*. London: Frank Cass.
Rosenstein-Rodan, P. 1943. 'Problems of industrialisation of Eastern and South-Eastern Europe'. *Economic Journal*, vol. 53, no. 3: 202–11.
Schive, C. 1993. 'Foreign investment and technology transfer in Taiwan'. In S. Lall, ed., *Transnational Corporations and Economic Development*. London: Routledge.
Scitovsky, T. 1954. 'Two concepts of external economies'. *Journal of Political Economy*, vol. 62, no. 2: 143–151.
Schumpeter, J. 1961. *The Theory of Economic Development*. London: Oxford University Press.
Shin, K. 1994. *An International Comparison of Competition Policy: USA, Japan, and Germany*. Seoul: Korea Development Institute (in Korean).
UNCTAD. 1993. *World Investment Report 1993*. Geneva: United Nations Conference on Trade and Development.
UNCTAD. 1995. *World Investment Report 1995*. Geneva: UNCTAD.
Wade, R. 1990. *Governing the Market*. Princeton: Princeton University Press.
Wade, R. 1996. 'Globalization and its limits: Reports on the death of the national economy are greatly exaggerated'. In S. Berger and R. Dore, eds., *National Diversity and Global Capitalism*. Ithaca and London: Cornell University Press.
Westney, E. 1987. *Imitation and Innovation: The Transfer of Western Organisational Patterns to Meiji Japan*. Cambridge: Cambridge University Press.
World Bank. 1987. *World Development Report, 1987*. New York: Oxford University Press.
World Bank. 1991. *World Development Report, 1991*. New York: Oxford University Press.
World Bank. 1993. *The East Asian Miracle*. New York: Oxford University Press.
World Bank. 1997. *World Development Report, 1997*. New York: Oxford University Press.
World Development. 1994, vol. 22, no. 4.
You, J. and H-J. Chang. 1993. 'The myth of free labour market in Korea'. *Contributions to Political Economy*, vol. 12: 29–46.
Yusuf, S. and R. Peters. 1985. 'Capital accumulation and economic growth: The Korean paradigm'. *World Bank Staff Working Papers* No. 712.

Chapter 9

Trade and the Industrial and Technological Development of ASEAN Countries

Thee Kian Wie

Although membership in the Association of Southeast Asian Nations (ASEAN) has since 1997 expanded to include all the Southeast Asian countries, except for Cambodia, this chapter focuses on the process of industrialization in the five founding member countries, Indonesia, Malaysia, the Philippines, Singapore and Thailand. This focus is warranted as the new members of ASEAN, Vietnam, Laos and Myanmar, are lagging far behind the others in economic and industrial development, even compared with the Philippines, which has been the laggard among the founding countries. It should also be borne in mind that the Malaysian federation, comprising Peninsular Malaysia, Sarawak and Sabah, was only established in 1963. Hence, when referring to Malaysia in the 1950s, we have in mind only the region commonly referred to as Peninsular Malaysia. For the sake of convenience we will refer to the five selected countries as the ASEAN countries, even though ASEAN was only established in 1967.

After a brief overview of the macroeconomic developments and trade regimes in the five ASEAN countries, the chapter sketches the rate and pattern of industrial growth and transformation and the export promotion efforts in the five countries. The following two sections deal with, respectively, the role of foreign direct investment (FDI) and that of small- and medium-scale enterprises (SMEs) in ASEAN manufacturing. The last section discusses the challenge facing the ASEAN countries in upgrading their industrial structures and technological capabilities. Meeting this challenge will be important to sustain their rapid industrial growth in the face of increasingly strong international competition, particularly after the trade liberalization following AFTA (ASEAN Free Trade Area) in 2003, APEC (Asia-Pacific Economic Cooperation) and the WTO (World Trade Organization) obligations. The concluding section summarizes the major points of the chapter and draws some policy implications.

Rapid Industrial Growth and Transformation: An Overview

During the past three decades, the ASEAN countries, with the exception of the Philippines, have achieved rates of industrial growth that have been among the highest for developing countries. As a group only the East Asian 'Tigers', particularly South Korea and Taiwan, have surpassed the industrial achievements of the ASEAN countries.

In the early 1950s economic activities in the ASEAN countries were still largely based on the primary sector, mainly agriculture, with mining also playing a significant role in Indonesia and Malaysia. During that period the ASEAN countries could be referred to as primary exporting countries, as the bulk of their exports consisted of primary commodities. Although Singapore, being based on entrepot trade and services, re-exported to its Southeast Asian neighbours manufactured products imported from the advanced industrial countries, it also re-exported to the industrial countries large amounts of imported primary commodities, which it had duly processed. Whatever manufacturing operations there were in the ASEAN countries in the 1950s consisted mainly of resource-processing activities and light consumer goods industries catering to the domestic market. Not surprisingly, manufactured exports were minuscule, if not non-existent.

The Philippines, in the early 1950s, was the first Southeast Asian country to embark on a deliberate import substituting pattern of industrialization. In the 1960s Malaysia, Singapore and Thailand followed suit. Actually, Singapore at the time already had highly developed activities to process the agricultural products it was importing from Indonesia and Malaysia. Only Indonesia, mired in a protracted dispute with the Netherlands, its former colonial ruler, about the status of West Irian (the present-day province of Papua) in the 1950s, internal political conflicts in the late 1950s and early 1960s, and then an armed conflict with the newly-established Malaysian federation and its allies (Britain, Australia and New Zealand), could not focus its efforts on economic development.

Despite the serious political problems, Indonesia's government in the early 1950s introduced an ambitious state-directed industrialization plan, the Economic Urgency Plan (EUP). The government attributed the economic backwardness of the country to the Dutch colonial government's reluctance to develop a modern manufacturing sector alongside the modern primary export activities (large-scale estates and mining). The EUP was partly based on an industrialization scheme designed by the colonial government in the early 1930s. It provided for the establishment of several large-scale, state-owned industrial plants, such as coconut flour, rubber re-milling, printing, cotton spinning, cement and caustic soda, to be financed by the newly-established State Industrial Bank (Bank Industri Negara, BIN). The new industrial plants were to be managed by state-owned enterprises (SOEs) in view of the shortage of indigenous Indonesian entrepreneurs. It was hoped that these state-owned plants could eventually be transferred to indigenous entrepreneurs or cooperatives or to government–private joint ventures (Anspach, 1969; Thee, 1996).

In addition to promoting large-scale industrialization, the Indonesian government also introduced some measures to promote small-scale, largely rural industries, notably through the Loan and Mechanization Programme. This programme contained various plans to provide direct assistance to small-scale industries, mostly located on the densely populated islands of Java and Madura (Paauw, 1963).

Despite these measures and subsequent half-hearted attempts at industrialization, however, none of Indonesia's industrialization plans could be realized because of the shortage of funds, including foreign exchange. Hence, by the mid 1960s the country's industrial landscape, consisting largely of resource-processing activities and a narrow range of light consumer goods industries, still looked very much like it had in the early 1940s before the Netherlands Indies was occupied by the Japanese army.

With relatively few benefits from primary export expansion for the population during the colonial period, it is not surprising that upon achieving political independence the ASEAN countries emphasized the need to change the structure of their economies. The leaders of the ASEAN countries strongly favoured industrialization to achieve a better balance between agriculture and manufacturing, and thereby strengthen the economic bases of their countries. Although Thailand had never been colonized, its leaders too attached great importance to industrialization, as its economic structure, largely dependent on agriculture, was similar to that of the other ASEAN countries. Moreover, because all the advanced countries had achieved higher standards of living as well as economic power through industrialization, the development of manufacturing was seen as the key to economic welfare and greater economic power.

In pursuing an import substituting pattern of industrialization, the ASEAN countries followed a path of industrialization similar to that taken earlier by the Latin American and South Asian countries. To support this import substituting pattern of industrialization, Malaysia and Singapore relied mainly on tariff protection; Indonesia, the Philippines and Thailand made extensive use of tariffs coupled with non-tariff protection (Ariff and Hill, 1985).

The relative openness of the economies of Malaysia, Singapore and Thailand, dating back to the colonial era for Malaysia and Singapore and to the British influence on Thailand's trade policy since the mid nineteenth century, made controls on foreign trade in these countries less attractive. Being open economies, the adverse effects of protection against imports on export interests would have become readily evident (Hill, 1996).

Initially import substitution did lead to high rates of industrial growth, but this growth could not be sustained after the completion of the 'easy' phase of import substitution. As a result, by the mid 1960s first Singapore and then by 1970 Malaysia, the Philippines and Thailand began to shift their industrialization strategies from import substitution to export promotion. Singapore's decisive shift to an export oriented strategy was a logical consequence of its separation from Malaysia and the subsequent loss of the expected larger domestic market. In Malaysia, the Philippines and Thailand, the shift to a more export oriented strategy was not as decisive, as import substitution policies continued to be pursued in the case of certain industries dependent on the domestic market (Ariff and Hill, 1985).

The anti-export bias of Malaysia's trade regime was less pronounced than that of its two neighbours, however, as it did not discriminate seriously against other traded goods, had relatively few non-tariff trade barriers (NTBs) and imposed a relatively low overall simple average tariff rate on manufacturing (Naya, 1988). Malaysia's initial export promotion efforts in the early 1970s also put a lot of emphasis on export processing zones (EPZs), which it operated with great success on the west coast of Peninsular Malaysia (Hill, 1995a). Although Thailand's tariff rates were higher than those of Malaysia, its import substitution policy was relatively mild (Naya, 1988). The Philippines had the longest commitment to import substituting industrialization (since the early 1950s) involving substantial protection for domestic producers of consumer goods. Thus elements of its protectionist policies continued to prevail to a larger extent than in either Malaysia or Thailand (Hill, 1995a). Consequently, the Philippines until recently found it difficult to make a decisive shift to export-oriented policies.

Among the ASEAN countries, Indonesia was pursuing the most inward-looking pattern of industrialization. This was evident in the mid 1970s, when the Indonesian government, buoyed by its vastly increased oil revenues, decided to sustain industrial growth by pushing the process of industrialization into the second stage of import substitution. This second phase involved the development of upstream industries, particularly basic, resource processing industries such as steel and aluminium, and engineering goods and its supporting industries (parts and components industries). The basic industries were to be built by the Indonesian government and funded by the vastly increased government revenues resulting from the oil booms of the 1970s.

A major factor in Indonesia's attraction to total import substituting industrialization could perhaps be attributed to what Professor Deepak Lal has referred to as the 'environment'. What Lal meant was that it was tempting for planners in developing countries with large populations and a fairly varied natural resource base, such as India and Indonesia, to push beyond primary import substitution and proceed with the secondary and tertiary phases of import substitution (Lal, 1988). With a large and rapidly expanding domestic market and a broad natural resource base, carrying out total import substitution in the early 1980s looked indeed financially feasible and desirable to Indonesia's policy makers.

It was only after the end of the oil boom in the early 1980s that the Indonesian government, after some hesitation, felt compelled to shift to a more export oriented strategy. This was imperative as non-oil exports had to be increased rapidly to offset the sharp decline in oil earnings. However, like the Philippines, Indonesia's shift to a more export oriented strategy was not as decisive as Singapore's, as import protection continued to be maintained in the case of certain industries. This was reflected in the persistence of significant inter-sector variations in the effective rates of protection enjoyed by the various industries. (Hill and Basri, 1996). As in most other countries, political opposition (by well-connected vested interests) has been the major obstacle to further trade liberalization in Indonesia. Moreover, continuing preferential treatment of certain industries, notably the ten designated state-owned strategic industries (including the high-tech aircraft industry), was being justified on the grounds of Indonesia's national interest (Hill and Basri, 1996).

By the early 1980s the economic costs of inward-looking policies and the benefits of export-led growth had become increasingly apparent. The ASEAN countries made a decisive shift to outward-looking policies, implemented through a succession of trade reforms. Malaysia, after Singapore, already had a strong outward-looking orientation as reflected by its relatively low import protection. Indonesia and the Philippines on the other hand, introduced wide-ranging and substantial trade reforms. The same applied to Thailand, also with a fairly open economy, which introduced a variety of trade reforms without many difficulties. Even the Philippines, apparently bogged down in import-substitution, introduced various trade reforms, although less extensive in scope (Hill, 1994).

During the past 15 years the ASEAN countries, except for the Philippines, have been able to sustain their rapid industrial growth, as indicated in Table 9.1. Indonesia's manufacturing sector has grown at double-digit rates, and both Malaysia's and Thailand's industrial growth has also been impressive. Singapore, being the most industrialized among the ASEAN countries, recorded a slower industrial growth than those three. The industrial performance of the Philippines, however, has been dismal until recently. It has not been able to build on its early push into industrialization in the 1950s, but instead experienced two decades of industrial stagnation. Only since the recent policy reforms introduced by President Ramos has Philippine manufacturing been growing more rapidly thanks to a greater inflow of foreign direct investment into this sector.

Table 9.1 ASEAN industrialization in comparative perspective, 1980–1995

Country	Manufacturing value added (MVA) (% millions US$)		Manufacturing average annual growth rate (%)		MVA as % of GDP		Manufacturing exports as % of total exports	
	1980	1994	1980–90	1990–95	1980	1995	1980	1993
Indonesia	10,133	41,186	12.6	11.2	13	24	2	53
Malaysia	5,054	22,387	8.9	13.2	21	33	19	65
Philippines	8,354	14,917	0.2	1.8	26	23	37	76
Singapore	3,415	18,119	6.6	8.3	29	27	50	80
Thailand	6,960	40,791	9.5	11.6	22	29	28	73

Source: World Bank (1997: Tables 4.1; 4.2; 4.6; and 4.8).

As a result of the rapid industrial growth the share of manufacturing in the gross domestic product of Indonesia, Malaysia and Thailand increased rapidly. Indonesia and Thailand, with manufacturing contributing 20–30 per cent of GDP, can be categorized as 'semi-industrial' countries according to UNIDO criteria, while Malaysia can already be classified as an 'industrial country', with manufacturing contributing more than 30 per cent of GDP.

The Philippines and Singapore, however, have been experiencing 'de-industrialization' as the share of their manufacturing sectors in GDP has declined. In the Philippines this process was caused by protracted industrial stagnation, but may soon be reversed as recent policy reforms take effect. Singapore's de-industrialization has taken place as rising land and labour costs have forced many manufacturing firms, particularly the subsidiaries of TNCs (transnational corporations), to relocate their operations overseas, notably in nearby Johore state, Malaysia, and in Batam and other adjacent islands of Riau province, Indonesia. Moreover, de-industrialization in

Singapore has taken place as the city-state, like Hong Kong, has become a post-industrial or services economy; with sophisticated services (e.g., financial services, telecommunications, tourism) contributing the largest share of GDP.

Export Promotion Efforts

The export promotion efforts of the ASEAN countries have also been successful over the past 15 years, as the bulk of their merchandise exports now consists of manufactured goods. The most striking example of a relatively successful shift to export oriented industrialization has been resource-rich Indonesia. In 1980 around 80 per cent of Indonesia's merchandise exports consisted of oil and gas (LNG), while its manufactured exports accounted for only 2 per cent of total exports. However, 15 years later the bulk of its exports consisted of manufactured exports. To a large extent this change can be attributed to the successful trade reforms introduced since the mid 1980s. To offset the bias against imports, the Indonesian government in May 1986 introduced a duty exemption and drawback scheme that enabled exporting firms (defined as firms exporting at least 65 per cent of their output) to procure inputs, whether imported or locally made, at international prices.

This opportunity is most important, as the experience of the East Asian newly industrializing economies (NIEs), particularly South Korea and Taiwan, has indicated. The establishment of what Little (1979: 14, 34) has referred to as 'almost free trade conditions for exporters' is a major factor in the rapid labour-intensive, export oriented industrialization in these countries.

Another important element of Indonesia's successful export promotion efforts was its supportive exchange rate policy, which kept the real effective exchange rate competitive. This was achieved by a managed floating rate by which the Bank of Indonesia, Indonesia's central bank, allowed the rupiah to depreciate by 4 per cent to 5 per cent on the average to offset the differential between Indonesia's higher inflation and the inflation rates of its major trading partners.

A third significant factor in the increase in Indonesia's manufactured exports has been enforced export substitution. Under this policy, exports of a number of primary products, specifically timber in the early 1980s and rattan in the late 1980s, were no longer permitted in unprocessed form. Following the ban on log exports, many wood-processing plants, particularly plywood and other wood panel plants, were set up by foreign as well as domestic investors in the timber-producing regions in Indonesia, notably on the islands of Sumatra and Kalimantan and in the other islands in Eastern Indonesia. Due to this enforced export substitution policy, Indonesia in the late 1980s became the largest plywood exporter in the world by virtue of its large (but rapidly dwindling) reserves of tropical hardwood. Similarly, after the ban on rattan exports in the late 1980s Indonesia became a significant exporter of rattan furniture.

A fourth important factor in the steady rise in Indonesia's manufactured exports has been the relocation since the late 1980s of footloose export oriented, labour-intensive industries from the East Asian NIEs, notably South Korea, Taiwan and Singapore, to the lower-wage countries in Southeast Asia, including Indonesia.

Indonesia's success in attracting foreign direct investment from the East Asian NIEs can be attributed to its successive deregulation policies, which improved the investment climate for private investors, including foreign investors. In addition, the trade reforms introduced since the mid 1980s led to a reduction in the anti-export bias of Indonesia's trade regime, making it more profitable for manufacturing firms to invest in export oriented activities (Thee, 1991). As a result, according to Bank of Indonesia estimates, the contribution of FDI firms (particularly Asian NIE firms) to Indonesia's non-oil exports, notably manufactured exports, rose from only 14 per cent in 1987 to almost 40 per cent in 1993 (Santoso Wibowo, 1995).

Resource-poor Singapore, on the other hand, was the first country to pursue a consistent export oriented industrialization strategy. And it has been the most successful in rapidly increasing its manufactured exports. For this reason Singapore has also been classified as one of the four East Asian newly industrializing economies (NIEs), along with Hong Kong, South Korea and Taiwan. Because Singapore has been extremely successful in attracting TNCs to fuel its export-oriented industrialization drive, the bulk of its manufactured output and exports have been generated by the subsidiaries of TNCs.

When Singapore's labour market grew increasingly tight by the late 1970s, the Singapore government made a determined effort to upgrade the country's industrial structure and comparative advantage, which had largely been based on light industries (garments and semiconductor assembly). The government intervened in the entry of foreign TNCs to steer them to invest in higher value added industries, (Lal, 1994). It also restructured its educational institutes to provide training in specific high-level technical skills required by the more skill- and technology-intensive industries (Lal, 1994). With a more developed and diversified industrial base, Singapore's export concentration is lower than that of its ASEAN neighbours.

Malaysia and Thailand, and even the slow-growing Philippines, have also been successful in diversifying their merchandise exports away from their earlier reliance on primary exports. In 1980 the bulk of merchandise exports from these three countries consisted of primary exports, but by 1993 manufactured exports accounted for close to 70 per cent or more of their total exports. More detailed information on the successful export diversification of the ASEAN countries is presented in Table 9.2.

The data in Table 9.2 show that in 1980 Indonesia, enjoying its second oil boom, obtained 96 per cent of its foreign exchange earnings from primary exports (predominantly oil and LNG), while manufactured exports accounted for only 3 per cent of export earnings. However, 13 years later Indonesia's manufactured exports accounted for 53 per cent of total export earnings due to the trade and other policy reforms introduced since end of the oil boom in the mid 1980s. The reduction if not elimination of price distortions as a result of the trade reforms enabled Indonesia to export those labour-intensive, low skill products in which it has a comparative advantage. As a result, the contribution of textile and garment exports to total exports rose from 1 per cent in 1980 to 17 per cent in 1993.

Nonetheless, the concentration level of Indonesia's manufactured exports is still relatively high; in 1992 not less than 48.5 per cent of its total manufactured exports consisted of only five products, plywood and veneers (21.6 per cent), woven synthetic fibre fabrics (8.4 per cent), footwear (8.0 per cent), women's outerwear (5.6 per cent), and men's outerwear (4.9 per cent) (Lall and Rao, 1995). In other words, almost half of Indonesia's manufactured exports consisted only of relatively vulnerable, low skill labour- and resource-intensive manufactured products—processed wood products, textiles and garments, and footwear. During the past few years, however, electronics exports have increased rapidly, although from a very low base.

Table 9.2 Structure of ASEAN countries' merchandise exports 1980–1993 (%)

	Merchandise (millions of $)		Fuels, minerals, metals (% of total)		Other primary exports (% of total)		Machinery & transport equipment (% of total)		Other manufactured exports (% of total)		Textile fibres, textiles & garments (% of total)	
	1980	1993	1980	1993	1980	1993	1980	1993	1980	1993	1980	1993
Indonesia	21,900	45,417	76	32	22	15	1	5	2	48	1	17
Malaysia	13,000	74,037	35	14	46	21	12	41	8	24	3	6
Philippines	5,740	17,502	21	7	42	17	2	19	35	58	7	9
Singapore	19,400	118,268	31	14	18	6	27	55	24	25	4	4
Thailand	6,510	56,459	14	2	58	26	6	28	22	45	10	15

Source: World Bank (1997: Table 4.8, pp. 158–60).

Like Indonesia, Malaysia, the Philippines and to a lesser extent Thailand, were by 1980 still highly dependent on primary exports. However, by 1993 these three countries had diversified their exports to such an extent that the bulk of their exports consisted of manufactured exports. In fact, Malaysia's industrial performance during the past quarter of a century can be rated as one of the best among the developing countries. During the period 1970–1990 its manufacturing sector grew at 10.3 per cent and during the period 1990–1993 at 13.2 per cent (Table 9.1), the best among the ASEAN countries. With manufactured exports reaching $48.1 billion in 1993 (Table 9.2), Malaysia had become the developing world's sixth largest exporter of manufactures, behind the four East Asian Tigers and China (Lall, 1996c).

Moreover, Malaysia's manufactured exports have to an increasing extent been technology based products. In fact, since the 1990s electronics and electrical products have accounted for nearly 60 per cent of Malaysia's manufactured exports. As a result, Malaysia has emerged as the world's largest exporter of semiconductors and among the largest exporters of disk drives, telecommunications apparatus, audio and video equipment, room air-conditioners, calculators, colour television sets, and various household electrical appliances (Lall, 1996b). This great reliance on electronics and electrical goods has set Malaysia apart from the large majority of newly-industrializing economies, such as India, China and Indonesia, which during their early phase of export oriented industrialization relied mainly on labour-intensive, low skill exports, such as textiles, garments and footwear. As such, Malaysia's pattern of manufactured export growth has been more similar to that of neighbouring Singapore, which during its phase of export oriented industrialization has also shifted rapidly to the export of high skill, technology based products, and then sustained its momentum by strategic interventions to promote further upgrading into high-technology products (Lall, 1996f).

Malaysia's export success has to a large extent been due to the establishment of export-processing zones (EPZs) along the west coast of Peninsular Malaysia, especially on the island of Penang. Beginning in the early 1970s a number of vertically integrated electronics TNCs, notably from the United States and Japan, set up consumer electronics assembly plants as part of the relocation of the labour-intensive elements of their operations to lower-wage countries in Southeast Asia. Under this strategy the electronics parts and components assembled in these countries were re-exported back for final-stage processing in the home countries of the principals. For this reason it is not surprising that a large part of Malaysia's and Singapore's manufactured exports consist of electronics, including consumer electronics, professional electronics equipment and to an increasing extent electronics components. At the same time, the increasingly tight labour market in Malaysia and Singapore and the subsequent erosion of their comparative advantage in labour-intensive, low skill products have reduced their textile and garment exports to only a small part of their total exports. However, like Indonesia, Malaysia's export concentration is rather high, as in 1992 its top five manufactured exports accounted for almost 42 per cent of its total manufactured exports. These were transistors and valves (22.8 per cent), telecommunication equipment and accessories (5.7 per cent), office machines and accessories (5.7 per cent), television receivers (3.4 per cent), and ships and boats (2.7 per cent) (Lall and Rao, 1995).

Criticisms have been levelled at EPZs for being export enclaves with few, if any, linkages to the domestic economies. Moreover, the manufactured exports are highly import-intensive, while the local value added is generally quite low. Despite the general validity of these criticisms, the assembly plants nevertheless provide a useful economic contribution by generating employment opportunities in countries with ample supplies of underemployed labour, as was the case in Malaysia and Singapore in the early 1970s, and by establishing a country's international reputation as an efficient export platform (Hill, 1995b). Moreover, over time EPZs can establish local linkages with the domestic economy in line with the development of the technical capabilities of local supplier firms. This has indeed been the case in Singapore, for example, in the electronics industry where the export oriented electronics TNCs since the early 1980s have established vertical linkages with local input suppliers (Lim and Pang, 1982: 586). Unlike Singapore, Malaysia has been less successful in fostering vertical linkages between the TNCs and local supplier firms. Hence, its EPZs are still export enclaves relatively isolated from the rest of the economy.

Although the structure of Malaysia's manufactured exports has become more skill-intensive, its manufacturing industries have not yet been able to achieve the design, linkage, and R&D capabilities acquired by the three East Asian Tigers (South Korea, Taiwan and Singapore). Even now, the operations of Malaysia's electronics and electrical goods industries still consist largely of assembly activities, while many of its consumer electronics and electrical goods are in the relatively mature stage of their product cycles. However, because of its favourable investment climate for FDI, electronics and electrical goods TNCs have stayed in Malaysia and upgraded their export oriented operations, using more complex, labour-saving technologies when wages rose as the country's labour market tightened (Lall, 1996c).

In recent years Thailand, too, has emerged as an increasingly important exporter of electronics products, textiles and garments, and processed food products. Industrial development in the Philippines has been sluggish during the past two decades, but it has also been able to increase its manufactured exports, although not as spectacularly as its ASEAN neighbours. As in Indonesia, the manufactured exports of the Philippines and Thailand still consist mostly of labour-intensive, relatively low skill and low technology products, notably textiles, garments and footwear. In recent years electronics exports, largely generated by the subsidiaries of electronics TNCs, have become increasingly important.

Foreign Direct Investment in ASEAN Manufacturing

Unlike Japan and South Korea and to a lesser extent Taiwan, which have tended to restrict foreign direct investment (FDI) into their economies, the ASEAN countries have in general welcomed it. As a result, FDI has played a much greater role in the economic development and industrialization of the ASEAN countries than in Japan and the two larger East Asian Tigers. This is clearly reflected in Table 9.3, which presents data on inward FDI as a percentage of gross domestic investment in the respective countries.

Table 9.3 Inward foreign direct investment as a percentage of gross domestic investment in four ASEAN countries and Japan, South Korea and Taiwan (1986–1992)

	1981–1985	1986–1990	1991	1992
Indonesia	1.0	2.0	3.7	4.1
Malaysia	10.8	10.6	23.9	-
Singapore	181.0	33.9	26.2	30.6
Thailand	3.2	5.9	5.6	-
Japan	0.1	-	0.1	0.2
South Korea	0.5	1.3	1.0	0.5
Taiwan	1.5	3.5	3.0	-

Source: Lall (1996a).

The policy stance restricting FDI in the NIEs was motivated primarily by a strong economic nationalism reflected by the strong desire to promote domestic enterprises and to build international competitiveness through the development of technological capabilities. The ASEAN countries, on the other hand, though not less nationalistic, had more modest technological ambitions and less desire to promote domestic enterprises (Lall, 1996a).

In general, the ASEAN countries to a lesser or greater degree have welcomed FDI. In fact, they have been among the top destinations of FDI since the mid 1980s. Within

ASEAN itself, Singapore, Malaysia, Indonesia and Thailand, respectively, received cumulative FDI inflows of US$31.0 billion, US$27.5 billion, US$13.4 billion and US$12.6 billion during 1984–1995 (Lall, 1997). Annual FDI inflows into the ASEAN region increased from around US$1.8 billion in 1985 to more than US$8.5 billion in 1992. After some stagnation in 1992/93, FDI surged again in 1994 and 1995 (Lall and Rao, 1995). FDI into the Philippines has gradually increased in recent years, particularly since the Philippine economy began to recover after Fidel Ramos became president, but annual FDI inflows are still below those of its ASEAN neighbours.

Despite the surge of FDI into ASEAN, the member countries during the early 1990s faced increasing competition from other rapidly growing Asian economies, notably China, which has become the top destination of FDI among Asian developing economies. In recent years, however, the rate of growth of FDI into China has slowed, even though in absolute terms FDI into China is still the largest among the developing countries. The reasons for the slower growth of FDI into China have been the abolition of some incentives for FDI in 1993 and the shift to a policy of selective promotion of FDI. On the other hand, FDI into the ASEAN countries has grown steadily, particularly in Indonesia, Malaysia and even the Philippines, (JETRO, 1997).

The data in Table 9.3 show that Singapore has been much more dependent on FDI than the other ASEAN countries. This is true even though Singapore, as one of the four East Asian NIEs (along with South Korea, Taiwan and Hong Kong), is industrially the most advanced among the ASEAN countries. Singapore's reliance on FDI is reflected by the fact that in the late 1970s, 70 per cent of its manufactured exports were generated by the subsidiaries of foreign TNCs, as compared with only 15 per cent for Korea and 20 per cent for Taiwan (Parry, 1988).

Singapore's high reliance on FDI does not mean that it was pursuing a laissez-faire policy towards FDI. On the contrary, the Singapore government targeted certain industries (and services) for promotion and used TNCs as the most appropriate tool to achieve its goals. When Singapore shifted to export oriented industrialization in the mid 1960s it actively sought to attract export oriented FDI by foreign TNCs. Similarly, as the Singapore government upgraded its industrial structure in the mid 1980s it actively intervened in foreign investment by guiding the TNCs to invest in higher value added activities (Lall, 1996a).

By contrast, Indonesia initially relied less on FDI than either Malaysia or Thailand. To a large extent the relatively low importance of FDI in Indonesia has been due to its aversion to foreign private capital investment dating back to its bitter colonial past. In fact, during its early years of independence in the 1950s Indonesia's foreign investment policy was perhaps of the greatest interest among its economic policies, as nowhere was Indonesia's determination to break with its colonial past more pronounced than in its hostile attitude and corresponding policy towards foreign investment (Lindblad, 1991). The Indonesian government prepared a foreign investment law in 1953, which was only enacted by parliament in 1958, the worsening climate against foreign investment led to a repeal of this law in 1959, after only one year in force (Thee, 1996).

In 1967, however, a new government in Indonesia enacted a new Foreign Investment Law that opened Indonesia's door wide to foreign investment. In 1968 a similar

Domestic Investment Law was enacted to encourage investments by domestic investors. The open-door policy towards foreign investment lasted for only a relatively brief period, however, as economic nationalism re-emerged in the early 1970s as a result of the concern about the perceived over-presence of Japanese direct investment. As a consequence, the Indonesian government felt it necessary to pursue increasingly restrictive policies towards foreign investment. The restrictive foreign investment policy was further bolstered by the oil boom, which provided huge revenues through the resource rent taxes levied on foreign oil companies. These windfall oil revenues enabled the Indonesian government to embark on the second stage of import substituting industrialization by promoting the establishment of a number of state-owned, large-scale, capital-intensive basic industries. Under these conditions foreign investment was not considered to be very important anymore to fuel Indonesia's industrialization. Not surprisingly, therefore, foreign investment was not a significant source of gross domestic investment (Table 9.3).

The end of the oil boom in the early 1980s prompted the Indonesian government to make another U-turn in its policy towards FDI. Because of its diminished fiscal capacity, the government was forced to turn once again to the private sector, including foreign investors, to undertake the necessary investments to sustain economic growth and industrialization. To this end the Indonesian government began in the mid 1980s to introduce a series of deregulation policies to improve the investment climate for foreign (and domestic) investors. In addition, trade reforms led to a reduction in the anti-export bias of the trade regime, making investment in export oriented activities more attractive. The outcome was a surge in FDI, notably by East Asian NIE firms that tended to invest in labour-intensive, low skill export industries such as garment and footwear manufacturing (Thee, 1991).

Since the early 1990s the Indonesian government, concerned about increasing competition from other Asian countries, including Thailand, China and Vietnam, has progressively dismantled its restrictive foreign investment regime. The government's substantial investment deregulation policy of June 1994 abolished the mandatory divestment rule that required foreign investors to divest their majority equity ownership to a minority equity share of maximum 49 per cent after a specified period of time. This mandatory divestment had been one of the basic principles of Indonesia's foreign investment policy since the mid 1970s, and had proved to be a hindrance to attracting more FDI into the country. Western investors were particularly concerned about losing management control over their operations after they had transferred majority equity ownership to their Indonesian partners. As a result, since the introduction of successive foreign investment deregulation measures in the late 1980s FDI has flowed into Indonesia in increasing amounts. Hence, the role of FDI as a source of gross domestic investment has steadily increased since the early 1990s, as shown in Table 9.3.

The foreign direct investment in the ASEAN countries since the mid 1980s has mostly taken place in the manufacturing sector and to a lesser extent the primary and services sectors. The FDI patterns do show some significant differences, depending on the comparative advantages of each country. In resource-rich Indonesia, for example, apart from outside the sizeable FDI in the important oil and gas sectors, FDI has largely taken place in natural resource-oriented industries, such as chemicals (27 per cent of total cumulative approved FDI) and paper industries (10 per cent). FDI in Malaysia has mostly been in light manufacturing and light engineering industries, such as transport equipment (19 per cent), basic metal goods (15 per cent), non-metallic minerals (12 per cent), and electronics and electrical goods (12 per cent). FDI patterns in Thailand are more diversified, however, as more fields of activity are open to FDI than in the other two countries. The largest share of FDI in Thailand has taken place in the trade and services sectors, accounting for 31 per cent of total approved FDI, followed by FDI in electrical appliances (16 per cent) and construction (9 per cent) (Lall and Rao, 1995). FDI in the other manufacturing and services industries together accounts for less than 8 per cent of the total.

While FDI in Singapore has from the outset been export oriented, FDI in the other ASEAN countries was initially oriented to the domestic market in view of the import substitution policies they pursued in the 1970s. As Malaysia and Thailand in the early 1980s, followed by Indonesia in the late 1980s and the Philippines in the early 1990s, increasingly shifted to export oriented policies, more and more FDI into these countries took place in export oriented activities (i.e., activities that export more than 50 per cent of their output). During the period 1984–1985, for example, only 24 per cent of the approved FDI projects in Malaysia were export oriented; by 1988–1990 this figure had risen to 82 per cent. For Thailand the comparable figures were, respectively, 16 per cent and 60 per cent. (Lall and Rao, 1995). Similarly, in Indonesia only 37 per cent of approved FDI projects were export oriented in 1986; by 1990 this figure had risen to 70 per cent (Thee, 1991).

To sustain the growth in manufactured exports the ASEAN countries will have to make a major effort to improve the investment climate for FDI, particularly as the recent currency crisis in the region has scared away a lot of foreign investors. This will require a stable, open and transparent policy framework underpinned by sound macroeconomic policies, and further streamlining of administrative procedures. Other critical elements are national treatment of foreign investment projects and a steady expansion and upgrading of the physical infrastructure and available human resources. The upgrading of human resources will, in turn, facilitate technology transfer from expatriate to local employees and encourage the shift from low value added to higher value added activities.

The Role of Small and Medium-Scale Industries

As in most other developing countries, small- and medium-scale industries (SMIs) play an important role in the ASEAN economies. They comprise the majority of manufacturing establishments and generate considerable employment. Many of these establishments make simple products that are cheap and therefore accessible to people on low income. To the extent that SMIs are located in rural areas, their development may stimulate the decentralization of economic activities, and offer off-farm employment for rural workers who cannot find jobs in agricultural activities.

SMIs also offer opportunities for the development of prospective entrepreneurs (Sandee, 1995).

Some Definitions

As the definition of SMIs differs in the various ASEAN countries and sometimes even within one country, it is necessary first to specify what SMIs are, before assessing their relative importance. For example, in Indonesia the Central Bureau of Statistics (CBS) defines small-scale industries as those industries in which establishments employ 5 to 19 paid workers, whereas medium-scale industries consist of establishments with 20 to 99 workers. Cottage industries consist of establishments employing fewer than 5 workers, including unpaid family workers. The Department of Industry and Trade, however, defines small industries as those whose establishments have a capital investment in machinery and other capital equipment (but excluding the value of land and buildings) of less than Rp600 million (equivalent to US$60,000 at the prevailing exchange rate of US$1 = Rp10,000 of early February 1998).

In Malaysia different government agencies also use different definitions. The Ministry of Trade and Industry (MITI) defines small manufacturing enterprises as those with net assets of less than RM500,000, and medium-scale manufacturing enterprises (MEs) as those with net assets ranging between RM500,000 and RM2.5 million. Another definition classifies small enterprises as enterprises employing fewer than 50 workers and medium-sized enterprises as enterprises having 50 to 199 workers (Meyanathan and Ismail, 1994).

Singapore, MEs are defined by the Small Industries Finance Scheme (SIFS) as enterprises with no more than S$1 million in fixed productive assets, including factory buildings, machinery, other capital equipment and tools (Soon, 1994).

Thailand is Industrial Finance Corporation of Thailand (IFCT) and the Small Industry Finance Office (SIFO) define a small manufacturing enterprise as one with fixed assets worth less than baht 10 milllion, and a medium manufacturing enterprise as one having fixed assets worth baht 10 million to 50 millon. The Bank of Thailand uses both net fixed assets and number of employees as criteria. A small enterprise is one with fewer than 50 workers, and a medium-sized enterprises is one employing between 50 and 299 workers (Thongpakde et al., 1994).

Despite the various definitions, the relative importance of SMIs can be assessed, as the most commonly used definitions do not differ substantially from one country to another. Hence, by taking account of these differences, it is possible to get at least a rough impression of the relative importance of the SMIs in the various ASEAN countries (Table 9.4).

The database of SMIs in the ASEAN countries is rather weak (except for Singapore), since these countries, like most other developing countries, do not collect data on a regular (e.g., annual) basis. The reason for this is the obvious difficulty in collecting reliable data on the very large number of SMIs geographically dispersed all over the country. In view of these difficulties developing countries only collect data on a decennial basis (e.g., the Economic Census on Non-Agricultural Enterprises held in

Indonesia in 1985 and 1995). There are usually also delays in publication, so that the data mau be a decade or more old (Hill, 1995b), as is the case with some of the data in Table 9.4.

Table 9.4 Relative importance of SMIs in the ASEAN countries (%)

	Establishments		Manufacturing value added		Manufacturing employment	
	SMIs	Total	SMIs	Total	SMIs	Total
Indonesia (1986)	93.0	100.0	17.8	100.0	67.3	100.0
Malaysia (1981)	98.1	100.0	50.5	100.0	54.1	100.0
Philippines (1986)	98.6	100.0	22.6	100.0	52.2	100.0
Singapore (1987)	79.7	100.0	17.8	100.0	35.9	100.0
Thailand (1987)	99.4	100.0	n.a.	100.0	57.0	100.0

Notes: Estimates on SMIs include cottage industries (CIs); n.a. = not available.
Source: Thee Kian Wie (1994).

Taking account of these qualifications, Table 9.4 shows that SMIs in the five ASEAN countries account for the bulk of manufacturing establishments operating in the country, ranging from 99 per cent in the Philippines and Thailand to 80 per cent in Singapore. In terms of manufacturing value added (MVA), however, the estimates range from 51 per cent for Malaysia to 18 per cent in Indonesia and Singapore. These figures indicate that large industries in the ASEAN countries generate the bulk of MVA.

SMIs also account for the larger share of manufacturing employment in the ASEAN countries, except for Singapore. The estimates of much larger shares of workers in the SMIs should be treated with some caution, however, because of the difficulties in estimating employment in the SMIs, particularly in small industries.

Promotional Policies for SMIs

Unlike the other ASEAN countries, which have directed their promotion policies toward the SMIs proper, Indonesia has focused on micro and small enterprises (MSEs), including cottage industries. The major direct promotion programmes for small enterprises (including cottage enterprises) in Indonesia have included directed credit and technical assistance. During the 1970s and 1980s the major directed credit programme was the Small Enterprise Development (KIK/KMKP) Programme, a nationwide subsidized credit scheme. This programme was terminated in early 1990 because of serious loan collection problems and high default rates (Thee, 1994b).

KIK/KMKP was replaced in early 1990 by the Small Enterprise Credit Scheme (Kredit Usaha Kecil, KUK), which required all commercial banks, including foreign and joint venture banks, to allocate 20 per cent of their loan portfolio to small enterprises. This percentage has recently been raised to 25 per cent of a bank's loan portfolio. Failure to achieve this percentage would lead to the imposition of fines by the Bank of Indonesia. The major difference with the KIK/KMKP scheme was that KUK charged market interest rates. The KUK scheme has not been very effective either, as banks, concerned about not achieving the required percentage, have not bothered to scrutinize loan applications carefully. As a result, a not inconsiderable part of the KUK credits allocated to small enterprises has been used for consumption rather than productive or investment purposes.

In view of the broad definition of SEs (defined as enterprises with net assets amounting to Rp600 million), and the perceived difficulties in getting access to KUK credits because of the inability of many small enterprises to offer adequate collateral, it has been the larger small enterprises rather than the smaller ones that have been able to obtain the bulk of KUK credits. Realizing these difficulties, the Indonesian government last year introduced the feasibility credit scheme (Kredit Kelayakan Usaha, KKU) to provide smaller amounts of credit to the really small enterprises (including cottage enterprises). On the assumption that these enterprises would not be able to provide collateral, the KKU scheme was set up so that credit could be obtained without any collateral if the enterprise could submit a plausible business feasibility proposal to the banks.

In addition to the nationwide credit schemes, a nationwide technical assistance programme for small industries (BIPIK Programme) was introduced in the early 1970s and carried out by the former Directorate-General of Small-Scale Industries, Department of Industry. Unfortunately, this technical assistance programme has not been successful either, as reflected by the low occupancy rates and relatively limited use of the Technical Service Centres (Unit Pelayanan Teknis, UPT) and the Small Industry Estates (Lingkungan Industri Kecil, LIK), as well as the low productivity of the SMIs in these estates. One reason for the lack of success is that the extension workers had little or no business or technical experience (Thee, 1994b).

Other policy measures to promote small and medium enterprises (SMEs) include the obligation for state-owned enterprises (SOEs) to allocate 1–5 per cent (recently reduced to 1–3 per cent) of their net profits to small enterprises and provide them with technical, managerial and marketing assistance. The idea was to enable the small enterprises to grow into commercially viable concerns, able to stand on their own and to obtain bank credit by offering adequate collateral. This programme has on the whole not been successful in the sense that most SOEs, with some notable exceptions, have limited themselves to channelling the required 1–5 per cent of their profits to the small enterprises without bothering to provide the necessary managerial, technical or marketing guidance. This is not necessarily the fault of the SOEs, many of which are inefficient and face enough difficulties themselves in surviving as commercial entities. They are not in a position—and do not have the necessary expertise—to provide guidance to small enterprises.

Aside from these programmes directed at all the SMEs, the Indonesian government in the late 1970s also introduced a programme to promote viable SMIs. This programme was the mandatory deletion programme (i.e., local content programme), which intended to foster vertical inter-firm linkages between the large, assembling industries, specifically the engineering goods industries, and local supplier industries, which consisted mostly of SMIs. The programme did not achieve its aims of nurturing capable small and medium-size subcontracting firms. In fact, the program has led either to the in-house manufacture of major components to be procured locally (which has therefore led to the vertical integration of the assembly firm and the newly-established local supplier firm) or, if manufactured out of house, to the local manufacture of the components by large supplier firms, often affiliated with large TNCs (Thee, 1994b: 110).

As the direct government promotion programmes (credit schemes and technical assistance programmes) have not been as effective as expected, the Indonesian government has turned to indirect mechanisms. The 'partnership' (*kemitraan*) scheme between large and small enterprises and SMEs is currently the major promotion vehicle. It is hoped that by requiring large enterprises to establish partnerships with small ones, mutually profitable strategic alliances can be established. However, the experience with the deletion programme indicates that a government, no matter how powerful, cannot force large enterprises to establish effective partnerships with SMEs if it is not in their interest to do so. These large businesses may go through the motions of establishing partnerships, and may even provide some aid (mostly financial), but the partnerships have not been effective in stimulating the development of viable SMEs.

Like Indonesia, Malaysia has for social reasons also spent a lot of effort on promoting SMEs, particularly the ones owned by indigenous (*Bumiputera*) Malaysians. The Malaysian government has introduced various promotion programmes, including financial assistance schemes and training, technical and marketing assistance. Some of these programmes were introduced as part of the more activist development approach adopted under the New Economic Policy (NEP) to redress the economic imbalance between the various ethnic groups in Malaysia.

The financial assistance programmes included the credit facilities provided by MARA (Majlis Amanah Rakyat); the Credit Guarantee Schemes for SMEs provided by the Credit Guarantee Corporation; and Central Bank Guidelines for Priority Sector Lending, including for SMEs. Other mechanisms are development finance institutions, including the construction of standard factory units in selected locations by the Malaysian Industrial Estates Limited (MIEL), a subsidiary of the Malaysian Industrial Development Finance (MIDF) institution, for sale to SMEs through rental, credit financing, and a lease and purchase scheme. In 1985 the Development Bank of Malaysia (Bank Pembangunan Malaysia, BPM) established the nursery factory scheme (NFS) to provide new factory units for rental at subsidized rates by new *Bumiputera* firms receiving financial assistance from the Bank (Meyanathan and Ismail, 1994).

Malaysia's training, technical and marketing assistance support for SMIs includes entrepreneurial development and business management training for the owners and managers of SMIs, and technical skills (extension) and marketing training to the employees and workers of SMIs. The entrepreneurial and business management training is provided by the Malaysian Entrepreneurial Development Centre, MARA, National Productivity Corporation and the Small Business Development Centre of the Agricultural University of Malaysia. Technical skills training and extension services are provided by the industrial extension unit of SIRIM (Standards and Industrial Research Institute of Malaysia), the small-scale industry section of the Forest Research Institute (for wood-based SMIs) and the Food Technology Division

(FTD) of MARDI (Malaysian Agricultural Research and Development Institute). In addition, marketing assistance to SMIs in the form of free or subsidized consulting services is provided by MARA, the Malaysian Entrepreneurship Development Centre (MEDEC) and the development finance institutions (Meyanathan and Ismail, 1994).

Despite the many promotion schemes for Malaysia's SMIs, these programmes have in general, just as in Indonesia, not been effective in raising the capabilities of the SMIs to become viable enterprises. As a result, Malaysia, like Indonesia, lacks a vibrant SMI sector (Meyanathan and Ismail, 1994). However, Malaysia—probably influenced by Singapore's success in establishing a mutually profitable partnership among government, TNCs and SMI subcontractors—may be pondering the same indirect promotion programme for SMEs by urging large enterprises, including foreign ones, to establish strategic alliances with SMIs.

SMIs in Singapore consist of small and medium enterprises that lack financial resources, as well as production and management skills. Although the Singapore government has introduced a wide array of schemes to assist SMIs, the local business sector has remained relatively underdeveloped, as the Singapore economy is still dominated by TNCs. However, the presence of many world class TNCs has also assisted the emergence of supporting industries, consisting largely of SMIs. In this respect the local industry upgrading programme (LIUP), initiated as a partnership between Singapore's Economic Development Board (EDB) and participating TNCs and their subcontractors, almost all SMIs, has been quite effective in promoting technology transfer from the TNCs to their subcontractor SMIs. To encourage TNCs to participate in this programme in an effective way, a substantial proportion of the costs they incur in training SMIs is being reimbursed by grants from the Skills Development Fund (SDF) (Soon, 1994).

Despite the relative success of the LIUP, however, Singapore still has a considerable number of manufacturing SMIs that are performing poorly, with low value added. The Singapore government, particularly the EDB, could, as in the SMI master plan, mount a multi-agency programme to upgrade these businesses. Given the hard-headed approach adopted by the Singapore government, however, it seems unlikely that the EDB, with its insistence that market forces should prevail, would contemplate measures to prop up substandard SMIs merely to ensure their survival. Allowing less competitive SMIs to fail could prompt the entrepreneurs and workers of these business to move into more productive sectors (Soon, 1994: 90).

SMIs in Thailand face the same constraints as in the other ASEAN countries—inadequate technical and management skills and little or no access to finance. Unlike the other ASEAN countries, however, the Thai government, despite some specific measures to support SMIs, has not articulated a firm policy initiative to promote these businesses. The Thai government has instead relied on market forces to encourage the establishment of vertical inter-firm and subcontracting linkages between large enterprises and SMIs. In view of the limited capabilities of many SMIs, however, many of the inter-firm linkages that have been established have been between different large enterprises, as happened in Indonesia, rather than between large enterprises and SMIs (Thongpakde et al., 1994).

Promoting Industrial and Technological Upgrading in the ASEAN Countries

There is a growing concern in the ASEAN countries that they cannot continue to rely on their traditional sources of comparative advantage—cheap labour and natural resources—to sustain their manufactured exports. Moreover, it will also not be easy for these countries to maintain the export competitiveness of their manufactured exports by relying mainly on exchange rate policies to keep their real effective exchange rate competitive. In fact, the recent severe currency crisis experienced by all the ASEAN countries has underlined the great difficulty in stabilizing exchange rates.

To sustain the rapid growth of their manufactured exports, the ASEAN countries will have to develop a more sustainable base for the international competitiveness of their manufacturing industries. This will require the further development of their industrial technology capabilities, which would in turn enable them to transform their narrow export base from unskilled labour- and resource-intensive manufactured exports to more skill- and technology-intensive ones.

The question arises as to what extent the ASEAN countries, particularly the three 'near NIEs'—Indonesia, Malaysia and Thailand—have been able to develop their industrial technology capabilities.

In 1993 UNCTAD's technology programme sponsored a comparative study to assess the contribution of technological capabilities to the export performance of two important export industries in three ASEAN countries: the traditional textile and garment industries, and the more modern electronics industry. The three ASEAN countries covered in the study were the countries tagged as the three 'near NIEs' or second generation NIEs: Indonesia, Malaysia and Thailand. For the sake of comparison, the two industrially more developed East Asian NIEs, South Korea and Taiwan, were also included in the UNCTAD study.

Findings of the Indonesian country study indicated that several of the domestic private, export oriented textile, garment and electronics firms had acquired the technological capabilities that are most necessary during the early stages of industrialization: *acquisitive* (investment), *operational* (production) and to a lesser extent *adaptive* (minor change) capabilities. Among these three categories of capabilities, the domestic private firms had mastered the operational (production) capabilities the best, that is those capabilities required for the efficient operation of a plant. However, it turned out that the more demanding *marketing, linkage* and *innovation* (major change) capabilities, which are crucial for achieving and improving international competitiveness, were generally still beyond the reach of these firms (Thee and Pangestu, 1994).

The inadequate technological capacity building pointed out by the study is not surprising, as Indonesia's manufacturing industries were only encouraged to become export oriented in the mid 1980s after the end of the oil boom. Before that the large majority of manufacturing firms were oriented to the domestic market and shielded from import competition by high protection, including tariff and non-tariff measures. During that period there was little incentive on the part of most manufacturers to raise their competitiveness by developing their technological capabilities.

The findings of the Malaysian country study indicated that the electronics industry had acquired considerable *operational* (production) and *adaptive* (minor change) capabilities and experience in the production process. In other words, by the early 1990s the Malaysian electronics industry had acquired sufficient operational capability to run a fairly sophisticated assembly of a wide range of electronics products. In many of the larger companies owned by the TNCs (transnational corporations)—for example the American-owned semi-conductor industry and the Japanese-owned TNCS—a high degree of automation was achieved (Salleh and Kassim, 1993).

The enhanced capability in the electronics industry has been limited, however. Local participation in the industry has remained relatively insignificant, since the industry is dominated by foreign TNCs. In addition, the development of local supplier industries has lagged because of their inadequate technological capabilities (Salleh and Kassim, 1993). Hence, despite its rapid progress, Malaysia's electronics industry still consists largely of assembling rather than full manufacturing activities.

The study points out that Malaysia's textile industry faces increasingly stiff competition from lower-wage countries, particularly Thailand, Indonesia, China, India and Pakistan. In view of this challenge, the industry needs to upgrade its technological capabilities to permit the production of higher value-added products, and scaling down of certain activities that are no longer competitive. In addition, Malaysia's textile industry is highly dependent on imported raw materials, specifically synthetic fibres. As a petroleum-producing country, Malaysia has the opportunity to expand into the synthetic fibre industry, but presently there is only one such company in the country (Salleh and Kassim, 1993).

There is considerable concern in Thailand, as well, that the growth of manufactured exports cannot be sustained. In fact, during the past few years Thailand's manufactured exports have been growing at a sluggish rate. Findings of the Thailand study indicate that as in Indonesia and Malaysia, the most important technological capabilities acquired by the Thai employees in the textile and electronics industries during their growing up stage in the 1970s were the *operational* or *production* capabilities. In the electronics industry these production capabilities included process operation and control, quality control of both inputs and outputs, training programmes to enhance human capital and employees' involvement, maintenance and calibration procedures relating to machinery and equipment, inventory controls, subcontracting, original equipment manufacturing, and input sourcing arrangements. These enhanced production capabilities resulted in lower defection rates and, consequently, lower production costs. Productivity was also enhanced by mass production made possible by the use of automated machines. As a result of these developments, Thailand's textile and electronics industries were quite competitive during this period (Poapongsakorn and Thongudai, 1993).

Since the early 1990s, however, rapid technological developments have taken place in the world textile industry. Mastery of new technologies, including the acquisition of new and expensive textile machinery and high quality raw materials, is imperative for maintenance of the international competitiveness of Thailand's textile industry (Poapongsakorn and Thongudai, 1993). Since the largest firms are in a better position to purchase these expensive machines, it is likely that the smaller firms will lose out.

The Thai study also found that the country's electronics industry has not been very successful in developing adequate technological capabilities, particularly the more demanding marketing, linkage and innovation (including design) capabilities, to sustain its electronics exports. The only innovations made thus far have been modifications in the circuit design of TV sets and the reverse engineering of a few consumer electronics products. To a large extent it has been the lack of marketing experience of these electronics firms, mostly consisting of foreign TNC subsidiaries or joint ventures with foreign companies, that has hampered their technological developments. In fact, all the marketing activities were carried out by the foreign parent companies, while the local subsidiaries or Thai partners were solely responsible for the assembly and production activities (Poaponsakorn and Thongudai, 1993).

Concluding Remarks

During the past few decades the ASEAN countries, except for the Philippines until recently, have experienced some of the fastest rates of growth among the developing countries. While initially this rapid growth took place under import substituting, protectionist trade policies, the costs and distortions caused by this regime and the need to earn foreign exchange eventually persuaded these countries to shift to an export oriented industrial strategy. Over time this outward orientation enabled the ASEAN countries to transform themselves from primary exporting to manufactures exporting countries. As the rapid growth of their manufactured exports is closely associated with these countries' rapid economic and industrial development, it has become imperative for them to sustain their manufactured exports.

However, in view of the recent sluggish growth of their manufactured exports, caused by increasing competition from other newly-exporting countries (NECs), including China, India, Bangladesh and Vietnam, the ASEAN countries will have no alternative but to improve the international competitiveness of their manufacturing industries. This could be achieved by developing the technological capabilities of their manufacturing industries. There is a role for governments in encouraging manufacturers to undertake the necessary investments in technological capacity building. To the extent that they have not already done so, the governments of the ASEAN countries will have to establish a conducive incentive system for manufacturing firms and assist these firms to raise their supply-side capabilities.

A conducive incentive system would include sound macroeconomic policies, a neutral or only mildly protectionist trade regime based on the reciprocity principle (e.g., that protection would only be given if the beneficiary firm was able to achieve a certain export target) and sound domestic competition policies.

While the right incentive system is a necessary condition for establishing a competitive business environment, it is not a sufficient condition for enabling manufacturers to develop their technological capabilities. The other major element is strengthening of the supply-side capabilities of manufacturing firms. Government steps in this direction should include increased investment in human capital through the expansion of education at all levels, particularly technical education, and the improvement of the quality of education.

The supply-side capabilities of manufacturing firms can also be raised by improving the capabilities of the domestic science and technology (S&T) institutes to provide needed technology support services to national industry. These services would include R&D, technical information, and metrology, standardization, testing and quality assurance (MSTQ) services. The experience of the Northeast Asian NIEs has indicated that such technology support services rendered by their domestic S&T institutes have been quite effective in raising the technological capabilities of their manufacturing enterprises, including their SMIs. However, it is precisely in enhancing supply-side capabilities—specifically skill formation and upgrading the effectiveness of S&T institutes–that the ASEAN countries, with the exception of Singapore, are still lagging behind the Northeast Asian NIEs.

References

Anspach, R. 1969. 'Indonesia'. In F. Golay et al., eds., *Underdevelopment and Economic Nationalism in Southeast Asia.* Ithaca: Cornell University Press.

Ariff, M. and H. Hill. 1985. *Export Oriented Industrialization: The ASEAN Experience.* Sydney: Allen & Unwin.

Hill, H. 1994. 'ASEAN economic development: An analytical survey – The state of the field'. *The Journal of Asian Studies*, vol. 53, no. 3 (August): 832–66.

Hill, H. 1995a. 'ASEAN industrialization: A stocktaker'. Paper presented at the Seminar '5o Tahun Indonesia Merdeka dan 40 Tahun Fakultas Ekonomi UGM. Yogyakarta, 15–16 September.

Hill, H. 1995b. 'Small-medium enterprise and rapid industrialization: The ASEAN experience'. *Journal of Asian Business*, vol. 11, no. 2: 1–30.

Hill, H. 1996. 'Towards a political economy explanation of rapid growth in Southeast Asia' Working Papers in Trade and Development, No. 2. Department of Economics, Research School of Pacific and Asian Studies, The Australian National University.

Hill, H. and M. Chatib Basri. 1996. 'The political economy of protection in LDCs: An Indonesian case study'. Oxford Development Studies, vol. 24, no. 3: 241–59.

JETRO. 1997. JETRO White Paper on Foreign Direct Investment,97–FDI Speeds Industrial Restructuring. Tokyo: Japan External Trade Organization.

Lal, D. 1988. 'Ideology and industrialization in India and East Asia'. In: H. Hughes, ed., *Achieving Industrialization in East Asia.* Cambridge: Cambridge University Press.

Lall, S. 1994. 'Industrial policy: The role of government in promoting industrial and technological development'. In UNCTAD Review 1994. Geneva: UNCTAD.

Lall, S. 1996a. 'Foreign Direct Investment Policies in the Asian NIEs'. In Lall, 1996c.

Lall, S. 1996b. 'Malaysia: Industrial success and the role of government'. In Lall, 1996c.

Lall, S. 1996c. *Learning from the Asian Tigers – Studies in Technology and Industrial Policy.* London: Macmillan Press.

Lall, S. 1997. 'Technology policies in Indonesia'. Paper presented at the Indonesia Update 1997 Conference. The Australian National University, Canberra, 19–20 September.

Lall, S. and Kishore Rao. 1995. Indonesia: Sustaining Manufactured Export Growth, Volume 1: Main Report, Revised Draft. August.

Lim, Linda Y.C., and Pang Eng Fong. 1982. 'Vertical linkages and multinational enterprises in developing countries'. *World Development*, vol. 10, no. 7 (July): 585–95.

Lindblad, J.Th. 1991. 'Foreign investment in late colonial and post-colonial Indonesia'. Economic and Social History in the Netherlands, No. 33: 183–208.

Little, I.M.D. 1979. The Experience and Causes of Rapid Labour Intensive Development in Korea, Taiwan, Hong Kong, and Singapore: The Possibilities of Emulation. Asian Employment Programme, Working Papers, WP II-1, ILO-ARTEP, February.

Meyanathan, S. and Muhd. Salleh Ismail. 1994. 'Malaysia'. In S.D. Meyanathan, ed., *Industrial Structures and the Development of Small and Medium Enterprise Linkages – Examples from East Asia*. EDI Seminar Series. Washington, D.C.: Economic Development Institute, The World Bank.

Meyanatha, S.D., ed. 1994. Industrial Structures and the Development of Small and Medium Enterprise Linkages – Examples from East Asia. EDI Seminar Series. Washington, D.C.: Economic Development Institute, The World Bank.

Naya, S. 1988, 'The role of trade policies in the industrialisation of rapidly growing Asian developing countries'. In H. Hughes, ed., *Achieving Industrialisation in East Asia*. Cambridge: Cambridge University Press.

Paauw, D. 1963. 'From colonial to guided economy'. In R. McVey, ed., *Indonesia*. New Haven: Human Relations Area Files (HRAF) series. New Haven: Yale University Press.

Parry, T.G. 1988. 'The role of foreign capital in East Asian industrialization, growth and development'. In H. Hughes, ed., *Achieving Industrialisation in East Asia*. Cambridge: Cambridge University Press.

Poapongsakorn, N. and Pawadee Thongudai. 1993. Technological Capability Building and the Sustainability of Export Success in Thailand's Textile and Electronics Industries. A research report presented at the UNCTAD Workshop on Technological Dynamism and R&D in the Exports of Manufactures of Developing Countries. Kuala Lumpur, 25–28 January.

Salleh, Ismail Muhd. and Hamzah Kassim. 1993. Technological Dynamism behind Malaysia's Successful Export Performance. Report for UNCTAD's Research Project on Technological Dynamism and R&D in the Exports of Manufactures from Developing Countries.

Sandee, H. 1995. 'Promoting small-scale enterprises in developing countries'. In Centre for Development Cooperation Services, Annual Report–University Development Cooperation, Vrije Universiteit, Amsterdam.

Santoso W.Y. 1995. 'The importance of foreign direct investment data on the balance of payments'. Paper presented at the Workshop on Foreign Direct Investment Data Base. Jakarta, 8 November.

Soon, Teck Wong. 1994. 'Singapore'. In Meyanathan and Saleh, 1994.

Tan, J.L.H. and Luo Zhaohong, eds. 1994. ASEAN-China Economic Relations-Industrial Restructuring in ASEAN and China. Institute of World Economics and Politics, Beijing and Institute of Southeast Asian Studies, Singapore.

Thee Kian Wie. 1991. 'The surge of Asian NIC investment into Indonesia'. *Bulletin of Indonesian Economic Studies*, vol. 27, no. 3 (December): 55–88.

Thee Kian Wie. 1994a. 'Indonesia'. In Meyanathan, 1994.

Thee Kian Wie. 1994b. Industrial Restructuring and the Role of Small- and Medium-Scale Enterprises in ASEAN with Special Reference to Indonesia. In Joseph L.H. Tan and Z.H. Luo, eds., *Industrial Restructuring in ASEAN and China Economic Relations*. Singapore: Institute of Southeast Asian Studies.

Thee Kian Wie. 1996. 'Economic policies in Indonesia during the period 1950–1965, in particular with respect to foreign investment'. In J.T. Lindblad, ed., *Historical Foundations of a National Economy in Indonesia, 1890s–1990s*. Amsterdam: Royal Netherlands Academy of Sciences (KNAW).

Thee Kian Wie and M. Pangestu. 1994. *Technological Capabilities and Indonesia's Manufactured Exports.* Final report prepared for the UNCTAD/SAREC Project on Technological Dynamism and R&D in the Exports of Manufactures from Developing Countries. Jakarta, January.

Thongpakde, Nattapong, Wisarn Pupphavesa and Pussarangsri. 1994. 'Thailand'. In Meyanathan, 1994.

World Bank. 1997. *World Development Indicators, 1997.* Washington, D.C.: The World Bank

PART FOUR

FINANCIAL POLICIES AND FINANCIAL SECTOR DEVELOPMENT

Chapter 10

Financial Policies and Financial Sector Development in Sub-Saharan Africa

Ernest Aryeetey and Machiko Nissanke

Sub-Saharan African countries have spent a considerable part of the last decade attempting reform of their financial sectors to facilitate the growth of savings (both private and public) and to increase the rate and returns of productive investment. The need to achieve substantial growth in private and public savings arose because the characteristic poor output growth is derived from low investments, which are largely a consequence of low levels and rates of savings (World Bank, 1989). Savings rates of 12.5 per cent of GDP on average in the 1980s were not only far below the East Asian average of 28.9 per cent, but far less than was desirable to achieve an average annual growth rate of 5 per cent for the 1990s.

A closer examination of the savings–investment nexus sheds more light on the non-sustainability of economic growth in these economies. In such reforming countries as Ghana, Malawi and Tanzania, national accounts show that the savings–investment gap has been widening throughout the last decade. The large increases in domestic investment rates recorded in Tanzania and Ghana, for example, have been supported by a significant rise in foreign savings. In Malawi also, where there was a higher investment rate, this was maintained above the average for SSA only with increased foreign savings flows.

The structure of the financial markets of SSA is a significant factor behind the inability to generate enough savings. Popiel (1994) has suggested that they are shallow, narrow and undiversified. This description is derived from the highly segmented nature of the financial markets in the region. Note that segmentation goes beyond a simple dichotomy of formal and informal institutions, as these two broad segments suffer from further divisions (Nissanke and Aryeetey, 1998). Each of the many different segments usually lends only to borrowers with distinct characteristics, and there is relatively little interaction among them. There are very few spillovers from formal to informal segments and even within the larger sectors. The high level of segmentation, with little prospect for efficiently allocating financial resources, makes it more appropriate to describe the markets as fragmented. But the fragmentation is a result of the high-risk environment in which transactions take place. The difficult access to information, characteristic of poor economies, is a major contributor to the situation.

The Search for Effective Financial Sector Reforms

In tackling the problem of shallow markets, early attempts in many SSA countries to bring about an efficient and equitable distribution of financial resources led to the adoption of repressive policies. These took the form of governments setting interest rates for bank lending and directing credit flows to specific sectors (or even entities and individuals in some cases). In the process, governments allocated large chunks of investible funds to themselves and other state-owned enterprises. The World Bank (1989) well documents the largely negative impact that these policies had on an already poor situation. The difficulties created for entire economies during in the 1980s led to the search for financial sector reforms, focusing on market liberalization.

But the efficacy of recent financial policies emphasizing liberalization also appears to be in severe doubt (Nissanke and Aryeetey, 1998). Their impact on financial intermediation has been substantially less than expected in a number of countries (World Bank, 1994a), and the many private investors continue to be starved of credit following the persistent shallowness of the markets. Savings rates remain low for both the public and private sectors in many SSA countries. The expected competition in financial markets has been slow in coming for many countries as interest rates reflect, more and more, increasing fragmentation in the markets.

There are various explanations for the difficulty of getting financial systems in SSA to produce significantly positive outcomes from the reform programmes. The World Bank (1994a: 8) suggests that policy reforms often did not go far enough:

> Financial reform lags behind as well. The financial position of the banking sector is weak because of poor macroeconomic management, which induces the monetization of fiscal deficits through the banks. It is also weak because of the slow pace of reform in the public enterprise sector. And it reflects continuing government interference in the management of the financial sector. A large share of bank lending still goes to the public enterprise sector, making it more difficult for the private sector to borrow.

Aryeetey et al. (1997) attribute the inadequate response from financial sector reforms in four SSA countries—Ghana, Malawi, Nigeria and Tanzania—to the fact that the policy reforms did not affect the structural and institutional barriers to interactions across different market segments. In explaining why market fragmentation persists after several years of reforms, they echo the view that reforms have been incomplete in some cases, but add that the reform programmes have not been accompanied by adequate complementary measures to address underlying institutional and structural constraints. They suggest that 'simply removing financially repressive policies is not sufficient to increase financial depth or to induce banks to reach a wider clientele' (p. 214).

The consequence of the inadequate reform outcomes is that the markets are not capable of raising the rates of domestic savings and investment. This chapter discusses a number of issues that need to be addressed in order to make the financial systems respond to stimuli for growth and diversification. Aside from discussing the scope of the problems facing SSA financial markets, the paper also highlights new insights into dealing with the problems in the light of the East Asian experiences. It is hoped that the debates those new insights generate will lead to serious research on how to tackle the problems.

We begin by highlighting the magnitude of the problem facing SSA financial markets, discussing savings mobilization and financial intermediation. We then show the problem from the demand side by introducing aspects of enterprise finance in SSA, and next analyse how the different risks facing lenders and borrowers condition institutional development. In discussing the institutional arrangements for mobilizing savings and for lending, we show how financial agents have developed mechanisms for limiting the risks they are exposed to, leading to market segmentation and information-constrained equilibrium. We show how the different segments are used by different groups of clients. Considering that one of the earlier approaches to countering the problems of shallow markets was to intervene with directed credit programmes, we discuss some assessments of such programmes in Africa, as well as the impact of financial liberalization on financial market performance and institution building, and the environment for regulating and supervising financial market operations. Issues of globalization and how they impinge on financial integration are also covered, as well as alternative paradigms for reforming the financial sector.

Savings Mobilization and Financial Intermediation in SSA

Before reforms, most banks in SSA countries faced severe financial difficulties that threatened their liquidity and solvency and hence the stability of the entire financial system. Contributing factors included undercapitalization, inadequate bank regulation and supervision, insufficient credit analysis, inappropriate sectoral policies, weak accounting and management systems, and rapid depreciation of the currency. Most banks were weak in their capacity for risk management. It is therefore not surprising that savings mobilization and financial intermediation in SSA are the lowest in the world, and have often been contrasted to East Asian countries where household and corporate savings have been among the highest in the world for the last three decades.

The situation has not improved significantly with the reforms governments pursued throughout the 1980s. The average M2/GDP ratio for SSA experienced only marginal increase, from 27.3 per cent in the period 1981–1985 to 26.6 per cent in 1986–1990. Although the share of credit to the public sector has declined in many countries, governments and public enterprises continue to receive the largest proportion of bank credit. Clearly, in most SSA countries, the expected positive effects from liberalization in savings mobilization and credit allocation have been slow to emerge. For example, Nissanke and Aryeetey (1998) show for the four countries they studied that even though radical changes occurred in the policy environment, with a general shift in policy from 'repressed' regimes toward 'liberalized' ones, their effects on savings mobilization and financial intermediation were generally disappointing. Table 10.1 shows period averages of three indicators of financial deepening proposed by King and Levine (1993): the M2/GDP ratio; the ratio of private sector credit to GDP; and the share of credit to the public sector (government and public enterprise) in total domestic credit.

Table 10.1 Indicators of financial deepening

Country	M2/GDP 1981–86	M2/GDP 1987–92	Private sector credit/GDP 1981–86	Private sector credit/GDP 1987–89	Public sector credit in total credit 1981–86	Public sector credit in total credit 1987–92
Ghana	14.6	15.0	2.37	4.14	86.32	74.53
Malawi	21.1	21.4	14.62	9.05	63.33	53.55
Nigeria	31.7	20.2	17.39	11.27	55.29	50.26
Tanzania	37.6	30.5	2.25	2.15	94.82	61.63

Source: Nissanke and Aryeetey (1998).

In Nigeria, for example, where poorly designed reform was undertaken without the necessary prerequisites, indicators of both savings mobilization and credit allocation showed a marked deterioration in the adjustment period (see Table 10.1). The difficulties experienced by the formal financial system after 1986/87 were clearly evident in the financial deepening indicators. The deterioration could be placed against the trend set before the liberalization attempts. The M2/GDP ratio increased steadily from 19 per cent in 1975 to 33 per cent in the mid-1980s. The ratio of (M2–M1)/GDP showed a similar rise, although the currency/M2 ratio remained around 26 per cent.

It is peculiar that Ghana's financial depth remains one of the lowest in SSA despite very comprehensive financial sector reforms. Formal sector credit to the private sector accounts for just over 4 per cent of GDP in the adjustment period. The public sector still accounts for three-quarters of total domestic credit. According to a World Bank study (Neal, 1988), in 1985 Ghana had one of the lowest ratios of M2/GDP (13.5 per cent) in the world. It was only better than that of Zaire. By 1992, Ghana's M2/GDP ratio had improved to reach 17.5 per cent, which was still low. It is evident that a significant recovery of the process of financial deepening has not begun yet. After several years of financial liberalization and costly bank restructuring, the financial deepening ratios are still far from the levels attained in the second half of the 1970s.

In the case of Malawi, the level of financial depth, while higher than Ghana's, has not experienced any positive development in the decade of reforms. We must add that the process of financial deepening has not proceeded rapidly, either. The M2/GDP ratio fluctuated between 20 per cent and 25 per cent over the period 1975–1992 without showing any definite trend.

Before embarking on reforms, Tanzania showed a marked increase in deposits mobilized by banking institutions in the late 1970s and early 1980s, when the M2/GDP ratio rose to over 40 per cent. This was far higher than the ratio attained in many other countries, as the average ratio for SSA was 25 per cent. The rapid growth indeed reflected a condition of monetary overhang as financial assets held by the non-bank public increased sharply as a result of the severe shortage of consumer goods in those years (Mayer and Collier, 1989). With economic reform and adjustment accompanied by considerable aid, the goods shortage was eased in 1984–1988 and the banking system suffered in savings mobilization.

Nor do the ratios for most SSA countries compare well internationally. The current average M2/GDP ratio of 25 per cent can be compared with 79 per cent in Malaysia and 46 per cent in Indonesia. Some of the better and steadier performers in SSA are Kenya with 37 per cent and Zimbabwe with 30 per cent.

In terms of the ability of formal financial systems to deliver credit, there is evidence in many SSA countries of diminishing access for the private sector. In Ghana, again Nissanke and Aryeetey (1996) report that while credit to the private sector by deposit-taking banking institutions (DMBs) increased after reforms began, reaching over one-third of total domestic credit in 1989/90, it experienced a decline in the 1990s as fiscal imperatives again started dominating credit allocation.

Malawi shows a better performance in the delivery of credit to the private sector than Ghana and many other SSA countries. For deposit money banks (DMB), the share of the private sector increased from around 60 per cent in the mid 1980s to over 80 per cent in the early 1990s. Over the same period the proportion of credit to central government and other public entities declined. However, Table 10.1 shows that as a proportion of GDP, credit flows to the private sector declined in the later period (1987–1992) by almost five percentage points compared with the earlier period (1981–1986). The decline is indicative of an initial convulsion experienced by the banking sector following the liberalization measures.

Table 10.1 again shows that in Nigeria, the public sector's absorption of credit was not as high as in Ghana and Tanzania, either before or after reforms began. However, when measured in relation to GDP, banking institutions mobilized fewer financial assets and granted less credit to the private sector in the adjustment period. Soyibo (1997) shows that financial liberalization was incorrectly sequenced, given the unstable macroeconomic environment and weak supervisory framework. Thus, it is not surprising that liberalization has not produced any significant positive trend in the aggregate financial indicators. There is indeed a large number of distressed financial institutions and growing non-performing loans. This has produced a sharp contraction of credit to the private sector, since government financing requirements have first claim on credit.

Here, too, Kenya is among the better performing African nations, with a credit/GDP ratio of 23 per cent. And again, international comparisons are unfavourable for SSA. The low credit/GDP ratios for African countries may be compared with 50 per cent in Indonesia and 75 per cent in Malaysia. There has not yet been a clear upward trend since the implementation of liberalization measures and bank restructuring to restore banks' commercial viability. Indeed, banks' asset portfolio management appears to have become more risk–averse since liberalization.

While the formal financial sectors have had difficulty mobilizing savings and providing credit for private sector development, the informal and semi-formal sectors have shown considerable growth in many SSA countries. Nissanke and Aryeetey (1998) report that deposits mobilized by savings and credit associations in Ghana did not show any major changes in the reform years, but those of savings collectors, a more commercially-oriented segment, rose significantly in the same period. Between 1990 and 1992, *susu* collectors[1] in Ghana steadily increased the sizes of their clientele. The number of urban collectors in Ghana increased by 48 per cent in the period. There were even more significant increases in both urban and rural Nigeria. The growth came from both the size of clientele for each collector and average nominal deposit sizes. Mayer et al. (1993) report significant savings mobilization activity among the *Kafos* of Gambia. Bagachwa (1996) and Chipeta and Mkandawire (1996b) also report considerable growth in Tanzania and Malawi, respectively.

Enterprise Finance

Having seen the supply-side problems, we turn now to the demand side. We discuss in this section the relationship between the methods of financing enterprises and the structures of those enterprises, particularly size. We first discuss the significance of finance as a constraint and then look at how firms deal with it.

Finance as a Constraint to Enterprise Development

A number of surveys, Biggs and Srivastave (1996) suggest that private sector operators generally perceive various constraints to their expansion as being 'beyond their immediate control' and relating to access to various services. The most frequently cited by the enterprises is the financial problem, however. Parker et al. (1995) provides survey evidence that credit is a major problem for micro- and small enterprises in Ghana, Malawi, Mali, Senegal and Tanzania (see Table 10.2).

Aryeetey et al. (1994) report that the problems receiving the most mention by firms of all sizes in their study of Ghana were:

- The absence or inadequacy of credit for working capital, which almost 40 per cent of the entire sample included among their top four constraints to expansion (23 per cent of respondents indicated that it was the most significant constraint to expansion).
- The lack of credit for the purchase of capital equipment was suggested by 37 per cent of the entire sample (21 per cent of respondents thought it was the most significant obstacle to expansion).

---

[1] *Susu* or *esusu* collection is the arrangement whereby an individual collector collects an agreed amount from each person in a group known only to that collector and returns the amount to the depositors at the end of an agreed period. This development has been described as 'mobile banking' by Miracle et al. (1980). It is believed to have evolved from the savings and credit associations (Aryeetey and Gockel, 1991). As a matter of fact, the expression *susu* is used in Ghana for both SCAs and the mobile banks, while in Nigeria *esusu* is used for both of those activities among certain ethnic groups.

Table 10.2 Firms facing financial constraints (per cent)

Ghana		Malawi		Senegal		Mali	
Micro	Small	Micro	Small	Micro	Small	Micro	Small
79	83	62	68	92	90	83	72

Source: Parker et al. (1995).

Indeed, smaller enterprises have a greater problem with credit than larger firms. As many as 42 per cent of the microenterprises Aryeetey et al. (1994) studied in Ghana listed credit for working capital among their major constraints, compared with 38 per cent of small-scale enterprises and 25 per cent of the medium-sized firms. A similar trend was observed with credit for equipment purchase. The results were generally seen to reflect an inverse relationship between size and demand for credit, as well as access. The authors observed that the success ratio for large firms applying for bank loans was almost 70 per cent, compared with 45 per cent for small-scale enterprises and 34 per cent for microenterprises. Smaller firms obviously tend to have greater problems with access to finance.

Aside from the general difficulty in obtaining the credit applied for, firms also often have difficulty with the way credit is packaged. In the Nissanke and Aryeetey (1998) study, firms, irrespective of size, showed some difficulty with interest rates and loan maturities. The study observed that minimum market rates at the time were on average eight percentage points above the preferred interest rates of enterprises. In Malawi, most entrepreneurs studied thought a loan at 30 per cent was only moderately useful for both new investment and working capital, which was very similar to the observations from Ghana. While many businesses found prevailing interest rates quite steep, they were often not considered to be the only significant factor driving decisions on borrowing. For many small African entrepreneurs, a 30 per cent interest rate, for example, would be acceptable if they had sufficient market control to ensure that they could pass their increased costs on to consumers. This was still possible in the early years of structural adjustment, when many firms enjoyed considerable monopolies and the flow of imports was limited. As adjustment took hold, however, increased competition made high interest rate loans difficult to service. But the achievement of real positive interest rates was a major objective of financial sector reforms. As the countries maintained high inflation rates, lending rates were forced up considerably, thus making the cost of borrowing unattractive in many situations. In Nigeria and Ghana, lending rates have exceeded 35 per cent for more than five years in the past decade.

There is some variation by firm size with respect to desired maturities. In Ghana, larger firms, often seeking fixed investment loans, prefer loans with longer maturities, averaging 48 months. Smaller firms are generally more interested in working capital loans that can be paid back within 18 months. But the average maturity of Ghanaian loans is six months, as in many countries. Furthermore, microenterprises generally find it difficult to provide any collateral. Owners of firms without landed property usually suggest that banks could take a lien on their equipment as an alternative source of collateral. Some micro–enterprises suggest that the best alternative would be the savings account of a guarantor (Aryeetey et al., 1994).

Financing Enterprises

Depending on the size of enterprises, there are considerable differences in financial services demanded and constraints faced in gaining access to finance. At the same time, financial sector development is closely linked to real sector development and its evolution follows a certain sequence in response to demand for new kinds of financial services as the real sector develops (Gurley and Shaw, 1967; Goldsmith, 1969; Gertler and Rose, 1994). In particular, an economy's financial structure follows an evolutionary path through demand–supply interactions. As enterprises grow and develop, they are expected to have more access to a variety of financing sources and they are able to switch from internal sources to external sources (Chuta and Liedholm, 1985; Nissanke, 1998).

In SSA, however, there is little evidence of this process taking place. Internal sources have continued to dominate finance, even long after operations have started. The recent studies of enterprise development by the World Bank (Regional Programme for Enterprise Development, RPED) in a number of countries, including Cameroon, Zimbabwe and Ghana, provide substantial material on how firms are financed in those countries. The most notable observation is the importance of suppliers' credit in the finance of African businesses.

The Zimbabwean RPED study showed that the majority of firms used owners' savings to finance start-up, as is generally the case with African businesses. As many as 71 per cent of the entire Zimbabwean RPED sample used owners' savings as the primary source of start-up capital. Table 10.3 indicates that the use of owners' savings was much more intense in the smaller operations, where loans from friends and relatives also made minor contributions of 8 per cent. When firms were already operating, retained earnings were cited by 63 per cent of the respondents across the size categories as the main source of funding.

Table 10.3 Sources of start-up finance by firm size in Zimbabwe (per cent)

Proportion of firms that used:	Micro	Small	Medium	Large	Mean
Own savings	90	80	58	52	71
Friends/relatives	13	2		11	8
Bank loan	3	14	9	9	10
Other	13	19	22	25	19
Number of observations	40	64	45	44	200

Source: World Bank, RPED study on Enterprise Finance in Zimbabwe, April 1995.

Various other sources of funding (loans from development finance institutions (DFIs), equity issues, advances from parent companies) were mentioned by 22 per cent, bank loans by 12 per cent and personal savings by 4 per cent as the main source of finance for investments. For existing microenterprises, however, personal savings of the owner still remain important, second only to retained earnings of the firm.

The African Employment Report (ILO, 1989) mentioned comparable results from ten African countries. The report indicated that about 65 per cent of start-up capital came from owners' savings and most of the remainder consisted of loans from family and friends.

Again in the Zimbabwean RPED study of manufacturing enterprises, the survey results for all firm categories show that suppliers' credit accounted for about 30 per cent of their outstanding balances. Altogether, this was the most important source of outside funds. Small and medium-sized firms were, however, more likely to benefit from such credit than microenterprises. Next in order of importance were loans from non-bank financial institutions (NBFIs), such as finance houses, building companies, pension funds and government credit programmes. They accounted for 28 per cent of total credit in-flows. These loans were found to benefit mostly large firms and only a few medium or small enterprises. No microenterprise benefited from such credit. The third most important source of funds was bank overdrafts (which were normally rolled–over in effect to become long-term credit) and bank loans, which provided 23 per cent and 14 per cent, respectively, of total enterprise credit. Again, bank loans generally benefited small and medium enterprises more than they did microenterprises. Larger firms in Zimbabwe made more use of formal finance, as less than 20 per cent of microenterprises reported ever having received a bank loan, in contrast to 75 per cent of larger firms.

Borrowing from informal sources was generally not found to be important, except for a few small enterprises. Client pre-payment for goods was also observed to be unimportant in Zimbabwe, which was quite different from what had been observed in the Ghana study (Cuevas et al., 1993). In Zimbabwe, most firms also gave and received trade credit. Microenterprises were found to be twice as likely to give credit to their customers as to receive credit from their suppliers.

Cuevas et al. (1993) observed from Ghanaian manufacturing enterprises' debt portfolio that 25 per cent of firms surveyed had no debt of any kind. For those with some outstanding debt, this was made up of bank overdrafts and loans, trade credit (including suppliers' credit and customer prepayments), and loans from family and friends.

Table 10.4 shows that as firm size rises, the use of bank credit also increases. For small and medium enterprises, trade credit overwhelmingly dominates. With trade credit, client pre-payment is more than twice as important as suppliers' credit. Suppliers' credit also appears more important for medium-sized enterprises (11–50 employees). Cuevas et al. (1993) suggest that this structure reflects not only the inefficiency of long-standing lending programmes targeted at small enterprises through formal banking institutions, but also the futility of firm-size targeting when large firms may be precisely the best conduit to increase liquidity among medium and small-scale firms through trade credit linkages.

Table 10.4 Portfolio composition by firm size: Average shares of sources of finance in total debt (per cent of total)

	Small	Medium	Large
Banks	7	24	66
Trade credit	66	64	32
Suppliers	20	36	21
Clients	46	28	10
Family and friends	27	12	2

Notes: Firm size by number of employees: small 1–10; medium 11–50; large 51+.
Source: Cuevas et al. (1993).

The investigation of sources of finance for capital investments by manufacturing firms as shown in Table 10.5 suggests that internal sources of funds, mainly retained earnings or personal savings, dominated for small and medium manufacturing firms, while bank credit and suppliers' credit were most important for large firms. Hence, Cuevas et al. (1993: 7) argue that 'this fact disputes the alleged decisiveness of bank credit as a factor in enterprise development'. However, further analyses of the data showed that large investments tend to be financed more by external sources (banks, trade credit, informal sources or equity) than small projects.

Table 10.5 Sources of finance for investments in capital stock in Ghana (per cent of total investment costs)

Source of finance	Small	Medium	Large
Internal	65.3	71.7	36.1
Banks	3.3	12.5	33.3
Suppliers' credit	4.7	0.0	30.6
Family/friends	10.0	15.8	0.0
Equity	16.6	0.0	0.0

Notes: Firm size by no. of employees: small 1–10; medium 11–50; large 51+.
Source: Cuevas et al. (1993).

Many studies of enterprise finance (e.g., RPED) suggest that medium-sized and small firms are likely to turn first to a bank for credit, but are not likely to find the bank finance they seek. It is estimated that there is a substantially larger credit-worthy demand for credit than banks would like to believe, but fewer credit-worthy projects than potential borrowers believe they have (Aryeetey et al., 1994). One country with many smaller firms obtaining loans is Malawi, where most of those firms were export-processing entities (Chipeta and Mkandawire, 1996b). In Tanzania, Bagachwa (1995) suggests that microenterprises have very little chance of being financed by banks, with the result that very few such enterprises approach banks.

We would generally have expected that under competitive conditions, firms that failed to secure formal loans would turn to the informal financial sector. Most studies, however, indicate very little use of informal finance (apart from start-up capital from family and friends), reflecting the highly segmented nature of financial markets. In the

Aryeetey et al. (1994) study of Ghana, only 8.1 per cent of the sample had ever sought a loan from a moneylender and 2.5 per cent had approached a *susu* operator for a similar facility. In Tanzania, where informal finance plays only a minor role as a credit substitute for formal sources in enterprise financing, more than 90 per cent of informal finance consisted of loans from friends and relatives (Blanc, 1997).[2]

Considering the relatively large number of rejected bank loan applications, these statistics indicate little spill over of unsatisfied demand into informal segments of the financial market. This is partly due to the narrow specialization of each segment of the informal financial sector, as discussed below. It is also attributable to the nature of the financial products/instruments they provide—the relatively high interest rates, short repayment periods and limited loan sizes. These characteristics make informal sources less appropriate for regular business transactions of industrial firms. Many firms viewed borrowing from informal commercial sources as a measure of last resort rather than a preferred means of regular finance. Thus, Blanc (1997) suggests that in the absence of organized informal credit mechanisms, firms resort to informal finance only as an ex-post response to short-term liquidity problems.

Risk Management with Imperfect Information and Financial Market Structure

As indicated earlier, there are generally two broad components of financial markets—the formal sector and the informal sector. These two sectors are divided into smaller segments, thus placing on one side the formal sector of bank and assorted non-bank financial institutions, while the informal sector is made up of a varied number of smaller segments. Some institutions may straddle the two broad sectors and have been generally described as semi-formal institutions (Aryeetey et al., 1997).

The fragmented financial markets we mentioned earlier are a consequence of the incomplete nature of those markets. The markets fail regularly as a result. This characteristic conditions the kind of transactions that take place, their cost, the selection of who can participate and hence the structure of the market. Considering that people demand savings and credit facilities because they expect a gain with time, it is essential to analyse market conditions and structures from the point of view of the conditions under which that gain will occur. These will be influenced by the nature of the *information* possessed by borrowers and lenders, depositors and deposit-takers on intertemporal conditions, and the *contract enforcement* possibilities on the financial markets.

In the framework that Stiglitz and Weiss (1981) developed, trading credit and savings in such an intertemporal manner is guided by behaviour whose analysis goes beyond the simple paradigm of competitive equilibrium and provides a new theoretical foundation for policy intervention in efforts to correct market failure. In addition to playing the role of intertemporal allocation of resources, credit transactions are seen to reflect the economic environment within which they occur. Since most of the

[2] Levy (1993) also reports that informal financing is less used by small enterprises in Tanzania than by those in Sri Lanka.

SSA environment is characterized by objective risk, with unpredictable variations in income as a result of weather and other exogenous processes, credit transactions are expected to take these into account. They must reflect transfers of resources in response to pervasive income shocks. The costly acquisition and asymmetric distribution of information are essential aspects of this environment. Increased risk resulting from inadequate information affects the transaction costs of lenders and forces them to adopt measures that will lead to incomplete information equilibrium. Carter (1988) shows that the profitability of bank lending is reduced with increasing risk, as in the case of small farms, which are assumed to be less productive than large farms.

In general, creditors and borrowers have adopted a number of ways of dealing with the described inherent risks and the poor contract enforcement mechanisms. One of the known methods is to develop a 'repeat lending' relationship that provides an incentive for borrowers to put up their best behaviour in order to qualify for future credit. This leads to a 'self-enforcing contract'. Another method is to develop group schemes that bring together lenders and borrowers with distinct socioeconomic characteristics. It is the availability of social sanctions to punish defaulters that is believed to compel repayment. There is evidence, however, that group arrangements do not always yield the most satisfactory results to a lender. Besley and Coate (1995) show that groups that have the characteristic of socially connecting people are more likely to be efficient than other groups. This would be a crucial point for explaining the difficulties of many of today's innovative schemes/micro-finance projects that rely on the group concept without having developed the required social capital in the community in which they operate. Indeed, in schemes that involve groups, loan repayment is enforced through the exclusion of defaulters from access to future credit transactions. This, of course, works if the relationship between borrower and lender is exclusive, which is so in many rural markets especially, and in most group arrangements that involve poor people.

It would appear that formal institutions obtain and assess information differently from informal and semi-formal units. Further more, while they all go through the processes of screening the information, monitoring projects and attempts to enforce contracts, they approach these functions differently from informal groups and agents, resulting in different transaction costs and different clients.

At a different level, however, policy makers intervene in the market to ensure that it works in a particular manner. Their interventions include attempts to socialize the risks involved, which can take the form of loan guarantees, taking over the ownership of financial institutions and a myriad of other credit allocation policies. In the rest of this section, we first discuss the types of institutions and clients (formal and informal), looking at ownership, management of institutions, clientele and size, and then show how they counter objective risk with their evolved structures.

Structure of Formal Financial Markets

When governments came face-to-face with incomplete markets at independence, their first reactions were usually to intervene. Thus, until recently, the dominant types of formal financial institutions in most SSA countries were state-owned commercial and development banks. Commercial banks were started in many countries in the colonial period as branches of larger banks in the colonizing economies. They were initially privately owned but had strong support from the colonial government as they helped provide financial assistance to the extractive industries that dominated colonial economies. In the former British colonies, Standard Bank and Barclays Bank dominated the markets. Throughout the former French colonies, on the other hand, *Societé Generale*, *Banque Nationale de Paris* and *Credit Lyonnais* provided the bulk of all financial services. In both anglophone and francophone Africa, institutions were preoccupied with supporting the export of raw materials to Europe. There was little consideration of the development of a broader-based economy.

Soon after independence, the authorities in most countries concerned themselves with financial sector development as a means of accelerating the growth of their economies. With support from the state, the ownership of commercial banks changed. The state participated fully in the setting up of commercial banks, and followed this up with the creation of development banks. The state's early involvement was not necessarily motivated by a need to counter the objective risks faced by the financial markets. The governments largely ignored the risks and decided that if the private sector was incapable of dealing with them, the state's resources could be used to get the markets functioning, irrespective of the cost.

In Tanzania, for example, the Arusha Declaration of February 1967 required the government to pursue policies that would transform the country into a socialist and self-reliant state. Subsequently, major industries, banking institutions, insurance and export-import businesses, most of which were foreign owned, were nationalized. New financial institutions that were established after 1967 became publicly owned. Popiel (1994) estimates that by the end of the 1970s, governments held—either directly or indirectly—a majority interest in more than half of SSA's banking institutions and a minority interest in 40 per cent of the remaining institutions. State intervention in the creation of commercial banks was intended to facilitate access to credit by indigenous small businesses, regardless of the costs. As this access did not materialize after the first few years of the creation of government-owned commercial banks, attention was focused on setting up development banks. These were to provide enterprises with long-term finance that commercial banks could not make available. They used government or donor lines of credit under various projects.

In the years that banks were largely owned by the state, their management tended to suffer significantly. State-owned commercial and development banks became institutions for distributing state largesse to favoured functionaries of the state and their cronies. A lot of the problems that many banks later had with their portfolios could be attributed to poor management of the institutions. Aside from the poor training that many bank officials had, having been rushed into rapidly expanding institutions, the interference from state officials in loan decision making did not allow for significant internal development aimed at enhancing efficiency. The management of most institutions was highly centralized, so that the management staff at head offices took most decisions on lending and other relevant matters.

Reforms have brought the privatization of a number of banks, and state control over many banks in a number of countries has been reduced extensively. In such countries as Ghana, Uganda, Tanzania and Nigeria, the private sector's increasing role in the financial sector is obvious. This has had considerable impact on management, and approaches to loan management appear to be better defined than they ever used to be. Issues of risk are much better considered now, as shown below in our discussion of how loans are screened and monitored and contracts enforced.

Several indicators of size suggest a smallness of the formal financial sector in SSA. Using the value of assets, it may be observed that financial institutions in SSA have always been the smallest in the world. While the average net financial assets of OECD countries was 188 per cent of GNP in 1985, that of Nigeria, a relatively large SSA economy, was only 49 per cent. The smallness of the sector in various countries is best seen in terms of lending to the private sector and in relation to informal sector lending. As shown earlier, the size of private sector credit in relation to GDP is extremely low in Ghana, at 3 per cent to 4 per cent, compared with 50 per cent in Indonesia and 75 per cent in Malaysia. Kenya has one of the better achievements in Africa at 23 per cent. In many countries, the formal sector is judged to be either smaller than or about the same size as the informal sector (Aryeetey, 1995; Nissanke and Aryeetey, 1998).

Dealing with Risk among Formal Institutions

The formal financial sector in SSA is yet to develop adequate mechanisms for countering the risks prevalent in many of the economies in question. The inadequacy helps explain why their asset and liability structures have not changed significantly long after reforms began (Nissanke and Aryeetey, 1998; Popiel, 1994). It also explains why financial intermediation is weak, making the sector still relatively small. The mechanisms in use, and their shortcoming, are described below.

Loan screening and client selection In screening loan applications, banks require much more comprehensive and reliable information than the informal sector does. Banks emphasize the feasibility of proposed projects, for which information must necessarily come from feasibility studies. Where information is not readily obtained from available documents, banks often enquire about the borrower from other sources, invariably amounting to asking other bankers about borrower indebtedness. This contrasts with the position of informal lenders, who usually seek information about the character of borrowers first, followed by their wealth positions (Nissanke and Aryeetey, 1998).

While banks often find documentary evidence attached to applications inadequate, they are not likely to be more successful in the search for personal information about borrowers. Similarly, when they attempt to obtain information on the integrity of borrowers, this is not likely to be forthcoming in many cases. When such information is lacking, bankers' judgements are based largely on their personal knowledge of the proposed projects or on major feasibility studies carried out by the banks themselves. The process of screening delimits the boundary of selection, allowing only relatively large firms to pass through.

In view of the difficulty in finding the relevant information, it is not too surprising that the clientele of banks has not changed much. Thus, before reforms in the mid 1980s, the clientele of most state-owned banks was mostly either parastatals or the governments themselves. In Ghana, Aryeetey et al. (1994) show that these banks lent mainly to state-owned enterprises (SOEs) and to senior government officials. For Tanzania, Collier and Gunning (1991: 533) point out that '...lending (was) determined by government priorities rather than market criteria'. Indeed, government directed banks to open branches in various areas and granted credit to institutions irrespective of the commercial considerations of risk and return. On the other hand, the foreign privately owned banks continued to lend mainly to the few large multinational enterprises. Less than 20 per cent of their portfolios in Ghana went to indigenous businesses. And, as we indicated earlier, more than a decade after the reforms began, the portfolios have not seen any significant structural changes.

The concept that lenders are more likely to enter into repetitive games as a form of screening is borne out by some bank lending patterns. But there is considerable variation in the type of client to receive this treatment. Soyibo (1996b) observes that in Nigeria, banks are more likely to have a longstanding relationship with their large clients than with small borrowers. In Ghana, large enterprises, with a higher likelihood of receiving loans, are more likely to be repeat borrowers (Aryeetey, 1996).

Loan monitoring The main form of monitoring for banks is to monitor the accounts. This was mainly a consequence of cost considerations, even though most banks have regulations that specify the frequency with which such visits must be undertaken. Banks only irregularly undertake project visits. The failure of banks to make extensive project visits need not be seen as an indication of little concern about the moral hazard involved in lending to small businesses. It is often due to pressure on banks to cut their costs as they try to reform. Also, many banks in Africa lack the required equipment for regular project visits. While most project officers know that they are required by internal regulations to visit projects regularly, they are constrained from doing so by lack of transport. This is particularly true for state-owned banks.

Contract enforcement There are significant variations in loan repayment among institutions in SSA. In general, state-owned banks are acknowledged to have the worst repayment records. Tanzania had some of the most disappointing bank loan repayment records before reforms, where poor loan repayment and contract enforcement characterized the banking system. About 94 per cent of the credit portfolio of the major state-owned commercial bank was found to be substandard, doubtful or rated as loss in 1991 (Eriksson, 1993). Despite the problems with default, very few banks in SSA foreclose on defaulting loans. In the 1980s this was not surprising since a large number of the defaulters were SOEs.

Structure of Informal/Semi-Formal Financial Markets

Most SSA countries have informal and semi-formal financial activities (Aryeetey, 1995). Various studies from different countries suggest a wide variety of informal savings and lending units. The prevalence of one institution or the other varies across countries, as indicated by Seibel and Parhusip (1992). This is because informal units are purpose-oriented. Bouman (1995) discusses the development contribution of informal finance in several African countries. Such units are found in both urban and rural areas and, depending on the socioeconomic goals of communities are developed to meet the demand for specific financial services. So long as there exists significant variation in the goals of different social groups and communities, there are likely to be different units. As these goals change with time, and the risks involved in meeting them change, the units are forced to change their operational structures, leading to the establishment of institutions that were not previously found in the countries.

Until recently, most informal financial institutions either only accepted deposits or only lent money. When they lent, this was done mainly to keep the deposits secure and returned to the depositors within the shortest possible time.[3] Since the funds of different lenders can hardly be substituted, the fragmented markets have difficulty intermediating between savers and investors. In not being able to allocate financial resources, they cannot always transform and distribute risks and maturities efficiently. As a consequence, the deposits mobilized by informal financial units as well as their credit facilities display specific differences in structure that make it possible to associate their demand and use with distinct socioeconomic groups.

Savings collectors are more commonly found in West Africa, in such countries as Nigeria, Benin, Togo and Ghana. In both Nigeria and Ghana they are the most signifycant informal deposit mobilizers in terms of the numbers of depositors involved and also sizes of deposits (Soyibo, 1996a; Aryeetey, 1994). The deposits mobilized by various units are targeted at specific uses by their depositors over relatively short periods. This makes financial intermediation rather difficult. The collectors sometimes provide 'advances' to some of their trusted clients. Other loan recipients include traders at local markets in need of short-term credit.

A major group of lenders consists of landlords, neighbours, friends and relative. But these seldom lend on a commercial basis. Despite this, many surveys of enterprise finance in SSA indicate that start-ups of micro-businesses in most countries are primarily funded from such sources.

Moneylenders are significant commercial lenders, often lending from surplus incomes earned from farming or trading. Since moneylender credit is usually the most expensive available, it is demanded mainly by persons without any other options. Moneylenders remain the only informal credit that does not require borrowers to satisfy specific group obligations.

Savings and credit associations, particularly the rotating ones (ROSCAs or *tontines*), are found in most SSA countries (Seibel, 1989). In Senegal they normally operate among salaried employees as well as market women. *Tontines* are more common in towns than in villages. Depositors use their savings for both investment and consumption (religious feasts, pilgrimage, etc.). In Ethiopia, Aredo (1993) studied a number of mutual assistance associations called *iddir* and the ROSCA-type units called *iqqub*. Many groups come together to provide wide-ranging mutual assistance,

---

[3] In many countries, the functions of informal savings mobilization and credit allocation are unrelated among the many segments. Hence, the volume of lending that is undertaken by the sector is not directly related to how much savings it can mobilize.

but in the end, most are dominated by the provision of financial services to members. Indeed, many groups for informal financial arrangements have been created by members primarily to encourage mutual assistance (not necessarily financial) to those members. They are indeed designed to perform mainly an insurance function.

Cooperatives and credit unions are the commonest non-indigenous semi-formal financial units found in many sub-Saharan African communities. In Tanzania, Bagachwa (1995) note that the cooperative movement or 'scheme' was the most significant deposit mobilizer in rural areas. The country had 485 urban-based savings and credit societies (SCS) or credit unions and 438 rural-based cooperatives. They mobilized the equivalent of 4 per cent of total commercial bank deposits in 1990.

A growing number of other semi-formal credit schemes (dominated by NGOs) has been introduced into SSA in the last decade. Webster and Fidler (1995) studied micro-finance institutions in eight West African nations and observed that there were countries with a good number of micro-finance programmes (including Mali, Guinea, Burkina Faso, The Gambia and Guinea Bissau), and others with very few (including Sao Tome, Chad, Mauritania and Sierra Leone). K-REP (Kenya Rural Enterprise Programme) in Kenya is probably the best known micro-finance scheme in Africa, where there are over 40 organizations involved in micro-finance projects. A number of evaluations of innovative and other micro-finance projects suggest that their practice has been less successful in Africa in terms of outreach and sustainability than in other developing economies (Christen et al. 1994).

Some private sector-led developments have also taken place in the area of non-bank finance recently. In Ghana, soon after the launching of economic reforms and the first signs of growth after many years of stagnation, *susu* companies emerged as new sources of semi-formal finance, guaranteeing their depositors credit after six months of regular deposits. Following their failure to meet these credit needs after significant increases in numbers requesting them, many of these companies folded up and were replaced by better organized savings and loan companies that had a greater link to the banking system. Similar institutional developments in Nigeria led to the creation of finance houses, which are private investment companies engaged in the provision of loans, hire purchase, equipment leasing, factoring, project financing and debt administration.

Despite the fragmented nature of informal finance, a number of studies have suggested that the sector is larger in its supply of credit to households than the formal sector (Aryeetey, 1995). The ability of individual units of the informal sector to carry on successfully in the reform years is derived from their ability to localize risks. But this localization within the units tends to fragment the market even further and restricts access to informal credit for many households and small businesses.

Dealing with Risk in the Informal/Semi-Formal Sector

Informal lenders will often lend only if they have the means to enforce the contract. Many such lenders do not make any pretences about evaluating projects. They simply accept the fact they do not have adequate information to form clear judgements about the outcomes of particular investments, except in obvious cases. Apart from this inadequacy, they are also aware that most of their borrowers have no intention of using the borrowed funds for economic ventures. A lot of the credit goes into consumption. These are some of the assumptions that underline the sector's mechanisms for assessing and dealing with risk, which are described below.

Loan screening In the informal sector, screening relies heavily on personal knowledge of borrowers, as Udry (1990) notes. In the semi-formal sector, a mixture of both good knowledge of the borrower and project documentary evidence is used, weighted in favour of good knowledge of the borrower. The development of these personal ties and the use of borrower proximity in decision making are mechanisms for countering the effects of both adverse selection and moral hazard.

But there are some geographical and other variations in the significance of these ties. There is some indication that the more rural the environment, the greater the need to personalize ties in confronting information asymmetry. This conforms to Udry's (1990) observations in northern Nigeria where agricultural lending among relatives, acquaintances, neighbours, etc., was the norm. The ties also vary between group arrangements and individually managed arrangements. In ROSCAs, where only members receive loans, all borrowers are known. Most of the remaining informal lenders only sometimes know the persons who apply for loans. In general, most successful applicants were personal acquaintances of lenders before they made their applications (Nissanke and Aryeetey, 1998). Repetition as a way of screening applications is usual with group arrangements, as the whole process becomes cyclical. It is not that common with other arrangements.

The concept of 'groups' is important as a loan screening tool. Its importance is best reflected in the way it restricts the expansion of group sizes (Bortei-Doku, 1988). Rapid expansion is expected to lead to high default rates as the concepts of 'peer pressure' and 'social stigma' become endangered.[4]

Some of the Asian literature suggests that interlinked credit markets are a major aspect of credit transactions (Yotopoulos and Floro, 1991). There is some variation in the use of interlinked transactions in SSA, however. The evidence of such interlinkages in informal credit markets is not very widespread in places like Ghana and Nigeria (Aryeetey, 1994; Soyibo, 1996a). For Tanzania, on the other hand, Bagachwa (1996) has reported that credit transactions are often linked to land titles. Thus the transactions effectively became ways of buying land in a system where land sales were not possible.

Loan monitoring It has been suggested that informal lenders have a better record on repayments than the formal sector mainly because of constant monitoring of the uses

[4] The risk of being stigmatized is directly related to the fact that issues of credit-taking and debt are considered to be private matters other parties need not know about (Adegboye, 1969; Chipeta and Mkandawire, 1996). The pressure on borrowers to repay is greater in view of the risk of being found out by relations and friends to be borrowers following delinquency in repayment. When credit becomes an open and communal affair, the shame of being 'found out' is no longer a burden for the borrower.

to which the loans are put (Yotopoulos and Floro, 1991). A number of studies into financial markets in Africa have observed very little serious monitoring by the informal sector, however, just as in the case of banks (Popiel, 1994; Nissanke and Aryeetey, 1998). We assume therefore that the better repayment record of informal lenders cannot be attributed to constant loan monitoring.

Very few informal and semi-formal lenders explicitly show interest in how loans are used (Nissanke and Aryeetey, 1998). This is because most of the loans are expected to be used for consumption expenditures. Half of credit unions in Ghana never monitor any loans and another 22 per cent only sometimes do (Aryeetey, 1994). Moneylenders and other informal groups have indicated they seldom visit the project sites of their borrowers. Presumably, when lending is localized there is no need for formal visits.

Loan repayment and contract enforcement Even though repayment trends in the semi-formal and informal sectors are usually much better, we have no reason to believe that it is the result of more 'aggressive' contract enforcement procedures, as suggested by Shipton (1991). There is little evidence of litigation in courts, contrary to what Shipton (1991) suggests for The Gambia. The informal sector does not do much differently from banks in enforcing contracts. The major difference between formal and informal contract enforcement is in relation to how collateral is treated by the two. In the situation of farmland being used as collateral, for example, a bank is less likely to foreclose on this than a rural moneylender would. A rural moneylender can always find relative to farm on land until a loan is repaid—an action that a bank cannot take without incurring additional costs. Hence, for borrowers facing the two sectors, collateral has different meanings that condition their attitudes towards repayment. They would not treat the threat of collateral confiscation by an informal lender lightly, since the informal contract can be enforced more easily.

Experiences with Directed Credit Programmes

Throughout the 1970s and early 1980s, the pursuit of directed credit programmes grew significantly in the developing world, involving a myriad of institutions, often fashioned after institutions to be found in the donor countries. For example, rural banks were set up in the Philippines, Vietnam and Ghana styled after the Farmers' Home Administration of the United States. A number of European countries actively supported the development of cooperatives all over SSA to provide loans to rural people. The World Bank and other large donors encouraged the creation of specialized development banks. In many countries, as we saw earlier, governments were encouraged to introduce policies that forced banks to lend a larger portion of their loan portfolio to small farmers.

There have been a number of evaluations of these programmes for several regions, including Africa (Adams and Von Pischke, 1995). These often tend to suggest that while some of the projects were successful in reaching the target groups of poor rural farmers, many more could not be sustained and folded up without having achieved their objectives. The relevance of the directed credit programmes to today's attempts to support microenterprise development is that the assumptions underlying them have not changed. 'In both cases, the target groups have been perceived to be too poor to afford new technologies in the absence of loans, and they have been unable to save for them' (Adams and Von Pischke, 1995). In addition to this basic assumption, small farmers were considered to require training and technical assistance, hence the need for appropriate technologies that would be conveyed to them. There was active discouragement of informal finance since it was not considered to have any development role.

The irony of the regime of directed credit was that in the design of programmes, considerable emphasis was placed on ensuring higher production from the units that received them, and very little attention was paid to the financial infrastructure that supplied the credit. One consequence was that many of the institutions made significant losses from outrageously high operating costs. A good illustration of the operations of directed credit programmes is provided by the DFIs of Malawi.

Malawi has a relatively large number of DFIs. The Industrial Development Bank (INDEBANK) started operations in 1972. It was set up to provide equity capital, as well as medium- and long-term loans for new and existing industries and agricultural ventures. It also had the objective of encouraging joint ventures with foreign partners. Until recently, it did not accept any deposits. As its shareholders included four foreign organizations, it had considerable access to external finance. The Malawi Development Corporation (MDC), established with equity participation of international financial institutions, acts as a holding company with investment in major Malawian firms. The Agricultural Development and Marketing Corporation (ADMARC) was instituted primarily to develop a marketing and distribution network for smallholder agriculture. It was also expected to promote agricultural and industrial sectors as an investment holding company. Malawi also has INDEBANK's offshoot, the Investment and Development Fund (INDEFUND), and the Small Enterprise Development Organization of Malawi (SEDOM). INDEFUND was targeted at medium-scale Malawian owned businesses to provide advisory and training services, as well as medium- and long-term loans for start-up and working capital. With financial assistance from the EU, SEDOM specializes in the provision of term loans, technical assistance and advisory services to small-scale enterprises owned by indigenous Malawians.

The Malawian DFIs have relied extensively on foreign resources for their operations, not the mobilization of domestic savings, and their financial performance has generally been unsatisfactory. While the larger DFIs have managed to generate positive, though minimal, pre-tax returns, the smaller institutions (INDEFUND and SEDOM), specializing in providing services to small and medium enterprises (SMEs), have frequently shown operating losses. Inadequate resources and staff shortages have made operational efficiency difficult for both institutions. In-house capacity to appraise, evaluate and monitor projects is judged to be inadequate (Chipeta and Mkandawire, 1996a). In the early years of its operations, INDEFUND had arrears as high as 40 per cent and cumulative losses amounting to kwacha 0.9 million at the end of 1986, compared with an annual income of kwacha 0.6 million and kwacha 4.8

million of capital employed. Its financial position has improved in the 1990s. SEDOM also faced a rising level of arrears in its overall portfolio throughout the 1980s. The transaction costs of INDEFUND and SEDOM are also known to be extremely high: in 1988 INDEFUND and SEDOM incurred costs of 0.67 kwacha and 0.44 kwacha, respectively, for every 1.00 kwacha lent.

The performance of the larger DFIs was not much better. Adam et al. (1992) suggest that poor project selection, weak management and high gearing were the main factors behind MDC's difficulties. While its crop marketing and distribution proved profitable, ADMARC experienced poor financial performance of its investment and development operations. INDEBANK promoted joint ventures with Press Holdings, ADMARC and MDC, which together formed about 60 per cent of its loan portfolio. It reported marginally higher pre-tax returns than MDC.

There have been attempts at reforms in recent years. INDEBANK has been given license to accept deposits, to float a local currency bond, to issue letters of credit and bankers acceptances, and to engage in other merchant activities. The portfolio of the DFIs was also restructured through a fairly comprehensive asset swap programme involving Press Holdings, ADMARC and MDC in 1984–1986. MDC and ADMARC were also encouraged to undertake a number of divestitures in 1984–1989.

It is the view of Adam et al. (1992), however, that the primary objective of the asset swaps was to control the losses of the politically strong Press Holdings. Hence the main benefits of the process accrued to Press Holdings at the expense of MDC, and to a lesser extent, ADMARC. Although the short-run effect of the asset swap was positive, the effect on the long-run health of portfolios is less certain.

The problems of the DFIs of Malawi are in no way peculiar to that country. For Tanzania, Bagachwa (1996) reports the difficulties of the Cooperative and Rural Development Bank (CRDB), which became illiquid and insolvent. Popiel (1994) reports that Côte d'Ivoire had to liquidate all of its DFIs in the 1980s.

The failure of targeting under directed credit programmes is amply illustrated by the decline of rural banks in Ghana.[5] Aside from the development banks, unit rural banks were set up beginning in 1976 in an attempt to mobilize funds for a market not catered for by established commercial banks. They were primarily intended for targeting credit to agriculture and the rural microenterprise sector. There are at the moment 124 of them. In the 1980s, while the growth of deposits with rural banks appeared encouraging, the proportion of total credit going to the agricultural sector declined in favour of other sectors. In 1985 credit to agriculture amounted to 54.4 per cent of total credit, but dropped to 41.0 per cent in 1987 and then to 34.0 per cent in 1988. The share of trading, on the other hand, rose from 12.9 per cent in 1985 to 25.9 per cent in 1988, while credit to cottage industry fell from 11.6 per cent to 6.0 per cent in 1987 and rose slightly to 7.6 per cent in 1988. As a matter of fact, between 1977 and 1988, the share of agriculture in total credit from rural banks was halved, while that for the commerce sector was doubled. The changes observed were the banks' approach to risk diversification, and the declining trends have continued to date:

---

[5] These are unit banks for specific rural areas and rely on local ownership and support. The central bank holds preference shares, equivalent to one-third of the initial share capital.

banks' portfolios are dominated by trading activities. The difficulties of the existing rural banks are reflected in the fact that Bank of Ghana classified only 60 as 'satisfactory' and another 47 as 'mediocre' in 1996. Eighteen banks continued to be distressed and did not operate.

The difficulties of many directed credit programmes in Africa have been discussed by Thomas (1993). In sum, while these programmes had relatively large costs, they had little positive impact on the magnitude of credit available to the target groups. The loans benefited mainly political structures and they became tools for funding politically motivated projects.

In more recent times, directed credit programmes have mainly taken the form of NGO schemes and other micro-finance projects. Evaluations of micro-finance projects generally examine the extent of their outreach activities and their drive towards self-sustainability (Yaron, 1992). Financial self-sustainability is achieved when the return on equity, net of any subsidy received, equals or exceeds the opportunity cost of funds. Outreach is measured on the basis of the type of clientele served and the variety of financial services offered, including the value and number of loans extended, the value and number of savings accounts, the type of financial services offered, the number of branches and village subbranches, the percentage of the total rural population served, the real annual growth of the institution's assets over recent years, and the participation of women as clients. Many such evaluations have questioned the sustainability of projects as well as their outreach (Webster and Fidler, 1995; Aryeetey, 1997).

Adams and Von Pischke (1995) warn in particular against allowing the common assumptions that underlie directed credit programmes to influence unduly a repetition of the policies and the definitions of beneficiary groups. They argue that the policies and practices that most hurt the directed credit schemes were: the loan guarantees to induce banks to lend to target groups, concessionary lines of credit to stimulate targeted lending, subsidized interest rates, absence of deposit mobilization, emphasis on large loans, and reliance on government and donor funds. The target groups were poorly defined to the extent that they were hardly well known to the lending agencies. The justification for pursuing particular projects had nothing to do with the risks involved in those projects, as the focus was more on the need for them. The consequence, as has been shown with the Malawian case above, was that only a small fraction of the targeted population was reached, the programmes were too expensive and too little revenue was collected. In addition, the beneficiaries of the subsidies that came with the interest rates were often not poor people. The loan recovery problems that were typical of directed programmes came from the little risk analysis that the institutions undertook. Adams and Von Pischke (1995) have suggested that only a few of the specialized agencies that have handled small farmer credit have proven to be durable. They saw their operations as having been rather brittle and unable to survive economic shocks, including high inflation.

The Impact of Financial Liberalization on Performance and Institute Building

The reaction to the problems of directed credit in the 1980s was to call for financial liberalization throughout the developing world (Caprio et al., 1994). As we mentioned earlier, however, financial liberalization has not proven to be the panacea to the problems of the financial sector in SSA. We showed that in a number of SSA countries, the functions of savings mobilization and financial intermediation have not fully recovered since reforms were initiated. Pervasive objective risk continues to be a major feature of the markets; the infrastructure for financial service delivery has not significantly improved, and the environment for regulation and supervision remains poor.

Thus, banks' balance sheets remain precarious. Even in Ghana and Malawi, where reforms have been relatively orderly, most banking institutions have not developed the capacity of risk management and still operate with an inadequate information base. They have become overly risk averse in their asset management, resulting in a credit crunch (Nissanke and Aryeetey, 1998). In Nigeria and Tanzania, banks' net worth deteriorated in the adjustment period through imprudent asset management. These contrasting trends conform to what Caprio et al. (1994) describe as characteristic responses to liberalization attempts, where banking institutions had been previously shielded from market forces by government intervention. Caprio et al. (1994) predict two different possible responses from banks: The first is to avoid all but the lowest risk. The second is a reckless expansion of lending, even to insolvent clients.

Various explanations have been advanced to explain the apparent failure of financial liberalization programmes to address the problems of SSA financial markets. As earlier indicated the most frequently mentioned explanation for the disappointing outcome of financial liberalization in SSA is the incompleteness of the reforms. The World Bank (1994) largely subscribes to this view and suggests that the continued poor financial performance is due to lack of progress on some of the reform measures. A major blame is placed on the use of financial systems to finance public sector activities, which is made possible by the continuing public sector ownership of a large part of the financial system.

Policy changes in the course of reforms in a number of countries have often been seen to be either ad hoc responses to emerging events or a reflection of low government commitment to reform measures (World Bank, 1994a). In contrast, favourable evaluations of some Asian liberalization experiences suggest that policy has been 'flexible and adaptable', while remaining firmly anchored in strategy taken by implementing agencies. In the Asian countries, policy responses to evolving circumstances have involved fine-tuning the pace of reform measures rather than ad hoc changes. Certainly, in several countries, better design and implementation procedure might have stalled some of the negative consequences of the reform.

In Nigeria, incorrect pace and sequencing in the initial reform years led to the crisis and eventual collapse of the financial system, necessitating several policy reversals (Soyibo, 1996b). The crisis made policy consistency and credibility critical issues. The comprehensiveness of this explanation is dented by other observations, however. In Ghana and Malawi, with more gradual reforms, the results are not different. The disappointing outcomes differ from the optimistic assertions initially made about liberalization and reform, which had raised unfounded expectations about the time frame within which positive effects could be generated. It is observed in the World Bank report (1994b) that the design of reform programmes sometimes placed too much faith in 'quick fixes'. Over-emphasis in reform programmes on the benefits of restructuring balance sheets and the re-capitalization of banks has also been criticized. It is further pointed out that the time it takes to improve financial infrastructure in an environment where the main borrowers (the government and the public enterprises) are financially distressed and institutionally weak was underestimated.

One area where there have been severe constraints to effective reform has been the macroeconomic environment. Despite some encouraging improvements reported in the adjustment period for some countries, the macroeconomic environment remains quite fragile. Macroeconomic stability is difficult to maintain in the face of external shocks and political pressures, which erode fiscal and monetary discipline. Unable to restrain inflation, authorities have had a hard time achieving positive real interest rates, despite increasing nominal rates. Indeed, unstable and high interest rates have further destabilized macroeconomic conditions in many countries. In several Asian countries, rising interest rates engendered a shift to interest-bearing deposits with longer maturities. In SSA, on the other hand, neither a marked growth in deposits nor clear improvement in the maturity structure has been observed after increases in nominal rates in countries with considerable macroeconomic instability (Nissanke and Basu, 1992). Ghana is a clear case of this experience.

Another major requirement for effective liberalization that has been missing in many SSA countries is a conducive environment for supervision and regulation of financial institutions. In SSA this environment is grossly inadequate and ineffectual, and there are few concerted genuine measures to build institutional capacity of regulatory systems, as discussed below. The systems must be transparent, accountable, and free from political interference and patronage. Infrastructural support systems such as the legal framework and information base have not been developed in many countries.

The human capacity problems remain immense. A study of the preparedness of banks for SME lending in Ghana after reforms were initiated (Duggleby, 1992) indicated that many banks were not comfortable with the capacity of their credit operations staff to make the key judgements involved in determining whether a project was viable and capable of repaying the credit out of cash flow. Most of the institutions studied expressed the need for further staff training to improve the quality and accuracy of project analysis as part of credit analysis. The management of the institutions particularly emphasized the need to upgrade skills in cost analysis and project sensitivity analysis. Testing project resilience to changes in market share, cost and prices was especially important because of the poor quality of available information. Determination of market adequacy and the actual liquidity position of the business were also areas where bankers indicated that skills needed upgrading.

Many banks in SSA do not have the capacity to market financial services in an increasingly competitive environment. Having come out of total government ownership only recently, such banks are particularly lacking in marketing skills, since they previously did not face competition or analyse projects on the basis of more than simple cash flows. The need to diversify their portfolios, especially those that previously concentrated on particular sectors, remains paramount, but they have not been sufficiently equipped to deal with them.

It is not surprising, therefore, as the World Bank's Policy Review Note (1994b) argues that complete interest rate deregulation should only be attempted when more stringent criteria than previously suggested are satisfied. In addition to stable macroeconomic conditions and adequate regulatory and supervisory systems, the criteria should include more sophisticated and solvent banking institutions with positive net worth and 'contestable' financial markets. The Bank maintains that where these conditions are not satisfied interest rates should not be subject to complete deregulation. They should instead be managed in the interim, with the move to market-determined rates as a longer-term objective. Many SSA countries do not meet the criteria for using market-determined rates in the manner applied in the last decade in several of those countries. Indeed, the financial sectors of SSA countries were largely not ready for full-scale liberalization and deregulation.

It is now widely accepted that financial reform is a lengthy process, requiring critical progress in institution building. For effective long-term reform programmes, it is important to gain a deeper understanding of banks' operating environments and their resulting behavioural characteristics. Unless the constraints that prevent improvements in banks' operations are reduced, it may take a long time for reforms to engender positive results.

Regulatory and Supervisory Environment

A number of studies into financial market development in SSA in the last decade suggest that the regulatory and supervisory environment has been quite poor, leading to many of the difficulties the markets have encountered (Popiel, 1994; Nissanke and Aryeetey, 1998). Poor regulation and supervision are partly blamed for the large number of non-performing assets found on the books of banks in the 1970s and 1980s.

In Nigeria, with a relatively larger financial market, the World Bank (1995) has reported major problems with banking supervision. Soyibo et al. (1997) have made similar comments about regulation and supervision in the Nigerian banking system. Referring to a report from the Nigerian Deposit Insurance Corporation, they wrote, 'One worrisome aspect of the result of liberalization of the financial sector in Nigeria is the extent of distress in the sector. The poor performance of distressed banks was traced to a number of factors, among which are: ineffective management, poor loans and advances administration, under-capitalization, owners' interference in management, board and management instability, poor internal controls and fraud' (Soyibo et al., 1997: 3). These strong views about the inadequacy of the regulatory and supervisory environment in Nigeria are further corroborated by Sobodu and Akiode (1998).

Prior to the financial sector reform programme in Ghana, enforcement of banking regulations was ineffective and supervision was weak. There tended to be greater focus on the banks' condition at a given point in time, rather than on strengthening management systems. The number of staff in the central bank's examination department was insufficient, and they did not have the skills needed to carry out comprehensive examination procedures (Duggleby et al., 1992). The situation in Tanzania was even worse (Bagachwa, 1996).

Popiel (1994) observes that in the francophone countries of the West African Monetary Union, the conditions for regulation and supervision were quite similar, leading to the widespread distress that banks suffered in the 1980s, with the severest form occurring in Benin where all banks simply shut down. This was primarily because central bank and other banking laws were largely outdated and the prudential framework no longer made any sense. The legal, regulatory and prudential frameworks were judged to lack strength, consistency and flexibility.

Under financial sector reforms in a number of countries, technical advice was sought to strengthen the supervision function of central banks. Management structure, staffing, training and compensation issues were reviewed. In Ghana, the Banking Law was amended to require that each bank be examined at least once a year. Regulation was extended to semi-formal financial institutions through the Rules and Regulations and Control Measures for the Establishment and Supervision of Savings and Loan Companies issued by the Bank of Ghana in 1990. This led to a new act for NBFIs. The same has been done in Uganda. Standard accounting and auditing principles were introduced in many countries.

While the measures are recognized as having gradually improved supervision and helped the banking sectors to regain some stability, it is also obvious that restructuring requirements for better credit analysis, portfolio management and capital adequacy have made most banks more reluctant to take risks. The result is that lending continues to be highly selective. Indeed, we recognize that an effective prudential regulatory and supervisory system is still missing in SSA countries. It is an essential requirement, since financial transaction through the banking system involves a significant externality through the act of offering deposits and money creation. It is important that monetary authorities maintain the solvency of deposit institutions and the stability of the monetary system through regulations of reserve requirements or risk adjusted capital adequacy ratios or supervision of the quality of banks' assets and portfolio. Supervision and regulation of financial institutions have remained grossly inadequate, while infrastructural support systems such as the legal framework are deficient, and banks' balance sheets remain problematic, even if better than they were a decade ago.

Globalization and Financial Integration

Aside from improving the domestic climate for mobilizing savings and providing credit, are there any changes that could be made in a more globalized framework? Despite the fact that foreign savings, largely official aid flows, continue to be important for SSA growth and development, there are few systematic ways for attracting private foreign savings to individual countries. In view of the peculiar risks of various countries, their ability to attract foreign savings is highly circumstantial and unstable.

Private capital flows, particularly foreign direct investment and portfolio equity, into the developing world grew remarkably after the mid 1980s. Their share in total private flows moved to an average 35 per cent and 13.5 per cent, respectively, in the period 1990–1996, up from 12 per cent and 1.2 per cent a decade earlier. The growth is generally attributed to the growing integration of markets and financial institutions, increased economic liberalization, and rapid innovation in financial instruments and technologies, particularly in the areas of computing and telecommunications. The reality for Africa, however, is that most of these growing flows are directed at Asia and Latin America. China alone accounted for 86 per cent of total FDI flows in 1995. Even though Nigeria is the second largest recipient of FDI, this is not diversified and is mainly restricted to the extractive sector of the economy, as is the case in Ghana.

A number of studies have suggested that for the majority of low-income countries that fail to attract foreign private capital, especially FDI, the small domestic market is the main bottleneck. But there are often other reasons for the relative absence of FDI, including the lack of rich natural resources. To counter this problem, there are often calls for regional integration in order to make the markets larger. For portfolio flows, on the other hand, an additional factor is the depth and stability of the financial markets. Countering this latter problem has led to calls for regional integration of a different sort—the integration of financial markets across country borders (Folkerts-Landau and Van Greuning, 1997).

It is interesting that a number of SSA countries with more internationally-oriented emerging financial markets have become interested in strengthening monetary co-operation and financial market infrastructure. The Franc Zone allows 13 countries to share a common currency with a common central bank. Zone members are moving steadily towards modernizing bank regulation, liberalizing markets, improving supervision and instituting indirect monetary instruments at the regional level. They are continuing to develop regional bond and equity markets, as well as regional pension and insurance regulations.

The argument for integrating financial market infrastructure in SSA is based on the notion that 'prudent cross-border lending and investment can diversify financial institutions' asset risks away from the small number of economic sectors that dominate so many national economies and that are prone to frequent shocks' (Folkerts-Landau and Van Greuning, 1997: 1). In Southern Africa, for example, it is argued that the concentration of economic activity in a small number of natural resources, e.g., tobacco in Malawi, cattle and diamonds in Botswana, copper in Zambia, ensures that banks are often largely exposed to only a few industries and crops. They could diversify their asset portfolios by investing abroad, a step that would help them to reduce their exposure to risk while increasing the volume of inflation-adjusted lending.

A further argument for regionalization of banking is that the new legislation and regulations from an outside body would act as an agency of restraint on national authorities when banking regulations have been harmonized. This would allow for coordinated supervision. Further benefits come from the possibility of leveraging country resources to mitigate small country concerns and the possibility of a coordinated response to financial crisis as happened with the problems created by the Meridien Bank failure.[6] Folkerts-Landau and Van Greuning (1997) provide many other reasons why such integration would improve the service delivery and efficiency of financial institutions in SSA.

The main approach recommended for integration is the institution of a regional supervising authority, which might be either private or public, charged with responsibility for off-site analysis of adherence to prudential rules and regulations on a regional basis. Such off-site supervision, which would entail processing returns and manipulating data, would lead to evaluating and interpreting individual banks' risk management processes as well as their performance. The supervisory authority would need to be well equipped with appropriate standards and regulations, as well as human capacity, in order to establish its credibility.

However, it should be noted that globalization of financial markets could present SSA countries an opportunity as well as a challenge. The experiences of East Asian countries are pertinent here again. On the one hand, globalized markets and regional dynamics helped many East Asian countries to attract foreign savings by way of direct and portfolio investments in the past. On the other hand, the events that have unfolded since 1997 in a number of East Asian countries, initially triggered by their financial and banking crisis, but evolving into serious currency and general economic crises, remind us how difficult it is to manage strategically the process of globalization in the interest of development of national economies.

Conclusion: Alternatives To Liberalization?

With the increasing realization that the aspirations of reforming countries have largely not been met, renewed interest in intervention in financial markets is being expressed (Stiglitz, 1994). The few empirical tests of the general equilibrium framework for complete markets in Africa, including Udry (1990) for Northern Nigeria and Deaton (1992) for Côte d'Ivoire, reject the implications for complete perfectly competitive markets. There are hardly any full-risk sharing institutions. Nissanke and Aryeetey (1998) have shown that in a number of countries, there are many individuals,

[6] Meridien BIAO was an international banking group whose umbrella bank was based in Luxembourg and treasury in the Bahamas. It started operations in a number of African countries in the mid 1980s as countries began reforms. The parent bank in Luxembourg held 75 per cent of total shares of the group, while Bahamas often held up to 55 per cent of the shares of Meridien BIAO in various countries. Meridien BIAO became exposed (deposit-wise) to Bahamas in a significant way. When Bahamas, being the treasury of the group, suffered severe over-exposure on its assets, this triggered a chain of financial distress within the group, affecting banks in Ghana, Nigeria, Swaziland and Zambia.

households and regions that are isolated from markets and mechanisms for borrowing and lending or insuring against risk. These situations suggest that there is considerable scope for intervention in SSA financial markets. Indeed, despite the evidence that interventions have their own problems, depending on how they are pursued, the movement towards intervention has grown stronger, particularly with various microfinance schemes being pushed into mainstream financing arrangements in many countries. Today, credit delivery systems appear to be gaining centre stage in many donor activities. The main research question becomes how governments should structure and design intervention in the financial markets.

In particular, targeting intervention is devised in order to reach the sections of the market that are not reached by existing institutions. The issue for many specialized schemes becomes one of how to equip institutions that can reach poor households and small enterprises at low cost to achieve a wider outreach. The activities of informal lenders throughout SSA suggest that they already target the poor (including women), even if they are not always successful. At the same time, the attempts by better-resourced innovative schemes to target the same poor people have not been any more successful. The following sections discuss some of the proposals for intervening in financial markets in order to ensure proper policy development and appropriate ways of targeting.

Financial Restraint?

Since governments in SSA are generally seen to have failed to provide the support needed to draw out a positive response from the financial sector to real sector needs, there has been some suggestion that the state play a more active role than the financial liberalization doctrine would imply. Hellman et al. (1997) put forward what they see as a new paradigm of 'financial restraint'. The ideas behind financial restraint are largely influenced by the experiences of high-performing East Asian economies, including the Japanese postwar experience.

Financial restraint policies aim at creating rents within the private sector. Rents are defined to mean the 'returns in excess of those generated by a competitive market' (Hellman et al., 1997). They differ from financial repression in the sense that the rents obtained from holding deposit rates and lending rates below the competitive equilibrium level go to private sector agents instead of the government. This is achieved by putting in place financial policies that regulate entry and direct competition. The imposition of different lending rates for different sectors serves to distribute the rents to the financial and real sectors. The rents are intended to reduce information-related problems that hamper perfectly competitive markets.

In order to differentiate between financial restraint and financial repression, a number of conditions must be satisfied. These include the existence of a stable macroeconomic environment with low and predictable inflation rates as well as positive real interest rates. (See Nissanke and Aryeetey, 1998, for detailed discussion on the difference between the two policy frameworks.) It is important that the policies of financial restraint do not lead to rent extraction by the government from the private sector.

In the basic analysis of financial restraint, it is argued that selective intervention through financial restraint creates 'franchise value for banks that induces them to become more stable institutions with better incentives to monitor the firms they finance and manage the risk of the loan portfolio'. Banks are expected to expand their deposit base following the creation of rents and then increase the extent of intermediation. Directed credit is expected to compensate for market deficiencies including the lack of long-term lending. Lower lending rates should induce a reduction in the agency problems of banks as adverse selection is reduced. It is suggested that in some East Asian economies, directed credit led to 'contest' effects among firms; if well structured such effects can provide even stronger incentives than competitive markets.

The proponents of financial restraint indicate that it is not a static policy instrument. It is suggested that the various sets of financial policies must be adjusted with time, depending on the performance of the financial markets and the economy in general. 'As financial depth increases, and, in particular, as the capital base of the financial sector strengthens, these interventions may be progressively relaxed and the economy may make the transition to a more classic "free markets" paradigm' (Hellman et al., 1997: 166).

Financial Systems Development Approach?

While financial sector liberalization is claimed to provide a broad policy framework within which financial institutions can seek to operate efficiently, it is not enough to ensure unhindered financial resource flows from surplus units to deficit units at low cost. In attempting to use financial flows for enterprise development, financial restraint may be considered as a possible alternative, if the institutional capacity for its implementation is in place. In practice, for low-income countries in SSA, this points to the need to develop a more comprehensive approach to institution building than has been envisaged so far in financial sector reforms.

Furthermore, there is need to consider answers to such questions as the following: Which credit and insurance delivery mechanisms might allow financial institutions to achieve a second best solution? What financial institutions are most accessible to the poor and how do these affect SSA production? Alternatively, what types of credit conditions are most agreeable with borrowers and what institutions are most suited for providing it?

Rashid and Townsend (1993) analyse the theoretical suggestions for answering these questions. They acknowledge that the exact design of any intervention would depend on the nature of the particular barrier to trading risks. In the past, however, the approaches that have been advocated for countering the problems of information asymmetry, including the acquisition of more information by banks and the strengthening of group schemes, have been tried unsuccessfully by both formal and semi-formal institutions, as we saw with the review of directed credit arrangements.

But the differentiated and inconclusive outcomes of reforms, as portrayed in such countries as Ghana and Nigeria, where financial reforms have not yet led to financial deepening, also show that other positive developments have emerged in the informal and semi-formal non-banking sector, partly due to economic recovery and also as a result of the more open environment. The semi-formal and informal sectors have shown greater adaptation to a changing environment and developed means for containing risk. These lead to the submission that aside from a closer relationship between the formal and informal sectors, there is little scope for allocating credit efficiently and equitably. One has to note the reservation of Besley (1995), however that such strengthened ties will not be a panacea for financial development. But the linkage has the potential of permitting banks to acquire more information as well as aiding semi-formal institutions to enforce contracts as outreach and sustainability are enhanced. The trick is to use, as much as possible, known and community-wide accepted indigenous institutions for retailing credit from formal institutions.

It is possible for the regulatory framework to be used to provide incentives for surplus units to do business with such deficit financial agents as those in the semi-formal and informal sectors. It is important that the regulatory framework is not seen to be punitive or tending to discourage innovation, as is the case in a number of countries. Central banks could develop incentive frameworks that encourage formal institutions to want to use semi-formal and other non-bank institutions for credit allocation and savings mobilization. Greater diversification in the management of reserves could be a useful mechanism for achieving such an objective. Thus, leasing companies, for example, could become good outlets for term finance for small expanding businesses, while savings and loan companies serve the purpose of providing working capital to smaller growing businesses and even other informal lenders.

The regulatory and supervisory systems could be of considerable importance in providing incentives to banks. If banks perceived that risk was considerably reduced by dealing with credible semi-formal and informal agents, they would be encouraged to use them. Effective regulation and supervision of semi-formal and informal institutions would tend to be problematic in some cases, however. But the ultimate outcome of such innovation could be considerable credit layering, among many other possibilities.

Having an effective regulatory framework requires concrete decisions on what to do about all segments of the financial system. Such decision making needs to be informed by sound judgement on types of regulation that are required for different types of institutions. Indeed for most SSA countries where administrators possess little knowledge of informal 'institutions' and are therefore ill equipped to monitor and regulate a large number of such organizations at a time, a considerable amount of self-regulation might be considered.

New institutions require appropriate incentives to go into 'new niches', as financial development strategies should be demand driven and sufficiently flexible to accommodate innovations. At the same time, sufficient supervision is required to avoid problems such as insider lending and misuse of funds or inadequate capital to meet obligations. The encouragement of other forms of financing, including the increasing use of equities, must be explored as new institutions emerge.

Institutional restructuring should aim at not only improving the capacity of bank staff to assess projects with appropriate skills, but also to understand the workings of the informal sector. Currently, considerable distrust, inadequate knowledge about the informal sector, prejudice in some cases, all create a risky environment for banks (Nissanke and Aryeetey, 1998). In developing policy to overcome this situation, a financial systems development approach that ensures the development of institutions and linkages that serve the identified segments should be adopted. Using policy to bring about such institutional development can be done with both the fiscal system and the regulatory and supervisory system to provide incentives for formal institutions and informal segments to overcome the current state of market fragmentation.

References

Adam, C., S. William, P. Cavendish and P.S. Mistry. 1992. *Adjusting Privatization.* London: James Currey Publishing Co.

Adam, C. and S. O'Connell. 1996. 'Aid, taxation and development: Analytical perspectives on aid effectiveness in sub-Saharan Africa'. Mimeo. Centre for the Study of African Economies, University of Oxford.

Adams, D.W. and J.D. Von Pischke. 1995. 'Microenterprise credit programs: Déja vu'. In F.J.A. Bouman and O. Hospes, eds., *Financial Landscapes Reconstructed.* Boulder: Westview Press.

Adegboye, R.O. 1969. 'Procuring loans by pledging cocoa trees'. *Journal of the Geographical Association of Nigeria*, vol. 12, nos. 1 and 2.

Aredo, D. 1993. *The Informal and Semi-Formal Financial Sectors in Ethiopia: A Study of the Iqqub, Iddir and Savings and Credit Cooperatives.* Research Paper No. 21. African Economic Research Consortium, Nairobi.

Aryeetey, E. 1994. *Financial Integration and Development in Sub-Saharan Africa: A Study of Informal Finance in Ghana.* Working Paper 78. Overseas Development Institute, London.

Aryeetey, E. 1995. *Filling the Niche. Informal Finance in Africa:* Nairobi: Heinemann/African Economic Research Consortium.

Aryeetey, E. 1996. *The Formal Financial Sector in Ghana After the Reforms.* Working Paper 86. Overseas Development Institute, London.

Aryeetey, E. 1997. 'Rural finance in Africa: Institutional developments and access for the poor'. *Proceedings of the Annual World Bank Conference on Development Economics 1996.* Washington, D.C.: The World Bank.

Aryeetey, E. and F. Gockel. 1991. *Mobilizing Domestic Resources for Capital Formation In Ghana: The Role of Informal Financial Markets.* Research Paper No. 3. African Economic Research Consortium, Nairobi.

Aryeetey, E., A. Baah-Nuakoh, T. Duggleby, H. Hettige and W.F. Steel. 1994. 'The supply and demand for finance among SMEs in Ghana'. *World Bank Discussion Paper* 251, Africa Technical Department, Washington, D.C.

Aryeetey, E., H. Hettige, M. Nissanke and W.F. Steel. 1997. 'Financial market fragmentation and reforms in four African countries'. *World Bank Economic Review*, vol. 11, no. 2.

Bagachwa, M.S.D. 1994. *Financial Integration and Development in sub-Saharan Africa: a Study of Informal Finance in Tanzania.* Working Paper 79. London: Overseas Development Institute.

Bagachwa, M.S.D. 1996. *Financial Integration and Development in Sub-Saharan Africa: A Study of Formal Finance in Tanzania.* Working Paper 87. Overseas Development Institute, London.

Besley, T.J. 1995. 'Savings, credit and insurance'. In J. Behrman and T.N. Srinivasan, eds., *Handbook of Development Economics*, Vol. 3A, *Handbooks in Economics*, vol. 9. Amsterdam: Elsevier Science, North Holland.

Besley, T.J., and S. Coate. 1995. 'Group lending, repayment incentives, and social collateral'. *Journal of Development Economics*, 46: 1–18.

Biggs, T. and P. Srivasatva. 1996. *Structural Aspects of Manufacturing in Sub-Saharan Africa: Findings from a Seven Country Enterprise Survey*. Africa Technical Discussion Paper No. 346, June. The World Bank, Washington, D.C.

Blanc, Xavier. 1997. 'Industrial change under structural adjustment: Tanzania 1993–96.' The African Regional Programme on Enterprise Development. Washington, D.C.: The World Bank.

Bortei-Doku, E. 1988. 'Mid-term evaluation of the People's Participation Project'. Mimeo. FAO Africa Regional Office, Accra.

Bouman, F.J.A. 1995. 'Informal rural finance: An Aladdin's lamp of information'. In F.J.A. Bouman and O. Hospes, eds., *Financial Landscapes Reconstructed*. Boulder: Westview Press.

Caprio, Gerald, Jr., Izak Atiyas and J. Hanson, eds. 1994. *Financial Reform: Theory and Experience*. Cambridge: Cambridge University Press.

Carter, M. 1988. 'Equilibrium credit rationing of small farm agriculture'. *Journal of Development Economics*, vol. 28, no. 1(February): 83–103.

Chipeta, C. and M. Mkandawire. 1996a. *Financial Integration and Development in Sub-Saharan Africa: The Informal Sector in Malawi*. Working Paper 85. Overseas Development Institute, London.

Chipeta, C. and M. Mkandawire. 1996b. *Financial Integration and Development in Sub-Saharan Africa: the Formal and Semi-Formal Financial Sectors in Malawi*. Working Paper 89. Overseas Development Institute, London.

Christen, R.P., E. Rhyne and R.C. Vogel. 1994. 'Maximizing the outreach of microenterprise finance: The emerging lessons of successful programs'. Consulting Assistance for Economic Reform (CAER) Paper. Washington, D.C.: IMCC.

Collier, P. and C. Mayer. 1989. 'The assessment: Financial liberalization, financial systems, and economic growth'. *Oxford Review of Economic Policy*, vol. 5, no. 4.

Collier, P. and J. W. Gunning. 1991. 'Money creation and financial liberalization in a socialist banking system: Tanzania 1983–1988'. *World Development*, vol. 19, no. 5: 533–38.

Cuevas, C., R. Hanson, M. Fafchamps, P. Moll and P. Srivastava. 1993. 'Case Studies of Enterprise Finance in Ghana'. RPED, The World Bank, Washington, D.C., March.

Chuta, E. and C. Liedholm. 1985. *Employment and Growth in Small-Scale Industry: Empirical Evidence and Policy Assessment from Sierra Leone*. New York: St. Martin's Press.

Deaton, A.S. 1992. 'Saving and income smoothing in Côte d'Ivoire'. *Journal of African Economies*, 1(1): 1–24.

Duggleby, T. 1992. 'Best practices in innovative small enterprise finance institutions'. In William F. Steel, ed., *Financial Deepening in Sub-Saharan Africa: Theory and Innovations*. Industry and Energy Department Working Paper, Industry Series Paper No. 62. Washington, D.C.: The World Bank.

Eriksson, G. 1993. 'Incidence and pattern of the soft budget in Tanzania'. Macroeconomic Studies No. 44/93. Sida Planning Secretariat, Stockholm.

Folkerts-Landau, E. and H. Van Greuning. 1997. 'The case for regional financial-market infrastructure in Africa'. Informal Discussion Paper, Country Department 1, Africa Region, The World Bank. May.

Gertler, M. and A. Rose. 1994. 'Finance, growth and public policy'. In G. Caprio, Jr., I. Atiyas and J. Hanson, eds., *Financial Reforms: Theory and Experience*. Cambridge: Cambridge University Press.

Goldsmith, R.W. 1969. *Financial Structure and Development*. New Haven and London: Yale University Press.

Gurley, J.G. and E. Shaw. 1967. 'Financial structure and economic development'. *Economic Development and Cultural Change*, 15, 3: 257–68.

Hellman, T., K.C. Murdock and J. Stiglitz. 1997. 'Financial restraint: Toward a new paradigm. In M. Aoki, H. Kim and M. Okumo-Fujiwara, eds., *The Role of Government in East Asian Economic Development*. Oxford: Clarendon Press.

King, R. and R. Levine. 1993. 'Finance, entrepreneurship, and growth'. Paper presented at the World Bank Conference, 8–9 February 1993.

ILO/Jobs and Skills Programme for Africa (JASPA). 1989. *African Employment Report 1988*. Addis Ababa.

Levy, Brian. 1993. 'Obstacles to developing indigenous small and medium enterprises: An empirical Assessment'. *The World Bank Economic Review*, vol. 7, no. 1: 65–83.

Meyer, R.l., G. Nagarajan and K. Ouattara. 1993. 'Financial Intermediation by NGOs – Implications for Indigenous Village Groups in The Gambia'. *American Journal of Agricultural Economics*, 75(5): 1300–35, December.

Miracle, M.P., D.S. Miracle and L. Cohen. 1980. 'Informal savings mobilization in Africa'. *Economic Development and Cultural Change*, vol. 28, no. 2.

Neal, Craig R. 1988. 'Macro-financial indicators for one hundred seventeen developing and industrial countries'. The World Bank, December 1988.

Nissanke, M. 1998. 'Financing enterprise development and export diversification in sub-Saharan Africa'. Paper presented at the UNCTAD Workshop on Economic Development and Regional Dynamics in Africa: Lessons from the East Asian Experiences. Mauritius, 4–5 December 1997.

Nissanke, M. and E. Aryeetey. 1998. *Financial Integration and Development in Sub-Saharan Africa*. London and New York: Routledge.

Nissanke M. and P. Basu. 1992. 'Improving domestic resource mobilization in LDCs'. Background Paper to UNCTAD LDC Report 1992. Mimeo. UNCTAD, Geneva.

Parker, R., R. Riopelle and W.F. Steel. 1995. 'Small enterprises adjusting to liberalization in five African countries'. *World Bank Discussion Papers* 271. Africa Technical Department Series. The World Bank, Washington, D.C.

Popiel, P.A. 1994. 'Financial systems in sub-Saharan Africa; A comparative study'. *World Bank Discussion Papers* 260. Africa Technical Department Series, The World Bank, Washington, D.C.

Rashid, M. and R.M. Townsend. 1993. 'Targeting credit and insurance: Efficiency, mechanism design and program evaluation'. Mimeo. The World Bank, Washington, D.C.

Seibel, H-D. and U. Parhusip. 1992. 'Linking formal and informal finance: An Indonesian example'. In D. Adams and D. Fitchett, eds., *Informal Finance in Low-Income Countries*. Boulder and Oxford: Westview Press, p. 239–48.

Seibel, H.D. 1989. 'Linking informal and formal financial institutions in Africa and Asia'. In Levitsky, ed., *Micro-Enterprises in Developing Countries*. London: Intermediate Technology Publications.

Shipton, P. 1991. 'Time and money in the western Sahel: A clash of cultures in Gambian rural finance'. In M. Roemer and C. Jones, eds., *Markets in Developing Countries: Parallel, Fragmented and Black*. San Francisco: International Center for Economic Growth and Harvard Institute for International Development.

Soyibo, A. 1996a. *Financial Linkage and Development in Sub-Saharan Africa: The Informal Financial Sector in Nigeria*. Working Paper 90. Overseas Development Institute, London.

Soyibo, A. 1996b. *Financial Linkage and Development in Sub-Saharan Africa: The Role of Formal Financial Institutions in Nigeria*. Working Paper 88. Overseas Development Institute, London.

Soyibo, A. 1996c. *TheTransmission of Savings to Investments in Nigeria*. Research Paper No. 48. African Economic Research Consortium, Nairobi.

Soyibo, A. 1997. 'Financial liberalization and bank restructuring in Sub-Saharan Africa: Some lessons for sequencing and policy design'. *Journal of African Economies*, vol. 6, no. 1, Supplement Part 2 (March), pp. 100–50, Oxford.

Soyibo, A., S.O. Alashi and M.K. Ahmad. 1997. 'The extent and effectiveness of banking supervision in Nigeria'. Paper presented at the AERC Biannual Research Workshop. Harare, 6–11 December.

Stiglitz, J.E. 1994. 'The role of the state in financial markets'. Proceedings of the World Bank Annual Conference on Development Economics, 1993.

Stiglitz, J.E. and A. Weiss. 1981. 'Credit rationing in markets with imperfect information', *American Economic Review*, 71.

Sobodu, O.O. and P.O. Akiode. 1998. *Bank Performance and Supervision in Nigeria: Analysing the Transition to a Deregulated Economy*. Research Paper No. 71. African Economic Research Consortium, Nairobi.

Thomas J.J. 1993. 'The informal financial sector: How does it operate and who are the customers?' In S. Page, ed., *Monetary Policy in Developing Countries*. London: Routlege.

Udry, C. 1990. 'Credit Markets in Northern Nigeria: Credit as Insurance in Rural Economy'. *World Bank Economic Review*, 4(3): 251–69.

Webster, L. and P. Fidler, eds. 1995. 'The informal sector and micro-finance institutions in West Africa'. Industry and Energy Division, Private Sector Development Department, The World Bank, Washington, D.C.

World Bank. 1989. *World Development Report 1989: Financial Systems and Development*. New York: Oxford University Press.

World Bank. 1994a. *Adjustment in Africa: Reforms, Results and the Road Ahead*. A World Bank Policy Research Report. Washington, D.C.: The World Bank.

World Bank. 1994b. 'Interest rate deregulation'. Policy Review Note. Mimeo. The World Bank.

World Bank. 1995. 'The Nigerian rural financial system: Assessment and recommendations'. Western Central Africa Department, Agriculture and Environment Division, January 26, report no 13911-UNI.

Yaron, J. 1992. 'Successful rural financial institutions'. *World Bank Discussion Papers* 150, Africa Technical Department Series, The World Bank, Washington, D.C.

Yotopoulos, P.A. and L. Floro. 1991. 'Transaction costs and quantity rationing in the informal credit markets: Philippine agriculture'. In M. Roemer and C. Jones, eds., *Markets in Developing Countries*. San Francisco: ICS Press.

Chapter 11

Financial Institution Building in Meiji Japan

Juro Teranishi

Financial markets in developing countries are plagued with serious market failures arising from information asymmetry, contract enforcement costs and incomplete markets. Creating financial institutions capable of effectively coping with these failures is indispensable for successful and sustainable growth, but eradicating the causes of market failures is a highly resource- and time-consuming process. Thus, the establishment of efficient financial institutions is not only one of the long-term objectives of economic policy, it is also an essential precondition for efficient resource allocation for the purpose of growth. It follows that there are two options for a developing economy in pursuit of financial institution building and growth.

One option is to establish modern financial institutions gradually, but aim at maximum resource mobilization for immediate growth. The other is to give priority to building up modern financial institutions at the possible cost of immediate inefficiency in resource allocation. The first option usually takes the form of a two-track approach in the sense of using the indigenous financial system along with modern institutions. With this approach, the financial system usually carries over indigenous elements, which are nonetheless liable to cause serious market failures in the future, although the short-term economic growth rate might be high. The second option is a turnpike approach, which, if successful, might eventually lead to a rapid growth following the establishment of modern institutions, although short-term costs due to the changeover from indigenous to modern systems could also be considerable.

Faced with these two options, Japan in the Meiji era (1868–1912)[1] seems to have adopted the former after 1880: It devoted significant resources to developing modern financial institutions, which it tried to adapt to existing socioeconomic conditions, but, at the same time, it relied heavily on traditional financial mechanisms and tried to modernize them.

The propose of this chapter is to deliberate on the costs and benefits of the approach adopted by Meiji Japan after 1880 and on the reasons for the choice of

[1] During the period before 1880, the Meiji government tried a big bang approach to establishing modern industries through direct intervention. However, the attempt failed since most of the state enterprises amassed serious deficits, and an act privatizing state enterprises was promulgated in 1880.

approaches. The chapter first gives an overview of Japan's financial development, then examines the process of establishing the banking and corporate systems and discusses the relationship between the formal and informal financial systems.

An Overview of Financial Development

Meiji Japan was basically an agrarian economy; some 69.7 per cent of the labour force worked in agriculture during 1872–1875 and 56.5 per cent during 1906–1910. The main exports were primary goods such as rice and coal, and indigenous industrial products related to agriculture, the most important being raw silk. The share of raw silk in total exports was 36.8 per cent during 1882–1891 and 26.1 per cent during 1902–1911. After the transplanting of modern industries, the cotton spinning industry became the leading modern exporter, with the share of cotton yarn reaching 34.5 per cent in manufacturing exports or 10.2 per cent in total exports in 1912.

Economic growth was stimulated by the introduction of new products and technology as well as of the expansion of markets brought by the opening of foreign trade and abolition of barriers to domestic trade. With the expansion of markets, factory production spread rapidly both in such indigenous industries as silk and processed food production and in modern industries such as cotton spinning and shipbuilding. At the same time, the number of modern companies increased steadily (Table 11.1). The government encouraged the establishment of companies by promulgating the Commercial Act (*Kyu-shoho*) in 1893 and revising it (*Shin-shoho*) in 1899.

Table 11.1 Number of production units, companies and factories (1896, 1905)

		Number of production units	Number of companies	Number of factories
Silk	1896	409,799	175	2,684
	1905	411,943	286	2,573
Cotton spinning	1896	63	58	81
	1905	82	41	214
Weaving	1896	660,409	60	954
	1905	448,609	175	2,397
Ceramics	1896	5,088	11	164
	1905	4,834	29	481
Lacquers	1896	5,016	-	5
	1905	5,442	12	20

Table 11.1 (contd)

		Number of production units	Number of companies	Number of factories
Vegetable oils	1896	9,381	20	30
	1905	10,808	25	-
Matches	1896	210	13	269
	1905	254	31	-
Brewing	1896	25,459	51	603
	1905	33,240	114	703

Note: A factory in 1896 was defined as an establishment with more than 10 workers. In 1905 it referred to establishments with more than 20 workers.
Source: Teikoku Tokei Nenan, Nos. 16 and 26.

Three kinds of private commercial banks were established, as shown Table 11.2. *Kokuritsu* banks (national banks) were private banks with note-issuing privileges. They were established by the National Banking Act in 1872 (revised in 1876) in imitation of national banks in the United States. *Shiritsu* banks (private banks) and quasi banks were established without such a privilege. The number of commercial banks was 312 in 1880... reaching a maximum in the prewar period of 2,646 in 1901. All three types of banks were integrated and classified as either ordinary or saving banks in 1890 when the Ordinary Bank Act (*Futsu-ginko-jorei*) and the Saving Bank Act (*Chochiku-ginko-jorei*) were enacted. At the same time, the note-issuing privilege of the national banks was abolished.

Table 11.2 Number of banks and their average capital

	Kokuritsu banks		*Shiritsu* banks		*Quasi* banks	
	Number	Average capital	Number	Average capital	Number	Average capital
1876	6	408	1	2,000	*	
1877	27	851	1	2,000	*	
1878	95	351	1	2,000	*	
1879	153	265	10	329	*	
1880	153	281	39	161	120	10
1881	148	303	90	116	369	16
1882	143	309	176	97	438	18
1883	141	315	207	99	573	21
1884	140	318	214	91	741	20
1885	139	320	218	86	744	21

Note: Units of average capital are thousand yen.
* Not known.
Source: Asakura (1961).

The financing method of fixed capital formation is shown in Table 11.3. It is calculated as the ratio of the flow amount of corporate bonds, equities and bank lending to the fixed capital formation of the economy. The residual is considered to represent financing by means of informal financial methods as well as retained earnings. Equity and bonds included in the calculation are confined to those issued by the private non-bank sector. Three findings are noteworthy:

- The share of financing by equity and bonds was low until after World War I.
- Bank borrowing became a stable source of investment funds after the 1896–1900 period.
- The share of the residual is very high, especially during the Meiji era.

Table 11.3 Sources of funds of private fixed capital formation (per cent)

	Bonds	Equity	Borrowings	Others
1881–1885	0.0	15.5	4.9	79.7
1886–1890	0.0	11.9	18.0	70.1
1891–1895	1.7	10.6	7.4	80.3
1896–1900	0.3	16.9	38.0	44.8
1901–1905	2.2	8.8	22.3	66.6
1906–1910	5.3	13.2	31.0	50.5
1911–1915	4.3	15.1	37.0	43.6
1916–1920	2.8	45.9	60.4	-9.1
1921–1925	14.6	19.3	36.3	29.9
1926–1930	18.0	30.3	16.1	35.6
1931–1935	6.1	30.0	-3.7	67.6
1936–1940	12.8	57.6	55.3	-25.7

Source: Private fixed capital formation is from *Long-term Economic Statistics*, Vol. 1. Sources of funds taken from Fujino and Teranishi (1998).

The supply of funds from the private sector is shown in Table 11.4. The percentage share of cash decreased quite rapidly toward the turn of the century and gradually thereafter, matched by the increase in the shares of claims on modern financial institutions, first on banks and then on insurance and trust companies. Table 11.5, showing the composition of deposits, has interesting implications. It can be seen that the share of time deposits was as low as 20 per cent, and increased sharply to 40 per cent during the period 1898–1913. At the same time, small demand deposits (*koguchi-toza yokin*) increased their share of deposits. The small demand deposits are composed of savings by middle class households as well as by small merchants and industrialists. Although it is not clear from the aggregate data in Table 11.5, we have some evidence that this type of deposit increased quite rapidly during 1893–1898 (Teranishi, 1982), so that one can say that the use of bank deposits as a store of value diffused to the public during 1893–1903.

Table 11.4 Percentage composition of financial assets of the private non-financial sector

	Cash	Deposits	Insurance	Securities and trust
1876–80	47.4	2.7		49.9
1881–85	29.9	12.4	0.0	57.6
1886–90	21.6	18.6	0.1	57.5
1891–95	21.1	20.9	0.2	51.7
1896–90	15.6	26.2	0.5	50.2
1901–05	10.3	30.6	0.9	47.1
1906–10	8.0	33.9	1.1	43.2
1911–15	6.2	33.5	1.9	42.6
1916–20	4.7	41.0	1.8	37.5
1921–25	3.5	36.1	3.2	41.2
1926–30	2.4	36.2	7.2	36.7
1931–35	2.1	35.5	10.5	36.5
1936–40	2.7	39.6	11.6	33.7

Notes: Excludes trade credits and claims in informal credit markets.
Source: Fujino and Teranishi (1998).

Table 11.5 Percentage composition of bank deposits

	Demand deposits	Small demand deposits	Saving deposits	Time deposits	Government deposits	Others
1878	37.2	-	-	26.2	19.5	17.1
1883	37.2	-	3.2	12.3	23.3	24.0
1888	33.4	-	6.4	21.8	20.7	17.7
1893	44.9	-	5.8	26.8	9.9	12.6
1898	36.4	14.4	9.1	22.5	5.2	12.4
1903	33.4	17.3	9.0	27.9	1.6	10.8
1908	27.3	18.2	10.0	33.7	1.8	9.0
1913	23.5	15.9	9.2	42.8	1.2	7.4
1918	20.5	18.4	7.3	46.6	1.3	5.9
1923	17.2	22.0	7.3	42.7	1.6	9.2
1928	12.7	18.6	9.1	48.4	-	11.2
1933	10.8	16.8	10.1	47.1	-	15.2
1938	13.3	17.1	8.7	45.3	-	15.6

Source: Teranishi (1982).

Finally, Figure 11.1 provides evidence of the regional integration of financial markets. The fall of the coefficient of variation of deposit rates among 47 prefectures toward the turn of the century is quite dramatic. The coefficients of variation of commodity prices (raw silk and rice) also declined during the same period. The main reason for this is the development of transportation (railway and marine) and communication (telephone and telegraph) systems.

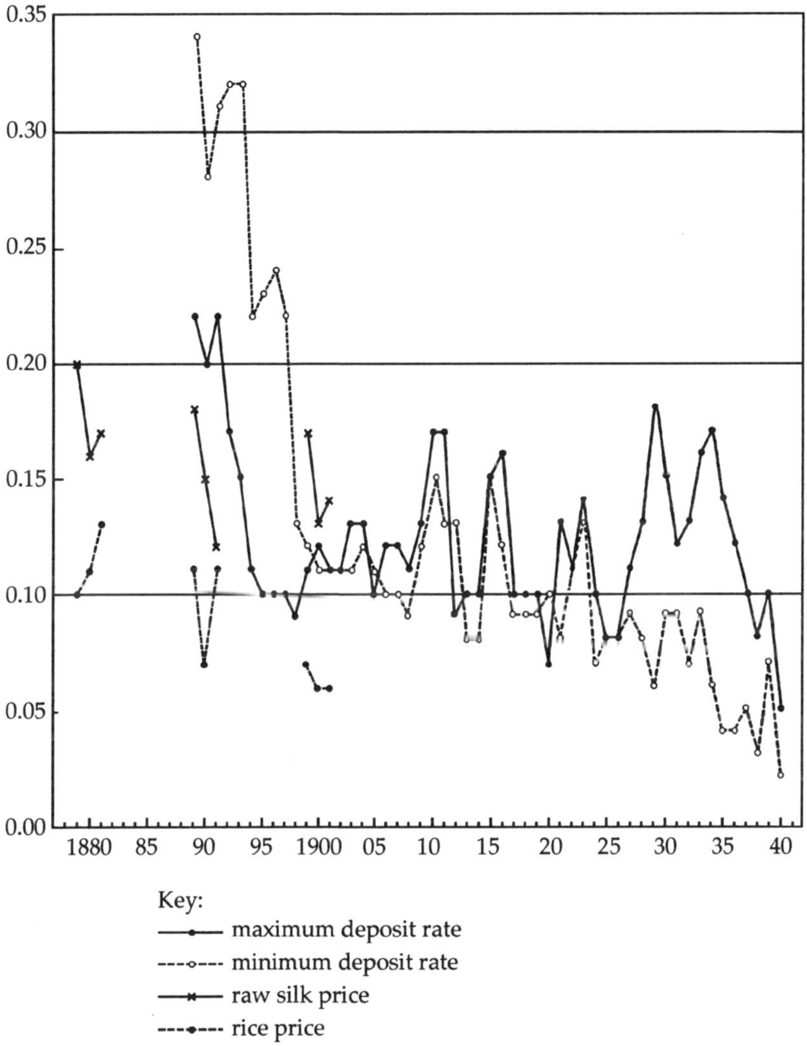

Figure 11.1 Coefficient of variation of regional deposit rates, raw silk price and rice price (source: Teranishi (1982))

Development of the Banking Sector

Private Sector Initiative and Implicit Subsidies

The government tried vigorously to develop a modern banking sector, but it was the strong response of the private sector to opportunities for profit that led to the remarkable expansion of the sector (Patrick, 1967).

The government provided significant incentives for the establishment of banks. The first were for the nationally-chartered private banks called *kokuritsu* banks. These were endowed with the privilege of issuing bank notes worth as much as 80 per cent of equity capital, backed by reserves of as much as 20 per cent of equity capital. This meant banks were able to obtain funds equal to as much as 60 per cent of equity capital at zero cost.[2] Moreover, those banks were also allowed to handle government deposits, which were also zero cost funds for banks. Since these conditions were very attractive, but an inflationary expansion of bank notes was to be avoided, the government rationed the bank equity capital of *kokuritsu* banks to the prefectures on the basis of a formula using prefectural population and tax payments as variables. With 88 per cent of tax revenues coming from land taxes in 1875, the formula meant that the rationing was implemented on the basis of agricultural production.[3]

These incentives brought the immediate establishment of 153 *kokuritsu* banks, and the predetermined ceiling of bank capital was reached in 1879. However, since bank capital was rationed according to regional agricultural production, performance varied widely among the banks. Banks in prefectures with active industrial and commercial sectors such as raw silk, textiles and processed food production were quite active, expanding lending and absorbing private deposits. Banks in purely agrarian regions were less active, holding a large part of their assets in the form of government bonds and idle cash.

Moreover, in view of the profitability of the banking business, there was a surge of requests to the government to establish banks after 1879. The government took a quite accommodating stance to the requests and generously allowed new banks to be established even though there was no legislation applicable to banks other than *kokuritsu* banks until 1893. These banks were conveniently classified into two types—*shiritsu* banks and quasi banks—depending on the degree of engagement in side businesses. The growth in the number and capital of these banks was seen in Table 11.2.

---

[2] According to the rules of the revised National Bank Act enacted in 1876, banks were also allowed to hold reserves in the form of government notes. Before the revision the note issue equity ratio was 0.6 and the resume equity ratio was 0.4, so that banks were allowed zero cost funds equivalent only to a maximum of 20 per cent of equity capital. Moreover, the government requested that reserves be held in gold specie, whose price relative to silver had been rapidly increasing in the world market.

[3] Some allowances were made for prefectures with foreign trade activities and active production.

The establishment of *shiritsu* banks and quasi banks was most significant in regions where indigenous industrial activities were active. Table 11.6 shows this through a comparison of the percentage share of three types of banks in regions having active industrial activities with the percentage share of the three types of banks in the rest of the regions. Table 11.7 shows a cross comparison of the performance of *kokuritsu* and *shiritsu* banks between two types of regions. It can be seen that *shiritsu* banks in regions with indigenous industrial sectors were more active than *shiritsu* banks in other regions or *kokuritsu* banks in any other region. Both the lending/total assets ratios and the private deposits/total assets ratios of *shiritsu* banks were higher than those of *kokuritsu* banks, and *shiritsu* banks in industrial regions were less dependent on government deposits than *kokuritsu* banks.

Table 11.6 Percentage composition of bank capital in two regions (1889)

	Indigenous industrial regions	Other regions
Kokuritsu banks	28.0	65.7
Shiritsu banks	32.4	23.5
Quasi banks	39.6	10.8

Notes: Indigenous industry regions are Tokai, Hokuriku and Tozan. Capital is authorized capital.
Source: Ministry of Finance, *Ginkokyoku-nenpo*.

Table 11.7 Comparison of balance sheets of banks in two regions (1889)

	Indigenous industrial regions	Other regions
Lending/total assets		
Kokuritsu banks	46.6	46.1
Shiritsu banks	77.1	79.5
Private deposits/total assets		
Kokuritsu banks	25.4	24.3
Shiritsu banks	32.1	41.7
Government deposits/total assets		
Kokuritsu banks	16.3	6.9
Shiritsu banks	9.5	15.5
Notes issued/total assets		
Kokuritsu banks	15.4	22.2
Shiritsu banks	0.0	0.0

Notes: Total assets refers to total funds equal to the sum of private and government deposits, capital and notes issued (*kokuritsu* banks only).
Source: Compiled by author.

The *kokuritsu* banks' low ratio of lending to total assets means that some of these banks had excess capacity during some periods after their founding. Since these excess capacities were eventually used as industrial activities became active in the regions in which they were located, the policy of establishing *kokuritsu* banks could be regarded as a supply-leading policy: the government had established banks before the start of full-scale industrialization (Patrick, 1967).

It seems that the government tried to make *kokuritsu* banks into a forerunner of or a model for modernization. They were the first joint-stock companies established in Japan, and the nation's first organizations to use modern accounting systems. Moreover, many of the founders of *kokuritsu* banks later became leaders of industrial society. To achieve such purposes the government offered very generous resources (implicit subsidies). Estimating the implicit subsidies related to the note-issuing privilege and dealings in government deposits by multiplying the time deposits rate by the sum of notes issued and government deposits, we obtain the results seen in Table 11.8. It can be seen that the banking sector, mainly *kokuritsu* banks,[4] was the largest recipient of subsidies among individual industries until the period 1886–1895.[5]

Table 11.8 Implicit and explicit subsidies to industries (100,000 yen)

	Industrial subsidies					Implicit subsidies to banks
	Construction	Railway	Marine transport	Others	Total	
1876–1880	15	-	3	0	17	19
1881–1885	15	1	2	6	24	43
1886–1895	16	4	1	12	33	26
1891–1895	25	6	10	1	42	20
1896–1900	4	1	39	4	48	12
1901–1905	1	9	48	18	76	7
1906–1910	3	2	87	64	156	13

Source: Teranishi (1982).

Coping with Market Failures

There seems to be no doubt that financial markets of Meiji Japan were seriously prone to market failures stemming from information asymmetry and the high costs of enforcing contracts. In coping with these problems, the Meiji government did not take any specific direct measures to reduce information gaps between *kokuritsu* banks and their borrowers or to enforce contracts between *kokuritsu* banks and

[4] Some of the large *shiritsu* banks also benefited by being able to use government deposits in their financial dealings.

[5] It must be noted that this calculation does not include implicit subsidies related to the privatization of state enterprises, which had been established during the early big bang approach (note 2). To the extent the selling prices of enterprises were lower than market prices, there should have some implicit subsidies. However, it is not easy to estimate the exact amount of such subsidies.

their customers. Instead, the government enlarged the concept of banks and collateral so as to accommodate and use traditional information and contracting mechanisms.

The government coped with the information asymmetry problem in the bank loan market by allowing entry of *shiritsu* and quasi banks rather than encouraging branching of *kokuritsu* banks. Most quasi banks were established by moneylenders who were also engaged in some kind of manufacturing and commercial business (Asakura, 1961). Moreover, money lending was an important side business for large merchants, warehouse owners and indigenous manufacturers, so these people were eager to use the term 'bank' in the names of their business. Therefore, most quasi banks continued to engage in side businesses. This practice characterized the activity of many of *shiritsu* banks also, although to a lesser degree. The enactment of the Ordinary Bank Act in 1890 did not drastically change this situation since it did not completely prohibit side businesses. Moreover, the Bank Act did not stipulate any minimum capital requirement for banks, so that minuscule banks, many set up by moneylenders, continued to appear.[6]

In this way, in order to cope with possible market failures caused by information asymmetry, the Meiji government used the information processing capabilities and accumulated information of traditional moneylenders by enlarging the concept of banks. In the process, a large portion of the informal lenders were gradually converted into modern financial institutions.

As for the market failures related to contract enforcement costs, one of the serious problems faced by banks was that newly established companies in modern industries did not have either reputation or sufficient assets to serve as collateral for bank borrowing. Moreover, new entrepreneurs with the expertise and ambition necessary for embarking on new businesses were usually not rich enough to offer collateral, apart from some progressive people among large traditional merchants and landlords. The remarkable measure taken by banks to cope with this problem was to lend to entrepreneurs who used company equity as collateral. An entrepreneur would offer equity from established company A as collateral to borrow from a bank. The entrepreneur would then subscribe to equity issue of company B using the borrowed money, and again borrow from banks using equity from company B as collateral, and so on. In this way, banks were able to siphon savings into new companies in the form of equity capital. Companies did not have to borrow from banks, but entrepreneurs borrowed in order to finance companies with equity capital.

The macroeconomic importance of this method of equity-collateral financing can be seen by the share of equity in the total collateral of *kokuritsu* banks. The average share of equity during 1893–1897 was 43.4 per cent,[7] and in 1896 it was as

[6] Regulations on minimum capital size became effective after around 1918, and the Banking Law promulgated in 1927 finally made the requirements mandatory.

[7] The share of other types of collateral are government bonds 10.5 per cent, real estate 16.1 per cent, rice and others 3.0 per cent, miscellaneous items 10.1 per cent, and credit lending 16.9 per cent.

high as 56.1 per cent. An impressive incident here is that the Bank of Japan took a measure to support this method. In 1885, in view of the prevalence of equity-collateral financing, the Bank of Japan introduced a new arrangement for rediscounting by designating equities of 13 railway companies as qualified collateral. Although the arrangement was illegal according to the Bank of Japan Law, which forbade lending with real estate or company equities as collateral, the Bank of Japan retained this system throughout the prewar years as an 'unavoidable convenient method' in order to help banks to adjust their liquidity position smoothly.

Another aspect of the high reliance on equity-collateral financing was the large share of equity financing of big firms. As Table 11.9 shows, large firms in Meiji were financed mainly by equity capital. (The proposition of high dependence on bank borrowings of Japanese firms is not applicable to the Meiji era.). At the same time, the share of reserves was extremely small, mainly because of the demand for high dividend ratios by stockholders, who had to pay interest on bank loans.

Table 11.9 Financing of large companies (per cent)

	1890	1895	1900	1905	1915	1925	1935
Equity capital /total assets							
Railway companies		90.3	91.4	84.4			
Cotton spinning companies	65.5	53.5	74.0	66.7	53.9		
Large companies (A)				67.1	72.0	67.2	72.8
Large companies (B)					53.4	47.0	46.7
Reserves / total assets							
Railway companies		1.4	1.8	3.0			
Cotton spinning companies	8.7	8.8	8.2	20.3	23.5		
Large companies (A)				14.7	17.1	15.1	19.3
Large companies (B)					15.7	16.9	14.8

Note: Sizes of sample of large companies (A) are 10,715 (1905), 22,202 (1915), 45,275 (1925) and 94,592 (1935); those of (B) are 49 (1915), 69 (1925) and 295 (1935).
Source: Teranishi (1982).

There were two underlying reasons for the prevalence and the tacit approval by the government of equity-collateral financing. First, in terms of reputation and assets, some of the individuals such as rich merchants and landlords were more qualified as bank customers than newly established firms. Second, the approval was apparently intended as a way of supply investible funds to potential investors who were not rich but endowed with entrepreneurship and vision for industrialization. Since many of the leaders of the newly established Meiji government were former warriors in the southwestern peripheral region and were not rich in pecuniary wealth, the latter reason cannot be neglected. Anyway, the practice of equity-collateral financing became less pronounced as companies (as well as former warrior-class leaders) established reputations and assets that could be used as collateral for bank loans. In other words, as time went on, companies themselves rather than individual entrepreneurs became customers of banks.

It must be noted that the policy of enlarging the concept of banks to virtual moneylenders incurred significant costs to the economy over a long period of time. Many small banks thus established operated as organ banks (*kikanginko*), lending to family businesses with interlocked directorships, and disregarding the benefits of risk diversification and disclosure of information. In the interwar period, the chronic instability of the financial system, partly caused by unsound banking practices, forced the government to subject the banking sector to drastic reform, as is touched upon in the concluding section of this paper.

Development of the Corporate System

The establishment of the modern corporate system was another important basis for financial system building in Meiji Japan.

As the number of companies increased steadily, the process of the separation of ownership and management proceeded. The share of companies with owner-executives declined from 48.8 per cent in 1900 to 17.4 per cent in 1928, with the decrease most pronounced in banks, heavy and chemical industries, and public utilities, and least pronounced in indigenous manufacturing and commerce (Teranishi, 1990). Despite the emergence of professional managers, however, many of the companies continued to be held by family groups. This is indicated by the large share of partnership companies as shown in Table 11.10.

Table 11.10 Types of corporations

	Joint-stock companies (*Kabushiki kaisya*)		Limited partnership companies (*Goshi kaisha*		Unlimited partnership companies (*Gomei kaisha*)	
	Number of corporations (1000s)	Average capital (thousand yen)	Number of corporations (1000s)	Average capital (thousand yen)	Number of corporations (1000s)	Average capital (thousand yen)
1896	2.6	138	1.7	17	0.3	37
1906	4.3	219	3.6	19	1.5	43
1916	7.5	279	7.5	21	3.2	60
1925	17.6	542	11.5	64	5.2	171
1925*	17.6	844	11.5	63	5.2	171
1935*	23.3	855	44.4	26	16.5	79

Notes: Capital of years with asterisk refers to authorized capital including unpaid-in portions.

Source: Japan Statistical Association, *Historical Statistics of Japan*, Vol. 4, Table 15-5-b and 15-5-c.

Even in 1906, joint-stock companies comprised less than half of all companies, and this situation continued throughout the prewar period. Although smaller than joint-stock companies, the scale of partnership companies rose rather rapidly until joint-stock companies, the scale of partnership companies rose rather rapidly until 1925. It is well known that *zaibatsu* firms continued to take the partnership system as their organizational base until the 1930s—Mitsubishi and Sumitomo Limited and Mitsui and Furukawa unlimited partnership.

The government did not take any policy measures to encourage joint-stock companies or discourage partnership companies. Only with respect to financial institutions—saving banks in 1922, trust companies in 1923 and ordinary banks in 1927—did partnership companies come to be forbidden.

Reducing Agency Costs

Since disclosure of information was insufficient, there was a high degree of moral hazard in the dealings of partnership companies with lender banks and small equity owners. The Meiji government was aware of this, but did not try to change the family ownership pattern in the corporate sector. Instead, the government changed the liability system of companies to reduce agency costs.

For one thing, until the promulgation of the Commercial Law in 1893, even joint-stock companies were subject to the unlimited liability system, except for some categories of companies stipulated by special legislation.[8] The 1893 Commercial Law adopted the western system, requiring joint-stock companies to be composed of limited liability memberships. It also stipulated that limited partnership companies were to be composed of members with either limited or unlimited liabilities, and unlimited partnership companies of members with unlimited liability only. However, when the law was revised in 1899 (the New Commercial Law), the liability system was strengthened again, so that limited partnership companies could not be established without some unlimited liability members.

The emphasis on family or group ownership during the Meiji era is clearly shown in the voting system of joint-stock companies. During the 1880s many joint-stock companies adopted the voting system, which curtailed the voting power of large stockholders (Imuta, 1976). In the case of *kokuritsu* banks, for example, shareholders received one vote for the first 10 shares they owned, one vote for every 5 additional shares they held up to 100 shares, and one vote for every 10 additional shares they owned over 100 shares. Such practices were not allowed after the enactment of the Commercial Law, and this seems to be one of the reasons for the subsequent growth of partnership companies, in which every member was given one vote regardless of the number of shares held.

After World War I, when the Japanese economy embarked on heavy and chemical industrialization, the corporate system based on partnerships became inefficient as a means of mobilizing savings from middle class investors. The

---

[8] *Kokuritsu* banks were subject to the limited liability system by the National Bank Act. The reason for this seems to be that prompt establishment of banks was given priority over the agency cost problem. *Shiritsu* banks, on the other hand, were subject to the unlimited liability system like other companies. This seems to be reasonable because agency costs related to deposit mobilization were more serious for *shiritsu* banks.

establishment of partnership companies was confined to small firms as is indicated by the declining average capitalization of partnership companies shown in Table 11.10. At the same time, the exclusive and closed system of *zaibatsu* firms became the target of social criticism, and these firms became obliged to convert themselves into joint-stock companies.

Incidentally, there is room for more in-depth research into the reasons for limiting voting power of large investors. One such reason seems to be the emphasis on family and group leadership, as we have already touched upon. Another reason may have been to give more control power to new leaders of the Meiji regime, whose wealth was small compared with rich merchants or landlords.

Informal Credit System

Formal financial institutions include banks, credit cooperatives and government financial institutions (*kangyo* ginko and *noko* ginko). Informal financial institutions include moneylending companies, moneylenders and pawnshops. The informal credit system comprises informal financial institutions, the lending activities of merchants, and private credit among relatives and acquaintances, including private rotating schemes.

The Share of Informal Credits

The informal credit system occupied an important position in the financial system in prewar Japan. Data on the farm and manufacturing sectors are available. Table 11.11 which focuses on the farm sector, Table 11.11 shows that the share of informal credit was as high as 92.8 per cent in 1888, but decreased rapidly to 64.3 per cent in 1911, and then to 52.7 per cent in 1932. The decrease in the share during the 1888–1911 period is most impressive. Since the share of private and other credits seems to have been stable, judging by the figures for 1911 and 1932, the decrease was apparently due primarily to the decrease in the shares of informal financial institutions and merchants.

Table 11.11 Borrowing by the farm sector (million yen; per cent in parentheses)

	Formal financial institutions	Informal financial institutions	Informal credits		Other credits
			Merchants	Private	
1888	9	-	120	-	-
	(7.2)	-	(92.8)	-	-
1911	287	161	12	333	12
	(35.7)	(20.0)	(1.5)	(41.4)	(1.5)
1932	2,602	474	-	2,422	-
	(47.3)	(8.6)	-	(44.1)	-

Source: Teranishi (1982).

Table 11.12 summarizes the share of borrowing by manufacturing firms in 1932 by firm size. A comparison of the percentages of the total manufacturing sector with those of the farm sector indicates three points worth noting:

- There is not much difference in the total shares of informal financial institutions and merchants (11.9 per cent in manufacturing and 8.6 per cent in farming).
- The share of merchants seems to be high in manufacturing, and the share of informal institutions is high in the farm sector (judged from the figures for 1911).
- The share of private and other credits is smaller in the manufacturing sector, and this is reflected in the higher share of formal financial institutions in the sector.

Table 11.12 Percentage composition of lenders by firm size (manufacturing sector, 1932)

Firm size (capital) (thousand yen)	Banks and others	Credit coopera-tives	Merchants	Informal financial institutions	Private credits and others
-0.1	9.2	2.4	3.9	10.6	73.9
0.1–0.5	3.8	4.7	18.0	24.0	45.6
0.5–1.0	4.5	5.0	21.5	21.2	42.2
1–2	12.3	6.9	21.2	25.0	34.7
2–5	19.7	9.3	20.0	22.2	28.8
5–10	27.6	8.7	18.9	21.6	23.2
10–50	37.6	4.9	20.4	14.4	22.5
50–100	37.8	1.5	18.8	18.0	23.8
100–500	51.6	1.0	15.8	5.8	25.8
500	62.9	0.4	6.0	0.6	30.1
Total	58.9	1.1	8.1	3.7	27.3

Notes: Data on manufacturing sector of Tokyo and Kobe. Banks and others includes trust companies and insurance companies. Merchants includes warehouses. Informal financial institutions is composed of moneylenders, pawnshops and *mujin*.
Source: *Kogyo chosasyo* of Tokyo-shi and Kobe-shi.

It is not easy to find aggregate figures for the informal credit system. However, for the year 1911, we have the data shown in Table 11.13. Data on moneylenders in Table 11.13, including pawnshops, are obtained from Shibuya (1952), although the coverage is confined to those with operating capital of more than 300 yen, which are subject to operating taxes. On the other hand, *noshomusho-tokei* (No. 28) gives company data as a sum of banks and money lending companies: 532 million yen (paid in capital) for 2,992 companies. Since the number and paid-in capital of banks (ordinary, savings, *noko*, and five special banks—*angyo*, *Kogyo*, *Taiwan*, *Chosen* and *Chosen-shokusan*) were 2,143 and 482 million yen, respectively, we can estimate the figures for moneylending companies as shown above. The figure for operating capital in the banking sector is the balance of lending by the bank sector shown in Fujino and Teranishi (1998).

Table 11.13 The informal credit system in Japan, 1911 (in million yen)

	Paid-in capital	Operating capital	No. of units
Banking sector	482	1,984	2,143
Money lending companies	50	-	849
Moneylenders and pawn shops	-	265	60,483

Notes: Moneylenders with company systems were called moneylending companies. After the late Meiji period, we may include *mujin* companies in the informal systems. However, these were converted into a formal system in 1914 when the *mujin* Act was enacted.
Source: Shibuya (1952); Fujino and Teranishi (1998)

Finally, let us check the relationship between the activities of informal lenders and the business cycle. Figure 11.2 shows the rates of increase of nominal GDP and operating capital of moneylenders. There seems to exist a negative relationship between the two series.

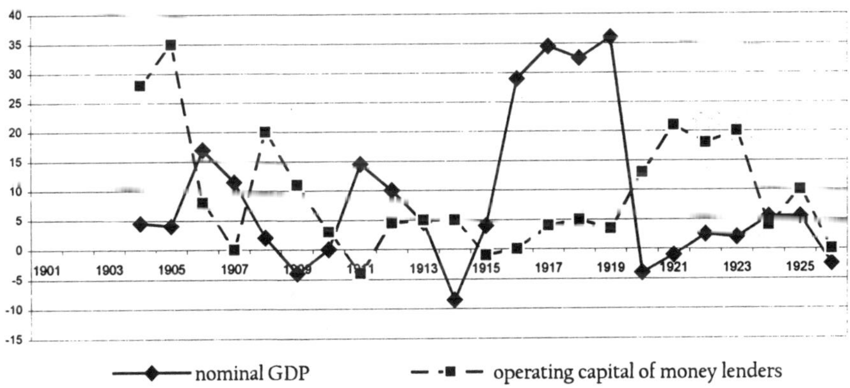

Figure 11.2 Rate of increase (per cent) of nominal GDP and operating capital of moneylenders

Note: Moneylenders with operating capital of more than 300 yen before 1914, and 1,000 yen after 1915.
Source: GDP from Ohkawa and Shinohara (1979); moneylender data from Shibuya (1962).

The coefficient of correlation during 1905–1914 is −0.28, and during 1915–1926, it is −0.50. The coefficient of the former period seems to be lowered by leads and lags of one year. This information implies the cyclic nature of the relative size of formal and informal financial activity. Informal credits proliferated during depression periods. During good periods, on the other hand, informal creditors lost their business opportunities and had to convert their informal financial claims into formal financial instruments (or simply hoarded in the form of cash?). Incidentally, it seems worth pointing out that the number of moneylenders does not show any clear cyclical movements.

Fragmentation and Linkage between the Formal and Informal Credit Systems

The informal credit system of Japan was segmented from the formal financial system, and significantly fragmented, especially during the early Meiji period.[9]

Fragmentation occurred in the relationship with modern (formal) financial institutions. First, ordinary moneylenders[10] never borrowed from banks, so the flow of funds from the formal financial sector was severed. Second, moneylenders in the early Meiji period usually did not hold time deposits at banks. Moreover, the security investments by moneylenders were mainly in war-related government bonds, the purchase of which was often compulsory, or equities of local firms with which they had some personal obligatory relationship. This meant that the flow of funds toward the formal sector was also limited.[11]

However, there were strong linkages between the informal credit system and the formal financial institutions in two respects. The first linkage was through merchants. Throughout the prewar period, merchants played an important role as mediators of bank credits to smaller producers. This occurred to some extent in rural regions. Rice merchants and fertilizer merchants were important lenders to farmers, and these merchants borrowed heavily from banks. For indigenous industrial production, the mediating role of merchants was more pronounced and crucial for the survival of firms. A typical and well-documented case was silk manufacturing; raw silk manufacturers could borrow from banks but they were also financially dependent on silk merchants.

More important was the role of merchants in financing small and medium-sized manufacturing. In general these manufacturers were unable to borrow from banks due to their lack of reputation and collateral, and they relied heavily on indirect financing through merchants. Table 11.12 shows that manufacturers in

---

[9] Refer to Aryeetey, Hettige, Nissanke and Steel (1997) for a discussion of the fragmentation and segmentation of informal credit markets in Africa.

[10] The term money lenders here refers to representative institutions in a broad sample of informal financial institutions including money lending companies and pawnshops. The behaviour of large money lending companies was a little bit different from the representative money lenders, and closer to that of banks. On the other hand, small pawnshops were only engaged in consumption loans and had no interface with banks in the lending market.

[11] The description is mainly based on the detailed case study of money lender *Sakurai* in Shibuya (1959), whose operating capital in 1912 was 53,000 yen, close to the national average of 44,000 yen.

Tokyo and Kobe with capitalization from 500–10,000 yen (2.7 workers on average) to 10,000–50,000 yen (13.8 workers on average) depended heavily on informal financial institutions as well as merchants. Table 11.14, on the other hand, shows that commerce and service sectors borrowed from banks more than proportionately with their production. It seems to follow that banks and informal financial institutions were brought into close interaction through the mediation of bank funds by merchants.

Table 11.14 Percentage composition of bank loans and NDP by industry

		Agriculture	Industry	Commerce and services	Others
1893	Bank loan	5.6	1.0	49.2	44.2
	NDP	40.6	13.4	35.0	11.0
1926	Bank loan	7.6	18.6	50.4	23.4
	NDP	23.6	20.7	34.6	21.1
1933	Bank loan	5.8	22.4	42.1	29.7
	NDP	18.8	26.0	34.5	20.7

Source: Teranishi (1982); Ohkawa and Shinohara (1979).

It is also interesting to note that as the firm size increased from 500–10,000 yen to 10,000–50,000 yen, the shares of both merchants and informal institutions remained stable at the 20 per cent level, while the share of banks and others increased and the share of private credits and others decreased steadily. This seems to imply that by 1932, when informal credit institutions had already significantly declined and indigenous industries had suffered a serious credit crunch, the remaining informal credit system and the mediation of funds by merchants were the last resorts for small and medium-sized firms. Incidentally, it is worth noting that manufacturing firms with from 500–1,000 yen to 10,000–50,000 yen in capital employed 54.2 per cent of the workers and accounted for 31.2 per cent of the output of the total manufacturing sector of Tokyo, Yokohama and Kobe. These firms engaged in indigenous industrial activities characterized by high dependence on apprenticed workers rather than hired labour or family workers.

The second linkage between the formal and informal financial sectors was the interaction and competition in lending markets. Although their main clients were peasants and minuscule manufacturers, moneylenders, especially of medium or above size, quite frequently dealt with some landlords and merchants. Since merchants and landlords were the banks' main customers, there ensued a competition between moneylenders and banks as the scale of operation of the latter expanded. In the next section, it will be shown that the moneylenders were eventually defeated in this competition, bringing their decline and subsequent conversion into interest earners.

Conversion and Exclusion of Informal Credit System

The fall in the share of informal credits in prewar Japan occurred through two processes: the conversion of informal into formal institutions, and the exclusion of the informal by the formal system.

The conversion of moneylenders into banks, especially quasi banks, played a crucial role in promoting the banking sector in rural areas. Such a conversion occurred not only before 1893, when the Ordinary Banking Act was promulgated; it continued afterward because the government did not regulate minimum bank capital effectively until 1918. The same thing happened with other modern financial institutions. For example, when the Trust Company law was enacted, the Saito family, a large moneylending company in Miyagi Prefecture, converted their moneylending business into *Sendai-shintaku* (trust) company.

Another case of conversion was *mujin* companies. *Mujingyo*, rotating credits operated by companies, emerged in the late Meiji era. In 1897, there were just seven such companies, with capital of 0.7 million yen, but the number increased quite rapidly thereafter, reaching 1,151 companies with a capital of 1.2 million yen in 1913 (Zenkoku Mujin-Shukaijo, 1938).[12] This led the government to promulgate the *Mujingyo* Act in 1914, converting informal financial activities into a formal system. In 1951, *mujin* companies were again converted into *sogo* banks with the right to collect deposits. More recently, after 1989, *sogo* banks were converted into ordinary (second-tier local) banks.

The process of exclusion of informal credits occurred through the interaction in the lending market between formal and informal institutions. As both banks and moneylenders expanded their operations, they came to compete with each other in the same loan markets, particularly landlords and merchants. During the early period of interaction, moneylenders had a strong competitive edge based on their channels of information, especially information accumulated through daily monitoring. As the information processing capability of banks improved, however, moneylenders were forced to lower lending rates to the level of the bank lending rates (Shibuya, 1956). This tendency was intensified by the spread of credit cooperatives, set up with the main aim of excluding moneylenders. Since credit cooperatives were established on the basis of regional and kinship relationships, they had considerable information strength, and were also supported by subsidized credits from the government financial system. Through this process, moneylenders were forced to shift their assets from money lending claims to investments in modern financial instruments such as time deposits and securities.

This process is eloquently described in detailed case studies by Shibuya (e.g., 1959, 1962), and is tested by Teranishi (1994) through estimation of the demand function of moneylending using prefectural cross-section data for the period 1921–1926. The calculation is as follows.

---

[12] Zenkoku Mujin-shukaijo, Zenkoku-mujin Guo Tokei (1938)

The demand for moneylending depends negatively on money lending interest rates and positively on the interest rate and the availability of alternative sources of funds. It is assumed that the availability of alternative sources of funds depends on the lending of credit cooperatives and banks. While credit cooperatives could lend with their pre-existing information channels, bank loans could be effected only through the expansion of branch offices and the accumulation of information through them. The accumulation of information by bank branches is approximated by a vintage index of bank branches V_i.

The period 1885–1920 is divided into six subperiods: 1885–1990, 1891–1996, 1897–1902, 1903–1908, 1909–1914 and 1915–1920 Each subperiod is represented by an index i (i = 1, ..., 6). Thus the vintage index V_i for 1921–1926 can be written as:

$$V_i = (A - B_i)/A \qquad (_i = 1, \ldots, 6)$$

where A is the average number of branch offices during 1921–1926 in each prefecture, and B_i is a similar number for the ith period. V_i is assumed to represent the share of branch offices established since the ith period among the total existing branches during 1921–1926. In Table 11.15, all variables except for V_is have the correct sign and are statistically significant. As for V_is, although V_1 and V_2 are not statistically significant, V_3–V_6 are significant, and V_4 yields the best results.

Table 11.15 Demand function for informal credit with vintage index (1921–1926 average) – Independent variables

Rate of interest on informal credits	Rate of interest on bank loans	Lending by credit cooperatives (per household)	Number of bank branches (per 100 households)	V_1	V_2	V_3	V_4	V_5	V_6	R^2
-0.005	0.013	-0.427	-0.024	0.031						0.22
(-1.97)*	(2.04)	(-2.91)	(-2.10)	(1.20)						
-0.004	0.010	-0.408	-0.025		-0.001					0.19
(-1.54)	(1.59)	(-2.74)	(-2.11)		(-0.001)					
-0.006	0.011	-0.372	-0.029			0.032				0.32
(-2.26)	(1.86)	(-2.56)	(-2.47)			(1.65)				
-0.006	0.010	-0.300	-0.027				0.044			0.37
(-2.29)	(1.74)	(-2.06)	(-2.48)				(2.44)			
-0.005	0.009	-0.321	-0.026					0.033		
(-1.94)	(1.58)	(-2.12)	(-2.33)					(1.77)		
-0.005	0.010	-0.310	-0.032						0.039	0.32
(-1.86)	(1.67)	(-1.95)	(-2.57)						(1.48)	

Note: t-values in parentheses.
Source: Teranishi (1994).

This suggests the following. For banks to do business in the informal sector, mere establishment of new branch offices was not sufficient. It was also necessary for them to establish information channels with customers and accumulate information through continuous monitoring. This was a time-consuming process, however, and during 1921–1926, new bank branches established after period four could not compete with moneylenders since the former were inferior to the latter in terms of accumulation of information. In other words, in prewar Japan, it took some 20 years for banks to develop their information capability to a level sufficient to cope with existing moneylenders.

Concluding Remarks

Financial system building in prewar Japan followed a gradual or two-track approach. The indigenous financial mechanism was used along with modern financial institutions. While the information processing capability of modern banks was promoted, the internalization of information in family or community systems was also kept intact. In order to avoid moral hazard or agency problems, unlimited liability rather than disclosure of family secrets was emphasized. By setting limits on the voting power of large shareholders, group-based leadership in corporate control was pursued. For the purpose of overcoming a lack of collateral to finance modern firms, the method of obtaining bank loans with equity collateral was used extensively, reducing contract enforcement costs. The informal credit system was not denied, but efforts were made to convert it into a modern category to the greatest extent possible.

One of the reasons for adopting such an approach was the need for maximum mobilization of resources through the financial system. The severe international tension with neighbouring countries like Korea, China and Russia made the rapid buildup of military power backed by economic strength an urgent task for Meiji Japan. Under these conditions, establishing a full-fledged modern financial institution was not necessarily the first priority. What was most important was to establish a system capable of mobilizing resources to support rapid economic and military expansion.

Another reason for the adoption of the two-track approach was that the maintenance of family or community ties was another aim of economic institution building in Meiji Japan. Family and community ties were considered to be fundamental bases for the governance of the political system of the Empire. Further, distributive interests in the Meiji economy were represented through regional interests during the period, and the mechanism for sharing incomes by family groups with regional and kinship ties or by communities was a basic micro ingredient for the working of such a system. In the same way, the sharing of residuals among stockholders and employees became a necessary microeconomic ingredient for the postwar high-growth economy, where distributive interests were represented by interests of each industrial sector (Teranishi, 1996).

However, characteristics of the Meiji financial system such as family ownership or internalization of information became serious impediments to the working of the economy in the inter-war period. The problems that erupted in the financial system, including unsound banking by organ banks, maturity mismatching and the collapse of money markets, monopolistic behaviour by large banks, disorder in corporate governance, and the like, became the major causes of the turmoil of the inter-war economy. The government was obliged to resort to drastic measures to restructure the financial system (Teranishi, 1997). The old Banking Law, promulgated in 1927, was a landmark. Two measures were introduced. First, the information disclosure requirement as well as monitoring by the government was intensified. The corporate form of banks was confined to joint-stock company, monitoring organizations of the Ministry of Finance and Bank of Japan were expanded, and the system for reporting to the government was strengthened. Second, the minimum capital requirement was drastically intensified. Out of the 1,283 ordinary banks existing in 1927, some 617 were requested to increase their capital base within five years. Moreover, the government did not allow increasing capitalization by means of new issuing of stocks in principle, but requested certain banks to merge with other banks as the method of increasing capitalization. The main purpose of the policy was to get out of the practice of organ banks and to promote the diversification of bank portfolios. With this policy, however, the customers of weaker banks that merged into large banks came to suffer seriously from the ensuing credit crunch. Most seriously hit were small and medium-sized manufacturing firms, which shared an important part of employment and production in the inter-war period. It was only after 1955 that a financial system capable of coping with the many problems related to catching up industrialization was finally established.

References

Aryeetey, E., H. Hettige, M. Nissanke and W. Steel. 1997. 'Financial market fragmentation and reforms in Ghana, Malawi, Nigeria, and Tanzania' *The World Bank Economic Review*, vol. 11, no. 2: 195–218.

Asakura, Kokichi. 1961. *Meiji-zenki Nihon Kinyu Kozo-shi* (Historical Analysis of Financial Structure of Early Meiji Japan). Tokyo: Iwanami-shoten.

Fujino, Shozaburo and Juro Teranishi. 1998. *Nihon Kinyu no Suryo Bunseki: 1872–1940* (Estimation and Analysis of Flow of Funds Accounts in Prewar Japan). Tokyo: Toyokeizai-shimposha.

Imuta, Toshimitsu. 1976. *Meijiki Kabushikikaisha Bunseki Josetsu* (An Analysis of Joint-Stock Companies in Meiji Japan). Tokyo: Yuhikaku.

Ministry of Finance, Ginkokyoku-nenpo. 1989. Annual Report of Banking Bureau of Ministry of Finance.

Ohkawa, Kasushi, et al. 1974. Kokumin-shotoku. Long-term Economic Statistics, vol. 1. Toyokeizai-shinposha.

Ohkawa, Kazushi and Miyohei Shinohara. 1979. *Patterns of Japanese Economic Development*. New Haven, Connecticut: Yale University Press.

Patrick, H. 1967. 'Japan'. In Rondo Cameron, ed., *Banking in the Early Stages of Industrialization – A Study in Comparative Economic History*. New York: Oxford University Press.

Shibuya, Ryuichi. 1959. 'Nosonkorikashi-shihon no Tenkaikatei' (Historical analysis of a moneylender in rural area). *Nogyo-sogokenkyu*, vol. 13 (1): 39–101; (2): 63–104; (3): 181–226.

Shibuya, Ryuichi. 1962. 'Wagakuni kashikingyo no Tokeiteki-Kosatsu' (A statistical analysis of moneylenders in Japan). *Nogyo-sogokenkyu*, vol. 16 (1): 175–92.

Teranishi, Juro. 1982. *Nihon no Keizaihatten to Kinyu* (Money, Capital and Economic Development in Japan). Tokyo: Iwanami-shoten.

Teranishi, Juro. 1990. 'Financial system and industrialization in Japan: 1900-1970.' *Banca nazionale del Lavore, Quarterly Review*, no. 174, September: 309–42.

Teranishi, Juro. 1994. 'Modernization of financial markets: An analysis of informal credit markets in prewar Japan'. *World Development*, vol. 22, no. 3: 312–15.

Teranishi, Juro. 1996. 'Industrial interests vs. class interests: Conflicts over income distribution in the economic development of Japan and Brazil'. Paper presented at the Round Table Conference of the International Economic Association, *The Institutional Foundation of Economic Development in East Asia*. Tokyo, 17–19 December.

Teranishi, Juro. 1997. 'Senkanki no Bunpai o meguru Seisaky-tairitsu to Kinyu Sisutemu' (Distributive conflicts, economic policy and financial system in prewar Japan). *Keizaikenkyu*, vol. 48, no. 4: 329–38.

Teikoku Tokei Nenan. *Annual Report of the Ministry of Statistics*, vol. 16 and 26.

Zenkoku Mujin-shukaijo. 1038. Senkoku-mujin-gyo. Tokei, Zenkoku Mujin-shukaijo.

PART FIVE

RURAL DEVELOPMENT, INCOME DISTRIBUTION AND POVERTY

Chapter 12

The State of Rural Poverty, Income Distribution and Rural Development in Sub-Saharan Africa

Ali Abdel Gadir Ali and Erik Thorbecke

The first section of this chapter derives a detailed rural profile of sub-Saharan Africa (SSA) from a new and highly disaggregated data set based on a large number of recent country household surveys. The profile is quite bleak. It reveals the significantly greater poverty, income inequality and agricultural stagnation in SSA as compared with Asia and other parts of the developing world. The discouraging rural socioeconomic profile raises two fundamental issues:

- Why did the rural sector in SSA evolve so differently for those in other regions, and particularly Asia?
- What are the main factors that caused contributed to or the particular rural development path followed by SSA in recent times?

To try to begin to answer these questions we explore the major factors that appear to have influenced the development path of the African rural sector. The first set of factors relates to the physical, technological and legal environment. The next set includes policies, institutions, and cultural and community norms affecting agriculture and the rural sector. Clearly, policies at the macroeconomic and sectoral levels have tended to discriminate heavily against agriculture, both directly and indirectly. In particular, the very divergent treatment of the agricultural surplus over time in SSA compared with Asia is brought to the fore. Examples of inappropriate institutions within the context of SSA that contributed to agricultural stagnation are given, and the contrast between the typical cultural and community norms prevailing in SSA and Asia is drawn. The chapter closes with some conclusions and policy recommendations.

The Rural Sector in SSA: A Profile

The following profile of the rural sector in SSA is based on the most recent household data set available for a sample of 16 SSA countries (see Annex Table 12.A1 for the countries involved and World Bank, 1997a, for further details). The total population of the sample countries was 278 million in 1993, which was about 47 per cent of the total population of SSA. The rural population in the sample represents 191 million, 69 per cent of the total population. Before looking at data and highlighting some trends, it should be emphasized that agricultural statistics in much of Africa are notoriously unreliable; consequently, drawing strong inferences from the data should be regarded as a somewhat perilous exercise. The more recent survey data are clearly more reliable but as will be shown shortly are not immune to serious errors.

Social and Consumption Indicators

The World Bank (1997a) provides information on five sets of indicators summarizing returns from household surveys: demographic (population below 15 years, number of households and average household size), education and literacy (net primary enrolment, net secondary enrolment and literacy rate), head of household (male headed households, female headed households, educational level of head and sector of employment of head), household expenditure (per capita expenditure, poverty line and food share in total expenditure), and household amenities (type of fuel for cooking, access to safe sanitation and access to water). Table 12.1 summarizes the most important characteristics of rural SSA and Annex Table 12.A1 provides some of the country details.

Table 12.1 Major characteristics of rural SSA in the 1990s

Indicator	Mean	Standard deviation
Average household size (no.)	6.34	1.83
Population below 15 years (%)	47.80	2.50
Net primary enrolment (%)	42.50	19.50
Male primary enrolment (%)	46.40	18.60
Female primary enrolment (%)	39.90	22.00
Literacy rate (%)	30.38	19.02
Male literacy rate (%)	43.75	21.54
Female literacy rate (%)	23.69	18.19
Female-headed households (%)	18.63	9.87
Heads in agro-pastoral activities (%)	78.56	11.95
Access to sanitation (%)*	53.73	30.73
Access to piped water (%)**	10.64	11.35

Notes: * information available for 11 countries, ** information available for 14 countries.
Source: Table 12.A1; World Bank (1997a).

The picture in Table 12.1 is of a rural sector with a fairly young population (48 per cent below the age of 15 years), heavy reliance on agriculture as a source of employment (79 per cent of the heads of households) and a high degree of deprivation: literacy rate of 30 per cent, access to sanitation for only 54 per cent of the population and access to piped water for only 11 per cent of the population.

As usual, however, the average picture hides a lot of variation among countries as indicated by the standard deviation. Thus, for example, taking the literacy rate as an indicator of educational achievement, we find that both Kenya and Tanzania have made commendable progress in rural education, with total literacy rates of 71 per cent and 70 per cent, respectively (81 per cent and 80 per cent rates for males and 63 per cent and 62 per cent for females, respectively). At the other extreme, Guinea (with a total literacy rate of only 10 per cent, male literacy rate of 23 per cent and female rate of only 1 per cent), Guinea-Bissau (12 per cent; 22 per cent and only 4 per cent for females) and Zambia (12 per cent, 6 per cent and 8 per cent) have a long way to go in this respect. Access to piped water, a proxy for rural health achievements, paints another extreme picture of deprivation in rural SSA for all countries. Of the 14 countries for which data are available, the highest achievement is recorded for Côte d'Ivoire, where 38 per cent of the rural population has access to piped water. In the Central African Republic and Guinea only 1 per cent of the rural population have access to piped water, while only 2 per cent in Guinea-Bissau, Tanzania and Uganda have such access. Both education and health indicators reflect not only the extent of rural deprivation but also the magnitude of the development challenge facing the continent.

Regarding the gender dimension of the indicators for the indicators for rural SSA it is not clear whether the 19 per cent of the households being headed by females is high. This category, we hasten to note, includes both the 'de facto female heads', which refers to households 'where the husband is not present and the wife is head by default', and the 'de jure female heads', which refers to house where the head 'has never been married, is divorced or widowed'. The de facto situation can capture some important socioeconomic processes such as migration. The highest incidence of female headed households is recorded for Guinea-Bissau with 43 per cent, followed by Kenya (32 per cent), Ghana (29 per cent), Uganda (25 per cent) and Central African Republic (24 per cent). The lowest incidence is recorded for Gambia (3 per cent) followed by Burkina Faso (8 per cent).

The gender dimension, as discrimination between the sexes, is usually discussed in terms of educational attainment. Table 12.1 shows a female literacy rate for rural SSA of 24 per cent compared with a male literacy rate of 44 per cent, which indicates gender discrimination. The difference between the two is statistically significant at the 5 per cent level. At the primary education level, however, the school enrolment ratios are 40 per cent for females and 46 per cent for males and the difference is not statistically significant. The gender bias in health observed in South Asia does not appear to be generally prevalent in Africa and this holds true for other indicators such as infant and child mortality (Appleton et al., 1996).

The picture of a fairly underdeveloped rural sector is further reinforced by a consideration of welfare standards as judged by per capita expenditure. Annex

Table 12.A2 provides the country details for our sample. At the aggregate level a summary is provided in Table 12.2.

Table 12.2 Average annual per capita expenditure in SSA 1993 (PPP 1985 dollars unless specified otherwise)

Indicator	National	Urban	Rural	Rural/ national (%)	Rural/ urban (%)	Rural food share (%)
Mean	513	829	380	74.6	48.5	58.2
Standard deviation	170	326	142	13.4	16.6	15.9

Source: Based on Annex Table 12.A2. Note that the percentage ratios in the last three columns are arithmetic means of the national percentage ratios from Annex Table 12.A2.

According to Table 12.2, the mean per capita expenditure for the sample countries was $513 per annum for 1993. This works out as $43 per person per month, which is 42.5 per cent above the international benchmark poverty line currently in use by, among others, United Nation Development Programme and the World Bank for international comparisons. This indicates that we are dealing with an overall depressed economic situation in SSA. Within this, we note that mean urban expenditure works out to $69 per person per month, while mean rural per capita expenditure is only $32 per person per month (only 7 per cent above the international poverty line). Compared with mean national per capita expenditure, the rural welfare indicator is 75 per cent of the national average. Urban expenditure is twice that of rural expenditure, indicating a fairly wide rural–urban gap.

Once again the aggregate picture hides wide variations among countries. Eight countries in the sample have a rural per capita monthly expenditure below the international poverty line of $30 per person per month: Burkina Faso, $22; CAR, $22; Gambia, $24; Guinea, $23; Guinea-Bissau, $24; Niger, $24; Tanzania, $20; Zambia, $16. Four countries have a rural per capita expenditure between $30 and $40 per person per month (Madagascar, $31; Senegal, $35; Sierra Leone, $36; Uganda, $35). The remaining four have a rural per capita expenditure of $40 per person per month or more (Côte d'Ivoire, $42; Ghana, $59; Kenya, $40; Nigeria, $53).

The share of food in rural expenditure averages 58 per cent for the sample. This varies from a low of 21 per cent for Côte d'Ivoire to a high of 78 per cent for Zambia. Of the 15 countries for which information is available, 10 have a food share in rural expenditure of 60 per cent or more. The shares for Côte d'Ivoire (21 per cent), Niger (29 per cent) and Ghana (37 per cent) are simply not credible; their shares are much lower than those of much more developed and richer countries and as such would refute Engel's Law. One possible hypothesis for the low shares reported by the World Bank (1997a) could be that they are based on the proportion of income spent on food expenditures rather than the proportion of food consumption including both food purchases and the imputed value of food consumption from own farm production out of total monetary and non-monetary income.[1]

A comparison of the indicators discussed above, as well as additional health (life expectancy and infant mortality rates) indicators for SSA and other developing regions, reveals clearly the relative underdevelopment of SSA.

Income Distribution and Inequality Measures: SSA Compared with Other Developing Regions

Comparisons based on national data The difficulties surrounding the use of income distribution data in developing countries have been addressed extensively in the literature (see, for example, Deininger and Squire, 1996; Fields, 1994; Chenet al., 1994; Ravallion, 1995). The crux of the matter is that such data are scarce and full of inconsistencies and that care should be exercised in using them. Deininger and Squire (1996: 567–71) specify minimum standards for the quality of income distribution data as: (a) the database must be an actual household survey; (b) the data, even if drawn from household surveys, must be based on a representative sample covering all of the population; and (c) the data source must be based on a comprehensive coverage of different income sources as well as population groups (see also Fields, 1989, 1994). Ravallion (1995) discusses the problems related to the comparability of data used in making cross-country comparisons of poverty.

To guard against such problems, and to maintain maximum comparability with the literature, Ali (1997) used the original data set of Chen et al. (1994). This set included 44 countries, three of which were European (then socialist), with a total of 63 income distribution observations, where 19 countries had two observations each. In use, the three socialist countries were excluded from the data set, leaving only 41 countries and 58 observations for regional comparisons. Table 12.3 summarizes the results in terms of averages over observations, where figures in parentheses are standard deviations.

It is an easy matter to check that there exists a statistically significant difference at the 5 per cent level of significance for all reported measures of inequality between sub-Saharan Africa and both South Asia and Asia. Thus, it will be safe to conclude that SSA exhibits more unequal distribution of income than either of the other two regions. However, there is no statistically significant difference between SSA and East Asia.[2]

---

[1] It is quite surprising that the World Bank (1997a) would uncritically publish such figures. In any case, the food share given for Côte d'Ivoire in the recent book by Grootaert (1996) distinguishes between consumption of food purchases and consumption of home produced food. He reports total food shares of 60 per cent for the 'extreme poor', 57 per cent for the 'mid-poor' and 47 per cent for the 'non-poor'. Even the food purchase shares of income (excluding consumption of home produced food) reported by Grootaert are higher than the World Bank estimate of 21 per cent, i.e., 22 per cent for the 'extreme poor', 29 per cent for the 'mid-poor' and 33 per cent for the non-poor' (Grootaert, 1996: Table 3.18).

[2] This, we believe, is an interesting result in its own right. Relating these results to the share of population living in rural areas tends to confirm the assumption frequently invoked in the

We note that these results are not qualitatively different from those reported by Deininger and Squire (1996: 383–85). To see this we summarize their results in Table 12.4.

Table 12.3 A summary of inequality measures: Averages by region (percentages of total consumption, except for last two columns)

Region (no. of countries)	No. of observations	Share of lowest 40%	Share of top 20%	Share of top 10%	Gini coefficient	Ratio of top 20% to lowest 40% *
SS Africa (16)	16	14.50	51.34	35.95	45.37	4.19
		(5.02)	(8.85)	(8.47)	(10.75)	(2.08)
East Asia (5)	9	16.76	47.01	31.33	40.02	2.96
		(2.88)	(5.17)	(5.18)	(06.21)	(0.89)
South Asia (5)	8	21.85	39.73	25.43	30.50	1.83
		(1.00)	(1.31)	(1.13)	(01.81)	(0.14)
Asia (10)	17	18.63	44.50	29.42	36.77	2.53
		(3.23)	(4.96)	(4.56)	(06.29)	(0.79)

*Mean of country ratios.
Source: Calculations by Ali (1997) based on Chen et al. (1994).

Table 12.4 Deininger and Squire inequality results for the 1990s: Averages by region (percentages of total consumption, except for last two columns)

Region (no. of countries)	No. of observations	Share of lowest 20%	Share of top 20%	Share of middle class (3rd and 4th quintile)	Gini coefficient	Ratio of top 20% to lowest 20%
SS Africa (14)	16	5.15	52.37	33.54	46.95	10.17
East Asia (9)	16	6.84	44.33	37.53	38.09	6.48
South Asia (4)	6	8.76	39.91	38.42	31.88	4.56
Asia (13)*	22	7.80	42.12	37.98	34.98	5.52

* The last row is a simple average of the two Asian regions and is meant to be indicative.
Source: Based on Deininger and Squire (1996: tables 12.5 and 12.6).

An interesting result reported by Deininger and Squire (1996) pertains to the behaviour of inequality over the decade. According to these results SSA inequality declined over the period 1960–1980 (from an average Gini ratio of 49.9 per cent in the 1960s to an average Gini ratio of 43.46 per cent in the 1980s) and increased thereafter to an average Gini ratio of 46.95 per cent in the 1990s. By contrast,

development literature that the more rural an economy is the more equal its distribution of income is likely to be.

inequality in East Asia first increased from a Gini ratio of 37.43 per cent in the 1960s to a Gini ratio of 39.88 per cent in the 1970s, before declining to 38.7 per cent in the 1980s and 38.09 per cent in the 1990s. The behaviour of inequality in South Asia was different; it declined over the period 1960–1970 (from a 36.23 per cent in the 1960s to 33.95 per cent in the 1970s) then increased to a Gini ratio of 35.01 per cent in the 1980s prior to declining again to an average of 31.88 per cent in the 1990s. Once again, given data limitations, these results should be taken as indicative rather than definitive.

Comparisons based on rural sector data Next we concentrate on the distribution of income within the rural sector. For this we report the results from a sample of 16 SSA countries for which information is available, as noted earlier. As is clear from Annex Table 12.A3, the income distribution information for SSA relates to the early 1990s and indeed for most of the countries it relates to 1993. The results are summarized in Table 12.5.

Table 12.5 Income distribution measures for rural SSA: A summary (percentages)

Inequality measure	Mean	Standard deviation	Minimum	Maximum
Share of lowest 40%	15.55	5.1	3.54	21.38
Share of top 20%	50.46	10.8	37.94	78.44
Gini coefficient	42.88	11.2	29.72	66.67
Ratio of top 20% to lowest 40%	4.5996	4.9	1.77	22.16

Source: Annex Table 12.A3.

The summary shows a fairly highly unequal distribution of income within the rural sector of SSA. However, it is important to note that the inequality in rural income distribution within most SSA countries is due to large inter-village income differences (itself the result of large climatic, agronomic and soil fertility differences) rather than to large intra-village income differences. As usual, being a summary, the picture hides much variation among countries in the sample. For all the inequality measures reported, however, Côte d'Ivoire comes out as having the most equal rural income distribution in SSA, with the highest share of income for the lowest 40 per cent of the population (21.38 per cent), the lowest share for the top 20 per cent of the rural population (37.93 per cent), the lowest Gini coefficient (29.72 per cent) and the lowest ratio of the share of the top 20 per cent to that of the lowest 40 per cent (1.77). At the other extreme, Sierra Leone comes out as having the most unequal rural distribution in SSA, with the lowest share of income for the lowest 40 per cent of its rural population (only 3.5 per cent) and the highest values for the remaining inequality measures as reported in the table.

The distribution of the sample countries on the basis of the mean of the inequality measures could be summarized as follows:

- Seven countries have a share of the lowest 40 per cent that is less than the mean (CAR, Guinea-Bissau, Kenya, Nigeria, Senegal, Sierra Leone and Zambia).
- Five countries have a share of the top 20 per cent that is greater than the mean (CAR, Guinea-Bissau, Kenya, Nigeria, Sierra Leone and Uganda).
- Six countries have a Gini coefficient greater than the mean (CAR, Guinea-Bissau, Kenya, Nigeria, Sierra Leone and Zambia).
- Three countries have a ratio of the top 20 per cent to the lowest 40 per cent greater than the mean (CAR, Guinea-Bissau and Sierra Leone).

This distribution implies that 48.5 per cent of the rural population of SSA live under conditions where the distribution of income is relatively highly unequal.

We next report, in Table 12.6 the results for the inequality of income in the Asian region. The available information on the distribution of income in the Asian rural sector is from a recent ILO compendium of data authored by Tabatabai (1996). This source provides quintile or percentile data suitable for further analysis for only five countries. However, since the countries in the sample include China, with its dominating share of population in rural Asia, the results could be taken as strongly indicative of the state of income distribution in the Asian rural sector.

Table 12.6 Income distribution measures for rural Asia: A sample of countries (percentages except for the last column)

Country (year)	Share of lowest 40%	Share of top 20%	Gini coefficient	Ratio of top 20% to lowest 40%
China (1988)	18.6	44.2	36.34	2.38
Indonesia (1987)	23.5	37.6	27.60	1.60
Malaysia (1984)	14.1	49.4	44.45	3.50
Nepal (1984/85)	25.5	35.2	23.78	1.38
Pakistan (1990/91)	16.5	47.3	40.99	2.87
Mean	19.6	42.7	34.63	2.35
Standard deviation	4.3	5.5	7.84	0.79

Source: Based on Tabatabai (1996).

In comparing the two tables (12.5 and 12.6) it is perhaps clear that the distribution of income in the Asian rural sector in the mid 1980s (with the exception of Malaysia) was significantly more equal than that prevailing in SSA at the beginning of the 1990s. Indeed, with a t-test it is an easy matter to show this result for all the reported inequality measures.

Extent and Incidence of Poverty in SSA

We report the poverty results for rural SSA in terms of the three well-known poverty measures: the head-count ratio (H: which measures the spread of poverty), the poverty-gap ratio (P_1: which measures the depth of poverty) and the squared poverty-gap ratio (P_2: which measures the severity of poverty).[3] The detailed country results are presented in Annex Table 12.A4 and summarized in Table 12.7. To generate comparable results we followed Chen et al. (1994) in using per person consumption expenditure denominated in 1985 purchasing power parity (PPP) dollars. Indeed, for the countries for which they report such figures we adjusted their results to the corresponding survey years using appropriate growth rates from the World Development Reports of the World Bank. For countries where such figures are not reported we used the original Summers and Heston (1991) results and adjusted them as appropriate. Note, however, that Chenet al. (1994) do not report mean consumption figures for rural and urban sectors. To obtain the rural sector figures we used the original sectoral ratios reported in the World Bank (1997a) summary of these surveys.

Table 12.7 SSA rural poverty in 1993: A summary

Poverty indicator	Mean	Standard deviation	Minimum	Maximum
Head-count (%)	58.72	12.16	34.42	77.57
Poverty-gap (%)	26.51	12.22	9.26	55.58
Squared PG (%)	15.89	11.01	3.55	45.86
Mean income ($)	380.00	142.00	191.00	706.00
Poverty line ($)	311.00	60.50	237.00	456.00

Source: Annex Table 12.A4.

Given rural per capita consumption expenditure, we estimated the relevant country poverty lines by using the estimated equation reported in Ali (1997) where the relationship between the poverty line and mean income is given by the following semi-log functional form (figures in parentheses are t-values):

$$\text{Ln } z = \underset{(100.9)}{5.181} + \underset{(18.3)}{0.00158}\,\mu - \underset{(-10.9)}{0.0000003485}\,\mu^2;\ R^2 = 0.96 \qquad (1)$$

Given Equation 1 and the rural distribution information, the rural poverty results are generated by Povcal, a programme developed by Chen et al. (1994) for calculating poverty measures from grouped data.

It is clear from Table 12.7 that at the beginning of the 1990s poverty in rural SSA was very widespread, with 59 per cent of the rural population living below a

---

[3] As is well known the three poverty measures are special cases of the Foster–Greer–Thorbecke (1984) measure defined as $P(\alpha) = 1/n\ \Sigma[(z - y_i)/z]^\alpha$, where z is the poverty line, y_i is the income (or expenditure) of poor person i and α is a non-negative poverty aversion parameter, and where the summation is over q poor persons. When α takes the values 0, 1 and 2, we get the head-count ratio, the poverty-gap ratio and the squared poverty-gap ratio, respectively.

poverty line of approximately $26 per month per person. SSA rural poverty is also found to be both deep, as reflected by a poverty-gap ratio of 27 per cent, and severe, as reflected by a squared poverty-gap ratio of 16 per cent. To further appreciate the extent of this poverty it can easily be shown that the average income of the poor in 1993 amounted to only $14 per person per month.

The spread, depth and severity of SSA rural poverty differ among countries as captured by the magnitude of the reported standard deviations. In terms of spread, Côte d'Ivoire ranks as the country with the least rural poverty with a head-count ratio of 38 per cent, CAR is the worst, with 78 per cent of its rural population living below a poverty line of $103 per person per annum (or only $9 per person per month). In terms of both depth and severity, Ghana ranks as the country with the least poverty (with a poverty-gap measure of 9.3 per cent and a squared poverty-gap measure of 3.6 per cent), while Sierra Leone ranks as the country with the worst rural poverty (with a poverty-gap measure of 55.6 per cent and a squared poverty-gap measure of 45.9 per cent).

Further, the distribution of the countries of the sample around the reported mean head-count ratio is such that eight countries have a ratio greater than the mean (Burkina Faso: 68 per cent; CAR: 78 per cent; Guinea: 61 per cent; Guinea-Bissau: 68 per cent; Niger: 60 per cent; Tanzania: 67 per cent; Zambia: 77 per cent). Four countries have poverty-gap and squared poverty-gap ratios greater than the mean (CAR, 46 per cent and 32 per cent; Guinea-Bissau, 40 and 28 per cent; Sierra Leone, 56 and 46 per cent; and Zambia, 40 and 26 per cent).[4]

How sensitive is SSA rural poverty to changes in mean income and the Gini coefficient? Table 12.8 provides indicative results of estimating a double-log relationship between the poverty measures and their growth and distribution determinants.

In terms of sensitivity to its major determinants, SSA rural poverty exhibits a pattern that is now becoming stylized for the three poverty measures used above. Thus the head-count ratio is relatively more responsive to growth in income compared with distribution, though in the case of rural poverty in SSA this difference is not great: a 1 per cent increase in income leads to half a percentage point reduction in poverty, while a 1 per cent increase in the Gini coefficient leads to an increase in poverty by 0.48 percentage point. The poverty-gap ratio and the squared poverty-gap measure are more sensitive to changes in the distribution than to changes in mean income. The elasticities of the two measures with respect

---

[4] No attempt has been made to compare these SSA results with ones for the Asia region due to lack of data that could be used to conduct a comparable exercise. Secondary results on rural poverty, such as the ones appearing in Ravallion and Sen (1996) for Bangladesh (1991/92: H = 52.9, P1 = 14.6, P2 = 5.6), Balisacan (1995) for Philippines (1991: H = 64.5, P1 = 22.82, and P2 = 10.42), and Ravallion and Bidani (1994) for Indonesia (1990: H = 23.58, P1 = 4.25, and P2 = 1.08) are not readily comparable to ours. Further, not all sources provide the information we require to use the distribution data reported in Table 12.7 to generate comparable poverty results. Tabatabai's (1996) compilation is not of much help; it is incomplete on poverty in the rural sector and sometimes does not report the most recent results, as in the case of Philippines where Balisacan (1995) is not used.

to the Gini coefficient are almost double those with respect to mean income (in absolute value). This is an important result for policy purposes. Given such elasticities, poverty alleviation through an extrapolation of the present growth pattern would take a very long time in SSA—as some simulation exercises we have done (but do not report here) reveal.

Table 12.8 The sensitivity of SSA rural poverty to growth and distribution (t-values are in parentheses)

Dependent variable	Constant	Log income	Log Gini coefficient	R^2
Log head-count ratio	5.2175	-0.5028	0.4792	0.93
	(14.33)	(-10.75)	(7.61)	
Log poverty-gap ratio	2.5105	-0.7648	1.3801	0.96
	(4.6)	(-10.92)	(14.63)	
Log squared poverty-gap ratio	0.2894	-0.9585	2.1116	0.96
	(0.35)	(-9.0)	(14.72)	

Poverty is an extremely elusive concept and essentially normative—depending on how the poverty line is defined. Given the paucity of reliable surveys in Africa and the intrinsic difficulty of making inter-country and interregional comparisons, only weak inferences relating to poverty trends can be made. A very recent and careful analysis of poverty trends in the developing world concluded that although the head-count ratio of poverty was still somewhat higher in 1993 in South Asia (43.1 per cent) than in SSA (39.1 per cent), the severity of poverty (according to the poverty-gap index) was significantly greater in the latter. In addition, SSA was the only developing region where poverty continued to increase—at least over the period 1987 to 1993. (See Table 12.5 in Ravallion and Chen, 1997.)

Food Output and Employment in Rural SSA

In a recent study, Khan (1997) documented the stagnation of the rural sector in SSA and its dismal performance compared with other developing regions. Table 12.9 summarizes the evidence.

The data in Table 12.9 show, first, that SSA is not the most rural of developing regions; that distinction belongs to South Asia where the share of the total population residing in rural areas was 74 per cent, compared with 69 per cent in SSA in 1994 (see row 1 of Table 12.9). Second, SSA was the only developing region recording a negative growth rate of food output per capita between 1963 and 1992 (i.e., -0.3 per cent) and a negative growth rate of agricultural labour productivity between 1980 and 1990 (-0.4 per cent). Particularly worrisome is the fact that in the four years since 1990, the rate of decline of labour productivity in agriculture accelerated greatly to 1.5 per cent per year (Khan, 1997). The fall in food output per capita becomes an even greater concern when it is seen in conjunction with another trend in SSA, i.e., a fall in the proportion of the rural labour force engaged in non-farm activities, at least when comparing the late 1980s with the mid 1960s (Khan, 1997: Table 2).

Table 12.9 Comparative indicators of the status and trends for the rural economy

	SSA	ESEA	SA	LAC	Mean
Rural population as % of total population (1994)	69	68	74	26	44
Agricultural labour as % of total labour force (1990)	68	68	64	26	37
Annual growth rate of rural population (1980–94)	2.26	0.56	1.79	−0.18	1.84
Annual growth rate of agricultural labour productivity (1980–90)	−0.4	1.9	2.7	1.8	3.9
Growth rate of food output per capita (1963–92)	−0.3	1.4	0.6	0.4	n.a.

Note: SSA = Sub-Saharan Africa, ESEA = East and Southeast Asia, SA = South Africa, LAC = Latin America and the Caribbean, MENA = Middle East and North Africa.
Source: Adapted from Khan (1997). Rows 1 and 2 are from World Bank (1996) and rows 3 and 4 are based on the data shown in World Bank (1996). Row 5 is from Table 2 in Platteau and Hayami (1998).

Third, the very strong demographic pressures to which Africa is subjected are indicated by the very high annual growth rate of the rural population of 2.26 per cent in the recent period. As Khan (1997) emphasizes, the evidence on trends in employment and productivity in agriculture and in employment in non-farm activities suggests that the growth of output in rural SSA was far short of what was necessary to provide employment to the growing rural labour force at either constant productivity or constant income and that consequently rural poverty is likely to have worsened.

Summary

The rather bleak rural profile we have painted reveals that SSA, in comparison with other regions, suffers from greater, more severe and more persistent poverty; more unequal distribution of income; declining food production per capita and agricultural labour productivity; and a continuing population explosion. The new entrants in the labour force cannot be absorbed productively in sufficient number either in rural non-farm activities or in urban activities, tending thereby to depress agricultural productivity.

Why did the rural sector in SSA evolve so differently than in other regions and particularly Asia? What are the main factors, proximate causes and constraints that help explain the particular rural development path followed by SSA in the last few decades? An attempt is made in the next sections to provide some answers to these questions.

Factors Influencing the Rural Development Path in SSA

In an important recent paper Platteau and Hayami (1998: 357) provide a comprehensive and systematic explanation of why 'Sub-Saharan Africa appears as the perfect counter-model to the East Asian experience'. The thesis they develop is rather convincing and one we generally subscribe to. Hence, we draw repeatedly on their contribution. At the same time, we bring up additional factors and issues and highlight further—and in some instances qualify and question—elements of their thesis. In a nutshell, their contention is that 'differences in population density are responsible, through short- or medium-term physical and economic effects or through (very) long-term social and cultural effects (effects on cultural values and norms mediated by social and family patterns) for most of the divergence observed between rural development performance in SSA and Asia' (p. 3).

A necessary qualification that has to be made at the outset is that 'SSA in the mid-1990s represents a mosaic' and that 'it is no longer possible, if it ever was, to talk of the continent as an undifferentiated whole' (World Bank, 1995: vii). The continent comprises one relatively giant country, Nigeria, with a population in excess of 100 million, one large country, Ethiopia (56 million) and a large number of very small countries, i.e., about a dozen SSA countries have populations of 6 million or less. To quote Oyejide (1999: 372)

> The typical African economy is small, in terms of both population and gross national products. Taken together the SSA region has a very limited human resource base, in spite of its rapidly growing population. Furthermore, these small economies suffer from inherent inflexibility and structural rigidities that constrain their ability to respond to external shocks. An important constituent of the rigid economic structures is agriculture. SSA's highly extensive and diversified farming systems have traditionally been based, essentially, on household food self-sufficiency. SSA's agricultural sector is further characterized by fragile soils, and is predominantly rain-fed and frequently exposed to unfavourable weather and other climatic conditions. Dynamism is severely limited by extremely low levels of technology and the lack of rural infrastructure such as roads and irrigation.

There is a whole constellation of factors that have influenced the path of African rural development. In what follows, we group these elements into three categories: the physical, technological and legal (mainly land tenure) environment; policies and institutions bearing on rural development; and cultural and community norms and customs.

Physical, Technological and Legal Environment

This category of factors includes access to land, quantity and quality of infrastructure, extent of market integration for agricultural products, and relative size of the marketable surplus. Others are agro-climatic diversity and technological constraints, and issues of land tenure and titling.

Access to land Access to land, quantity and quality of infrastructure, extent of market integration for agricultural products, and relative size of the marketable surplus. Others are agro-climatic diversity and technological constraints, and land tenure and titling.

The initial resource endowment, particularly in terms of access to land, is likely to be a crucial determinant of the pattern of agricultural development a country or region will follow. Platteau and Hayami (1998) provide evidence that Asia, as compared with Africa, is characterized by scarcity of land resources relative to population and labour force. As they put it (p. 4):

> The high population density and the unfavorable land–labour ratio have induced more intensive land use, resulting in high percentages of land used for agricultural production....by building better land infrastructure...above all, irrigation. The better land infrastructure created suitable conditions for the introduction of modern land-saving technologies such as high-yielding varieties and chemical fertilizer.

If the amount of arable land per agricultural worker is taken as a measure of access to land, Platteau and Hayami (1998) show ratios ranging from 0.3 (hectares of arable land to agricultural workers) in East Asia to 0.8 in South Asia (and 0.5 for the whole of Asia) and 1.2 in Africa in the early 1990s. Khan (1997), using somewhat different sources, comes up with somewhat different estimates, i.e., 0.43 for Asia (with 0.20 for China and 0.73 for India) contrasting with 0.96 for SSA. Khan (1997, Table 5) demonstrates the wide diversity of land endowments among African countries ranging from a ratio of 0.27 in Kenya to 1.88 in Nigeria, which prompts him to state that 'this overall measure of land endowment hides a great deal of difference among individual countries of SSA. In many countries land scarcity is worse than the Asian average and in some it is as bad as in quintessentially land-scarce China' (p. 8). Furthermore, Khan argues that 'once the higher cropping intensity due to irrigation and the better land quality in Asia is taken into account, the relative advantage of SSA over Asia...becomes much narrower. ... [and] SSA should perhaps be considered just as land scarce as India' (p. 8).

Even if the contrast in relative land access between Africa and Asia is signifycantly less pronounced today than some authors would argue, the initial conditions that prevailed in the past—say, at the outset of the post colonial era and before the greater population growth trends in Africa than in Asia reduced the differential in the land/worker ratio over time—would appear to be consistent with greater land scarcity in Asia as a stylized fact.

Quantity and quality of infrastructure There is a great scarcity of physical infrastructure in SSA—particularly road networks within rural areas (as well as farm to market roads) and between rural and urban areas. There is also tremendous underinvestment in irrigation projects; (only 4.6 per cent of SSA agricultural land is irrigated, compared with 38.4 per cent in Asia (Khan, 1997: Table 5). The quantity and quality of the road network play a crucial role in facilitating trade at all levels (intraregional, interregional, and international). This network is tremendously underdeveloped in SSA and is a major cause of a) the very high transportation costs that prevail; b) the high price spreads between initial agricultural producer prices and ultimate consumer prices; c) segmented agricultural product markets; and d) very limited market orientation on the part of the small African farmers who produce largely for subsistence with low marketable surpluses.

Very large interregional and inter-country differences in the extent of transport infrastructure can be observed.[5] Ahmed and Rustagi (1984) documented the underdeveloped stage of road infrastructure in Africa. Africa possesses only between 0.01 to 0.11 kilometres of road per square kilometre of land area compared with 0.30 to 0.45 kilometres of road per square kilometre of land area in Asian countries.[6] Furthermore, as of the early 1980s, only about 10 per cent of the road network in African countries consisted of paved roads compared with about 35 per cent of such roads in Asia. The relatively poor state of physical infrastructure in much of SSA compared with Asia is directly related to another characteristic of the physical environment, mainly the much lower population density in the former.

Asian countries are likewise significantly better off in terms of railways and river transport networks. Because of greater reliance on trucks and railways in Africa, the import content of transportation marketing costs in Kenya and Tanzania, for example, is about 50 per cent compared with an estimated average import intensity of only 17 per cent in Indonesia and Bangladesh (Ahmed and Rustagi, 1984: 4.3). The absolute transport costs in marketing were also found to be twice as high in Africa compared with selected Asian countries. To this list, Platteau and Hayami (1998) add the low quality of rural roads in Africa, noting that about half the rural road network requires 'substantial rehabilitation'.

There is evidence of more intensive land cultivation following population growth occurring in specific African settings. In the Machakos region of Kenya, four positive effects of population growth have been identified: increased food needs; increased labour supply; increased interaction of ideas leading to new technologies; and economies of scale in the provision of social and physical infrastructure (Tiffen et al., 1994). According to these authors, 'These effects in the medium or long term can outweigh the negative effects of population growth, at least at the levels of population density which we have discussed...' (Tiffen et al., 1994: 266).

The mechanisms through which population growth affect land intensification and agricultural output are a) a fall in the per capita costs of providing infrastructure; b) economies of scale for the exchange, storage and processing of knowledge (such as schools and extension services; and c) greater efficiency of the activities of private traders due to greater population density.

[5] Much of the evidence comes from the excellent paper by Ahmed and Rustagi (1984). Both Thorbecke (1992) and Platteau and Hayami (1996) rely extensively on the Ahmed and Rustagi (1984) paper. The summarized evidence that follows is based on Thorbecke (1992) supplemented by more recent evidence unearthed by Platteau and Hayami (1996).

[6] Quoting from more recent sources, Platteau and Hayami (1996) mention that in the early 1990s, Africa (i.e., a group of 18 countries) had only one-sixth the rural roads density per square kilometre of land as India.

In short, all these interrelated factors—together with technological constraints and discriminatory policies against agriculture (which are discussed subsequently)—go a long way in explaining the essentially stagnant agricultural production picture in SSA over the last three decades or so.[7]

Extent of market integration for agricultural products Market integration can take different forms: spatial integration, inter-temporal integration and inter-commodity integration. In the present discussion, the emphasis is on spatial integration.[8] A market is spatially integrated when price differences between any two regions (or markets) that trade with each other just equal transfer (mainly transportation) costs. Alternatively, markets are spatially segmented if the interregional price differences are less than their transfer costs. Integrated markets have been defined as 'markets in which prices of differentiated products do not behave independently' (Monke and Petzel, 1984: 482). The assumption is that identical products are differentiated by location.

Markets are centred on specific items to be exchanged, such as wheat, rice or maize. Each item has its own set of characteristics, actors and environmental settings. Since the marketing chain between producers (farmers) and ultimate consumers may involve many intermediaries, it is useful to think in terms of specific commodity systems. During the marketing process, agricultural commodities gain in value as they are moved through space, held over time and transformed. Each commodity system has its own particular marketing chain, network and set of transactions corresponding to the functions performed by different actors as the commodity progresses from producer to final consumer (Thorbecke, 1992).

In evaluating the extent of market integration and the efficiency along a commodity system (marketing chain) and interregionally, two types of price spread indicators suggest themselves. The price spread between the producer and consumer ends of a commodity system represents the overall marketing margin. Its relative magnitude, as well as its decomposition among components, yields insights about the efficiency of the product market and the degree of integration among the various configurations constituting the marketing chain. A second category of price spreads, i.e., spatial price spreads, reflects the differences in prices obtaining in various regional markets at a particular time.

These two types of price spreads in food grain markets were estimated for five African and four Asian countries by Ahmed and Rustagi (1984).[9] Three major empirical findings emerge from an analysis of the data:

---

[7] These factors were systematically discussed in a paper by Thorbecke (1992) on 'The anatomy of agricultural product markets and transactions in developing countries', which drew comparisons between Africa and Asia.

[8] This subsection is based on Section 4.2 of Thorbecke (1992).

[9] Their results are summarized in their Table 2, p. 3.4, and cover the following countries: Nigeria, Malawi, Tanzania, Kenya, Sudan, Indonesia, India, Bangladesh and the Philippines. Depending on the country, the following food grains were used: maize, rice, sorghum and wheat.

- Average producer prices as a percentage of final consumer prices in the African countries ranged from 30 to 60 per cent; in Asia they ranged from 75 to 90 per cent. Thus, African farmers received a significantly smaller proportion of final consumer prices of marketed food grains than did their Asian counterparts.
- The regional price differences within each country were substantially larger in Africa than in Asia; in some African countries the lowest price in one region was only one-fourth to one-third that of the highest price in another region. In contrast, the corresponding ratio in Asia ranged from 64 to 83 per cent.
- The absolute size of the regional price spread in Africa was significantly larger than the marketing margin (i.e., the producer/consumer price spread).

From this quantitative analysis, Ahmed and Rustagi (1984: 109) conclude:

> Many markets may not be linked with one another in African countries because of high transport costs resulting from poor transport and communication infrastructure or government restrictions. In the Asian countries, the regional price spreads are quite close to the marketing margins, which indicates that the markets scattered over various regions are probably well integrated with one another.

The example of Zaire may be enlightening. In a detailed study of sectoral investment priorities in Zaire, Koné and Thorbecke (1998: 303) found that:

> Owing to chronic transport and marketing problems, about 40 per cent of total production is consumed by the farmers themselves, while urban markets are increasingly supplied by imports. Clearly, there is great potential for increased production in agriculture through exports and further increase in domestic demand once the major obstacles, both on the production and the distribution side, are removed.

However, the producer/consumer and interregional price spreads are determined not only by transportation and marketing costs; they are also influenced by government taxes, profit margins of parastatals and private traders, and transaction costs. Ahmed and Rustagi (1984) concluded that almost two-thirds of the higher marketing costs in Africa compared with Asia are accounted for by transport and transaction costs. The latter reflect the greater degree of government intervention in grain marketing in Africa, through such measures as bans on the interregional movement of commodities by private traders and a variety of licensing schemes imposed on these same traders.

At this stage, we can summarize the main factors that have been found to be responsible for Africa's relatively low levels of market infrastructure development and market integration compared with Asia, and the associated marketing inefficiencies and significantly greater price spreads. (See Ahmed and Rustagi, 1984; FAO, 1992, particularly p. 226.) These factors are:

- The much lower population density in most African countries (15 to 30 persons per square kilometre, compared with 500–750 persons per square kilometre in Asia) results in a wider dispersion of production and consumption centres in Africa.
- Road, railway and river transport systems are generally much less developed in Africa than in Asia, as some of the earlier statistics indicated.
- Transport modes in Africa are less diversified and more import intensive.
- Some African countries generate a small volume of marketable surplus in food grains because of the predominance of subsistence production, which reduces the scope for scale economies in transport and marketing (an issue that is examined in the next subsection).
- A bimodal structure in agriculture is typical of many African countries, which results in market dualism.
- Economies of scale in Asian marketing have enabled separate specialization in transport services and grain trade, whereas in Africa the more typical pattern is for truckers to combine transport services with wholesaling and retailing.
- The more extensive spread of rural electrification in Asia allows more small-scale milling and processing to occur close to the production location with concomitant lower transportation costs.

Relative size of the marketable surplus It is well known that on the whole, the relative size of the marketable surplus (i.e., the proportion of farm household output sold out of total farm household production) is significantly higher in Asia than in SSA. As the World Bank (1997b: 31) emphasized, most farmers in SSA operate on a small scale, 'often producing commodities that, because of their type and small quantities, are not part of the market economy. In Côte d'Ivoire, Ghana and Malawi, the rural poor grow 60 per cent of their food; in Tanzania the poor produce 50 per cent of what they consume'. In other words, African small farmers tend to be much more subsistence oriented than their Asian counterparts.

Why is the proportion of farm household output consumed within the farm household typically larger in SSA than in Asia and, conversely, why is the size of the relative marketable surplus smaller? To answer this question, we have to analyse the behaviour of peasant households in terms of their reliance on intra-household (non-market) transactions vs. market transactions. In other words, how do farm households decide on the extent to which they engage in intra-farm household transactions such as production for own consumption, and family farm labour applied to own farm production, as opposed to participating in transactions in existing market configurations for the same items?

De Janvry et al. (1991) have provided a formal framework within which this question can be answered.[10] They start by offering an interpretation of market failure for food and labour that is specific to the household and not to the commodity. They proceed to derive within an integrated farm household model

[10] The description that follows is based on Thorbecke (1993).

(acting as a producing and a consuming unit) the household response to changes in the price and productivity of cash crops, changes in the price of manufactured and consumption goods, the levying of a monetary tax, and availability of new technological opportunities in the production of food. They postulate that for commodities such as food and labour that can be sold and bought by peasant households, the sale price is a fraction of the purchase price.

In turn, the width of this band depends on a whole set of transaction costs (such as transportation costs and marketing margins). 'The poorer the infrastructure, the less competitive the marketing systems, the less information is available, and the more risky the transactions, the greater the size of this band' (de Janvry et al., 1991: 1402). When the shadow price of a product, or of labour produced and used by a farm household, falls within this price band, no trade takes place and the household reverts to self-sufficiency (subsistence) and relies on intra-household transactions.

The key finding is that the chronic inelasticity of supply response—particularly within the context of SSA—may be explained 'as a structural feature associated with missing markets and not as an inherent behavioural trait of peasants' (de Janvry et al., 1991: 1410). This implies that a number of specific characteristics of the environmental element such as the previously discussed large price spread from farm gate to ultimate consumer, reflecting high transportation and transaction costs and the scarcity of road infrastructure, operate as binding constraints on the behaviour of actors within the farm household configuration. In turn, the more inelastic supply response in the African context, relative to Asia, can be attributed to the fact that most, if not all, environmental and physical elements are less structurally rigid in the latter case.

The key policy implication that flows from this analysis is how to relax the structural constraints (i.e., yielding an upward shift and narrowing the price band) so as to elicit greater market responsiveness on the part of peasant actors. de Janvry et al. (1991) mention a number of potentially desirable interventions, such as infrastructure investment, increased competitiveness among local merchants, better access for peasants to credit markets, technology transfer, and a more elastic and lower-priced supply of manufactured consumption goods such as textiles, footwear, processed foods and some inputs. We shall return to these policy implications in the last section of this paper.

Agro-climatic diversity and technological constraints It has been well documented that the 'physical environment for agriculture (and cattle rearing) in SSA is marked by an exceptional diversity of agro-climatic and soil characteristics, of farming systems and socioeconomic conditions' (Platteau and Hayami, 1998: 19). This diversity is not only across SSA countries but also within countries and even regions. Another characteristic of SSA agricultural production is that it occurs almost completely on rain-fed land—less than one-twentieth of the total arable land is irrigated. Still another feature is the lack of congruence between the large number of locally produced foodstuffs (such as coarse grains) and the preferred foodstuffs (such as wheat and rice) that are largely imported (Oyejide, 1999).

Given these characteristics, SSA is at a great technological disadvantage compared with Asia. The Green Revolution technologies have been extremely successful in creating new and highly productive varieties of rice, wheat and maize grown on irrigated land, but have had only very limited success with improved varieties of other crops applicable to rain-fed land. Thus, given the diversity of products grown in SSA on rain-fed land that is itself agronomically heterogeneous, a standard technical package comparable to single rice varieties (such as IR36) that worked so well in Asia has no chance to succeed within the context of SSA (Platteau and Hayami, 1998).

What is perhaps surprising is that notwithstanding the bleak picture described above, there is evidence that expenditures on agricultural research have had high returns in SSA. In a study of total factor productivity (TFP) in SSA agriculture—based on a data set of physical output aggregates (where different products are converted into wheat-equivalent units) and corrected for artificial price and exchange-rate effects—Block (1994) found that after 15 years of stagnation, African agricultural TFP increased substantially during the mid 1980s, growing at about 2 per cent per year from 1983 to 1988.[11] In turn, taking the real exchange rate depreciation as a proxy for policy reform (i.e., adjustment), his suggested finding is that policy reform *and* lagged research expenditures explain most of the improvement in agricultural TFP growth. One possible explanation for the very limited expenditures on agricultural research in SSA, according to Block (1994) is that cuts in domestic absorption following structural adjustment programmes have come largely from public investment—a critical source of funding for agricultural research. This issue is discussed in Thorbecke and Koné (1995).

The condition described above also helps explain 1) the 'pitifully low level of fertilizer consumption in SSA', amounting to only 14 per cent per hectare of the average consumption in low-income developing countries in 1992–1993 (Khan, 1997); and 2) the very limited scope of extension services provided in the light of the topographic and physical constraints.

Land tenure and titling The typical land tenure pattern in SSA is collective land ownership at the village or tribe level. Village chiefs allocate land to individual members of the community who maintain their land use rights throughout their lifetimes and often can pass them on to their descendants. This pattern is in distinct contrast with the Asian model, where small farmer-cultivators own their land.

There is a school of thought—perhaps best reflected by the World Bank—that subscribes to the so-called Evolutionary Theory of Land Rights (ETLR) as

---

[11] Incidentally, TFP is defined as the difference in the growth rate of real product and the growth rate of real factor input. Therefore, a positive growth rate of TFP means that resources are used more efficiently in agriculture but not necessarily that total real output actually increased. However, it is fair to state that many studies have found very low or even negative TFP rates for SSA. Once again the earlier warning relating to the very low quality of African statistics and particularly agricultural output statistics should be borne in mind.

being applicable to SSA in largely the same way that it applies to other parts of the world. According to this thesis, growing population pressure and increasing commercialization of agriculture have given rise to changes in land tenure practices toward enhanced individualization of tenure (Platteau, 1996: 32). In turn, land titling and the security of tenure would create the necessary incentives for small farmers in Africa to invest in their land through a variety of activities such as land leveling, terracing and other types of improvements that would increase yields and output. In other words, the absence of clear titling and property rights is seen as a major institutional constraint to the growth of agricultural production in SSA.

In a very incisive piece, Platteau (1996) shows that the ETLR, based on the theory of induced innovation, does not lead to the expected institutional innovation in the form of land titling in the African context. Platteau (1996) demonstrates that in order to be valid the theory requires two crucial conditions to be fulfilled. First, new technical packages must be available to create attractive investment opportunities for people willing and able to invest, and, second, efficiency and equity considerations must be separable. Since neither of these conditions hold in SSA, enhanced land titling will not evolve endogenously as an induced institutional innovation.

If in the specific setting of SSA, land titling is not to evolve naturally, what about imposing it by fiat? Platteau (1996) provides strong arguments against the alteration of customary rights under the aegis of governments. In a nutshell, he argues that titling is undesirable for several reasons. For one thing, sections of local populations face a serious risk of being denied legal recognition of their customary rights to land during the registration process; this is especially true of vulnerable groups such as women who have traditionally enjoyed subsidiary or derived (usufruct) rights to land. This point is echoed in a recent study by Lastarria-Cornhiel (1997: 1329) on the impact of privatization on gender and property rights in Africa, which concluded: 'It is under the increasing transformation of customary tenure systems to market-based, individualized tenure systems that women's limited but recognized land rights may be ignored and consequently lost'.

Moreover, since most of the people in SSA continue to adhere strongly to the traditional ethical principle that land ought to belong to the 'sons of the village', a separation of land ownership from land use and the assignment of transfer of land to strangers are bound to arouse deep seated feelings of injustice. The problem of registering land is complicated even further because of limited administrative capabilities, which is likely to invite corruption. Finally, the empirical evidence on the relationships among land rights, land improvements and agricultural yields in SSA is generally inconclusive—a conclusion also reached by Pinckney and Kimuyu (1994), who flatly state that 'land titling is unimportant for development; governments should invest scarce fiscal and managerial resources in other areas'.

In short, individual land titling and property rights within much of the context of SSA are not the panacea that supporters claim.

Policies and Institutions

We have noted the policy and institutional bias against agriculture in many countries in SSA. Among the issues in this category are treatment of agricultural surpluses, and a wide range of inappropriate institutions.

Policies and the agricultural surplus The major mechanism for obtaining the resources needed for industrialization at an early stage of development is the intersectoral transfer out of agriculture. It is important to identify the major components of this transfer. A first component consists of the resources that tend to flow out of agriculture, automatically, through the market mechanism wherever the rate of return on resources is higher in agriculture than in nonagriculture (typically in the incipient industrial sector). Teranishi (1997) has called this flow a 'market-based resource shift'. In addition, there are resource flows that are policy-induced through the direct intervention of the government. Therefore, it is useful to make a distinction, as Teranishi (1997) does between market based resource flow and policy based resource flow; the latter can be broken further into net direct taxation, net indirect taxation and infrastructure investment in agriculture.

Typically developing countries tax their agricultural sectors heavily through both direct and indirect taxation. Direct taxation usually occurs when the internal terms of trade are turned against agriculture through such interventions as artificially low consumer prices for food and high input prices, e.g., the hidden rice tax through high fertilizer prices in Taiwan. Indirect taxation consists mainly of the impact of an over-valued exchange rate on agricultural tradeables.

In a careful empirical study of intersector resource flows, Teranishi (1997) showed that there was no significant difference in the (high) degree of direct and indirect taxation on agriculture among the four regions, East Asia, South Asia, Latin America and SSA, but that the regional differences in infrastructure investment in agriculture were enormous. Teranishi (1997: 289) concluded:

> In East Asia, the adverse effects of indirect taxation (real exchange rate over-valuation and industrial protection) and direct taxation of agriculture were counterbalanced by government efforts in agricultural development, particularly in the area of infrastructure investment, resulting in the relatively low level of total policy-based resource shift from agriculture.

The explanation that is given for the radically different treatments of agriculture in Asia and in SSA and the consequent widely disparate performances is that in SSA governments used 'divisible benefits' in a very selective way to keep or win over agricultural actors who supported the incumbent political regimes regardless of their contribution to production. Furthermore, Teranishi (1997) provides an interesting political economy explanation of why small farmers in SSA, in contrast with those in East Asia, do not react collectively against the effects of policies detrimental to agriculture. The answer lies in the shifting mode of cultivation of small African farmers, which does not provide incentives to invest in land improvement, a situation made worse by the fact that most small farmers do not own their land, again in contrast with Asia. Given the very different production and tenure conditions in East Asia, incentives for small farmers to resist policies detrimental to agriculture are much larger in Asia than in Africa.

In the 1980s, the Development Center of the Organization for Economic Cooperation and Development (OECD) embarked on a large-scale research project to evaluate the effects of policies and institutions on agricultural performance over time in six poor developing countries: Mali and Burkina Faso in West Africa, Kenya and Tanzania in East Africa, and Nepal and Sri Lanka in Asia. Six case studies using the same conceptual framework were undertaken for this project.[12] For each of these countries, a careful attempt was made to measure the agricultural surplus (i.e., the net transfer out of agriculture) over time. The main lesson to be drawn from the experience of a large set of developing countries (including the six listed above) was summarized by Thorbecke and Morrisson (1989: 1490):

> The process of capturing the surplus is quite delicate. The goal should be to generate a reliable and continuous flow of net resources from agriculture into the rest of the economy throughout much of the structural transformation. A lesson learned from those countries which were most successful in achieving both growth and equity throughout their development history is that a continuing gross flow of resources should be provided to agriculture in the form of such elements as irrigation, inputs, research and credit, combined with appropriate institutions and price policies to increase this sector's productivity and potential capacity of contributing an even larger flow to the rest of the economy. It is much easier to extract a net surplus from increasing production than from stagnant or falling output.

One interesting finding of the comparative analysis is that in those countries in which foodstuff prices were most depressed as a result of the actions of the government, aggregate output either fell or stagnated. In Tanzania, for example, the sheer magnitude of the burden imposed on both the domestic food crop and the cash crop export sectors was shown to have short-circuited the development process and, more specifically, jeopardized the desired industrialization. The ridiculously low regulated food prices in the official market led to a booming parallel market where at one time prices were 11 times higher than the official food price.

Likewise in Nigeria, agriculture was seen as a sector to be squeezed and taxed with impunity to provide an agricultural surplus to finance the incipient industrial sector. The contrast between Nigeria and Indonesia—both large oil exporting countries—in the treatment of agriculture is enlightening. In particular, the divergent macroeconomic policies followed by these countries had very different impacts on agricultural performance. From the outset Indonesia supported its agricultural sector, indirectly, through regular devaluations to maintain an equilibrium exchange rate and, more directly, through large- scale investment in irrigation, other physical infrastructure and a fertilizer subsidy scheme, among others.

---

[12] For a synthesis and lessons of these studies, see Lecaillon et al. (1987).

Nigeria, in contrast, has squeezed agriculture unmercifully since its independence, directly, through the regional and, later, national marketing boards, and indirectly, through the negative impact of distorted trade and exchange rate policies on domestic agricultural production. By dogmatically holding on to a fixed nominal exchange rate that led to a grossly over-valued real exchange rate, Nigeria caught a massive dose of the Dutch disease, which Indonesia largely escaped. Nigeria's over-valued exchange rate discriminated strongly against agricultural exports, which remained stagnant for a long period of time (Thorbecke, 1998).

Institutions Institutions in addition to policies can affect agricultural and rural performance in a major way. The following review provides a few examples of inappropriate institutions in SSA that contributed significantly to the dismal performance of the agricultural sector.

Perhaps the most extreme example of inappropriate organizations and institutions is the forced 'villagization' and collectivization programme imposed in Ethiopia; this wreaked havoc with agricultural production incentives (Khan, 1997). In Tanzania, the Arusha Declaration of 1967 signified a complete break with the previous relatively free enterprise regime. It emphasized socialism and self-reliance. In addition to a passive process of nationalization of private enterprises in urban and rural areas, the Ujamaa movement was introduced in the rural areas. During 1967–1973, agricultural production remained in private hands, but distribution channels were rapidly taken over by the state. In the next phase (1973–1982) the 'villagization' programme was further accelerated, leading to massive resettlement and dislocation. The government intervened increasingly on both the production and distribution sides. This helped trigger a vicious circle of cumulatively worsening agricultural performance, as described in Lecallion et al. (1987).

Sahn and Sarris (1994) conducted a study of the evolution of states, markets and civil institutions in rural Africa based largely on four countries (Guinea, Malawi, Mozambique and Tanzania). They concluded that state mandated and sponsored systems of production, which ironically had been built upon an exploitative colonial legacy, failed dismally. Production and yields plummeted in some cases, and stagnated in others. In all four countries (and in most other) analysed 'the state tried either to modify/strengthen inherited centralized controls from the West or to adopt authoritative socialist institutions from Eastern Europe' (p. 286). Sahn and Sarris (1994: 286) conclude: 'Why was there such uniformity in neglecting indigenous organizations and arrangements? The answer seems to be first, the need to create centrally controlled financial resources, and second, the imperative of maintaining a contented political base, defined as the urban elite, rather than the peasantry that was the real backbone of the economy'.

A final example of a misguided government initiative to modernize agriculture occurred in the 1970s in Nigeria: foreign companies wee allowed to acquire large-scale interests in the sector. The initiative involved a number of complementary policies: removal of import duties on tractors and provision of subsidies for tractor hiring; large-scale investment in irrigation and other public works; and subsidized credit. The notion was to bypass the traditional small farmer and encourage the emergence of a new class of commercial farmers. These measures artificially lowered the price of capital and thereby triggered an inappropriately induced technological change (Thorbecke, 1998). Khan (1997) gives additional examples of policies and institutions favouring employment-hostile techniques and activities. For example, in Kenya, the system of incentives in the late 1980s favoured the use of tractors and heavy machines and discriminated against the use of less mechanized techniques, e.g., hand tools and ox-drawn ploughs.

It should be emphasized, however, that in many instances in the face of government failure or market failure regional and community institutions evolved successfully to fill a vacuum. This is particularly true of rural informal credit institutions such as friends and family and rotating savings and credit associations. Furthermore, there are instances of regional and local governments playing a major role in promoting regional rural development (Côte d'Ivoire is such a country where the structure of local governments is strong).

Cultural and Community Norms

The differences in cultural and community norms and customs between SSA and Asia and their impact on the divergent rural development paths followed by these two regions in recent times have been perceptively analysed by Platteau and Hayami (1996). Their thesis can be summarized as follows:

- Cultural and social norms under land-abundant conditions in Africa compared with land- scarce Asia have constrained capital accumulation.
- 'The critical role of community as an economic organization is to guide its members to voluntary cooperation...to insure the subsistence of all members'.
- In Asia, high population density has shaped community norms so as to prevent free riders from depleting scarce natural resources, in contrast with land-abundant Africa where norms did not adapt quickly enough to prevent serious degradation.
- Rural communities in SSA are 'typically tribal, lineage-based societies' relying on 'production activities characterized by spatial mobility such as shifting cultivation and nomadic grazing', in contrast with 'strongly immobile village communities based on settled agriculture in much of Asia' (p. 24).
- 'Since land commands relatively low value in SSA, private property rights on land have not become well established', resulting in little social stratification based on unequal land ownership.
- As a consequence, tribal communities in SSA are characterized by strong egalitarianism; no causal link is seen between effort applied and resulting output success is attributed to 'luck' and hence it is expected that some type of balanced reciprocity norm should lead to redistribution from alleged 'lucky' to 'unlucky' individuals.
- Asian rural communities are based on conjugal owner-cultivator farm households living together in villages and having to cooperate for their security and

survival, leading to the emergence of community norms based on cooperative and collective actions to conserve common property resources.

- Under those circumstances reciprocity norms evolved in Asia and were consistent with the acceptance and full recognition of the link between effort and outcome (such as the yield- increasing effects of careful water control), in contrast with the redistribution norms in Africa that tend to deny the relationship between effort and outcome.

The bottom line of the Platteau–Hayami (1996) thesis is that the redistribution norms in SSA have growth-retarding effects that contrast with the growth-enhancing effects of reciprocity norms in the Asian rural sector.

Conclusions and Some Policy Implications

The bleak rural profile sketched above revealed that SSA, compared with other developing regions, suffers from more severe and persistent poverty, a more unequal distribution of income, declining food production per capita, and a continuing population explosion. This chapter attempted to provide at least some answers to the question of why the rural sector in SSA evolved so differently from those in other regions and particularly Asia.

We scrutinized and identified a whole constellation of factors that help explain the particular development path followed by SSA in the last three or four decades. In a nutshell, the relatively lower population density and greater spatial distribution of population in SSA compared with Asia presented major obstacles to the provision of an adequate rural infrastructure network. The greatly underdeveloped road network, in turn, was a major contributor to the very high transportation costs that are observed the high price spreads between initial agricultural producer prices and ultimate consumer prices, the segmented agricultural product markets, and the very limited market-orientation on the part of small-scale African farmers who produce largely for subsistence with low marketable surpluses. Superimposed on these factors is the great diversity of agro-climatic and soil characteristics and farming systems within SSA, as well as within individual countries, which presented a further obstacle to sustained agricultural growth. In particular, no standard technological package—similar to the Green Revolution high-yielding varieties of rice and wheat that have been so successful in Asia—was available and could succeed in an agronomically heterogeneous, essentially rain-fed African setting.

At the same time, we reported evidence that in some specific African settings the impact of population growth on population density has led to a significant process of land intensification resulting in increased yields and a reversal of agricultural stagnation.

Compounding the negative effects of physical and technological factors on rural and agricultural development in SSA were almost universal government policies and institutions that discriminated against agriculture. A large agricultural surplus was squeezed out of agriculture that contributed directly to agricultural stagnation. In contrast with Asia, the adverse effects of indirect and direct taxation on agriculture were not counterbalanced by a reverse flow into agricultural development, particularly into rural infrastructure and irrigation.

Many inappropriate institutions, such as the ill-fated 'villagization' experiments in Tanzania and Ethiopia and attempts to modernize agriculture through reliance on large farms and capital intensive techniques in Nigeria and Kenya, also contributed to the dismal performance of the agricultural sector.

Here again one should not overlook a whole set of indigenous institutions that have sprung up at the local and community level to remedy at least partially the vacuum left by government and market failures. There is also evidence in some SSA countries that governments are increasingly taking over the role of promoting rural development.

Finally, a case can be made that the very different physical and socioeconomic settings prevailing in SSA and Asia have led to the evolution of different norms—in the former case, growth-retarding and in the latter case, growth-enhancing. More specifically, the abundant land and corporate land tenure conditions in Africa constrained capital accumulation and helped foster egalitarian redistribute norms, in contrast with the land-scarce and individual property rights conditions in Asia that encouraged cooperative actions and reciprocity norms.

It goes beyond the scope of this paper to come up with a detailed policy and institutional agenda to remedy the rather discouraging state of rural development in SSA. At best a few suggestions may be in order.

The first observation that needs to be made is that recent reforms under the various structural adjustment programmes followed by SSA countries, at both macroeconomic and sector specific levels, have substantially reduced the anti-agricultural bias in the heavy direct and indirect taxation of agriculture. As a consequence of these reforms, the prices of agricultural tradeables (following devaluations) increased significantly. In addition, the improved rural–urban terms of trade are likely to result in favourable direct and indirect effects on rural non-agricultural activities through the strong demand and supply linkages between the latter and agricultural activities.

However, getting the prices right is, at best, only one blade of a pair of scissors. There is strong evidence that the growth of total factor productivity in SSA is highly correlated with public expenditures on agricultural research and that such expenditures tended to be further curtailed during the adjustment process. Likewise, an inadequate transportation and distribution network can raise the marketing and other transaction costs so much that even in the presence of attractive prices, farmers' incentives to increase output vanish and they revert largely to producing for their own subsistence.

The dilemma faced by adjusting countries is how to balance short-term cuts in public expenditures with the long-term need for improving the physical infrastructure and financing agricultural research. Given the very limited public resource base that these countries can tap, it appears that a partial solution to this dilemma lies in a change in the composition of external funding. One specific avenue suggests itself, that is, increasing the share of agricultural sector adjustment loans (SECALs) while reducing that of generalized programme loans (SALs) in the World Bank lending portfolio and in the portfolios of bilateral donors. The main advantage is that transfers embedded in agricultural SECALs contribute directly to the building of physical infrastructure projects and the funding of an agricultural research network (i.e., a tangible productive counterpart) instead of taking the form of undifferentiated programme and balance of payments support. When properly designed, agricultural sector loans need not reduce the conditionality leverage, but rather would allow these requirements to be expressed in much more concrete and specific terms (Thorbecke, 1995).

Improving the prospects for better infrastructure investment and the funding of agricultural research could provide the complementary second blade of the scissors needed to render price incentives effective and, thereby, increase supply responsiveness on the part of African farmers.

There is some scepticism about the potential scope for expanding the exports of primary commodities in SSA, but it seems likely that the agricultural export sector will be required to carry the main burden of moving African agriculture forward in the medium term. In a context where the projected growth in world demand for primary and agricultural commodities is very limited. It is important to recall that Africa has lost a significant share of most of these products to other regions in recent times. Nevertheless, with appropriate policies and complementary measures, SSA should be able to recapture a part of these losses and thus the potential scope for African agricultural export growth is higher than the anticipated growth of world demand. Estimates of short- and long-run revenue elasticities of major SSA commodities suggest that the 'adding-up' problem that most critics point at may hold for some commodities (such as cocoa and, to a lesser extent, coffee, sisal, tea and tobacco), but certainly not for all commodities. Furthermore, there appears to be some scope for expanding African production in commodities such as cut flowers that face relatively high income elasticities of demand.

Insofar as the domestic food crops sector is concerned, even a part of it could benefit from higher farm gate prices as some presently non-tradeable products could become tradeables. For example, rice and maize farmers in some settings could engage in import substitution. In the case of producers of subsistence food crops, Platteau and Hayami (1996) advocate the desirability of undertaking mini Green Revolutions in a limited number of food crops through concentration of government infrastructure investments and support services in favourable, high potential areas in tandem with a strategy of promoting export cash crops.

This is an interesting suggestion. However, one obvious issue that this high potential strategy raises is how feasible would it be within many small African countries. Conversely, how strong would the interregional and international spillover effects of successful experiments in large countries (such as Nigeria and the Congo) be on the rest of SSA?

References

Ahmed, R. and N. Rustagi. 1984. 'Agricultural marketing and price incentives: A comparative study of African and Asian countries'. International Food Policy Research Institute.

Ali, A.A.G. 1997. 'Dealing with poverty and income distribution issues in developing countries: Cross regional experiences'. *Journal of African Economies*, vol. 7, supplement 2, December 1998: 77–115.

Appleton, S., J. Hoddinott and J. Mackinnon. 1996. 'Education and Health in sub-Saharan Africa', *Journal of International*, vol 8, no. 3, (May-June 1996): 308–39.

Balisacan, A.M. 1995. 'Anatomy of poverty during adjustment: The case of Philippines'. Economic Development and Cultural Change, vol. 44, no. 1, (October 1995): 33–62.

Block, S.A. 1994. 'A new view of agricultural productivity in sub-Saharan Africa'. *American Journal of Agricultural Economics*, vol. 3, no. 76 (August): 619–24.

Chen, S., G. Datt and M. Ravalllion. 1994. 'Is poverty increasing in the developing world?' *Review of Income and Wealth*, vol. 40: 359–76 (December).

de Janvry, A., M. Fafchamps and E. Sadoulet. 1991. 'Peasant household behaviour with missing markets: Some paradoxes explained'. *The Economic Journal*, vol. 101, November: 1400–17.

Deininger, K. and L. Squire. 1996. 'A new data set measuring income inequality'. *World Bank Economic Review*, vol. 10, no. 3: 565–91.

Fields, G.S. 1994. 'Poverty and income distribution: Data for measuring poverty and inequality changes in developing countries'. *Journal of Development Economics*, vol. 44: 87–102.

Fields, G.S. 1989. 'Changes in poverty and inequality in developing countries'. *World Bank Research Observer*, vol. 4: 167–85.

FAO. 1992. *Agricultural Price and Marketing Policy: Government in the Market*. Policy Analysis Division, ESPT. Rome: Food and Agriculture Organization.

Foster, J., J. Greer and E. Thorbecke. 1984. 'A class of decomposable poverty measures'. *Econometrica*, vol. 52, no. 3 (May): 761–66.

Grootaert, C. 1996. *Analyzing Poverty and Policy Reform, The Experience of Côte d'Ivoire*. Avebury: Aldershot.

Khan, A.R. 1997. *Reversing the Decline of Output and Productive Employment in Rural sub-Saharan Africa*. Issues in Development Discussion Paper 17. Geneva: International Labour Office.

Koné, S. and E. Thorbecke. 1998. 'Sectoral investment priorities for renewed growth in Zaire'. In D.E. Sahn, ed., *Economic Reform and the Poor in Africa*. Oxford: Clarendon Press.

Lastarria-Cornhiel, S. 1997. 'Impact of privatization on gender and property rights in Africa'. *World Development*, vol. 25, no. 8 (August): 1317–33.

Lecaillon, J., C. Morrisson, H. Schneider and E. Thorbecke. 1987. *Economic Policies and Agricultural Performance of Low-Income Countries*. Paris: OECD Development Centre.

Monke, E., and T. Petzel. 1984. 'Market integration: An application to international trade in cotton'. *American Journal of Agricultural Economics*, vol. 66, no. 4: 481–87.

Oyejide, T. Ademola. 1999. 'What can sub-Saharan Africa learn from the Taiwanese development experience?' In E. Thorbecke and H. Wan, ed., *Taiwan's Development Experience: Lessons on Roles of Government and Market*.

Pinckney, T.C. and P.K. Kimuyu. 1994. 'Land tenure reform in East Africa: Good, bad or unimportant?' *Journal of African Economies*, vol. 3, no. 1 (April): 1–28.

Platteau, J.-P. 1996. 'The evolutionary theory of land rights as applied to Sub-Saharan Africa: A critical assessment'. *Development and Change*, vol. 27, no. 1 (January): 29–86.

Platteau, J.-P. and Y. Hayami. 1998. 'Resource endowments and agricultural development:

Africa vs. Asia'. In Y. Yayami and M. Aoki, eds., *The Institutional Foundation of East Asian Economic Developmen: Proceedings of the International Economic Association Conference, Tokyo.* New York: Macmillan Press and St. Martin's Press Inc.

Ravallion, M. 1995. 'Issues in measuring and modelling poverty'. Unpublished paper. The World Bank, Washington, D.C.

Ravallion, M., and B. Bidani. 1994. 'How robust is a poverty profile?' *World Bank Economic Review*, vol. 8, no. 1: 75–102.

Ravallion, M., and S. Chen. 1997. 'What can new survey data tell us about recent changes in distribution and poverty?' *World Bank Economic Review*, vol. 11, no. 2 (May): 357–82.

Ravallion, M., and B. Sen. 1996. 'When methods matter: Monitoring poverty in Bangladesh'. *Economic Development and Cultural Change. Economic Development and Cultural Change*, vol. 44, no. 4 (July): 761–92.

Sahn, D.E. and A. Sarris. 1994. 'The evolution of states, markets, and civil institutions in rural Africa'. *The Journal of Modern African Studies*, 32(2): 279–303.

Summers, H., and A. Heston. 1991. 'The Penn World Table (Mark 5): An extended set of international comparisons, 1950–1988'. *Quarterly Journal of Economics*, vol. CVI(2): 327–68.

Tabatabai, H. 1996. *Statistics on Poverty and Income Distribution: An ILO Compendium of Data.* Geneva: International Labour Organization.

Teranishi, J. 1997. 'Sectoral resource transfer, conflict, and macro stability in economic development: a comparative analysis'. In N. Aoki, Y.-K. Kim, and N. Okuno-Fujiwara, eds., *The Role of Government in East Asian Economic Development, Comparative Institutional Analysis.* Oxford: Clarendon Press.

Thorbecke, E. 1998. 'The institutional foundations of macroeconomic stability: Indonesia vs. Nigeria'. In Y. Hayami and M. Aoki, eds., *The Institutional Foundation of East Asian Development: Proceedings of the International Economic Association Conference, Tokoyo.* New York: Macmillan Press and St. Martin's Press Inc.

Thorbecke, E. 1995. 'Causes of African development stagnation: Policy diagnosis and policy recommendations for a long-term development strategy'. In J.-C. Berthelemy, ed., *Whither African Economies.* Paris: OECD Development Centre.

Thorbecke, E. 1993. 'Impact of state and civil institutions on the operation of rural markets and nonmarket configurations'. *World Development*, vol. 21, no. 4.

Thorbecke, E. 1992. *The Anatomy of Agricultural Product Markets and Transactions in Developing Countries.* Working Papers No. 43. Institute for Policy Reform, Washington, D.C., July.

Thorbecke, E. and S. Koné. 1995. 'The impact of stabilization and structural adjustment programmes on performance in sub-Saharan Africa'. In J.-C. Berthélemy, ed., *Whither African Economics?* Paris: OECD Development Centre.

Thorbecke, E. and C. Morrisson. 1989. 'Institutions, policies and agricultural performance: A comparative analysis'. *World Development*, vol. 17, no. 9 (September).

Tiffen, M., M. Mortimore and F. Gichuki. 1994. *More People, Less Erosion: Environmental Recovery in Kenya.* Chichester: John Wiley & Sons.

World Bank. 1997a. *African Development Indicators.* Washington, D.C.: The World Bank.

World Bank. 1997b. *Development in Practice, Taking Action to Reduce Poverty in Sub-Saharan Africa.* Washington, D.C.: The World Bank.

World Bank. 1996. *Status Report on Poverty in Sub-Saharan Africa 1996.* (Draft). International and Social Policy Group, Africa Region. Washington, D.C.: The World Bank.

World Bank. 1995. *A Continent in Transition: Sub-Saharan Africa in the Mid-1990s.* Africa Region. Washington, D.C.: The World Bank.

Annex: Development Indicators for Sub-Saharan Africa

Table 12.A1 Characteristics of the African rural sector

Country	Household size (persons)	Literacy rate (%)	Male literacy rate (%)	Female literacy rate (%)	Female-headed households (%)	Employment head (% in agriculture)
Burkina Faso	8.1	4.0	2.0	4.0	8.0	86.0
CAR	4.5	30.0	47.0	14.0	24.0	82.0
Côte d'Ivoire	5.4	33.0	39.0	27.0	12.0	83.0
Gambia	11.4	43.0	63.0	24.0	3.0	80.0
Ghana	4.6	43.0	57.0	31.0	29.0	56.0
Guinea	6.5	10.0	23.0	1.0	16.0	84.0
Guinea-Bissau	7.3	12.0	22.0	4.0	43.0	87.0
Kenya	5.2	71.0	81.0	63.0	32.0	74.0
Madagascar	4.9	51.0	57.0	15.0	19.0	91.0
Niger	7.1	36.0	53.0	21.0	11.0	88.0
Nigeria	4.8	33.0	39.0	27.0	14.0	73.0
Senegal	9.0	33.0	56.0	15.0	14.0	74.0
Sierra Leone	5.9	27.0	37.0	19.0	14.0	15.0
Tanzania	6.3	70.0	80.0	62.0	11.0	81.0
Uganda	4.9	21.0	28.0	14.0	25.0	84.0
Zambia	5.5	12.0	16.0	8.0	23.0	89.0

Source: Calculations based on World Bank (1997a).

Table 12.A2 Mean annual per capita expenditure in sub-Saharan Africa: 1993 (in PPP 1985 dollars unless specified otherwise)

Country	National	Urban	Rural	Rural/ National ratio	Rural/ Urban ratio	Rural share of food in expenditure (%)
Burkina Faso	368	908	267	0.73	0.29	59
CAR	402	625	261	0.65	0.42	61
Côte d'Ivoire	667	717	500	0.75	0.70	21
Gambia	535	831	290	0.54	0.35	60
Ghana	796	986	706	0.89	0.72	37
Guinea	379	586	277	0.73	0.47	62
Guinea-Bissau	367	551	288	0.78	0.52	n.a.
Kenya	640	1,690	476	0.74	0.28	56
Madagascar	481	867	376	0.78	0.43	72
Niger	312	527	289	0.93	0.55	29
Nigeria	674	727	641	0.95	0.88	68
Senegal	846	1,481	423	0.50	0.29	65
Sierra Leone	641	871	437	0.68	0.50	69
Tanzania	302	439	245	0.81	0.56	72
Uganda	450	865	415	0.92	0.48	64
Zambia	345	589	191	0.55	0.32	78

Source: Calculations based on World Bank (1997a) and Summers and Heston (1991) and their Internet database.

Table 12.A3 Inequality measures for rural Africa (percentages unless stated otherwise)

Country	Share of lowest 40%	Share of top 20%	Gini coefficient	Ratio of top 20% to bottom 40%	Survey year	Sample size (number)
Burkina Faso	18.37	45.71	38.70	2.4883	1995	5,912
CAR	8.00	67.43	64.11	8.4288	1993	4,462
Côte d'Ivoire	21.38	37.93	29.72	1.7741	1995	520
Gambia	17.90	41.75	35.21	2.3324	1993/94	1,185
Ghana	20.00	41.75	33.98	2.0875	1992	2,945
Guinea	20.06	40.82	32.61	2.0349	1993/94	1,680
Guinea-Bissau	8.33	59.79	56.68	7.1777	1991	1,178
Kenya	12.61	56.10	51.26	4.4489	1992/93	6,352
Madagascar	16.87	46.81	40.24	2.7748	1993	2,557
Niger	21.20	39.60	31.47	1.8679	1993	2,024
Nigeria	13.82	52.71	47.80	3.8140	1992	5,276
Senegal	15.00	50.00	40.27	3.3333	1991	4,158
Sierra Leone	3.54	78.44	66.67	22.1582	1989/90	2,244
Tanzania	19.76	41.40	33.81	2.0951	1993	2,762
Uganda	18.34	56.67	37.98	3.0900	1993	6,395
Zambia	13.67	50.40	45.60	3.6869	1993	3,900

Source: Calculations based on World Bank (1997a) and Summers and Heston (1991) and their Internet database.

Table 12.A4 Poverty measures in rural Africa: 1993 (percentages unless stated otherwise)

Country	μ(PPP 1985)	z (PPP 1985)	Gini coefficient	Head-count ratio	Poverty-gap ratio	FGT (2)
Burkina Faso	276	268	38.70	67.97	26.42	12.93
CAR	261	251	64.11	77.57	45.69	31.94
Côte d'Ivoire	500	359	29.72	38.42	10.45	3.76
Gambia	290	273	35.21	56.30	22.86	12.67
Ghana	706	456	33.98	34.56	9.26	3.55
Guinea	277	268	32.61	60.96	22.27	10.46
Guinea-Bissau	288	273	56.68	68.20	39.90	28.45
Kenya	476	349	51.26	58.52	25.79	14.55
Madagascar	376	307	40.24	54.67	21.04	11.04
Niger	289	273	31.47	59.84	19.79	8.78
Nigeria	641	424	47.80	48.12	19.75	10.89
Senegal	423	326	40.27	49.67	21.77	12.25
Sierra Leone	437	332	66.67	70.70	55.58	45.86
Tanzania	245	256	33.81	66.85	25.94	12.93
Uganda	415	323	37.98	50.19	17.51	8.25
Zambia	191	237	45.60	77.02	40.14	25.76

Source: Calculations based on the World Bank (1997a) and Summers and Heston (1991) and their Internet database.

Chapter 13

Rural Development, Income Distribution and Poverty Alleviation: A Northeast Asian Perspective

Toshihiko Kawagoe

Though per capita average income has long been a commonly used index of economic development, in recent decades more attention has been paid to income distribution and the poverty level because of the recognition that rapid economic growth is often associated with growing inequality in income distribution. The characteristics of the poor form another critical issue. The poor are often concentrated in rural areas. They earn their daily bread from agriculture and are often left behind during progress without enjoying the fruits of development.

This common wisdom has not applied to the Northeast Asian economies, however. East Asian economies are now a centre of rapid growth in the world economy. A highly acclaimed report by the World Bank (1993: 28–9), *The East Asian Miracle*, argued:

> High-performing Asian economies (HPAEs),[1] led by Japan] grew more rapidly and more consistently than any other groups of economies in the world from 1960 to 1990.....[They] have also achieved unusually low and declining levels of inequality...

Among these HPAEs, the economies of Northeast Asia, i.e., Japan, Republic of Korea and Taiwan, China (hereafter referred as Korea and Taiwan, respectively), are the forerunners of the 'miracle' economies, which have joined or almost approached the group of high-income economies.[2]

As common characteristics of the HPAEs, six features are pointed out (World Bank, 1993: 27–60): dynamic agricultural sectors; rapid growth of exports; rapid demographic transitions, i.e., low rate of population growth; high investment and domestic saving rates; human capital creation; and rapid productivity growth. As the forerunners of the HPAEs, Northeast Asian economies had attained most of

---

[1] HPAEs are Japan, the four tigers (Hong Kong, the Republic of Korea, Singapore and Taiwan, China) and three newly industrializing economies from ASEAN (Indonesia, Malaysia and Thailand).

[2] The high-income economies had GNP per capita of US$8,956 or more in 1994 (World Bank WDR, 1996: 181).

these features by the early postwar period or even before. Dynamic agricultural growth was already observed by the mid nineteenth century in Japan, where population growth rate was moderate. The agricultural sectors in Korea and Taiwan had also grown rapidly by the early twentieth century. As an example, Japan had become the largest exporter of cotton piece goods by the 1930s (Howe, 1996). By the early 1950s, all of these features were sufficiently evident in the Northeast Asian economies.

Furthermore, the inequality of income distribution was already low in Northeast Asia in the late 1950s. This is partly because a drastic land reform was implemented and the distribution of wealth and income was equalized in rural sectors in these economies. Since then, in spite of the rapid economic growth, the income distribution has not worsened, which is another feature in HPAEs and not consistent with the implication of the well known hypothesis of Kuznets (1955).

In the early 1950s, before their 'miraculous' success, the economies in Northeast Asia were poor agricultural states. The per capita GNP was only $200 in Japan, $128 in Korea and $196 in Taiwan at that time. These figures are not so different from those in African countries, such as $116 in Egypt.[3] The GDP share of agriculture was still as high as 18 per cent in Japan, 32 per cent in Taiwan and 50 per cent in Korea. If we include the income accrued from traditional rural industries and other activities of primary industries in the rural income, the share of the rural sectors in the economy would be much larger. The share of the agricultural labour force was also high. In Japan, 45 per cent of the workers were engaged in farming in 1950, and 56 per cent in Taiwan in 1952.[4]

The Japanese economy recovered quickly from the devastation caused by World War II. Since then Japan has attained rapid economic growth. In the 1960s the annual growth rate reached 11 per cent, though the economy entered a mature stage in the mid 1970s. This astounding growth was followed by Taiwan and then by Korea. Per capita GDP has now reached US$34,630 in Japan, US$11,604 in Taiwan and US$8,260 dollars in Korea.[5] Japan's per capita GDP is the second highest in the world and Taiwan's between New Zealand and Portugal. Korea is the top runner of upper-middle income countries.

Here several questions arise. How could Northeast Asian economies attain a highly equitable society at such an early stage of shared growth? How has the rural sector contributed to the rapid growth? What roles did the governments play in rural development in order to realize these 'miracles'? The purpose of this chapter is to try to find answers to these questions and to explore the rural origins of the Northeast Asian miracle.

In the next section, environmental and demographic constraints in Northeast Asia are examined and an Asian mode of rural economic activities is identified. Then, the analysis is applied to explore what sorts of rural communal rules and

---

[3] Data references in US dollars in 1953 for Korea and in 1952 for others. The figure in Egypt depicts GDP per capita (IMF, 1996; CEPD, 1995).
[4] Kayo (1977: 6), CEPD (1995).
[5] Current US dollars in 1994 (World Bank, 1996; CEPD, 1995).

rural organizations have evolved under this Asian mode. The chapter next reviews Northeast Asian experiences, showing how the inequality of income distribution was improved and poverty alleviated at early stages of modern economic growth, and examines how these achievements could be attained in these economies. The discussion is then extended to explore the role of agriculture in the process of economic growth, with reference to the historical experiences in Japan. The government's role in economic growth is discussed in relation to rural development.

The discussion in this chapter focuses on the early stage of the economic development of the Northeast Asian economies, from the late nineteenth century to the early post World War II period, because poverty and income inequality issues were almost completely solved by the 1950s.

Institutional Features of Rural Communities in Northeast Asia

Japan and Korea bind the northern edge of the rice growing area in Asia. The Japanese archipelago and the Korean peninsula are located in temperate monsoon Asia. This area is characterized by hot and humid summer seasons and cold winter seasons. Annual rainfall is 1,000 to 2,000 mm, average temperature is 10 to 15 degrees centigrade. Like other monsoon areas in Asia, in Northeast Asia, rice cultivation has traditionally been the most dominant activity in the rural communities. Oshima (1987: 18) argues:

> Asians had no choice but to evolve paddy rice agriculture over many centuries since no other crop was suited to the pattern of rainfall and humidity of monsoon Asia.

Rice has supported densely populated habitations in the region as the staple food.[6] Furthermore, the intensive rice cultivation system in the region required strict coordination and collective actions of the farm operations, which have formed a communal rule in the Northeast Asian rural sectors that may be called an 'Asian model' of rural economic activities.

A Mode of Rural Economic Activities

Asian rice is one of the cultivated rice species, *Oryza sativa*, that is now grown throughout the world, though it originated from the Ganges plain, which was very warm and humid with a strong monsoon rhythm in the rainfall pattern.[7] In the home area, rainfall is generally adequate for the main rice crop and thus it is still

---

[6] Rice is the most important staple in the Northeast Asian diet. For example, in Japan in the early 1930s, 61 per cent of daily intake of calories and 44 per cent of daily intake of protein came from rice.

[7] There is another rice species, *Oryza glaberrima*, that originated in West Africa and is cultivated in the high rainfall zone of the home region (Barker and Herdt with Rose, 1985).

often grown under rain-fed conditions (Barker and Herdt with Rose, 1985). On the other hand, in Northeast Asia, especially in Japan and Korea, the climate was primarily not favourable for rice cultivation, because of the limited quantity of rainfall and the cool weather, which constrained populations to plant only one rice crop during the several months centred around a hot summer season.[8] Therefore, possible farming systems have been and continue to be [rice]–[secondary crops] or only one rice crop and the land is left fallow during the winter seasons. Low temperature and insufficient sunlight in summer seasons were and at times still are a major cause of cold weather damage. For example, in Japan, during the hundred years from 1892 to 1991, 26 years were recorded as years of cold weather damage.[9] Lack of sufficient rainfall in early summer often causes droughts. Typhoons in autumn often cause flooding and severely damage plants just before the harvest.

In order to overcome these climatic constraints, tremendous efforts were made by peasants, landlords and governments over the centuries. Large- and small-scale irrigation systems were constructed and maintained by rural communities in order to guarantee a stable supply of water and provide even stricter control of water levels including drainage of wet paddy fields. Seed varieties were improved to add features such as cold tolerance and/or early ripening. The invention of cold tolerant varieties enabled farmers to plant rice in northern regions and thus the northern limits of rice were gradually extended. Early-ripening varieties avoided the risk to harvest during the typhoon seasons in autumn. Through these efforts, a highly productive farm sector has evolved, which could feed the dense populations in these economies. As early as the beginning of the twentieth century, paddy yield per hectare had already reached 3 metric tons in Japan. By around the mid 1930s the yield in Japan approached 4 tons, while the yield in Taiwan and Korea was also enhanced to reach 2.5 and 2.3 tons, respectively (Hayami and Ruttan, 1985).

The high yield, however, could not be realized without intensive and intricately coordinated farm management. Collective actions among villagers were also critical. In Northeast Asia, like other Asian monsoon regions, the rainfall pattern is unevenly concentrated in the several months of summer. Above all, there are large variations in the year-round temperature. The season that is suitable for rice cultivation is limited and the farmers have to follow a rigid farming schedule. In order to achieve high yields, they normally prepare seedling beds, transplanting them instead of broadcast planting. Harvesting was done carefully with sickles before the introduction of machinery like harvesters and combines in the 1970s. Transplanting and harvesting require heavy labour inputs, which must be completed within limited periods due to the climatic constraints. Thus, there were two peaks of heavy work, when all family members, old and young, male and female, had to be mobilized. Furthermore, labour was mutually exchanged between neighbours and relatives in order to obtain complementary labour forces.

---

[8] In Taiwan, with the aid of irrigation double cropping of rice is possible and the farming system of [rice]–[rice]–[secondary crops] can be applied on an annual basis.

[9] Calculated from the data of Japan Food Agency (1996: 73–4).

Irrigation water was distributed on the basis of a plan coordinated by village members. Important decisions on farming were basically made by individual farmers under well established land property rights. However, whenever the peasants took action, they were urged to achieve a consensus among the neighbouring villagers. The rural ethic was to keep good and harmonious relations among community members.

> The heavy demand for workers during the busy seasons had a favorable impact on diligence and propensity to work... Even more important was the impact of monsoon agriculture on attitudes toward cooperation, consensus, and harmonious relations, in contrast to the individualism and competition inherent in Western capitalistic agriculture (Oshima, 1987: 29–30).

Another critical factor that enabled Asian countries to sustain a high population density was that wet paddy rice can be planted consecutively every year without leaving the land fallow or introducing rotation with other crops. This enabled farmers to produce the most economically productive crop, usually rice, with full use of their operational arable land every year. Thus, rice can support many more people per hectare than upland crops such as wheat and maize. Consecutive planting also strengthened the bonds between farmers and their land. The farmer's land-specific know-how and skills were accumulated gradually through year-by-year operations. Under such conditions, coupled with limited land resource availability, it would be natural that the consciousness of the rights on land, property or holdings emerged at an early period. The land property issues will be reviewed in the next section.

Now, let us examine how these highly intensive rice cultures developed in Northeast Asia, while referring to the historical experiences of Japan. Japanese agriculture, like that in Taiwan and Korea, was traditionally shouldered by the peasantry and comprised a large number of small family farms that engaged in rice farming. This characteristic, inherited from the Tokugawa feudal era (the seventeenth to the mid-nineteenth century), was retained over the period of modern economic growth even after the Meiji Restoration in 1868. From the early stage of economic development until the mid 1910s, labour was relatively abundant and land was the major constraint to agricultural production. Efforts to improve agricultural development aimed to facilitate the substitution of labour for land.

Kelly and Williamson (1974) argued that three key factors were unique in Japanese agricultural development at this period:

- A more inelastic supply of land
- Low population growth
- High rate of technological changes

In fact, forest area accounts for 67 per cent of the total land area, whereas arable land occupies only 12 per cent. Room for opening new arable land was almost exhausted by the beginning of the modern economic growth period.

Permanent pasture and meadows are negligible, reflecting the fact that little animal husbandry developed. Since the country is densely populated, the crop land area per capita is only 0.04 hectare, which is among the lowest for industrial countries, but common among the Northeast Asian economies (Table 13.1).

Table 13.1 **International comparisons of land area by type and crop land per capita, 1994**

	Total land area (1000 sq. km)	% distribution of				Population (millions)	Crop land per capita (ha/person)
		Farmland		Forest	Other		
		Crop land	Permanent pasture				
Northeast Asia:							
Japan	377	12	2	63	24	125	0.04
Korea	99	21	1	66	12	45	0.05
Taiwan	36	24	-	52	24	21	0.04
Africa:							
Kenya	569	8	37	2	53	27	0.17
Ghana	228	19	37	42	2	17	0.25
Latin America:							
Brazil	8,457	6	22	66	6	159	0.32
Argentina	2,737	10	52	22	16	35	0.78
Europe, North America and Oceania:							
France	550	35	19	20	25	58	0.33
Denmark	42	56	7	12	25	5	0.47
USA	9,159	21	26	32	21	263	0.73
Australia	7,644	6	54	19	19	18	2.56

Notes: Crop land is the sum of arable land and orchards. Data on Taiwan are for the year 1994.

Sources: World Bank, *World Development Report* (1997); ADB (1996) for Taiwan.

In prewar Japan,[10] though the population growth rate accelerated during the process of modern economic growth,[11] it was still moderate at an annual average of 1.2 per cent.[12] During this period, the number of farms in Japan remained roughly constant at 5.5 million and the gainful workers in agriculture were about 14 million to 15 million.

---

[10] Prewar means the period since Meiji Restoration in 1868 to the end of the Second World War in 1945.

[11] The annual population growth rate during 1730–1872 (the latter half of the Tokugawa era) was 0.02 per cent (Hayami and Miyamoto, 1988).

[12] Data refer to the annual average of the 1885–1940 period.

Limited arable land per capita meant small sizes of farm operations in Northeast Asia. In Japan the average farm size has been as small as around 1 hectare. Arable land per farm worker was only about 0.4 ha. After World War II, both the number of farm households and the farmland area decreased, owing to out-migration of household members from agriculture to industrial sectors and the conversion of farmland to residential property and for industrial purposes. Even today there are 3.4 million farm households on the 5 million hectares of farmland; 70 per cent of the farm households operate on less than 1 hectare of farmland (Table 13.2).[13]

Table 13.2 Changes in the number of farm households by operational land area and average farm size in Japan, Korea and Taiwan

	Number of farm households (1,000)	Size distribution of farms (%)					Average farm size (ha)
		Less than 0.5 ha	0.5 to 1.0 ha	1.0 to 2.0 ha	Larger than 2.0 ha	Total	
Japan:							
1941	5,499	33.4	30.0	27.0	9.6	100	1.07
1955	6,043	38.5	32.7	22.9	5.9	100	0.99
1960	6,057	38.3	31.7	23.6	3.8	100	1.00
1970	5,402	38.0	30.2	24.1	7.8	100	1.09
1980	4,661	41.6	28.1	21.2	10.0	100	1.17
1990	3,835	40.9	27.6	20.6	10.9	100	1.37
Korea:							
1994	1,558	30.7	28.8	28.4	12.2	100	1.31
Taiwan:							
1994	808						1.08

Note. Since the definition of farm households in Japan changed in 1990, the data in 1990 cannot be directly compared with the data in previous years

Sources: Japan: JMAFF (1992). Korea: KSY (1996). Taiwan: CEPD (1995).

Labour productivity in agriculture *(Y/L)* can be expanded into the following equivalent:

$$\frac{Y}{L} \equiv \frac{Y}{A} \cdot \frac{A}{L}$$

where Y, L, *A* denote agricultural output, agricultural labour input and farmland area, respectively. Then, *Y/A* denotes land productivity, i.e., yield per hectare, and *A/L* denotes land–labour ratio, i.e., operational farmland area per worker. Small

[13] According to JMAFF (Japan, Ministry of Agriculture, Forestry and Fisheries), the definition of farm households is a household that operated farming on the farmland of 0.1 hectare or more, or sold more than 150,000 yen (gross value) of farm produce during the previous year of a survey.

farm size meant low land–labour ratio. The labour productivity is the product of land productivity and the land–labour ratio. In order to raise labour productivity in agriculture, either land productivity or the land–labour ratio must be raised. In Northeast Asia, efforts were geared to raising land productivity through the development and use of bio-chemical technologies, represented by seed improvements and intensive application of fertilizers. As a result, in 1980, land productivity in Japan was ten times higher and in Taiwan 16 times higher than US land productivity figures. However, the labour productivity in Japan and Taiwan was still only one-tenth and one-twentieth of that in the United States. This is because the land-labour ratio has been low, i.e., the operational size of farmland has remained very small (Kawagoe and Hayami, 1983).

Japanese agriculture has mainly relied on irrigated rice culture. Throughout the prewar period, the major farm products were rice, which occupied an overwhelming position in Japanese agriculture, followed by sericulture and wheat. Livestock had a negligible share.[14] After the war, though the share of rice dropped gradually, it still occupied about 30 per cent in 1990, while that of livestock and vegetables increased to 27 per cent and 22 per cent, respectively. Changes in dietary patterns brought this shift. The share of sericulture, which was the second most important product in 1920, has dropped drastically to almost nil in 1990. The production structure reflects the use of farmland. Of the 5 million hectares of farmland, 54 per cent is wet paddy field, while permanent pasture is only 13 per cent, since livestock production was introduced relatively recently (Table 13.3).

Table 13.3 Paddy and upland field in Japan, Korea and Taiwan, 1994

	Cultivated land area (000 ha)		
	Total	Paddy field	Upland field
Japan	5,083	2,764	2,318
	(100)	(54)	(46)
Korea	2,033	1,267	766
	(100)	(62)	(38)
Taiwan	872	461	411
	(100)	(53)	(47)

Note: Percentage distributions of paddy and upland fields are shown in parentheses.
Sources: Japan: JMAFF (1996); Korea: KSY (1996); Taiwan: CEPD (1995).

Communal Rules and Rural Organizations

Northeast Asian agriculture is characterized by a highly labour intensive rice culture under high population densities and thus severe constraints on arable land. This has meant small size farm operations. Property rights on land have been established and individual farmers are responsible for their farm operations and

[14] This is because Buddhism prohibited eating meat, and the habit of using dairy products hardly developed.

management. However, this does not mean the farmers could always make their own decisions about their operations freely based on profit maximizing rules as assumed in capitalistic economies. Their activities are interdependent with those of other members of the same community. Farmers often cooperate in farm operations to internalize production externalities, such as coordinating the distribution of irrigation water and jointly spraying pesticide at a village level. Smith (1959: 209) described Japanese agriculture in the Tokugawa era thus:

> Because rice must be made to stand in water much of the growing season to get maximum yields, there was need in nearly every village for an extensive system of ditches, dams, dikes, ponds, tunnels, and water gates. Since these could be constructed and maintained only by community effort, their use was subject to community control. A rice farmer never owned or controlled all of the essential means of production himself, ...

In this respect, farmers had to follow the rules set up at the community level. Furthermore, peasants often worked collectively for their mutual benefit. For example, in order to ease the heavy workload during the peak season, they often exchanged labour without relying on market transactions. These transactions were done reciprocally within small groups of neighbours and relatives. Communal rules, formed under the tightly connected community through locational affinity and kinship, governed the whole mode of rural activities. In Asia, community is not only a place where people live, but it provides a cooperative and mutually dependent production system of traditional agriculture (Kawagoe, Ohkama and Bagyo, 1992).

A Northeast Asian model of communal rules In order to identify the characteristics of rural economic activities in Northeast Asia in relation to the communal rules, let us examine a simple comparative model. Suppose economic activities in a rural community, such as farming and forestry, comprise two stages, 'Input (Decision)' and 'Output (Distribution)'. Input is a process by which community members plan and implement economic activities individually or collectively. Then, the outcome of the input process is obtained by individual members or shared with other members on the basis of the rules in the community. In the diagram in Figure 13.1, the economic activities are shown vertically from top to bottom, while prevailing communal rules are shown horizontally. In a capitalistic economy, which has been developed in the Western nations, individual members decide their 'input' by themselves at their own risk, while observing market signals. Each member basically takes the complete results obtained from their 'input', both benefits and losses, by themselves. This model may be called a 'capitalistic model' and is represented by a vertical arrow at the right side of the square. In contrast, a 'socialistic model' would be drawn as another vertical arrow at the left-hand side of the square. In a pure socialistic community, 'input' is made by the community or an authority that represents the community and 'output' is shared among the community members.

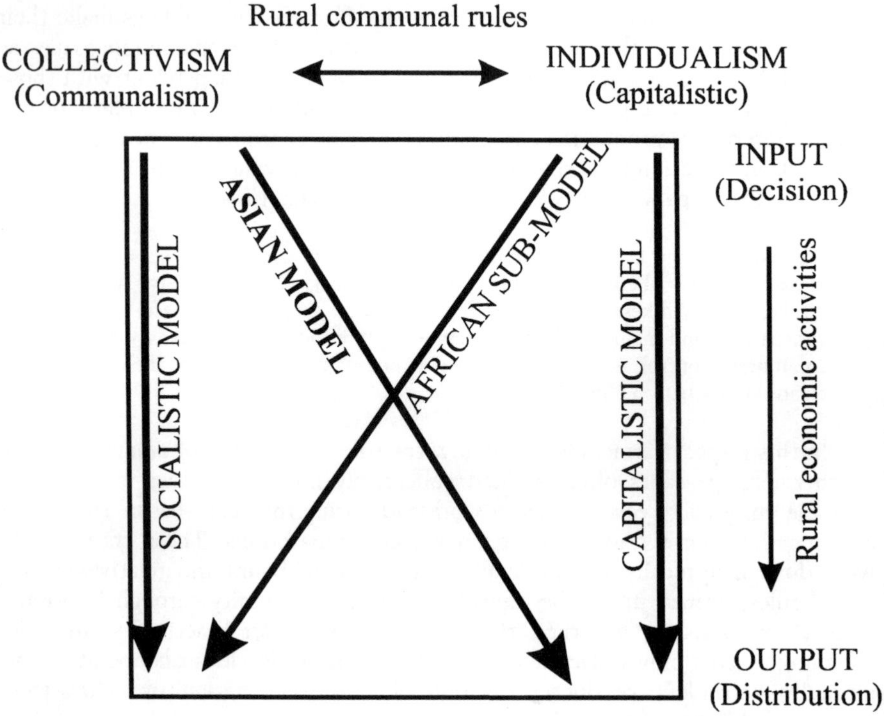

Figure 13.1 Asian model of rural communal rules in economic activities

In this case, the '(Northeast) Asian model' of rural community rules is a diagonal arrow from the upper left corner to the lower right corner. In Northeast Asia, 'input' is made on the base of the communal rules but the 'output' is obtained by the individuals. Finally, another diagonal arrow from upper right to lower left can be drawn. This arrow reflects a community where the members take action individually, but the 'output' is shared among the community members. The last mode would be observed in a society where land resources are abundant and the members' activities are not so interdependent, but they are at a subsistence level and the output must be shared for security. This model may be applicable to some land abundant areas in Africa, while the Asian model can be applied to relatively densely populated African economies.

Rural organizations Now, we will examine how rural organizations have developed in Northeast Asia, while referring to the historical experiences of Japan. Since the early stage of development, various spontaneous organizations emerged in rural communities, such as rotating credit associations and farmers' unions. The latter are now well-known as *Nokyo* or JA, a nationwide network of farmers' cooperatives in Japan.

In rural communities in developing economies there are various informal financial institutions for mobilizing scarce capital. Rural people often rely on informal credit such as loans from informal lenders and traders, or they borrow money from relatives and neighbours. Rotating credit associations are a kind of spontaneous informal financial institution for mutual saving. Found widely in the developing economies of Asia, they include the *hui* in Central China, *ho* in Vietnam and *arisan* in Indonesia (Geertz, 1962; Kawagoe et al., 1992). In Japan such activities were widely found in the prewar period and were known as *ko* or *tanomoshi* dating back to as early as the thirteenth century.

There are large variations in the rules, scale and organizational sophistication of the associations, but the basic principle is similar. First, participants organize a rotating credit association and set up rules. Then, a lump sum fund comprising fixed contributions from each participant is distributed at fixed intervals and as a whole to each participant in turn. The general structure of the associations is constant whether the fund is in kind or in cash; whether the order in which the participants receive the fund is determined by lot, by agreement or by bidding; and whether the association is composed of any professions (Geertz, 1962). The rotating credit associations in Japan have evolved into modern financial institutions as mutual banks, credit associations or unions. In a society represented by the 'Asian model', such as Northeast Asian rural communities, strong communal rules govern the tightly connected society with locational affinity and kinship and peoples live together over generations in the same places and cooperate for their daily life. In these communities, the possibility of default is limited and institutions like rotating credit associations developed into modern financial institutions.

In a society where peasants have cooperated at various stages of their activities, it is natural that they also organize various groups in order to seek scale economies in their farm operations, marketing their produce and purchasing farm inputs. In Japan, two different types of rural institutions were organized at the early stage of modern economic growth in the late nineteenth century. These were industrial associations (*sangyo kumiai*) and agricultural groups (*nokai*). The Industrial associations were engaged in economic activities, such as marketing, purchasing and/or credit arrangements, while the agricultural groups mostly provided advice on improved farming technologies.

The industrial associations first appeared in the early Meiji era and their numbers grew significantly by the turn of the century. Most of them were credit or marketing associations. The credit associations had grown out of the rotating credit associations established in the Tokugawa era. The marketing associations were organized by groups of farmers, traders or manufacturers. During the latter part of the Tokugawa era farmers had developed various cottage industries, thus their marketing activities for their production flourished in rural areas. The marketing associations were set up by the traders in the same business for the purpose of quality control and joint marketing of the merchandise, such as tea and raw silk thread, which were important export products of Japan at that time.

The origins of the agricultural groups are traced back to farmers' workshops (*nodankai*), which began from around the 1870s as spontaneous gatherings of progressive farmers and landlords. Since the Tokugawa era, there were veteran farmers, called *rono*, who were experts at farming, and paternalistic landlords. They introduced new farming techniques and invested in the infrastructure. By the Meiji Restoration, the feudal system, governed by the Tokugawa shogunate and *daimyo* was replaced by a modern centralized government. Under the feudal system, peasants were not formally allowed to leave their land and farming technologies were often banned for transfer to other regions. These obstacles were removed under the new order government and the interaction between different regions of the country grew with the rapid development of the commercial economy.

Under these conditions, the landlords and *rono* actively exchanged the information on new techniques and new plant varieties through the farmers' workshops.[15] They were proud of acting as village leaders and patrons of the peasants. In 1881 these workshops operated separately but were organized into the Greater Japan Agricultural Associations (*Dai Nippon Nokai*) under the government policy to encourage agricultural production.

The rural organizations, such as industrial associations and farmers associations, were spontaneous and private institutions. Until the 1910s, the Japanese government adopted non-intervention policies in private enterprise and gave them legal status through legislation.[16] However, from the mid 1920s, under growing social unrest, the government tended to use the agricultural associations for implementation of a variety of agricultural policies. For example, the official loan for fertilizer purchase and the promotion of the Rural Economy Revival Plan (*Nosangyoson keizai kosei keikaku*) were both implemented through the agricultural associations.[17] The use of agricultural associations for the implementation of the plan encouraged farm households to become members and make use of the services. The agricultural associations themselves took the opportunity to expand their organizations under government protection. During the progress of the war on the Asian continent and the War in the Pacific, the government control on agriculture strengthened, while the agricultural associations became the implementing agency for government controls in the wartime economy (Kawagoe,

---

[15] In 1883 more than 500 workshops were organized (Kawagoe, 1993c).

[16] In 1899, the Agricultural Associations Law (*Nokai ho*) was enacted and the agricultural groups were legalized as Agricultural Associations. The demands by these agricultural groups, such as the provisions of compulsory membership and the right to levy compulsory membership fees were rejected, but provisions on subsidies were included in the law. The industrial associations were legalized in 1900 by the enactment of the Industrial Association Law (*Sangyo kumiai ho*).

[17] The Rural Economy Revival Plan (1932~) was a comprehensive economic policy implemented to help the impoverished rural population during the agricultural crises caused by worldwide depression and the Great Depression of 1929. The Revival Plan included provisions for low interest loans, price supports for agricultural products, implementation of public works projects in rural areas and so on (Kawagoe, 1996b).

1996b). The function of the farmers organization as the government's agency was thus created during the wartime period. It was retained throughout the postwar period, when the agricultural associations and other institutions were reorganized into Farmers Coöperatives (*Nokyo*).

Income Distribution and Poverty Alleviation

The core of the miracle in East Asia is characterized by high performing Asian economies that have achieved unusually low and declining levels of inequality while sustaining rapid economic growth (World Bank, 1993).

Income Distribution in Northeast Asia

As far as the Northeast Asian economies are concerned, they had already achieved a highly equitable income distribution at the beginning of their rapid economic growth. The declining inequality in these economies was brought about by various factors, such as postwar agrarian reforms, tax systems and various job opportunities in rural areas. After a brief comparative analysis, review the historical changes in income distribution in Japan and then we will explore how these equitable income distributions were attained in the Northeast Asian economies.

An international comparison The inequality of income distribution is measured by size distribution of income or Gini coefficients. The former is a commonly used method in which the total population is divided into successive quintiles or deciles, according to ascending income levels; it measures what proportion of the total income in an economy accrues to each group. The percentage shares of each group are further aggregated into a single index, such as the ratio of income share of the highest income group to that of the lowest. The Gini concentration ratio, or more simply Gini coefficient, measures the aggregated inequality index varying from perfect equality (=0) to perfect inequality (=1). The Gini coefficient for economies with highly unequal income reveals a 0.5 to 0.7 coefficient, while economies with relatively equitable income distribution typically show a 0.20 to 0.35 coefficient (Todaro, 1997).

In Table 13.4, the inequality index, Gini coefficients and size distribution of income (measured as the ratio of income share of the highest quintile income group to that of the lowest quintile) are shown for several economies. It is apparent that the Gini coefficient for many economies in Africa and Latin America lie between 0.5 and 0.6, indicating the highly unequal nature of the income distribution in these economies. On the other hand, Northeast Asian economies since the 1960s reveal relatively equitable distributions, with between 0.3 and 0.36 Gini coefficients (Table 13.4a). The size distribution index shows a clearer contrast between African/Latin American economies and East Asian economies. The index of the former group is more than 10, while the latter is 4 to 6 (Table 13.4b).

Table 13.4 Comparisons of income distribution for selected economies

(a) Gini coefficient

	Year	Gini coefficient	Sources		Year	Gini coefficient	Sources
Japan	1937	0.55	(1)	Brazil	1989	0.60	(6)
	1956	0.31	(2)	Chile	1994	0.57	(6)
	1985	0.36	(3)	Colombia	1991	0.51	(6)
				Venezuela	1990	0.54	(6)
Korea	1965	0.34	(4)				
	1982	0.36	(4)	Botswana	1986	0.54	(6)
				Côte d'Ivoire	1988	0.40	(6)
Taiwan	1953	0.56	(5)	Kenya	1992	0.54	(6)
	1980	0.30	(5)	South Africa	1993	0.62	(6)
	1961	0.36	(5)				

Sources: (1) Minami (1996); (2) Wada (1975); (3) Mizoguchi and Terasaki (1995); (4) Leipziger et al. (1992); (5) Kuo (1983); (6) Deininger and Squire (1996).

(b) Income share

	Year	Ratio of income share[a]	Sources		Year	Ratio of income share[a]	Sources
Japan	1979	4.3	(7)	Brazil	1983	26.1	(7)
				Chile			
Korea	1965	7.3	(4)	Colombia	1988	13.3	(7)
	1982	6.3	(4)	Venezuela	1987	10.8	(7)
Taiwan	1953	20.5	(5)	Botswana	85/86	22.4	(7)
	1980	4.2	(5)	Côte d'Ivoire	1986	10.5	(7)
	1961	11.6	(5)	Kenya	1987	20.6	(8)
				South Africa			

Note: [a] Ratio of income share of top 20 per cent to bottom 20 per cent.
Sources: (2) Mizoguchi and Terasaki (1995); (4) Leipziger et al. (1992); (5) Kuo (1983); (7) World Bank (1990); (8) Campos and Root (1996).

Historical changes in income distribution in Japan When and how were the equitable distributions realized in Northeast Asian economies? Before World War II, the inequality of income distribution in Japan was much higher than in the postwar period. According to a recent estimate by Minami (1996), the inequality worsened over the prewar period, especially the 1920s and 1930s. The Gini coefficients were estimated to be around 0.4 to 0.43 at the turn of the century, increasing to 0.51 in the 1920s andreaching 0.55 by the end of the 1930s. Income was more unevenly distributed in urban areas than in rural areas and the increase of the inequality was caused by worsened intra-urban and rural–urban income distributions.

The intra-urban inequality, i.e., inequality among urban dwellers, was attributed to the wage differences between the formal and informal sectors. The major source of the rural–urban inequality was the income gap between farm and non-farm sectors. Enlarged inequality in the 1920s and 1930s was attributed to impoverishment of the farm sector, which was severely depressed by the postwar recession and the successive worldwide depression.

The level of income disparity in Japan was greatly reduced after World War II. In fact, estimated Gini coefficients of 0.313 in 1956 (Wada, 1975) and 0.376 in 1962 (Mizoguchi and Terasaki, 1995) meant drastic improvement in income distribution, if we compare them with that of 0.547 in 1937 (Minami, 1996). Wartime regulations and postwar economic reforms contributed to this improvement. The devastation caused by World War II virtually destroyed the wealth of the urban rich. The postwar land reform drastically improved the distribution of land ownership, and thus improved the wealth and income distribution in rural areas. The property tax system also contributed to the reallocation of wealth

Rural Poverty and Agrarian Reforms

Agricultural land reforms implemented after World War II in Northeast Asia largely contributed to improved income distribution and poverty alleviation in the rural communities. Prior to the discussion on the land reforms, we will briefly review the land tenure system and poverty in rural areas in prewar Japan.

The land tenure system, tenancy disputes and rural poverty in prewar Japan In the early part of the Meiji era, one-third of the farmland was owned by various sizes of landlords and owner farmers. Though most of them were small landowners, large farming landlords played an important role in rural development. They introduced new farming techniques and invested in the infrastructure. They actively exchanged information on new techniques and new plant varieties. As noted earlier, they were proud of their role as village leaders and patrons for the peasants. By the beginning of the twentieth century, however, these paternalistic landlords had disappeared and were replaced by parasitic landlords, who merely sought rents. At the same time, the land under tenancy reached nearly half of the farmland.[18]

The operations of tenant farmers were smaller than the average and these farmers had to pay nearly half of their produce as land rent to landlords. The tenant farmers, who occupied one-third of the farm households, formed the class of the rural poor. Beginning in the 1920s, deflationary policies and the world depression pushed agricultural prices and farm incomes down, seriously affecting the farm sector, especially small tenant farmers. The agricultural crisis in the 1930s was caused by a rapid decline of farm prices. Tenancy disputes became a common phenomenon in rural areas, resulting in social unrest and conflicts throughout the 1920s and 1930s. A reformist group of bureaucrats attempted to solve tenancy problems in order to remove the root cause of the disputes. But it was difficult to improve the tenants' economic and social status, due to strong opposition from the conservatives who had conflicting interests (Kawagoe, 1993b). Drastic agrarian reform was thus not realized until the conservatives' political and economic power was suppressed by the defeat in the war and strong support was given by the Supreme Commander for the Allied Powers of the occupation forces (SCAP).

Postwar land reform in Northeast Asia The low inequality of income distribution in Northeast Asian economies is largely attributed to the drastic agricultural land reform in the postwar period. In Japan the reform was implemented from 1946 to 1950 under the strong guidance of SCAP. In Taiwan, after the rent reduction programme in 1949, redistribution of public and private lands to tenant farmers was carried out in 1953 (Kuo, 1983). In Korea, land reform was implemented in 1947 under US initiatives. After the Korean War, it was done again by the Korean government (Campos and Root, 1996). These land reforms were implemented successfully and represent rare cases in the history of agrarian reform.

Land reform is basically a political issue that seeks to achieve or prevent change in the agrarian structure. At the same time, land reform can be an economic issue that brings a change in the production structure in agriculture. However, there is no general agreement on the definition of agricultural land reform. In a broad sense, ' a [land] reform is an institutional innovation promoted by the ruling order in an attempt to overcome economic or political contradictions without changing the dominant social relations' (de Janvry, 1981: 384–5).

More specifically, land reform aims to change the modes of production and the land tenure system, which consequently brings change to the class structure and political control of the state. Persistent inequality in income distribution and rural poverty can be modified through the reform, if it is properly designed and drastically implemented. Land reforms can take various forms depending on the mode of agricultural production.

Peasant operations prevail in Northeast Asia. Under these operations, the major style of production is the small family farm that mainly produces food crops

---

[18] The heavy land tax burden compelled small owner-farmers to sell their land when the prices of agricultural produce declined and they could not afford to pay the tax in cash.

for own consumption. The surplus, if available, is sold at the market. The concept of peasants who allocate resources for subsistence without regard to price signals (Chayanov, 1926; Wharton, 1969) does not apply to the peasants in this mode. In the modern world, even in villages remote from urban centres, peasants are integrated with the market economy to the extent that market prices determine their farming decisions, just as those made by modern entrepreneurs. In this respect, it may be hard to differentiate peasant farming from modern commercial farming. Peasant farming retains a self-sufficient nature in farm production and decisions on which crops should be planted. These are decided in relation to household activities, while commercial farms determine their farm operations solely in relation to the markets (Kawagoe, 1996a). The land reform in peasant production takes the form 'land to tillers', that is, property rights on the farmland are transferred from landlords to the cultivators of the soil.[19] The reforms implemented in Northeast Asian economies in the 1940s and 1950s were reforms along this line.

In Japan the land reform was carried out between 1946 and 1950. When the Japanese land reform programme was designed, there was a strong belief among the policy makers of the Japanese government, as well as those of SCAP, that landlordism was the source of a multitude of evils that could only be corrected by establishing owner farmers.[20] Throughout the five years of reforms, all tenanted land owned by absentee landlords, and a portion of the village landlords' land, was compulsorily purchased by the government and sold to the tenant farmers.[21] As a result of the reform, more than 90 per cent of the farmland under tenancy came into cultivators' hands. The number of tenant farmers, who had occupied one-third of the farms before the reform, was reduced to 4 per cent, while that of owner farmers increased from 52 per cent to 92 per cent (Table 13.5). Thus, most of the community members in the rural society became owner farmers, which brought equalized assets and income distributions among the members in the rural community. The Gini coefficient of the income distribution in the prewar period was around 0.5. It declined to 0.35 after the reform.[22]

Major factors behind the success of the drastic land reform included the existence of the superior power of SCAP. But the landlords' political and economic power had already been undermined by various regulations on land during the

---

[19] This reform may be called an Asian model, while the reform called the Latin America model includes the transformation of semi-feudal estates with bonded labour into capitalist estates with hired labour (Hayami et al., 1990).

[20] SCAP was under the influence of the liberal Jeffersonian tradition of agrarian reform, which regarded the family farm, owned and operated by cultivators, as the only sound foundation of social equity and political stability.

[21] The land price paid to landlords was reduced to a negligible level by rapid inflation, since the purchase price was fixed at the 1945 price level.

[22] The Gini coefficient of income distribution over the local town and villages was estimated to be 0.45 to 0.55 in 1937 (Minami, 1994), while the figure decreased to 0.35 on the national average during the postwar period (Mizoguchi and Terasaki, 1995).

war. Japanese land reform was a great political success.[23] The reform contributed to democratization and social and political stability in postwar Japan. In fact, the conservative Liberal Democratic Party, which was supported by the rural community, retained its dominance in the Diet and remained the ruling party for nearly 40 years after the reforms were implemented. The reforms also contributed to an increase in education and therefore to human capital accumulation. Before the reforms, the household expenditures of tenant farmers were substantially lower, especially in such categories as education, health care and social relationships. After the reforms, former tenant farmers could afford to spend more for the education of their children. Equitable income distribution enabled the society to accumulate human capital through more equal opportunities for education, which contributes to economic growth (Williamson, 1993).

Table 13.5 **Changes in the farmland area and the number of farm households by land tenure status in Japan, 1941–1955**

(a) Farmland area (thousand hectares)

Year	Owner	(%)	Tenant	(%)	Total	(%)
1941	3,099	(54)	2,660	(46)	5,759	(100)
1947	3,006	(60)	1,964	(40)	4,970	(100)
1949	4,274	(87)	643	(13)	4,917	(100)
1955	4,678	(91)	462	(9)	5,140	(100)

(b) Number of farm households (thousand farms)

Year	Owner[b] (%)	Owner cum tenant (%)	Tenant cum owner (%)	Tenant (%)	Total[c] (%)
1941	1,656 (31)	1,123 (21)	1,093 (20)	1,516 (28)	5,412 (100)
1947	2,154 (36)	1,183 (20)	997 (17)	1,574 (27)	5,909 (100)
1949	3,564 (57)	1,735 (28)	458 (7)	489 (8)	6,247 (100)
1955	4,200 (70)	1,308 (22)	285 (5)	239 (4)	6,043 (100)

Notes:

a. Owner: Farmers who own more than 90 per cent of their cultivating land. Owner cum tenant and Tenant cum owner: Farmers who own 50 to 90 per cent and 10 per cent to 50 per cent of their cultivating land, respectively. Tenant: Farmers who own less than 10 per cent of their cultivating land.

b. Include farming landlords, who rented out more than 1 hectare.

c. Data in each category do not add up to the total, as farmers who do not cultivate farmland are included in the total; these were 23,816 in 1941, 1,386 in 1947 and 663 in 1949.

Sources: Kayo (1977); NKTG (pp. 646–7, table 26).

---

[23] It should be noted, however, that the reform did not change the basic structure of agricultural production. The land reform transferred land ownership from landlords to tillers of the soil. Thus small tenant farmers became small owner cultivators without any significant change in average farm size. This caused serious difficulties in adjusting the agricultural production structure into a modern one during the rapid economic growth after the mid 1950s. See Kawagoe (1996a) for further discussions.

In Taiwan, substantial investment in the agricultural infrastructure was made in the colonial period. However, the distribution of farmland remained highly skewed during the prewar period. Around one-third of farmers were tenant cultivators and more than half the farmland was under tenancy. Tenant farmers, like Japanese tenants, had to pay nearly half their output under unstable short-term contracts. Judging from the still high Gini coefficient of 0.56 in 1953 (Feiet al., 1979), when the land reform was already in progress, it is natural to consider that the income distribution in prewar Taiwan was very unfavourable. Land reform was carried out through three steps. First, farm rents were reduced and tenant rights were enhanced in 1949.

Second, public land was sold to tenant farmers in 1949. The public land, about a quarter of the arable land, was formerly owned by Japanese. Finally, in 1953, the compulsory sale of the landlords' land was implemented. The private land in excess of specified amounts was sold to the government and then resold to tenant farmers. The landlords were paid 70 per cent in land bonds and 30 per cent in the industrial stock of four public enterprises formaly owned by the Japanese. This arrangement encouraged the landlord class to participate in industrial development (Fei et al., 1979). After the reform, more than 60 per cent of the farmers were owner cultivators and tenanted land decreased to only 14 per cent (Table 13.6). Successful land reform was attained, because 'it could be imposed by a government free of obligations and ties to the landowning class' (Fei et al., 1979: 39).

Table 13.6 Changes in the farmland area and the number of farm households by land tenure status in Taiwan, 1939–1955

(a) Farmland area (thousand hectares)

Year	Owner		Tenant		Total	
1939	364	(44)	464	(56)	828	(100)
1948		(56)		(44)		(100)
1955	743	(85)	130	(15)	873	(100)

(b) Number of farm households (thousand farms)

Year	Owner		Owner cum tenant		Tenant		Total	
1939	138	(32)	133	(31)	159	(37)	430	(100)
1950	230	(36)	166	(26)	242	(38)	638	(100)
1955	433	(59)	176	(24)	125	(17)	733	(100)
1970	768	(77)	114	(13)	88	(88)	880	(100)

Notes: Farm households in 1970 are estimated by the distribution of farm population by land tenure status.

Sources: Fei et al. (1979); CEPD (1995).

Rural–Urban Migration, Off-Farm Jobs and Poverty Alleviation

Successful land reforms greatly improved the income distribution among members of the rural community in Northeast Asia. However, land reform was not the only cause of highly equalized societies in the region. In the process of economic growth, the income gap between farm and non-farm sectors widens. This is because labour productivity improvements in the industrial sector are greater than those of the traditional agricultural sector. The widened income gap itself is a cause of growing inequality of income distribution between rural and urban sectors, and as well, induces rural to urban migration as an adjustment process of the wage gap. However, as is often observed in developing economies, there is not sufficient capacity to absorb labour in the industrial sector, as most migrants flood into the urban informal sector. Although the urban informal sector plays important roles in generating employment and income for the urban poor (ILO, 1972, 1974), the expansion of the informal sector solves neither inequality nor poverty problems. Even worse, excessive inflow of labour forms urban slums where poor people are crowded in to unsanitary conditions. The coexistence of the generously paid modern sector and the impoverished informal sector can be a cause of social and political unrest.

In Northeast Asia, though rural to urban migration was the norm, agricultural sector dynamism also allowed these countries to retain a labour force in the rural sector. In prewar Japan, the annual population growth rate was moderate at 1.2 per cent.[24] Natural growth of the population was higher in the rural areas than in the urban sectors, but the size of the agricultural labour force remained almost stable, only slightly declining from 15 million to 14 million during the prewar period. The number of farms also remained roughly constant at 5.5 million.[25] Accordingly, about 350,000 to 400,000 members of the rural population were transferred to non-farm sectors annually. This was not a constant process, however. In the upswing phase of the economy, the growth rate of the labour force increased in the industrial sectors and in the downswing phase, relatively more workers entered agriculture (Ohkawa and Rosovsky, 1973). While acting as the absorbent of the labour pool, the rural sector continually supplied labour to non-farm sectors at an annual rate of 2 per cent to 4 per cent. The share of the agricultural labour force was more than 80 per cent in the 1870s; it declined gradually to around 50 per cent by the 1930s.

Japanese agriculture retained a relatively large share of the labour force, compared with 19 per cent in the United States in 1940, 16 per cent in Germany in 1933 and 6 per cent in England in 1938 (Smith, 1959). However, the large agricultural labour share does not always mean that the rural sector in Japan was impoverished

---

[24] Since emigration or immigration was negligible, the natural rate of the population growth explains the whole demographic pattern. Calculated from LTES 2 (Long-Term Economic Statistics of Japan).

[25] As the frontier for new farmland disappeared, farmland also remained constant at about 6 million hectares. Thus the average farm size was around 1 hectare throughout the period.

by abundant labour. There were extensive opportunities for labour absorption in the rural sector. The intensive nature of the irrigated rice culture in Northeast Asia could sustain a large amount of the labour force. Japanese agriculture grew at the annual compound rate of 1.6 per cent in the late nineteenth century, which accelerated to 2.0 per cent at the beginning of the twentieth century and continued until the 1920s (Hayami et al., 1991). Furthermore, uneven distribution of labour requirements under monsoon agriculture enabled farmers to engage in various off-farm jobs during lean seasons. It was common in prewar Japan for farmers to produce farming tools, handicrafts and processed foodstuffs during these periods. These products were traded not only within rural areas, but also in towns and cities, which were easily accessible in the densely populated environment. Rural marketing of various farm produce was often shouldered by peasants as a side job. These off-farm activities in rural areas contributed to alleviating poverty, though the inequality of income distribution was still large and many of the rural habitants were poor in the prewar period.[26, 27]

After World War II, especially in the 1960s and later, off-farm jobs of farm households contributed highly to reducing the inequality of the income distribution in Japan. In 1946, just after the war, the number of farm labourers temporarily increased to 18 million (Kayo, 1977). This was because the industrial sectors and cities were damaged or destroyed by the war and many people moved to rural areas and engaged in farming to obtain food. When the economy recovered and began to grow rapidly in the 1950s, a large number of farm workers left to non-farm sectors, while the farm sector again acted as a buffer of the labour demand fluctuations in the industrial sector. However, the out-flow of the labour force did not always take the form of migration of whole families. Instead, farmers engaged in off-farm jobs as part-timers, while they continued their farm operations. Although the number of workers mainly engaged in agriculture declined to nearly one-third of the number in the early 1950s. The decrease was compensated for by an increase in the number of workers supplementarily engaged in farming. The total number of farms, therefore, decreased slowly. This is because non-farm employment opportunities increased rapidly in rural areas.

As discussed above, off-farm activities were already the norm in the prewar period, while job opportunities became more widespread during the period of

---

[26] This rural dynamism in industrialization and commercialization was already the norm in the Tokugawa era. In advanced areas, close to large cities, many peasants produced cash crops, since increased rice yields enabled peasants to diversify into various cash crops. Rural based cottage industries became pervasive in these areas. In the seventeenth century, regional specialization progressed. For example, nearly 40 per cent of the merchandise was produced in the suburban areas of the large cities (Miyamoto, 1988), while the remote areas specialized in the production of rice and other staple crops. The inter-regional specialization was supported by inter-regional marketing. Specialization or diversification in agricultural production enabled rural entrepreneurs to act as marketing agents (Kawagoe, 1998).

[27] The important role of rural marketing and industrial activities is also seen in Java. See Hayami and Kawagoe (1993).

rapid economic growth beginning in the 1950s. Construction of highways, factories and housing boomed. The public investments in rural areas provided lots of employment opportunities for farmers as construction workers. Development of transport networks expanded the commutable distance with progress in motorization, enabling farm household members to engage in off-farm jobs in modern sectors. These off-farm jobs allowed farm households to attain incomes comparable to those of non-farm households. Until the beginning of the 1960s, the average income per family member in farm households had been about 30 per cent lower than that of non-farm workers' households. This disparity narrowed and the former exceeded the latter in the mid 1970s (Table 13.7); thus, the problem incurred by the inequality of income distribution was nearly solved in postwar Japan.

Table 13.7 Comparison of income between farm households and urban workers' households in Japan, 1952–1990 (Unit: 000 yen per household member per year)

		1952	1960	1970	1980	1990
Farm household:						
Farm income	(1)	31 (66)	38 (49)	104 (32)	216 (17)	274 (14)
Off-farm income	(2)	13 (28)	34 (43)	181 (56)	810 (64)	1,280 (65)
Pension, etc.[a]	(3)	3 (6)	6 (7)	41 (12)	245 (19)	423 (21)
Total (1)+(2)+(3)	(4)	46 (100)	77 (100)	326 (100)	1,271 (100)	1,976 (100)
Urban household income:	(5)		115	357.8	1112.4	1710.1
Relative income (4)/(5)	(6)		0.67	0.91	1.14	1.16

Note: [a] Includes private grants, subsidies, insurance and transfer from members who work away from home.
Sources: JMAFF (1995); JMAFF (1974) for 1952.

A similar story applied to Taiwan. In Taiwan, the successful land reform, increase in multiple cropping and diversification all caused farm income to become more equally distributed. The growth of rural industries offered additional income opportunities to farm households, especially the poorer ones.

> Given the spatially dispersed pattern of industrial location, the growth of rural-based industries and services offered new opportunities for employment and investment. All the advantages of such a decentralized pattern of industrial location—for example, those related to agricultural modernization arising from direct contact with industrial activity, to avoiding the costs associated with labor dislocation and transport, and to reducing urban congestion and social overhead expenditure' (Fei et al., 1979: 315).

The share of off-farm income in farm households dramatically increased, from 3 per cent in 1966 to 73 per cent in 1979. Rapid labour absorption, especially of unskilled labour, from the mid 1960s and industrial decentralization were essential factors contributing to the reduction of income inequality in Taiwan (Kuo, 1983). We should also note that as was the case in Japan, most farmers engaged in non-farm activities on a part-time basis and were available for farm operations during the peak labour times for agriculture (Fei et al., 1979).

Rural Development and Economic Growth

Dynamic rural sectors in Northeast Asia not only contributed to poverty alleviation and equalization of income distribution, they also played important roles in industrialization and economic development. As the industrial sector modernizes, it needs various resources such as capital, workers and entrepreneurs. In most developing countries, primary industries occupy an overwhelming position in the economy, so these resources must be recruited mainly from the rural sector.

The Role of Agriculture in Economic Growth

We explore the roles agriculture can play in economic development, while referring to the experiences of prewar Japan. Prominent among these are capital formation and supply of labour and food.

Capital formation Among the various roles of the rural sector in economic development, one important role is the contribution to capital formation in industry. The net capital transfer from the rural sectors can be assumed to be the sum of the net market based transfer and net government based transfer. The former comprises the resource transfer based on private financial activities, such as the savings of rural people, private investments by urban dwellers in rural areas and the portfolio selection of landlords. The government based transfer is composed of three elements: the first is net direct taxation on the rural sector, which is taxes minus subsidies, including border measures, on the economic activities in the rural sectors. The second is net indirect taxation, which is de facto taxation on the rural sectors caused by such factors as over-valued exchange rates and protection of the industrial sectors. The third is public investment in rural infrastructure (Teranishi, 1997). Thus the contribution of the rural sector in capital formation in industry is determined by the combination of private market activities and government policies.

In the early Meiji period agriculture was the most important and nearly the sole source of fiscal revenue for the Japanese government.[28] In fact, by around 1880 the farm sector shouldered as much as 91 per cent of the tax revenue of the central and local governments. Though the share of the farm sector had declined gradually in the course of economic growth, it still occupied 70 to 50 per cent until the mid 1910s (Tobata and Ohkawa, 1956). The government's financial basis was established by the Land Tax Revision in the 1880s. During the Tokugawa era, rice was a

---

[28] Just after the Meiji Restoration, primary industry accounted for 45 per cent of the net domestic product and 73 per cent of the labour force (Hayami et al., 1991). In this respect, agriculture was the most important sector at that time.

major source of income for the government and the financial base rested largely on the rice tax levied in kind on the peasants. Under the tax in kind system, the government's revenue inevitably varied with the fluctuation of rice prices. The new government, therefore, implemented the Land Tax Revision. By this revision, the traditional rice tax was replaced by a modern land tax based on land value and paid in cash. Though the Land Tax Revision (1873–1881) was a huge project, which required the equivalent cost of the annual government budget, it enabled the government to rest on a more stable and secure foundation of fiscal revenue. But the tax burden on the farmlands was as high as 40 per cent of the gross value added, which was almost comparable to the feudal taxes during the Tokugawa era (see the Annex).

Resource transfer via private channels also played an important role in sustaining capital formation in industrial sectors. Land rent paid to landlords was transferred to non-farm sectors through such instruments as stocks and public bonds. Savings rates of farm households were around 10 per cent in the prewar period and the net outflow to non-farm sectors is estimated to have been half of the savings (Tobata and Ohkawa, 1956). Though the tax burden was heavy, as will be discussed below, the government transferred much of the collected taxes back to rural sectors, in ways such as public investment in rural infrastructure, research, extension and education. This public investment, coupled with dynamic private activities in the rural sectors, assured the rapid growth of agriculture, which enabled a balanced growth between farm and non-farm sectors in prewar Japan.

Labour supply In the process of economic development, the rural sectors are major suppliers of the labour force to industrial sectors. As discussed in the previous section, the Japanese rural sector had continuously supplied labour to non-farm sectors. The role of the rural sector was not limited to the function of labour supplier. It acted as the absorbent of the labour forces, responding to uneven demand of the industrial sector in long-term expansion and contraction phases. The rural sector absorbed more or less of the labour force depending on opportunities in the urban sectors.

Another consideration is related to human capital. The labour migration from rural to industrial sectors should not be enumerated by a mere head count, but attention should also be paid to the quality of labour. The development of industry could be constrained by the quality of the labour supplied by the rural sector. In Northeast Asia, due to urgent labour requirements and the tight schedule in the peak seasons, peasants were compelled to depend on their neighbours and relatives for group work (the Asian mode discussed above). Under these circumstances, attitudes toward cooperation, consensus and harmonious relations were important and thus evolved the tradition of working and living harmoniously, reinforced by the system of Confucian ethics (Oshima, 1987).

Integration of rural sectors into commercial markets and development of rural industries accustomed the peasants to responding or engaging in comercialized activities, while recognizing pecuniary incentives such as prices and wages:

> The agricultural labor force had been unwittingly preparing for the transition to factory employment. Commercial farming had taught peasants to respond with alacrity to monetary incentives, but at the same time agriculture had not changed so much as to destroy the habit of loyalty and obedience. (Smith, 1959: 212).

In Japan, thus, the rural sector could continually supply qualified and well-trained labour to the modern sectors. In the early Meiji era the share of non-farm labour was as small as less than 20 per cent, while in the mid 1920s it increased to more than half of the total labour force.

Exports and foreign currency earnings The critical role of foreign trade in modern economic development, a Kuznets prerequisite, is well recognized. Agricultural exports are primary growth engines and foreign currency earners until manufacturing exports overtake them. Japanese exports continuously grew more rapidly than the world average. Though this rapid export growth was sustained by the manufacturing industries, the role of agricultural exports in the early stage of the development process was critical. The share of agricultural products in total exports was more than 80 per cent in the early Meiji period, and still occupied 40 per cent in the mid 1920s. Government intervention in agricultural trade was limited until the 1920s.[29] For example, the import tariff on rice was adopted and often revised, but in most cases was less than 10 per cent. It was rare that any tariff on rice imports exceeded 20 per cent.

Among the agricultural exports, raw silk was the most important product; it occupied 30 to 40 per cent of the export share. Next to rice, sericulture was the most dominant sector in the prewar agriculture. In the late 1920s, when the silk export reached its peak, as many as 2 million farm households were engaged in sericulture and the planted area of mulberry trees extended to 600,000 hectares. Sericulture was thus an important source of cash income for Japanese farmers.

Food supply When a low-income economy begins to grow, the rise of income brings with it increased population growth, resulting in an accelerated increase in food demand. The income elasticity of food demand has a positive value at the early stage of economic development. The population increase, coupled with increased consumption per capita, means expanded food demand. If the growth of agricultural production cannot keep up with the expanding demand, the economy has to rely on imported food—and using foreign currency that might be applied to capital formation for further economic growth.

Under the policy of seclusion for more than two centuries during the Tokugawa era, self-sufficiency of rice had been maintained. After the opening of

---

[29] The free trade policy at that time does not mean that the Japanese government observed laissez-faire by principle. The Treaty of Amity and Commerce of 1858 (revised in 1866) restrained the maximum tariff rate to 5 per cent. After the substantial revision of the Treaty in 1911, tariff autonomy was recovered and the overall tariff rate was gradually raised in order to protect certain industries or merely to raise fiscal revenue (Howe, 1996).

the country during the Restoration, food demand continually increased. For example, per capita annual consumption of rice was about 100kg in the 1870s; this increased to 130–150kg by the end of the nineteenth century and reached a peak of 170kg by the mid 1910s. As a result, the country was forced to import rice from abroad. The share of imported rice gradually increased from around 1 per cent of the total consumption in the late nineteenth century to around 10 per cent in the 1930s. On the other hand, agriculture grew at a relatively high pace of 1.6 per cent per year during the late nineteenth century, accelerating to 2 per cent during the first two decades of this century. In fact, the production of rice nearly doubled during the half century following the Meiji Restoration. Sustainable agricultural growth in Japan meant the country did not have to rely heavily on imported food. The share of food in total imports remained at 10 to 20 per cent throughout the prewar period.

The Role of Governments in Rural Development

In HPAEs, wealth sharing mechanisms intended to raise the standard of living of the people were designed precisely to obtain the broad support of the people (Campos and Root, 1996). In Northeast Asia rural development policies, such as land reform, investment in education, investment in rural infrastructure, and public agricultural research and extension, were adopted and effectively worked in alleviating poverty, reducing the inequality of income distribution and raising the standard of living of the rural population. Successful rural development enabled these economies to attain rapid economic growth. Let us now examine what the governments in Japan and other northeast Asian economies have done in developing rural sectors.

Human capital development Human capital accumulation through education is important in economic development. HPAEs are well known for their heavy investment in education, especially primary and secondary schooling (Campos and Root, 1996). In the case of Japan, the government established a compulsory education system as early as the 1870s and encouraged the diffusion of primary education. In 1884 the number of children who had never attended primary school was 31 per cent for males and 66 per cent for females. By 1901, however, the ratio was drastically reduced, to 5 per cent for males and 16 per cent for females (LTES 2, 1988). In prewar Taiwan and Korea, Japanese colonial rulers introduced extensive primary and vocational education in the early twentieth century. By the mid 1940s the primary enrolment in public schools exceeded 50 per cent (Oshima, 1993). Furthermore, 'the inclusion of Confucian moral and work education...contributed to a strong work ethic... With fairly well-developed human resources, East Asia got a quick start when the postwar era began' (Oshima, 1993: 185).

In the postwar period educational levels were further raised in the Northeast Asian economies. Many people began to enter universities, technical colleges and vocational schools. Though primary school enrolment reached almost 100 per cent in the mid 1960s, secondary and tertiary enrolment has reached a very high level during the past three decades (Table 13.8). In Taiwan, the expenditure for education, science and culture accounted for more than 13 per cent of the budget during 1954–1968, increasing to 15 per cent by 1980 (Kuo, 1983).

In Japan, higher education institutions were established in the late nineteenth century. 'Through the public schools and universities, many men and some women who were country-born rose to important positions in banking, industry, politics, education, letters, government, and so on. Indeed, an astonishing proportion of Japan's leaders in the past century have been men who reached adolescence in village environments' (Smith, 1959: 213). Thus, with the government's positive role in education investment, the rural sector could supply not only a labour force, but entrepreneurs, engineers and many other talented people who were inevitably required for the modern economic development at that time.

Table 13.8 Education in Northeast Asia and other regions

	Percentage of age group enrolled in education					
	Primary		Secondary		Tertiary	
	1965	1992	1965	1992	1965	1992
Japan	100	102	82	96	13	30
Korea	100	101	35	93	6	48
Taiwan	97	100				
High income economies	104	103	62	97	21	55
Low & middle income economies	78	95	22	39	3	8
East Asia	88	117	23	55	1	5
Sub-Saharan Africa	41	72	4	24	0	-

Sources: World Bank (1990, 1997); CEPD (1995)

Public agricultural research Agricultural dynamism is a critical factor in balanced economic development. In Japan, the government had already founded agricultural colleges as early as the 1870s. The National Agricultural Experimental Institute was founded in 1893 and by the end of the century most local governments had opened agricultural experiment stations. During the Tokugawa era, there was no nationwide research network. Instead, landlords and experienced farmers played a leading role in improving agricultural technology. They found improved varieties of rice, invented new tools and improved farming methods. With the establishment of public research institutions, these technologies were generalized on the basis of modern scientific methods and were diffused throughout the country through the network of the experiment stations. The public investment in agriculture and rural communities sustained the rapid agricultural growth in the late nineteenth and early twentieth centuries.

Rural infrastructure investment Public investment in rural infrastructure also plays a critical role in sustaining rural development, and thus alleviating poverty and reducing income disparities. Agricultural investment, such as irrigation, land improvement and post-harvest facilities, advances agricultural growth. In Northeast Asia, under strong population pressure on limited land resources, when room for expansion of the cultivated area had been nearly exhausted in the 1910s and 1920s, massive irrigation and land improvement projects were implemented. These investments enabled farmers to raise land productivity with improved, fertilizer-responsive rice varieties and high levels of fertilizer application (Kikuchi and Hayami, 1978). As discussed in the previous section, such dynamism allows the agricultural sector to supply various resources to non-farm sectors for economic development.

Not only proximate investment in agriculture, but more general public investment in rural infrastructure, such as railroads, highways, bridges and communication networks, contributes to generating employment and income opportunities for rural populations. This in turn alleviates excessive out-migration to the urban sectors. It also facilitates the development and integration of a nationwide market of farm produce. In Japan the railroad system began with only 29 kilometres of track between Tokyo and Yokohama in 1872. This was soon extended to 2,200 kilometres in 1890 and to 6,000 kilometres in 1900, and exceeded 20,000 kilometres in the mid 1920s. Rolling stock kilometres[30] increased from 18 million in 1890 to more than 2 billion in the 1920s.[31] The railroad network promoted the integration of local markets segmented since the Tokugawa era and induced competition among producing areas. Through the market competition, quality controls on rice were promoted and qualitative and quantitative standards were established in each region. This reduced marketing costs and facilitated agricultural development through a more efficient allocation of resources (Kawagoe, 1998).

Summary and Conclusions

In Northeast Asia, climatic and demographic constraints compelled peasants to engage in labour intensive rice culture and extensive off-farm job activities. Sustaining a high yield of rice demands rigid time schedules of farm operations with a heavy workload during the peak seasons. These requirements had a favourable impact on the diligence and propensity to work. Due to severe resource constraints on land caused by high population density, the peasants were obliged to obey communal rules for achieving consensus, and to keep harmonious and cooperative relations among community members. From this evolved the tradition of working and living in harmony. The community was not only a place where people lived; it provided a cooperative and mutually dependent production system of traditional agriculture. At the same time, property rights on the land were well-established. The Asian model of rural economic activities evolved, demonstrating

[30] The distance between railroad stations × the number of freight cars that pass.
[31] The figures are calculated from Table 17, LTES 12 (1965: 204–5).

collectivity in the activities and individualism in distribution. The attitudes toward cooperation enabled the peasants to accommodate themselves to jobs in modern factories when they migrated to the industrial sectors. The Northeast Asian rural sectors therefore could supply hard-working and cooperative workers for the process of modern economic growth.

Northeast Asian countries achieved a highly equitable income distribution at the beginning of their rapid economic growth. The declining inequality in these economies was brought about by various factors and rural poverty was eliminated by postwar agrarian reforms coupled with wide job opportunities in rural areas. The drastic agricultural land reform in the postwar period transferred the property rights of land from landlords to cultivators of the soil and contributed largely to equalizing the distribution of wealth and income in rural sectors. The impact of the reform was not limited to the direct redistribution effect. As a result of the reforms, former tenant farmers could afford to spend more for the education of their children, which contributed to the accumulation of human capital and consequently to economic growth. Another important factor that contributed to reducing rural inequality and poverty was the existence of extensive job opportunities in the rural sector. Through the intensive nature of the irrigated rice culture, the region itself sustained its labour force and off-farm activities in rural districts generated large income and employment opportunities for the rural population.

The dynamic rural sector in Northeast Asia not only contributed to poverty alleviation and the equalization of income distribution, but also played important roles in industrialization and economic growth. In the process of modernization, the industrial sector needed various resources such as capital, workers and entrepreneurs, which were mainly recruited from the rural sector. Human capital accumulation through education and public investment in rural infrastructure enabled North Asian economies to sustain growth and played an important role in their economic development. This also played a critical role in sustaining rural development, thus alleviating poverty and reducing income disparities. All these factors contributed to the rapid economic growth seen in Northeast Asian economies.

References

Adelman, I. and S. Robinson. 1978. *Income Distribution Policy in Developing Countries: A Case Study for Korea.* Oxford: Oxford University Press.

Asian Development Bank. 1996. *Key Indicators of Developing Asian and Pacific Countries*. Oxford University Press: London.

Barker, R. and R.W. Herdt, with B. Rose. 1985. *The Rice Economy of Asia*. Washington, D.C.: Resources for the Future.

Campos, J.E. and H.L. Root. 1996. *The Key to the Asian Miracle: Making Shared Growth Credible.* Washington, D.C.: Brookings Institution.

CEPD 1995. *Taiwan Statistical Data Book*. Taipei: Council for Economic Planning and Development, Republic of China.

Chayanov, A.V. 1966. original publication 1926. *The Theory of Peasant Economy*. Edited by Daniel Thorner, B. Kerblay R.E.F. Smith. Homewood: Ill.: Richard D. Irwin.

de Janvry, A. 1981. 'The role of land reform in economic development: Policies and politics'. *American Journal of Agricultural Economics*, vol. 63 (May): 384–92.

Dore, R.P. 1959. *Land Reform in Japan*. London: Oxford University Press.

Fei, J.C., G. Ranis and S.W.Y. Kuo. 1979. *Growth with Equity: The Taiwan Case*. Oxford: Oxford University Press.

Deininger, K. and L. Squire. 1996. 'New ways of looking at old issues: Inequality and growth'. World Bank, Washington, D.C. mimeo.

Geertz, C. 1962. 'The rotating credit association: A "middle ring" in development'. *Economic Development and Cultural Change*, vol. 10, no. 3: 241–63.

Hayami, A. and M. Miyamoto, eds. 1988. *Keizai Shakai no Seiritsu: 17–18th Century* (Formation of the economy in the 17-18th century), *Nihon Keizai-shi* (Japanese economic history), Vol. 1. Tokyo: Iwanami Shoten.

Hayami, Y. and T. Kawagoe. 1993. *The Agrarian Origins of Commerce and Industry: A Study of Peasant Marketing in Indonesia*. London and New York: Macmillan and St. Martin's Press.

Hayami, Y., Ma. A.R. Quisumbing and L.S. Adriano. 1990. *Toward an Alternative Land Reform Paradigm: A Philippines Perspective*. Manila: Ateneo de Manila University Press.

Hayami, Y. and V.W. Ruttan. 1985. *Agricultural Development: An International Perspective*. Revised edition. Baltimore: Johns Hopkins University Press.

Hayami, Y. et al. 1991. *The Agricultural Development of Japan: A Century's Perspective*. Tokyo: University of Tokyo Press.

Howe, C. 1996. *The Origins of Japanese Trade Supremacy: Development and Technology in Asia from 1540 to the Pacific War*. London: Hurst & Company.

ILO. 1972. *Employment, Incomes and Equality: A Strategy for Increasing Productive Employment in Kenya*. Geneva: International Labour Office.

ILO. 1974 *Sharing in Development: A Programme of Employment, Equity and Growth for the Philippines*. Geneva: International Labour Office.

IMF. 1996. *International Financial Statistics*. CD-ROM June 1996 version. Washington, D.C.: International Monetary Fund.

Japan, Food Agency. 1996. *Beibaku Data Book* (Data book on rice and wheat) 1996 version. Tokyo:

Japan, Ministry of Agriculture, Forestry and Fisheries. 1992. Nogyo Census Ruinen-Tokeisho. (Cumulative Statistics of Agricultural Census). Statistics and Information Department, JMAFF.

Kayo, N. ed. 1977, *Kaitei Nihon Nogyo Kiso Tokei* (Basic statistics on Japanese agriculture, revised version). Tokyo: Norin Tokei Kyokai.

Kawagoe, T. 1993a. 'Land reform in postwar Japan'. In J. Teranshi and Y. Kosai, eds., *Japanese Experiences of Economic Reform*. London: Macmillan.

Kawagoe, T. 1993b. 'Dergulation and protectionisim in Japanese agriculture'. In J. Teranshi and Y. Kosai, eds., *Japanese Experiences of Economic Reform*. London: Macmillan.

Kawagoe, T. 1993c. 'Shokuryo Kanri Seido to Nokyo' (Food Control System and Farmers' Cooperatives) in *Gendai Keizai Sisutemu no Genryu* (The Origins of Japanese Economic System) Tetsuji Okazaki and Masahiro Okuno, Tokyo: Nihon Keizai Shinbun-sha, eds., (English version 'The Food Control System and Nokyo' in Tetsuji Omazaki and

Masahiro Okuno-Fujiwara eds., *The Japanese Economic System and Its Historical Origins.* Oxford: Oxford University Press, 1999).

Kawagoe, T. 1996a. 'Agricultural land reform in Japan: Reconsideration of the issues'. Discussion paper No. S-17, Center for Asian and Pacific Studies, Seikei University.

Kawagoe, T. 1996b. 'The origins of agricultural protectionism in Japan'. A paper presented at the Department Seminar of Economic History, Australian National University, 13 September 1996.

Kawagoe, T. 1998. 'Technical and institutional innovations in rice marketing in Japan'. In Hyung-Ki Kim and Yujiro Hayami, eds., *Toward the Rural-Based Development of Commerce and Industry: Selected Experiences from East Asia.* Washington, D.C.: The World Bank.

Kawagoe, T. and Y. Hayami. 1983. 'The production structure of world agriculture: An inter-country cross-section analysis'. *Developing Economies*, 21: 189–206.

Kawagoe, T., K. Ohkama and Al Sri Bagyo. 1992. 'Collective actions and rural organizations in a peasant economy in Indonesia'. *Developing Economies*, 30 (September): 215–35.

Korea Statistical Yearbook (KSY). 1996. Seoul: National Statistical Office, Republic of Korea.

Kelley, A.C., and J.G. Williamson. 1974. *Lessons from Japanese Development: An Analytical Economic History*. Chicago: University of Chicago Press.

Kikuchi, M. and Y. Hayami. 1978. 'Agricultural growth against a land resource constraint: A comparative history of Japan, Taiwan, Korea and Philippines'. *Journal of Economic History*, 38 (December): 839–64.

Kuo, S.W.Y. 1983. *Taiwan Economy in Transition*. Boulder: Westview Press.

Kuznets, S. 1955. 'Economic growth and income inequality'. *American Economic Review*, 45 (March): 3–28.

Leipziger, D.M., D. Dollar, A.F. Shorrocks and S.Y. Song. 1992. *The Distribution of Income and Wealth in Korea*. EDI Development Studies. Washington, D.C.: The World Bank.

LTES 1: Ohkawa, Kazushi, Nobukiyo Takamatsu and Yuzo Yamamoto. 1974. *Kokumin shotoku* (National income), vol. 1, in *Estimates of Long-term Economic Statistics of Japan since 1868*. by Kazushi Ohkaw, Miyohei Shinohara, and Mataji Umemura. Tokyo: Toyo Keizai Shipo-sha.

LTES 2: Umemura, Mataji, Keiko Akasaka, Ryoshin Minami, Nobukiyo Takamatsu, Kurotake Arai and Shigeru Itoh. 1988. *Rodoryoku* (Manpower), vol. 2, ditto.

LTES 8: Ohkawa, Kazushi, Tsutomu Noda, Nobukiyo Takamatsu, Saaburo Yamada, Minoru Kumazaki, Yuichi Shoinoya and Ryoshin Minami. 1967. *Bukka* (Prices), vol. 8, ditto.

LTES 9: Umemura, Mataji, Saburo Yamada, Yujiro Hayami, Nobukiyo Takamatsu and Minoru Kumazaki. 1966. *Noringyo* (Agriculture and Forestry), vol. 9, ditto.

LTES 12: Minami, Ryoshin. 1965. *Tetsudo to Denryoku* (Railroads and electric utilities), vol. 12, ditto.

Minami, Ryoshin. 1994. 'Senzen Nihon no Shotoku Bunpu: Suikei to Bunseki (Income distribution in rural areas in prewar Japan: Estimation and analysis)'. *Keizai Kenkyu* (Economic Review), 45(3). Tokyo: Economic Research Institute, Hitotsubashi University.

Minami, Ryoshin. 1996. *Nihon no Keizaihatten to Shotokubunpu* (Economic growth and income distribution in Japan). Economic Research Monograph 45, Hitotsubashi University. Tokyo: Iwanami Shoten.

Miyamoto, Matao. 1988. *Kinsei Nihon no Shijyo Keizai* (Market economies in modern Japan). Tokyo: Yuhikaku.

Mizoguchi, Hiroyuki, and Terasaki Yasuhiro. 1995. 'Kakei no Shotokubunpu hendo no Keizai Shakai oyobi Sangyokozo-teki Yoin (Changes in household income distribution in relation to socioeconomic and industrial structure)'. *Keizai Kenkyu* (Economic Review) 46 (1). Tokyo: Economic Research Institute, Hitotsubashi University.

Nishikawa, Shunsaku. 1985. *Nihon Keizai no Seicho-shi* (History of growth in the Japanese economy). Tokyo: Toyo Keizai Shinpo Sha.

NKTG: Nochi Kaikaku Kiroku Iinkai, ed. 1951. *Nochi Kaikaku Tenmatsu Gaiyo* (Summary accounts of the land reform). Tokyo: Nosei Chosa Kai; reprint, Tokyo: Ochanomizu Shobo, 1977.

NKSS: Nochi Kaikaku Shiryo Hensan Iinkai, ed. 1982. *Nochi Kaikaku Shiryo Shusei* (Collected documents on land reform), vol. 14 GHQ/ESCAP documents. Tokyo: Nosei Chosa Kai, Ochanomizu Shobo.

Ohkawa, Kazushi, and Henry Rosovsky. 1973. *Japanese Economic Growth: Trend Acceleration in the Twentieth Century*. Stanford, California: Stanford University Press.

Oshima, Harry T. 1987. *Economic Growth in Monsoon Asia*. Tokyo: University of Tokyo Press.

Oshima, Harry T. 1993. *Strategic Processes in Monsoon Asia's Economic Development*. Baltimore: Johns Hopkins University Press.

Smith, T.C. 1959. *The Agrarian Origins of Modern Japan*. Stanford, California: Stanford University Press.

Teranishi, Juro. 1997. 'Rural sector and development policy: Another aspect of rapid growth with stability in East Asia'. Paper presented at the World Bank Workshop on Political Economy of Rural Development Strategies, 5–6 May 1997.

Tobata, Seiichi, and Kazushi Ohkawa. 1956. *Nihon no Keizai to Nogyo* (Japanese economy and agriculture) Upper Volume. Tokyo: Iwanami Shoten.

Todaro, M.P. 1997. *Economic Developmen,*. Sixth edition. London and New York: Longman.

Wada, R.O. 1975. 'Impact of economic growth on the size distribution of income: The postwar experience of Japan'. In *Income Distribution, Employment and Economic Development in Southeast and East Asia*, Vol. 2. Tokyo: Japan Economic Research Center; Manila: Council for Asian Manpower Studies.

Walinsky, L.J., ed. 1977. *Agrarian Reform as Unfinished Business: The Selected Papers of Wolf Ladejinsky*. Oxford: Oxford University Press.

UNDP. 1997. *Human Development Report 1997*. New York: Oxford University Press.

Wharton, C.R. 1969. *Subsistence Agriculture and Economic Development*. Chicago: Aldine.

Williamson, J.G. 1993. 'Human capital deepening, inequality, and demographic events along the Asia Pacific Rim'. In Naohiro Ogawa, Gavin W. Jones, and Jeffrey G. Williamson eds. *Human Resources in Development along the Asia-Pacific Rim*. Oxford: Oxford University Press.

World Bank. 1993. *The East Asian Miracle: Economic Growth and Public Policy*. Oxford: Oxford University Press.

World Bank. 1990. *World Development Report*. Oxford: Oxford University Press.

Annex: Tax Burden of the Farmland after the Land Tax Revision in Japan

The Land Tax Revision[32] set the annual national tax rate (T_N) initially at 3 per cent of the land value, allowed up to 1 per cent of the land value to be imposed as local tax (T_L) by village authorities. The land value of a farmland (V) was calculated by the following formula:

$$V = \left(aPY - \left(T_N + T_L\right) \cdot V\right) / r \tag{1}$$

where P and Y are the producer price of rice and the output of rice from the land, respectively. As 15 per cent of the output value was deducted as the cost for current inputs, such as seed, fertilizer and chemicals, a was set to 0.85 and aPY represents the annual gross value added obtained by farming on the land. The tax deducted gross value added, i.e., annual net income of the land, was discounted by 6 per cent of the discount rate (r).

Equation 1 can be rewritten as

$$V = aPY / \left(T_N + T_L + r\right) \tag{2}$$

which gives the land value as a taxable standard. Hence

$T_N = 0.03,\ T_L = 0.01,\ r = 0.06$ and $T_N + T_L + r = 0.1$. Equation 2 means the land value was set to ten times the annual gross value added.

Since the annual total tax payment is $\left(T_N + T_L\right) \cdot V$, the taxation rate (TR) is

$$TR = \left(T_N + T_L\right) \cdot V / aPY = \left(T_N + T_L\right) / \left(T_N + T_L + r\right) \tag{3}$$

Hence TR=0.4, which means the burden of the tax on the land was as high as 40 per cent of the gross value added, which was almost comparable to the tax rate during the Tokugawa era.

[32] This Annex draws on Nishikawa (1985).

Chapter 14

Rural Development, Income Distribution and Poverty Decline in Southeast Asia

Anne Booth

This chapter[1] is in four parts. The first sets out some key stylized facts of agricultural and rural development in Southeast Asia since the 1970s, and the second part summarizes recent research on poverty and income distribution in Southeast Asia, and presents a synthesis of the main findings. The third part relates these findings to the evidence on economic growth and structural transformation in several Southeast Asian countries, and contrasts the Southeast Asian experience with that of Taiwan and South Korea. The fourth part discusses lessons the Southeast Asian experience may have to offer African countries.

Agricultural Growth and Rural Development in Southeast Asia

It is well known that while arable land has been declining relative to population in most parts of the world since the 1950s, there are very striking differences in trends in agricultural output per capita. In most of Asia food output and total agricultural output per capita has been increasing, although the rate of growth have been faster in East Asia (including Southeast Asia) than in South Asia. In sub-Saharan Africa, by contrast, food output per capita has been declining since the mid-1970s (Platteau and Hayami, 1998: Table 12.2). The differences between the Asian and the African outcomes are in large part due to the different rates of population growth on the one hand, and different trends in yields growth on the other. Although food output per unit of arable land rose in much of Africa between 1963 and 1992, the rate of increase has been slower than in much of Asia, while rates of population growth have been considerably faster.

About these broad facts there can be little dispute. But a problem with much of the literature comparing agricultural development in Asia and Africa is that it is very aggregated. 'East Asia' is usually treated as one block, which ignores the very

[1] This chapter is a revised version of Booth (1998). It does not attempt to cover the years 1998–2002 in any detail, momentous although they have been for several countries in Southeast Asia.

considerable heterogeneity of a region that encompasses China, North and South Korea, Taiwan, Indonesia, Thailand, Vietnam, Laos, Cambodia, the Philippines, Malaysia, and Myanmar (Burma). One aim of this chapter is to explore the growth and distributional experiences of the major agricultural economies of Southeast Asia in detail in order to bring out both the differences within the region, and the differences between Southeast Asia and other parts of East Asia such as Taiwan. It will be shown that these differences are considerable, especially in their distributional outcomes. Rather than regarding the 'East Asian experience' as a universal success story, it will be argued that the record of agricultural and rural development policies is a very mixed one, producing both successes and failures. Indeed, even within countries, there are often marked disparities in outcomes between regions. This should not be surprising given the different bio-physical conditions in different parts of Southeast Asia and the very different policies pursued towards agriculture in both the colonial and the post-independence eras.

Following the classic paper by Myint (1967), it is often argued that the economies of Southeast Asia can be divided into the 'inward-looking' and the 'outward-looking', depending on the trade and exchange rate policies they have adopted, and their stance towards foreign investment, foreign aid and borrowing. In some respects this remains a useful distinction, but as far as agricultural policies are concerned it is probably more helpful to distinguish between those governments that have treated the agricultural sector mainly as a source of tax revenues, and those governments that have viewed it as an engine of growth, to be supported through subsidies and other policy interventions. But even this distinction frequently breaks down as most governments in Southeast Asia, in both colonial times and more recently, have adopted very different policies in different parts of the agricultural sector. Important export crops have been taxed through export taxes, which usually depressed the prices received by local producers, while at the same time other producers (or even the same producers) have been assisted through provision of infrastructure at low or zero prices, subsidized inputs and subsidized credit. Indeed it has been said with some justification that no country in Southeast Asia has pursued an integrated rural development policy. Rather, they have adopted an uncoordinated bundle of crop-specific policies, which have themselves often varied considerably over time.

The outcome of this very mixed approach towards agricultural and rural development since the mid 1970s is shown in Table 14.1. In per capita terms, agricultural output grew at close to, or over, two per cent per annum in most parts of Southeast Asia from 1974 to 1984. In Malaysia agricultural output growth in per capita terms accelerated over the decade from 1985 to 1996, but in the Philippines the poor growth performance of the earlier decade continued. Elsewhere in Southeast Asia there has been a trend towards slower growth in agricultural output per capita, although only in Laos has growth actually been negative. The reasons for the trends shown in Table 14.1 vary considerably by country. In Thailand, where a high proportion of agricultural output growth in the past has been due to the expansion of cultivated area, rather than to growth in yields, the slowdown of growth since the mid-1980s is in part attributable to the fact that there is now little land left with arable potential that is not already under some form of cultivation.[2] Furthermore the government has become alarmed at the rate of deforestation over the past three decades and is now trying to replant land that was earlier cleared for grazing or cultivation. Many Thai agricultural economists have urged that the government respond to these challenges by adopting policies designed to increase yields, especially for crops such as rice. In spite of some reforms through the 1980s that were intended to increase farm-gate prices and thus the profitability of using fertilizer and new varieties of seed, rice yields in Thailand remain well below those in most other parts of the region (Table 14.1).

Table 14.1 **Annual average growth of per capita agricultural output, 1974-1984 and 1985-1996**

	Average annual growth rate of per capita agricultural output		Paddy yields tons/ha. (average 1994–96)
	1974–1984	1985–96	
Indonesia	2.2	1.6	4.4
Laos	4.2	-0.5	2.6
Malaysia	1.0	1.3	3.1
Myanmar	2.8	0.7	3.2
Philippines	0.7	0.6	2.8
Thailand	1.8	0.7	2.4
Vietnam	2.8	2.4	3.6

Sources: *FAO Production Yearbooks*, 1985 (Vol. 39), 1996 (Vol. 50), Table 10.

Most other countries in Southeast Asia have been more successful in disseminating new yield-increasing technologies in smallholder agriculture, especially in the food crop sector[3]. Malaysia in particular has also had considerable success in increasing yields for smallholder tree crops such as rubber. Those countries that adopted the new rice varieties earliest (especially the Philippines) did experience rapid output growth but this slowed down once most farmers in well-irrigated areas were operating near the technology frontier. Further yields growth would have required investment in irrigation and through the 1980s successive governments in the Philippines were unable to make such investments (Balisacan, 1989). In Indonesia the rapid adoption of new rice and corn varieties led to rapid growth of output but again output growth slowed once farmers operating in the more favourable bio-physical environments had achieved maximum yields. In Vietnam, where dissemination of new rice varieties only occurred in the 1980s, and where government reforms after 1986 gave much greater production responsibility to

[2] A detailed examination of the sources of growth in the rice sector in different parts of Asia between 1930 and 1980 is given in Barker and Herdt (1985: 46–53).

[3] For discussions of agricultural policy and its effects in the 1970s and 1980s in Thailand, Malaysia and the Philippines respectively see Siamwalla and Setboonsarng (1991), Jenkins and Lai (1991), and Intal and Power (1991).

individual households, output growth per capita has been sustained at a high rate through the 1990s.

While there is broad agreement about the main causes of agricultural output growth in Southeast Asia since the 1970s, there has been far more debate about the consequences of that growth for income distribution and poverty decline in rural areas. Has agricultural growth led to growing disparities in income and wealth within rural areas? Or has the sluggish performance in the agricultural sector since the mid-1980s in rapidly industrializing countries such as Indonesia, Malaysia and Thailand led to greater polarization between urban and rural areas? To what extent has rapid growth in the non-agricultural sectors created more off-farm employment opportunities for farm households, especially for the poorer groups in rural areas, as happened in Taiwan? And what have been the consequences for the proportion of the rural populations living below the poverty line? In fact the evidence indicates that the answers to these questions in Southeast Asia vary considerably by country and by region.

Trends in Poverty and Income Distribution in Southeast Asia: A Synthesis of Recent Research

Comparing income distribution across countries is extremely difficult, as data are often derived from different sources, which are not directly comparable. Even where data are derived from household income and expenditure surveys (HIES) that are broadly similar in design, the results are often flawed because of under-enumeration of some social groups or regions. Within Southeast Asia, the data most frequently used for estimating indicators of inequality in the distribution of income or expenditure are from household income and expenditure surveys. Ahuja et al. (1997: Table 3.2) estimated Gini coefficients from a number of HIES in Southeast Asia; for several countries they compared data from two points in time. Their results show a very mixed picture, with considerable variations in the Gini coefficient both across countries and over time. Only in Thailand was there evidence of a marked increase in expenditure inequalities; in other countries in the region the Gini coefficient has either stayed roughly constant or declined.[4] There was a tendency for inequality to be lower in the poorest countries in the region (the Lao PDR and Vietnam), although there was little difference between Vietnam and Indonesia, despite Indonesia's per capita GDP being over twice as high in the mid-1990s.

The Gini coefficients reported in Ahuja et al. (1997) are of course national averages, and in the larger countries disguise considerable regional variations. In Indonesia, the Central Bureau of Statistics has published estimates of the Gini coefficient of per capita consumption expenditures by province over the 1990s. In

[4] A recent, as yet unpublished, study by two economists at the Thai Development Research Institute (TDRI) estimates that the Gini coefficient of household incomes rose from 0.43 to 0.54 between 1975 and 1992. Since 1992 it has been roughly constant.

1996 estimates varied from 0.36 in Jakarta to 0.25 in Jambi in Sumatra.[5] In reality the difference in income distribution between urban and rural areas in Indonesia may be greater than the estimates from HIES show, as many experts consider that the HIES consistently under enumerate income and expenditures of the upper income groups in urban areas, while many among the urban poor may not be enumerated at all if they lack official urban residence cards. The tendency for the Gini coefficient to be higher in more urbanized regions is also evident in the Philippines (Balisacan, 1993: Table 3). But in Thailand, the data from the 1988 HIES indicate that the Gini coefficient is lower in the Bangkok region than in the poorer and far more rural regions of the North and Northeast (Tinakorn, 1995: Table 10.5). This might be due to the abundance of relatively well paid factory and service sector jobs in the Bangkok region compared with, for example, the North, where access to lucrative non-agricultural employment is more limited and many people still depend on agriculture for the bulk of their income.

Trends in Regional Income Disparities

Inter-personal disparities in income and expenditures are only one aspect of income inequality in Southeast Asia. Much research has been carried out on the extent of regional inequalities and their changes over time. In Indonesia a number of studies have estimated changes over time in the population-weighted coefficient of variation of provincial GDP and provincial consumption expenditures.[6] The study by Akita and Lukman (1995) shows that inter-provincial variations in per capita GDP declined considerably between 1975 and 1992, largely because of stagnating oil production. This has meant that since the mid-1970s, per capita GDP in the oil-rich provinces has been growing more slowly than for the country as a whole, and far more slowly than in those provinces (mainly Java-Bali) that have benefited from the rapid growth of the manufacturing sector and the modern service sector. As these tended to be relatively poor provinces in the mid 1970s, the overall disparity in provincial GDP has narrowed.

Virtually all the work on regional disparities in Indonesia has been carried out at the provincial level, but recently the Central Bureau of Statistics released a comprehensive set of regional GDP data at the district *(kabupaten/kotamadya)* level for Indonesia. Given that the three largest provinces in Indonesia each have populations in excess of 30 million people, it is important to investigate the extent of intra-provincial disparities. Preliminary analysis indicates that they are substantial and in some provinces have been increasing over time, especially in Java where the concentration of industrial growth in large connurbations surrounding Jakarta and Surabaya and the development of other industrial centres (such as the port of

[5] Expenditure for Consumption of Indonesia per Province (Jakarta: Central Bureau of Statistics, 2000: 27).

[6] Often referred to as the Williamson coefficient, as the technique was first used to estimate regional income disparities by Williamson (1965).

Cilacap on the south coast of Central Java) have inevitably led to some increase in intra-provincial disparities in GDP. The emergence of such disparities is an inevitable consequence of the industrialization process but it will just as inevitably lead to movements of people away from the relatively stagnant rural areas towards the large connurbations where jobs in both manufacturing and the service sector are more plentiful.

In Thailand, a large literature has accumulated over the years on regional disparities in development and in particular on the gap between the Greater Bangkok region and the Northeast region. However, recent work indicates that by the latter part of the 1990s, 'the overwhelming share of inequality in Thailand arises due to income variations across individuals residing within the same region—not differences in mean income across regions (World Bank, 2001: 28). The implications of this finding for policies are clear; although reducing inequalities between regions will have some effect on overall inequality, it is much more important to tackle those factors that lead to high levels of inter-personal inequality within regions.

Trends in Urban–Rural Disparities

Urban–rural disparities in household income and expenditures in most parts of Southeast Asia are substantial and in several countries appear to have been increasing over time. In most parts of Southeast Asia for which data are available there has been an increase in the disparity between GDP per capita in the capital city and in the country as a whole (Table 14.2). In Thailand and Indonesia in the mid-1990s per capita GDP in Bangkok and Jakarta was over three times as high as the national average, while in Indonesia and the Philippines per capita consumption expenditures in the capital were more than double those of the country as a whole. In Vietnam the disparity in consumption expenditures between Hanoi and the national average was only 37 per cent but it was much higher for Ho Chi Minh City (Saigon).

There are several reasons for the wide (and often increasing) gap between capital cities and the national average, both in GDP and in per capita consumption expenditures, in Southeast Asia. The capital city is of course the seat of government and the great majority of politicians and senior civil servants are located there.[7] In addition, most large companies, whether domestic, multinational or joint venture, have their national head offices in the capital city, and thus a high proportion of senior managers are to be found there. Capital cities usually have a large number of high schools, universities, hospitals, and research institutes and laboratories, and thus attract a disproportionate number of highly skilled professsionals. In Southeast Asia most capital cities are either ports or located close to

[7] It is not true that the majority of civil servants are located in the capital city; in Indonesia only 9.4 per cent of the estimated 4 million permanent civil servants are located in Jakarta. But a much higher proportion of the senior ones are in the capital, while many of those in the regions are relatively poorly paid teachers, health workers, etc.

ports and have better transport infrastructure, and so attract a disproportionate number of manufacturing industries. The extreme example is the Bangkok Metropolitan Region, which in the late 1980s accounted for 78 per cent of all manufacturing value added in Thailand. This concentration of the fastest growing sector of the economy in one region inevitably led to a faster growth of GDP and of personal incomes in the Bangkok region. Tinakorn (1995: Table 10.5) estimated that the Bangkok region accounted for less than 15 per cent of the total population in 1988, but 32 per cent of total household income.

Table 14.2 Ratio of per capita GDP and personal consumption expenditures (PCE) in capital city to national average

	GDP	PCE
Philippines		
1984	2.7	1.80
1994	2.49	2.05
Indonesia		
1984	2.29	2.07
1994	3.70	2.34 (1993)
Thailand		
1984	2.90	1.70 (1981)
1994	3.41 (1993)	1.74
Malaysia		
1987	1.74 (1988)	1.67[a]
Vietnam		
1993	n.a	1.37 (2.60)[b]

Notes:
a Peninsular Malaysia only
b Figure in brackets shows the ratio of personal consumption expenditure in Ho Chi Minh City (Saigon) to the national average.
Sources: National income accounts and HIES from the countries shown, as reported in Statistical Yearbooks, and national planning documents.

Trends in Sectoral Productivity Disparities

A further aspect of inequality in Southeast Asia that is related to urban–rural inequalities concerns the ratio of agricultural productivity (output per worker) to non-agricultural productivity, or the share of agricultural value added in GDP divided by the ratio of the agricultural labour force to the total labour force (Table 14.3). There are very considerable variations in this ratio across Southeast Asia, and also in the extent to which it has changed over time, that reflect differences in both the agricultural share of GDP and the agricultural share of the labour force. With the exception of Myanmar (Burma), every country in the region has experienced a decline in both these shares since the early 1970s. But the rates of decline in the output and labour force shares have been far from uniform. By 1994 Thailand still had 56 per cent of its labour force in agriculture, but only 11.5 per cent of GDP accrued from agriculture, so that productivity per worker in agriculture was only 21 per cent of output per worker in the economy as a whole. In Malaysia the decline in the agricultural share of its GDP between 1970 and 1990 was accompanied by a larger decline in the agricultural share of the labour force, so that output per worker in agriculture in 1990 was 72 per cent of the national average.

Table 14.3 Ratio of agricultural output per agricultural worker to average output per worker in Southeast Asian economies

	Agricultural productivity ratio	Percentage of GDP from agriculture	Percentage of the labour force in agriculture
Philippines			
1971	0.59	29.6	50.4
1994	0.49	22.4	46.1
Burma			
1976/77	0.73	47.5	65.3
1993/94	0.97	63.2	65.2
Vietnam			
1994	0.40	28.7	72.2
Malaysia			
1970	0.60	31.4	52.6
1990	0.72	18.6	26.0
Indonesia			
1971	0.67	43.6	64.8
1994	0.37	17.3	46.1
Thailand			
1971	0.36	28.6	79.2
1994	0.21	11.5	56.0

Source: National accounts data, as published in Statistical Yearbooks and Labour Force Surveys.

Given that output per agricultural worker in Thailand is such a small proportion of average output per worker in the economy as a whole, it is hardly surprising that rural–urban income disparities are high, and that overall household income inequalities have increased over the years of rapid GDP growth. Of course it can be argued that many agricultural households in Thailand, and in other parts of Southeast Asia, are deriving a substantial part of their incomes from non-agricultural sources and from remittances from family members working in cities, and this mitigates the impact of low agricultural incomes. This argument is examined further in the next section. It can also be argued, with some plausibility, that the agricultural labour force in Thailand is overstated relative to other countries in the region, not least because of the very high numbers of women reported as working in agriculture as unpaid family workers. But even allowing for these factors, there can be little doubt that economic growth in Thailand over the past four decades has exhibited a high degree of urban bias. The reasons for this are discussed further below.

Trends in the Distribution of Wealth

Almost all the discussion of economic inequalities in Southeast Asia has been concerned with inequalities in the distribution of household income and expenditures. This, of course, reflects the fact that data on both are available for most countries in the regions from HIES, often for more than one point in time. There has been relatively little scholarly discussion on trends in the distribution of wealth, because it is so difficult to get any reliable information. Wealth taxes are not levied anywhere in the region and although the Malaysian government has monitored trends in share ownership by ethnic group since the early 1970s, such information tells us nothing about the distribution of share ownership within ethnic groups and how it might have changed over time. Critics of the New Economic Policy in Malaysia point out that although there has been an increase in the total value of share capital owned by indigenous Malay (*bumiputera*) groups, most of these shares are in fact controlled either by a few politically well-connected individuals, or by holding companies closely connected to the ruling party.[8]

The lack of good data on the distribution of wealth in Southeast Asia has not prevented a lively discussion emerging in the press and in the scholarly community about the emergence of large conglomerates controlled by individuals and families whose personal wealth, while difficult to measure with accuracy, is considered to run to hundreds of millions, or in some cases, billions of dollars. Certainly there can be little doubt that the number of multi-millionaires in many parts of the region is growing, although the absolute numbers are still small. Considerable excitement was generated in Indonesia in the late 1980s when a list of the 40 largest domestic conglomerates was published in a leading Jakarta business magazine. A very high proportion were controlled by Indonesians of Chinese descent, many of whom were closely connected with senior politicians. Most of the rest were controlled by members of the President's immediate family. In Thailand, Malaysia and the Philippines, it is also the case that a high proportion of

---

[8] See Jomo (1990) for an elaboration of this argument.

the large conglomerates are controlled by ethnic Chinese, many of whom enjoy close ties with leading politicians.[9]

The emergence of powerful conglomerates controlled by ethnic Chinese, together with the growing numbers of 'crony capitalists' who owe their wealth to their ability to exploit family connections has led some commentators to claim that capitalism in Southeast Asia is 'ersatz', and has no real roots in indigenous society (Yoshihara, 1988). Certainly there can be little doubt that the presence of very wealthy Chinese families in what are still quite poor societies gives rise to tensions, especially in Indonesia where religious differences further accentuate the gap between the wealthy Chinese and the mass of the indigenous population. Of course not all Chinese are wealthy and, throughout Southeast Asia, there are millions of small Chinese businesspeople who may not be much better off than many indigenous urban dwellers. But at the same time it is often difficult to separate discussion of inequalities in wealth from a more overtly racist debate over the disproportionate share of private sector assets alleged to be controlled by the Chinese.

The declining share of GDP accounted for by agriculture in most parts of the region has meant that in recent years little attention has been paid to inequalities of wealth in rural areas. This is perhaps unfortunate as data on the distribution of agricultural land are available from agricultural censuses and surveys for several countries, but little attempt has been made to compare them on a systematic basis. It has frequently been argued in the literature that the Philippines has a much more skewed distribution of land than other parts of Southeast Asia; indeed a common argument is that the Philippines has a 'Latin American' distribution of land rather than an 'Asian' one.

In fact, an examination of the data on the distribution of holdings by size in Thailand, Indonesia and the Philippines from the Agricultural Censuses of 1978, 1983 and 1980, respectively, indicates that while there is a smaller proportion of total land in holdings under one hectare in the Philippines than in Indonesia, there is not a great difference in the proportion of total land in holdings over ten hectares (Table 14.4). The Indonesian distribution is a bimodal one, with over half the land in holdings under three hectares, and a further 20 per cent in holdings over ten hectares. This distribution evolved over time as a result of the emergence of large estates on the one hand, and population pressure leading to land fragmentation, on the other. In all three Southeast Asian countries, the distribution of land is very different from that in Taiwan, where in 1975 almost 80 per cent of agricultural land was in holdings under three hectares. The implications of this difference are discussed further in the next section.

[9] See Yoshihara (1988) and Hill (1996: 107–110) for a discussion of the role of conglomerates in Indonesia. A valuable set of papers on the emergence of a local capitalist class in Southeast Asia can be found in McVey (1992).

Table 14.4 **Distribution of land by holding size: Philippines, Indonesia, Thailand and Taiwan**

Holding size	Philippines		Indonesia		Thailand	Taiwan	
(Hectares)	1971	1980	1973	1983	1978	1960	1975
Under 1.0	1.9	3.8	25.0	22.7	2.3	33.4	39.0
1–3	22.2	25.9	32.6	35.3	19.3	51.5	48.0
3–5	23.7	21.2	11.1	12.9	17.8	10.5	9.2
5–10 [a]	18.3	23.1	8.8	9.8	36.3	4.6	3.8
Over 10	33.9	26.0	22.5	19.3	24.3		
TOTAL	100.0	100.0	100.0	100.0	100.0	100.0	100.0

Notes: a. Data for Taiwan include land in all holdings over five hectares.
Source: Ranis and Stewart (1993: Table 10); Censuses of Agriculture for Thailand, Indonesia and the Philippines.

Declining Incidence of Poverty

Poverty estimates have been made for a number of Southeast Asian countries since the 1950s. Household income and expenditure surveys (HIES) with a reasonable national coverage were first carried out in the Philippines and Peninsular Malaysia in the 1950s, and in Thailand, Indonesia, and Singapore in the 1960s. In these five countries HIES have been carried out at regular intervals since then so that it is possible to monitor trends in poverty over three decades. The most common approach adopted by scholars and government agencies was to set a national poverty line and measure the number of households or individuals that fell beneath that line (the head-count measure). As other approaches to the measurement of poverty have been developed in the theoretical literature, these have been applied in Southeast Asia, although the head-count measure remains the most widely used, especially in the official literature.

The incidence of poverty is the result of the average level of household income or expenditure on the one hand, and its distribution on the other. In those economies where real per capita household incomes/expenditures have been rising over time, the incidence of poverty is likely to have fallen, unless inequalities have increased substantially. As we have seen, inequalities have indeed been increasing in some Southeast Asian economies and this has mitigated the impact of household expenditure growth on poverty decline. But in the economies for which we have reliable data since the 1960s, the evidence indicates that real per capita consumption expenditures have been growing in real terms, and this offers prima facie grounds for expecting that the head-count incidence of poverty has fallen (Table 14.5). The data suggest that at least since the 1970s, the decline should have been particularly rapid in Singapore, Thailand, Malaysia and Indonesia, as these are the countries where growth in household expenditures have been most rapid.

Table 14.5 Annual average growth in real per capita consumption expenditures[a]

	1950–59	1960–69	1970–79	1980–92
Myanmar[b]	2.9	1.0	1.5	-0.1
Indonesia	n.a.	0.8	5.6	2.5
Malaysia	n.a.	n.a.	4.3	2.3
Philippines	3.8	1.8	2.1	0.6
Singapore	n.a.	2.3	4.8	4.4
Thailand	n.a.	4.7	3.5	4.7
Vietnam	n.a.	n.a.	n.a.	3.0[c]

Notes: a. Calculated by fitting an exponential trend to the annual data.
b. Data refer to the financial years from 1961/62 to 1969/70, 1970/71 to 1979/80 and 1980/81 to 1989/90. Per capita consumption expenditures given in the source documents include both private and government consumption.
c. Data refer to 1986–1990. Per capita consumption expenditures given in the source documents include both private and government consumption.
Sources:
Burma: 1950/1 to 1959/60: Government Printing and Stationery Office, *Economic Survey*, 1958, 1960, 1962; 1961/2 to 1991/92: Ministry of Planning and Finance, *Report to the Pyithu Hluttaw*, various issues between 1977/78 and 1985/86; Ministry of Planning and Finance, *Review of the Financial Economic and Social Conditions for 1992/93*
Thailand: National Statistical Office, *Statistical Yearbook of Thailand*, various issues. Office of the National Economic and Social Development Board, *National Income of Thailand (New Series), 1970–87; National Income of Thailand Rebase Series 1980–1991*
Indonesia. 1960–79, Central Bureau of Statistics, *National Income of Indonesia*, 1960–68, 1969–73, 1973–78, 1975–80. After 1980, unpublished data from World Bank sources were used.
Vietnam: *Vietnam Economy 1986-91 Based on the System of National Accounts*, Statistical Publishing House, 1992; *Statistical Yearbook 1995*, Hanoi: Statistical Publishing House
Malaysia: Department of Statistics, *Yearbook of Statistics*, 1984, 1989, 1993 Ministry of Finance, *Economic Report*, vols. 5–22
Singapore: Department of Statistics, *Yearbook of Statistics, Singapore*, various years; Department of Statistics, *Economic and Social Statistics, Singapore*. 1960–82
Philippines: 1950–72: National Economic and Development Authority, *Philippine National Income Series Number 5, The National Income Accounts CY 1946–75 (Link series)*, 1973–89, National Statistical Coordination Board, *Philippine Statistical Yearbook 1990, 1994*.

A useful set of estimates of the head-count measure of poverty in Asia have recently been provided by the World Bank (Ahuja et al., 1997: Table 2.1). These estimates have the merit of being at least roughly comparable across countries, in that they are calculated on the basis of a uniform poverty line of one US dollar per day, adjusted for differences in the price level. They confirm that in Malaysia,

Thailand and Indonesia both the head-count and poverty-gap measures of poverty have declined since the 1970s, and the absolute numbers of poor people have also declined. In the Philippines, where growth in per capita consumption expenditures was much slower in the 1970s and 1980s, there has been some decline in the head-count measure of poverty, but the absolute numbers of poor people increased between 1975 and 1993. The use of a low poverty line of one dollar a day gives an estimate of the head-count measure of poverty of under 1 per cent in the more affluent countries (Malaysia and Thailand), compared with 26 per cent in the Philippines.

A considerable literature on poverty measurement exists in all these countries, and in most of them several different poverty lines have been proposed.[10] But the finding that the incidence of poverty has declined is quite robust, regardless of the poverty line used. The poverty estimates prepared by the Central Bureau of Statistics in Indonesia show a continual decline in the head-count measure, and in the numbers of poor in both urban and rural areas between 1976 and 1996 (Booth, 2000: Table 3). The official estimates of poverty in Malaysia contained in the planning documents also show a steady decline since the 1970s; this finding is accepted even by those who argue that the poverty lines used in the official estimates may not have been comparable over time (Jomo, 1990: 145–54). The estimates of the incidence of poverty in the Philippines prepared by the National Statistical Coordination Board also show a decline between 1988 and 1994, although outside the national capital region, the decline was insufficiently rapid to prevent the number of households below the poverty line from rising.[11] Although there has been criticism of the official poverty estimates in both Malaysia and Indonesia, all independent estimates concur that there has in fact been a decline in the incidence of poverty, whatever the poverty measure used.[12]

Poverty in Urban and Rural Areas

The World Bank study referred to above argues that poverty in most parts of Asia is predominantly a rural problem. According to their estimates, in Malaysia, Indonesia and Thailand, well over 80 per cent of the poor were located in rural areas in the late 1980s or early 1990s (Ahuja et al., 1997: Table 2.4). But this finding depends crucially on the poverty line used; the poverty estimates prepared by the Central Bureau of Statistics (CBS) in Indonesia show that by 1996, some 31 per cent of the poor were in urban areas. The CBS estimates for urban Indonesia in

---

[10] In Malaysia, Thailand and the Philippines, the poverty lines used in official analyses of poverty are considerably higher than the dollar a day line used by the World Bank. Thus the incidence of poverty is higher than that shown in Ahuja et al. (1997).

[11] The official data on poverty in the Philippines are published in the annual publication, *Philippines Statistical Yearbook* (Manila: National Statistical Coordination Board). A critique of the official figures is provided by Balisacan (1997).

[12] See Jomo (1990: 145ff) for a discussion of the Malaysian estimates; Booth (1993) examines the literature on poverty measurement in Indonesia.

1996 were prepared on the basis of an urban poverty line that was 40 per cent higher than the rural one. Whether in fact this is a true reflection of the difference in cost of a basket of basic needs between urban and rural areas in Indonesia is a matter of some controversy. Certainly there can be little doubt that the cost of location-specific goods and services (housing, health care, education, transport) is higher in urban areas but whether the differential is sufficient to justify the difference in the poverty line is far from clear. In contrast to the CBS poverty line for Indonesia, the official poverty line for Malaysia was the same in both urban and rural areas, although higher in Sabah and Sarawak than in West Malaysia.[13]

Although it is obvious that a higher urban poverty line, relative to the rural one, will lead to a higher proportion of the poor being located in urban areas, it should be stressed that the basic finding of the World Bank, that poverty in Asia is predominantly rural, remains robust, even when a higher urban poverty line is used. Even in a region such as Java, where the rural population declined in absolute terms, at least until 1998, and urbanization has proceeded rapidly, the Central Bureau of Statistics found that 60 per cent of the poor were still located in rural areas in 1996. Of course this could well change in the early decades of the next century. Indeed, the issue of the appropriate way to estimate urban and rural poverty lines in Asia remains a difficult one, and its resolution will obviously affect the direction poverty policies take in coming decades. At the moment the attention of most governments in the region is still on rural poverty, but as urbanization proceeds, and a higher proportion of the poor are located in urban and urban-fringe areas, it is likely that urban poverty alleviation policies will be given greater priority.

Poverty and Ethnicity

A sensitive issue in several parts of Southeast Asia relates to the ethnic composition of the poor. Often there are deep economic and cultural divides between indigenous and migrant populations. Certainly these divisions concern the Chinese minorities, but the Chinese dimension is only one among several. In the East Malaysian state of Sabah, for example, and in the contiguous Indonesian province of East Kalimantan, there are deep cultural, religious and economic divisions between the indigenous populations and migrants from West Malaysia and Java. For obvious political reasons, most governments in Southeast Asia have been reluctant to present poverty estimates broken down by ethnicity; only in Malaysia have such estimates been a routine feature of official poverty analysis since the 1970s. As would be expected, the incidence of poverty among the Malay population has been higher than among the Chinese or the Indians, and these disparities remained large in spite of the overall decline in the incidence of poverty between the 1970s and the 1990s. Indeed the percentage of the poor accounted for by Malays increased between 1970 and 1987 (Table 14.6). In the East Malaysian state of Sabah, the incidence of poverty in 1989 was higher among the indigenous

[13] See Government of Malaysia (1994: 59) for details.

ethnic groups than among either the Malays or the Chinese, although the highest incidence of poverty was found among Philippine immigrant households, who accounted for 11.6 per cent of all households but 16.5 per cent of all poor households (Hashim, 1995: Table VII-29).

Table 14.6 **Poverty incidence and breakdown of poor households in Peninsular Malaysia by race, 1970–1987**

	Malay	Chinese	Indian	Others	Total
Incidence of poverty (% of households below the poverty line)					
TMP 1970	64.8	26.0	39.2	44.8	49.3
Anand 1970[a]	51.4	14.7	24.8	40.3	n.a
Shari 1973	63.4	29.7	39.9	42.9	49.7
Shari 1973 (EPU)	51.2	17.8	25.7	28.6	37.5
FMP 1976	46.4	17.4	27.3	33.8	35.1
HES 1980 (EPU)	33.1	10.6	11.4	27.0	23.4
MTRFMP 1984	25.8	7.8	10.1	22.0	18.4
MTRFMP 1987	23.8	7.1	9.7	24.3	17.3
Percentage distribution of poor households					
TMP 1970	73.8	17.2	7.9	1.1	100.0
Anand 1970[a]	78.1	12.9	8.0	1.0	100.0
Shari 1973	71.5	19.8	8.1	0.6	100.0
Shari 1973 (EPU)	76.7	15.8	6.9	0.5	100.0
FMP 1976	75.5	15.9	7.8	0.8	100.0
HES 1980 (EPU)	78.9	15.1	4.7	1.2	100.0
MTRFMP 1984	80.4	13.6	5.2	0.7	100.0
MTRFMP 1987	81.0	12.7	5.5	0.8	100.0

Notes: a. Calculated using the $25 per capita per month poverty line.
Sources: *Third Malaysia Plan*, Table 9.6; Anand (1983), Table 4.3; Shari (1979), Table 3; *Fourth Malaysia Plan*, Table 3.5; *Report of the 1980-2 Household Expenditure Survey*; *Mid-term Review, Fifth Malaysia Plan*, Table 3.7.

Poverty by Educational Attainment

In Southeast Asia, as in most other parts of the world, there is a strong positive correlation between income and education. Household surveys show that the higher the education level of the household head, the higher the household income. Thus the incidence of poverty declines sharply by educational level of household head (Ahuja et al., 1997: 85–87). There is also a strong correlation between household income and participation in education, especially at the post-primary level. In

1989 in Indonesia only 1.9 per cent of children aged 16–18 in the poorest decile of the population (according to expenditure) were enrolled in senior high school; the enrollment rate for the top decile was 69 per cent (Ahuja et al., 1997: Table 2.5). In Thailand in 1985, most (96 per cent) children aged 13 to 18 from professional and business homes were enrolled in secondary schools but only 14.5 per cent of children from farm households (Myers and Chalongphob, 1992: Table 4.3). The surge in post-primary enrolments in Thailand over the 1990s led to greater participation by children from lower income households in secondary and vocational education, but the percentage of university students drawn from the lowest income quintile barely increased (World Bank, 2001: 34–5).

Thus even in those parts of Southeast Asia that have seen rapid growth in post-primary enrolments in the 1990s, participation in higher education is still very much a function of income, while lifetime earnings are still much higher for tertiary graduates. The tight link between education and income operates mainly through occupational choice; tertiary qualifications are necessary to gain access to most professional, technical and administrative occupations and these are usually the most highly remunerated. And as the Thai data make clear, children of parents in these occupational groups are far more likely to be enrolled in universities than those from poor rural backgrounds.

Poverty and Gender

There is now a large literature on gender and poverty in many parts of the world. In advanced countries such as the USA there is strong evidence that the incidence of poverty is higher in female-headed households. But in Southeast Asia, the evidence indicates virtually no relationship between the gender of the household head and the incidence of poverty; in fact in most countries for which data are available, the incidence of poverty was higher in male-headed households (Ahuja et al., 1997: Table 2.10; World Bank, 2001: 43). In most parts of the region, female-headed household are a small percentage of the total; only in Vietnam do they account for more than 20 per cent. In those areas where many adult males regularly migrate to urban areas or abroad to find work, their wives, often in receipt of remittances that make the household relatively well off, become the temporary household heads.

It is quite possible that substantial intra-household gender inequalities exist in the allocation of food, clothing and access to education and health care, although on this issue as well the evidence suggests that male–female disparities are less glaring than in South Asia, West Asia and much of Africa.[14] Gender disparities in school enrollment rates are less pronounced in Southeast Asia than in many other parts of the developing world, and female infant and child mortality rates tend to be lower than for males. In addition son-preference is less marked in

[14] See UNDP (1997: 150ff) for more details on gender disparities by country.

Thai and Javanese cultures than in China or India, and there is very little evidence of abortion of female foetuses.[15]

Poverty by Region

The evidence for Thailand, Indonesia, the Philippines and Malaysia, and most recently Vietnam, all show very substantial regional disparities in the extent of poverty. Usually the head-count measure of poverty is lower in urban than rural areas, although this depends on the extent to which the urban and rural poverty lines differ. In Indonesia over the 1980s, the official poverty estimates show a higher incidence of poverty in urban areas, because of the much higher poverty line in use in urban areas. In Malaysia, where the same poverty line is used throughout the country (except in Sabah and Sarawak), the incidence of poverty in the latter part of the 1980s was higher in predominantly rural states such as Kedah, Kelantan and Terengganu than in more highly urbanized ones such as Selangor and Penang.[16] In Thailand, the incidence of poverty has historically been much higher in the Northeast than in other regions, and lowest in the Bangkok region (Tinakorn, 1995: Table 10.6).

The reasons for these pronounced differences in the regional incidence of poverty are examined in more detail in the next section. As would be expected, the incidence of poverty by region in most Southeast Asian countries is highly correlated with average per capita consumption expenditures. But the correlation with per capita regional GDP is less good, especially in those countries such as Indonesia and Malaysia where large disparities in regional GDP arise from the presence of mining and other extractive industries. As the profits from these activities often do not stay in the region but flow to the central government, or to foreign companies, it is quite possible for states or provinces with high per capita GDP relative to the national average to also have high incidences of poverty.

In Indonesia the province of Irian Jaya had a per capita GDP 1995 that was 60 per cent higher than the national average, but the head-count incidence of poverty (as estimated by the CBS) was almost twice as high as the national average in 1996, and indeed higher than in any other province except West Kalimantan and East Timor[17]. The oil and timber rich Indonesian province of East Kalimantan has a per capita GDP comparable to the contiguous Malaysian states of Sabah and Sarawak, but the average per capita household expenditure was much lower, and thus the incidence of poverty was much higher (Table 14.7). And within Malaysia, the incidence of poverty in the state of Terengganu (where there are substantial off-shore oil fields) in 1987 was estimated to be 36 per cent compared with the

[15] See Wongboonsin and Ruffolo (1995) for a discussion of sex preferences in Thailand, Indonesia and the Philippines, as well as in other parts of Southeast Asia.

[16] See Government of Malaysia (1989: Table 3.4).

[17] Another set of regional poverty lines for Indonesia was generated by Bidani and Ravallion (1993). They use a rather different poverty line, but also show that several provinces outside Java have a higher headcount measure of poverty than the provinces of Java.

national average of 17.3 per cent, despite a per capita GDP that was over 50 per cent above the national average.[18]

Table 14.7 Poverty, per capita expenditure and per capita GDP in Indonesian provinces and Malaysian states, 1995–1997

	Percentage below the Malaysian poverty line[a]		GDP per capita (US$)
	1995	1997	1995
Sabah	26.2	22.1	2,518
Sarawak	10.0	7.5	3,350
Kedah	12.1	11.5	2,591
Johor	3.2	1.6	3,879
	Percentage below the Malaysian poverty line (1996)		GDP per capita 1995
	100%	50%	
Aceh	89.0	40.6	1,493
Riau	76.5	23.6	2,380
East Kalimantan	76.5	33.7	4,100

Notes: a. Poverty lines as reported in Government of Malaysia (1999), The Sabah poverty line, converted at the 1996 exchange rate, is used to calculate the incidence of poverty in East Kalimantan. The Peninsular Malaysia poverty line is used to estimate the incidence of poverty in Aceh and Riau.

Sources: GDP data for states of Malaysia from Government of Malaysia (1999: Table 2.7); Poverty data from Government of Malaysia (1999: Table 3.2). GDP data for provinces of Indonesia from Central Bureau of Statistics (1998: Table 11.1). Poverty estimates made using data from Central Bureau of Statistics (1997: Table 10.2.11).

The Impact of Accelerated Growth and Structural Transformation on Poverty and Inequality

Having examined the evidence on trends in poverty and distribution in Southeast Asia in recent decades, I now turn to the literature on the causal factors involved. Given that for a constant distribution of income, poverty decline is a function of income growth, we would expect that the faster average household incomes or expenditures rise, the faster poverty is likely to decline. Broadly, this seems to have been true in Southeast Asia, although as Ahuja et al. (1997: Table D1) point out, there has been considerable variation in the elasticity of change in the head-count measure of poverty with respect to changes in the mean consumption in Southeast Asia in the two decades from 1975 to 1995. The elasticity was actually positive for Thailand between 1975 and 1985, indicating that rising incomes were associated with a rising head-count incidence of poverty. But between 1985 and 1995 the estimate was negative and almost two, showing that a given increase in mean

[18] Government of Malaysia (1989: Tables 3.4 and 3.5).

income led to a decline in poverty of twice the magnitude. The elasticity was negative and well above unity for Indonesia in this decade as well, but much lower in the Philippines.

In a purely statistical sense, the size of the elasticity depends on two factors, the density function near the poverty line, which determines the mass of people who can cross it when the cumulative frequency curve of the population by income group shifts to the right, and the changes in the distribution of income that occur during, and might induce, such a shift. The more the growth process is 'pro-poor' in the sense that those below the poverty line benefit more in terms of income growth than those above it, the greater the value of the elasticity. The estimates prepared by Ahuja et al. (1997) suggest that the growth process in Thailand switched from being very anti-poor in 1975–1985 to being very pro-poor in 1985–1995, while that in Indonesia was pro-poor in both decades but more so in the latter one. What explains these differences? Given that most of the poor are located in rural areas in both Thailand and Indonesia, it seems reasonable to assume that changes in rural income growth must be an important explanation. I first discuss the relationship betwen agricultural growth and poverty decline in Southeast Asia, before going on to look at broader issues of linkages between urban and rural growth and their implications for rural income distribution and living standards.

The Relationship between Agricultural Growth and Poverty Decline

Several attempts have been made using cross-sectional regression analysis to examine the correlates of rural poverty by region in several countries in Southeast Asia. Balisacan (1993: Table 9) pooled 1985 and 1988 HIES data and regressed the incidence of rural poverty (both head-count and poverty-gap measures) by region in the Philippines on a number of explanatory variables including the size distribution of farm holdings, average farm size, the proportion of agricultural land irrigated, the incidence of tenancy, the degree of urbanization and the road density. The last two variables were considered proxies for access to markets and availability of off-farm employment. He also included a year dummy to reflect the macroeconomic difficulties in 1985. He found that only the land distribution variable and the year dummy were consistently significant in all his estimates. The average holding size was significant in some but not all of the estimating equations, while the irrigation variable was significant in the poverty gap regressions. He concluded that his findings supported the commonly held view in the Philippines that the more skewed the distribution of land, the higher the incidence of poverty, but did not offer much support for the argument that tenancy per se was an important determinant of poverty.

In a cross-sectional regression for Indonesia using 1993 data, Booth (2000: Table 11) found that average farm size, value added in smallholder agriculture per hectare, and the proportion of total agricultural value added in agriculture accruing from food crops together accounted for 63 per cent of the observed variation in rural poverty by province. The signs on the first two variables were negative, while that on the third variable was positive, indicating that the less diversified smallholder agriculture was, the higher rural poverty was likely to be. Both this result and that of Balisacan for the Philippines emphasized the importance of access to land as a determinant of rural poverty. Recent research on causes of poverty in Thailand also shows that average holding size is strongly negatively related to rural poverty (World Bank, 2001: 48).

These cross-sectional studies, while offering some useful evidence on the correlates of poverty by region, do not really help much in explaining trends in the incidence of poverty over time, or indeed why there appears to be little relationship in some parts of Southeast Asia, such as the Philippines, between agricultural growth and trends in rural poverty. It has already been shown that in most parts of Southeast Asia, growth of agricultural output in per capita terms has slowed since the mid-1980s compared with the years from 1974 to 1984 (Table 14.1). What impact has this trend had on poverty and income distribution in rural areas? There is evidence that when agricultural output actually contracts, as it did in 1985/86 in Thailand, the impact on rural poverty may be severe, regardless of trends in the rest of the economy.[19] In Indonesia the official figures published by the Central Bureau of Statistics show that the rate of decline in the numbers of rural poor slowed after 1984, compared with the years from 1976 to 1984. It is likely that this was related to the slowdown in agricultural growth, although the causal mechanisms are still far from clear.

On the other hand, a sustained increase in agricultural output does not necessarily lead to a commensurate decline in rural poverty. Certainly in the case of the Philippines in the period from 1965 to 1980, rapid growth in agricultural output was not in itself a sufficient condition for a decline in poverty. Bautista (1992: 38) contrasted the Philippine experience with that of Taiwan in the 1960s and 1970s when in spite of comparable growth in agricultural output, the extent of rural poverty in the Philippines did not decline at anything like the rate observed in Taiwan. Bautista argued that the inequitable sharing of the benefits from the new rice technologies, the lack of any technological progress in rain-fed rice or non-rice food crops, and the domination of export-oriented agriculture by large estates and multi-national food processing companies all contributed to the failure of agricultural growth to lead to more rapid poverty alleviation. At the same time, the continued emphasis in the industrial sector on import substitution behind high tariff and non-tariff barriers meant that non-agricultural employment growth was slow and concentrated in the Metro Manila area. The over-valuation of the peso discriminated against export producers in both agriculture and industry, and although the selective export incentives adopted during the 1970s did induce some expansion of exports, the resulting output growth was not rapid enough to compensate for slow domestic demand. In addition, the over-valued currency made adoption of labour-displacing agricultural technologies (such as chemical herbi-

[19] Value added in crop agriculture in Thailand contracted between 1985 and 1987, and only recovered in 1988. Total value added in agriculture was constant over these three years.

cides rather than manual weeding) privately profitable to many farmers, thus depriving rural labourers of employment opportunities.

The Philippine experience in the 1970s can be compared with that of Indonesia. During the oil boom the government protected the non-oil traded goods sectors in a variety of ways from the effects of 'Dutch disease'. The rice sector received substantial input subsidies (irrigation and fertilizer), while the manufacturing sector was heavily protected through tariffs and quantitative import restrictions. Because a large part of the oil revenues were absorbed domestically and used for a variety of government infrastructure projects, the construction sector grew rapidly, as did demand for transport and other services. This growth led to more employment opportunities for rural people, and these opportunities, combined with the rapid growth in rice production, resulted in rural expenditures increasing in Java by almost six per cent per annum in real per capita terms between 1976 and 1981 (Booth, 1992: Table 10.2). The rapid growth in real expenditures in Java was not accompanied by any marked deterioration in distribution so the incidence of poverty in rural Java declined rapidly over these years.

Changing Employment Patterns, Income Diversification, Urban–Rural Linkages and Poverty Decline

Bautista's discussion of the impact of agricultural growth and diversification on poverty decline in the Philippines indicates that broader economy-wide policies can play a crucial role in determining the impact of a given rate of economic growth on rural incomes. An important channel through which developments in other parts of the economy affect the agricultural sector is through the provision of off-farm employment opportunities in rural areas, a topic that has generated a considerable literature in Southeast Asia in recent years.[20] In their study of linkages between the agricultural and non-agricultural sectors in the Philippines, Ranis et al. (1990: 76–7) stressed that agricultural output does increase rural non-agricultural employment, while at the same time 'increasing the extent and modernization of rural nonagricultural activity raises agricultural productivity by changing attitudes and incentives, improving markets, and improving supplies of inputs'.

They went on to argue that:

> ...for linkages in both directions, the extent of linkage effects depends not only on the quantity of employment and production in each sector, but also on the nature of sectoral output. In the case of agriculture to industry linkages, the extent of rural nonagricultural activity is influenced by the income distribution arising in agriculture. A more egalitarian agriculture generally absorbs more labor into agriculture and consequently increases the total level of consumption linkages and also the extent to which consumption expenditure is met by local production of appropriate goods, instead of imports or the centralized production of elite goods.

[20] See in particular the papers in Mukhopadhyay and Lim (1985) and Shand (1986).

> Labor absorption in agriculture also depends on the extent of agricultural mechanization and the crop composition of output.
>
> ....For industry-to-agriculture linkages, the evidence presented in this study shows that it is necessary to differentiate between types of non-agricultural activity. Traditional nonagricultural activities...do not appear to have significant linkage effects in raising agricultural productivity. However, the presence of 'modern' nonagricultural activities in rural areas in the Philippines, as well as improved roads and greater proximity to urban centers, are associated with increases in agricultural productivity.

In a subsequent paper, Ranis and Stewart (1993) contrast the development of both types of linkages in Taiwan and the Philippines. They point out that the growth of rural non-agricultural employment was much faster in Taiwan than in the Philippines, and by 1980 some 67 per cent of the rural labour force in Taiwan was employed in non-agricultural activities. The comparable figure for the Philippines in 1985 was 33 per cent. They argue that the more egalitarian distribution of rural income in Taiwan compared with the Philippines meant that a smaller proportion of total rural expenditures went to imported goods or luxury goods made in urban areas. The rapid expansion of Taiwanese manufactured exports also served to boost rural incomes, in that a significant proportion were processed agricultural products and even those produced in export processing zones and bonded warehouses used locally produced inputs often supplied by small industries located in rural areas.

Thus 'Taiwan's macro and sectoral policies were favourable to strong rural linkages, with good agricultural growth, a relatively egalitarian land and rural distribution of income, the generous provision of rural infrastructure, as well as an export orientation which was substantially rural-based' (Ranis and Stewart, 1993: 98). As a result, over the years from 1962 to 1980, rural non-agricultural incomes in Taiwan grew over three times as fast as agricultural incomes.[21] In the Philippines in the two decades from 1965 to 1985, agricultural incomes grew almost as fast on an annualized basis as in Taiwan, but the growth of non-agricultural rural incomes was very much slower. Thus what Ranis and Stewart term the 'linkage ratio' was much lower in the Philippines. The more skewed distribution of income in the Philippines, combined with the more capital-intensive, urban-biased nature of the industrialization process, meant that a given amount of agricultural growth created fewer non-agricultural employment opportunities in rural areas.

There is some evidence that what Ranis and Stewart found for the Philippines also applies in other parts of Southeast Asia, even in those countries such as Thailand and Indonesia where overall growth rates have been more rapid over the past two decades. The data on growth of agricultural household income in Thailand cited by Onchan (1990: Table 2.13) show that income from non-agricultural

---

[21] Fei et al. (1979: 315) argue that non-agricultural income was more evenly distributed than agricultural income in Taiwan, and thus the growth in farm household income from rural industries and services made a considerable contribution to the decline in inequality in farm household income that occurred over the 1960s.

sources grew about 38 per cent faster than income from agricultural sources over the 1970s (Table 14.8). In Indonesia, evidence from the 1983 and 1993 agricultural censuses indicates that the growth of off-farm income of agricultural households was only about 24 per cent faster than the growth in income from the agricultural holdings. A comparison of Indonesia and Thailand over these different time periods is justified because real per capita GDP (in 1985 dollars corrected for purchasing power difference) increased by a similar rate. In Taiwan in the five years from 1965 to 1970 (when real per capita GDP again grew at about the same rate) the linkage ratio was considerably higher. As in the Philippines, it is probable that the skewed distribution of land and the pronounced urban bias of the industrialization process in both countries explain the lower linkage ratio.[22] In both Indonesia and Thailand, data from agricultural censuses show that a much lower proportion of land is in smallholdings, and a higher proportion of agricultural land is in holdings over five hectares compared with Taiwan (Table 14.4).

The growth of non-agricultural employment in rural areas in both Indonesia and Thailand also appears to be following the Philippine rather than the Taiwanese pattern. In Indonesia, the growth of the manufacturing labour force has been rapid since 1971 (although from a small base), but much of the growth has occurred in urban areas (Table 14.9). In Thailand (perhaps surprisingly given that such a high proportion of manufacturing value added accrues from the Bangkok region) the growth of the manufacturing labour force has been slightly faster in rural than in urban areas between 1980 and 1995 (Table 14.9). But in both urban and rural areas the growth was markedly slower than in Taiwan between 1966 and 1980. The steep decline in the proportion of the rural labour force employed in agriculture in Taiwan over these years has not occurred in more recent decades in either Thailand or Indonesia. In spite of the fact that per capita GDP (in constant ICP dollars) in Taiwan in 1980 was about the same as in Thailand in 1995, the proportion of the rural labour force in agriculture was almost twice as high in Thailand.

---

[22] There is also some controversy in the literature on off-farm employment in Southeast Asia regarding the impact that such employment has on the distribution of rural incomes. Fei et al. (1979: 315–17) argue that in Taiwan, non-agricultural income was more evenly distributed than agricultural income, and thus over time the growth of employment opportunities in rural industries and services made a substantial contribution to greater equity. Evidence from the 1993 agricultural census in Indonesia would indicate that off-farm incomes have increased overall farm household income inequality in Indonesia (see Booth, 2002).

Table 14.8 Linkage ratios and the percentage of total farm income accruing from off-farm employment

	Linkage ratio[a]	Per capita GDP (initial year)[b]	Percentage of farm income from off farm sources	
			Initial year	Final year
Taiwan (1962–80)	3.55	1364	25	60
Philippines (1965–85)	0.94	1248	45	56
Taiwan (1962–72)	2.99	1364	40	60
Thailand (1971/2–1982/83)	1.38	1507	46	59
Indonesia (1984–93)	1.24	1602	45	50
West Java	1.34		58	65
Yogyakarta	1.35		58	64
Central Java	1.54		50	59
West Sumatra	1.60		48	58
Bali	1.70		41	55

Notes:
a. Percentage growth in off-farm incomes over the period shown divided by growth in farm incomes.
b. ICP dollars in 1985 prices adjusted for changes in the terms of trade. Data taken from Penn World Tables (version 5.6).
Source: Taiwan (1962–80) and the Philippines: Ranis and Stewart (1993), Tables 9 and 14. Taiwan (1962–72): Ho (1986), Table 4.2. Thailand: Onchan (1990), Table 2.13; Indonesia: Central Bureau of Statistics (1987, 1995).

Another way of viewing different employment outcomes in Southeast Asia compared not only with Taiwan but also with Japan and South Korea is to look at the share of the non-agricultural labour force employed in services rather than in industry. It has long been accepted that for any given agricultural share of the labour force, the service share of the non-agricultural labour force (SSNALF) has tended to be higher in modern industrializing economies compared with the historical experience of Japan, Western Europe, and the USA. This is frequently attributed to the fact that manufacturing industry is inherently more capital-intensive in modern times than was the case in the nineteenth century; another reason given is that public services including education absorb a larger share of the labour force in many contemporary developing countries than was the case in Europe or the USA a century ago (Berry, 1978). While this may well be true, there is a striking difference in the SSNALF between the Philippines, Malaysia, Thailand and Indonesia on the one hand, and Taiwan, South Korea and Japan, on the other, in the post 1950s era. If we compare Thailand in 1978 with Taiwan in 1969, when per capita GDP was roughly similar, not only was the proportion of the labour force in agriculture much higher, but the SSNALF was considerably lower (Booth, 1999b: Table 9).

Table 14.9 Annual growth of manufacturing employment

	Rural	Urban	% of rural labour force in agriculture	
Taiwan				
1956–66	5.0	4.9	1956	70
1966–80	10.3	9.4	1980	33
Philippines				
1967–75	0.6	1.4	1967	75
1975–88	2.0	4.8	1988	67
Indonesia				
1971–80	5.9	9.7	1971	75
1980–95	3.2	8.8	1995	61
Thailand				
1980–95	6.4	5.7	1980	82
			1995	64

Source: Ranis and Stewart (1993: Tables 5 and 8); Indonesia: *Population Census of Indonesia 1971 (Series D)*, 1980 (Series S2); *Inter-censal Population Survey 1995, Series S2*. Thailand: *Report of the Labour Force Survey*, July-September 1980, 1995

The significance of the higher SSNALF in Southeast Asia is that service occupations tend to be very diverse with a much greater variation in remuneration compared with industrial jobs. To the extent that people in Thailand or the Philippines are leaving agriculture for relatively poorly remunerated work in services, the overall distribution of earnings and income is likely to be more skewed than in Taiwan, where the falling employment share of agriculture was reflected to a greater extent in increased employment in industry. The greater capacity of the Taiwanese and South Korean industrial sectors to absorb labour is often claimed to be due to their high degree of export orientation, an argument that is reviewed below. But it is worth noting that in spite of the high level of the SSNALF in all four Southeast Asian economies in recent years, only in Thailand is there clear evidence of worsening income inequality. What other factors account for the Thai outcome?

Access to Education, and Its Effect on Inequalities in Income

We have seen that poverty and educational attainment are inversely correlated in most parts of Southeast Asia and that children from poor backgrounds, especially in rural areas, are less likely to go on to secondary and tertiary education, or even in some areas to complete primary school, than are children from more affluent, urban backgrounds. It could be argued that this has been true in most societies in the early stages of industrialization. But comparisons of trends in educational enrolments and educational expenditures across Asia reveal considerable differences, in spite of broadly similar levels of real per capita GDP. If we compare Thailand in 1992 with South Korea and Taiwan in 1980, when per capita GDP (in 1985 ICP dollars) was roughly similar, the gross secondary enrolment ratio in Thailand was markedly lower than that of either of the others (Booth, 1999a: Table 1). On the other hand the Philippines in 1992 had a much higher secondary enrolment ratio than either South Korea or Taiwan when those countries had a similar level of per capita GDP.

Thailand's poor record on post-primary education was widely recognized among policy makers by the late 1980s, and during the 1990s considerable government effort was devoted to increasing educational participation rates, especially in the 12–17-year age groups. By 1999, 69 per cent of young people in these age groups were enrolled in lower and upper secondary school (Ministry of Education, 1999: Table 3). But the problem for Thailand, as for other countries which have only recently committed themselves to the goal of universal nine-year education, is that many young people who left school with at most having completed primary education will be in the labour force for years or indeed decades to come. They will find it increasingly difficult to compete in a labour market that will demand more skilled workers in order to permit the Thai industrial sector to move into export markets for more sophisticated manufactured goods and services. The Thai predicament can be contrasted with countries such as Taiwan and South Korea, where

> educational expansion took place ahead of demand, delivering new cohorts of appropriately skilled workers for each phase of industrialization. This allowed rising average wages to be underwritten by growing productivity, and moderate or declining wage differentials (Ahuja et al., 1997: 53).

But providing education ahead of demand also has its problems, as the Philippine case illustrates. Indeed, the Philippines emerged into independence with probably the most favourable educational legacy of any of the former colonies in Southeast Asia. This advantage was then squandered by decades of macroeconomic mismanagement, which meant that by the mid 1990s per capita GDP (in ICP dollars) was even lower than in Indonesia, where the Dutch colonial legacy in the educational sector had been far more meagre. The Indonesian government has made considerable progress in increasing access to education at all levels in the five decades since independence, but government educational expenditure as a proportion of GDP remains low in comparison to most other Asian countries (Booth, 1999a: Table 1). In Indonesia, critics of current educational policies argue that low expenditure per student leads to poor quality education, which in turn will affect the quality of the labour force for decades to come.

Open Trade Regimes, Rapid Export Growth, Income Distribution and Poverty Alleviation

In Singapore and Malaysia, and more recently in Thailand and Indonesia, the undoubted decline in the incidence of poverty that has occurred since the 1960s is often ascribed to the open, liberal or 'outward-looking' policies that have allowed these economies to grow in line with their comparative advantage and rapidly absorb labour in manufacturing industries, leading to accelerated growth in production of both traded and non-traded goods. The problem with this argument is that it often leads to a *post hoc ergo propter hoc* type of reasoning: the decline in poverty was accompanied by an open policy regime, so therefore the open policy regime must have caused the decline in poverty. The generalization therefore follows that open, outward looking policy regimes always lead to a reduction in poverty.

The Southeast Asian experience would indicate that this sort of generalization is far too facile. It is quite possible for a country that has been growing rapidly as a result of 'open' macroeconomic policies still to have a considerable poverty problem in particular regions or sectors. This appears to have been the case in Thailand, where in spite of the very rapid growth since the 1960s, the incidence of poverty in the Northeast of the country was still high in comparison with other parts of the country in the early 1990s (Tinakorn, 1995: Table 10.6).[23] The main reason was that the economy of the Northeast continued to rely primarily on agriculture. Although the rapid growth of the manufacturing and tertiary sectors has led to a sustained fall in the share of agriculture in Thai GDP, the proportion of the labour force giving agriculture as its primary source of income remains high. The result is that labour productivity in the agricultural sector is much lower than in other parts of the economy, and this gap widens when, for climatic or other reasons, agricultural production or prices fall below their long-term trend, as happened in the mid 1980s. Thus poverty remained high in the Northeast even when other parts of the country were booming, and this was an important reason for the rise in income inequality that occurred.

What Are the Lessons from Southeast Asia?

Are there any useful lessons the Southeast Asian experience can give to other parts of the developing world, and especially those countries in sub-Saharan Africa that emerged from colonialism with similar economic structures? The main purpose of this paper has been to bring out both the successes and the failures of the Southeast Asian experience, and to point out both the positive and the negative lessons the region offers. While per capita agricultural output growth has been positive virtually everywhere in Southeast Asia over the decades from 1970 to 1996,

[23] More recent work by economists at the Thai Development Research Institute suggests that after the crisis of 1997/98, the incidence of poverty in the Northeast region increased rapidly as many unemployed workers returned home.

the growth trend was downwards. Slower agricultural growth rates do not necessarily signal slower growth in rural incomes if rural households can secure access to off-farm employment. There is plenty of evidence that by the mid 1980s, such employment was providing a substantial share of total income for many rural households in Indonesia, the Philippines, Thailand and Malaysia. But the rate of growth of off-farm income was slower, relative to agricultural incomes on average than was the case in Taiwan from 1960 to 1980.

Certainly no country in Southeast Asia would seem to exemplify 'redistribution with growth' as well as Taiwan, but it may well be that Taiwan is an exceptional case that for a number of reasons cannot be used as a role model by other countries, in Asia or elsewhere. Taiwan began the process of rapid growth and structural change in the late 1950s with an unusual set of initial conditions, including a well-educated population, and an egalitarian distribution of income and land.[24] Thailand and Malaysia have had rapid economic growth, but existing income disparities among individuals, regions and ethnic groups have remained considerable and in Thailand have become wider over time. Indonesia managed to sustain rapid growth over three decades from 1967 to 1997, in spite of considerable fluctuations in the terms of trade, but urban–rural disparities have been growing and so have income disparities within urban areas. Although there is little evidence on income disparity by ethnic group in Indonesia, it is widely thought that the Chinese minority has benefited disproportionately from economic growth, and that the gap between their incomes and those of the indigenous majority has widened. In the Philippines, where economic growth over the 1980s was very slow, inequality in household income remained high, with little change over the early part of the 1990s.

Over the past two decades, most countries in Southeast Asia have experimented with some form of targeted anti-poverty policy, whether it be labour intensive public works, land reform, land settlement or rural credit policies. In almost all cases the results have been mixed. Although there is considerable evidence that both labour-intensive public works and land settlement schemes have increased the incomes of the poor, careful and objective appraisals indicate that in almost all cases the programmes could have been more cost-effective in the sense that with more accurate targeting the same allocation of funds could have produced a greater pay-off in terms of poverty alleviation.[25] In some cases, of course, it is obvious that poverty alleviation was not the only, or even the main, goal of the particular programme. For example, in the case of the Thai Rural Jobs Creation Programme, the greater allocation of funding to the central region was at

[24] Rodrik (1995) examines the impact of 'initial conditions' on economic growth in both Taiwan and South Korea. Booth (1999b) contrasts initial conditions in Southeast Asia with those in Taiwan and South Korea.

[25] See Poot (1979) and Krongkaew (1987) for a discussion of the implementation of the Rural Jobs Creation Programme, and Esmara (1987) for a review of labour intensive public works programmes in Indonesia. Mangahas (1987b) compares the experience of Thailand and the Philippines.

least partly due to political considerations. In the case of both the Indonesian and the Vietnamese land settlement programmes, political and strategic imperatives have clearly influenced the choice of settlement sites, the choice of settlers and the way in which the settlement programmes have been implemented.[26] Had poverty alleviation considerations been paramount, different sites could have been chosen, and the settlement programmes implemented in different ways. In many parts of Indonesia's Outer Islands, and in East Malaysia, poverty alleviation will in future require that more attention be paid to upgrading technology and productivity on existing farms.

Targeting poverty programmes is inevitably very much a matter of trial and error, and given the many political and strategic considerations that influence decision making in most countries it is unlikely that any one programme will ever have a dramatic impact on rural poverty. The Southeast Asian experience demonstrates that the abolition of policies such as export taxes that depress prices of key staples can also have a significant positive impact on farm incomes, although again the impact of such policies on poverty is more difficult to assess. If the crops are cultivated by poor farm households, then the poor households will benefit directly from increased farm-gate prices. Landless households also benefit from the increased employment that is likely to be generated from an increase in cultivator incomes, although the extent of the benefit will depend on a number of factors, including the extent of agricultural mechanization and the consumption patterns of land-owning farm households.

It is arguable that public perceptions about the distribution of the benefits of growth are at least as important as the evidence (often of doubtful quality) as to what has actually happened. It is indisputable that many millions of people in Southeast Asia feel that the growth process has been inequitable and that small minorities, usually concentrated in urban areas and often with close links to powerful politicians, have benefited far more than the rest of the population. It is probably inevitable that a slowdown in economic growth combined with increasing public unrest over what are perceived to be large income disparities will lead to more populist economic policies being adopted by governments throughout the region, policies that could in turn lead to growing fiscal deficits and even slower economic growth. This is very much the Latin American 'disease', to which most East Asian economies have in the past been considered immune.[27] Whether they will continue to be immune in the future remains to be seen.

---

[26] The Indonesian transmigration was the largest and most controversial of all transmigration schemes in Southeast Asia. Hardjono (1977, 1986) reviews the history and implementation of this programme. Desbarats (1987) looks at the history of land settlement in Vietnam, and King (1986) looks at land development schemes in East Malaysia. Most of the recent literature on land reform in Southeast Asia has dealt with the Philippines; valuable insights are given in Mangahas (1985, 1987a) and Putzel (1992).

[27] Alesina and Rodrik (1994) develop a model which suggests that 'there will be strong demand for redistribution in societies where a large section of the population does not have access to the productive resources of the economy. Such conflict over distribution will generally harm growth'. Their empirical results show that inequality in income and land

References

Ahuja, V., B. Bidani, F. Ferreira and M. Walton. 1997. *Everyone's Miracle? Revisiting Poverty and Inequality in East Asia*. Washington, D.C.: The World Bank.

Akita, Takahiro and Rizal Affandi Lukman. 1995. 'Interregional inequalities in Indonesia: A sectoral decomposition analysis for 1975–92'. *Bulletin of Indonesian Economic Studies*, vol. 31(2): 61–82.

Alesina, A. and D. Rodrik. 1994. 'Distributive politics and economic growth'. *Quarterly Journal of Economics*, vol. 109 (May): 465–85.

Anand, S. 1983. *Inequality and Poverty in Malaysia: Measurement and Decomposition*. New York: Oxford University Press for the World Bank.

Balisacan, A. 1989. 'Philippine agricultural development in historical perspective'. In M. Montes and H. Sakai, eds., *Philippine Macroeconomic Perspectives, Developments and Policies*. Tokyo: Institute of Developing Economies.

Balisacan, A. 1993. 'Agricultural growth, landlessness, off-farm employment and rural poverty in the Philippines'. *Economic Development and Cultural Change*, vol. 41(3), April: 533–62.

Balisacan, A. 1997. 'Getting the story right: Growth, redistribution and poverty alleviation in the Philippines'. *Philippine Review of Economics and Business*, vol. XXXIV(1), June: 1–35.

Barker, R. and R.W. Herdt. 1985. *The Rice Economy of Asia*. Washington, D.C: Resources for the Future.

Bautista, R. 1992. *Development Policy in East Asia: Economic Growth and Poverty Alleviation*. Singapore: Institute of Southeast Asian Studies.

Berry, A. 1978. 'A positive interpretation of the expansion of urban services in Latin America, with some Colombian evidence'. *Journal of Development Studies*, vol. 14(2): 210–31.

Bidani, B. and M. Ravallion. 1993. 'A regional poverty profile for Indonesia'. *Bulletin of Indonesian Economic Studies*, vol. 29(3): 37–68.

Booth, A. 1992. 'Income distribution and poverty'. In Anne Booth, ed., *The Oil Boom and After: Indonesian Economic Policy and Performance in the Soeharto Era*. Singapore: Oxford University Press.

Booth, A. 1993. 'Counting the poor in Indonesia'. *Bulletin of Indonesian Economic Studies*, vol. 29(1): 53–84.

Booth, A. 1998. 'Rural development, income distribution and poverty decline in Southeast Asia'. Paper prepared for the African Economic Research Consortium, Nairobi.

Booth, A. 1999a. 'Education and economic development in Southeast Asia: Myths and Realities'. *ASEAN Economic Bulletin*, vol. 16(3): 290–306.

Booth, A. 1999b. 'Initial conditions and miraculous growth: Why is South East Asia different from Taiwan and South Korea?' *World Development*, vol. 27(2), February: 301–21.

Booth, A. 2000. 'Poverty and inequality in the Soeharto era: An assessment'. *Bulletin of Indonesian Economic Studies*, vol. 36(1): 73–104.

Booth, A. 2002. 'Changing role of non-farm activities in agricultural households in Indonesia: Some insights from the agricultural censuses'. Mimeo.

---

distribution is negatively associated with subsequent growth. The message for South East Asia would appear to be that some measure of income and asset redistribution is essential for sustained growth. At the very least governments should make an effort to ensure equality of access to the education system.

Central Bureau of Statistics. 1987. *Sensus Pertanian 1983, Seri I: Sampel Pendapatan Petani*. Jakarta: Central Bureau of Statistics.

Central Bureau of Statistics. 1994. *Penduduk Miskin dan Desa Tertinggal 1993: Metodologi dan Analisis*. Jakarta: Central Bureau of Statistics.

Central Bureau of Statistics. 1995a. *Sensus Pertanian 1993, Seri D1: Pendapatan Rumahtangga Pertanian dan Indikator Sosial Ekonomi*. Jakarta: Central Bureau of Statistics.

Central Bureau of Statistics. 1995b. *Sensus Pertanian 1993, Seri B1: Sensus Sampel Rumahtangga Pertanian Pengguna Lahan*. Jakarta: Central Bureau of Statistics.

Central Bureau of Statistics. 1995c. *Sensus Pertanian 1993, Seri D1: Pendapatan Rumahtangga Pertanian dan Indikator Sosial Ekonomi*. Jakarta: Central Bureau of Statistics.

Central Bureau of Statistics. 1997. *Statistik Indonesia (Statistical Yearbook of Indonesia) 1996*. Jakarta: Central Bureau of Statistics, June.

Central Bureau of Statistics. 1998. *Statistik Indonesia (Statistical Yearbook of Indonesia) 1997*. Jakarta: Central Bureau of Statistics, June.

Central Board of Statistics. 2000. *Expenditure for Consumption of Indonesia Per Province 1999*. Jakarta: Central Board of Statistics, January.

Desbarats, J. 1987. 'Population redistribution in the Socialist Republic of Vietnam'. *Population and Development Review*, 13(1): 43–76.

Esmara, H. 1987. 'Creating employment through labour-intensive public works programmes'. *Philippine Review of Business and Economics*, vol. 14(3 and 4): 215–36.

Fei, John C. H., G. Ranis and Shirley W.Y. Kuo. 1979. *Growth with Equity: The Taiwan Case*. New York: Oxford University Press.

Government of Malaysia. 1989. *The Mid-term Review of the Fifth Malaysia Plan*. Kuala Lumpur: National Printing Department.

Government of Malaysia. 1994. *The Mid-term Review of the Sixth Malaysia Plan*. Kuala Lumpur: National Printing Department.

Government of Malaysia. 1999. *The Mid-term Review of the Seventh Malaysia Plan*. Kuala Lumpur: National Printing Department.

Hardjono, J. 1977. *Transmigration in Indonesia*. Kuala Lumpur: Oxford University Press.

Hardjono, J. 1986. 'Transmigration: Looking to the future'. *Bulletin of Indonesian Economic Studies*, vol. 22(2), August: 28–53.

Hashim, S. 1995. *Poverty and Income Inequality in Malaysia*. PhD dissertation, University of London.

Hill, H. 1996. *The Indonesian Economy since 1966*. Cambridge: Cambridge University Press.

Ho, S.P.S. 1978. *Economic Development of Taiwan 1860–1970*. New Haven: Yale University Press.

Ho, S.P.S. 1979. 'Decentralized industrialization and rural development: Evidence from Taiwan'. *Economic Development and Cultural Change*, vol. 28(1), October: 77–96.

Ho, S.P.S. 1986. 'Off-farm employment and farm households in Taiwan'. In R.T. Shand, ed., *Off-farm Employment in the Development of Rural Asia*. Canberra: National Centre for Development Studies, Australian National University.

Intal, P. and J.H. Power. 1991. 'Philippines'. In A.O. Krueger, M. Schiff and A. Valdes, eds., *The Political Economy of Agricultural Pricing Policy*, Volume 2. Baltimore: Johns Hopkins University Press.

Jenkins, G.P. and A. Kwok-Kong Lai. 1991. 'Malaysia'. In A.O. Krueger, M. Schiff and A. Valdes, eds., *The Political Economy of Agricultural Pricing Policy*, Volume 2. Baltimore: Johns Hopkins University Press.

Jomo, K.S. 1990. *Growth and Structural Change in the Malaysian Economy*. London: Macmillan.

Khoman, S. 1993. 'Education policy'. In Peter Warr, ed., *The Thai Economy in Transition*. Cambridge: Cambridge University Press.

King, V. 1986. 'Land settlement schemes and the alleviation of rural poverty in Sarawak, East Malaysia: A critical commentary'. *Southeast Asia Journal of Social Science*, vol. 14(1): 71–99.

Krongkaew, M. 1987. 'The economic and social impact of Thailand's rural job creation programs'. *Philippine Review of Business and Economics*, vol. 14(3 and 4): 237–72.

Mangahas, M. 1985. 'Rural poverty and Operation Land Transfer'. In R. Islam, ed., *Strategies for Alleviating Poverty in Rural Asia*. Bangkok: ILO-ARTEP.

Mangahas, M. 1987a. 'The political economy of land reform and distribution in the Philippines'. In *Agrarian Reform: Experiences and Expectations*. Manila: Center for Research and Communication.

Mangahas, M. 1987b. 'Rural employment creation in the Philippines and Thailand'. In *Rural Employment Creation in Asia and the Pacific*. Manila: Asian Development Bank.

Ministry of Education. 1999. Education Statistics in Brief 1999, Bangkok: Bureau of Policy and Planning, Ministry of Education.

McVey, R., ed. 1992. *Southeast Asian Capitalists*. Ithaca: Cornell University Modern Southeast Asia Programme.

Mukhopadhyay, S. and Chee Peng Lim, eds., 1985. *The Rural Non-farm Sector in Asia*. Kuala Lumpur: Asian and Pacific Development Centre.

Myers, C.N. and Chalongphob Sussangkarn. 1992. *Educational Options for the Future of Thailand: A Synthesis*. Bangkok: Thai Development Research Institute.

Myint, Hla. 1967. 'The inward and outward-looking countries of South East Asia'. *Malayan Economic Review*, vol. XII (1), April: 1–13.

Onchan, T. 1990. *A Land Policy Study*. Bangkok: Thai Development Research Institute Foundation.

Platteau, J-P. and Y. Hayami. 1998. 'Resource endowments and agricultural development: Africa and Asia'. In Y. Hayami and M. Aoki, eds., *The Institutional Foundations of East Asian Economic Development*. London: Macmillan for the International Economic Association.

Poot, Huib. 1979. 'Evaluation of the Tambon Development Programme in Thailand'. Mimeo. Bangkok: ILO-ARTEP.

Putzel, J. 1992. *A Captive Land: The Politics of Agrarian Reform in the Philippines*. London: Catholic Institute for International Relations.

Ranis, G. and F. Stewart. 1987. 'Rural linkages in the Philippines and Taiwan'. In Frances Stewart, ed., *Macro-Policies for Appropriate Technology in Developing Countries*. Boulder: Westview Press.

Ranis, G. and F. Stewart. 1993. 'Rural non-agricultural activities in development: Theory and application'. *Journal of Development Economics*, vol. 40: 75–101.

Ranis, G., F. Stewart and E. Angeles-Reyes. 1990. *Linkages in Developing Economies: A Philippine Study*. San Francisco: International Center for Economic Growth.

Rodrik, D. 1995. 'Getting interventions right: How South Korea and Taiwan grew rich'. *Economic Policy*, no. 20, April: 55–107.

Shand, R.T., ed. 1986. *Off-farm Employment in the Development of Rural Asia*. Canberra: National Centre for Development Studies, Australian National University.

Shari, I. 1979. 'Estimation of poverty lines and the incidence of poverty in Peninsular Malaysia, 1973'. *Philippine Economic Journal*, vol. XVIII(4): 418–49.

Siamwalla, A. and S. Setboonsarng. 1991. 'Thailand'. In A.O. Krueger, M. Schiff and A. Valdes, eds., *The Political Economy of Agricultural Pricing Policy*, Volume 2. Baltimore: Johns Hopkins University Press.

Tinakorn, P. 1995. 'Industrialization and welfare: How poverty and income distribution are affected'. In Medhi Krongkaew, ed., *Thailand's Industrialization and its Consequences*. London: Macmillan.

UNDP. 1997. *Human Development Report 1997*. New York: Oxford University Press for the United Nations Development Programme.

Williamson, J.G. 1965. 'Regional development and the process of national development: A description of the patterns'. *Economic Development and Cultural Change*, vol. 13: 3–45.

Wongboonsin, K. and Vipan Prachuabmoh Ruffolo. 1995. 'Sex preference for children in Thailand and some other South-East Asian countries'. *Asia-Pacific Population Journal*, vol. 10(3): 43–62.

World Bank. 1988. *Indonesia: The Transmigration Program in Perspective*. Washington, D.C.: The World Bank.

World Bank. 2001. *Thailand Social Monitor: Poverty and Public Policy*. Washington, D.C.: The World Bank, November.

Yoshihara, K. 1988. *Ersatz Capitalism in Southeast Asia*. Kuala Lumpur: Oxford University Press.

Index